OUR HAVEN *and* OUR STRENGTH

ספר תהלים

OUR HAVEN *and* OUR STRENGTH

The BOOK *of* PSALMS

With a New Translation and Commentary by

Martin Samuel Cohen

AVIV PRESS NEW YORK 2004/5764

Library of Congress Cataloging-in-Publication Data
Bible. O.T. Psalms. English. Cohen. 2003.
Our haven and our strength : the book of Psalms / with a new translation and commentary by Martin Samuel Cohen.
p. cm.
Text of Psalms in English and Hebrew; commentary in English.
ISBN 0-916219-22-4
1. Bible. O.T. Psalms—Commentaries. I. Title: Book of Psalms. II. Cohen, Martin Samuel, 1953– III. Bible. O.T. Psalms. Hebrew. 2003. IV. Title.

BS1424.C594 2003
223'.2077—dc22

2003063033

Cover painting: "Heaven and Earth" © 2003 Myra Mandel
Published by Aviv Press
An Imprint of the Rabbinical Assembly
3080 Broadway
New York, NY 10027

Designed by Adrianne Onderdonk Dudden
English composition by Duke & Company, Devon, Pennsylvania
Hebrew composition by El Ot, Tel Aviv, Israel
Text type: Fairfield, Cochin, and Hadassah
Display type: Barbedor and Meiri
Printed in the United States of America

CONTENTS

INTRODUCTION

Throughout the generations, no book has been more valuable as a constant source of inspiration to Jewish people everywhere than the Book of Psalms. Printed and bound over and over in countless editions since the dawn of printing, the Psalter—called in Hebrew *Sefer Tehillim* or, both colloquially and affectionately, just *Tillim*—has been the literary companion of Jewish pilgrims seeking a life in God for so long that it seems reasonable to say that no one book, not even the Torah itself, has been drenched with more tears or recited with more spiritual enthusiasm by Jewish men and women in pursuit of the comfort, encouragement, or solace of faith.

The Book of Psalms is, at first blush, an unlikely candidate for such avid interest. For one thing, the specific reason for which the book was created is unknown, as are the identities and dates of the poets who composed its poems. Nor are the poems themselves, suffused as so many of them are with obscure references and antique oracles, uniformly easy to decipher. Yet, with all the baggage any ancient book inevitably must carry along with it into the modern world, the Psalter somehow retains more than enough of its ancient majesty and deeply engaging style to speak to the spiritual needs of modern readers the world over.

Sefer Tehillim is a book of popular prophecy. Returning over and over in countless passages to the notion that average supplicants can reasonably hope to hear the voice of God, the psalmists seem to find it entirely plausible for people to seek communion with the Divine not merely by praying *to* God, but by expecting and awaiting a response *from* God as well. Auditory perception is only part of the story, however, and there are also passages in the Book of Psalms that speak frankly about the possibility of experiencing God visually. The language is sometimes tantalizingly obscure, especially when a poet writes vaguely about gazing on the beauty of God or the face of God or the light of God's face. However, the basic concept is the same in those passages as it is when a poet talks boldly, and unapologetically, simply of seeing God. Indeed, one of the basic assumptions of the poets of the Psalter seems to have been that the reality of God's basically unfathomable existence in the world may never prevent the pious from stepping back from the challenging—and more than slightly unsettling—truth that faith, to be real and not feigned, must always be hewn with the same sensory tools we human beings use to perceive and interpret the rest of our world. In the end, we know only of one kind of knowledge . . . just as we know only of one kind of truth and of one kind of love.

Nothing will ever take the place of encountering the psalms in the original Hebrew, but the poetry of the Psalter is accessible in translation and, to the extent that every translation is inevitably some kind of commentary, there may even be some benefit that will accrue to readers of Hebrew from inspecting the psalms in translation. For its part, the English presented in this book hovers somewhere between a literal translation and a paraphrase of the Hebrew original: words have been added to elucidate passages that would otherwise be difficult, or even impossible, for the average reader to seize without them and any number of obscure words and turns of phrase have been translated based on some amalgam of context, etymology, and informed guesswork, or with reference to the comments of the classical Jewish commentators. Indeed, although I have endeavored to convey the meaning, implicit or explicit, of the Hebrew in good English, and nothing more, the integrity of the experience of reading the Psalms in translation will be preserved as long as the reader bears in mind both that many passages can bear alternate interpretations, and also that many verses that read clearly in English are actually so obscure as to be almost unintelligible in the original. It also bears saying that this edition of the Psalms is intended not for scholarly, but for devotional, use by men and women interested in undertaking the recitation of psalms as part of a spiritual regimen of contemplative prayer and focused reading. To facilitate this way of using the Psalter, I have refrained from footnoting the many passages throughout the book that could be translated in different ways. Nor have I indicated which specific commentator inspired the translation of each specific verse, if any did. Still, readers encountering an unexpected translation and curious about its source will most often find the answer to their question in the commentaries of Radak (Rabbi David Kimhi, c. 1160–c. 1235) and the Meiri (Rabbi Menachem ben Solomon, 1249–1316), who, along with the efforts of the better known commentators Rashi (1040–1105) and Ibn Ezra (Rabbi Abraham Ibn Ezra, 1089–1164), have provided me with the exegetical base on which my own translation is built. In textual matters and with respect to the textual traditions known under the general rubric of *masorah,* I have generally followed the observations of the *Minḥat Shai* of Rabbi Yedidiah Solomon Raphael ben Abraham Norzi (1560–1616).

The English translation of each psalm is accompanied by an original introduction. Countless introductions and commentaries to the Book of Psalms already exist, some rooted in questions of vocabulary, grammar, and syntax, and others primarily focused on the countless historical questions that arise from the book. I have chosen a different path, however, and have tried to introduce each psalm in a way that will be of use primarily to people trying to use the poems of the Psalter to deepen their spirituality and religious sensitivity, and—in the traditional Jewish way—to seek God through the words and phraseology of Scripture. How successful this effort has been —or, indeed, if it has been successful at all—will only be clear to the men and women who attempt to use this book of *Tillim* as part of their ongoing efforts to know God, to feel their days and nights suffused with the presence of God, and to commune personally and effectively with the poetic presence of the Divine through the medium of these ancient verses. If any of them finds the path to communion with the God of Israel slightly less crooked because of my work, I will be amply satisfied.

One of the more novel features of this translation has to do with the question of gender-based language, and I would like to address that issue in this introduction as well. The classical texts of the Bible invariably use masculine nouns, pronouns, and verbs to refer to the Almighty. And although Scripture does specifically note that Eve was created in the image of God no less than was Adam, it seems entirely clear that the average citizen of ancient Israel generally thought of God in masculine terms: as a king rather than as a queen, as a celestial master rather than as a heavenly mistress, as a divine father rather than as a holy mother. In our day, people are either so used to hearing masculine language with respect to God that they hardly notice it, or they are offended by the notion that God, who both faith and common sense tell us must logically exist in divine reality no more with reference to a specific gender than with reference to the limitations of time or space, should invariably be described with terms that are specifically masculine. Continuing a trend that has been going on for some time among the faithful in both Jewish and non-Jewish circles, I have attempted to avoid any gender-based language with respect to God in my translation of the psalms. Attempting to avoid gender-specific language without deforming the feel of the original Hebrew has been difficult, however, and readers will have to forgive the occasional infelicitous turn of phrase rooted in the simple, but incredibly potent, fact that English only uses gender-neutral pronouns to denote animate beings under very specific and circumscribed conditions.

In a category by itself is the four-letter name of God called the *shem hameforash* or the *shem havayah* in Hebrew. Although it is invariably used as a proper name in Hebrew, we no longer know precisely how it was pronounced in ancient times and, as a result—and also as a nod to its ineffable holiness—this personal four-letter name of God is not pronounced at all in Jewish liturgical settings, where the name *Adonai* is almost always substituted for it. However, *Adonai* is simply the Hebrew word meaning "my Lord"—in the plural to denote respect—and it is, therefore, not really any less gender-specific in Hebrew than its translation would be in English. Different editors and authors in recent years have tried to solve this problem in different ways. Some English books simply give *Hashem* (literally, "the name") in place of the *shem havayah,* which has the double advantage of being totally gender-neutral and also of corresponding to the way at least some English-speaking Jews actually do refer to God in common speech. Other books print *Adonai* in place of the four-letter name, but this technique would not suit a translation of the Book of Psalms because the actual Hebrew word *adonai* appears regularly in the Psalter as a divine title in its own right. (To minimize confusion, I have written out "Adonai" in English letters in the translation only where that specific word appears in the Hebrew text.)

With respect to the best way to present the actual four-letter name, however, I weighed a number of different options and chose in the end to remain as faithful as possible to the Hebrew (without contravening my own effort to present a gender-neutral text) by printing the four-letter name in Hebrew characters within the English translation. When reading psalms as part of worship or study, or as part of a regimen of devotional meditation, readers of the translation anxious to come as close as possible to the experience of reading the Psalms in Hebrew should say *Adonai* when they see the Hebrew name; in less spiritually charged contexts, they should say *Hashem*. Indeed, since seeing the four-letter name and saying something else is the way Jewish readers of the original Hebrew respond to the name of God, there is no obvious reason why readers of the English translation should not have the experience of encountering, and dealing with, the divine name in the same way. For the sake of consistency, I have also printed the four-letter name in Hebrew letters in the occasional verse cited in translation or transliteration in the introductory comments to each psalm.

There is, however, an exception to this rule that pertains when the *shem havayah* appears directly before or after the actual Hebrew word *adonai*. In such cases, the divine name should be pronounced *Elohim* (the Hebrew word meaning

"God")—as, for example, at Psalms 69:7 and 71:5 (where the combination yields *Adonai Elohim*) or at Psalms 109:21, 140:8, or 141:8 (where it yields *Elohim Adonai*). *Elohim* itself as a divine title does not appear before or after the actual word *adonai* anywhere in the Psalter.

Yah, a shorter form of the *shem havayah* consisting of its first two letters alone, appears a dozen and a half times in the Book of Psalms. Lacking the ultimate sanctity of its longer version, this shortened divine name is simply pronounced as written. Yet as a nod to its derivative sanctity, I have printed it too in Hebrew letters both in the translation and the introductory comments.

I would like to add a note about the gender of the psalmists themselves. Although the Book of Chronicles (at 1 Chronicles 25:5–6) makes the specific point that both men and women served as choral singers in the First Temple, it is not known if women were similarly enfranchised in Second Temple days, when the Book of Psalms was created as an anthology of ancient and contemporary hymns and prayers. (Psalm 68 does make reference to female Temple musicians, but the poet is formally describing First Temple times and could only possibly have been describing the day-to-day reality in contemporary Jerusalem as well.) It is, however, the case that only masculine forms are used wherever the psalmists refer to themselves with gender-specific pronouns or verbs. For the sake of not having constantly to refer to the poets whose hymns form our Psalter as "he or she," I have therefore followed the lead of the ancients themselves and referred to the psalmists with masculine pronouns. Having said that, I must add that there is no inherent reason to assume that there were no women among the authors of those psalms that do not refer to their authors as men. Nor is it impossible to imagine that women poets may have felt obligated to write as though they were men for the sake of having their poetry taken seriously.

There are many words and phrases in the Book of Psalms —and especially in the superscriptions to many of the psalms— that refer to the specific way in which the psalms were sung in ancient times, but the precise meaning of these musical terms is mostly unknown. In this translation, I have mostly left untranslated terms that convey their imprecise meanings clearly enough in transliteration. For example, it is obvious from the context in Psalm 150 that an *ugav* is a kind of musical instrument (and this is especially so when the passage is compared to Job 21:12 and 30:31, and to Genesis 4:21, where the term also appears). Yet arbitrarily to name a modern instrument in the translation—as though there were any particular reason to think of an *ugav* as an oboe or a set of panpipes—is more than just slightly misleading. The same applies to the famous word *selah,* which appears scores of times in the Psalter. It appears to be a kind of choral indication, perhaps marking the places in which singers were to hold a note for effect, or perhaps a place in which the choristers were to breathe. I have left the word untranslated to indicate that, in the end, we do not know what precisely the term was meant to denote.

Many of the psalms have superscriptions of various sorts. In translating these, I have tried to capture the spirit of the original even where the Hebrew could bear alternate explanations. When obscure words that sound as though they could possibly be a song title appear in the superscription of a psalm, I have translated those words as though they were there to indicate that the psalm was to be sung to a well-known melody, a song with which the reader was expected to be familiar. It would be wonderful somehow to recover these long-lost tunes, if that is what those words really mean, but, even without knowing that with any certainty, translating these words as putative song titles can still serve to provide readers with ongoing reminders that the psalms were meant to be sung rather than recited or read silently. Other psalms make specific reference to the kind of musical instrument the poet wished to be used to accompany his song.

The masoretic scholars who fixed the text of the psalms noted a certain number of places in the book where words written one way were to be read differently. In this edition, these words are printed in the body of the text of the Psalter as they are to be read and the original forms, the so-called *ketiv* form of the words, appear in footnotes at the bottom of the page. Also, readers will note that I have presented the Hebrew text of the psalms in sections designed to correspond to the English translation, rather than to the original masoretic presentation of the text. Readers fluent in Hebrew will find it interesting, perhaps, to compare the way the text "feels" when presented in the traditional textual blocks to the way it is presented here; those relying more strongly on the English, I suspect, will find the way the Hebrew is printed in this edition more conducive to comparison with the translation, however, and thus more useful. I have also retained (and footnoted) certain peculiarities in the masoretic Hebrew text that occasioned interesting midrashic comments by the ancients. (In this regard, see, e.g., the explanation in *Midrash Tehillim* 27:7 of the dots that appear over and under some of the letters of the word *lulei* at Psalm 27:13, or the explanation in *Vayikra Rabbah* 13:5 of the raised *ayin* at Psalm 80:14.) I have not bothered to reproduce other grammatical or punctuational masoretic notes that would not be of interest to any but the most erudite scholars of the Hebrew text, nor have I culled the masoretic footnotes that do appear in this volume from a single source.

Almost half the psalms are attributed to King David, and another two and a half dozen are attributed to other famous or obscure biblical personalities. Since it seems likely that at least most of these psalms are products of a much later age than David's, the simplest way to explain these superscriptions is to assume that the psalms attributed to David were either written in David's homage or composed as poetic responses to specific incidents in his life. As the ascriptions of other psalms—to Moses, Solomon, Asaph, Heman, Ethan, Jeduthun, and the sons of Korach—appear to fall into the same category, I have tried to capture the ambiguity of the Hebrew in English without passing absolute judgment on the meaning of the original. Thus the superscription to the twenty-third psalm, *mizmor ledavid,* is given as "a psalm of David" and left at that. Although the psalmists clearly identified most strongly with the image of the young David as a persecuted musician fleeing from the unjustified wrath of his mad king and clinging to faith in God throughout years of danger and uncertainty, there are also other specific incidents in David's life that inspired certain particular psalms. Moderns, I think, will profit best from this aspect of the Psalter not by becoming focused on the historical issue of whether David did or did not write this or that specific poem, but by familiarizing themselves with the story of his life to the point that they too can appreciate the vivid images that so inspired the ancient psalmists to focus their fears, their hopes, and their intense faith in divine deliverance through the prism of the biblical story of King David's life.

Regardless of the historical origin of specific psalms, that is certainly how their latter-day admirers have read these poems for millennia and it is, I think, how we may most profitably read them ourselves as well.

Finally, I wish formally to thank the many people who have helped me bring this project to fruition. Foremost among them I would like to mention: Jonathan Slater, Michael Graetz, and Stephen Chaim Listfield, who read and commented upon early drafts; Ira Stone, who proposed this book as one of the opening projects of the Aviv Press; Amy Gottlieb, who provided superb editorial advice and who set the stage for the Aviv Press imprint; Michelle Kwitkin-Close, who provided expert copy-editing and proofreading; Adrianne Onderdonk Dudden, who designed the book; Myra Mandel, who supplied the cover image; Richard Weisman, of Duke & Company, who typeset the English text; Shaul Akri, of El Ot, who typeset the Hebrew; and Jim Harris, of G&H Soho, who printed the book. I am grateful to them all.

With every passing year, the Book of Psalms becomes more central to my understanding both of what it means to be a Jew and what it means to be a human being. I know I am the richer for having traveled down this path and it is in that spirit that I present this Psalter, this *Tillim,* to my readers.

M.S.C.
Roslyn, New York
1 Kislev 5764
יום השנה הכ״ד
לפטירת אמי מורתי ע״ה וז״ל

יְהִי רָצוֹן קוֹדֶם אֲמִירַת תְּהִלִּים

אֱלֹהֵינוּ הַמִּסְתַּתֵּר הַשּׁוֹכֵן בָּעֲרָפֶל,
מְקוֹר חַיַּי אֲשֶׁר בְּאוֹרְךָ אֶרְאֶה אוֹר,
אֲדוֹן כָּל הָאָרֶץ שֶׁאַתָּה לִי מַחֲסֶה וָעֹז,
יְהִי רָצוֹן מִלְּפָנֶיךָ שֶׁתְּחָנֵּנִי וְשֶׁתְּבָרְכֵנִי כִּי אֵלֶיךָ
אֶקְרָא בֶּאֱמֶת וּבְיֹשֶׁר לֵבָב וְשֶׁתָּבִיא אוֹתִי אֶל
הֵיכַל קָדְשֶׁךָ וְרוּחַ קָדְשְׁךָ אַל תִּקַּח מִמֶּנִּי.
הַאֲזִינָה אֱלֹהִים תְּפִלָּתִי וְאַל תִּתְעַלַּם מִן
הַמִּזְמוֹרִים וְהַתְּהִלּוֹת שֶׁאֲנִי אֶקְרָא, שֶׁכָּל אֶחָד
מֵהֶם הוּא שִׁיר הַלֵּל וָשֶׁבַח לְאֵל עֶלְיוֹן, אֲדוֹן כָּל
הָאָרֶץ וּמַלְכִּי בַקֹּדֶשׁ.
בָּרוּךְ אַתָּה יהוה, מֶלֶךְ מְהֻלָּל בַּתִּשְׁבָּחוֹת.

A Prayer before the Devotional Recitation of Psalms

O elusive God, shrouded in cloud and mystery,
O sacred Source of life and perception,
O God of all the earth, my haven and my strength,
May it be Your will to be gracious unto me, to bless me as I call out to You in sincerity and candor, and to usher me into Your holy palace.
May Your holy spirit never depart from me.
Give ear to my prayers and listen to my recitation of these holy psalms, each one of which is a sacred song of praise to You, O God of the universe and my holy Sovereign.
Blessed are You, Almighty God, Sovereign of the Universe to whom all praise is due.

ספר תהלים

The BOOK *of* PSALMS

א

אַשְׁרֵי־הָאִישׁ אֲשֶׁר לֹא הָלַךְ בַּעֲצַת רְשָׁעִים וּבְדֶרֶךְ
חַטָּאִים לֹא עָמָד וּבְמוֹשַׁב לֵצִים לֹא יָשָׁב׃ 2 כִּי
אִם־בְּתוֹרַת יְהוָה חֶפְצוֹ וּבְתוֹרָתוֹ יֶהְגֶּה יוֹמָם
וָלָיְלָה׃
3 וְהָיָה כְּעֵץ שָׁתוּל עַל־פַּלְגֵי מָיִם אֲשֶׁר פִּרְיוֹ ׀ יִתֵּן
בְּעִתּוֹ וְעָלֵהוּ לֹא יִבּוֹל וְכֹל אֲשֶׁר־יַעֲשֶׂה יַצְלִיחַ׃
4 לֹא־כֵן הָרְשָׁעִים כִּי אִם־כַּמֹּץ אֲשֶׁר־תִּדְּפֶנּוּ רוּחַ׃
5 עַל־כֵּן ׀ לֹא־יָקֻמוּ רְשָׁעִים בַּמִּשְׁפָּט וְחַטָּאִים בַּעֲדַת
צַדִּיקִים׃ 6 כִּי־יוֹדֵעַ יְהוָה דֶּרֶךְ צַדִּיקִים וְדֶרֶךְ
רְשָׁעִים תֹּאבֵד׃

To readers familiar with the angst and anguish of so many of the psalms, it may come as a bit of a surprise to learn that the Psalter begins with, of all things, a definition of happiness. But there is not really anything all that anomalous about the opening of the first psalm: twenty-five times in the course of nineteen different poems, different psalmists repeat the famous word *ashrei* ("happy is" or "happy are") and finish the phrase with yet another definition of human happiness. One poet, for example, suggests that the truly happy are those who take refuge in God. Another writes, rather intrepidly, that happiness comes from being among those God deigns to punish for their sins. A third passage suggests that the key is always to find one's greatest source of help and support in God. Yet another insists that the secret to achieving happiness in life rests in coming both to fear God *and,* perhaps as a result, to be seized by intense longing to observe the commandments diligently and properly. Still other subgroups within society are called happy by different poets: those who are guileless, those who know the sound of the *shofar,* those whom God chooses to draw near to the sacred presence of the Divine. And the author of the first psalm has an opinion of his own, also boldly stated: "Happy is the person who refuses to follow the counsel of the wicked and who neither pursues the path of sinners nor sits in the company

1

Happy is the person who refuses to follow the counsel of the wicked and who neither pursues the path of sinners nor sits in the company of buffoons, [2]but whose delight is in the teaching of יהוה, who ponders that teaching day and night.

[3] Such a person is like a tree planted by flowing waters that gives forth its fruit at the right time of year and whose foliage does not wither; such a person succeeds at every undertaking.

[4] The wicked, however, are a different story: they are just the kind of chaff a gust of wind can easily blow away.

[5] For this reason the wicked dare not stand up in court, nor sinners in the congregation of the righteous—[6]for יהוה knows the way of the righteous, but the way of the wicked leads to ruin.

of buffoons, but whose delight is in the teaching of יהוה, who ponders that teaching day and night."

Indeed, by contrasting individuals who attain happiness in that way with the wicked, our poet is offering us his definition of happiness *and* righteousness—and, at the same time, challenging us to respond with our own set of questions. Is righteousness merely the absence of depraved company, or is it a quality to be cultivated in its own right? Is righteousness that somehow fails to bring happiness in its wake by definition flawed or false? Or is "happiness" merely the name for the specific kind of satisfaction that righteousness brings to the righteous?

The Psalter opens up by prompting us to consider that ordinary people can attain happiness simply by living their lives in such a way so as to come ever closer to God by choosing as twin life-tasks the avoidance of evil and the study of God's word. By framing his poem this way, the poet is asking his readers to decide if they concur or, if they do not, to decide how they would prefer to define the happiness we all spend so much time and energy seeking, even *without* having a specific definition of it in mind at all.

ב

לָמָּה רָגְשׁוּ גוֹיִם וּלְאֻמִּים יֶהְגּוּ־רִיק׃
[2] יִתְיַצְּבוּ ׀ מַלְכֵי־אֶרֶץ וְרוֹזְנִים נוֹסְדוּ־יָחַד עַל־יְהוָה
וְעַל־מְשִׁיחוֹ׃
[3] נְנַתְּקָה אֶת־מוֹסְרוֹתֵימוֹ וְנַשְׁלִיכָה מִמֶּנּוּ עֲבֹתֵימוֹ׃
[4] יוֹשֵׁב בַּשָּׁמַיִם יִשְׂחָק אֲדֹנָי יִלְעַג־לָמוֹ׃ [5] אָז יְדַבֵּר
אֵלֵימוֹ בְאַפּוֹ וּבַחֲרוֹנוֹ יְבַהֲלֵמוֹ׃ [6] וַאֲנִי נָסַכְתִּי
מַלְכִּי עַל־צִיּוֹן הַר־קָדְשִׁי׃
[7] אֲסַפְּרָה אֶל חֹק יְהוָה אָמַר אֵלַי בְּנִי אַתָּה אֲנִי
הַיּוֹם יְלִדְתִּיךָ׃ [8] שְׁאַל מִמֶּנִּי וְאֶתְּנָה גוֹיִם נַחֲלָתֶךָ
וַאֲחֻזָּתְךָ אַפְסֵי־אָרֶץ׃ [9] תְּרֹעֵם בְּשֵׁבֶט בַּרְזֶל כִּכְלִי
יוֹצֵר תְּנַפְּצֵם׃
[10] וְעַתָּה מְלָכִים הַשְׂכִּילוּ הִוָּסְרוּ שֹׁפְטֵי אָרֶץ׃
[11] עִבְדוּ אֶת־יְהוָה בְּיִרְאָה וְגִילוּ בִּרְעָדָה׃
[12] נַשְּׁקוּ־בַר פֶּן־יֶאֱנַף ׀ וְתֹאבְדוּ דֶרֶךְ כִּי־יִבְעַר כִּמְעַט
אַפּוֹ אַשְׁרֵי כָּל־חוֹסֵי בוֹ׃

The second psalm has at its core the idea that showing reverence to the king of Israel is a way of acknowledging the sovereignty of God and that treason, therefore, is both a crime and a sin. Indeed, when the poet imagines God referring to the king as a "son," he does so to prompt readers to take note of the fact that the king serves as a link between God and people that is not only strong, but also ancient, permanent, and unconditional. His unstated corollary—that sedition is not mere folly, but blasphemy as well—is both provocative and potent, but can these ancient notions still be meaningful today for modern readers?

The psalmist believes that God's sovereignty is more legitimate—and thus more defensible—than the claim to kingship of any earthly monarch, but Israel today has no earthly regent for the pious to revere. We continue to call God our Sovereign, but can moderns come to faith by embracing that aspect of divine reality? Can the contemplation of any earthly regent, even those few left with real political power, still serve as a stepping-stone towards the

2

Why are the nations so overwrought? Why are the peoples of the world sputtering such nonsense? [2] The kings of the earth have taken a stance, the rulers of the countries of the world conspiring together against יהוה and against the king, God's anointed prince.
[3] "Let us break our bonds," they have declared. "Let us cast off our chains."
[4] But God who dwells in heaven only laughs. Indeed, Adonai mocks them, [5] then, enraged, speaks to them and terrifies them with divine wrath by declaring: [6] "I have appointed My king on Zion, My holy mountain."
[7] And the king has his own story to relate. "Let me tell it precisely," he says. "'You are my son,' יהוה said to me. 'I have fathered you this very day. [8] Ask what you wish of Me and I shall grant it, for the nations of the world are your inheritance and the very ends of the earth are yours to possess. [9] You shall rule over them like a shepherd possessed of an iron staff. You shall crush them as a potter might smash a defective pot.'"
[10] Be wise, therefore, O kings; be chastened, O judges of the earth.
[11] Serve יהוה in awe; give yourselves over to joyful worship to the point of trembling.
[12] Adore the king God calls "son," lest God be enraged and you come to ruin, for it takes but little to kindle the wrath of the Almighty. Happy, on the other hand, are those who take refuge in God.

acquisition of faith in God? Or is thinking of the messianic age as a future era of divine sovereignty enough to lead us to accept God as the force for ordered governance in the world as it exists in its pre-redeemed state? In the end, the poet leaves us with a provocative question to consider: is the concept of divine sovereignty archaic and vestigial, or can it still function as a meaningful conceptual framework for citizens of modern, democratic states seeking to achieve communion with God?

ג

מִזְמוֹר לְדָוִד בְּבָרְחוֹ מִפְּנֵי ׀ אַבְשָׁלוֹם בְּנוֹ:

2 יְהוָה מָה־רַבּוּ צָרָי רַבִּים קָמִים עָלָי:

3 רַבִּים אֹמְרִים לְנַפְשִׁי אֵין יְשׁוּעָתָה לּוֹ בֵאלֹהִים סֶלָה:

4 וְאַתָּה יְהוָה מָגֵן בַּעֲדִי כְּבוֹדִי וּמֵרִים רֹאשִׁי:

5 קוֹלִי אֶל־יְהוָה אֶקְרָא וַיַּעֲנֵנִי מֵהַר קָדְשׁוֹ סֶלָה:

6 אֲנִי שָׁכַבְתִּי וָאִישָׁנָה הֱקִיצוֹתִי כִּי יְהוָה יִסְמְכֵנִי:

7 לֹא־אִירָא מֵרִבְבוֹת עָם אֲשֶׁר סָבִיב שָׁתוּ עָלָי:

8 קוּמָה יְהוָה ׀ הוֹשִׁיעֵנִי אֱלֹהַי כִּי־הִכִּיתָ אֶת־כָּל־אֹיְבַי לֶחִי שִׁנֵּי רְשָׁעִים שִׁבַּרְתָּ:

9 לַיהוָה הַיְשׁוּעָה עַל־עַמְּךָ בִרְכָתֶךָ סֶּלָה:

Most people seeking to find a life in God would consider it ideal to be surrounded on all sides by supportive, caring, and encouraging friends . . . and only slightly less ideal to be left alone to pursue the spiritual path towards communion with God in blissful solitude. The author of the third psalm, however, is neither surrounded by friends nor peacefully alone: he is dogged from every direction by enemies who oppose him, loathe him, and mock his longing for salvation in God as superstition and folly. In his terror, he invites his audience to think of him as a latter-day David fleeing Jerusalem when Absalom briefly gained the upper hand in his rebellion against his father's rule. David was enraged at his son's audacious behavior, but when Absalom later paid for his sedition with his life, David's tears were no less bitter than those of any bereaved father. Indeed, it seems plausible that the poet has chosen to recall this particular event in David's life because he felt himself to be in an analogous situation: he was totally enraged at his enemies not because they were strangers to him, but because they were people he would have preferred to like, even perhaps to love, and his anger was therefore tinged with sadness . . . and deep regret.

3

A psalm of David as he fled from Absalom, his son.

[2] O יהוה, how numerous are my foes! How many oppose me!

[3] How many insist that my life cannot be redeemed in God, *selah*!

[4] But You, יהוה, are a shield before me, my source of dignity and pride.

[5] It is to יהוה, who will answer me from the holy mountain of God, that I raise my voice in prayer, *selah*.

[6] I lay down and slept, then woke up when I felt יהוה pressing down on me.

[7] And so do I not fear the myriads who surround me, who have set themselves against me.

[8] Rise up, O יהוה. Deliver me, O my God, by striking my enemies' jaws and shattering the teeth of the wicked.

[9] For as salvation comes from יהוה, so may Your blessing come to Your people, *selah*.

People seeking a life in God often feel that they are laboring mightily for things the world insists it respects, yet actually considers quirky, slightly peculiar goals for normal people. Could the poet's prayer for the physical torment of his enemies be a literary echo of the frustration all people seeking a life in God feel when they first realize that they are on their own . . . and that the world is not only generally apathetic to spiritual yearning, but often overtly hostile to the kind of ritual activity or religious discipline that sets those who seek God apart from their co-citizens? Could the poet be responding to the slightly disorienting realization that most people—including many who would describe themselves as religious—prefer God to be both silent and invisible, no matter how loudly or emotionally they protest precisely to the contrary?

ד

לַמְנַצֵּחַ בִּנְגִינוֹת מִזְמוֹר לְדָוִד׃

2 בְּקָרְאִי עֲנֵנִי ׀ אֱלֹהֵי צִדְקִי בַּצָּר הִרְחַבְתָּ לִּי חָנֵּנִי וּשְׁמַע תְּפִלָּתִי׃

3 בְּנֵי־אִישׁ עַד־מֶה כְבוֹדִי לִכְלִמָּה תֶּאֱהָבוּן רִיק תְּבַקְשׁוּ כָזָב סֶלָה׃

4 וּדְעוּ כִּי־הִפְלָה יְהוָה חָסִיד לוֹ יְהוָה יִשְׁמַע בְּקָרְאִי אֵלָיו׃

5 רִגְזוּ וְאַל־תֶּחֱטָאוּ אִמְרוּ בִלְבַבְכֶם עַל־מִשְׁכַּבְכֶם וְדֹמּוּ סֶלָה׃

6 זִבְחוּ זִבְחֵי־צֶדֶק וּבִטְחוּ אֶל־יְהוָה׃

7 רַבִּים אֹמְרִים מִי־יַרְאֵנוּ טוֹב נְסָה־עָלֵינוּ אוֹר פָּנֶיךָ יְהוָה׃ 8 נָתַתָּה שִׂמְחָה בְלִבִּי מֵעֵת דְּגָנָם וְתִירוֹשָׁם רָבּוּ׃ 9 בְּשָׁלוֹם יַחְדָּו אֶשְׁכְּבָה וְאִישָׁן כִּי־אַתָּה יְהוָה לְבָדָד לָבֶטַח תּוֹשִׁיבֵנִי׃

For most people, belief in God alone doesn't make it any more bearable to compare a miserable present with a happy past.

The poet of the fourth psalm has a very good memory when it comes to spiritual matters. He recalls, for instance, how his faith in God was often sufficient to grant him respite from his woes in past times of trouble. He remembers the deep sense of gratitude to God he always feels when the new crop of grain or the year's new wine is brought to market. Indeed, it is precisely the recollection of that sense of profound, penetrating beholdenness that the poet appears to feel challenged to weigh against the current reality he encounters in the course of his daily life.

Mocked for his faith by men of fraudulent piety whose worship is prompted solely by the desire to get the Almighty to serve them in some way or another, the poet is both unnerved and sincerely moved by the beneficence of the God

4 For the choral conductor, a psalm of David.
[2] O my God of righteousness, answer me when I call out. Just as in the past You granted me relief when I was in dire straits, so now be gracious unto me and hear my prayer.
[3] O humanity that so loves emptiness and so ardently chases after falsehood, how long will my glorious soul know only shame, *selah*?
[4] Know rather that יהוה recognizes the faithful. יהוה will hear when I cry out.
[5] To those faithful, I say: Tremble, but do not sin! Say this in your hearts while you lie on your beds and otherwise be still, *selah*. [6] Offer sacrifices of righteousness and trust in יהוה.
[7] Many ask, "Who will show us goodness?" To them I respond by saying to God: Shine on us the light of Your face, O יהוה, [8]as You once put joy in my heart when there was a surfeit of grain and new wine. [9]Let me both lie down and sleep in peace, for You alone, O יהוה, can grant me safety.

who sustains him in his honest faith. And his point is as cogent as it is slightly encouraging: the very same God who so loathes self-serving false piety logically must also be the One that allows those few whose worship is truly prompted by sincere and honest faith to lie down in peace and sleep calmly through the night. Indeed, when the poet writes *imru vilvavkhem al mishkavkhem vedomu selah* ("Say this in your hearts while you lie on your beds and otherwise be still, *selah*"), he is signaling that his poem is a nighttime psalm to be recited by those who have come to realize that even something as seemingly ordinary as being possessed of the inner tranquility necessary to lie down at night and fall asleep peacefully is a gift from God and, as such, an appropriate focus for potentially productive meditation.

ה

לַמְנַצֵּחַ אֶל־הַנְּחִילוֹת מִזְמוֹר לְדָוִד׃

2 אֲמָרַי הַאֲזִינָה ׀ יְהֹוָה בִּינָה הֲגִיגִי׃ 3 הַקְשִׁיבָה
לְקוֹל שַׁוְעִי מַלְכִּי וֵאלֹהָי כִּי־אֵלֶיךָ אֶתְפַּלָּל׃
4 יְהֹוָה בֹּקֶר תִּשְׁמַע קוֹלִי בֹּקֶר אֶעֱרָךְ־לְךָ וַאֲצַפֶּה׃
5 כִּי ׀ לֹא אֵל חָפֵץ רֶשַׁע ׀ אָתָּה לֹא יְגֻרְךָ רָע׃
6 לֹא־יִתְיַצְּבוּ הוֹלְלִים לְנֶגֶד עֵינֶיךָ שָׂנֵאתָ
כָּל־פֹּעֲלֵי אָוֶן׃ 7 תְּאַבֵּד דֹּבְרֵי כָזָב אִישׁ־דָּמִים
וּמִרְמָה יְתָעֵב ׀ יְהֹוָה׃
8 וַאֲנִי בְּרֹב חַסְדְּךָ אָבוֹא בֵיתֶךָ אֶשְׁתַּחֲוֶה אֶל־הֵיכַל
קָדְשְׁךָ בְּיִרְאָתֶךָ׃
9 יְהֹוָה ׀ נְחֵנִי בְצִדְקָתֶךָ לְמַעַן שׁוֹרְרָי *הַיְשַׁר לְפָנַי
דַּרְכֶּךָ׃
10 כִּי אֵין בְּפִיהוּ נְכוֹנָה קִרְבָּם הַוּוֹת קֶבֶר־פָּתוּחַ
גְּרוֹנָם לְשׁוֹנָם יַחֲלִיקוּן׃

v. 9 הושר כתיב

The psalmist who wrote the poem we know as the fifth psalm lived a narrow existence hemmed in on one side by his abiding faith in God's goodness and mercy and, on the other, by a corrupt government of hypocritical, dishonest officials who (for reasons the poet delicately omits) are out for blood. The poet alludes only vaguely to the specifics of his situation, but even those few allusions paint a scary enough picture. *Kever patuaḥ geronam,* he writes: he has been denounced to the civil authorities by men whose "throats are gaping graves" that house not living truth, but decaying, putrid lies. And there is no end to the eloquence these false accusers can muster when they put their mind to denouncing the innocent. Indeed, the poet—himself no amateur when it comes to the effective use of language—writes almost comically of his libelers as devoting themselves to nothing so seriously as the making of their tongues smoothly eloquent. Worst of all is that the authorities have taken their slander seriously and have sent out agents to lie in wait, to observe the comings and goings of the poet, and to prepare the state's case against the psalmist as effectively as possible by watching to see what he does with the hours of his day. And what is it that the poet actually spends his days doing? He comes to the Temple and worships God as the Destroyer of falsehood, as the Enemy of liars, as the divine Loather of the arrogant, the boastful, and the morally depraved, and as the celestial Abhorrer of violence and deceit. The irony is exquisite, but the poet

5

For the conductor, to be accompanied on the *neḥilot,* a psalm of David.

[2] Give ear to my words, יהוה, and consider my thoughts. [3]Listen to the sound of my supplication, O my Sovereign, my God, for it is to You that I pray.

[4] יהוה, hear my voice in the morning, for it is in the morning that I set out my prayers before You and wait for Your response.

[5] You are not, after all, a God who wishes to be served with wickedness; indeed, You cannot abide evil. [6]The debauched cannot stand in Your sight; You loathe doers of iniquity. [7]You bring liars to ruin; O יהוה, the violent and the deceitful, You abhor.

[8] But as for me, I shall come to Your house imbued with a sense of the vastness of Your mercy. I shall bow down towards Your holy shrine imbued with the awe due You.

[9] יהוה, lead me forward in Your righteousness to save me from those who are watching me. Make straight Your path before me.

[10] For there is no honesty in their mouths; their innards are stuffed with schemes. Their throats are gaping graves; their only concern is making their lying tongues smoothly eloquent.

refuses to wallow in it, preferring to make his point far more effectively simply by praying aloud that God guide him to righteousness and straighten the path he seems destined to walk . . . whether he wishes to or not.

For all people of faith, God exists in many different roles and capacities, but it is not at all unusual for one of these aspects of divine reality to come to the fore in an individual's consciousness and become the touchstone of that person's personal belief system. And so it is for the poet, whose belief in God is total and complete, but for whom God exists in an especially potent and meaningful way as a source of refuge from the unfairness and villainy of the world. In short, the poet exists in an endless night of fear and disorientated worry, but remains convinced that God will be there when the night ends and dawn comes, and also that his prayers will be heard . . . and answered kindly and effectively in that longed-for morning.

[11] הַאֲשִׁימֵ֨ם ׀ אֱֽלֹהִ֗ים יִפְּלוּ֮ מִֽמֹּעֲצ֫וֹתֵ֥יהֶ֑ם בְּרֹ֣ב
פִּ֭שְׁעֵיהֶם הַדִּיחֵ֑מוֹ כִּי־מָ֥רוּ בָֽךְ׃
[12] וְיִשְׂמְח֨וּ כָל־ח֪וֹסֵי בָ֡ךְ לְעוֹלָ֣ם יְ֭רַנֵּנוּ וְתָסֵ֣ךְ עָלֵ֑ימוֹ
וְֽיַעְלְצ֥וּ בְ֝ךָ֗ אֹהֲבֵ֥י שְׁמֶֽךָ׃ [13] כִּֽי־אַתָּה֮ תְּבָרֵ֪ךְ צַ֫דִּ֥יק
יְהוָ֑ה כַּ֝צִּנָּ֗ה רָצ֥וֹן תַּעְטְרֶֽנּוּ׃

Although few modern readers will have had the experience of being arrested and indicted for crimes of which they are totally innocent, we may wish to react to the fifth psalm by considering our responses to specific disasters with which we have had to deal: living through the unwarranted loss of a job, suffering the death of a beloved parent, or enduring the searing pain that comes from rejection by a lover or (perhaps even worse) by a friend. No living person can permanently avoid misery, but the ancient poet has his spiritual descendants in those who find themselves drawn closer to faith in God by the troubles and travails of their lives. Readers

[11] Condemn them, O God, and make them fall from their lofty councils. Remove them because of their many sins, for they have rebelled against You.

[12] On the other hand, let all who seek refuge in You rejoice; may they forever be glad. May You shelter them, so that those who love Your name come to exult in You—[13]for You always bless the righteous, O יהוה. You crown them with favor as though it were a protective shield.

seeking to use the fifth psalm as the basis for meditation and purposeful introspection regarding their own religious lives, therefore, will want to test themselves against the poet's model and ask, if they find the results of their analysis troubling, why it is that they have failed to seek comfort in God precisely when they have needed it the most. At their most effective, the psalms can function as mirrors into which we moderns can peer to see ourselves all the more clearly . . . if we have the courage to look without flinching and to react honestly to what we see.

ו

לַמְנַצֵּ֣חַ בִּ֭נְגִינוֹת עַֽל־הַשְּׁמִינִ֗ית מִזְמ֥וֹר לְדָוִֽד׃
2 יְֽהוָ֗ה אַל־בְּאַפְּךָ֥ תוֹכִיחֵ֑נִי וְאַל־בַּחֲמָתְךָ֥ תְיַסְּרֵֽנִי׃
3 חָנֵּ֥נִי יְהוָה֮ כִּ֤י אֻמְלַ֫ל אָ֥נִי רְפָאֵ֥נִי יְהוָ֑ה כִּ֖י נִבְהֲל֣וּ
עֲצָמָֽי׃ 4 וְ֭נַפְשִׁי נִבְהֲלָ֣ה מְאֹ֑ד *וְאַתָּ֥ה יְ֝הוָ֗ה
עַד־מָתָֽי׃
5 שׁוּבָ֣ה יְ֭הוָה חַלְּצָ֣ה נַפְשִׁ֑י ה֝וֹשִׁיעֵ֗נִי לְמַ֣עַן חַסְדֶּֽךָ׃
6 כִּ֤י אֵ֣ין בַּמָּ֣וֶת זִכְרֶ֑ךָ בִּ֝שְׁא֗וֹל מִ֣י יֽוֹדֶה־לָּֽךְ׃
7 יָגַ֤עְתִּי בְּֽאַנְחָתִ֗י אַשְׂחֶ֣ה בְכָל־לַ֭יְלָה מִטָּתִ֑י
בְּ֝דִמְעָתִ֗י עַרְשִׂ֥י אַמְסֶֽה׃
8 עָֽשְׁשָׁ֣ה מִכַּ֣עַס עֵינִ֑י עָ֝תְקָ֗ה בְּכָל־צוֹרְרָֽי׃
9 ס֣וּרוּ מִ֭מֶּנִּי כָּל־פֹּ֣עֲלֵי אָ֑וֶן כִּֽי־שָׁמַ֥ע יְ֝הוָ֗ה ק֣וֹל
בִּכְיִֽי׃ 10 שָׁמַ֣ע יְ֭הוָה תְּחִנָּתִ֑י יְ֝הוָ֗ה תְּֽפִלָּתִ֥י יִקָּֽח׃
11 יֵבֹ֤שׁוּ וְיִבָּהֲל֣וּ מְ֭אֹד כָּל־אֹיְבָ֑י יָ֝שֻׁ֗בוּ יֵבֹ֥שׁוּ רָֽגַע׃

v. 4 ואת כתיב

The poet presents himself as a sick man lying in bed and contemplating the progress of his disease. His eyesight is becoming perceptibly worse with every successive day. He can hardly speak without groaning in pain. Tears flow freely from his eyes at the slightest provocation. He imagines he can actually feel his bones becoming brittle and weak as the tumors spread. Yet the poet/patient's disease has not destroyed his faith in God's healing power. On the contrary: the author of the sixth psalm implies with passion in his voice that his disease, for all it has ravaged his body, has only strengthened his faith and made him more, not less, secure in his belief that, in the end, true relief and real peace can only come from God.

Indeed, the jagged syntax of the poet's anguished cry, *ve'atah* יהוה *ad matai* ("How long will You . . . O יהוה!") can successfully inspire even the most

6

For the choral conductor, a psalm of David to be accompanied on the eight-stringed lyre.

[2] יהוה, neither rebuke me in Your anger nor cause me to suffer as a result of Your divine wrath.

[3] Instead, be gracious to me, O יהוה, for I am wretched. Heal me, יהוה, for I am terrified down to my bones; [4]even my soul is profoundly terrified. How long will You . . . O יהוה!

[5] Return, יהוה, and grant relief to my soul; save me for the sake of Your mercy.

[6] For there is no possibility of praising Your name after death; in Sheol, who will give thanks to You?

[7] My moaning has exhausted me; I drench my couch every evening so totally that I have practically melted my bed away with my tears.

[8] My eyesight is fading, actually wasting away, because of the anger I feel directed towards me by my foes.

[9] Depart from me, you doers of iniquity, for יהוה has heard the sound of my crying. [10]יהוה has heard my supplication; יהוה shall accept my prayer.

[11] May all my enemies be ashamed and terrified; may they relent and, even just for a moment, be ashamed.

jaded readers to confront and consider the way we moderns tend to think about illness. Does the fear of sickness bring us closer to God? Does illness itself make us more or less certain that God is the ultimate source of healing? Do we think of ill health as the curse it appears at first blush to be? Or could infirmity, as something that has the potential to bring people closer to God, be some kind of subtle blessing? To long for sickness is insane, but the glory of intelligence suffused with faith lies precisely in the human ability to derive spiritual benefit even from the least wanted burden.

ז

שִׁגָּיוֹן לְדָוִד אֲשֶׁר־שָׁר לַיהוָה עַל־דִּבְרֵי־כוּשׁ בֶּן־יְמִינִי:
2 יְהוָה אֱלֹהַי בְּךָ חָסִיתִי הוֹשִׁיעֵנִי מִכָּל־רֹדְפַי וְהַצִּילֵנִי: 3 פֶּן־יִטְרֹף כְּאַרְיֵה נַפְשִׁי פֹּרֵק וְאֵין מַצִּיל:
4 יְהוָה אֱלֹהַי אִם־עָשִׂיתִי זֹאת אִם־יֶשׁ־עָוֶל בְּכַפָּי:
5 אִם־גָּמַלְתִּי שׁוֹלְמִי רָע וָאֲחַלְּצָה צוֹרְרִי רֵיקָם:
6 יִרַדֹּף אוֹיֵב ׀ נַפְשִׁי וְיַשֵּׂג וְיִרְמֹס לָאָרֶץ חַיָּי וּכְבוֹדִי ׀ לֶעָפָר יַשְׁכֵּן סֶלָה:
7 קוּמָה יְהוָה ׀ בְּאַפֶּךָ הִנָּשֵׂא בְּעַבְרוֹת צוֹרְרָי וְעוּרָה אֵלַי מִשְׁפָּט צִוִּיתָ:
8 וַעֲדַת לְאֻמִּים תְּסוֹבְבֶךָּ וְעָלֶיהָ לַמָּרוֹם שׁוּבָה:
9 יְהוָה יָדִין עַמִּים שָׁפְטֵנִי יְהוָה כְּצִדְקִי וּכְתֻמִּי עָלָי:
10 יִגְמָר־נָא רַע ׀ רְשָׁעִים וּתְכוֹנֵן צַדִּיק וּבֹחֵן לִבּוֹת וּכְלָיוֹת אֱלֹהִים צַדִּיק:
11 מָגִנִּי עַל־אֱלֹהִים מוֹשִׁיעַ יִשְׁרֵי־לֵב:

Who precisely the poet had in mind when he imagined his poem as an ode that David might have sung to Cush the Benjaminite is not known, but the ancient rabbis thought that he might have meant us to think of Saul, who was indeed of the tribe of Benjamin and whose father was named Kish. There is, however, no way to know with any certainty if that was the poet's intention and, although some of the details in the poem do indeed match the story of David and Saul, others just as clearly do not. In any case, the poet has an enemy who will stop at nothing to bring him down as he pursues him with the vigor and enthusiasm of a ravenous lion chasing after a defenseless antelope in the wild. The poet stops just short of saying why precisely his foe loathes him so intensely, but we do learn that the foe's hatred is groundless and totally unwarranted . . . and that it cannot possibly be justified as a reasonable response to anything the poet has done or any crime he may have actually committed. We also learn that the poet is certain that God punishes people like his foe by bringing their evil plans crashing down on their own heads, by having them fall into pits they have dug as traps for others, and by having their complex, dastardly plots eventually give birth to the kind of falsehood and dishonesty that end up ruining their own lives. Moreover, the poet asserts that God has an arsenal of weapons at the ready to use to bring down those who earn the wrath of the divine Judge and that this

7 A *shigayon* hymn that David sang to יהוה in response to the words of Cush the Benjaminite.

[2] יהוה, my God, I have sought refuge in You;
deliver me from all my pursuers and save me—
[3]lest he, their leader, tear me apart like a lion
might his prey, lest he break me into pieces
and there be none to save me.

[4] O יהוה, my God, if I have done this sin of which I have been accused, if there is wrongdoing in my hands, [5]if I have dealt unfairly with the one who now wishes to do me ill, that one of my foes whom I once pointlessly rescued, [6]then let my enemy pursue my soul and seize it; let him fling me to the ground and trample the life out of me, so that he forces my glorious soul to dwell forever in the dust, *selah.*

[7] Rise up, יהוה, in divine rage. Come forward in anger against my enemies and carry out on my behalf the verdict You have decreed.

[8] Should the assembly of peoples surround You to denounce me, simply return to heaven without heeding their plea.

[9] May יהוה render a just verdict against the nations, but may יהוה judge me in accordance with my innocence and my guilelessness.

[10] Would that evil itself could finish off the wicked and the righteous be established, for God, who knows the innermost secrets of the human heart and mind, is just.

[11] I rely on God, my shield, the Savior of the upright of heart.

arsenal includes arrows, swords, bows, and assorted other "instruments of death."

The depth of the poet's anger is palpable and, in its own way, deeply provocative: surely, most will think, a deeply religious man should pray for his enemy's conversion to the way of goodness and tolerance rather than for his annihilation at the hands of the *El zo'em,* the furious God of unbridled rage! Without knowing what led the poet to pen his ode to divine vengeance, however, readers should be cautious in forming strong opinions about the validity of his emotional plea for revenge. Nevertheless, the contemplation of this psalm can be spiritually productive if it prompts us to reconsider the timid, half-

12 אֱלֹהִים שׁוֹפֵט צַדִּיק וְאֵל זֹעֵם בְּכָל־יוֹם׃
13 אִם־לֹא יָשׁוּב חַרְבּוֹ יִלְטוֹשׁ קַשְׁתּוֹ דָרַךְ וַיְכוֹנְנֶהָ׃
14 וְלוֹ הֵכִין כְּלֵי־מָוֶת חִצָּיו לְדֹלְקִים יִפְעָל׃
15 הִנֵּה יְחַבֶּל־אָוֶן וְהָרָה עָמָל וְיָלַד שָׁקֶר׃
16 בּוֹר כָּרָה וַיַּחְפְּרֵהוּ וַיִּפֹּל בְּשַׁחַת יִפְעָל׃
17 יָשׁוּב עֲמָלוֹ בְרֹאשׁוֹ וְעַל־קָדְקֳדוֹ חֲמָסוֹ יֵרֵד׃
18 אוֹדֶה יְהוָה כְּצִדְקוֹ וַאֲזַמְּרָה שֵׁם־יְהוָה עֶלְיוֹן׃

hearted way society generally responds to pure evil in the world. There are, after all, many elaborate government-funded programs designed to rehabilitate criminals and return them to society "cured" of their propensity to do wrong, but the poet's words dare us to evaluate how society responds to those so utterly given over to sin that rehabilitation is not a viable option. With the example of the Shoah to contemplate, surely no decent person need profess uncertainty that pure

[12] God is a righteous Judge, a furious God who dispenses justice every day, [13] a God who, should the guilty not repent, will sharpen the divine sword to mete out justice, a God who will bend and make ready the divine bow.

[14] God has prepared instruments of death for such a guilty party, even transforming plain arrows into flaming ones.

[15] Behold, the sinner plots wrongdoing; he conceives treachery and gives birth to lies.

[16] He digs a pit and makes it deep, then falls into the trap he himself has fashioned.

[17] His plots come back onto his own head, his violent schemes landing on his own skull.

[18] But I shall give thanks to יהוה in accordance with God's justice; in song shall I celebrate the name of יהוה Most High.

evil might actually exist in the world. Why is it then, the poet prompts us to ask, that otherwise savvy, sophisticated citizens of the world are so strangely timid about responding to absolute evil with unyielding, uninhibited fury?

לַמְנַצֵּחַ עַל־הַגִּתִּית מִזְמוֹר לְדָוִד׃
2 יְהוָה אֲדֹנֵינוּ מָה־אַדִּיר שִׁמְךָ בְּכָל־הָאָרֶץ
אֲשֶׁר־תְּנָה הוֹדְךָ עַל־הַשָּׁמָיִם׃
3 מִפִּי עוֹלְלִים ׀ וְיֹנְקִים יִסַּדְתָּ עֹז לְמַעַן צוֹרְרֶיךָ
לְהַשְׁבִּית אוֹיֵב וּמִתְנַקֵּם׃
4 כִּי־אֶרְאֶה שָׁמֶיךָ מַעֲשֵׂי אֶצְבְּעֹתֶיךָ יָרֵחַ וְכוֹכָבִים
אֲשֶׁר כּוֹנָנְתָּה׃ 5 מָה־אֱנוֹשׁ כִּי־תִזְכְּרֶנּוּ וּבֶן־אָדָם
כִּי תִפְקְדֶנּוּ׃
6 וַתְּחַסְּרֵהוּ מְּעַט מֵאֱלֹהִים וְכָבוֹד וְהָדָר תְּעַטְּרֵהוּ׃
7 תַּמְשִׁילֵהוּ בְּמַעֲשֵׂי יָדֶיךָ כֹּל שַׁתָּה תַחַת־רַגְלָיו׃
8 צֹנֶה וַאֲלָפִים כֻּלָּם וְגַם בַּהֲמוֹת שָׂדָי׃ 9 צִפּוֹר
שָׁמַיִם וּדְגֵי הַיָּם עֹבֵר אָרְחוֹת יַמִּים׃
10 יְהוָה אֲדֹנֵינוּ מָה־אַדִּיר שִׁמְךָ בְּכָל־הָאָרֶץ׃

The psalmist who wrote the eighth psalm looks out at the world and is overcome with the majesty of God's creation. The sun, the moon, and the stars in the heavens, the oxen and sheep in the fields, the fish in the sea, the birds flying overhead in the blue sky—all these things merely make the poet more confirmed in his conviction that God made the world. Of all the various things of the world, however, nothing surpasses, or even comes close to surpassing, the wonder that is the human being. Indeed, even a tiny baby that can neither speak nor walk reminds the poet that no foe, no matter how formidable, can ever best the God who created human beings only slightly less splendid than angels.

The poet is not only speaking *of* the world, however, but also *to* the world. And, indeed, the majestic words with which the poet begins and ends his poem, *mah adir shimkha bekhol ha'aretz* ("How mighty is Your name in all the earth"), prompt us almost unavoidably, even after millennia, to evaluate the nature of our belief in God the Creator. Is this belief mere dogma or a self-evident truth that comes to us directly from our contemplation of the world? Given that our world differs from the psalmist's only in the most superficial, cosmetic ways and that the glories of nature—the majestic heavens and the

8 For the conductor, a psalm of David to be accompanied on the *gittit.*

[2] יהוה, our Ruler, how mighty is Your name in all the earth; how mighty are You, You who have set Your splendor over the heavens.

[3] You begin to make manifest Your might with the first breaths of infants and nursing babes, acting so early on because of Your foes to defuse enemy and avenger.

[4] When I see Your heavens—the work of Your fingers, the moon and stars that You have established—I cannot but exclaim, [5]"What are human beings that You should remember them, the children of Adam that You should even take note of them?"

[6] Nevertheless, You have made humans just a little less marvelous than divine beings, crowning them with glory and splendor.

[7] Indeed, You have granted them the right to rule over the work of Your hands, over all that You have placed beneath their feet: [8]sheep and oxen and all other animals, even the beasts of the field and [9]the birds of the heavens and the fish of the sea, everything that swims through the ocean's currents.

[10] יהוה, our Ruler, how mighty is Your name in all the earth.

endless sea, for example—remain now just as they were then, the challenge laid down by the poet's great enthusiasm for God will sound no less provocative to moderns than it presumably did to the psalmist's original audience. Moderns unsure how exactly to respond to that challenge would do well to begin by considering the question that is at the heart of the matter: do we consider the splendors of the natural universe to be baubles to admire (sometimes) and ignore (mostly), or do we take them seriously as rungs on the ladder that human beings—armed only with their sensory ability to perceive and decipher the world—can climb towards communion with God the Creator?

ט

לַמְנַצֵּחַ עַלְמוּת לַבֵּן מִזְמוֹר לְדָוִד׃
2 אוֹדֶה יְהוָה בְּכָל־לִבִּי אֲסַפְּרָה כָּל־נִפְלְאוֹתֶיךָ׃
3 אֶשְׂמְחָה וְאֶעֶלְצָה בָךְ אֲזַמְּרָה שִׁמְךָ עֶלְיוֹן׃
4 בְּשׁוּב־אוֹיְבַי אָחוֹר יִכָּשְׁלוּ וְיֹאבְדוּ מִפָּנֶיךָ׃
5 כִּי־עָשִׂיתָ מִשְׁפָּטִי וְדִינִי יָשַׁבְתָּ לְכִסֵּא שׁוֹפֵט צֶדֶק׃
6 גָּעַרְתָּ גוֹיִם אִבַּדְתָּ רָשָׁע שְׁמָם מָחִיתָ לְעוֹלָם וָעֶד׃
7 הָאוֹיֵב ׀ תַּמּוּ חֳרָבוֹת לָנֶצַח וְעָרִים נָתַשְׁתָּ אָבַד זִכְרָם הֵמָּה׃
8 וַיהוָה לְעוֹלָם יֵשֵׁב כּוֹנֵן לַמִּשְׁפָּט כִּסְאוֹ׃ 9 וְהוּא יִשְׁפֹּט־תֵּבֵל בְּצֶדֶק יָדִין לְאֻמִּים בְּמֵישָׁרִים׃
10 וִיהִי יְהוָה מִשְׂגָּב לַדָּךְ מִשְׂגָּב לְעִתּוֹת בַּצָּרָה׃
11 וְיִבְטְחוּ בְךָ יוֹדְעֵי שְׁמֶךָ כִּי לֹא־עָזַבְתָּ דֹרְשֶׁיךָ יְהוָה׃
12 זַמְּרוּ לַיהוָה יֹשֵׁב צִיּוֹן הַגִּידוּ בָעַמִּים עֲלִילוֹתָיו׃
13 כִּי־דֹרֵשׁ דָּמִים אוֹתָם זָכָר לֹא־שָׁכַח צַעֲקַת *עֲנָוִים׃
14 חָנְנֵנִי יְהוָה רְאֵה עָנְיִי מִשֹּׂנְאָי מְרוֹמְמִי מִשַּׁעֲרֵי מָוֶת׃ 15 לְמַעַן אֲסַפְּרָה כָּל־תְּהִלָּתֶיךָ בְּשַׁעֲרֵי בַת־צִיּוֹן אָגִילָה בִּישׁוּעָתֶךָ׃

v. 13 עניים כתיב

We tend to think of geopolitics as a modern concern, but the ancient world was no less alive with politics and political intrigue than is our world today. Indeed, the world in which the psalmists lived and labored had its superpowers and client states, its uneven balance between dominator countries and their victim nations, its uneasy alliances between parties of unequal strength, and its hopeful unions of smaller states hoping to accomplish with diplomacy what none of them could ever manage to achieve with military might. The psalmist, looking out at the world and surveying its complex set of political alliances and intrigues, is visited by the sudden realization that any number of political realities could successfully be expressed as spiritual truths as well. He notes that nations, for all their bluster, seem to come and go, leaving behind ruined cities and legacies so flimsy that, even a generation or two later, no one can quite recall those nations' official names. Furthermore, the poet realizes that, more often than not, the nations of the world end up vanishing into the whirlwind of history as a result of wars they themselves have provoked. *Tav'u goyim beshaḥat asu,* he writes: these nations dig pits carefully, subtly, with the

9

For the conductor, a psalm of David to the tune of "On the Death of the Son."

[2] I shall give thanks to יהוה with all my heart; I shall tell all Your wonders.

[3] I shall rejoice and exult in You; I shall sing of Your name, O Most High.

[4] When my enemies retreat, they stumble and disappear from Your presence [5]because You have executed justice and judgment for me; You sit on the throne of a righteous judge.

[6] You scold nations and destroy the wicked; You erase their names for ever and always.

[7] The enemy is utterly gone, their camps are eternal ruins; because You uprooted their cities, their memory is permanently lost.

[8] But יהוה will sit enthroned forever, readying the divine throne for judgment, [9]then judging the world in righteousness and rendering a just verdict to the peoples of the earth.

[10] And so is יהוה a refuge for the downtrodden, a refuge in times of trouble; [11]therefore do those who know Your name trust in You, for You will never abandon any who seek You, O יהוה.

[12] Sing to יהוה, who dwells in Zion; tell God's deeds among the nations, [13]for the One who requites spilt blood will remember the suffering of the miserable and will not forget their cries.

[14] Be gracious unto me, יהוה, and see my suffering at the hands of those who hate me; lift me up from the gates of death, [15]that I might sing all Your praises in the gates of Daughter-of-Zion, that I might rejoice in Your salvation.

greatest skill . . . and then fall right into them and drown, disappearing without ever finding the strength to climb out and reestablish themselves with any lasting success.

It is the poet's special insight to realize that this aspect of the fate of nations is actually quite similar to the fate of the wicked of the world who plot mischief and carry it out, only to be swept away in the swift currents of violence they themselves have unleashed. Indeed, the poet wishes to assert that God governs the world precisely by allowing both individuals and nations to come to faith or to distance themselves from it at will. They can thus either provide themselves with permanence or deprive themselves of any possibility of per-

16 טָֽבְע֣וּ ג֭וֹיִם בְּשַׁ֣חַת עָשׂ֑וּ בְּרֶֽשֶׁת־ז֥וּ טָ֝מָ֗נוּ נִלְכְּדָ֥ה רַגְלָֽם׃
17 נ֤וֹדַ֨ע ׀ יְהוָה֮ מִשְׁפָּ֪ט עָ֫שָׂ֥ה בְּפֹ֣עַל כַּ֭פָּיו נוֹקֵ֣שׁ רָשָׁ֑ע הִגָּי֥וֹן סֶֽלָה׃
18 יָ֣שׁ֣וּבוּ רְשָׁעִ֣ים לִשְׁא֑וֹלָה כָּל־גּ֝וֹיִ֗ם שְׁכֵחֵ֥י אֱלֹהִֽים׃
19 כִּ֤י לֹ֣א לָ֭נֶצַח יִשָּׁכַ֣ח אֶבְי֑וֹן תִּקְוַ֥ת *עֲ֝נִיִּ֗ים תֹּאבַ֥ד לָעַֽד׃
20 קוּמָ֣ה יְ֭הוָה אַל־יָעֹ֣ז אֱנ֑וֹשׁ יִשָּׁפְט֥וּ ג֝וֹיִ֗ם עַל־פָּנֶֽיךָ׃
21 שִׁ֘יתָ֤ה יְהוָ֨ה ׀ מוֹרָ֗ה לָ֫הֶ֥ם יֵדְע֥וּ ג֑וֹיִם אֱנ֖וֹשׁ הֵ֣מָּה סֶּֽלָה׃

v. 19 ענוים כתיב

manence by embracing or rejecting the only true source of constancy in the world: the Eternal One who is the Author of history, yet whose own existence is, by definition, extrahistorical. And as it once was, so is it still: in our own day, the greatest powers have imposed themselves on the world, only to be swept away within years in wars they themselves began. Does the contemplation of the fates of those

[16]The nations have drowned in a pit they themselves once dug; their own feet are ensnared in a net they themselves hid.

[17] יהוה executes judgment and becomes known in the world when the wicked individual is ensnared by the work of his own hands, *higayon selah.*

[18]The wicked shall descend straight to Sheol together with all those nations who have forgotten God, [19]for the destitute shall not be forgotten forever nor shall the hopes of the miserable always be for naught.

[20]Rise up, יהוה, and let not humanity become too arrogant; indeed, may the nations be judged before You.

[21] Instill a sense of fear in them, O יהוה; may the nations come to know that they are naught but mortal beings, *selah.*

nations bring us closer to God? Or do we find our faith weakened by the fact that these depraved regimes came into existence in the first place? In the end, do we moderns find greater satisfaction seeking God *in* history . . . or blaming God *for* history?

י לָמָה יְהוָה תַּעֲמֹד בְּרָחוֹק תַּעְלִים לְעִתּוֹת בַּצָּרָה:

2 בְּגַאֲוַת־רָשָׁע יִדְלַק עָנִי יִתָּפְשׂוּ ׀ בִּמְזִמּוֹת זוּ
חָשָׁבוּ:

3 כִּי־הִלֵּל רָשָׁע עַל־תַּאֲוַת נַפְשׁוֹ וּבֹצֵעַ בֵּרֵךְ נִאֵץ ׀
יְהוָה:

4 רָשָׁע כְּגֹבַהּ אַפּוֹ בַּל־יִדְרֹשׁ אֵין אֱלֹהִים
כָּל־מְזִמּוֹתָיו:

5 יָחִילוּ *דְרָכָיו ׀ בְּכָל־עֵת מָרוֹם מִשְׁפָּטֶיךָ מִנֶּגְדּוֹ
כָּל־צוֹרְרָיו יָפִיחַ בָּהֶם:

6 אָמַר בְּלִבּוֹ בַּל־אֶמּוֹט לְדֹר וָדֹר אֲשֶׁר לֹא־בְרָע:

7 אָלָה פִּיהוּ מָלֵא וּמִרְמוֹת וָתֹךְ תַּחַת לְשׁוֹנוֹ עָמָל
וָאָוֶן:

8 יֵשֵׁב ׀ בְּמַאְרַב חֲצֵרִים בַּמִּסְתָּרִים יַהֲרֹג נָקִי עֵינָיו
לְחֵלְכָה יִצְפֹּנוּ:

9 יֶאֱרֹב בַּמִּסְתָּר ׀ כְּאַרְיֵה בְסֻכֹּה יֶאֱרֹב לַחֲטוֹף עָנִי
יַחְטֹף עָנִי בְּמָשְׁכוֹ בְרִשְׁתּוֹ:

10 *יִדְכֶּה יָשֹׁחַ וְנָפַל בַּעֲצוּמָיו *חֵיל כָּאִים:

v. 5 דרכו כתיב

v. 10 ודכה כתיב, חלכאים כתיב

Given that the tenth psalm has no superscription, that the ninth and tenth psalms taken together appear to present a single acrostic poem (albeit a corrupted one), and that the ancient Greek version of the Bible presents both poems as a single literary unit, it would be reasonable to consider the tenth psalm merely to be the end of the ninth. However, one could also make a rational case for considering it on its own merits and evaluating its eighteen verses as a poetical work unto itself. For one thing, that is how tradition has bequeathed it to us. And although the tenth psalm shares the ninth's fascination with the way God rules the affairs of the world while still granting humanity the right to choose between good and evil, this poem has an entirely different focus: the ninth psalm is largely concerned with the fate of hostile nations, while the tenth is specifically focused on the nature and fate of the wicked individual. Indeed, the description of the wicked in the tenth psalm is one of the most developed and interesting in the entire Psalter and puts forth the theory that villainy in all its various manifestations invariably springs from one single principle that has taken root in the hearts of villains: that there is no God. From this one idea, the poet suggests, flow the rest of villains' most cherished beliefs: that laws universally consid-

10

Why do You stand at a distance, יהוה? Why do You hide Yourself in times of trouble?

[2] The wicked may arrogantly pursue the poor, but they will end up ensnared in the very plots they devise.

[3] Thus, when the wicked individual utters some words of formal praise to God for having fulfilled some depraved desire, or if he should break bread and say a blessing, all he really does is scorn יהוה.

[4] The wicked individual, consumed by arrogance and anger, will never seek God; indeed, at the base of all his wicked plots is one single principle: there is no God.

[5] And what else of this wicked individual? His ways continually prosper. He considers Your laws to be too ethereal for his consideration. As for his enemies, his total concern is to snort now and then in their direction.

[6] He says in his heart, "I shall never totter; indeed, I shall endure from generation to generation and not face retribution."

[7] His mouth is filled with oaths that are naught but fraud and deceit; beneath his tongue fester oppression and iniquity.

[8] He sits hidden in secret ambush in obscure courtyards, the better to murder the innocent and fix his eyes on the helpless.

[9] He lies in wait in a secret place like a lion camouflaged in its lair, lying in wait until the opportunity presents itself to seize a poor person; he can seize a poor person simply by pulling in his net.

[10] He stoops down and creeps forward, the better to fall on the helpless with his gang of thugs.

ered to be of divine origin do not concern them, that they bear no responsibility to others of God's creatures, that their success in life is (and always will be) the result of their own ability to impose their will on others. The rest of their sins—the fraud, calumny, and violence, the willingness to ambush and kidnap, the disregard for the plight of the orphan, the bogus benedictions and phony, hypocritical prayers—are also all functions of this single principle. Indeed, when the psalmist writes *ein elohim kol mezimotav* ("at the base of all his wicked plots is one single principle: there is no God"),

11 אָמַר בְּלִבּוֹ שָׁכַח אֵל הִסְתִּיר פָּנָיו בַּל־רָאָה לָנֶצַח׃
12 קוּמָה יְהוָה אֵל נְשָׂא יָדֶךָ אַל־תִּשְׁכַּח *עֲנָוִים׃
13 עַל־מֶה ׀ נִאֵץ רָשָׁע ׀ אֱלֹהִים אָמַר בְּלִבּוֹ לֹא תִּדְרֹשׁ׃
14 רָאִתָה כִּי־אַתָּה ׀ עָמָל וָכַעַס ׀ תַּבִּיט לָתֵת בְּיָדֶךָ עָלֶיךָ יַעֲזֹב חֵלְכָה יָתוֹם אַתָּה ׀ הָיִיתָ עוֹזֵר׃
15 שְׁבֹר זְרוֹעַ רָשָׁע וָרָע תִּדְרוֹשׁ־רִשְׁעוֹ בַל־תִּמְצָא׃
16 יְהוָה מֶלֶךְ עוֹלָם וָעֶד אָבְדוּ גוֹיִם מֵאַרְצוֹ׃
17 תַּאֲוַת עֲנָוִים שָׁמַעְתָּ יְהוָה תָּכִין לִבָּם תַּקְשִׁיב אָזְנֶךָ׃ 18 לִשְׁפֹּט יָתוֹם וָדָךְ בַּל־יוֹסִיף עוֹד לַעֲרֹץ אֱנוֹשׁ מִן־הָאָרֶץ׃

v. 12 ענוים כתיב

he is merely provoking us to ask if we truly believe that crime is what results when an individual refuses to accept the reality of God into his or her life. If not, how do we explain the willingness of so many people in the world to be cruel, even merciless, and to inflict almost indescribable suffering on others, often without even a twinge of conscience? Reading the tenth psalm provides a chance to ask ourselves a simple, profound question: what is it, other than behavior, that actually distinguishes the saint from the fiend?

[11] He says in his heart, "God has forgotten to note my misdeeds and has turned away the divine face; God will never see a thing."

[12] Rise up, O יהוה; God, lift up Your hand and forget not the humble.

[13] Wherein has the evil individual scorned God? In that he has said in his heart that You will not investigate his doings.

[14] You surely see the trouble and anger they cause; You surely see more than enough to give them a slap with Your hand. The helpless rely on You; You are the One who helps orphans.

[15] Break the arms of the wicked; search out their wickedness until there is no more to find.

[16] יהוה is Sovereign for ever and always; the heathen nations are vanished from God's land.

[17] You will listen to the desires of the humble, O יהוה; ready their hearts and let Your ears hear their plea [18]so that You may decide for the orphan and the downtrodden. May the wicked no longer terrorize any of this earth.

יא

לַמְנַצֵּחַ לְדָוִד
בַּיהוָה ׀ חָסִיתִי אֵיךְ תֹּאמְרוּ לְנַפְשִׁי *נוּדִי הַרְכֶם
צִפּוֹר:
2 כִּי הִנֵּה הָרְשָׁעִים יִדְרְכוּן קֶשֶׁת כּוֹנְנוּ חִצָּם עַל-
יֶתֶר לִירוֹת בְּמוֹ-אֹפֶל לְיִשְׁרֵי-לֵב: 3 כִּי-הַשָּׁתוֹת
יֵהָרֵסוּן צַדִּיק מַה-פָּעָל:
4 יְהוָה ׀ בְּהֵיכַל קָדְשׁוֹ יְהוָה בַּשָּׁמַיִם כִּסְאוֹ עֵינָיו
יֶחֱזוּ עַפְעַפָּיו יִבְחֲנוּ בְּנֵי אָדָם:
5 יְהוָה צַדִּיק יִבְחָן וְרָשָׁע וְאֹהֵב חָמָס שָׂנְאָה נַפְשׁוֹ:
6 יַמְטֵר עַל-רְשָׁעִים פַּחִים אֵשׁ וְגָפְרִית וְרוּחַ
זִלְעָפוֹת מְנָת כּוֹסָם:
7 כִּי-צַדִּיק יְהוָה צְדָקוֹת אָהֵב יָשָׁר יֶחֱזוּ פָנֵימוֹ:

v. 1 נודו כתיב

A shot rings out in the night from a villain's unseen hiding place. A decent citizen, a mother of four walking peacefully in the street, falls to the ground dead. In a moment, her earrings and her wallet are gone, as well as her wedding band and the silver locket with the pictures of her parents she had lately taken to wearing around her neck. For her family, her death is a tragedy. For the law enforcement officials of her city, it is a challenge. For her murderer, it is part of a night's work either to be regretted later on or not. For the rest of the world, it is a horror to be read about, bemoaned, and then explained away as just another instance of senseless urban mayhem. For the pious, however, the news of her death initiates a series of different questions. Does God rule the world? (But if so, then why are innocent women murdered for their jewelry?) Does God reward the righteous and punish the wicked? (But if so, why do the police so often fail to make any arrests in cases of random, unprovoked violence?) Does religious faith require that we maintain our belief that the world was fashioned by a

11 For the conductor, a psalm of David.

Since you know I find my refuge in יהוה, why do you address me as though I were a scared little bird, saying, "Flee to your mountain aerie, birdie"?

[2–3] For what can the righteous do when evil men are already bending their bows and positioning their arrows on taut cords as they prepare to shoot at the decent in the dark, when the foundations of goodness are already crumbling all around them?

[4] They can have faith that יהוה, who resides in the holy Temple—יהוה, whose throne is in heaven—is possessed of eyes that see more than well enough to test the mettle of Adam's descendants.

[5] And that יהוה, testing the righteous, but loathing the wicked and those who love violence, [6] will rain down hot coals, fire, and sulphur on the wicked. Thus shall winds of terror be their lot.

[7] But in that יהוה, being righteous, loves righteousness in others, their faces shall yet behold our upright God.

God who is its never-failing source of goodness and justice? (But if it does, then why does God allow the world to appear, at least sometimes, to be totally devoid of both?) The psalmist's response to each set of questions is simply to embrace both possibilities and refuse to flee to the sanctuary of disbelief like a scared little bird. His psalm urges us to accept that paradox is not the enemy of faith, but something that can propel us to new levels of insight into a God who is not bound by the rules of logic that govern the world below. Seeking refuge in faith need not be a way of ignoring the world or distancing ourselves from it, but it can be a way of deciphering the world . . . and, ultimately, of seeking the Creator through the contemplation of creation in all its great complexity and infuriating, maddening inconsistency.

לַמְנַצֵּחַ עַל־הַשְּׁמִינִית מִזְמוֹר לְדָוִד׃
2 הוֹשִׁיעָה יְהוָה כִּי־גָמַר חָסִיד כִּי־פַסּוּ אֱמוּנִים
מִבְּנֵי אָדָם׃ 3 שָׁוְא ׀ יְדַבְּרוּ אִישׁ אֶת־רֵעֵהוּ שְׂפַת
חֲלָקוֹת בְּלֵב וָלֵב יְדַבֵּרוּ׃
4 יַכְרֵת יְהוָה כָּל־שִׂפְתֵי חֲלָקוֹת לָשׁוֹן מְדַבֶּרֶת
גְּדֹלוֹת׃ 5 אֲשֶׁר אָמְרוּ ׀ לִלְשֹׁנֵנוּ נַגְבִּיר שְׂפָתֵינוּ
אִתָּנוּ מִי אָדוֹן לָנוּ׃
6 מִשֹּׁד עֲנִיִּים מֵאַנְקַת אֶבְיוֹנִים עַתָּה אָקוּם יֹאמַר
יְהוָה אָשִׁית בְּיֵשַׁע יָפִיחַ לוֹ׃
7 אִמֲרוֹת יְהוָה אֲמָרוֹת טְהֹרוֹת כֶּסֶף צָרוּף בַּעֲלִיל
לָאָרֶץ מְזֻקָּק שִׁבְעָתָיִם׃
8 אַתָּה יְהוָה תִּשְׁמְרֵם תִּצְּרֶנּוּ ׀ מִן־הַדּוֹר זוּ לְעוֹלָם׃
9 סָבִיב רְשָׁעִים יִתְהַלָּכוּן כְּרֻם זֻלֻּת לִבְנֵי אָדָם׃

The combination of hypocrisy and eloquence is especially potent in the wicked. The poet knows this and declares his enemies to be both duplicitous liars who speak "out of both sides of their hearts"—the biblical equivalent of speaking out of both sides of one's mouth—and also smooth, effective orators who have allowed their talents to overwhelm their humility to the extent that they can ponder their own oratory skills and then, forgetting God, ask: *mi adon lanu* ("Who could ever be our master?").

The Bible suggests that Adam established his mastery over the beasts by naming them. The idea sounds reasonable precisely because we realize that the way to conquer anything—even an inchoate fear or anxiety—is to name it . . . and thus deny it the terrifying format of the unnamed, the unidentified, or the unspecified. The power inherent in the ability to speak, therefore, is awesome. Indeed, one of the reasons the Bible teaches us that God created the world with a word is to remind us that no tool as potent as language has ever been devised or will ever be invented. For his part, though, the poet is interested in comparing the speech of the wicked with the speech of God. He notes that the former speak in order to dominate the world by bringing the people

12 For the conductor, a psalm of David to be accompanied on the eight-stringed lyre.

[2] Grant salvation, יהוה, for the pious are lacking, for faith is vanished from humanity; [3]people, speaking out of both sides of their hearts at the same time, speak dishonestly to each other in a language of smoothly spoken lies.

[4] May יהוה cut off such smooth-talking lips and such boastful tongues [5]that say: "With our eloquence, we shall prevail. With skill at language such as ours, who could ever be our master?"

[6] יהוה says, "I shall now respond to the plunder of the poor, to the groaning of the poverty-stricken. I shall grant salvation to those who are the most rudely insulted."

[7] The words of יהוה are pure words, no less pure than refined silver purified seventy times over in an earthen smelter.

[8] You, יהוה, will guard the poor and protect them always from a sinful generation that appears never to end.

[9] For when the wicked walk about with impunity, it is as though they are boasting about their successful degradation of humanity.

to whom they are speaking into line and by intimidating the less well-spoken among them. God, on the other hand, speaks as a way of allowing human beings, to whom thought unformulated in language is barely perceptible, to conceive of divinity in the only medium in which they can truly conceive of anything more complex than color, sensation, or taste.

Speaking a word, any word, can build a bridge to God, or, to the extent it encourages its speaker to feel a sense of mastery over the things of the world, it can create a barrier between the speaker and God. Only a fool, however, would attempt to defuse the challenge by declining to speak altogether.

יג

לַמְנַצֵּחַ מִזְמוֹר לְדָוִד׃

[2] עַד־אָנָה יְהוָה תִּשְׁכָּחֵנִי נֶצַח עַד־אָנָה ׀ תַּסְתִּיר
אֶת־פָּנֶיךָ מִמֶּנִּי׃

[3] עַד־אָנָה אָשִׁית עֵצוֹת בְּנַפְשִׁי יָגוֹן בִּלְבָבִי יוֹמָם
עַד־אָנָה ׀ יָרוּם אֹיְבִי עָלָי׃

[4] הַבִּיטָה עֲנֵנִי יְהוָה אֱלֹהָי הָאִירָה עֵינַי פֶּן־אִישַׁן
הַמָּוֶת׃ [5] פֶּן־יֹאמַר אֹיְבִי יְכָלְתִּיו צָרַי יָגִילוּ כִּי
אֶמּוֹט׃

[6] וַאֲנִי ׀ בְּחַסְדְּךָ בָטַחְתִּי יָגֵל לִבִּי בִּישׁוּעָתֶךָ אָשִׁירָה
לַיהוָה כִּי גָמַל עָלָי׃

There's an old story rabbis like to tell about the man who complains bitterly to his rabbi that his prayers are never answered. The rabbi listens sympathetically, then asks in that wise rabbinic way if the man has ever considered that all his prayers have indeed been answered . . . but that the answer has simply been "no." The story has a certain cogency, but very few people are going to find it an adequate response to the silence of God. The author of the thirteenth psalm, for example, was so depressed and unhappy by God's silence that he could only give voice to his frustration by asking some very tough questions that go straight to the heart of the rationality of prayer. Why is God silent? Why doesn't God prefer those who pray to those who ignore religion entirely? Why is there no obvious correlation between prosperity and an individual's devotion to prayer? Is it possible that these questions have no answers at all?

The poet's willingness to end his poem as he does suggests a useful way to begin to address all these issues at once. Yet the poet's point is actually a simple one: that prayer is a ritual and can only be successfully understood as such. This may seem like a banal observation, but its implications are far more

13

For the conductor, a psalm of David.

[2] Up to what point are You going to ignore me completely, יהוה? Up to what point are You going to continue to hide Your face from me?

[3] Up to what point will I have to spend my days cramming advice into my soul and worry into my heart? Up to what point will my enemy be able to dominate me?

[4] Look to me and answer me, O יהוה, my God. Grant my eyes some light, lest I fall asleep and die, [5] lest my enemy say, "I have vanquished him," and others of my enemies rejoice at my downfall.

[6] As for me, I trust in Your mercy. My heart rejoices at the prospect of Your salvation. I sing to יהוה, who has already done so much for me.

challenging than might seem at first to be the case. It is one thing, after all, to note that all Jewish rituals have at their core some aspect of God's existence that Scripture wishes us to embrace . . . and that fundamental to engaging God in prayer is the notion that God exists not merely as distant celestial energy, but as a close Partner-in-dialogue for those courageous enough to divest themselves totally of arrogance and egotism before setting forth to seek God in prayer. That much may seem fairly obvious (at least to people who profess to hold arrogance and egotism in disdain), but the idea has a corollary that even the most skilled pray-er will find at least slightly disorienting: that prayer is best understood, therefore, as an exercise in developing faith in the above-mentioned concept of God as an attainable Partner-in-dialogue, not as a mere propitiatory technique designed to assist those who do it well in getting God to grant this or that favor in return. The idea is of God as Friend, and as the caring Listener whose willingness to engage human beings in dialogue grants meaning to human language . . . not as some sort of celestial machine that dispenses blessings on demand. The idea is that prayer is the language of love, not debt.

יד

לַמְנַצֵּחַ לְדָוִד
אָמַר נָבָל בְּלִבּוֹ אֵין אֱלֹהִים הִשְׁחִיתוּ הִתְעִיבוּ
עֲלִילָה אֵין עֹשֵׂה־טוֹב׃
2 יְהוָה מִשָּׁמַיִם הִשְׁקִיף עַל־בְּנֵי־אָדָם לִרְאוֹת הֲיֵשׁ
מַשְׂכִּיל דֹּרֵשׁ אֶת־אֱלֹהִים׃ 3 הַכֹּל סָר יַחְדָּו
נֶאֱלָחוּ אֵין עֹשֵׂה־טוֹב אֵין גַּם־אֶחָד׃
4 הֲלֹא יָדְעוּ כָּל־פֹּעֲלֵי אָוֶן אֹכְלֵי עַמִּי אָכְלוּ לֶחֶם
יְהוָה לֹא קָרָאוּ׃
5 שָׁם ׀ פָּחֲדוּ פָחַד כִּי־אֱלֹהִים בְּדוֹר צַדִּיק׃
6 עֲצַת־עָנִי תָבִישׁוּ כִּי יְהוָה מַחְסֵהוּ׃
7 מִי־יִתֵּן מִצִּיּוֹן יְשׁוּעַת יִשְׂרָאֵל בְּשׁוּב יְהוָה שְׁבוּת
עַמּוֹ יָגֵל יַעֲקֹב יִשְׂמַח יִשְׂרָאֵל׃

This poem appears twice in the Book of Psalms: here and, with some minor variations (and one major one), as the fifty-third psalm as well. In both versions, however, the poet is clearly grappling with the same crippling sense of loneliness and alienation that he feels as a result of attempting to maintain his faith in a cold, unsympathetic world. Is he merely using hyperbole when he implores the Almighty to look down from heaven to see if there is even one wise soul in the world who bothers seeking God within the warp and woof of human life? Or does the poet truly live such a wretched, desolate existence that he seriously wonders if there *are* any people of real faith in the world—not merely people who *profess* faith, but people who truly *do* believe, whose every waking effort is somehow motivated by the desire to seek God, to find God, and to bring the palpable, physically real presence of God into their lives? The poet's question is probably rhetorical, but perhaps even this kind of bleak disconnectedness from the world has its own reward for the alienated. Faith, after all, thrives in its own patch of soil and rarely blossoms on an assembly line or in a crowded room. Indeed, living at the confluence of desire and hope, faith derives its staying

14 For the conductor, a psalm of David.
The scoundrel says in his heart, "There is no God," and thus do his people behave corruptly and perpetrate abominable schemes; no one does good.

[2] Meanwhile, יהוה surveys humanity from heaven to see if there is anyone on earth wise enough to seek God, [3]but all have gone off together to plot depravity. No one does good, not even one single soul.

[4] Do not all sinners know that they court disaster when they devour my people as though they were eating bread, when they fail to cry out to יהוה?

[5] In the end, they will know fear, for God dwells in the company of the righteous.

[6] In the meantime, I say this to the wicked: "You scorn the counsel of the poor, thereby denying that יהוה is their haven."

[7] Whenever will the salvation of Israel come to us from Zion? When יהוה restores the nation's fortunes, Jacob will rejoice, Israel will exult.

power precisely from the union of deep longing for God and a sense that, just possibly, the God for whom we yearn exists in some way related to the metaphors we use to speak about the divine realm.

The poet looks at the world and is so totally seized with pessimism that he is moved to conclude that not even one single soul in it does good. (Of course, he himself is part of the world and so the fact that he personally does good cancels out his blanket indictment of humanity.) In the end, however, hope submerged in despair is a subcategory of hope, not of despair. And although prayer suffused with despair risks yielding sarcasm, prayer rooted in hope almost inevitably creates stirrings of incipient love. And, for all he professes deep, unyielding pessimism, one has the sense that the poet was not totally unaware that his poem was a kind of prayer . . . and that its message was far more one of hope than of cynicism.

טו

מִזְמוֹר לְדָוִד

יְהוָה מִי־יָגוּר בְּאָהֳלֶךָ מִי־יִשְׁכֹּן בְּהַר קָדְשֶׁךָ׃

2 הוֹלֵךְ תָּמִים וּפֹעֵל צֶדֶק וְדֹבֵר אֱמֶת בִּלְבָבוֹ׃

3 לֹא־רָגַל ׀ עַל־לְשֹׁנוֹ לֹא־עָשָׂה לְרֵעֵהוּ רָעָה וְחֶרְפָּה לֹא־נָשָׂא עַל־קְרֹבוֹ׃

4 נִבְזֶה ׀ בְּעֵינָיו נִמְאָס וְאֶת־יִרְאֵי יְהוָה יְכַבֵּד נִשְׁבַּע לְהָרַע וְלֹא יָמִר׃

5 כַּסְפּוֹ ׀ לֹא־נָתַן בְּנֶשֶׁךְ וְשֹׁחַד עַל־נָקִי לֹא־לָקָח עֹשֵׂה אֵלֶּה לֹא יִמּוֹט לְעוֹלָם׃

In our world, the word "religious" is generally used to denote the ritually observant individual. It is, therefore, all the more surprising to read the fifteenth psalm: when the poet asks who may live on God's mountain or tarry in God's tent, he is merely using the poetic language of his time and place to ask what constitutes the truly religious person and, by then answering his own question, to challenge us to re-evaluate our own sense of what constitutes being right with God. And who *does* the poet imagine God suffering to dwell on the holy mountain? People who don't lie. People who don't slander their neighbors. People who don't harm others. People whose words are their bonds, even when they later regret those words. People who don't take bribes. People who don't seek to profit from the misery of the poor by charging interest when they lend them money. People who hold in contempt the individual whose conduct is degrading and corrupt, and who refuse to make endless excuses for poor conduct or base, decadent behavior in others.

By omitting the most well-known rituals of "religious" life from his list, the poet is suggesting that those rituals have meaning only when those who perform them use them to express the ethical values they hold meaningful and

15 A psalm of David.

Who may dwell in Your tent, יהוה? Who may reside at Your holy mountain?

[2] One who walks with integrity and acts with righteousness and speaks truth in his heart.

[3] One who does not slander with his tongue or do evil to another or bring shame to any member of his family.

[4] One who holds the depraved in contempt, who shows honor to those who fear יהוה, and who never reneges on an oath, even when it turns out contrary to one's own best interests.

[5] One who never charges interest when lending money or takes a bribe concerning the innocent. Whoever does these things will never totter.

dear . . . and to worship the God they revere as the source of those values. To adopt a regimen of punctilious observance without embracing the core values of morality and faith has no meaning at all: such people, the poet is saying, do not get to sojourn, even briefly, in the holy tent or on God's sacred mountain. Religion isn't magic and, as a result, the rituals of faith only "work" when an individual uses them as tools to fashion a kind of personal temple dedicated to the worship of God out of the bricks of morality, decency, and ethical goodness. And an equally profound part of the poet's message is the unstated corollary of that thought—that rituals devoid of such spiritual intent are meaningless gestures whose performance risks engendering the type of self-satisfied spiritual complacency that actually leads *away from,* not *towards,* God. Moderns contemplating this ancient poem will do well to allow it to stir them to consider whether they evaluate ritual activity solely on whether it does or doesn't reflect honest yearning for God, or whether they allow themselves to be impressed by mere pageantry and pomp . . . and by blind obedience to detail.

טז

מִכְתָּם לְדָוִד
שָׁמְרֵנִי אֵל כִּי־חָסִיתִי בָךְ׃
2 אָמַרְתְּ לַיהוָה אֲדֹנָי אָתָּה טוֹבָתִי בַּל־עָלֶיךָ׃
3 לִקְדוֹשִׁים אֲשֶׁר־בָּאָרֶץ הֵמָּה וְאַדִּירֵי כָּל־חֶפְצִי־
בָם׃ 4 יִרְבּוּ עַצְּבוֹתָם אַחֵר מָהָרוּ בַּל־אַסִּיךְ
נִסְכֵּיהֶם מִדָּם וּבַל־אֶשָּׂא אֶת־שְׁמוֹתָם
עַל־שְׂפָתָי׃
5 יְהוָה מְנָת־חֶלְקִי וְכוֹסִי אַתָּה תּוֹמִיךְ גּוֹרָלִי׃
6 חֲבָלִים נָפְלוּ־לִי בַּנְּעִמִים אַף־נַחֲלָת שָׁפְרָה עָלָי׃
7 אֲבָרֵךְ אֶת־יְהוָה אֲשֶׁר יְעָצָנִי אַף־לֵילוֹת יִסְּרוּנִי
כִלְיוֹתָי׃
8 שִׁוִּיתִי יְהוָה לְנֶגְדִּי תָמִיד כִּי מִימִינִי בַּל־אֶמּוֹט׃
9 לָכֵן ׀ שָׂמַח לִבִּי וַיָּגֶל כְּבוֹדִי אַף־בְּשָׂרִי יִשְׁכֹּן
לָבֶטַח׃ 10 כִּי ׀ לֹא־תַעֲזֹב נַפְשִׁי לִשְׁאוֹל לֹא־תִתֵּן
חֲסִידְךָ לִרְאוֹת שָׁחַת׃
11 תּוֹדִיעֵנִי אֹרַח חַיִּים שֹׂבַע שְׂמָחוֹת אֶת־פָּנֶיךָ
נְעִמוֹת בִּימִינְךָ נֶצַח׃

Although some of the individual psalms are probably older than the epoch of the Second Temple, it seems undeniable that the Psalter itself dates back to the days when the Second Temple stood in Jerusalem. That being the case, we can assume that many of the psalmists were associated with the Levites who served as Temple singers and, indeed, their words fit nicely with much of what we know of the Levitical role in Temple days. Readers must resist the temptation to idealize, however, and must remember that the citizens of ancient Jerusalem appear to have been just as divided into political factions as are modern-day Jews. Indeed, the fact that there was no love lost between

16

A golden-song of David.

Guard me, O God, for in You do I seek refuge.

[2] I say to יהוה, "You are Adonai; I find no good in my life greater than You."

[3] As to the mighty and so-called holy ones of this earth, all my desire is that [4] their sorrows be many; in that they rush towards perversity, neither shall I take part in their bloody libations nor even let their names pass my lips.

[5] יהוה is my allotted portion, the cup given to me; You support me in the pursuit of my destiny.

[6] The estate that has passed to me is among the most pleasant; indeed, my inheritance pleases me intensely.

[7] I shall bless יהוה, my source of counsel, even though my conscience tortures me all night long.

[8] I place יהוה before me always; with God at my right hand, I shall not totter.

[9] Therefore does my heart rejoice and my glorious soul exult. Even my flesh dwells secure in the belief that [10] You would never abandon me to Sheol, that You would never allow Your pious follower to face the grave on his own.

[11] Teach me the way of life, for I am sated with joy in Your presence; indeed, I perceive eternal bliss in Your right hand.

priest and Levite in those days surfaces several times in the Torah and has its echoes in the Psalter as well. The author of the sixteenth psalm, for example, does not actually name his personal foes as Temple priests, but he does drop some fairly broad hints about their identity: they are widely thought of as holy folk, they wield great power, and they regularly worship by pouring out libations of blood. Modern readers can enjoy the poet's faith even despite his cryptic language, however: he condemns his enemies (fairly or unfairly) as hypocrites and phonies, yet refuses to pay for his candor with his own hope in God's essential goodness.

יז

תְּפִלָּה לְדָוִד
שִׁמְעָה יְהוָה ׀ צֶדֶק הַקְשִׁיבָה רִנָּתִי הַאֲזִינָה
תְפִלָּתִי בְּלֹא שִׂפְתֵי מִרְמָה׃
2 מִלְּפָנֶיךָ מִשְׁפָּטִי יֵצֵא עֵינֶיךָ תֶּחֱזֶינָה מֵישָׁרִים׃
3 בָּחַנְתָּ לִבִּי ׀ פָּקַדְתָּ לַּיְלָה צְרַפְתַּנִי בַל־תִּמְצָא זַמֹּתִי
בַּל־יַעֲבָר־פִּי׃
4 לִפְעֻלּוֹת אָדָם בִּדְבַר שְׂפָתֶיךָ אֲנִי שָׁמַרְתִּי אָרְחוֹת
פָּרִיץ׃
5 תָּמֹךְ אֲשֻׁרַי בְּמַעְגְּלוֹתֶיךָ בַּל־נָמוֹטּוּ פְעָמָי׃
6 אֲנִי קְרָאתִיךָ כִי־תַעֲנֵנִי אֵל הַט־אָזְנְךָ לִי שְׁמַע
אִמְרָתִי׃
7 הַפְלֵה חֲסָדֶיךָ מוֹשִׁיעַ חוֹסִים מִמִּתְקוֹמְמִים
בִּימִינֶךָ׃
8 שָׁמְרֵנִי כְּאִישׁוֹן בַּת־עָיִן בְּצֵל כְּנָפֶיךָ תַּסְתִּירֵנִי׃
9 מִפְּנֵי רְשָׁעִים זוּ שַׁדּוּנִי אֹיְבַי בְּנֶפֶשׁ יַקִּיפוּ עָלָי׃
10 חֶלְבָּמוֹ סָּגְרוּ פִּימוֹ דִּבְּרוּ בְגֵאוּת׃
11 אַשֻּׁרֵינוּ עַתָּה *סְבָבוּנוּ עֵינֵיהֶם יָשִׁיתוּ לִנְטוֹת
בָּאָרֶץ׃

v. 11 סבבוני כתיב

The David whose exploits so inspired the poets of the Psalter is almost never the proud, victorious king of Israel, but rather the terrified fugitive fleeing from King Saul's wrath long before being acclaimed or recognized as the legitimate monarch of his people. Indeed, it is that image of an innocent David fleeing the death sentence pronounced against him by a paranoid, wrathful Saul that seems to have spoken most eloquently to the poets whose poetry makes up our Book of Psalms, and the author of the seventeenth psalm was no exception. The point, however, is not that the poet himself harbored royal pretensions of the kind that could have put him in danger of being arrested on charges of sedition or treason. It does sound, however, as though he may have held certain opinions that placed him—and probably many of his colleagues in the poets' guild—outside the pale of what then passed for normal religious sentiment.

What specifically might have been the opinions that placed the poet in such danger? He skirts around the issue for most of his poem, but finally comes out with it in the final strophe of his ode to terror assuaged in faith when he admits to believing that it is possible for ordinary people like himself to experi-

17 A prayer of David.

Hear my just plea, O יהוה, and listen to my joyous hymn; give ear to this prayer of mine uttered by lips untainted with guile.

[2] Let my judgment come forth from You; let Your eyes see nothing but my decency.

[3] You have tested my heart; You have examined me by night. You have analyzed my behavior and found nothing amiss; whatever evil plots I may have considered, none actually exited my mouth.

[4] As an individual, I have acted only in accordance with the word of Your lips; I have kept myself from the ways of the depraved.

[5] My legs have held firm to Your paths; my feet have never slipped.

[6] I call upon You to answer me, O God; incline Your ear to me and hear my words.

[7] Astound me with Your mercies, O God, You who save with the divine right hand those who take refuge in You from aggressors.

[8] Guard me as carefully as the pupil of Your eye. Hide me in the shadow of Your wings [9]from the wicked who would rob me and from bloodthirsty enemies who surround me.

[10] They have stopped up their hearts with fat; their mouths speak only arrogance.

[11] They are already grabbing at our legs; their eyes are fixed on us, the better to push us down to the earth.

ence communion with God. More to the point, he finds it perfectly possible to imagine that he will eventually merit the experience of gazing on the image of God—and not in a dream-state trance, but in a waking vision in the manner of the prophets of old.

This notion—that ordinary people can experience sensory communion with God—will probably sound reasonable enough to most modern readers. The poet and his fellow Levites, however, appear to have promulgated their belief in the plausibility of attaining that kind of intimate, sensory communion with the divine realm at their own peril. Indeed, the author of the seventeenth psalm has acquired an enemy for himself whom he can only describe as a wild beast lying in a dark cave waiting patiently for his unsuspecting victim to pass innocently by. And the poet's

12 דִּמְינוֹ כְּאַרְיֵה יִכְסוֹף לִטְרוֹף וְכִכְפִיר יֹשֵׁב
בְּמִסְתָּרִים׃
13 קוּמָה יְהוָֹה קַדְּמָה פָנָיו הַכְרִיעֵהוּ פַּלְּטָה נַפְשִׁי
מֵרָשָׁע חַרְבֶּךָ׃
14 מִמְתִים יָדְךָ ׀ יְהוָֹה מִמְתִים מֵחֶלֶד חֶלְקָם בַּחַיִּים
*וּצְפוּנְךָ תְּמַלֵּא בִטְנָם יִשְׂבְּעוּ בָנִים וְהִנִּיחוּ יִתְרָם
לְעוֹלְלֵיהֶם׃
15 אֲנִי בְּצֶדֶק אֶחֱזֶה פָנֶיךָ אֶשְׂבְּעָה בְהָקִיץ תְּמוּנָתֶךָ׃

v. 14 וצפינך כתיב

enemy is not just violent and wily, but also more than prosperous enough to possess all the trappings of material success: a belly full of gourmet delicacies, a nursery full of babies, and enough wealth to spend all he wishes and still have plenty to leave to his heirs.

For his part—and undaunted by his adversary's prosperity—the poet places his faith in God. He knows that his prosperous enemy has a heart encased in fat and a mouth filled not with wisdom and humility, but with arrogance and vanity. He knows that his is the right path, and he also knows, with the certainty and faith born of quiet confidence, that it is he, and not his foe, who will end up with the more profound sense of God's saving presence in his life.

Perhaps the poet wrote to prompt his audience to consider and evaluate

[12] The enemy is like a lion yearning to rip apart his victim, like a lion cub dwelling in a secret lair.

[13] Rise up, O יהוה, to meet and defeat him; save my soul from a wicked man with Your sword.

[14] O יהוה, may Your hand save me from my fellow human beings, from those people of this world whose portion is so rich in this life, whose bellies You fill up with rare delicacies, who are blessed with children, who have so much that they can bequeath large estates even to their infants.

[15] In justice shall I behold Your face; I shall be sated with a waking vision of Your image.

their reactions to the financial prosperity of the wicked, or perhaps he had some other, less obvious motive. In either event, we moderns can very profitably ask just that question of ourselves. Do we find our faith weakened, or merely challenged, by wealthy people who openly and brazenly dismiss the need to worship God as an irrelevant, superfluous superstition? If the point of observance is to prod God into granting specific boons and gifts, then how do we explain the fact that so many pious people seem doomed to live lives of permanent penury? It is, after all, one thing to pay glib lip service to the idea that a life in God is its own reward. The question the poet is posing, however, is infinitely more disturbing to ponder: he is asking his readers to consider if they would—or could—still hold fast to that idea if they were suddenly asked to do so from the depths of misery, illness, hunger, poverty, and want.

יח

לַמְנַצֵּחַ ׀ לְעֶבֶד יְהֹוָה לְדָוִד אֲשֶׁר דִּבֶּר ׀ לַיהֹוָה אֶת־דִּבְרֵי הַשִּׁירָה הַזֹּאת בְּיוֹם ׀ הִצִּיל־יְהֹוָה אוֹתוֹ מִכַּף כָּל־אֹיְבָיו וּמִיַּד שָׁאוּל׃

2 וַיֹּאמַר אֶרְחָמְךָ יְהֹוָה חִזְקִי׃

3 יְהֹוָה סַלְעִי וּמְצוּדָתִי וּמְפַלְטִי אֵלִי צוּרִי אֶחֱסֶה־בּוֹ מָגִנִּי וְקֶרֶן יִשְׁעִי מִשְׂגַּבִּי׃

4 מְהֻלָּל אֶקְרָא יְהֹוָה וּמִן־אֹיְבַי אִוָּשֵׁעַ׃

5 אֲפָפוּנִי חֶבְלֵי־מָוֶת וְנַחֲלֵי בְלִיַּעַל יְבַעֲתוּנִי׃

6 חֶבְלֵי שְׁאוֹל סְבָבוּנִי קִדְּמוּנִי מוֹקְשֵׁי מָוֶת׃

7 בַּצַּר־לִי ׀ אֶקְרָא יְהֹוָה וְאֶל־אֱלֹהַי אֲשַׁוֵּעַ יִשְׁמַע מֵהֵיכָלוֹ קוֹלִי וְשַׁוְעָתִי לְפָנָיו ׀ תָּבוֹא בְאָזְנָיו׃

8 וַתִּגְעַשׁ וַתִּרְעַשׁ ׀ הָאָרֶץ וּמוֹסְדֵי הָרִים יִרְגָּזוּ וַיִּתְגָּעֲשׁוּ כִּי חָרָה לוֹ׃

9 עָלָה עָשָׁן בְּאַפּוֹ וְאֵשׁ מִפִּיו תֹּאכֵל גֶּחָלִים בָּעֲרוּ מִמֶּנּוּ׃

10 וַיֵּט שָׁמַיִם וַיֵּרַד וַעֲרָפֶל תַּחַת רַגְלָיו׃

11 וַיִּרְכַּב עַל־כְּרוּב וַיָּעֹף וַיֵּדֶא עַל־כַּנְפֵי־רוּחַ׃

12 יָשֶׁת חֹשֶׁךְ ׀ סִתְרוֹ סְבִיבוֹתָיו סֻכָּתוֹ חֶשְׁכַת־מַיִם עָבֵי שְׁחָקִים׃

The desire to experience God in the simple, sensory way human beings perceive each other is mentioned so often in the Psalter that it may be considered one of the book's major themes. That said, it is surprising to note how few of the psalms actually describe not mere *longing* to know God experientially (rather than solely intellectually), but the actual *experience* of entering into the realm of mystic, sensually perceptible knowledge of the divine. The author of the eighteenth psalm (which also appears, with some slight changes, as the twenty-second chapter of the Second Book of Samuel) not only mentions the specifics of his mystic encounter with God, however, but also intertwines his account of that experience with the other great theme of the Psalter: the desire for God to help in vanquishing, even annihilating, merciless enemies of whom one is utterly terrified. This poem is therefore, if not quite totally unique, then certainly of special importance among the psalms.

The poet's description of prophetic-style communion with God has parallels and echoes in many other passages in the Bible (most notably in the lovely psalm that is preserved in the second chapter of the Book of Jonah), but it can also easily stand on its own as an independent account of the poet's mystic journey. He begins by chanting God's praises, deriving from the experience

18

For the conductor Eved-יהוה, the words of the psalm David sang to יהוה on the day יהוה finally saved him from the hand of all his enemies and from the grasp of Saul.

[2] He said, "I love you, O יהוה, my Strength.

[3] יהוה, You are my crag, my fortress, and my source of deliverance, my God, the rock in whom I trust, my shield and the horn of my salvation, my refuge.

[4] 'God is to be praised,' I cried out, O יהוה; 'Indeed, I know I shall be saved from my enemies.'

[5] The bonds of death constrained me; the rivers of Belial terrified me.

[6] The bonds of Sheol encompassed me; the snares of death came out to greet me.

[7] In my trouble, I called out to יהוה, supplicating before the God who hears my voice from within the divine palace as my supplication comes into God's presence, into God's ears.

[8] The earth trembled and quaked; the very foundations of the mountains quivered and shook as God responded to my plight with rage.

[9] Smoke rose in God's nostrils and consuming fire appeared in God's mouth; coals began to glow as a result of the divine presence.

[10] God bent the heavens and descended, dense fog billowing out from beneath the divine feet.

[11] Riding on a cherub, God flew aloft, coasting along on the wings of the wind.

[12] All around the divine residence, God cast secret divine darkness consisting of dark heavenly clouds filled with water.

the strength to proclaim with conviction that he will live to vanquish his earthly foes. Then, feeling himself becoming submerged in the sea, he enters into his trance state. As he sinks in the deep waters, however, he becomes so tangled up in seaweed that he knows he will never be able to escape. And then, just when he feels that he is on the verge of dying, a new chasm of experience opens up and he finds himself in the divine throne room. The earth begins to quake and, as the ground trembles, a series of terrifying images begins to pass before the poet's astounded eyes. The heavens bend down towards earth. Stones embedded in the ground begin to glow from the intense heat of God's presence. Darkness

13 מִנֹּגַהּ נֶגְדּוֹ עָבָיו עָבְרוּ בָּרָד וְגַחֲלֵי־אֵשׁ:
14 וַיַּרְעֵם בַּשָּׁמַיִם ׀ יְהוָה וְעֶלְיוֹן יִתֵּן קֹלוֹ בָּרָד
וְגַחֲלֵי־אֵשׁ:
15 וַיִּשְׁלַח חִצָּיו וַיְפִיצֵם וּבְרָקִים רָב וַיְהֻמֵּם:
16 וַיֵּרָאוּ ׀ אֲפִיקֵי מַיִם וַיִּגָּלוּ מוֹסְדוֹת תֵּבֵל מִגַּעֲרָתְךָ
יְהוָה מִנִּשְׁמַת רוּחַ אַפֶּךָ:
17 יִשְׁלַח מִמָּרוֹם יִקָּחֵנִי יַמְשֵׁנִי מִמַּיִם רַבִּים:
18 יַצִּילֵנִי מֵאֹיְבִי עָז וּמִשֹּׂנְאַי כִּי־אָמְצוּ מִמֶּנִּי:
19 יְקַדְּמוּנִי בְיוֹם אֵידִי וַיְהִי יְהוָה לְמִשְׁעָן לִי:
20 וַיּוֹצִיאֵנִי לַמֶּרְחָב יְחַלְּצֵנִי כִּי חָפֵץ בִּי:
21 יִגְמְלֵנִי יְהוָה כְּצִדְקִי כְּבֹר יָדַי יָשִׁיב לִי:
22 כִּי־שָׁמַרְתִּי דַּרְכֵי יְהוָה וְלֹא־רָשַׁעְתִּי מֵאֱלֹהָי:
23 כִּי כָל־מִשְׁפָּטָיו לְנֶגְדִּי וְחֻקֹּתָיו לֹא־אָסִיר מֶנִּי:
24 וָאֱהִי תָמִים עִמּוֹ וָאֶשְׁתַּמֵּר מֵעֲוֺנִי: 25 וַיָּשֶׁב־
יְהוָה לִי כְצִדְקִי כְּבֹר יָדַי לְנֶגֶד עֵינָיו:
26 עִם־חָסִיד תִּתְחַסָּד עִם־גְּבַר תָּמִים תִּתַּמָּם:

descends on the celestial palace, but this thick, soupy dark is illuminated almost immediately by hailstones of fire and by lightning bolts that suddenly surround the poet. And then, just as he begins to adjust to the terrifying weather, the poet feels God sending for him, lifting him out of the waters and actually saving him from his foes. What happens then, when the poet finally finds himself in the presence of God? He does not tell us precisely; we know only that he leaves the divine presence some time later imbued with certainty that he will prevail over his enemies.

Was the point of the experience, then, for the poet to use his mystical knowledge of God to reassure himself that he will yet manage to escape from his foes? It certainly may have been, but modern readers may prefer to focus on the poet's actual description of his mystic experience of God. Dying in God, drowning in God, feeling oneself approaching the very threshold of Sheol only to be delivered at the last moment by God's saving hand—these are all attempts to explain something that the poet clearly considered more or less indescribable. Readers may therefore feel prompted to consider their own experiences of the Divine in the same light. When we moderns say that we long to know God, do we mean that we truly yearn to love God and to experience God's love? To die (or rather, *almost* to die) and experience last-minute deliverance in God? To feel God's saving presence actually freeing us from the bonds of death? Do we truly yearn for God's totally present presence or only

[13] But then those holy clouds suddenly dissipated in the magnificent splendor of the divine presence and were replaced by a mixture of hailstones and smoldering coals.

[14] And then יהוה thundered forth from heaven; God Most High spoke as the hailstones and smoldering coals began to fall.

[15] God sent divine arrows to scatter those clouds, countless bolts of lightning that sorely discomfited them.

[16] Streams of water became visible as the very foundations of the world were revealed at Your rebuke, יהוה, at a blast of air from Your nostrils.

[17] God sent down from on high and took me, lifting me up from deep waters, [18]saving me from my mighty enemy, saving me from those stronger than myself who hate me.

[19] They had at me in a calamitous day, but יהוה was my support, [20]taking me from my dire straits to a wide place, granting me respite from my foes as a sign of pleasure in me.

[21] יהוה dealt with me according to my own righteousness, returning unto me a reward commensurate with the purity of my hands, [22]for I have kept the ways of יהוה and have not betrayed my God with wicked deeds.

[23] Indeed, as all God's laws are ever before me and as I have never ignored any of the holy statutes, [24]as I am guileless before God and as I keep myself far from the sins to which I am drawn, [25]יהוה has paid me back according to my righteousness, rewarding me according to the purity of my hands before God's eyes.

[26] With the pious, You act with piety. With the guileless, You act without guile.

for some sort of ill-defined, fuzzy feeling that God probably exists? Do today's readers of the psalms want to perceive God fully present in the context of everyday life as it is actually lived by ordinary people . . . or merely to function as a kind of soothing balm to be brought out and slathered on when the going gets rough?

Answering these questions honestly will be, at the very least, unsettling for most readers today. But trying to answer difficult questions honestly can also be a productive, useful experience . . . and an account like the one presented by the poet whose poem is

27 עִם־נָבָ֥ר תִּתְבָּרָ֑ר וְעִם־עִ֝קֵּ֗שׁ תִּתְפַּתָּֽל׃

28 כִּֽי־אַ֭תָּה עַם־עָנִ֣י תוֹשִׁ֑יעַ וְעֵינַ֖יִם רָמ֣וֹת תַּשְׁפִּֽיל׃

29 כִּֽי־אַ֭תָּה תָּאִ֣יר נֵרִ֑י יְהֹוָ֥ה אֱ֝לֹהַ֗י יַגִּ֥יהַּ חָשְׁכִּֽי׃

30 כִּֽי־בְ֭ךָ אָרֻ֣ץ גְּד֑וּד וּ֝בֵֽאלֹהַ֗י אֲדַלֶּג־שֽׁוּר׃

31 הָאֵל֮ תָּמִ֪ים דַּ֫רְכּ֥וֹ אִמְרַ֣ת יְהֹוָ֣ה צְרוּפָ֑ה מָגֵ֥ן ה֝֗וּא
לְכֹ֤ל ׀ הַחוֹסִ֬ים בּֽוֹ׃

32 כִּ֤י מִ֣י אֱ֭לוֹהַּ מִבַּלְעֲדֵ֣י יְהֹוָ֑ה וּמִ֥י צ֝֗וּר זוּלָתִ֥י
אֱלֹהֵֽינוּ׃

33 הָאֵ֣ל הַמְאַזְּרֵ֣נִי חָ֑יִל וַיִּתֵּ֖ן תָּמִ֣ים דַּרְכִּֽי׃ 34 מְשַׁוֶּ֣ה
רַ֭גְלַי כָּאַיָּל֑וֹת וְעַ֥ל בָּ֝מֹתַ֗י יַעֲמִידֵֽנִי׃

35 מְלַמֵּ֣ד יָ֭דַי לַמִּלְחָמָ֑ה וְֽנִחֲתָ֥ה קֶֽשֶׁת־נְ֝חוּשָׁ֗ה
זְרוֹעֹתָֽי׃

36 וַתִּתֶּן־לִי֮ מָגֵ֪ן יִ֫שְׁעֶ֥ךָ וִימִינְךָ֥ תִסְעָדֵ֑נִי וְֽעַנְוַתְךָ֥
תַרְבֵּֽנִי׃

37 תַּרְחִ֣יב צַעֲדִ֣י תַחְתָּ֑י וְלֹ֥א מָ֝עֲד֗וּ קַרְסֻלָּֽי׃

38 אֶרְדּ֣וֹף א֭וֹיְבַי וְאַשִּׂיגֵ֑ם וְלֹא־אָ֝שׁ֗וּב עַד־כַּלּוֹתָֽם׃

39 אֶ֭מְחָצֵם וְלֹא־יֻ֣כְלוּ ק֑וּם יִ֝פְּל֗וּ תַּ֣חַת רַגְלָֽי׃

40 וַתְּאַזְּרֵ֣נִי חַ֭יִל לַמִּלְחָמָ֑ה תַּכְרִ֖יעַ קָמַ֣י תַּחְתָּֽי׃

41 וְֽאֹיְבַ֗י נָתַ֣תָּה לִּ֣י עֹ֑רֶף וּ֝מְשַׂנְאַ֗י אַצְמִיתֵֽם׃

our 18th psalm, therefore, can serve as a kind of wake-up call for latter-day readers even *more* than it can serve as an interesting glimpse into somebody else's spirituality. The poet does not have a feeling that God probably exists, after all, but is possessed rather of the absolutely unshakable belief that God is no less real than anything else in the world. Moreover, God doesn't merely exist as some sort of ocean of cosmic being in the poet's conception, but as an active, vital force in the lives of people such as himself. His descriptive language may be a bit hard for moderns to take literally—although it seems certain that the poet meant seriously to describe an actual encounter with the divine realm he himself experienced. It would be a mistake, however, for moderns to focus on this or that specific detail as a way of avoiding the challenge inherent in the psalm itself: since the poet, a human being, knew God experientially (and not merely intellectually), sensually (and not merely theoretically), and in the context of absolutely perceptible reality (and not in the rarified realm of myth, poetry, symbol, or metaphor), it must therefore actually be possible to have such an experience. But if that is the case, then moderns will have to deal with the relationship of that fact to the state of their own belief. Why is it so easy for religious people in our world to relegate this kind of knowledge of God to the spiritual lives of

[27] With the pure, You act with purity. But with the stubbornly willful, You act with cunning.

[28] Thus will You save an impoverished people and bring humility to those with haughty eyes. [29] And thus will You light my lamp; יהוה, my God, shall illuminate my darkness.

[30] With You, I can outrun a battalion; with the help of my God, I can scale a wall.

[31] God's way is guileless and the word of יהוה is well-tested; indeed, God is a shield for all who seek refuge in faith.

[32] For what God is there other than יהוה? What rock is there aside from our God?

[33] Yea, the very God who girds my loins with courage shall make guileless my path; [34] indeed, that very God will make my feet no less swift than a deer's and set me upon the high places of my land.

[35] God has trained my hands for war so well that my arms can bend even a copper-plated bow.

[36] You bestow on me the shield of Your salvation; Your right hand supports me and the humility You inspire in me gives me the strength of many.

[37] You make sturdy my steps beneath me; my feet do not slip.

[38] I shall pursue my enemies and overtake them; I shall not return before annihilating them totally.

[39] I shall crush them so that they never rise again; they shall fall beneath my feet.

[40] You gird me with the courage for war; You will vanquish for me all who oppose me.

[41] You have made my enemies flee so that I can decimate those remaining foes who hate me.

other (usually long-dead) people . . . or to categorize it as "mystic," and thus irrelevant to the spiritual lives of normal, rational people such as themselves? Perhaps there is a bit of spiritual cowardice in the whole enterprise: by treating the psalmist's kind of encounter with the divine realm as unrepresentative of the ways average people may know God, they are essentially making their own kind of passive, challengeable faith sound reasonable and acceptable almost by default. But by insisting that God cannot be heard, cannot be seen . . . and *certainly* cannot be encountered with

42 יְשַׁוְּעוּ וְאֵין מוֹשִׁיעַ עַל־יְהוָה וְלֹא עָנָם:
43 וְאֶשְׁחָקֵם כְּעָפָר עַל־פְּנֵי־רוּחַ כְּטִיט חוּצוֹת
אֲרִיקֵם:
44 תְּפַלְּטֵנִי מֵרִיבֵי עָם תְּשִׂימֵנִי לְרֹאשׁ גּוֹיִם עַם
לֹא־יָדַעְתִּי יַעַבְדוּנִי:
45 לְשֵׁמַע אֹזֶן יִשָּׁמְעוּ לִי בְּנֵי־נֵכָר יְכַחֲשׁוּ־לִי:
46 בְּנֵי־נֵכָר יִבֹּלוּ וְיַחְרְגוּ מִמִּסְגְּרוֹתֵיהֶם:
47 חַי־יְהוָה וּבָרוּךְ צוּרִי וְיָרוּם אֱלוֹהֵי יִשְׁעִי: 48 הָאֵל
הַנּוֹתֵן נְקָמוֹת לִי וַיַּדְבֵּר עַמִּים תַּחְתָּי: 49 מְפַלְּטִי
מֵאֹיְבָי אַף מִן־קָמַי תְּרוֹמְמֵנִי מֵאִישׁ חָמָס
תַּצִּילֵנִי:
50 עַל־כֵּן ׀ אוֹדְךָ בַגּוֹיִם ׀ יְהוָה וּלְשִׁמְךָ אֲזַמֵּרָה:
51* מַגְדִּיל יְשׁוּעוֹת מַלְכּוֹ וְעֹשֶׂה חֶסֶד ׀ לִמְשִׁיחוֹ
לְדָוִד וּלְזַרְעוֹ עַד־עוֹלָם:

v. 51 מגדל כתיב

reference to the kind of descriptive language we find in the 18th psalm, we moderns create a kind of depressing cycle of rationalization and spiritual self-denigration. Indeed, we end up convincing ourselves that, since God cannot *really* be known or perceived in the normal way people know and perceive the things they truly, unequivocally believe to exist, it must therefore be reasonable to believe more profoundly and unyieldingly in the reality of our shoes or our feet than in the reality of God.

Reading the 18th psalm, one of the masterpieces of biblical literature and one of the greatest of all the psalms, can provide moderns with the ideal opportunity to question those assumptions and beliefs. In the normal course of events, people do not find it pleasant to entertain the possibility that they have settled for what they thought they could get, rather than striving to attain what they could actually achieve. Countless novels and screenplays have been written about the consequences of someone making that unsettling discovery about his or her professional or romantic life, but dramatically fewer about the

[42] They shall cry out, but none will save them; they may finally even call out to יהוה, but God will not answer them.

[43] I shall grind them up and scatter them like dust thrown into the wind; I shall hollow them out until they are no firmer than the mud in the streets.

[44] You shall save me from my opponents among the people; You shall make me the head of nations such that a people I barely know will serve me.

[45] They will hear only a rumor of my might and they will obey me; alien forces will be as naught before me.

[46] Indeed, alien forces will crumble and the survivors will burst out of their besieged battlements.

[47] יהוה lives; blessed be my Rock. May the God of my salvation be exalted, [48]God who grants me revenge on my foes, who subdues nations beneath me, [49]who rescues me from my enemies —and even from those of my own people who rise up against me, who saves me from the violent individual.

[50] Therefore do I give thanks to You among the nations, O יהוה. Therefore do I sing hymns to Your name, to the One [51]who makes great the saving acts granted to the king who rules by divine right, who deals mercifully with the prince anointed at God's behest, with David and with his descendants forever."

consequences of coming to that realization with respect to the life of the spirit. To a certain extent, that has to do with the nature of Western culture —but it has proved to be a fortunate happenstance for moderns formally devoted to religion, but far happier having their basic assumptions about the potential for knowing and encountering God left unchallenged. As a result, there is a sort of unavoidable wistfulness that accompanies the experience of reading a psalm like the 18th seriously as we are prompted to wonder, even just for a moment, if we are being wise or foolish in settling for what passes in our world for the attainable fruits of religious endeavor that normal people feel rational expecting in return for their spiritual efforts.

יט

לַמְנַצֵּחַ מִזְמוֹר לְדָוִד׃

2 הַשָּׁמַיִם מְסַפְּרִים כְּבוֹד־אֵל וּמַעֲשֵׂה יָדָיו מַגִּיד הָרָקִיעַ׃

3 יוֹם לְיוֹם יַבִּיעַ אֹמֶר וְלַיְלָה לְּלַיְלָה יְחַוֶּה־דָּעַת׃

4 אֵין אֹמֶר וְאֵין דְּבָרִים בְּלִי נִשְׁמָע קוֹלָם׃

5 בְּכָל־הָאָרֶץ ׀ יָצָא קַוָּם וּבִקְצֵה תֵבֵל מִלֵּיהֶם לַשֶּׁמֶשׁ שָׂם אֹהֶל בָּהֶם׃ 6 וְהוּא כְּחָתָן יֹצֵא מֵחֻפָּתוֹ יָשִׂישׂ כְּגִבּוֹר לָרוּץ אֹרַח׃ 7 מִקְצֵה הַשָּׁמַיִם ׀ מוֹצָאוֹ וּתְקוּפָתוֹ עַל־קְצוֹתָם וְאֵין נִסְתָּר מֵחַמָּתוֹ׃

8 תּוֹרַת יְהוָה תְּמִימָה מְשִׁיבַת נָפֶשׁ עֵדוּת יְהוָה נֶאֱמָנָה מַחְכִּימַת פֶּתִי׃

9 פִּקּוּדֵי יְהוָה יְשָׁרִים מְשַׂמְּחֵי־לֵב מִצְוַת יְהוָה בָּרָה מְאִירַת עֵינָיִם׃

The ancient poet lies on his back somewhere in ancient Judah and contemplates the nighttime sky. As would any modern in a similar position on a dark and starry night, he is moved, first, by the immensity of creation. But another thought takes hold almost immediately as the poet is seized by the realization that the earth, despite its feeling of endless vastness, is really only one tiny speck in the endless sea of being that is the known universe. And finally, overwhelmed by the grandeur of the heavens—and inspired either by his own poetic nature or by the sense that he is experiencing a kind of mystic vision (and perhaps by both)—the poet goes one step further and imagines that he can somehow actually hear the universe speaking aloud to him personally and directly.

And what, then, does the poet hear the heavens saying? Of their own immensity or beauty or indescribable grandeur—the very qualities that must have inspired him in the first place—he hears nothing at all. Whether that surprises him nor not, he does not say. But what he does hear clearly inspires him to poetic rapture and, as the poet hears the heavens proclaiming the glory of their Creator, the God of the heavens and the earth, he is moved to write one of the most famous of all the psalms. We can no longer know with any certainty if the poet, like so many others in ancient times, thought of the stars in the sky as living beings. But whatever he may have imagined the stars actually were, the more important detail is that the poet imagines he can hear them speaking of themselves not as miniature sparkling divinities or as the twinkling souls of dead heroes, but rather as prime examples of the handiwork

19 For the conductor, a psalm of David.
[2] The heavens tell of the glory of God; indeed, the firmament recounts the work of God's hands.
[3] Each day expresses this to the next day, just as each night conveys this thought to the next night; [4] indeed, without those celestial voices in the background as inspiration, no mortal could utter even a single word on the topic.
[5] This description of God's celestial glory extends through the entire world, its words inspired by heavens that extend as far as the ends of the earth. It is in the heavens, after all, that God pitched a tent for the sun so that it might go forth every morning [6] like a bridegroom leaving his nuptial chamber, like a top athlete delighted to run a race. [7] Its starting place is at the very edge of the heavens and its celestial circuit goes to their other end; none may hide from the sun's heat.
[8] The teaching of יהוה is perfect, restoring the soul. The testimony of יהוה is reliable, making wise the simple.
[9] The precepts of יהוה are just, making glad the heart. The heritage of יהוה is pure, illuminating the eyes.

of God. Indeed, as the poet lies still and looks into the sky, he is suddenly possessed of the insight that anything truly honest said about God the Creator must somehow be a reaction to (or a reflection of) the glory of the Divine that all people may perceive through the contemplation of the physical universe. Day speaks to day and night to night as the sun passes through the one and behind the other, leaving in its tracks evidence of God's awesome creative power so splendid that nothing on earth—not even an athlete's boundless pride upon winning a difficult race or the intense satisfaction a bridegroom feels on the morning following his wedding—can equal its splendor.

Having made this point, however, the poet then goes off in an entirely different direction, praising the commandments, precepts, and laws that God has bestowed upon humanity. The precise connection between the first and second parts of the psalm is not obvious, but the poet's point is probably that it is by observing God's laws and ordinances that human beings can become true creatures of God, servants of the Divine no less faithful to the laws and stric-

10 יִרְאַת יְהֹוָה | טְהוֹרָה עוֹמֶדֶת לָעַד מִשְׁפְּטֵי־יְהֹוָה אֱמֶת צָדְקוּ יַחְדָּו׃

11 הַנֶּחֱמָדִים מִזָּהָב וּמִפַּז רָב וּמְתוּקִים מִדְּבַשׁ וְנֹפֶת צוּפִים׃

12 גַּם־עַבְדְּךָ נִזְהָר בָּהֶם בְּשָׁמְרָם עֵקֶב רָב׃

13 שְׁגִיאוֹת מִי־יָבִין מִנִּסְתָּרוֹת נַקֵּנִי׃

14 גַּם מִזֵּדִים | חֲשֹׂךְ עַבְדֶּךָ אַל־יִמְשְׁלוּ־בִי אָז אֵיתָם וְנִקֵּיתִי מִפֶּשַׁע רָב׃

15 יִהְיוּ לְרָצוֹן | אִמְרֵי־פִי וְהֶגְיוֹן לִבִּי לְפָנֶיךָ יְהֹוָה צוּרִי וְגֹאֲלִי׃

tures given *them* than the planets and stars are to the physics of the created universe.

Did the poet write specifically to challenge his readers to ponder why it is that obedience to specific rules and regulations is presented in Scripture as the medium through which the average individual can experience communion with God? He could well have, and his answer—that obedience to divine law is a sign of subservience so potent that the truly obedient will inevitably come, at least eventually, to feel themselves living in the shadow of God—is a theory moderns can more than profitably ponder in the context of their own religious lives. Moreover, the poet's other concept—that obedience to the unalterable law of Scripture makes one part of a universe that operates according to immutable principles—has its own logic and, in some ways, may be of even more use to readers seeking to justify their observance in a purely rational way. One way or the other, moderns can use the

[10] The fear of יהוה, when pure, will endure forever.
The laws of יהוה are truth, entirely righteous.
[11] They are more valuable than any kind of gold,
no matter how much, and more sweet than
the honey of the date-palm or the honeycomb.
[12] And so Your servant is careful to observe them,
for there is great reward in keeping them.
[13] Who can understand the extent of one's own
errors? Cleanse me, therefore, from unknown
sins.
[14] Save Your servant also from the arrogant; let
them not rule over me, so that I may remain
guileless and be innocent of great wrongdoing.
[15] May the words of my mouth and the meditation
of my heart be acceptable before You, O יהוה,
my Rock and my Redeemer.

nineteenth psalm to stimulate contemplation of the place of the observant individual in the physical universe . . . and also to provoke some very interesting questions. Does religious observance require that the pious act like mindless automatons, the human equivalent of stars and planets whirling around endlessly in the heavens according to laws they have no choice but to obey? Or does the concept that God may be known through the observance of laws perhaps ennoble the human beings who observe those laws precisely because they feel themselves, unlike the unintelligent planets, to have *chosen* to do so? The stars and the planets are no less splendid today than they were in the psalmist's time, but can moderns still look towards heaven and hear them speak of God?

כ

לַמְנַצֵּחַ מִזְמוֹר לְדָוִד׃
2 יַעַנְךָ יְהוָה בְּיוֹם צָרָה יְשַׂגֶּבְךָ שֵׁם | אֱלֹהֵי יַעֲקֹב׃
3 יִשְׁלַח־עֶזְרְךָ מִקֹּדֶשׁ וּמִצִּיּוֹן יִסְעָדֶךָּ׃
4 יִזְכֹּר כָּל־מִנְחֹתֶךָ וְעוֹלָתְךָ יְדַשְּׁנֶה סֶלָה׃
5 יִתֶּן־לְךָ כִלְבָבֶךָ וְכָל־עֲצָתְךָ יְמַלֵּא׃
6 נְרַנְּנָה | בִּישׁוּעָתֶךָ וּבְשֵׁם־אֱלֹהֵינוּ נִדְגֹּל יְמַלֵּא
יְהוָה כָּל־מִשְׁאֲלוֹתֶיךָ׃
7 עַתָּה יָדַעְתִּי כִּי הוֹשִׁיעַ | יְהוָה מְשִׁיחוֹ יַעֲנֵהוּ
מִשְּׁמֵי קָדְשׁוֹ בִּגְבֻרוֹת יֵשַׁע יְמִינוֹ׃
8 אֵלֶּה בָרֶכֶב וְאֵלֶּה בַסּוּסִים וַאֲנַחְנוּ | בְּשֵׁם־יְהוָה
אֱלֹהֵינוּ נַזְכִּיר׃
9 הֵמָּה כָּרְעוּ וְנָפָלוּ וַאֲנַחְנוּ קַמְנוּ וַנִּתְעוֹדָד׃
10 יְהוָה הוֹשִׁיעָה הַמֶּלֶךְ יַעֲנֵנוּ בְיוֹם־קָרְאֵנוּ׃

What are the greatest of God's blessings? The author of the twentieth psalm penned an extended prayer for the welfare of his king, the anointed prince of Israel, and, in so doing, he created a list of the choicest favors he imagines God can grant. Most moderns will find his wish-list reasonable: that God respond to his king's prayers both in word and deed, that God ordain the success of his various political and military undertakings, that God accept all his ritual worship as though it were a sacrificial offering of the finest suet, that God make any advice given the king correct (at least after the fact), and that God save the king from earthly enemies who place their trust in military hardware rather than in the saving power of the Divine. The poet was writing a prayer for his king's welfare, but by enumerating the blessings he hopes God will grant his sovereign, he effectively challenges his latter-day audience to consider which of God's blessings they themselves consider the most desirable. The poet does not, after all, pray for his king's health, wealth, or sexual contentment, but rather that God find the

20

For the conductor, a psalm of David.

[2] יהוה will answer you on a day of trouble; the name of the God of Jacob will set you high and safe from danger.

[3] God will send you help from the Sanctuary, aiding you from Zion.

[4] God will remember all your grain offerings and will consider all your wholly burnt sacrifices as though they were made of pure fat, *selah.*

[5] God will grant you whatever your heart wishes and make right all the advice you give.

[6] We shall rejoice in your salvation, expressing our joy by praising God's name; יהוה will fulfill all your requests.

[7] Now I know that יהוה has saved the anointed one of God and will answer him from holy heaven with the redemptive might of the divine right hand.

[8] Some trust in chariots and others in horses, but we shall always recall the saving might of the name of יהוה, our God.

[9] Those others will bend and fall, whereas we shall rise up and remain ever strong.

[10] O יהוה, save us! May Sovereign God answer us on the day we call out.

king worthy to be an instrument of divine governance in the world specifically by virtue of his deeply sincere faith.

Is that what moderns, even pious ones, desire the most deeply? Is the greatest hope of religious people in our own world that God perceive the depth of feeling behind even the most banal ritual acts? Do the lives of the ritually observant inevitably affirm that all the great and small blessings that might come to an individual are necessarily the collective function of being right with God? Is it possible for moderns truly to believe that all the trappings of human happiness are merely simple or elaborate consequences of successful, heartfelt worship?

כא

לַמְנַצֵּחַ מִזְמוֹר לְדָוִד׃

2 יְהֹוָה בְּעָזְּךָ יִשְׂמַח־מֶלֶךְ וּבִישׁוּעָתְךָ מַה־*יָּגֶיל מְאֹד׃

3 תַּאֲוַת לִבּוֹ נָתַתָּה לּוֹ וַאֲרֶשֶׁת שְׂפָתָיו בַּל־מָנַעְתָּ סֶּלָה׃

4 כִּי־תְקַדְּמֶנּוּ בִּרְכוֹת טוֹב תָּשִׁית לְרֹאשׁוֹ עֲטֶרֶת פָּז׃

5 חַיִּים ׀ שָׁאַל מִמְּךָ נָתַתָּה לּוֹ אֹרֶךְ יָמִים עוֹלָם וָעֶד׃

6 גָּדוֹל כְּבוֹדוֹ בִּישׁוּעָתֶךָ הוֹד וְהָדָר תְּשַׁוֶּה עָלָיו׃

7 כִּי־תְשִׁיתֵהוּ בְרָכוֹת לָעַד תְּחַדֵּהוּ בְשִׂמְחָה אֶת־פָּנֶיךָ׃

8 כִּי־הַמֶּלֶךְ בֹּטֵחַ בַּיהֹוָה וּבְחֶסֶד עֶלְיוֹן בַּל־יִמּוֹט׃

9 תִּמְצָא יָדְךָ לְכָל־אֹיְבֶיךָ יְמִינְךָ תִּמְצָא שֹׂנְאֶיךָ׃

10 תְּשִׁיתֵמוֹ ׀ כְּתַנּוּר אֵשׁ לְעֵת פָּנֶיךָ יְהֹוָה בְּאַפּוֹ יְבַלְּעֵם וְתֹאכְלֵם אֵשׁ׃

11 פִּרְיָמוֹ מֵאֶרֶץ תְּאַבֵּד וְזַרְעָם מִבְּנֵי אָדָם׃

12 כִּי־נָטוּ עָלֶיךָ רָעָה חָשְׁבוּ מְזִמָּה בַּל־יוּכָלוּ׃

13 כִּי תְּשִׁיתֵמוֹ שֶׁכֶם בְּמֵיתָרֶיךָ תְּכוֹנֵן עַל־פְּנֵיהֶם׃

14 רוּמָה יְהֹוָה בְעֻזֶּךָ נָשִׁירָה וּנְזַמְּרָה גְּבוּרָתֶךָ׃

v. 2 יתיר י׳

Like the twentieth psalm, the twenty-first is a prayer for the welfare of the poet's king. Unfortunately, we cannot know whether this was an ancient hymn even in the days when the Psalter was being put together (for there was no king of the House of David who ruled over Israel in the period of the Second Temple) or a latter-day reverie about what it would be like for Israel once again to have a legitimate king. Nonetheless, modern readers can still feel profitably provoked by this "royal psalm" if they allow it to goad them into considering their own feelings about the concept of divine sovereignty. The traditional liturgy, after all, consistently acknowledges God as the Sovereign of the universe, but most worshipers rarely stop to consider what, precisely, that notion implies. Do people today truly feel governed by God in the manner of faithful subjects of a supremely powerful king? If we do, then must not the sense most of us have that we function freely in the world be merely an illusion born of human arrogance? But if *that* actually were the case, then what could it possibly mean for Scripture to urge us to choose one path in life over any other one?

By presenting his king's trust in God as parallel to the trust the king's subjects place in him, the poet is suggesting an alternate answer. The nobility

21

For the conductor, a psalm of David.

[2] O יהוה, the king rejoices in Your strength;
how intensely does he exult in Your salvation!

[3] You have granted him his heart's desire, not
denying him any spoken request, *selah.*

[4] For You greet him with blessings of goodness;
You set a crown of gold upon his head.

[5] He asked You for life and You granted it to him,
offering him length of days for ever and always.

[6] His glory in Your salvation is great; You made
him worthy of splendor and majesty.

[7] For You have bestowed permanent blessings
upon him, allowing him to take joyful pleasure
in the presence of Your face.

[8] For the king trusts in יהוה and, indeed, because
of his faith in the mercy of the Most High,
he shall not totter.

[9] Your hand will be the equal of all Your enemies;
indeed, Your right hand will vanquish those who
hate You.

[10] You will make the moment Your presence is made
manifest as terrifying to them as a fiery oven;
יהוה will swallow them up with divine anger
and fire shall consume them.

[11] Their fruit shall vanish from the earth, their seed
from humanity.

[12] For they planned evil against You, hatching plans
they could never actually bring to fruition.

[13] But You still made them flee, pulling back Your
bowstring and taking aim directly at their faces.

[14] Rise up in Your great strength, O יהוה. We shall
sing and chant hymns to Your might.

inherent in the assumption that God may be sought and worshiped through obedience to divine law flows directly, after all, from the fact that we are capable of sin, but choose to live differently. For their part, the subjects of a powerful monarch also have the capacity to disobey their sovereign's commands . . . but, unless they are very naive or very foolish, they must always weigh the plausible consequences of such disobedience against its potential benefits before deciding how to proceed. Perhaps the psalmist's model, then, although antiquated, will not be too far off the mark for moderns attempting to know God through faithfulness, fidelity, and fealty to law.

לַמְנַצֵּחַ עַל־אַיֶּלֶת הַשַּׁחַר מִזְמוֹר לְדָוִד:
2 אֵלִי אֵלִי לָמָה עֲזַבְתָּנִי רָחוֹק מִישׁוּעָתִי דִּבְרֵי שַׁאֲגָתִי:
3 אֱלֹהַי אֶקְרָא יוֹמָם וְלֹא תַעֲנֶה וְלַיְלָה וְלֹא־דוּמִיָּה לִי:
4 וְאַתָּה קָדוֹשׁ יוֹשֵׁב תְּהִלּוֹת יִשְׂרָאֵל: 5 בְּךָ בָּטְחוּ אֲבֹתֵינוּ בָּטְחוּ וַתְּפַלְּטֵמוֹ:
6 אֵלֶיךָ זָעֲקוּ וְנִמְלָטוּ בְּךָ בָטְחוּ וְלֹא־בוֹשׁוּ:
7 וְאָנֹכִי תוֹלַעַת וְלֹא־אִישׁ חֶרְפַּת אָדָם וּבְזוּי עָם:
8 כָּל־רֹאַי יַלְעִגוּ לִי יַפְטִירוּ בְשָׂפָה יָנִיעוּ רֹאשׁ: 9 גֹּל אֶל־יְהוָה יְפַלְּטֵהוּ יַצִּילֵהוּ כִּי חָפֵץ בּוֹ:
10 כִּי־אַתָּה גֹחִי מִבָּטֶן מַבְטִיחִי עַל־שְׁדֵי אִמִּי:
11 עָלֶיךָ הָשְׁלַכְתִּי מֵרָחֶם מִבֶּטֶן אִמִּי אֵלִי אָתָּה:
12 אַל־תִּרְחַק מִמֶּנִּי כִּי־צָרָה קְרוֹבָה כִּי־אֵין עוֹזֵר:
13 סְבָבוּנִי פָּרִים רַבִּים אַבִּירֵי בָשָׁן כִּתְּרוּנִי: 14 פָּצוּ עָלַי פִּיהֶם אַרְיֵה טֹרֵף וְשֹׁאֵג:

Many of the psalmists whose poems were incorporated in the Book of Psalms wrote of their misery, their dejectedness, their physical infirmity, and their despair, but only a very few of them managed to compose odes to anguish as deeply potent as the twenty-second psalm. Indeed, generations of readers have found it almost impossible to read this poem without being overwhelmed by empathy and sympathy for the plight of the poet, whose remark that he has turned into a worm is not meant to evoke an image of Kafkaesque metamorphosis as much as the simple fact that the poet perceives the world to be as interested in his suffering as the average passer-by would be concerned about a squashed centipede lying underfoot.

As little shy as he is miserable, the poet describes his problems in detail. He is terribly sick. His bones have become brittle and disjointed. His heart is fibrillating so constantly that his irregular heartbeat reminds him of a candle's flickering flame. He suffers from such violent diarrhea that his internal organs feel as though they have totally liquified. He has enough strength left to hold his writing tablet and his pen, but not much more than that. And on top of all that, his mouth is so terribly dry that his tongue keeps sticking to the roof of his mouth. But the poet is not solely the victim of unfortunate physical infirmity. Like so many others in the poetic guild, he has violent, predatory enemies who will stop at nothing to bring him down. Only this poet's enemies do not have to bother lurking in the dark to ambush him, for his illness has

22

For the conductor, a psalm of David to the tune of "The Doe at Dawn."

[2] My God, my God, why have You abandoned me? Why are the words I roar in agony so distant from effecting my salvation?

[3] I cry out all day, O my God, but You do not answer; I cry out all night, not letting even a single moment pass in silence.

[4] You, O Holy One, You who are enthroned upon the praises of Israel, [5] in You did our ancestors place their trust; they trusted in You and You delivered them.

[6] They cried out to You and escaped harm; they trusted in You and were not disappointed.

[7] But I am more of a worm than a human being, an insult among people and an object of national scorn.

[8] All who see me mock me, curling their lips in scorn, shaking their heads in disgust as if to say, [9] "Let him carry his troubles to יהוה who, so delighting in him, will rescue him and save him."

[10] But it was You who brought me forth from the womb, You who made me secure while I was still a suckling infant at my mother's breast. [11] Indeed, I have been dependent on You since the womb; You were my God when I was still in my mother's belly.

[12] Therefore, be not far from me now, for trouble is near and there is no one to help.

[13] Many oxen surround me; the bulls of Bashan are encircling me. [14] They open their mouths in my direction like ravenous, roaring lions.

already brought him so low that he will die soon enough on his own without any outside help.

And so the poet lies on what he presumes is his deathbed and contemplates his lot. He hears his enemies gathering around him, jokingly casting lots to see which of them will inherit which of his diseased rags. He thinks of them now as dumb oxen, now as vicious dogs, now as ravenous lions. The images shift in the poet's mind as the fever mounts, but his faith in God is amazingly unaffected by the circumstances of the hour. Incredibly, the poet does not blame God for his misery, preferring instead to recall the intense security he once felt as an infant nestled in his mother's protective bosom as he suckled at her

15 כַּמַּיִם נִשְׁפַּכְתִּי וְהִתְפָּרְדוּ כָּל־עַצְמוֹתָי הָיָה לִבִּי
כַּדּוֹנָג נָמֵס בְּתוֹךְ מֵעָי׃
16 יָבֵשׁ כַּחֶרֶשׂ ׀ כֹּחִי וּלְשׁוֹנִי מֻדְבָּק מַלְקוֹחָי וְלַעֲפַר־
מָוֶת תִּשְׁפְּתֵנִי׃ 17 כִּי־סְבָבוּנִי כְּלָבִים עֲדַת מְרֵעִים
הִקִּיפוּנִי כָּאֲרִי יָדַי וְרַגְלָי׃
18 אֲסַפֵּר כָּל־עַצְמוֹתָי הֵמָּה יַבִּיטוּ יִרְאוּ־בִי׃
19 יְחַלְּקוּ בְגָדַי לָהֶם וְעַל־לְבוּשִׁי יַפִּילוּ גוֹרָל׃
20 וְאַתָּה יְהוָה אַל־תִּרְחָק אֱיָלוּתִי לְעֶזְרָתִי חוּשָׁה׃
21 הַצִּילָה מֵחֶרֶב נַפְשִׁי מִיַּד־כֶּלֶב יְחִידָתִי׃
22 הוֹשִׁיעֵנִי מִפִּי אַרְיֵה וּמִקַּרְנֵי רֵמִים עֲנִיתָנִי׃
23 אֲסַפְּרָה שִׁמְךָ לְאֶחָי בְּתוֹךְ קָהָל אֲהַלְלֶךָּ׃
24 יִרְאֵי יְהוָה ׀ הַלְלוּהוּ כָּל־זֶרַע יַעֲקֹב כַּבְּדוּהוּ וְגוּרוּ
מִמֶּנּוּ כָּל־זֶרַע יִשְׂרָאֵל׃
25 כִּי לֹא־בָזָה וְלֹא שִׁקַּץ עֱנוּת עָנִי וְלֹא־הִסְתִּיר פָּנָיו
מִמֶּנּוּ וּבְשַׁוְּעוֹ אֵלָיו שָׁמֵעַ׃
26 מֵאִתְּךָ תְּהִלָּתִי בְּקָהָל רָב נְדָרַי אֲשַׁלֵּם נֶגֶד יְרֵאָיו׃

breast. Surely, he reasons, that sense of invulnerability was a gift from God for which he was then too innocent to be grateful, but which he can now recall with a sense of absolute beholdenness. As he recalls that God especially loves the prayers of the downtrodden and brokenhearted, the poet finds that the taunts of the wicked do not phase him. And then, when he finally realizes that the terminal nature of his illness has brought him closer to God than he had been—or perhaps was ever likely to be—as a healthy person, his courage transforms an ode to personal calamitous misery into a work of profound spiritual truth.

As moderns used to thinking of sickness and disease as catastrophes to be avoided at all cost, we may feel prompted by the poet's confession to ask ourselves how we feel about the contention that anything that leads an individual to God is, by definition, at least a kind of a blessing. To say just that is almost ordinary, but, given that it is so often the contemplation of human frailty that finally leads a person to faith, the twenty-second psalm also challenges us to ask a shocking question: can moderns stop fearing infirmity long enough to praise God for any antidote to the insane delusion of invulnerability that holds most people back from embracing faith in God with absolute trust, abiding love, and deep, unyielding conviction?

Moderns tend to think about faith as a kind of quirky genetic trait, like eye color or innate musical ability, that manifests itself in some people and not in

[15] My innards are as liquid as water and my bones are separating one from the other; my heart feels like so much molten wax dribbling down into my bowels.

[16] My palate is as brittle as a potsherd, my tongue is stuck to my gums. You have set me down in the dust of death, [17]for dogs have surrounded me and a congregation of evildoers has encompassed me; like lions, they are at my hands and my feet.

[18] I take stock of my bones while they look on and stare.

[19] They are already dividing up my clothing, casting lots to see which of them ends up with which of my garments.

[20] But You, O יהוה, be not distant from me; You who are my strength, hurry to my aid.

[21] Save my soul from the sword, my inmost self from the dog's hand; [22]save me from the lion's mouth and answer me before I am impaled on the horns of oxen.

[23] I shall proclaim Your name to my brethren; I shall praise You in the midst of the congregation.

[24] All you who fear יהוה, praise God. All you who are of Jacob's seed, honor God. All you of the seed of Israel, fear God.

[25] For God neither scorns nor abhors the prayer of the poor man. God will never hide the divine face from him and will listen when he cries out.

[26] From You comes all my praise in the great congregation; I shall honor my vows before those who fear God.

others with little or no reference to those people's moral worthiness or spiritual histories. To a certain extent, it may be true that there is some sort of predisposition to religious faith. Far more relevant, however, is an individual's willingness to struggle towards spiritual wholeness in God *both* by embracing those specific character traits capable of nurturing faith within the human heart *and* by jettisoning those traits inimical to religious development. Every individual will, of course, have to identify the specific qualities that will abet or disable his or her personal growth towards God, but the lesson for all to learn from contemplating the 22nd psalm is, perhaps, that the human personality is nowhere near as mal-

27 יֹאכְלוּ עֲנָוִים ׀ וְיִשְׂבָּעוּ יְהַלְלוּ יְהוָה דֹּרְשָׁיו יְחִי
לְבַבְכֶם לָעַד׃
28 יִזְכְּרוּ ׀ וְיָשֻׁבוּ אֶל־יְהוָה כָּל־אַפְסֵי־אָרֶץ וְיִשְׁתַּחֲווּ
לְפָנֶיךָ כָּל־מִשְׁפְּחוֹת גּוֹיִם׃ 29 כִּי לַיהוָה הַמְּלוּכָה
וּמֹשֵׁל בַּגּוֹיִם׃
30 אָכְלוּ וַיִּשְׁתַּחֲווּ ׀ כָּל־דִּשְׁנֵי־אֶרֶץ לְפָנָיו יִכְרְעוּ
כָּל־יוֹרְדֵי עָפָר וְנַפְשׁוֹ לֹא חִיָּה׃
31 זֶרַע יַעַבְדֶנּוּ יְסֻפַּר לַאדֹנָי לַדּוֹר׃ 32 יָבֹאוּ וְיַגִּידוּ
צִדְקָתוֹ לְעַם נוֹלָד כִּי עָשָׂה׃

leable as moderns tend to think. Indeed, there is nothing quite as impermeable as the various barriers life itself erects around the great goals of human spiritual development, making them elusive in the extreme for most people. We are not, therefore, in a position to turn away from those things life does give us as tools we might use to fashion a life in and of God for ourselves. Some of these tools—intelligence, sensitivity, empathy, and creativity, for example—are positive, desirable things that no one would consider spurning. But, as the poet knew, others are things like frailty, dependency, and a deep sense of obligation, indebtedness, and subservience—things that people generally prefer to avoid, even to shut totally out of their lives. The poet, however, has learned to look askance at nothing—not even at despair

[27] The humble will eat and be sated; those who seek God will render praise to יהוה. May your hearts forever beat strong!

[28] May even those who live at the very ends of the earth remember and return unto יהוה. And may all the families of the nations bow down before You, [29]for sovereignty belongs to יהוה, the God who rules over nations.

[30] The well-fed of the world will eat and bow down; all who must descend into the dust, even those whose souls God will not restore to life, will kneel down before God.

[31] Their progeny will worship God as well and tell of the great deeds of Adonai to the next generation; [32]they will go and tell of God's righteousness, of what God once did for a newborn nation.

and worry—that can lead to spiritual growth. He has come to understand that people grow towards God in different ways, along different roads, endowed with different gifts, and possessed of different tools. The location of those roads and tools, he knows, is hard enough to discern. But to locate them and then to spurn them because one feels somehow obliged by the culture of one's society to do so . . . that, the poet is saying, is as much folly as it is tragedy.

כג

מִזְמוֹר לְדָוִד
יְהוָה רֹעִי לֹא אֶחְסָר׃ 2 בִּנְאוֹת דֶּשֶׁא יַרְבִּיצֵנִי
עַל־מֵי מְנֻחוֹת יְנַהֲלֵנִי׃ 3 נַפְשִׁי יְשׁוֹבֵב יַנְחֵנִי
בְמַעְגְּלֵי־צֶדֶק לְמַעַן שְׁמוֹ׃
4 גַּם כִּי־אֵלֵךְ בְּגֵיא צַלְמָוֶת לֹא־אִירָא רָע כִּי־אַתָּה
עִמָּדִי שִׁבְטְךָ וּמִשְׁעַנְתֶּךָ הֵמָּה יְנַחֲמֻנִי׃
5 תַּעֲרֹךְ לְפָנַי ׀ שֻׁלְחָן נֶגֶד צֹרְרָי דִּשַּׁנְתָּ בַשֶּׁמֶן רֹאשִׁי
כּוֹסִי רְוָיָה׃
6 אַךְ טוֹב וָחֶסֶד יִרְדְּפוּנִי כָּל־יְמֵי חַיָּי וְשַׁבְתִּי
בְּבֵית־יְהוָה לְאֹרֶךְ יָמִים׃

The poet lies down to sleep and dreams of himself as a lamb grappling with the exquisite ambivalence inherent in wanting to serve in God's holy Temple, yet knowing that the lambs who serve God in that place usually do so by being slaughtered, by having their blood poured out as divinely ordained libations, and by having their lifeless carcasses burnt to ash. Yet what can the poet do if not praise God? His life as a lamb, at least so far, has been good and he feels deeply beholden to his Shepherd for all the blessings he enjoys, blessings that encompass everything a lamb could possibly need. And what are these blessings precisely? Plenty of cool water to drink. Endless tracts of grassy pastureland in which to meander and graze. An ongoing regimen of healthy exercise under the watchful eye of a Guardian whose staff is there to fight off wolves, not to strike the sheep when the darkness of a mountain pass temporarily immobilizes them with fear or when the contemplation of their destiny unnerves them and fills them with feelings of crippling anxiety.

23 A psalm of David.

I want for nothing, for יהוה is my shepherd; [2]it is God who lets me lie down in pastures of grass and who leads me to calm waters [3]to restore my spirit, who walks me in level pastures as befits a shepherd of sound reputation.

[4]Even though I must sometimes pass through dark valleys, I fear no harm for You are with me; indeed, Your crook and Your walking stick are sources of constant comfort for me.

[5]You set a table for me in the presence of my enemies; You have anointed my head with so much fine oil that I feel like an overflowing cup.

[6]Nothing but goodness and mercy pursue me all the days of my life; indeed, I feel certain that I shall dwell in the House of יהוה for days without end.

Modern readers who feel similarly ambivalent about their own role in the service of God will find it easy to identify with the lamb's dilemma. It is, after all, quite easy to *wish* to serve God because of the great blessings that come from currying favor with the divine realm, but it is another thing entirely to face the darker side of yearning for God and to accept that there will be enormous challenges to face as a result of choosing to live a life in God. Serving God means abandoning sin. Serving God means abandoning arrogance. Serving God means not serving other masters, some of whom pay very well. Serving God means being a servant, with all the good and bad that status entails. Serving God means wanting to live forever in God's sacred House—yet knowing at the same time that no sheep ever offers anything of value to God in that holy place other than its life. And serving God also means committing oneself to nothing else—to no other cause or master—quite as strongly or sincerely or passionately as one dedicates one's life to the sacred service of the Divine.

כד

לְדָוִד מִזְמוֹר
לַיהוָה הָאָרֶץ וּמְלוֹאָהּ תֵּבֵל וְיֹשְׁבֵי בָהּ׃ 2 כִּי הוּא
עַל־יַמִּים יְסָדָהּ וְעַל־נְהָרוֹת יְכוֹנְנֶהָ׃
3 מִי־יַעֲלֶה בְהַר יְהוָה וּמִי־יָקוּם בִּמְקוֹם קָדְשׁוֹ׃
4 נְקִי כַפַּיִם וּבַר לֵבָב אֲשֶׁר לֹא־נָשָׂא לַשָּׁוְא נַפְשִׁי
וְלֹא נִשְׁבַּע לְמִרְמָה׃
5 יִשָּׂא בְרָכָה מֵאֵת יְהוָה וּצְדָקָה מֵאֱלֹהֵי יִשְׁעוֹ׃
6 זֶה דּוֹר *דֹּרְשָׁיו מְבַקְשֵׁי פָנֶיךָ יַעֲקֹב סֶלָה׃
7 שְׂאוּ שְׁעָרִים ׀ רָאשֵׁיכֶם וְהִנָּשְׂאוּ פִּתְחֵי עוֹלָם
וְיָבוֹא מֶלֶךְ הַכָּבוֹד׃
8 מִי זֶה מֶלֶךְ הַכָּבוֹד יְהוָה עִזּוּז וְגִבּוֹר יְהוָה גִּבּוֹר
מִלְחָמָה׃
9 שְׂאוּ שְׁעָרִים ׀ רָאשֵׁיכֶם וּשְׂאוּ פִּתְחֵי עוֹלָם וְיָבֹא
מֶלֶךְ הַכָּבוֹד׃
10 מִי הוּא זֶה מֶלֶךְ הַכָּבוֹד יְהוָה צְבָאוֹת הוּא מֶלֶךְ
הַכָּבוֹד סֶלָה׃

v. 6 דרשו כתיב

The Bible tells the story of how Jacob wrestled with God and then named the place of their encounter Peniel (meaning "Face of God") to memorialize his experience of intimate, sensory communion with the Divine. Attempts to obfuscate that tradition, however—or even to deny it outright—are as old as the biblical text itself (in which the name of the place is altered to the obscure Penuel almost immediately). The psalmists took the story seriously, however, and the Psalter is, in a certain sense, the poetic chronicle of their attempts to see the face of God for themselves and to bask in the sacred glow of the light thrown off by the divine countenance. Indeed, it was probably against the background of that story that the poets' special kinship to Jacob developed: although Isaac's name appears in the psalms just once and there are only a

24

A psalm of David.
The world and its fullness, the earth and its inhabitants—everything belongs to יהוה,
[2]who laid its foundation upon the seas and set it firm upon its many rivers.
[3]Who may go up onto the mountain of יהוה?
And who may stand in that holy place?
[4]One who has clean hands and a pure heart.
One who has never falsely taken a vow by his life nor sworn a duplicitous oath.
[5]That person will receive a blessing from יהוה,
a righteous blessing from the God of salvation.
[6]This is the generation of those who seek God,
of those who seek Your face in the style of Jacob, *selah.*
[7]Lift up your heads, O gates. Lift yourselves up,
O portals of eternity, so that our glorious Sovereign may enter.
[8]And just who is our glorious Sovereign? יהוה,
valiant and heroic. יהוה, heroic in battle.
[9]Lift up your heads, O gates. Lift up your heads,
O portals of eternity, so that our glorious Sovereign may enter.
[10]And just who is our glorious Sovereign? יהוה
of the celestial legions is our glorious Sovereign, *selah.*

handful of verses in which Abraham is mentioned, Jacob's name appears about three dozen times because his life story, more than his father's or grandfather's, combined the psalmists' two favorite themes: the terror of brethren-turned-enemies and the deep desire to experience God not merely intellectually, but through the senses as well.

Many psalmists imply almost unambiguously that they consider this wholly perceptible God to exist in a relationship of potential intimacy with all humanity, thus challenging their latter-day readers to ask and, if they dare, to answer a simple question: if God can speak, why does society condemn as insane any who claim to hear the divine voice?

כה

לְדָוִד
אֵלֶיךָ יְהֹוָה נַפְשִׁי אֶשָּׂא:
2 אֱלֹהַי בְּךָ בָטַחְתִּי אַל־אֵבוֹשָׁה אַל־יַעַלְצוּ אֹיְבַי לִי:
3 גַּם כָּל־קֹוֶיךָ לֹא יֵבֹשׁוּ יֵבֹשׁוּ הַבּוֹגְדִים רֵיקָם:
4 דְּרָכֶיךָ יְהֹוָה הוֹדִיעֵנִי אֹרְחוֹתֶיךָ לַמְּדֵנִי:
5 הַדְרִיכֵנִי בַאֲמִתֶּךָ ׀ וְלַמְּדֵנִי כִּי־אַתָּה אֱלֹהֵי יִשְׁעִי אוֹתְךָ קִוִּיתִי כָּל־הַיּוֹם:
6 זְכֹר־רַחֲמֶיךָ יְהֹוָה וַחֲסָדֶיךָ כִּי מֵעוֹלָם הֵמָּה:
7 חַטֹּאות נְעוּרַי ׀ וּפְשָׁעַי אַל־תִּזְכֹּר כְּחַסְדְּךָ זְכָר־לִי־אַתָּה לְמַעַן טוּבְךָ יְהֹוָה:
8 טוֹב וְיָשָׁר יְהֹוָה עַל־כֵּן יוֹרֶה חַטָּאִים בַּדָּרֶךְ:
9 יַדְרֵךְ עֲנָוִים בַּמִּשְׁפָּט וִילַמֵּד עֲנָוִים דַּרְכּוֹ:
10 כָּל־אָרְחוֹת יְהֹוָה חֶסֶד וֶאֱמֶת לְנֹצְרֵי בְרִיתוֹ וְעֵדֹתָיו:
11 לְמַעַן־שִׁמְךָ יְהֹוָה וְסָלַחְתָּ לַעֲוֺנִי כִּי רַב־הוּא:
12 מִי זֶה הָאִישׁ יְרֵא יְהֹוָה יוֹרֶנּוּ בְּדֶרֶךְ יִבְחָר:
13 נַפְשׁוֹ בְּטוֹב תָּלִין וְזַרְעוֹ יִירַשׁ אָרֶץ:

Although most of the themes that dominate the twenty-fifth psalm also appear in many other poems in the Psalter, two of the poet's remarks set this psalm and its author apart from the others.

First, the poet's reference to the sins of his youth is as candid as it is anomalous: more openly than most of the other psalmists, this poet is prepared to attribute the suffering of his adulthood to the sins of his younger years. The poet begs God not to recall those transgressions—and then asks that God recall instead *not* the poet's own acts of worship and good deeds throughout the years, but rather God's own quality of goodness and kindness. Moved by the poet's candor, the reader cannot but wonder what the unspecified sins of the author's youth that continued to exert such an influence on his spiritual bearing as an adult may have been. Were they instances of ritual neglect? Or, as is so typical of adolescence, were they sins of sexual impropriety or disrespectful behavior towards parents or teachers? Or was the poet possibly an adult-style villain whose violent misdeeds reasonably continued to haunt him all the days of his life?

The actual nature of those sins cannot be known, but the second theme that sets the twenty-fifth psalm apart from the other poems of the Psalter might well point readers in the right direction. Four times the poet returns to the theme of shame, wishing aloud at the very beginning of his poem and then

25 (A psalm) of David.

I lift up my soul to You, O יהוה.

[2] My God, let me not be ashamed, for I have put my trust in You; let my enemies not exult in my downfall.

[3] Similarly, may all those who trust in You not be ashamed; instead, let those who betray You without reason be ashamed.

[4] Make Your ways known to me, O יהוה; teach me Your paths.

[5] Guide me with Your truth and teach me, for You are the God of my salvation and it is in You that I place my trust every day.

[6] O יהוה, remember Your compassion and Your mercy, for they are everlasting, [7]but remember not the sins and indiscretions of my youth; remember me in accordance with Your great mercy for the sake of Your own goodness, O יהוה.

[8] יהוה is good and just and therefore does God instruct sinners in the way, [9]guiding the humble to judge justly and teaching them the way of God.

[10] All the paths of יהוה are mercy and truth to those who keep the divine covenant and its testimonies.

[11] For the sake of Your name, יהוה, forgive my sin though it be great.

[12] Who is the individual who fears יהוה, if not the one God instructs in the right way to choose? [13]Such a soul will abide in goodness and his descendants shall inherit the earth.

again at the end that he not be shamed in public because of his decision to renounce the evil ways of his youth and embrace faith in God. He even prays that those who trust in God not know shame, but that those who betray the innocent be shamed both in public and before God.

Was there something in the poet's past that he recalled later in life not so much with regret or pain as with shame and embarrassment? Readers will naturally ask themselves both that question and its devotional corollary: when we think back to the errors and misdeeds of our own younger years, are we merely regretful or are we truly ashamed of having acted contrary to the word of God? Shame, after all, has a very poor reputa-

14 סוֹד יְהוָה לִירֵאָיו וּבְרִיתוֹ לְהוֹדִיעָם׃
15 עֵינַי תָּמִיד אֶל־יְהוָה כִּי הוּא־יוֹצִיא מֵרֶשֶׁת רַגְלָי׃
16 פְּנֵה־אֵלַי וְחָנֵּנִי כִּי־יָחִיד וְעָנִי אָנִי׃
17 צָרוֹת לְבָבִי הִרְחִיבוּ מִמְּצוּקוֹתַי הוֹצִיאֵנִי׃
18 רְאֵה־עָנְיִי וַעֲמָלִי וְשָׂא לְכָל־חַטֹּאותָי׃ 19 רְאֵה
אוֹיְבַי כִּי־רָבּוּ וְשִׂנְאַת חָמָס שְׂנֵאוּנִי׃
20 שָׁמְרָה נַפְשִׁי וְהַצִּילֵנִי אַל־אֵבוֹשׁ כִּי־חָסִיתִי בָךְ׃
21 תֹּם־וָיֹשֶׁר יִצְּרוּנִי כִּי קִוִּיתִיךָ׃
22 פְּדֵה־אֱלֹהִים אֶת־יִשְׂרָאֵל מִכֹּל צָרוֹתָיו׃

tion in modern life. People speak of shame almost as though it were itself something to be ashamed of, almost as though feeling ashamed of oneself or one's actions unavoidably points to an embarrassing lack of self-confidence or self-assurance. But the poet leads his readers down a different path by prompting them to consider the implications of his discovery that feeling deeply ashamed can lead one back to God. If this is so—and any-

[14] Membership in the council of יהוה is reserved for those who fear God; indeed, it is to them that the terms of the divine covenant are made known.

[15] My eyes are constantly towards יהוה, who will free my feet from the foes' net.

[16] Turn to me, O my God, and be gracious unto me; for I am alone and miserable.

[17] The troubles of my heart have swollen into a litany of woe; bring me forth from my calamities.

[18] See my misery and my suffering and forgive all my sins. [19] See how numerous my enemies are, and the groundless hatred with which they hate me.

[20] Guard my soul and save me; may I not be ashamed of having sought refuge in You.

[21] Guilelessness and decency will protect me, for I have put my hope in You.

[22] O God, redeem Israel from all of its troubles.

one who has ever truly felt ashamed of intemperate or vulgar behavior will find it almost impossible to argue with the poet's basic premise—then shame must be considered a positive force in life, perhaps even a kind of blessing. This is clearly the poet's conviction. But is it one moderns can embrace?

כו

לְדָוִד ׀
שָׁפְטֵנִי יְהֹוָה כִּי־אֲנִי בְּתֻמִּי הָלַכְתִּי וּבַיהֹוָה
בָּטַחְתִּי לֹא אֶמְעָד׃
2 בְּחָנֵנִי יְהֹוָה וְנַסֵּנִי *צָרְפָה כִלְיוֹתַי וְלִבִּי׃
3 כִּי־חַסְדְּךָ לְנֶגֶד עֵינָי וְהִתְהַלַּכְתִּי בַּאֲמִתֶּךָ׃
4 לֹא־יָשַׁבְתִּי עִם־מְתֵי־שָׁוְא וְעִם־נַעֲלָמִים לֹא
אָבוֹא׃
5 שָׂנֵאתִי קְהַל מְרֵעִים וְעִם־רְשָׁעִים לֹא אֵשֵׁב׃
6 אֶרְחַץ בְּנִקָּיוֹן כַּפָּי וַאֲסֹבְבָה אֶת־מִזְבַּחֲךָ יְהֹוָה׃
7 לַשְׁמִעַ בְּקוֹל תּוֹדָה וּלְסַפֵּר כָּל־נִפְלְאוֹתֶיךָ׃
8 יְהֹוָה אָהַבְתִּי מְעוֹן בֵּיתֶךָ וּמְקוֹם מִשְׁכַּן כְּבוֹדֶךָ׃
9 אַל־תֶּאֱסֹף עִם־חַטָּאִים נַפְשִׁי וְעִם־אַנְשֵׁי דָמִים
חַיָּי׃ 10 אֲשֶׁר־בִּידֵיהֶם זִמָּה וִימִינָם מָלְאָה שֹּׁחַד׃
11 וַאֲנִי בְּתֻמִּי אֵלֵךְ פְּדֵנִי וְחָנֵּנִי׃
12 רַגְלִי עָמְדָה בְמִישׁוֹר בְּמַקְהֵלִים אֲבָרֵךְ יְהֹוָה׃

v. 2 צרופה כתיב

At the heart of the twenty-sixth psalm rests the notion that the existence of evil people in the world constitutes a spiritual challenge to people of good will in a far more potent way than it exists as a theological dilemma to be grappled with at a safe distance by philosophers and scholars. The poet cannot hold back from mentioning the various groups of villains and thugs whose company he assiduously avoids. They are people of deceit, secret sinners, wicked evildoers, murderers, bribe-takers, and schemers, but the poet's own hands are clean and he is more than ready for God's judgment.

Indeed, for all his psalm reads as a kind of poetic self-justification, it also challenges readers to decide if they would look forward to that kind of divine scrutiny with the same equanimity as the poet does. The world, after all, is

26

(A psalm) of David.
Judge me, O יהוה, for I have walked guilelessly and, trusting in יהוה, I shall never slip.
[2] Test me, יהוה, and examine me; evaluate my head and my heart.
[3] For evidence of Your mercy is ever before my eyes; I walk about possessed of faith in Your truth.
[4] I do not sit with deceitful people and neither do I go about with those who hide themselves away to sin in secret.
[5] Indeed, I loathe the company of evildoers and shall never sit down with the wicked.
[6] Instead, I shall wash my hands clean, then circle Your altar, O יהוה, [7]to join in with the thanksgiving choir in singing of Your wondrous deeds.
[8] יהוה, I love this dwelling that is Your House, this place in which Your glory dwells.
[9] Gather not my soul up into the company of sinners, nor take my life along with people who spill blood, [10]whose hands are filled with licentiousness, whose right hands are filled with bribes.
[11] For I go about guilelessly; therefore, redeem me and be gracious unto me.
[12] My foot stands on level ground; I shall bless יהוה among the assembled masses.

surely as filled now with malign evildoers as it was in the poet's day. Do we understand avoiding their company to be an act of divine worship? Do we countenance the way society appears to insist on explaining (or rather, explaining away) the existence of evil people as a kind of flaw in God's creation, rather than as an opportunity for decent individuals to commune with God by renouncing depravity and embracing goodness? The poet had no doubts about his own innocence in God's eyes and had no qualms whatsoever about saying so explicitly. How many of us would dare say as much about ourselves?

לְדָוִד ׀
יְהוָה ׀ אוֹרִי וְיִשְׁעִי מִמִּי אִירָא יְהוָה מָעוֹז חַיַּי
מִמִּי אֶפְחָד׃
2 בִּקְרֹב עָלַי ׀ מְרֵעִים לֶאֱכֹל אֶת־בְּשָׂרִי צָרַי וְאֹיְבַי
לִי הֵמָּה כָשְׁלוּ וְנָפָלוּ׃
3 אִם־תַּחֲנֶה עָלַי ׀ מַחֲנֶה לֹא־יִירָא לִבִּי אִם־תָּקוּם
עָלַי מִלְחָמָה בְּזֹאת אֲנִי בוֹטֵחַ׃
4 אַחַת ׀ שָׁאַלְתִּי מֵאֵת־יְהוָה אוֹתָהּ אֲבַקֵּשׁ שִׁבְתִּי
בְּבֵית־יְהוָה כָּל־יְמֵי חַיַּי לַחֲזוֹת בְּנֹעַם־יְהוָה
וּלְבַקֵּר בְּהֵיכָלוֹ׃
5 כִּי יִצְפְּנֵנִי ׀ *בְּסֻכֹּה בְּיוֹם רָעָה יַסְתִּרֵנִי בְּסֵתֶר אָהֳלוֹ
בְּצוּר יְרוֹמְמֵנִי׃
6 וְעַתָּה יָרוּם רֹאשִׁי עַל־אֹיְבַי סְבִיבוֹתַי וְאֶזְבְּחָה
בְאָהֳלוֹ זִבְחֵי תְרוּעָה אָשִׁירָה וַאֲזַמְּרָה לַיהוָה׃
7 שְׁמַע־יְהוָה קוֹלִי אֶקְרָא וְחָנֵּנִי וַעֲנֵנִי׃
8 לְךָ ׀ אָמַר לִבִּי בַּקְּשׁוּ פָנָי אֶת־פָּנֶיךָ יְהוָה אֲבַקֵּשׁ׃
9 אַל־תַּסְתֵּר פָּנֶיךָ ׀ מִמֶּנִּי אַל־תַּט בְּאַף עַבְדֶּךָ עֶזְרָתִי
הָיִיתָ אַל־תִּטְּשֵׁנִי וְאַל־תַּעַזְבֵנִי אֱלֹהֵי יִשְׁעִי׃

v. 5 בסכה כתיב

The author of the twenty-seventh psalm has a wish (or perhaps more than one) and he has no hesitation about expressing himself forcefully, yet somehow also ambiguously, on the point. *One* thing does he ask of God, he writes, but then continues to explain that that one thing will lead to two separate goals: he wishes to dwell in the Temple forever so as to gaze on the beauty of God and to tarry permanently in God's presence.

Each of these notions has its own history, but the last is the least clear. (The Hebrew word translated here as "tarry" is *levakker,* a slightly obscure term used at 2 Kings 16:15 to denote some sort of obeisance at the Temple altar.) Even without understanding the full force of *levakker,* however, it is easy to understand that the poet wants to cultivate experiential, rather than merely intellectual, knowledge of God. And this, in turn, explains why the one thing he wants and the two boons attaining it will bring in its wake are actually one great spiritual goal in his mind: to dwell in God's physically perceptible presence, to gaze upon the beauty of God's perceptibly existent self-manifestation, and to worship God in the fullest, most perceptibly real way possible are

27 (A psalm) of David.

If יהוה is my light and my salvation, whom need I fear? If יהוה is the stronghold of my life, of whom then should I be frightened?

[2] When evildoers draw near to me to devour my flesh, when my enemies and foes approach, they stumble and fall.

[3] Should a platoon camp against me, my heart shall not know fear; should war be declared against me, even then shall I remain confirmed in my faith.

[4] One boon have I asked of יהוה and I request it now anew: that I be permitted to dwell in the House of יהוה all the days of my life, so that I might gaze on the beauty of יהוה and tarry forever in the divine sanctuary.

[5] For God will surely conceal me in the Temple—the divine *sukkah*—on a day of evil, hiding me in that protective tent, lifting me up onto a rock.

[6] Indeed, as I offer up the kind of sacrifice attended by trumpet blasts in God's tent, I can see my head lifted up higher than any of the enemies who surround me; I shall sing and chant hymns to יהוה.

[7] Hear my voice, יהוה, when I cry out; be gracious unto me and answer me.

[8] I heard my heart say, "Seek me" to You, but surely it is I who need to seek out Your face, יהוה.

[9] That being the case, hide not Your face from me. Turn not from Your servant in anger, for You are my help; neither forsake nor leave me, O God of my salvation.

merely different ways the poet has found to express the desire to know God through the senses rather than solely through the intellect. Indeed, although each of these things is mentioned one way or another throughout the Psalter, it is the special insight of the author of this psalm that they are, in the end, the same thing . . . or perhaps different aspects of the same thing. Indeed, the poet's point is that experiencing God emotionally, through the senses, and devotionally are *such* intensely interrelated experiences that none of them can bear ultimate meaning in the absence of the other two.

10 כִּֽי־אָבִ֣י וְאִמִּ֣י עֲזָב֑וּנִי וַֽיהֹוָ֣ה יַאַסְפֵֽנִי׃
11 ה֤וֹרֵ֥נִי יְהֹוָ֗ה דַּ֫רְכֶּ֥ךָ וּ֭נְחֵנִי בְּאֹ֣רַח מִישׁ֑וֹר לְ֝מַ֗עַן שֽׁוֹרְרָֽי׃
12 אַֽל־תִּ֭תְּנֵנִי בְּנֶ֣פֶשׁ צָרָ֑י כִּ֥י קָֽמוּ־בִ֥י עֵֽדֵי־שֶׁ֝֗קֶר וִיפֵ֥חַ חָמָֽס׃
13* לׅׄ֗וּׅׄלֵׅׄ֗אׅׄ הֶ֭אֱמַנְתִּי לִרְא֥וֹת בְּֽטוּב־יְהֹוָ֗ה בְּאֶ֣רֶץ חַיִּֽים׃
14 קַוֵּ֗ה אֶל־יְה֫וָ֥ה חֲ֭זַק וְיַאֲמֵ֣ץ לִבֶּ֑ךָ וְ֝קַוֵּ֗ה אֶל־יְהֹוָֽה׃

v. 13 נקוד מלמטה ומלמעלה חוץ מן ו׳ שלא נקוד אלא מלמטה

Readers may feel challenged to ask themselves to what extent their own religious lives bear out this truth. We live in a world in which we consider it quite normal to be devoted intensely to the rituals of religious observance even without feeling able, let alone obliged, to explain the riddle of God's presence in the world. Similarly, there are people in our modern world who profess to believe wholeheartedly in God's existence, but who desist entirely (or almost entirely) from the formal worship of the Divine. In yet a third category are people who have convinced themselves that faith in God and allegiance to the service of God are rendered neither pointless nor absurd by God's apparent refusal ever actually to be seen or heard by mortals in this world. In his own way, the poet is simply asking us, his latter-day readers, to evaluate the spiritual worth of belonging to any of these categories and to draw whatever conclusions we can with respect to the

[10] For although my father and my mother have left me, יהוה shall gather me in.

[11] Teach me Your way, O יהוה, and guide me on the level path in order to confound all those who are watching my every move.

[12] Give me not into the hand of my enemies, for false witnesses out to inspire violence have risen up against me.

[13] Perhaps they would have already vanquished me, had I not believed it to be my lot to look upon the goodness of יהוה in the land of the living.

[14] Hope in יהוה! Be strong and may your heart be of good courage; hope in יהוה!

worth of our own spirituality.

The twenty-seventh psalm is read in the synagogue service twice a day during the month preceding Rosh Hashanah and throughout the entire season of the autumn penitential holidays. At the time of year when people find their thoughts turning more and more frequently to their relationship with God, it is both bold and brave to read the twenty-seventh psalm over and over as part of public worship, almost as though its message were in need of intense inculcation. And what is that message? Simply that God may be known even today in the normal way human beings know each other, that God must be served to be known, and that even the most assiduous performance of rites and rituals must be deemed meaningless in the absence of faith in a God who can be encountered, not merely obeyed.

כח

לְדָוִד
אֵלֶיךָ יְהוָה | אֶקְרָא צוּרִי אַל־תֶּחֱרַשׁ מִמֶּנִּי פֶּן־
תֶּחֱשֶׁה מִמֶּנִּי וְנִמְשַׁלְתִּי עִם־יוֹרְדֵי בוֹר:
2 שְׁמַע קוֹל תַּחֲנוּנַי בְּשַׁוְּעִי אֵלֶיךָ בְּנָשְׂאִי יָדַי
אֶל־דְּבִיר קָדְשֶׁךָ:
3 אַל־תִּמְשְׁכֵנִי עִם־רְשָׁעִים וְעִם־פֹּעֲלֵי אָוֶן דֹּבְרֵי
שָׁלוֹם עִם־רֵעֵיהֶם וְרָעָה בִּלְבָבָם:
4 תֶּן־לָהֶם כְּפָעֳלָם וּכְרֹעַ מַעַלְלֵיהֶם כְּמַעֲשֵׂה
יְדֵיהֶם תֵּן לָהֶם הָשֵׁב גְּמוּלָם לָהֶם:
5 כִּי לֹא יָבִינוּ אֶל־פְּעֻלֹּת יְהוָה וְאֶל־מַעֲשֵׂה יָדָיו
יֶהֶרְסֵם וְלֹא יִבְנֵם:
6 בָּרוּךְ יְהוָה כִּי־שָׁמַע קוֹל תַּחֲנוּנָי:
7 יְהוָה | עֻזִּי וּמָגִנִּי בּוֹ בָטַח לִבִּי וְנֶעֱזָרְתִּי וַיַּעֲלֹז לִבִּי
וּמִשִּׁירִי אֲהוֹדֶנּוּ:
8 יְהוָה עֹז־לָמוֹ וּמָעוֹז יְשׁוּעוֹת מְשִׁיחוֹ הוּא:
9 הוֹשִׁיעָה אֶת־עַמֶּךָ וּבָרֵךְ אֶת־נַחֲלָתֶךָ וּרְעֵם
וְנַשְּׂאֵם עַד־הָעוֹלָם:

The poet's yearning to hear the voice of God is so intense that he believes enduring divine silence to be almost unbearably painful. He is adept at all the rituals and ethical practices of his faith: he lifts up his hands towards the Holy of Holies, he recites his prayers faithfully, and he assiduously avoids the company of hypocrites and wrongdoers. All that may be praiseworthy, but the poet's point is *precisely* that living in a world in which God can be served and worshiped, but not actually heard, would be a kind of living death.

Modern readers will find the poet's point easiest to seize if we respond to his poem by asking ourselves if we believe that God *ever* speaks to individual

28

(A psalm) of David.

I cry out to You, יהוה; my Rock, be not deaf to my supplication. For if You are silent to my plea, then I will be as those already gone down to the pit.

[2] Hear the sound of my supplications as I cry out to You, as I lift up my hands towards the innermost chamber of Your sanctuary.

[3] Draw me neither to the wicked nor to doers of iniquity, people who speak of peace with their friends while their hearts are filled with evil.

[4] Pay them back in accordance with their actions and their evil deeds. Punish them in accordance with the work of their hands; give them their just desserts.

[5] For they understand neither the doings of יהוה nor the work of God's hands; may God destroy them and never rehabilitate them.

[6] Blessed be יהוה for hearing the sound of my supplications.

[7] יהוה is my strength and my shield; in God does my heart trust and in God am I helped. Let my heart exult, so that I may express my gratitude to God with my song.

[8] יהוה is a source of strength to the faithful and a stronghold of salvation to the divinely anointed prince.

[9] Save Your people and bless Your inheritance; shepherd them and sustain them forever.

human beings. Believing in an all-powerful God who cannot speak is illogical, after all—but faith in a God who *can,* but simply *will not,* speak is not really any less so. The poet could not bear the thought of living with God's silence. His latter-day audience will begin to understand him best by pondering why we moderns find it so reasonable—and so little difficult—to believe in a quiet God.

כט

מִזְמוֹר לְדָוִד
הָבוּ לַיהוָה בְּנֵי אֵלִים הָבוּ לַיהוָה כָּבוֹד וָעֹז׃
2 הָבוּ לַיהוָה כְּבוֹד שְׁמוֹ הִשְׁתַּחֲווּ לַיהוָה בְּהַדְרַת־קֹדֶשׁ׃
3 קוֹל יְהוָה עַל־הַמָּיִם אֵל־הַכָּבוֹד הִרְעִים יְהוָה עַל־מַיִם רַבִּים׃
4 קוֹל־יְהוָה בַּכֹּחַ קוֹל יְהוָה בֶּהָדָר׃
5 קוֹל יְהוָה שֹׁבֵר אֲרָזִים וַיְשַׁבֵּר יְהוָה אֶת־אַרְזֵי הַלְּבָנוֹן׃
6 וַיַּרְקִידֵם כְּמוֹ־עֵגֶל לְבָנוֹן וְשִׂרְיֹן כְּמוֹ בֶן־רְאֵמִים׃
7 קוֹל־יְהוָה חֹצֵב לַהֲבוֹת אֵשׁ׃
8 קוֹל יְהוָה יָחִיל מִדְבָּר יָחִיל יְהוָה מִדְבַּר קָדֵשׁ׃
9 קוֹל יְהוָה | יְחוֹלֵל אַיָּלוֹת וַיֶּחֱשֹׂף יְעָרוֹת וּבְהֵיכָלוֹ כֻּלּוֹ אֹמֵר כָּבוֹד׃
10 יְהוָה לַמַּבּוּל יָשָׁב וַיֵּשֶׁב יְהוָה מֶלֶךְ לְעוֹלָם׃
11 יְהוָה עֹז לְעַמּוֹ יִתֵּן יְהוָה | יְבָרֵךְ אֶת־עַמּוֹ בַשָּׁלוֹם׃

Although widely thought to be an ancient hymn accepted into the Psalter centuries after its composition, the twenty-ninth psalm must have appealed mightily to those ancients who cultivated ongoing auditory communion with God. The Book of Psalms, after all, is studded with passages which record the various oracles the authors of specific psalms felt themselves actually to have heard, and the twenty-ninth psalm is nothing less than an ode to the experience of hearing the (no less real than recondite, no less attainable than elusive) voice of God.

29

A psalm of David.

Render unto יהוה, O divine beings, render glory and strength unto יהוה.

[2] Render unto יהוה the glory due the divine name; bow down low to יהוה in the splendor of the Sanctuary.

[3] The voice of יהוה goes out over the waters; the God of glory thunders forth. יהוה thunders forth over the multitude of waters.

[4] The voice of יהוה is powerful; the voice of יהוה is splendid.

[5] The voice of יהוה can destroy cedars; indeed, יהוה can demolish all the cedars of Lebanon.

[6] Alternately, our God can make those cedars dance like romping calves or make Lebanon and Sirion gambol about like young oxen.

[7] The voice of יהוה can hew flames of fire.

[8] The voice of יהוה can make a desert tremble; יהוה can even make tremble the Kadesh Desert.

[9] The voice of יהוה can make ewes dance or defoliate entire forests; within God's Sanctuary, however, its full force exists only to say, "Glory."

[10] יהוה reigned at the time of the flood and יהוה will reign for all time.

[11] יהוה gives strength unto the people of God; may יהוה ever bless the people of God with peace.

Seven times the poet returns to the phrase *kol* יהוה ("the voice of יהוה"), in each instance describing its wondrousness in more and more extravagant terms. Readers will inevitably feel prompted to ask themselves what they think it would be like actually to experience divine speech. Would it be akin to a lover's whisper or a mother's kiss . . . or would it be the kind of blast of intense divinity that really could defoliate a forest or make a desert tremble? More to the point: what do an individual's specific expectations about hearing God's voice say about the specific nature of that person's faith . . . and about the likelihood that that person will ever hear God speak?

ל

מִזְמוֹר שִׁיר חֲנֻכַּת הַבַּיִת לְדָוִד׃
2 אֲרוֹמִמְךָ יְהוָה כִּי דִלִּיתָנִי וְלֹא־שִׂמַּחְתָּ אֹיְבַי לִי׃
3 יְהוָה אֱלֹהָי שִׁוַּעְתִּי אֵלֶיךָ וַתִּרְפָּאֵנִי׃ 4 יְהוָה
הֶעֱלִיתָ מִן־שְׁאוֹל נַפְשִׁי חִיִּיתַנִי *מִיָּרְדִי־בוֹר׃
5 זַמְּרוּ לַיהוָה חֲסִידָיו וְהוֹדוּ לְזֵכֶר קָדְשׁוֹ׃ 6 כִּי רֶגַע
בְּאַפּוֹ חַיִּים בִּרְצוֹנוֹ בָּעֶרֶב יָלִין בֶּכִי וְלַבֹּקֶר רִנָּה׃
7 וַאֲנִי אָמַרְתִּי בְשַׁלְוִי בַּל־אֶמּוֹט לְעוֹלָם׃
8 יְהוָה בִּרְצוֹנְךָ הֶעֱמַדְתָּה לְהַרְרִי עֹז הִסְתַּרְתָּ פָנֶיךָ
הָיִיתִי נִבְהָל׃ 9 אֵלֶיךָ יְהוָה אֶקְרָא וְאֶל־אֲדֹנָי
אֶתְחַנָּן׃ 10 מַה־בֶּצַע בְּדָמִי בְּרִדְתִּי אֶל־שָׁחַת
הֲיוֹדְךָ עָפָר הֲיַגִּיד אֲמִתֶּךָ׃ 11 שְׁמַע־יְהוָה וְחָנֵּנִי
יְהוָה הֱיֵה עֹזֵר לִי׃
12 הָפַכְתָּ מִסְפְּדִי לְמָחוֹל לִי פִּתַּחְתָּ שַׂקִּי וַתְּאַזְּרֵנִי
שִׂמְחָה׃ 13 לְמַעַן ׀ יְזַמֶּרְךָ כָבוֹד וְלֹא יִדֹּם יְהוָה
אֱלֹהַי לְעוֹלָם אוֹדֶךָּ׃

v. 4 מיורדי כתיב

It is hard to imagine anyone as overwhelmed with gratitude for a miraculous cure from illness as the author of the thirtieth psalm. Other psalmists write of being sick unto death, but this poet writes that he actually felt himself entering Sheol, the great common grave of mortal humanity. Yet although he clearly saw himself on the verge of being lowered into the pit, it turned out to have been a false alarm and, instead of joining the dead in their dank kingdom, he lived. Amazed at his recovery and overwhelmed with gratitude, he explains his good fortune theologically, not medically: he turned to God and God answered him. His answer leaves us with the satisfying image of God granting him a full recovery and turning his misery to joy, literally (or at least figuratively) ripping off his hospital gown

30

A psalm-song of David composed upon the dedication of the House of God.

[2] I exalt You, יהוה, for You have drawn me up and have not given my enemies cause to rejoice over my downfall.

[3] יהוה, my God, I called out to You and You healed me; [4]יהוה, You have brought my soul up from Sheol and granted me life when I was already practically in the grave.

[5] May the faithful chant hymns to יהוה and give thanks to God's holy name, [6]for divine anger lasts but a moment, yet life is extended in accordance with God's will; one can lie down for the night weeping, yet rise up singing hymns of joy.

[7] I declare with tranquil certainty that I shall never again totter.

[8] יהוה, You had previously granted me the strength to stand up like a mighty mountain, so I was duly terrified when You hid Your face; [9]I cried out to You, יהוה, and made supplication before Adonai, saying: [10]"What would be the profit in me being silenced, in me descending into the pit? Will dust give You thanks? Can it tell of Your truth? [11]Hear me, O יהוה, and be gracious unto me. יהוה, be my help . . ."

[12] And, indeed, You did turn my mourning into dancing; You pulled off my sackcloth and girded me instead with happiness, [13]that my soul might sing out to You and not be silent. יהוה, my God, I shall declare my gratitude to You forever.

and replacing it with the kind of outfit one would normally wear to go dancing, but readers will understand the poet best if they pause to contemplate the implications of finding in God the source of healing. Why is it, then, that today's faithful so often *dis*courage very sick people from praying to God for recovery? Do they assume that God, whose omnipotence they claim not to doubt, would never actually alter the apparently inexorable course of terminal illness?

לא

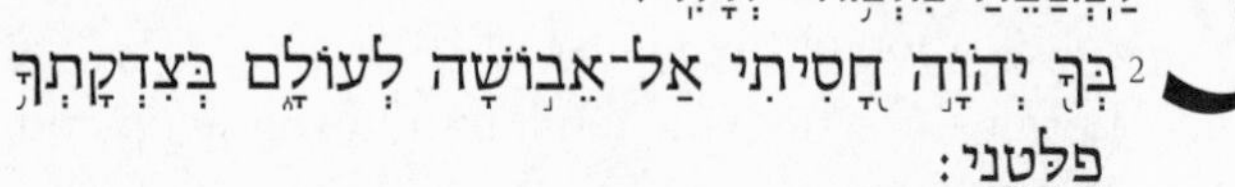

לַמְנַצֵּחַ מִזְמוֹר לְדָוִד׃
2 בְּךָ יְהוָה חָסִיתִי אַל־אֵבוֹשָׁה לְעוֹלָם בְּצִדְקָתְךָ
פַלְּטֵנִי׃
3 הַטֵּה אֵלַי ׀ אָזְנְךָ מְהֵרָה הַצִּילֵנִי הֱיֵה לִי ׀ לְצוּר־
מָעוֹז לְבֵית מְצוּדוֹת לְהוֹשִׁיעֵנִי׃ 4 כִּי־סַלְעִי
וּמְצוּדָתִי אָתָּה וּלְמַעַן שִׁמְךָ תַּנְחֵנִי וּתְנַהֲלֵנִי׃
5 תּוֹצִיאֵנִי מֵרֶשֶׁת זוּ טָמְנוּ לִי כִּי־אַתָּה מָעוּזִּי׃
6 בְּיָדְךָ אַפְקִיד רוּחִי פָּדִיתָה אוֹתִי יְהוָה אֵל אֱמֶת׃
7 שָׂנֵאתִי הַשֹּׁמְרִים הַבְלֵי־שָׁוְא וַאֲנִי אֶל־יְהוָה
בָּטָחְתִּי׃
8 אָגִילָה וְאֶשְׂמְחָה בְּחַסְדֶּךָ אֲשֶׁר רָאִיתָ אֶת־עָנְיִי
יָדַעְתָּ בְּצָרוֹת נַפְשִׁי׃ 9 וְלֹא הִסְגַּרְתַּנִי בְּיַד־אוֹיֵב
הֶעֱמַדְתָּ בַמֶּרְחָב רַגְלָי׃
10 חָנֵּנִי יְהוָה כִּי צַר־לִי עָשְׁשָׁה בְכַעַס עֵינִי נַפְשִׁי
וּבִטְנִי׃
11 כִּי כָלוּ בְיָגוֹן חַיַּי וּשְׁנוֹתַי בַּאֲנָחָה כָּשַׁל בַּעֲוֺנִי
כֹחִי וַעֲצָמַי עָשֵׁשׁוּ׃
12 מִכָּל־צֹרְרַי הָיִיתִי חֶרְפָּה וְלִשְׁכֵנַי ׀ מְאֹד וּפַחַד
לִמְיֻדָּעָי רֹאַי בַּחוּץ נָדְדוּ מִמֶּנִּי׃
13 נִשְׁכַּחְתִּי כְּמֵת מִלֵּב הָיִיתִי כִּכְלִי אֹבֵד׃ 14 כִּי

The author of the thirty-first psalm feels he could bear the scorn of strangers or the casual loathing of anonymous passers-by with stoic equanimity. He could even perhaps adapt to the ongoing fear of physical violence, but the situation in which the poet actually finds himself is far worse than that. For one thing, he feels certain that his enemies are plotting not merely to do him ill, but to do him in: he indicts them (perhaps only slightly prematurely) of attempting to murder him. And to make matters even more painful, the enemies of whom the poet speaks are not strangers, but people well-known to the poet, individuals he calls "neighbors" and "acquaintances" with the bitter sarcasm of the betrayed. Has the poet already been seized by those who wish him such grievous evil? He makes passing reference to his guards as impotent nothings, but then fails to mention them even one more time. He does, however, write about having been caught in a net of some sort as though he had been hunted down like a wild animal. And, indeed, if he had been ambushed, captured, and held in some secret dungeon, then the poet's repeated references to God as his fortress made of rock, his stronghold,

31

For the conductor, a psalm of David.

[2] In You, יהוה, have I sought refuge, may I never be ashamed; rescue me, therefore, with Your righteousness.

[3] Incline Your ear towards me, save me quickly; become my stone-fortified stronghold, my fortress of deliverance, [4]for You are my rock and my fortress and You will lead me forward and guide me for the sake of Your name.

[5] Bring me forth out of the trap that they have set for me, for You are my source of strength.

[6] Into Your hand I commend my spirit; redeem me, O יהוה, O God of truth.

[7] I despise the guards as barely existent breaths of nothingness; instead, I trust in יהוה.

[8] Once You take note of my distress, I shall exult and rejoice in Your mercy; You know the suffering of my soul [9]and will not let me be imprisoned by the enemy. Indeed, You will grant me a wide open space in which to stand.

[10] Be gracious unto me, יהוה, for I am in dire straits; my eye, my soul, even my belly, are weak with worry.

[11] For my life is given over entirely to suffering, my years to groaning; my strength has waned in accordance with my sins and even my bones have become weak.

[12] Because of all my enemies, I have become the very embodiment of ill ease to my neighbors, something truly fearful to my acquaintances; people who see me outdoors wander off when they notice me coming.

[13] I am as forgotten from their hearts as a dead person; I have become a lost object in their

his citadel, and his pavilion would be even more moving as the words of a man hunted and pursued like a fox in the forest, then confined against his will by guards who, despite the poet's sarcasm, must have been strong enough (or at least well enough armed) to keep him where they wished him to be kept for as long as they wanted. He would not be a metaphoric or symbolic detainee, therefore, but an actual prisoner being held by actual kidnappers—but whose poem would nonetheless not be one of despair. Without any hint of irony, the poet proclaims his certainty that God will

שָׁמַעְתִּי ׀ דִּבַּת רַבִּים מָגוֹר מִסָּבִיב בְּהִוָּסְדָם יַחַד
עָלָי לָקַחַת נַפְשִׁי זָמָמוּ׃

[15] וַאֲנִי ׀ עָלֶיךָ בָטַחְתִּי יְהוָה אָמַרְתִּי אֱלֹהַי אָתָּה׃

[16] בְּיָדְךָ עִתֹּתָי הַצִּילֵנִי מִיַּד־אוֹיְבַי וּמֵרֹדְפָי׃

[17] הָאִירָה פָנֶיךָ עַל־עַבְדֶּךָ הוֹשִׁיעֵנִי בְחַסְדֶּךָ׃

[18] יְהוָה אַל־אֵבוֹשָׁה כִּי קְרָאתִיךָ יֵבֹשׁוּ רְשָׁעִים
יִדְּמוּ לִשְׁאוֹל׃

[19] תֵּאָלַמְנָה שִׂפְתֵי שָׁקֶר הַדֹּבְרוֹת עַל־צַדִּיק עָתָק
בְּגַאֲוָה וָבוּז׃

[20] מָה רַב טוּבְךָ אֲשֶׁר־צָפַנְתָּ לִּירֵאֶיךָ פָּעַלְתָּ לַחוֹסִים
בָּךְ נֶגֶד בְּנֵי אָדָם׃

[21] תַּסְתִּירֵם בְּסֵתֶר פָּנֶיךָ מֵרֻכְסֵי אִישׁ תִּצְפְּנֵם בְּסֻכָּה
מֵרִיב לְשֹׁנוֹת׃

[22] בָּרוּךְ יְהוָה כִּי־הִפְלִיא חַסְדּוֹ לִי בְּעִיר מָצוֹר׃

[23] וַאֲנִי ׀ אָמַרְתִּי בְחָפְזִי נִגְרַזְתִּי מִנֶּגֶד עֵינֶיךָ אָכֵן
שָׁמַעְתָּ קוֹל תַּחֲנוּנַי בְּשַׁוְּעִי אֵלֶיךָ׃

[24] אֶהֱבוּ אֶת־יְהוָה כָּל־חֲסִידָיו אֱמוּנִים נֹצֵר יְהוָה
וּמְשַׁלֵּם עַל־יֶתֶר עֹשֵׂה גַאֲוָה׃

[25] חִזְקוּ וְיַאֲמֵץ לְבַבְכֶם כָּל־הַמְיַחֲלִים לַיהוָה׃

save him and bring him forth from the predicament into which he has blundered. He declares openly, and not at all cynically, that God is his fortress, his rock, his safe house. The poet's slanderers will end up silent in their graves, but their victim will live in his faith, sure both of the good stored up for the faithful and of the dire fate that will befall their tormentors.

Moderns considering these ancient lines will be either perplexed or inspired by them, but they will find them stimulating in either case. For most moderns, after all, it would be a challenge not only to find a personal path to the poet's kind of bedrock, unflinching faith in the Almighty, but even just to find a way of embracing the conviction that such a path actually could exist . . . or that the poet's kind of faith actually could. The word "faith" is mostly used in our day to refer to ideas and dogmatic assertions that cannot be scientifically or rationally demonstrated to be true and that, therefore, have to be accepted—if they are to be accepted at all—without the benefit of clear, unequivocal proof that they mirror reality. Yet, although most moderns tend to dismiss insistence on the truth of unproven theories as whiney and inconsequential, scientists

minds. [14]And I have heard the slanderous things all those people say about me; indeed, there is nothing but horror all around me as they organize against me. They are plotting to kill me, [15]but I trust in You, יהוה; I say, "You are my God."

[16] In Your hand are the seasons of my life; save me from my enemies and persecutors.

[17] Let the light of Your face shine upon me, Your servant; in Your mercy, save me.

[18] יהוה, may I not know shame because I have called upon You; on the contrary: may the wicked know shame and may they rot silently in Sheol.

[19] May their lying lips be silenced, those lips that speak audacious libel about a righteous person with arrogance and contempt.

[20] What great goodness have You hidden away for those who fear You; how mightily have You labored in public on behalf of those who put their trust in You.

[21] You hide them in the hidden folds of Your divine face from the secret plottings of other people; You protect them in a protective shelter from malicious slander.

[22] Blessed be יהוה, who has shown wondrous mercy to me in a city under siege.

[23] Although in my haste I might have said, "I am excised from Your field of vision," the truth is that You do hear the sound of my supplication when I call out to You.

[24] Love יהוה, all you faithful, for יהוה is the Guardian of faith who more than amply requites those who act arrogantly.

[25] Be strong and let your hearts be firm, all you who hope in יהוה.

and mathematicians *do* in fact accept any number of unproven assertions as axioms—not because they can be scientifically demonstrated, but merely because they appear always and invariably to be true. Since the poet's faith in God appears to be absolute and unshakable, then, it must also be the case that that kind of totally secure belief in God's existence has to be possible . . . and could be embraced, therefore, by any individual capable of fashioning a life in which faith in God, even when sorely tested, appears always to mirror reality.

לב

לְדָוִד מַשְׂכִּיל
אַשְׁרֵי נְשׂוּי־פֶּשַׁע כְּסוּי חֲטָאָה׃
2 אַשְׁרֵי אָדָם לֹא יַחְשֹׁב יְהוָה לוֹ עָוֺן וְאֵין בְּרוּחוֹ רְמִיָּה׃
3 כִּי הֶחֱרַשְׁתִּי בָּלוּ עֲצָמָי בְּשַׁאֲגָתִי כָּל־הַיּוֹם׃
4 כִּי ׀ יוֹמָם וָלַיְלָה ׀ תִּכְבַּד עָלַי יָדֶךָ נֶהְפַּךְ לְשַׁדִּי בְּחַרְבֹנֵי קַיִץ סֶלָה׃
5 חַטָּאתִי אוֹדִיעֲךָ וַעֲוֺנִי לֹא־כִסִּיתִי אָמַרְתִּי אוֹדֶה עֲלֵי פְשָׁעַי לַיהוָה וְאַתָּה נָשָׂאתָ עֲוֺן חַטָּאתִי סֶלָה׃
6 עַל־זֹאת יִתְפַּלֵּל כָּל־חָסִיד ׀ אֵלֶיךָ לְעֵת מְצֹא רַק לְשֵׁטֶף מַיִם רַבִּים אֵלָיו לֹא יַגִּיעוּ׃
7 אַתָּה ׀ סֵתֶר לִי מִצַּר תִּצְּרֵנִי רָנֵּי פַלֵּט תְּסוֹבְבֵנִי סֶלָה׃
8 אַשְׂכִּילְךָ ׀ וְאוֹרְךָ בְּדֶרֶךְ־זוּ תֵלֵךְ אִיעֲצָה עָלֶיךָ עֵינִי׃
9 אַל־תִּהְיוּ ׀ כְּסוּס כְּפֶרֶד אֵין הָבִין בְּמֶתֶג וָרֶסֶן עֶדְיוֹ לִבְלוֹם בַּל קְרֹב אֵלֶיךָ׃
10 רַבִּים מַכְאוֹבִים לָרָשָׁע וְהַבּוֹטֵחַ בַּיהוָה חֶסֶד יְסוֹבְבֶנּוּ׃
11 שִׂמְחוּ בַיהוָה וְגִילוּ צַדִּיקִים וְהַרְנִינוּ כָּל־יִשְׁרֵי־לֵב׃

This famous psalm, which Jews everywhere recite on Yom Kippur, turns on a paradox: the poet knows he has sinned before God and feels too ashamed to speak openly of his transgressions, yet his situation only deteriorates for as long as he remains silent. When, on the other hand, he confesses his sins to God, owning up to them openly and acknowledging them with regret and deep, unabashed contrition, he feels the forgiveness of God coming over him and comforting him. And he doesn't *only* experience relief from his suffering, but he is also vouchsafed an unexpected oracle from God telling him to stop behaving like a mule

32

A wise-song of David.
Happy is one whose transgression is overlooked, whose sin is glossed over.
[2] Happy is the one to whom יהוה does not attribute any iniquity, the one not even slightly fraudulent of spirit.
[3] While I did not speak, my bones eroded away as I moaned all day long.
[4] When Your hand weighed down on me day and night, my sap turned sour as if I were a piece of dried out summer fruit, *selah.*
[5] But now I declare my sins to You without hiding any of my iniquities. When I say, "I admit my transgressions to יהוה," You will declare my iniquitous sins overlooked, *selah.*
[6] For this reason the faithful pray to You when the opportunity presents itself; only let the flood of great waters not reach those who turn to You in prayer.
[7] You are my hiding place; You saved me from my enemy. You allowed me to escape joyfully; You surrounded me and spoke to me, saying, *selah,*
[8] "I will enlighten you and teach you on which path you should walk; I shall advise you well, for My eye is upon you.
[9] Be not like a horse or a mule that has no understanding, a foolish beast that needs its 'ornaments'—its bit and bridle—to stop it from approaching you."
[10] The wicked will suffer great pains, but one who trusts in יהוה will be surrounded by mercy.
[11] Rejoice in יהוה. Be glad, O you righteous; exult, O you upright of heart.

that only knows to turn this way and that when its master yanks on the bit in its mouth. God, the poet learns, can control human behavior that same way, but that is not how divine justice is *inevitably* dispensed in the world. There is another way to live in God's favor, he now knows: the way of *teshuvah,* of repentance, of turning wholeheartedly to God while both suffused with contrition and fortified with the unyielding will to sin no more.

לג

רַנְּנוּ צַדִּיקִים בַּיהוָה לַיְשָׁרִים נָאוָה תְהִלָּה׃
2 הוֹדוּ לַיהוָה בְּכִנּוֹר בְּנֵבֶל עָשׂוֹר זַמְּרוּ־לוֹ׃
3 שִׁירוּ לוֹ שִׁיר חָדָשׁ הֵיטִיבוּ נַגֵּן בִּתְרוּעָה׃ 4 כִּי־יָשָׁר דְּבַר־יְהוָה וְכָל־מַעֲשֵׂהוּ בֶּאֱמוּנָה׃
5 אֹהֵב צְדָקָה וּמִשְׁפָּט חֶסֶד יְהוָה מָלְאָה הָאָרֶץ׃
6 בִּדְבַר יְהוָה שָׁמַיִם נַעֲשׂוּ וּבְרוּחַ פִּיו כָּל־צְבָאָם׃
7 כֹּנֵס כַּנֵּד מֵי הַיָּם נֹתֵן בְּאֹצָרוֹת תְּהוֹמוֹת׃
8 יִירְאוּ מֵיהוָה כָּל־הָאָרֶץ מִמֶּנּוּ יָגוּרוּ כָּל־יֹשְׁבֵי תֵבֵל׃ 9 כִּי הוּא אָמַר וַיֶּהִי הוּא־צִוָּה וַיַּעֲמֹד׃
10 יְהוָה הֵפִיר עֲצַת גּוֹיִם הֵנִיא מַחְשְׁבוֹת עַמִּים׃
11 עֲצַת יְהוָה לְעוֹלָם תַּעֲמֹד מַחְשְׁבוֹת לִבּוֹ לְדֹר וָדֹר׃
12 אַשְׁרֵי הַגּוֹי אֲשֶׁר־יְהוָה אֱלֹהָיו הָעָם ׀ בָּחַר לְנַחֲלָה לוֹ׃
13 מִשָּׁמַיִם הִבִּיט יְהוָה רָאָה אֶת־כָּל־בְּנֵי הָאָדָם׃
14 מִמְּכוֹן־שִׁבְתּוֹ הִשְׁגִּיחַ אֶל כָּל־יֹשְׁבֵי הָאָרֶץ׃
15 הַיֹּצֵר יַחַד לִבָּם הַמֵּבִין אֶל־כָּל־מַעֲשֵׂיהֶם׃

The poet sits quietly and contemplates the hordes of soldiers and horses that pass through Jerusalem on a daily basis. And, indeed, no matter how many pilgrims come to the holy city and no matter how packed the Temple courts are with pious locals and worshipers from afar, the city always seems like an armed camp to the poet. The king's infantry, in fact, is so vast and his mounted troops so numerous that one could easily believe that the security of the people rests on the might of the royal cavalry rather than on faith in God. But the poet knows a secret, one that might well sound seditious—or at least suspect—to most of his countrymen, but which he is prepared to share with his readers. Kings, he has learned, do not escape with their lives from battles they are losing because they have enormous armies backing them up and covering their escapes. And neither do they survive because of their horses, no matter how many thousands they may have ready for war. Indeed, the poet has lighted upon a truth that might escape even the most respectful observer of the military: in the end, true security only comes from faith in God . . . and particularly from the cultivation of faith in a God who knows the innermost secrets of the human heart, who *made* the heart so as to be able to see into its most private chambers, and who is therefore capa-

33

Rejoice in יהוה, you righteous, for praise is delightful for the upright to enjoy.

[2] Give thanks to יהוה with a lyre; sing to God with a ten-stringed *nevel.*

[3] Sing unto God a new song accompanied by shouts of joy, [4]for the word of יהוה is just and all that God has wrought is done in good faith.

[5] God loves righteousness and justice; the whole earth is filled with the mercy of יהוה.

[6] At a word from יהוה, the heavens were made; at a gust of divine breath, all their host of heavenly bodies were fashioned.

[7] God gathered the waters of the sea together in a vast pool, setting the ocean depths in special vaults.

[8] The whole earth holds יהוה in awe; all the world's inhabitants revere God, [9]who said that the world should be and it was, who commanded that it endure and it did.

[10] יהוה annuls the advice of nations and overrides the plans of alien peoples, [11]but the advice of יהוה will always stand, as will those thoughts that derive directly from the divine heart.

[12] Happy is the nation whose God is יהוה, the people God chose as the divine portion.

[13] יהוה looks down from heaven and sees all humanity; [14–15]from the divine residence, God, who fashioned the human heart in all its complexity and who knows the deeds of all people, observes all the world's populace.

ble of discerning the true motives behind all human behavior. And the poet also knows something else: that it is simple enough to mouth slogans and platitudes, but quite something else truly to accept the idea of a God by whose grace even mighty kings are saved.

Modern readers of the thirty-third psalm may well feel prompted to respond to the poet's ancient words by asking themselves where, precisely, they put their own trust, their own faith, and their own hope. Most readers, of course, will not be generals who command armies or sovereign monarchs at war with hostile enemy nations, but rather ordinary people seeking in the psalms a way of coming to understand God, to fear God,

16 אֵין הַמֶּלֶךְ נוֹשָׁע בְּרָב־חָיִל גִּבּוֹר לֹא־יִנָּצֵל
בְּרָב־כֹּחַ׃ 17 שֶׁקֶר הַסּוּס לִתְשׁוּעָה וּבְרֹב חֵילוֹ לֹא
יְמַלֵּט׃
18 הִנֵּה עֵין יְהוָה אֶל־יְרֵאָיו לַמְיַחֲלִים לְחַסְדּוֹ׃
19 לְהַצִּיל מִמָּוֶת נַפְשָׁם וּלְחַיּוֹתָם בָּרָעָב׃
20 נַפְשֵׁנוּ חִכְּתָה לַיהוָה עֶזְרֵנוּ וּמָגִנֵּנוּ הוּא׃
21 כִּי־בוֹ יִשְׂמַח לִבֵּנוּ כִּי בְשֵׁם קָדְשׁוֹ בָטָחְנוּ׃
22 יְהִי־חַסְדְּךָ יְהוָה עָלֵינוּ כַּאֲשֶׁר יִחַלְנוּ לָךְ׃

and to feel the eye of God upon themselves. They will be average citizens attempting to convince themselves that their chances for deliverance from the dangers of the world depend on their faith in God rather than on wealth, status, or power. How can a psalm help its readers come to this kind of deep, abiding faith? The poet thinks that acknowledging God as the Creator of the world, then contemplating God as the true source of power and deliverance in that world, would be a good place to start. The journey is long, the poet knows, but not impossible . . . and not any longer for commoners than for kings.

[16] Kings are not saved because of their great armies and neither do heroes escape defeat because of their great strength. [17]Indeed, horses are false guarantors of salvation and one will never escape danger because of great strength alone.

[18] But the eye of יהוה is on those who fear God and who hope that God, prompted by feelings of divine mercy, [19]will save their souls from death and sustain them in times of famine.

[20] Our soul waits for יהוה, our source of help and our shield.

[21] In God do our hearts rejoice, for in God's holy name do we place our trust.

[22] May Your mercy, יהוה, be upon us just as we have put our hope in You.

לד

לְדָוִד בְּשַׁנּוֹתוֹ אֶת־טַעְמוֹ לִפְנֵי אֲבִימֶלֶךְ וַיְגָרְשֵׁהוּ
וַיֵּלַךְ:
2 אֲבָרְכָה אֶת־יְהוָה בְּכָל־עֵת תָּמִיד תְּהִלָּתוֹ בְּפִי:
3 בַּיהוָה תִּתְהַלֵּל נַפְשִׁי יִשְׁמְעוּ עֲנָוִים וְיִשְׂמָחוּ:
4 גַּדְּלוּ לַיהוָה אִתִּי וּנְרוֹמְמָה שְׁמוֹ יַחְדָּו:
5 דָּרַשְׁתִּי אֶת־יְהוָה וְעָנָנִי וּמִכָּל־מְגוּרוֹתַי הִצִּילָנִי:
6 הִבִּיטוּ אֵלָיו וְנָהָרוּ וּפְנֵיהֶם אַל־יֶחְפָּרוּ:
7 זֶה עָנִי קָרָא וַיהוָה שָׁמֵעַ וּמִכָּל־צָרוֹתָיו הוֹשִׁיעוֹ:
8 חֹנֶה מַלְאַךְ־יְהוָה סָבִיב לִירֵאָיו וַיְחַלְּצֵם:
9 טַעֲמוּ וּרְאוּ כִּי־טוֹב יְהוָה אַשְׁרֵי הַגֶּבֶר יֶחֱסֶה־בּוֹ:
10 יִרְאוּ אֶת־יְהוָה קְדֹשָׁיו כִּי אֵין מַחְסוֹר לִירֵאָיו:
11 כְּפִירִים רָשׁוּ וְרָעֵבוּ וְדֹרְשֵׁי יְהוָה לֹא־יַחְסְרוּ
כָל־טוֹב:
12 לְכוּ־בָנִים שִׁמְעוּ־לִי יִרְאַת יְהוָה אֲלַמֶּדְכֶם:
13 מִי־הָאִישׁ הֶחָפֵץ חַיִּים אֹהֵב יָמִים לִרְאוֹת טוֹב:
14 נְצֹר לְשׁוֹנְךָ מֵרָע וּשְׂפָתֶיךָ מִדַּבֵּר מִרְמָה:
15 סוּר מֵרָע וַעֲשֵׂה־טוֹב בַּקֵּשׁ שָׁלוֹם וְרָדְפֵהוּ:
16 עֵינֵי יְהוָה אֶל־צַדִּיקִים וְאָזְנָיו אֶל־שַׁוְעָתָם:

The poet knows God neither as a philosophical theory nor as a spiritual truth, but as part of his day-to-day reality, as a feature of the actual world in which he lives and works. His poem, in turn, reflects his sense of the Divine: the poet knows God not through the mind—or at least not *solely* through the mind—but through the senses as well. He hears the voice of God in his ears. As part of a community of fellow seekers, he has felt the light of God's face warming his own face as he experiences divine communion. He can even taste God's presence in his mouth and, although he stops short of explaining precisely what he means by such an unusual assertion, the basic concept is clear enough: the poet's God is neither poetry nor philosophy, but reality no less perceptible than any other thing the poet deems truly and absolutely to exist.

And how is one to attain that kind of intimacy with the divine presence? The poet has some ideas along those lines too, but his instructions may surprise latter-day readers. Shun evil, he suggests, and do good. Avoid slander and calumny. Pursue peace in every aspect of daily life and do not be content to live in a world of strife and unhappiness. Divest yourself of arrogance

34 (A psalm) of David, composed when he changed his demeanor before Abimelech, who banished him as a result, whereupon he left.

[2] I bless יהוה at all times; the praise of God is always in my mouth.

[3] My soul shall vaunt itself in יהוה; let the humble hear and rejoice.

[4] Ascribe greatness to יהוה with me; let us together exalt the divine name.

[5] Look to me: I sought יהוה, who answered me and saved me from all my worst fears.

[6] Look to the others: they directed their gaze towards God and were illuminated; may their faces never again be pale.

[7] For even if a poor person cries out, יהוה will hear and redeem him from all his woes; indeed, [8]the angel of יהוה will set up camp around those who fear God to make them safe.

[9] Taste and see how good is יהוה; happy is the one who trusts in God.

[10] The saints hold יהוה in awe, for God-fearers will never suffer want; [11]even lions must occasionally know poverty and hunger, but those who seek יהוה will never lack for any good thing.

[12] O children, come and listen to me and I will instruct you in the awe due to יהוה.

[13] Are you the individual who yearns for life, a lover of days who yearns to see goodness?

[14] Guard your tongue from evil and your lips from speaking deceit.

[15] Avoid evil and do good; solicit peace and pursue it actively.

[16] The eyes of יהוה are on the righteous; God's ears are ever open to hear their cries.

and the haughty sense of superiority to which the spiritually adept so often find themselves falling prey, for God hates people who are full of themselves and is especially accessible to the brokenhearted of this world, to the downcast of spirit, and to the miserable who turn *to,* rather than *from,* God in their misery. These, the poet is saying, are the most useful tools with which anyone can attempt to build a life in God.

Readers of the thirty-fourth psalm may wish to allow themselves to be provoked by its stirring cadences into considering the effect their own

17 פְּנֵי יְהֹוָה בְּעֹשֵׂי רָע לְהַכְרִית מֵאֶרֶץ זִכְרָם׃
18 צָעֲקוּ וַיהֹוָה שָׁמֵעַ וּמִכָּל־צָרוֹתָם הִצִּילָם׃
19 קָרוֹב יְהֹוָה לְנִשְׁבְּרֵי־לֵב וְאֶת־דַּכְּאֵי־רוּחַ יוֹשִׁיעַ׃
20 רַבּוֹת רָעוֹת צַדִּיק וּמִכֻּלָּם יַצִּילֶנּוּ יְהֹוָה׃ 21 שֹׁמֵר כָּל־עַצְמוֹתָיו אַחַת מֵהֵנָּה לֹא נִשְׁבָּרָה׃
22 תְּמוֹתֵת רָשָׁע רָעָה וְשֹׂנְאֵי צַדִּיק יֶאְשָׁמוּ׃
23 פּוֹדֶה יְהֹוָה נֶפֶשׁ עֲבָדָיו וְלֹא יֶאְשְׁמוּ כָּל־הַחֹסִים בּוֹ׃

religious observance has had on the state of their souls. Has it induced more humility or more arrogance into those souls? Has the search for God made them feel more eager to do good in the world or more scornful of those of less punctil-

[17]The face of יהוה is ever set against those who do evil so that their name be extirpated from the earth; [18]יהוה listens when the righteous cry out, then saves them from all their troubles.

[19]Indeed, יהוה is ever close to the brokenhearted, ever scrupulous to save the downtrodden of spirit; [20]no matter how many disasters befall the righteous, יהוה will save them from them all, [21]caring so zealously for each of their bones that not even one shall be broken.

[22]For, in the end, evil itself will kill the wicked, and those who hate the righteous will themselves be annihilated.

[23]יהוה will redeem the souls of the servants of God, so that those who put their trust in God will never face annihilation.

ious observance? Has hewing to a regimen of ritual observance helped them embrace the pursuit of peace or given them leave to feel good about ignoring it entirely? Have they unintentionally fallen into the trap of allowing their piety to engender destructive hubris, egotism, and insolence, and thus to drive them away from God . . . just precisely as they appear to the outside world to be seeking communion with the Divine more fervently than ever?

לה

לְדָוִד ׀
רִיבָה יְהוָה אֶת־יְרִיבַי לְחַם אֶת־לֹחֲמָי׃
2 הַחֲזֵק מָגֵן וְצִנָּה וְקוּמָה בְּעֶזְרָתִי׃
3 וְהָרֵק חֲנִית וּסְגֹר לִקְרַאת רֹדְפָי אֱמֹר לְנַפְשִׁי
יְשֻׁעָתֵךְ אָנִי׃
4 יֵבֹשׁוּ וְיִכָּלְמוּ מְבַקְשֵׁי נַפְשִׁי יִסֹּגוּ אָחוֹר וְיַחְפְּרוּ
חֹשְׁבֵי רָעָתִי׃
5 יִהְיוּ כְּמֹץ לִפְנֵי־רוּחַ וּמַלְאַךְ יְהוָה דּוֹחֶה׃
6 יְהִי־דַרְכָּם חֹשֶׁךְ וַחֲלַקְלַקּוֹת וּמַלְאַךְ יְהוָה רֹדְפָם׃
7 כִּי־חִנָּם טָמְנוּ־לִי שַׁחַת רִשְׁתָּם חִנָּם חָפְרוּ
לְנַפְשִׁי׃
8 תְּבוֹאֵהוּ שׁוֹאָה לֹא יֵדָע וְרִשְׁתּוֹ אֲשֶׁר־טָמַן תִּלְכְּדוֹ
בְּשׁוֹאָה יִפָּל־בָּהּ׃
9 וְנַפְשִׁי תָּגִיל בַּיהוָה תָּשִׂישׂ בִּישׁוּעָתוֹ׃
10 כָּל עַצְמוֹתַי ׀ תֹּאמַרְנָה יְהוָה מִי כָמוֹךָ מַצִּיל עָנִי
מֵחָזָק מִמֶּנּוּ וְעָנִי וְאֶבְיוֹן מִגֹּזְלוֹ׃
11 יְקוּמוּן עֵדֵי חָמָס אֲשֶׁר לֹא־יָדַעְתִּי יִשְׁאָלוּנִי׃

Many are the sorrows that afflict people in the course of their lives. Some are grievous, others less so. Some feel almost insurmountable, while others can be borne and eventually transformed from torturous present into nightmarish past.

For the poet whose ancient ode is our thirty-fifth psalm, the experience of betrayal by a friend was something that no amount of rationalization could neutralize . . . and something he could only work through in the context of his faith in God. Unlike other psalmists who write vaguely about the hostile environments in which they were obliged to live and work, this poet holds nothing back and describes his situation in a way that is as shocking as it is deeply pathetic. Someone, or some group of people, is trying to kill him. Too cowardly actually to murder him themselves, they have sought refuge from their weakness in the perversion of justice: they have denounced him to the authorities and accused him falsely of capital crimes.

The poet's situation, however, is as ironic as it is tragic because his foes are not erstwhile enemies, but former friends. These are people for whose good health he actually used to fast and pray, people whose ill fortune so affected his sense of inner calm that he himself went around looking more like someone whose mother had died than like someone whose friends were going through a difficult patch. But the past is not so easily erased by the present and, even

35

(A psalm) of David.

Struggle, O יהוה, with those who struggle with me; fight against those who fight against me.

[2] Make firm my shield and buckler and rise up to be my source of help.

[3] Empty Your scabbard of its sword and latch it closed as You go forth against my pursuers; say to my soul, "I am your salvation."

[4] May those who seek to take my soul be ashamed and embarrassed; may those who wish me ill be forced to retreat and may their faces turn pale in fear.

[5] May they be like chaff in the wind as the angel of יהוה shoves them aside.

[6] May their path be one of darkness and slipperiness as the angel of יהוה pursues them, [7]for they laid their net over a pit to seize me for no reason; for no reason at all did they dig a pit to take my life.

[8] May catastrophe come upon my enemy unawares; may the net he hid for me capture him instead and may he fall in it, thus himself suffering the planned catastrophe.

[9] As for me, my soul will find gladness in יהוה and rejoice in God's salvation.

[10] All my bones shall say, "Who is like You, O יהוה, who saves the poor from those stronger than they, who saves the poor and the destitute from whomever would rob them?"

[11] Violent thugs—perjurers—rise up and ask me about things of which I know nothing.

now, he thinks of the people who gnash their teeth at him in the street and leer at him with the most sarcastic, threatening looks not merely as lapsed acquaintances, but as former friends, even as some kind of ex-brothers. And now that the truth has come out, the poet can barely keep from drowning in the misery generated by contemplating the treachery of his former intimates. Indeed, when the poet passionately calls on God to wake up and look after the administration of justice in this perverse world, his words echo not only with hurt and resignation, but also with anger—anger generated by perfidy at the hands of people he once loved and trusted, whose company he once

12 יְשַׁלְּמוּנִי רָעָה תַּחַת טוֹבָה שְׁכוֹל לְנַפְשִׁי׃ 13 וַאֲנִי ׀
בַּחֲלוֹתָם לְבוּשִׁי שָׂק עִנֵּיתִי בַצּוֹם נַפְשִׁי וּתְפִלָּתִי
עַל־חֵיקִי תָשׁוּב׃
14 כְּרֵעַ כְּאָח־לִי הִתְהַלָּכְתִּי כַּאֲבֶל־אֵם קֹדֵר
שַׁחוֹתִי׃
15 וּבְצַלְעִי שָׂמְחוּ וְנֶאֱסָפוּ נֶאֶסְפוּ עָלַי נֵכִים וְלֹא
יָדַעְתִּי קָרְעוּ וְלֹא־דָמּוּ׃
16 בְּחַנְפֵי לַעֲגֵי מָעוֹג חָרֹק עָלַי שִׁנֵּימוֹ׃
17 אֲדֹנָי כַּמָּה תִּרְאֶה הָשִׁיבָה נַפְשִׁי מִשֹּׁאֵיהֶם
מִכְּפִירִים יְחִידָתִי׃
18 אוֹדְךָ בְּקָהָל רָב בְּעַם עָצוּם אֲהַלְלֶךָּ׃
19 אַל־יִשְׂמְחוּ־לִי אֹיְבַי שֶׁקֶר שֹׂנְאַי חִנָּם יִקְרְצוּ־עָיִן׃
20 כִּי לֹא שָׁלוֹם יְדַבֵּרוּ וְעַל רִגְעֵי־אֶרֶץ דִּבְרֵי מִרְמוֹת
יַחֲשֹׁבוּן׃ 21 וַיַּרְחִיבוּ עָלַי פִּיהֶם אָמְרוּ הֶאָח ׀ הֶאָח
רָאֲתָה עֵינֵינוּ׃

sought, and whose beneficence he once took totally and absolutely for granted.

Modern readers will understand the ancient bard best if they focus on the poet's sense that the only hope for escaping the machinations of one's enemies lies in the cultivation of faith. The poet, after all, is not responding to his former friends' disloyalty by hiring a lawyer (much less an assassin), but by writing a psalm to God. Like the author of the thirty-first psalm, he writes openly about the way he was ambushed with some sort of net laid secretly over a pit his enemies had dug in the ground. But God is the poet's safety net, his refuge from fear, worry, and the terrifying possibility that his foes will denounce him successfully enough to secure a conviction against him that will carry the death penalty. Readers who feel comfortable nodding to the poet's trusting faith will do better to ask themselves what they really think of his response to disaster. Is the psalmist being deeply pious or deeply foolish to respond to his enemies' machinations by seeking refuge in God? Should he be spending his time writing poetry or should he be scrambling to denounce his foes to the authorities? Surely people who report a crime to the police rather than to God are not considered blasphemers, but how then shall we react to the poet's analysis of where his best chances lie? Is he behaving like a saint or an idiot, like a *tzaddik* or a total fool?

And there is another issue for moderns to contemplate as they ponder the verses of the 35th psalm as well. The poet has been betrayed by his former circle of friends and acquaintances. He has been denounced, insulted, threat-

[12] They repay me evil for good and bring me nothing but bereavement, [13]even though I went around in sackcloth when they were ill, afflicting my own soul with fasting on their behalf. Would that I could take my prayers back now!

[14] I went around as though they were my brothers or friends; in their times of trouble, I went about bent and depressed as one who mourns for a mother.

[15] But now they get together to rejoice when they see me limping, a group of degenerates gathering together in my regard, although they think I know nothing of it. They are tearing me to shreds and they will not desist.

[16] As the most scornful of mocking insults, they grind their teeth in my direction.

[17] Adonai, how much more of this will You have to see? Restore my soul from the threat of destruction at their hands, my unique being from that pride of lions.

[18] Amidst the many, I give thanks to You; among a mighty people, I shall praise You.

[19] May my lying enemies not gloat at my downfall; may those who hate me for no reason not wink their eyes insultingly in my direction.

[20] For they speak not of peace; indeed, all they do is hatch evil plots against the peaceful inhabitants of the land, [21]opening their mouths wide against me and saying, "Hurrah! Hurrah! Our own eyes have seen his downfall!"

ened, and degraded. Yet, unlike many moderns would, he does not appear to harbor the slightest worry that he himself might be the party ultimately responsible for his own disaster. He does not identify even slightly with his ex-comrades. He does not appear, even for a moment, to entertain the possibility that they are in the right and he is in the wrong. Nor does he mention any lingering hope for reconciliation, or for a return to the world—the false, but familiar and secure world—in which those he now knows as enemies appeared in the role of supportive, caring friends. In other words, the poet sounds grateful to know things as they truly are, not regretful that he has been disabused of his fantasies about the world (and the comfort and ease those fantasies brought in their satisfying, but ultimately illusory, wake). Moreover, he

22 רָאִיתָה יְהוָה אַל־תֶּחֱרַשׁ אֲדֹנָי אַל־תִּרְחַק מִמֶּנִּי
23 הָעִירָה וְהָקִיצָה לְמִשְׁפָּטִי אֱלֹהַי וַאדֹנָי לְרִיבִי׃
24 שָׁפְטֵנִי כְצִדְקְךָ יְהוָה אֱלֹהָי וְאַל־יִשְׂמְחוּ־לִי׃
25 אַל־יֹאמְרוּ בְלִבָּם הֶאָח נַפְשֵׁנוּ אַל־יֹאמְרוּ
בִּלַּעֲנוּהוּ׃
26 יֵבֹשׁוּ וְיַחְפְּרוּ ׀ יַחְדָּו שְׂמֵחֵי רָעָתִי יִלְבְּשׁוּ־בֹשֶׁת
וּכְלִמָּה הַמַּגְדִּילִים עָלָי׃
27 יָרֹנּוּ וְיִשְׂמְחוּ חֲפֵצֵי צִדְקִי וְיֹאמְרוּ תָמִיד יִגְדַּל
יְהוָה הֶחָפֵץ שְׁלוֹם עַבְדּוֹ׃
28 וּלְשׁוֹנִי תֶּהְגֶּה צִדְקֶךָ כָּל־הַיּוֹם תְּהִלָּתֶךָ׃

sounds totally at his ease wishing ill for his enemies *regardless* of how he once thought of them. As a result, the poet sounds more angry than pathetic, more secure in his faith than rattled by his former friends' perfidy. He has, to say it simply, moved on. And when he curses his foes with shame, misery, and woe, he appears to mean every word.

Moderns, trained from childhood on to assume that there are two sides to every coin, will want to ask themselves if they have it in them to denounce evil when it crosses their path without first exhausting themselves to find excuses for the perpetrators of that evil. Identification with the aggressor is not a modern malady *per se,* but it is a feature of the lives of all those who, even when evil is being directed against them personally, still find it troubling to turn to God in wholehearted prayer for the triumph of good and the annihilation of evil.

[22] In that You surely have seen all this, יהוה,
be not silent; Adonai, be not distant from me.
[23] Wake up and rouse Yourself to justice on my behalf, O my God; Adonai, take up my struggle.
[24] Judge me according to Your justice, יהוה, my God; let them not gloat over me.
[25] Let them not say in their hearts, "Hurrah! By our souls, he had it coming." Let them not say, "We have swallowed him alive."
[26] Let the reward for those who rejoice at my troubles be a mixture of shame and embarrassment; let those who vaunt themselves over me wear garments woven of shame and disgrace.
[27] But may those who wish justice for me be glad and rejoice; may they always have cause to say, "Great is יהוה, who wishes always for the peace of a servant of God."
[28] Then shall my tongue too speak of Your justice and sing Your praise all day long.

The biblical accounts of the wars undertaken by the Israelites to rid the land of its former inhabitants, though gory and gruesome, have the same lesson at their core: that complacency in the eradication of evil is a sin against God, and that it is always moral and right to work for the defeat of wickedness. Moderns generally vacillate between dismissing these lessons as archaic (and therefore irrelevant) and accepting them as theoretically valid (but wholly impractical in terms of how the world actually functions). The psalmist points to a different way entirely, however. Leading by example, he writes to teach his readers that there is nothing base about hating treachery and disloyalty . . . nor is there anything peculiar or unjustifiable about praying that God reward the just and punish those who rejoice at the suffering of a righteous man.

לו

לַמְנַצֵּ֬חַ ׀ לְעֶֽבֶד־יְהֹוָ֬ה לְדָוִֽד׃
2 נְאֻֽם־פֶּ֣שַׁע לָ֭רָשָׁע בְּקֶ֣רֶב לִבִּ֑י אֵֽין־פַּ֥חַד אֱ֝לֹהִ֗ים לְנֶ֣גֶד עֵינָֽיו׃ 3 כִּֽי־הֶחֱלִ֣יק אֵלָ֣יו בְּעֵינָ֑יו לִמְצֹ֖א עֲוֺנ֣וֹ לִשְׂנֹֽא׃ 4 דִּבְרֵי־פִ֭יו אָ֣וֶן וּמִרְמָ֑ה חָדַ֖ל לְהַשְׂכִּ֣יל לְהֵיטִֽיב׃ 5 אָ֤וֶן ׀ יַחְשֹׁ֗ב עַֽל־מִשְׁכָּ֫ב֥וֹ יִ֭תְיַצֵּב עַל־דֶּ֣רֶךְ לֹא־ט֑וֹב רָ֝֗ע לֹ֣א יִמְאָֽס׃
6 יְ֭הֹוָה בְּהַשָּׁמַ֣יִם חַסְדֶּ֑ךָ אֱ֝מ֥וּנָתְךָ֗ עַד־שְׁחָקִֽים׃
7 צִדְקָֽתְךָ֨ ׀ כְּֽהַרְרֵי־אֵ֗ל מִ֭שְׁפָּטֶךָ תְּה֣וֹם רַבָּ֑ה אָֽדָם־וּבְהֵמָ֖ה תוֹשִׁ֣יעַ יְהֹוָֽה׃
8 מַה־יָּקָ֥ר חַסְדְּךָ֗ אֱלֹ֫הִ֥ים וּבְנֵ֥י אָדָ֑ם בְּצֵ֥ל כְּ֝נָפֶ֗יךָ יֶחֱסָיֽוּן׃
9 יִ֭רְוְיֻן מִדֶּ֣שֶׁן בֵּיתֶ֑ךָ וְנַ֖חַל עֲדָנֶ֣יךָ תַשְׁקֵֽם׃
10 כִּֽי־עִ֭מְּךָ מְק֣וֹר חַיִּ֑ים בְּ֝אוֹרְךָ֗ נִרְאֶה־אֽוֹר׃
11 מְשֹׁ֣ךְ חַ֭סְדְּךָ לְיֹדְעֶ֑יךָ וְ֝צִדְקָתְךָ֗ לְיִשְׁרֵי־לֵֽב׃
12 אַל־תְּ֭בוֹאֵנִי רֶ֣גֶל גַּאֲוָ֑ה וְיַד־רְ֝שָׁעִ֗ים אַל־תְּנִדֵֽנִי׃
13 שָׁ֣ם נָ֭פְלוּ פֹּ֣עֲלֵי אָ֑וֶן דֹּ֝ח֗וּ וְלֹא־יָ֥כְלוּ קֽוּם׃

The picture the poet draws of the wicked scheming to do ill to the good is a familiar one, but he has an exceptional insight to share regarding its deeper meaning. *Ki imkha mekor ḥayyim,* he writes, *be'orkha nireh or:* "For the source of life is with You; indeed, it is only in Your light that we may see light at all." The words sound wise and deep, but the success of the poet's effort will be measured by the degree to which he inspires his audience to consider the mystery behind his apparently simple message. Is all that we know of worldly things merely a reflection of the way they exist in God? Is light itself, the medium in which we see everything we perceive visually, only recognizable as a reflection of the light of God? Is the same true of life itself,

36 For the conductor Eved-יהוה, (a psalm) of David.
[2] A speech given only in the interior chambers of my heart about the way sin comes naturally to the wicked: "The fear of God is invisible before their eyes; [3]indeed, they glide smoothly along, pausing only for their eyes to seek out opportunities for their favorite sin: to hate. [4]The words of their mouths are iniquity and fraud; they have long since stopped seeking wisdom or doing good. [5]They plot iniquity in their beds, then plant themselves in the path of wickedness; they are not repulsed by evil."

[6] יהוה, Your mercy resides in heaven, Your faithfulness in the skies; [7]Your righteousness is as unshakable as the mighty mountains, Your justice as endless as the watery, unfathomable deep. You grant salvation, יהוה, both to human beings and animals.

[8] Your mercy is so very precious, O God; humanity can ever seek refuge in the shadow of Your wings.

[9] They luxuriate in the fatty fare of Your house; You grant them to drink from Your rivers of delight.

[10] For the source of life is with You; indeed, it is only in Your light that we may see light at all.

[11] Draw Your mercy over those who know You and Your righteousness over the upright of heart.

[12] Keep the feet of the arrogant from trampling me; may the hand of the wicked not drive me to a life of wandering.

[13] There shall the doers of iniquity fall; pushed down, they shall never rise again."

the poet challenges his readers to ask: do we only perceive ourselves as being alive because we see our existence as somehow reflecting the reality of the God whom we acclaim as the Life of the Universe? And this as well: the issue for us to ponder is not so much whether *God* exists, but whether *existence* exists—or rather, if what we know of existence can bear any meaning at all outside of faith in God.

לז

לְדָוִ֨ד ׀

אַל־תִּתְחַ֥ר בַּמְּרֵעִ֑ים אַל־תְּ֝קַנֵּ֗א בְּעֹשֵׂ֥י עַוְלָֽה׃ 2 כִּ֣י
כֶ֭חָצִיר מְהֵרָ֣ה יִמָּ֑לוּ וּכְיֶ֥רֶק דֶּ֝֗שֶׁא יִבּוֹלֽוּן׃ 3 בְּטַ֣ח
בַּ֭יהוָה וַעֲשֵׂה־ט֑וֹב שְׁכָן־אֶ֝֗רֶץ וּרְעֵ֥ה אֱמוּנָֽה׃
4 וְהִתְעַנַּ֥ג עַל־יְהוָ֑ה וְיִתֶּן־לְ֝ךָ֗ מִשְׁאֲלֹ֥ת לִבֶּֽךָ׃
5 גּ֣וֹל עַל־יְהוָ֣ה דַּרְכֶּ֑ךָ וּבְטַ֥ח עָ֝לָ֗יו וְה֣וּא יַעֲשֶֽׂה׃
6 וְהוֹצִ֣יא כָא֣וֹר צִדְקֶ֑ךָ וּ֝מִשְׁפָּטֶ֗ךָ כַּצָּהֳרָֽיִם׃
7 דּ֤וֹם ׀ לַיהוָה֮ וְהִתְח֪וֹלֵֽל ל֥וֹ אַל־תִּ֭תְחַר בְּמַצְלִ֣יחַ
דַּרְכּ֑וֹ בְּ֝אִ֗ישׁ עֹשֶׂ֥ה מְזִמּֽוֹת׃
8 הֶ֣רֶף מֵ֭אַף וַעֲזֹ֣ב חֵמָ֑ה אַל־תִּ֝תְחַ֗ר אַךְ־לְהָרֵֽעַ׃ 9 כִּֽי־
מְ֭רֵעִים יִכָּרֵת֑וּן וְקֹוֵ֥י יְ֝הוָ֗ה הֵ֣מָּה יִֽירְשׁוּ־אָֽרֶץ׃
10 וְע֣וֹד מְ֭עַט וְאֵ֣ין רָשָׁ֑ע וְהִתְבּוֹנַ֖נְתָּ עַל־מְקוֹמ֣וֹ
וְאֵינֶֽנּוּ׃ 11 וַעֲנָוִ֥ים יִֽירְשׁוּ־אָ֑רֶץ וְ֝הִתְעַנְּג֗וּ עַל־רֹ֥ב
שָׁלֽוֹם׃
12 זֹמֵ֣ם רָ֭שָׁע לַצַּדִּ֑יק וְחֹרֵ֖ק עָלָ֣יו שִׁנָּֽיו׃ 13 אֲדֹנָ֥י
יִשְׂחַק־ל֑וֹ כִּֽי־רָ֝אָ֗ה כִּֽי־יָבֹ֥א יוֹמֽוֹ׃
14 חֶ֤רֶב ׀ פָּתְח֣וּ רְשָׁעִים֮ וְדָרְכ֪וּ קַ֫שְׁתָּ֥ם לְ֭הַפִּיל עָנִ֣י

The poet has produced a long, rambling poem that, judging from its slightly off-kilter acrostic style, has probably not come down to us entirely as the author originally composed it. Nevertheless, the main points of the poet's message are still quite easy to isolate and identify. The earth is God's to bequeath to any individual found worthy of the bequest. And although the world is full of arrogant scoundrels who fully expect to inherit the earth and its riches, it is really the righteous who will become the heirs of the world. Furthermore, this inheritance will come to the righteous not as an unearned blessing, but in partial recompense for the suffering they endure during their lifetimes of doing good.

Again and again the poet returns to the question of inheriting the earth, each time adding a new wrinkle. Evildoers will be cut off—from happiness, from peace, and from God. On the other hand, people who hope for salvation in God will inherit the earth that God made, as will the humble of spirit. (Indeed, despite the fact that the world is full of self-important narcissists who expect to receive every one of God's blessings, the reality the poet perceives is precisely the opposite: God will favor the humble of spirit with dominion over the earth because *they*—and not the arrogant—will be judged worthy in God's eyes.) The blessed of God shall also inherit the earth, the poet

37 (A psalm) of David.

Be not bothered by evildoers; be not envious of doers of iniquity, [2]for they shall soon all die like dried out grass, withering as even the greenest lawn eventually must. [3]Trust instead in יהוה and do good; dwell in the land and graze in fields of faith. [4]Take pleasure in יהוה and God will grant you all of your heart's desires.

[5] Entrust יהוה with your needs; trust in the God who will then act on your behalf, [6]who will produce justice for you as visible as light itself, a judgment no less just than the light of the afternoon is bright.

[7] Be silent before יהוה and place your trust in God; do not be bothered by a successful person if you know him to be a schemer.

[8] Give up on anger and abandon rage; avoid irritation, for it leads to doing evil—[9]and evildoers will be cut off. Those who place their hope in יהוה, on the other hand, will inherit the earth.

[10] Soon the wicked will vanish entirely; you will consider the place in which they were, but they will be gone from it. [11]In turn, the humble will inherit the earth; they shall revel in a surfeit of peace.

[12] The wicked scheme against the righteous and gnash their teeth towards them in scorn. [13]Adonai, seeing this, laughs at them, knowing full well that the day is coming for them to face judgment.

[14] The wicked draw their swords and bend their bows to bring down the poor and the impover-

continues, implying subtly—or perhaps not so subtly—that the limited dominion human beings exercise over worldly things is neither patrimony nor right, but a gift that comes to them from the God who both made the world and the things in it. Moreover, those cursed by God will inherit nothing at all. Indeed, the poet remarks over and over, those cursed by God will not only end up inheriting nothing at all of value or worth, but they will end up totally cut off from the flow of human history as well. Indeed, the poet understands existence itself as a blessing from God to be cherished, not an ontological right to be mostly ignored or, when occasionally acknowledged, then still taken totally for granted.

וְאֶבְיוֹן לִטְבוֹחַ יִשְׁרֵי־דָֽרֶךְ׃ 15 חַרְבָּם תָּבוֹא בְלִבָּם
וְקַשְּׁתוֹתָם תִּשָּׁבַֽרְנָה׃
16 טוֹב מְעַט לַצַּדִּיק מֵהֲמוֹן רְשָׁעִים רַבִּים׃ 17 כִּי
זְרוֹעוֹת רְשָׁעִים תִּשָּׁבַרְנָה וְסוֹמֵךְ צַדִּיקִים יְהוָֽה׃
18 יוֹדֵעַ יְהוָה יְמֵי תְמִימִם וְנַחֲלָתָם לְעוֹלָם תִּהְיֶֽה׃
19 לֹא־יֵבֹשׁוּ בְּעֵת רָעָה וּבִימֵי רְעָבוֹן יִשְׂבָּֽעוּ׃
20 כִּי רְשָׁעִים ׀ יֹאבֵדוּ וְאֹיְבֵי יְהוָה כִּיקַר כָּרִים כָּלוּ
בֶעָשָׁן כָּֽלוּ׃
21 לֹוֶה רָשָׁע וְלֹא יְשַׁלֵּם וְצַדִּיק חוֹנֵן וְנוֹתֵֽן׃ 22 כִּי
מְבֹרָכָיו יִירְשׁוּ אָרֶץ וּמְקֻלָּלָיו יִכָּרֵֽתוּ׃
23 מֵיְהוָה מִֽצְעֲדֵי־גֶבֶר כּוֹנָנוּ וְדַרְכּוֹ יֶחְפָּֽץ׃ 24 כִּי־יִפֹּל
לֹא־יוּטָל כִּֽי־יְהוָה סוֹמֵךְ יָדֽוֹ׃
25 נַעַר ׀ הָיִיתִי גַּם־זָקַנְתִּי וְלֹא־רָאִיתִי צַדִּיק נֶעֱזָב
וְזַרְעוֹ מְבַקֶּשׁ־לָֽחֶם׃ 26 כָּל־הַיּוֹם חוֹנֵן וּמַלְוֶה
וְזַרְעוֹ לִבְרָכָֽה׃
27 סוּר מֵרָע וַעֲשֵׂה־טוֹב וּשְׁכֹן לְעוֹלָֽם׃ 28 כִּי יְהוָה ׀

Finally, the poet returns a final time to the theme of inheriting the world and notes that, in the end, all the above categories can be subsumed under the general principle that the righteous shall inherit the world and live in it forever. Indeed, this notion—that righteous people who give liberally to the poor and lend funds freely to those in need will always be blessed of God—is at the heart of the poet's conception of the world. Getting slightly carried away, he professes never to have seen a righteous person begging for bread. Does the poet really expect his readers to believe this unlikely declaration? Has he truly never come across a decent person who has not prospered in the world or who needs gifts of charity to survive? Has he never met a kind individual who has hardly inherited anything at all, let alone the earth and its wealth? Perhaps the poet is thinking more spiritually than materially: since an ever stronger sense of dedication to the cause of righteousness is the great gift that God bestows upon the righteous, the true riches they possess cannot be taken from them by earthly thieves or brigands. Furthermore, since their hunger is for God, they are never hungry in any but the least important sense of the word (namely, the physical sense). Indeed, as the blessed ones of God, they can never be thought of as poor by anyone who thinks of God's blessings as the ultimate in human wealth.

Sensitive readers will also be prompted to wonder if there truly are people in the world who hew to this definition of prosperity. Assuming they do exist,

ished, to slaughter those who walk an upright path. [15]Their swords will end up plunged into their own hearts, however, and their bows will be broken.

[16]The righteous are happier with a little than they would be with the fortune of many wicked people,[17]for the arms of the wicked shall be broken, while יהוה is the support of the righteous.

[18]יהוה knows how the guileless spend their days and ensures that their inheritance will remain theirs forever. [19]They will not suffer shame in hard times, but will be satisfied even in times of famine.

[20]The wicked, on the other hand, shall perish and the enemies of יהוה shall vanish as though they were only huge clouds; they shall dissipate like so much smoke.

[21]The wicked person borrows, but does not pay back, but the righteous person gives charity graciously. [22]Indeed, people blessed of God will inherit the earth, while those whom God curses will be cut off.

[23]It is due to יהוה that a man's steps are made firm and his way finds favor. [24]He may falter, but will never be cast away entirely, for יהוה supports his hand.

[25]I was a child and now I have grown old, but I still have never seen a righteous individual abandoned by God or the offspring of that person begging for bread. [26]All day long, the righteous lend to the poor graciously and consequently are their offspring blessed.

[27]Swerve away from evil and do good and thus shall you abide forever, [28]for יהוה loves justice

are they our heroes and our models? Or do we think of people who refuse to equate wealth with money as crazy or pathetic . . . or both? Modern readers of the thirty-seventh psalm can effectively use its recitation as a springboard for considering how they actually do feel about wealth. Certainly, most moderns pay regular lip service to the notion that giving oneself over to the all-consuming, relentless quest for money is a sign of spiritual degeneration. Yet how many of us would ever honestly consider someone who moves down the corporate ladder to a position that carries a far smaller salary, but which

אֹהֵב מִשְׁפָּט וְלֹא־יַעֲזֹב אֶת־חֲסִידָיו לְעוֹלָם
נִשְׁמָרוּ וְזֶרַע רְשָׁעִים נִכְרָת׃ 29 צַדִּיקִים יִירְשׁוּ־
אָרֶץ וְיִשְׁכְּנוּ לָעַד עָלֶיהָ׃
30 פִּי־צַדִּיק יֶהְגֶּה חָכְמָה וּלְשׁוֹנוֹ תְּדַבֵּר מִשְׁפָּט׃
31 תּוֹרַת אֱלֹהָיו בְּלִבּוֹ לֹא תִמְעַד אֲשֻׁרָיו׃
32 צוֹפֶה רָשָׁע לַצַּדִּיק וּמְבַקֵּשׁ לַהֲמִיתוֹ׃ 33 יְהוָה
לֹא־יַעַזְבֶנּוּ בְיָדוֹ וְלֹא יַרְשִׁיעֶנּוּ בְּהִשָּׁפְטוֹ׃
34 קַוֵּה אֶל־יְהוָה ׀ וּשְׁמֹר דַּרְכּוֹ וִירוֹמִמְךָ לָרֶשֶׁת אָרֶץ
בְּהִכָּרֵת רְשָׁעִים תִּרְאֶה׃
35 רָאִיתִי רָשָׁע עָרִיץ וּמִתְעָרֶה כְּאֶזְרָח רַעֲנָן׃
36 וַיַּעֲבֹר וְהִנֵּה אֵינֶנּוּ וָאֲבַקְשֵׁהוּ וְלֹא נִמְצָא׃
37 שְׁמָר־תָּם וּרְאֵה יָשָׁר כִּי־אַחֲרִית לְאִישׁ שָׁלוֹם׃
38 וּפֹשְׁעִים נִשְׁמְדוּ יַחְדָּו אַחֲרִית רְשָׁעִים נִכְרָתָה׃
39 וּתְשׁוּעַת צַדִּיקִים מֵיְהוָה מָעוּזָּם בְּעֵת צָרָה׃
40 וַיַּעְזְרֵם יְהוָה וַיְפַלְּטֵם יְפַלְּטֵם מֵרְשָׁעִים וְיוֹשִׁיעֵם
כִּי חָסוּ בוֹ׃

affords far more time for contemplative prayer, meditation, and study, as having received a wonderful gift?

The quest for material wealth is the cornerstone of modern life. Indeed, this is so much so that the efforts of those countries that have tried to adopt economic systems *not* based on the relentless quest for money have foundered on the shoals of the unfortunate reality that the unyielding desire for material prosperity appears to be *exactly* what motivates most people to work hard. To buck that trend is to renounce most of what society considers sacred; to declare it invalid and unacceptable entirely is to step into a bracing stream in which very few others wade even occasionally. Yet the poet whose poem is our 37th psalm appears totally secure in his belief that the righteous will always be happier even with a little than they ever could be with the fortunes amassed by the wicked of this world.

Of course, there is no inevitable connection between wealth and wickedness . . . and the poet seems aware of that as well. He has little to say, for example, about the great deal of good that wealthy, decent people can do with their money. Instead, he prefers to focus his withering gaze on the huge fortunes of the iniquitous and to compare them to the little that most of the righteous people in his world have as their estates. Indeed, by *formally* comparing the wicked to the righteous in his poem, but *actually* talking about the practical difference to the world between the negligible importance of the vast fortunes

and will never abandon the pious; they shall be preserved forever, but the offspring of the wicked shall be cut off. [29]The righteous, however, shall inherit the earth and dwell upon it forever.

[30]The mouths of the righteous utter words of wisdom and their tongues speak words of justice. [31]The teaching of their God is in their hearts and, as a result, their legs do not stumble.

[32]The wicked scout out the righteous and make plans to slay them, [33]but יהוה will neither abandon the latter into the hands of the former nor allow them to be convicted when tried on false charges.

[34]Place your hope in יהוה and keep to God's path so that you may be exalted and inherit the earth. Indeed, when the wicked are cut off, that is just what you will see.

[35]I saw a powerful wicked man leaving himself totally exposed like a relaxed citizen with nothing to fear, [36]but he passed away and was no longer; I sought him, but he was no longer to be found.

[37]Guard the innocent and look after the upright, for there will be a happy destiny for the peaceful. [38]Sinners, however, will be destroyed all together, their very destiny cancelled.

[39]The deliverance of the righteous comes from יהוה, their fortress in times of trouble.

[40]יהוה will help them and save them, indeed save them from the wicked and deliver them, for their trust is in God.

of the wicked and the profound impact on the world effected by the righteous even despite their modest estates the poet only makes his point that much more forceful. Being rich, he is saying, is value-neutral—neither good *nor* bad—because, in the end, it is neither the rich *nor* the poor who will inherit the earth, but those righteous people devoted body and soul to the worship of God and to the pursuit of deeds of kindness towards other people. They are the ones who give charity graciously. They are the ones who lend funds to people even less well off than they themselves are. They are the ones who, content with their lot, praise God for what they do have instead of endlessly blaming God for what they lack. And in the end, it is they, the poet feels certain, who will inherit the earth.

מִזְמוֹר לְדָוִד לְהַזְכִּיר׃
2 יְהוָה אַל־בְּקֶצְפְּךָ תוֹכִיחֵנִי וּבַחֲמָתְךָ תְיַסְּרֵנִי׃
3 כִּי־חִצֶּיךָ נִחֲתוּ־בִי וַתִּנְחַת עָלַי יָדֶךָ׃
4 אֵין־מְתֹם בִּבְשָׂרִי מִפְּנֵי זַעְמֶךָ אֵין־שָׁלוֹם בַּעֲצָמַי
מִפְּנֵי חַטָּאתִי׃
5 כִּי־עֲוֺנֹתַי עָבְרוּ רֹאשִׁי כְּמַשָּׂא כָבֵד יִכְבְּדוּ מִמֶּנִּי׃
6 הִבְאִישׁוּ נָמַקּוּ חַבּוּרֹתָי מִפְּנֵי אִוַּלְתִּי׃
7 נַעֲוֵיתִי שַׁחֹתִי עַד־מְאֹד כָּל־הַיּוֹם קֹדֵר הִלָּכְתִּי׃
8 כִּי־כְסָלַי מָלְאוּ נִקְלֶה וְאֵין מְתֹם בִּבְשָׂרִי׃
9 נְפוּגוֹתִי וְנִדְכֵּיתִי עַד־מְאֹד שָׁאַגְתִּי מִנַּהֲמַת לִבִּי׃
10 אֲדֹנָי נֶגְדְּךָ כָל־תַּאֲוָתִי וְאַנְחָתִי מִמְּךָ לֹא־נִסְתָּרָה׃
11 לִבִּי סְחַרְחַר עֲזָבַנִי כֹחִי וְאוֹר עֵינַי גַּם־הֵם אֵין
אִתִּי׃
12 אֹהֲבַי ׀ וְרֵעַי מִנֶּגֶד נִגְעִי יַעֲמֹדוּ וּקְרוֹבַי מֵרָחֹק
עָמָדוּ׃ 13 וַיְנַקְשׁוּ ׀ מְבַקְשֵׁי נַפְשִׁי וְדֹרְשֵׁי רָעָתִי
דִּבְּרוּ הַוּוֹת וּמִרְמוֹת כָּל־הַיּוֹם יֶהְגּוּ׃
14 וַאֲנִי כְחֵרֵשׁ לֹא אֶשְׁמָע וּכְאִלֵּם לֹא יִפְתַּח־פִּיו׃
15 וָאֱהִי כְּאִישׁ אֲשֶׁר לֹא־שֹׁמֵעַ וְאֵין בְּפִיו
תּוֹכָחוֹת׃

The poet is a sick man, but his enemies have not granted him any respite from their relentless persecution because of his infirmity. Just to the contrary, the poet suggests: his foes have seized the opportunity presented them by his illness to persecute him all the more vigorously.

The poet's description of his own condition, including a carefully presented catalogue of symptoms, is so interesting in its own right, however, that we can conjecture that the poet was not solely interested in speaking to his enemies through his poem. Indeed, it seems reasonable to imagine that the psalmist hoped his readers would be able to use their sympathy for such a tortured individual as a means of communing with him across the barriers of time and space . . . and of learning something profound about the human condition from the contemplation of his sorry lot. And his condition truly is grievous. His flesh is weak. He feels pain within his bones. His body is covered with festering, probably gangrenous, wounds. He suffers from some sort of curvature of the spine that makes him almost completely bent over. His heart fibrillates wildly, denying him any sense of well-being. He can, at least on occasion, actually feel his strength ebbing. And his eyesight is

38

A memorial psalm of David.

[2] יהוה, neither rebuke me on account of Your anger nor cause me to suffer on account of Your rage, [3]for Your arrows have rained down on me and Your hand has come down hard upon me.

[4] There is no healing for my flesh because of Your fury; there is no peace in my bones because of my sin.

[5] Indeed, my iniquities have piled up higher than my head; if they were a physical burden, they would be too heavy for me to bear.

[6] My wounds have become putrid and foul because of my own wrongdoing.

[7] I am incredibly bowed and bent; I walk about all day in darkness, [8]for my insides are filled with fever and there is no healing for my flesh.

[9] I feel faint and terribly crushed down; I cry out as an expression of the groaning of my heart.

[10] Adonai, everything I desire is known to You and neither is my sighing hidden from You.

[11] My heart is twisting, my strength has left me; the light is gone from my eyes.

[12] Seeing my illness, my friends and companions stand back; even my relations stand far away, [13]while those who would murder me devise plots against me, and those who wish me ill hatch schemes and speak deceitfully about me all day long.

[14] As though deaf, I hear nothing; I am like a mute who has no reason to open his mouth. [15] Indeed, I am precisely like someone who cannot hear or rebuke anyone by speaking.

failing too, as is his hearing. Indeed, when he writes that he is as good as deaf, he probably means that although he can still hear some sounds, he may as well be profoundly deaf for all the good it does him. On top of all that, he feels faint much of the time, as though some force outside his body were attempting to crush him, to beat him down, and perhaps even to kill him altogether. And he feels a kind of burning in his chest cavity as well. What a diagnostician would make of all these symptoms is not the point, however, as much as the poet's self-diagnosis:

16 כִּֽי־לְךָ יְהֹוָה הוֹחָלְתִּי אַתָּה תַעֲנֶה אֲדֹנָי אֱלֹהָֽי׃
17 כִּֽי־אָמַרְתִּי פֶּן־יִשְׂמְחוּ־לִי בְּמוֹט רַגְלִי עָלַי
הִגְדִּֽילוּ׃
18 כִּֽי־אֲנִי לְצֶלַע נָכוֹן וּמַכְאוֹבִי נֶגְדִּי תָמִֽיד׃
19 כִּֽי־עֲוֺנִי אַגִּיד אֶדְאַג מֵֽחַטָּאתִֽי׃ 20 וְֽאֹיְבַי חַיִּים
עָצֵמוּ וְרַבּוּ שֹׂנְאַי שָֽׁקֶר׃ 21 וּמְשַׁלְּמֵי רָעָה תַּחַת
טוֹבָה יִשְׂטְנוּנִי תַּחַת *רָֽדְפִי־טֽוֹב׃
22 אַל־תַּֽעַזְבֵנִי יְהֹוָה אֱלֹהַי אַל־תִּרְחַק מִמֶּֽנִּי׃
23 חוּשָׁה לְעֶזְרָתִי אֲדֹנָי תְּשׁוּעָתִֽי׃

v. 21 רדופי כתיב

he is drowning in sin and wrong-doing, and his various ailments are merely the physical manifestation of God's displeasure.

Nonetheless, the poet's faith remains intact. His friends and relatives, disgusted by his festering wounds, have abandoned him. His enemies, delighted by his sickness, are already taking advantage of his weakness to denounce him and to lay snares to entrap him. But the poet knows that God will always be with him and, despite everything, he places his hope, his faith, and his destiny in God's caring hands.

Modern readers will inevitably feel challenged by the ancient poet's words to evaluate their own feelings about illness. If illness brings us closer to a sense of the destiny we all share in God, then why does the prospect of infirmity unnerve us so? Indeed, can anything that brings an individual closer

[16] Nevertheless have I put my hope in You, יהוה. I believe that You will answer me, Adonai, my God, [17]for I say to myself, "If You were not to answer, it would be tantamount to allowing my enemies to rejoice over my downfall, to allowing them to grow in stature simply because my foot slipped."

[18] My pain never leaves me, yet mentally I am a sturdy beam of a person. [19]But even as I confess my iniquity, I worry because of my sin; [20]my enemies are flourishing and multiplying greatly, while those who groundlessly hate me are becoming many. [21]Those who repay good with evil loathe me because I pursue goodness.

[22] Do not abandon me, יהוה; become not distant from me, O my God.

[23] Hurry to my aid, Adonai, divine source of my salvation.

to God be other than a boon? But why then do we consider the sick cursed by their illnesses, when it is precisely the pain and fear engendered by those infirmities that so often lead the sick to embrace (or to re-embrace) faith in God? The poet knows constant pain, but his response is to seek refuge in faith, not to blame God for his endless suffering . . . or for the treachery of his violent, scheming enemies. To most people, the poet's piety will sound exemplary. But can he serve as a practical role model for moderns as well?

לט

לַמְנַצֵּחַ *לִידוּתוּן מִזְמוֹר לְדָוִד׃

2 אָמַרְתִּי אֶשְׁמְרָה דְרָכַי מֵחֲטוֹא בִלְשׁוֹנִי אֶשְׁמְרָה
לְפִי מַחְסוֹם בְּעֹד רָשָׁע לְנֶגְדִּי׃ 3 נֶאֱלַמְתִּי דוּמִיָּה
הֶחֱשֵׁיתִי מִטּוֹב וּכְאֵבִי נֶעְכָּר׃

4 חַם־לִבִּי ׀ בְּקִרְבִּי בַּהֲגִיגִי תִבְעַר־אֵשׁ דִּבַּרְתִּי
בִּלְשׁוֹנִי׃

5 הוֹדִיעֵנִי יְהוָה ׀ קִצִּי וּמִדַּת יָמַי מַה־הִיא אֵדְעָה
מֶה־חָדֵל אָנִי׃ 6 הִנֵּה טְפָחוֹת ׀ נָתַתָּה יָמַי וְחֶלְדִּי
כְאַיִן נֶגְדֶּךָ אַךְ־כָּל־הֶבֶל כָּל־אָדָם נִצָּב סֶלָה׃

7 אַךְ־בְּצֶלֶם ׀ יִתְהַלֶּךְ־אִישׁ אַךְ־הֶבֶל יֶהֱמָיוּן יִצְבֹּר
וְלֹא־יֵדַע מִי־אֹסְפָם׃

8 וְעַתָּה מַה־קִּוִּיתִי אֲדֹנָי תּוֹחַלְתִּי לְךָ הִיא׃

9 מִכָּל־פְּשָׁעַי הַצִּילֵנִי חֶרְפַּת נָבָל אַל־תְּשִׂימֵנִי׃

10 נֶאֱלַמְתִּי לֹא אֶפְתַּח־פִּי כִּי אַתָּה עָשִׂיתָ׃

11 הָסֵר מֵעָלַי נִגְעֶךָ מִתִּגְרַת יָדְךָ אֲנִי כָלִיתִי׃

v. 1 לידיתון כתיב

The poet, deeply aware of the indescribable pain that words spoken in anger or haste can bring to others, took an oath not to speak at all. And so he was silent, refusing even to speak good words, lest they somehow be misconstrued and inadvertently cause offense or harm. He held out for some time, but the strain of maintaining his silence—especially in the presence of the wicked—was too great to bear and, in the end, the poet spoke.

And what words broke forth from his mouth after he could be still no longer? No less than the truth about the human condition, conceived here as a set of dour realities that came to the poet during his self-imposed exile from the realm of communicative speech. Life is fleeting in the extreme, a path little more than a few handbreadths long, a bag of days not even mostly full. Life is a sojourn among strangers, something Jews—being descended from nomads and wanderers—should be able to seize especially easily. Human life exists, but as something no more profoundly real than an exhaled breath or a shadow. Indeed, most people think of worldly things as having real existence and their shadows as mere silhouettes, each one a kind of dark penumbra that attests to the reality of something that exists far more profoundly than it itself ever can or will. But, the poet avers, just the opposite is true: shadows are far more suggestive of the way worldly things actually exist than are the things that cast them. And the same is true of human beings and the shadows

39

For the conductor, for Jeduthun, a psalm of David.

[2] I said I would guard my ways lest I sin with my tongue, [3]that I would guard my mouth with a muzzle as long as a wicked person was present. And so, although my pain was ghastly, I was completely silent, refusing to say even good things aloud.

[4] But when my heart was hot within me, when my brain was on fire and I could control my tongue no longer . . . I did speak.

[5] "יהוה," I said, "make my end and the number of my days known to me so that I might know just how mortal I truly am. [6]For You have made my days so few that they should be measured in handspans; my world is nothing before You. Indeed, for all that people might hold themselves erect, their strength is naught but breath, *selah*.

[7] A person walking about is thus a mere image; the struggles of people, mere breath. They pile up baubles, but have no idea who will gather them up after they die.

[8] How I now wait, Adonai; all my hope is for You.

[9] You have saved me from all my sins; make me not into the object of the scoundrel's scorn.

[10] As long as You acted on my behalf, I was mute, not even opening my mouth.

[11] Remove Your plague from me; I have used the last of my strength to survive the rage of Your hand.

their bodies cast: as much as people may think of themselves as existing fully in the real world, all that the truly insightful among them can honestly claim to be are ghostly specters that bear vague allusion to the God who made them. In the end, the poet knows, the universe itself is nothing more than the outline of God's will to create as it dances slowly across a reality no human can ever truly comprehend in any but the most elementary, pedestrian way.

To have remained silent long enough to have come to such awful truths must have been an awesome experience for the poet. Indeed, the poet's description of how he felt himself bursting with the need to speak them aloud is the ultimate description of the creative impulse as it exists

12 בְּֽתוֹכָ֨חֽוֹת עַל־עָוֺ֨ן ׀ יִסַּ֬רְתָּ אִ֗ישׁ וַתֶּ֣מֶס כָּעָ֣שׁ
חֲמוּד֑וֹ אַ֤ךְ הֶ֖בֶל כָּל־אָדָ֣ם סֶֽלָה׃
13 שִֽׁמְעָ֥ה־תְפִלָּתִ֨י ׀ יְהֹוָ֡ה וְֽשַׁוְעָתִ֨י ׀ הַאֲזִינָה֮
אֶֽל־דִּמְעָתִ֗י אַֽל־תֶּ֫חֱרַ֥שׁ כִּ֤י גֵ֣ר אָנֹכִ֣י עִמָּ֑ךְ תּ֝וֹשָׁ֗ב
כְּכָל־אֲבוֹתָֽי׃
14 הָשַׁ֣ע מִמֶּ֣נִּי וְאַבְלִ֑יגָה בְּטֶ֖רֶם אֵלֵ֣ךְ וְאֵינֶֽנִּי׃

within the breasts of true artists (as opposed to egotists and hacks, who proclaim things to the world only for the sake of garnering the respect and admiration of their audiences).

Modern readers of the thirty-ninth psalm, however, will find themselves inspired to ask about more than just the nature of creativity. What do we think we are acquiring with all our endless hustling about? Does the fact that none of us can say with certainty what will happen to our estates after we die really deprive us of the pleasure of owning things? More to the point: can we echo the poet's words *ger anokhi imakh* ("I am a stranger in Your land")

[12] With rebukes regarding sin, You bring suffering to a man; You made his treasures melt away as though they were the wool that moths eat. But, of course, human beings are just breath, *selah.*

[13] Hear my prayer, יהוה; listen to my supplication. Let silence not be Your response to my tears, for I am a stranger in Your land, an alien abroad just as were all my ancestors.

[14] Leave me be, that I might gather some strength before I too depart and am no more."

and truly feel like strangers and sojourners in God's world? We usually think of alienation from the world as a form of mild mental illness, but perhaps the poet's point is that feeling disconnected from the world and its things is a sign of wisdom, not of mental fragility . . . that seeing ourselves as shadows of God's will to create may reasonably be taken as a sign of our readiness to divest ourselves of fantasy and see things as they truly are . . . that understanding our lives to be at most a handful of days is, in the end, the first real step towards God that most of us can hope to take.

מ

לַמְנַצֵּחַ לְדָוִד מִזְמוֹר׃

2 קַוֹּה קִוִּיתִי יְהוָה וַיֵּט אֵלַי וַיִּשְׁמַע שַׁוְעָתִי׃ 3 וַיַּעֲלֵנִי ׀ מִבּוֹר שָׁאוֹן מִטִּיט הַיָּוֵן וַיָּקֶם עַל־סֶלַע רַגְלַי כּוֹנֵן אֲשֻׁרָי׃ 4 וַיִּתֵּן בְּפִי ׀ שִׁיר חָדָשׁ תְּהִלָּה לֵאלֹהֵינוּ יִרְאוּ רַבִּים וְיִירָאוּ וְיִבְטְחוּ בַּיהוָה׃

5 אַשְׁרֵי הַגֶּבֶר אֲשֶׁר־שָׂם יְהוָה מִבְטַחוֹ וְלֹא־פָנָה אֶל־רְהָבִים וְשָׂטֵי כָזָב׃

6 רַבּוֹת עָשִׂיתָ ׀ אַתָּה יְהוָה אֱלֹהַי נִפְלְאֹתֶיךָ וּמַחְשְׁבֹתֶיךָ אֵלֵינוּ אֵין ׀ עֲרֹךְ אֵלֶיךָ אַגִּידָה וַאֲדַבֵּרָה עָצְמוּ מִסַּפֵּר׃

7 זֶבַח וּמִנְחָה ׀ לֹא־חָפַצְתָּ אָזְנַיִם כָּרִיתָ לִּי עוֹלָה וַחֲטָאָה לֹא שָׁאָלְתָּ׃

8 אָז אָמַרְתִּי הִנֵּה־בָאתִי בִּמְגִלַּת־סֵפֶר כָּתוּב עָלָי׃

9 לַעֲשׂוֹת רְצוֹנְךָ אֱלֹהַי חָפָצְתִּי וְתוֹרָתְךָ בְּתוֹךְ מֵעָי׃

10 בִּשַּׂרְתִּי צֶדֶק ׀ בְּקָהָל רָב הִנֵּה שְׂפָתַי לֹא אֶכְלָא יְהוָה אַתָּה יָדָעְתָּ׃

11 צִדְקָתְךָ לֹא־כִסִּיתִי ׀ בְּתוֹךְ לִבִּי אֱמוּנָתְךָ וּתְשׁוּעָתְךָ אָמָרְתִּי לֹא־כִחַדְתִּי חַסְדְּךָ וַאֲמִתְּךָ לְקָהָל רָב׃

The poet, the ultimate iconoclast, dared to stand up—either in the Temple itself or somewhere in its general vicinity—and proclaim to a crowd of smug worshipers the unsettling truth that the prophet Samuel once confided to King Saul: God *endures* sacrifice and libation, but *desires* obedience, fealty, allegiance, and love rather than an endless procession of burnt carcasses and spilt blood. For his efforts, the poet was put in jail, lowered (like Jeremiah in his day) into a pit filled with slimy mud, then left there to ponder his wretched situation. Yet, although he must have expected to die of exposure, starvation, or dehydration, the poet was eventually released from prison and he acclaimed this as an act of divine deliverance. His incarceration did nothing to alter his behavior, however: the poet returned to his former soapbox with the word of God churning and roiling about in his gut and resumed his preaching to the vast congregation of worshipers who were gathering to participate in the elaborate Temple ceremonial. *Retzeh* יהוה *lehatzileni,* he must now pray: O יהוה, may it be Your will to save me . . . this

40

For the conductor, a psalm of David.

[2] I hoped to be saved and יהוה answered me, turning to me and hearing my plea, [3]then lifting me from the slimy mud of my cacophonous prison pit and, making steady my legs, setting my feet upon a rock [4]and putting a new song in my mouth, an ode of praise to our God; indeed, many saw my deliverance and, awe-struck, were thus inspired to trust in יהוה.

[5] Happy is the man who makes faith in יהוה his stronghold, who turns not to the brazen or to those who embrace falsehood.

[6] You have done many things, O יהוה my God; Your wonders and plans for us are too numerous to be listed before You. Yet I will tell them and speak of them anyway, knowing all the while that they are too many to relate.

[7] You have opened my ears to a great secret: that You have no desire for animal sacrifice and grain offerings, that You never asked that wholly burnt offerings or sin offerings be offered to You.

[8] As a result of that experience, I said, "Since I have come in the guise of a scroll with writing all over me, [9]I naturally desire to do Your will, my God; Your teaching is planted deep within my bowels."

[10] I proclaimed justice in a great congregation without holding back my lips; but this, יהוה, You already know.

[11] I left nothing of Your righteousness behind in my heart; of Your faithfulness and deliverance I spoke freely, holding back nothing of Your mercy and truth from the great congregation.

time as well. Will he be arrested again? That certainly seems likely. Will God deliver him a second time from prison? That, apparently, remains to be seen, but the fortieth psalm is the prayer of a man who has paid an awful price for proclaiming the word of God, and who is willing to face paying it again for the sake of being true to the experience of God's presence in his life.

Modern readers of this ode to resigned suffering will want to focus on the poet's conception of himself as a walking scroll. He sees himself not so much as *a* Torah, but as *torah* itself: the word of

12 אַתָּה יְהוָה לֹא־תִכְלָא רַחֲמֶיךָ מִמֶּנִּי חַסְדְּךָ
וַאֲמִתְּךָ תָּמִיד יִצְּרוּנִי׃

13 כִּי אָפְפוּ עָלַי רָעוֹת עַד־אֵין מִסְפָּר הִשִּׂיגוּנִי
עֲוֺנֹתַי וְלֹא־יָכֹלְתִּי לִרְאוֹת עָצְמוּ מִשַּׂעֲרוֹת רֹאשִׁי
וְלִבִּי עֲזָבָנִי׃

14 רְצֵה־יְהוָה לְהַצִּילֵנִי יְהוָה לְעֶזְרָתִי חוּשָׁה׃

15 יֵבֹשׁוּ וְיַחְפְּרוּ ׀ יַחַד מְבַקְשֵׁי נַפְשִׁי לִסְפּוֹתָהּ יִסֹּגוּ
אָחוֹר וְיִכָּלְמוּ חֲפֵצֵי רָעָתִי׃

16 יָשֹׁמּוּ עַל־עֵקֶב בָּשְׁתָּם הָאֹמְרִים לִי הֶאָח ׀ הֶאָח׃

17 יָשִׂישׂוּ וְיִשְׂמְחוּ ׀ בְּךָ כָּל־מְבַקְשֶׁיךָ יֹאמְרוּ תָמִיד
יִגְדַּל יְהוָה אֹהֲבֵי תְּשׁוּעָתֶךָ׃

18 וַאֲנִי ׀ עָנִי וְאֶבְיוֹן אֲדֹנָי יַחֲשָׁב לִי עֶזְרָתִי וּמְפַלְטִי
אַתָּה אֱלֹהַי אַל־תְּאַחַר׃

God encapsulated within the confines of human existence. And his need to preach the truth about God and Israel openly and freely is a function of the way he feels this distillation of communicative divinity bubbling up inside him and forcing him to pay it heed. Moderns will want to compare that kind of perceptible, overwhelming sensory experience of God with the kind of wan belief that passes for faith in God in our faithless world. Do we cultivate the experience of God in our own lives in any but the most banal,

[12] You are יהוה; do not hold back Your compassion from me now. May Your mercy and truth continue to protect me.

[13] For innumerable evils surround me; my sins have at last caught up with me. I cannot see them, but they outnumber the hairs on my head; my heart is failing me.

[14] O יהוה, may it be Your will to save me; יהוה, hasten to my aid.

[15] Let those who are seeking to destroy my soul be both ashamed and humiliated; may they whose desire is to do me evil retreat and be mortified.

[16] May they who greet my misery with calls of "Hurrah! Hurrah!" be shamed, then destroyed altogether.

[17] But may all who seek You rejoice and be glad; may those who love the prospect of Your deliverance always say, "יהוה be great."

[18] And as for poor, indigent me—Adonai, consider my wretched situation, for You are my help and my refuge. O my God, do not delay!

least potentially transformational way? Do we moderns think it possible actually to be God's *torah*? Do we even aspire to, let alone actually ever attain, that kind of intimacy with the God to whom we pray, whose commandments we keep, and whose service is theoretically the whole motivating factor behind our spiritual lives?

A version of the last five verses of this psalm appears elsewhere in the Psalter as the seventieth psalm.

מא

לַמְנַצֵּחַ מִזְמוֹר לְדָוִד׃

2 אַשְׁרֵי מַשְׂכִּיל אֶל־דָּל בְּיוֹם רָעָה יְמַלְּטֵהוּ יְהוָה׃

3 יְהוָה ׀ יִשְׁמְרֵהוּ וִיחַיֵּהוּ *וְאֻשַּׁר בָּאָרֶץ וְאַל־תִּתְּנֵהוּ בְּנֶפֶשׁ אֹיְבָיו׃

4 יְהוָה יִסְעָדֶנּוּ עַל־עֶרֶשׂ דְּוָי כָּל־מִשְׁכָּבוֹ הָפַכְתָּ בְחָלְיוֹ׃

5 אֲנִי־אָמַרְתִּי יְהוָה חָנֵּנִי רְפָאָה נַפְשִׁי כִּי־חָטָאתִי לָךְ׃

6 אוֹיְבַי יֹאמְרוּ רַע לִי מָתַי יָמוּת וְאָבַד שְׁמוֹ׃

7 וְאִם־בָּא לִרְאוֹת ׀ שָׁוְא יְדַבֵּר לִבּוֹ יִקְבָּץ־אָוֶן לוֹ יֵצֵא לַחוּץ יְדַבֵּר׃

8 יַחַד עָלַי יִתְלַחֲשׁוּ כָּל־שֹׂנְאָי עָלַי ׀ יַחְשְׁבוּ רָעָה לִי׃ 9 דְּבַר־בְּלִיַּעַל יָצוּק בּוֹ וַאֲשֶׁר שָׁכַב לֹא־יוֹסִיף לָקוּם׃

10 גַּם אִישׁ־שְׁלוֹמִי ׀ אֲשֶׁר־בָּטַחְתִּי בוֹ אוֹכֵל לַחְמִי הִגְדִּיל עָלַי עָקֵב׃

11 וְאַתָּה יְהוָה חָנֵּנִי וַהֲקִימֵנִי וַאֲשַׁלְּמָה לָהֶם׃

12 בְּזֹאת יָדַעְתִּי כִּי־חָפַצְתָּ בִּי כִּי לֹא־יָרִיעַ אֹיְבִי עָלָי׃ 13 וַאֲנִי בְּתֻמִּי תָּמַכְתָּ בִּי וַתַּצִּיבֵנִי לְפָנֶיךָ לְעוֹלָם׃

14 בָּרוּךְ יְהוָה ׀ אֱלֹהֵי יִשְׂרָאֵל מֵהָעוֹלָם וְעַד הָעוֹלָם אָמֵן ׀ וְאָמֵן׃

v. 3 יאשר כתיב

The first book of the Psalter ends with a poem describing the most painful of all acts of treachery: betrayal not by an enemy or a jealous foe, but by a friend. By the poet's own admission, this individual was someone he had trusted, someone who had eaten in his home, a person whom he had once called *ish shelomi,* a man devoted to his own peace, to his well-being and welfare, to his health and comfort. But this former man of peace joined the poet's foes when he, the poet, was ill and therefore especially vulnerable and weak. Betrayal by a former friend is shocking enough, but it is the poet's response to his former friend's perfidy that will strike most moderns as even more surprising: he is moved by such stunning disloyalty not to blame God for the sordid ways of the world, but to cleave all the more strongly to his faith. Moreover, he sees in his situation not only disaster, but also blessing: the failure of his enemies' efforts to bring him down has already strengthened

41

For the conductor, a psalm of David.

[2] Happy is one who takes the lot of the wretched to heart; יהוה will help him escape on a day of evil.

[3] יהוה will guard him and grant him life; he will be considered a happy man in the land. O God, deliver him not into the hands of his enemies.

[4] יהוה will help him on his sickbed, even turning his mattress for him in times of illness.

[5] But as for me, I say, "יהוה, be gracious unto me; heal me for I have sinned against You."

[6] My enemies, speaking evil of me, ask, "When will he die and his name be forgotten?"

[7] If one of them comes to visit, he speaks naught but falsehood; his heart gathers iniquitous lies into it, then, when he goes outside, he declaims them freely.

[8] All those who hate me gather together to whisper about me; they scheme about me, plotting to do me evil, muttering, [9]"Pestilence is infecting him; once he lies down, he will rise up no more."

[10] Even my own former friend, someone in whom I once put my trust, someone who regularly ate my bread—he too turned on his heel and fled from me.

[11] But you, יהוה, be gracious unto me and raise me up that I might pay them back.

[12] For precisely in seeing my enemies fail to harm me shall I know that You take delight in me; [13]indeed, You support me in my guilelessness and grant that I stand forever in Your presence.

[14] Blessed be יהוה, the God of Israel, for as long as the universe has existed and will continue to exist, amen and amen.

his trust in God's goodness and will continue to do so. Even treachery, the poet knows, can have a positive aspect if it brings the betrayed closer to God. Moderns mostly find it simple to pay lip service to that kind of thinking. But the spiritual value of reading the forty-first psalm lies in its ability to prod readers into asking if they have ever been able to think in these terms when they have actually encountered betrayal and disloyalty in their own lives . . . or if they find the poet's point profound only when they are able to apply it to the lives of other people.

מב

לַמְנַצֵּחַ מַשְׂכִּיל לִבְנֵי־קֹרַח׃

2 כְּאַיָּל תַּעֲרֹג עַל־אֲפִיקֵי־מָיִם כֵּן נַפְשִׁי תַעֲרֹג אֵלֶיךָ אֱלֹהִים׃

3 צָמְאָה נַפְשִׁי ׀ לֵאלֹהִים לְאֵל חָי מָתַי אָבוֹא וְאֵרָאֶה פְּנֵי אֱלֹהִים׃

4 הָיְתָה־לִּי דִמְעָתִי לֶחֶם יוֹמָם וָלָיְלָה בֶּאֱמֹר אֵלַי כָּל־הַיּוֹם אַיֵּה אֱלֹהֶיךָ׃

5 אֵלֶּה אֶזְכְּרָה ׀ וְאֶשְׁפְּכָה עָלַי ׀ נַפְשִׁי כִּי אֶעֱבֹר ׀ בַּסָּךְ אֶדַּדֵּם עַד־בֵּית אֱלֹהִים בְּקוֹל־רִנָּה וְתוֹדָה הָמוֹן חוֹגֵג׃

6 מַה־תִּשְׁתּוֹחֲחִי ׀ נַפְשִׁי וַתֶּהֱמִי עָלָי הוֹחִילִי לֵאלֹהִים כִּי־עוֹד אוֹדֶנּוּ יְשׁוּעוֹת פָּנָיו׃

7 אֱלֹהַי עָלַי נַפְשִׁי תִשְׁתּוֹחָח עַל־כֵּן אֶזְכָּרְךָ מֵאֶרֶץ יַרְדֵּן וְחֶרְמוֹנִים מֵהַר מִצְעָר׃

8 תְּהוֹם אֶל־תְּהוֹם קוֹרֵא לְקוֹל צִנּוֹרֶיךָ כָּל־מִשְׁבָּרֶיךָ וְגַלֶּיךָ עָלַי עָבָרוּ׃

9 יוֹמָם ׀ יְצַוֶּה יְהוָה ׀ חַסְדּוֹ וּבַלַּיְלָה *שִׁירוֹ עִמִּי תְּפִלָּה לְאֵל חַיָּי׃

v. 9 שירה כתיב

The poet is at war with his own soul: he personally feels drawn towards God, but his soul, responding to the taunts and barbs of threatening foes, is feeling downcast and depressed. The poet, wishing to shake off his doldrums, calls out repeatedly to his soul—imploring it to ignore the vulgar insults of hooligans who neither know nor care to know anything of God and instead to choose a life lived in God and devoted to the service of God. For the savvy reader, however, the fact that the poet has chosen to frame his poem as a kind of dialogue does not obfuscate the fact that what we are really reading about is an inner debate within the poet's psyche. He wants to believe. He wants to put his faith totally in God. He wants to long for communion with God as passionately and singlemindedly as an ibex wandering through the parched wilderness on an unbearably hot day yearns to find a stream of cool water from which to drink.

On some level, the poet already yearns for God honestly and openly, but there is another portion of his inner self with which he must also deal, another piece of the inner landscape he must traverse on his way to spiritual wholeness. And this piece of the road passes through Doubt and Uncertainty just as

BOOK TWO

42

For the conductor, a wise-song of the Korachides.

[2] As a stag yearns for streams of cool water, so does my soul yearn for you, O God.

[3] Indeed, my soul thirsts for God, for the living God, saying, "When shall I come and see the face of God?"

[4] Tears are my bread day and night as scoundrels say to me all day long, "Where *is* your God?"

[5] Their question prompts me to remember so many things, to pour my heart out in anguish as I recall what it was like to walk up to the House of God singing songs of joy and thanksgiving with a crowd of friends in the midst of a truly festive multitude.

[6] Why so downcast, my soul, so that you whine about my lot? Hope instead in the God to whom I continue to give thanks, in the God whose face is salvation.

[7] O my God, my soul within me is downcast; thus must I recall You from the land of Jordan, from Hermonim, from Mount Mizar.

[8] Deep calls to deep at the sound of Your torrents; all Your breakers and waves have washed over me.

[9] By day יהוה commands that divine mercy be with me and by night, a divine song, a prayer to the God of my life.

surely as through Yearning and Desire. But neither Doubt nor Uncertainty constitutes the most treacherous stretch of road between the poet and his God, however, because the route also passes through Recollection. And it is there, in the realm of recollective memory, that the poet finds the most arduous part of the journey to lie. Indeed, for all he has grown to be a spiritually mature adult, the poet cannot stop remembering the happier days of his younger years and, in so doing, is forced to confront the awful, disturbing truth that the quest for a life in God has not brought him prosperity, fame, and unbridled happiness . . . but just the opposite: a life of ridicule and insult.

On top of all that, the poet's road to God also passes through Fear. Indeed, he suggests that he has already experienced the presence of God in the palpable, sensory way cultivated by the psalmists' guild, and he knows that the

10 אוֹמְרָ֤ה ׀ לְאֵ֥ל סַלְעִי֮ לָמָ֪ה שְׁכַ֫חְתָּ֥נִי לָֽמָּה־קֹדֵ֥ר
אֵלֵ֗ךְ בְּלַ֣חַץ אוֹיֵֽב׃
11 בְּרֶ֤צַח ׀ בְּֽעַצְמוֹתַ֗י חֵרְפ֥וּנִי צוֹרְרָ֑י בְּאָמְרָ֥ם אֵלַ֥י
כָּל־הַ֝יּ֗וֹם אַיֵּ֥ה אֱלֹהֶֽיךָ׃
12 מַה־תִּשְׁתּ֬וֹחֲחִ֨י ׀ נַפְשִׁי֮ וּֽמַה־תֶּהֱמִ֪י עָ֫לָ֥י הוֹחִ֣ילִי
לֵ֭אלֹהִים כִּי־ע֣וֹד אוֹדֶ֑נּוּ יְשׁוּעֹ֥ת פָּ֝נַ֗י וֵאלֹהָֽי׃

knowledge of God can be as terrifying an experience as it is a satisfying one. He remembers the feeling of being totally vulnerable, the sensation of drowning in God, of being lost at sea like Jonah (who also had the horrifying experience of just barely escaping death by drowning on his journey to fulfilling his own destiny in God, as did the Israelites on their way to Sinai). Worse still, the poet's tortured road to spiritual fulfillment also passes through Worry in that, for all its intensity, his yearning for God cannot make him forget that God, at least most of the time, appears to be totally unconcerned with his problems. And, since the search for communion with an unseen God will always be an unsettling, confusing experience for practical

[10] I say to God, "O my rock, why have You forgotten me? Why must I walk in darkness under the pressure of the enemy?"

[11] With the intent to murder, my foes insult me down to my bones when they say to me all day long, "Where *is* your God?"

[12] Why so downcast, my soul? Why do you whine about my lot? Hope instead in the God to whom I continue to give thanks, in my God, the One in whom my face finds salvation.

people, the poet's uncertainty about the ultimate nature of his spiritual path is part of that worry as well.

Moderns who bring their own ambivalence about religion to their spiritual lives will find a kindred spirit in the author of the forty-second psalm, especially if they allow his words to prompt the asking of a deep, challenging question: can we moderns harness the creative energy generated by conflicting certainties about the nature of the Divine to propel us further along our spiritual paths towards communion with the elusive God of Israel? Or are we doomed, as so often seems the case, to be paralyzed by uncertainty, almost as though respect for spiritual honesty and intellectual candor were somehow to be incompatible with living a life totally given over to yearning for redemption in God?

מג

שָׁפְטֵנִי אֱלֹהִים | וְרִיבָה רִיבִי מִגּוֹי לֹא־חָסִיד
מֵאִישׁ־מִרְמָה וְעַוְלָה תְפַלְּטֵנִי:
2 כִּי־אַתָּה | אֱלֹהֵי מָעוּזִּי לָמָה זְנַחְתָּנִי לָמָּה־קֹדֵר
אֶתְהַלֵּךְ בְּלַחַץ אוֹיֵב:
3 שְׁלַח־אוֹרְךָ וַאֲמִתְּךָ הֵמָּה יַנְחוּנִי יְבִיאוּנִי אֶל־הַר־
קָדְשְׁךָ וְאֶל־מִשְׁכְּנוֹתֶיךָ:
4 וְאָבוֹאָה | אֶל־מִזְבַּח אֱלֹהִים אֶל־אֵל שִׂמְחַת גִּילִי
וְאוֹדְךָ בְכִנּוֹר אֱלֹהִים אֱלֹהָי:
5 מַה־תִּשְׁתּוֹחֲחִי | נַפְשִׁי וּמַה־תֶּהֱמִי עָלָי הוֹחִילִי
לֵאלֹהִים כִּי־עוֹד אוֹדֶנּוּ יְשׁוּעֹת פָּנַי וֵאלֹהָי:

The forty-third psalm is clearly related to the poem that precedes it in the Psalter: it has much of the same imagery and its final verse appears in both poems. Yet it also has its own message to impart, one slightly different from the longer forty-second psalm. The poet is downcast, his soul and his psyche at odds with each other about how to proceed towards God. The poet's problems, however, are not all internal and, for all he truly yearns for God, his innermost self is also suffering under the weight of oppression, and specifically from the oppressive taunting of one particular, unnamed individual. Then, as he is struggling to overcome his own doubts and fears, the psalmist suddenly has an insight into his own spirituality. In his mind's eye, he can imagine what it would be like were the Light and Truth of God to come out of the Temple in the guise of divine messengers and take him by the hand into the House of God on God's holy mountain. He can almost see the two of them, Truth and Light, leading him to the altar in the Temple forecourt where, instead of being

43 Render judgment for me, O God, and plead my case against an impious nation; grant me refuge from a man of fraud and deceit.

2 If You are my God and my fortress, why have You forsaken me? Why must I walk about in darkness under the scrutiny of an enemy?

3 Send me Your light and Your truth, for they will guide me and bring me to Your holy mountain, to Your sacred residence on earth.

4 There will I approach the altar of God; there will I approach the God who is the essence of my joy and gladness. There will I give thanks to God, to my God, with a song I will accompany on a lyre.

5 Why so downcast, my soul? Why do you whine about my lot? Hope instead in the God to whom I continue to give thanks, in my God, the One in whom my face finds salvation.

moved to sacrifice an ox, he is so overwhelmed by feelings of almost unbearable happiness in God that he can only respond by lifting up a lyre and singing a hymn of praise.

Modern readers of the forty-third psalm will want to focus on the idea of Light and Truth coming in the guise of angels to guide them gently towards God. Where could we moderns look for such angels in our world? How could we recognize them as divine messengers? Would we have the courage to go along with them to the House of God, to Jerusalem? Perhaps some of us would and some of us wouldn't, but the poet has another question for us to ponder as well, one that only appears at first easier to answer: can we imagine joy in God so intense that it can only be expressed in song?

מד

לַמְנַצֵּחַ לִבְנֵי־קֹרַח מַשְׂכִּיל׃

2 אֱלֹהִים ׀ בְּאָזְנֵינוּ שָׁמַעְנוּ אֲבוֹתֵינוּ סִפְּרוּ־לָנוּ
פֹּעַל־פָּעַלְתָּ בִימֵיהֶם בִּימֵי קֶדֶם׃

3 אַתָּה ׀ יָדְךָ גּוֹיִם הוֹרַשְׁתָּ וַתִּטָּעֵם תָּרַע לְאֻמִּים
וַתְּשַׁלְּחֵם׃

4 כִּי לֹא בְחַרְבָּם יָרְשׁוּ־אָרֶץ וּזְרוֹעָם לֹא־הוֹשִׁיעָה
לָּמוֹ כִּי־יְמִינְךָ וּזְרוֹעֲךָ וְאוֹר פָּנֶיךָ כִּי רְצִיתָם׃

5 אַתָּה־הוּא מַלְכִּי אֱלֹהִים צַוֵּה יְשׁוּעוֹת יַעֲקֹב׃

6 בְּךָ צָרֵינוּ נְנַגֵּחַ בְּשִׁמְךָ נָבוּס קָמֵינוּ׃

7 כִּי לֹא בְקַשְׁתִּי אֶבְטָח וְחַרְבִּי לֹא תוֹשִׁיעֵנִי׃

8 כִּי הוֹשַׁעְתָּנוּ מִצָּרֵינוּ וּמְשַׂנְאֵינוּ הֱבִישׁוֹתָ׃

9 בֵּאלֹהִים הִלַּלְנוּ כָל־הַיּוֹם וְשִׁמְךָ ׀ לְעוֹלָם נוֹדֶה
סֶלָה׃

10 אַף־זָנַחְתָּ וַתַּכְלִימֵנוּ וְלֹא־תֵצֵא בְּצִבְאוֹתֵינוּ׃

The circumstances under which the forty-fourth psalm was written have been endlessly debated by modern commentators, but the spiritual lesson the poet has to teach his readers can be appreciated independently of whatever specific incident may have prompted its composition. The poet begins by celebrating God as the Author of History, a concept modern readers may find irreconcilably at odds with the notion of human beings having free will and thus possessing the unrestricted ability to create their own destinies. And although readers may wonder why the poet appears not to have felt the problem as acutely as they do, the notion that individuals in this world can decide freely how to behave does not appear to have struck the psalmist as impossible to square with the notion of a God who guides the history of the world, even in an absolute sort of way.

Our poet begins by noting that the conquest of the Land of Israel in the days of Joshua was less a result of Joshua's great military prowess than it was a function of God's decision to disinherit the indigenous peoples of Canaan and replace them with the Israelites. But now the nation faces a new situation: military defeat by vengeful, maniacal foes who, to hear the poet tell it, plunder and slaughter at will. The poet, however, faithful to the core, is prepared to accept this merely as the other side of the doctrinal coin: if God is the ultimate Arbiter of military matters, then the nation's defeat must reflect divine will no less accurately than did its earlier successes.

Modern readers will probably find that kind of faith both uplifting and a bit

44 For the conductor, a wise-song of the Korachides.

[2] O God, with our own ears we have heard our parents tell us what You wrought in ancient times for our people.

[3] Your hand drove out the indigenous nations of the Holy Land and planted our ancestors there in their stead; You dealt with those peoples harshly, summarily sending them away.

[4] For our ancestors did not acquire the land by conquering it with the sword and neither did their own arm bring them salvation, but rather were both these things wrought by Your right arm, by Your arm, by the light of Your face when You showed them favor.

[5] You are my Sovereign, O God; decree, therefore, the salvation of Jacob.

[6] By virtue of our faith in You shall we gore our enemies; in Your name we shall crush those who rise up against us.

[7] For I do not trust in my bow and neither do I imagine that it is my sword that delivers me; [8] it is You who have delivered us from our enemies all along and dealt out shame to those who hated us.

[9] To God do we sing hymns of praise all day long; forever shall we give thanks to Your name, *selah*.

[10] Nonetheless, You have now forsaken us and shamed us by not going forth with our armies.

puzzling, but the poet's closing plea for divine mercy cannot but inspire. In the end, seeking to resolve the paradox of human free will in a world governed by the Author of History is perhaps the most maddening of all spiritual riddles. Those ancients who managed to solve it, or at least to resolve it to their own spiritual satisfaction, and especially those who, like the psalmist, were able to do so within the context of their own personal, experiential knowledge of God—are thus easy to admire. But can moderns emulate them as well?

In any event, most moderns are of two minds about the whole issue. Yearning endlessly for the freedom to chart our own paths in life and to make the decisions that will affect us personally, yet also very pleased to have the Author of History around to blame when things go awry, we moderns bring

11 תְּשִׁיבֵנוּ אָחוֹר מִנִּי־צָר וּמְשַׂנְאֵינוּ שָׁסוּ לָמוֹ:
12 תִּתְּנֵנוּ כְּצֹאן מַאֲכָל וּבַגּוֹיִם זֵרִיתָנוּ:
13 תִּמְכֹּר עַמְּךָ בְלֹא־הוֹן וְלֹא־רִבִּיתָ בִּמְחִירֵיהֶם:
14 תְּשִׂימֵנוּ חֶרְפָּה לִשְׁכֵנֵינוּ לַעַג וָקֶלֶס לִסְבִיבוֹתֵינוּ:
15 תְּשִׂימֵנוּ מָשָׁל בַּגּוֹיִם מְנוֹד־רֹאשׁ בַּלְאֻמִּים:
16 כָּל־הַיּוֹם כְּלִמָּתִי נֶגְדִּי וּבֹשֶׁת פָּנַי כִּסָּתְנִי: 17 מִקּוֹל מְחָרֵף וּמְגַדֵּף מִפְּנֵי אוֹיֵב וּמִתְנַקֵּם:
18 כָּל־זֹאת בָּאַתְנוּ וְלֹא שְׁכַחֲנוּךָ וְלֹא־שִׁקַּרְנוּ בִּבְרִיתֶךָ:
19 לֹא־נָסוֹג אָחוֹר לִבֵּנוּ וַתֵּט אֲשֻׁרֵינוּ מִנִּי אָרְחֶךָ:
20 כִּי דִכִּיתָנוּ בִּמְקוֹם תַּנִּים וַתְּכַס עָלֵינוּ בְצַלְמָוֶת:
21 אִם־שָׁכַחְנוּ שֵׁם אֱלֹהֵינוּ וַנִּפְרֹשׂ כַּפֵּינוּ לְאֵל זָר:
22 הֲלֹא אֱלֹהִים יַחֲקָר־זֹאת כִּי הוּא יֹדֵעַ תַּעֲלֻמוֹת לֵב:

more than a touch of ambivalence to the issues the psalmist presents for his readers' consideration. The poet, for his part, sounds certain that Sovereign God has the ability to decree the salvation of Jacob without having to bend any immutable laws of nature . . . and without having to withdraw the gift of free will granted to human beings as part of their basic human nature in the first place.

One plausible way to understand the poet's stance would be to presume that God grants *individuals* the freedom to choose how to behave and in what direction to take their own lives, while charting with a much firmer divine hand the courses *nations* take towards the fulfillment of their national destinies. Given the open, unselfconscious way the poet expresses himself, this approach sounds vaguely plausible, especially in the context of a Bible filled with stories depicting a God who has no difficulty intervening in history on a national and international level, but who clearly wishes to be worshiped by individuals who voluntarily alter the way they would normally dress, eat, and conduct themselves in the workplace and at home for the sake of demonstrating their allegiance to God on even the most banal, ordinary level of daily life.

For Jews living after the Shoah, however, this way of resolving the issue will be dramatically more challenging than it might otherwise have been. Still, the thoughtful contemplation of the 44th psalm can nevertheless be a useful framework for coming to terms with the issue of the Holocaust as well. The poet writes that "All this has come upon us, yet we have not forgotten You nor

[11] You have left us to retreat from the foe, thus allowing those who hate us to take our goods as spoil for themselves.

[12] You have made us like sheep destined to be eaten; You have scattered us among the nations.

[13] You have sold Your people for a pitiable price, not even bothering to haggle with the enemy to get the best price for them.

[14] You have made us a source of embarrassment to our neighbors, a symbol of scorn and derision in the eyes of those who surround us.

[15] You have made us a paradigm of rejection among the nations, a reason for the countries of the earth to shake their heads in dismay.

[16] Disgrace is my companion all day long; shame covers my face [17] when I hear the voices of people who insult and taunt me, when I find myself in the company of enemy and vengeful foe.

[18] All this has come upon us, yet we have not forgotten You nor have we denied our covenant with You.

[19–20] Despite the fact that You have banished us to a den of jackals and covered us with deathly darkness, our hearts have not turned back nor have our feet swerved from Your path.

[21] If we were to forget the name of our God and spread out our hands to an alien god, [22] would God, who knows all the secrets of the human heart, not learn of it?

have we denied our covenant with You," and he sounds quite resolute in his conviction: God's immutable reality and absolute reliability make absurd any effort to unravel the theological riddle of divine inactivity during the Shoah by imagining a God uncertain about the eternal, inviolate nature of the covenant with Israel. Such a solution—predicated on the assumption that God's promise to function as the ultimate Guardian of Israel is conditional, and that God therefore bears no absolute responsibility for the welfare of the Jewish people and its continued existence—would be so far out of step with the spiritual reality the poet knows that he simply cannot go off in that direction, not even theoretically. Indeed, when he asks, "Why do You hide Your face? Why are You ignoring our pain and our suffering?" he is proposing

23 כִּֽי־עָ֭לֶיךָ הֹרַ֣גְנוּ כָל־הַיּ֑וֹם נֶ֝חְשַׁ֗בְנוּ כְּצֹ֣אן טִבְחָֽה׃
24 ע֤וּרָה ׀ לָ֖מָּה תִישַׁ֥ן ׀ אֲדֹנָ֑י הָ֝קִ֗יצָה אַל־תִּזְנַ֥ח לָנֶֽצַח׃
25 לָֽמָּה־פָנֶ֥יךָ תַסְתִּ֑יר תִּשְׁכַּ֖ח עָנְיֵ֣נוּ וְֽלַחֲצֵֽנוּ׃
26 כִּ֤י שָׁ֣חָה לֶעָפָ֣ר נַפְשֵׁ֑נוּ דָּבְקָ֖ה לָאָ֣רֶץ בִּטְנֵֽנוּ׃
27 ק֭וּמָֽה עֶזְרָ֣תָה לָּ֑נוּ וּ֝פְדֵ֗נוּ לְמַ֣עַן חַסְדֶּֽךָ׃

an approach to post-Holocaust theology moderns would do well to consider.

By suggesting that it is the horror of the Shoah that needs to be contemplated and evaluated against the background of the ongoing, permanent relationship between God and Israel (rather than the other way around), he is saying something challenging and invigorating about the nature of Jewish history. The poet knows God to exist. He knows, and believes absolutely, that his God is all-knowing and all-powerful. His response to the disasters that have befallen his people, therefore, is to call out to God in anguish and beg for a respite from the misery the debacle has brought in its wake. It doesn't occur to him to question the nature of God's reality, any more than it would strike him to question the existence of his nation's enemies. Reality is as one finds it in the world, the poet is saying. And if God is part of that reality, then the solution to even the thorniest riddle of divine action and inaction in human history cannot be predicated on any uncertainty about God's ability to act unilaterally and forcefully in the world.

By the end of his poem, the poet has failed to say whether he is writing in the middle of national crisis and is calling out to God to intervene on the nation's behalf, or whether he is writing long after the fact to suggest that the way to deal with national disaster always is to call out to God in confidence and with hope. Whatever its original historical context, though, the 44th psalm will serve for moderns as the ultimate litmus test for the cogency and reasonability of any approach to theology after the Shoah. In the end, the poet chose to write his ode to the paradox of Jewish suffering in the form of a psalm to God rather than a paean to the basic unfathomability of the world. His message, therefore, was primarily one of hope rather than despair . . . and in the end, that has to be the most inspiring detail of all.

[23] Indeed, it is precisely because of our faith in You that we were massacred all day long, granted no more consideration than sheep destined for slaughter.

[24] Wake up, Adonai! Why do You sleep? Rouse Yourself! Forsake us not forever!

[25] Why do You hide Your face? Why are You ignoring our pain and our suffering?

[26] Our souls are prostrate in the dust, our bellies pressed onto the ground in abject supplication.

[27] Rise up to aid us and redeem us in accordance with Your mercy.

מה

לַמְנַצֵּחַ עַל־שֹׁשַׁנִּים לִבְנֵי־קֹרַח מַשְׂכִּיל שִׁיר יְדִידֹת׃

2 רָחַשׁ לִבִּי ׀ דָּבָר טוֹב אֹמֵר אָנִי מַעֲשַׂי לְמֶלֶךְ לְשׁוֹנִי עֵט ׀ סוֹפֵר מָהִיר׃

3 יָפְיָפִיתָ מִבְּנֵי אָדָם הוּצַק חֵן בְּשְׂפְתוֹתֶיךָ עַל־כֵּן בֵּרַכְךָ אֱלֹהִים לְעוֹלָם׃

4 חֲגוֹר חַרְבְּךָ עַל־יָרֵךְ גִּבּוֹר הוֹדְךָ וַהֲדָרֶךָ׃

5 וַהֲדָרְךָ ׀ צְלַח רְכַב עַל־דְּבַר־אֱמֶת וְעַנְוָה־צֶדֶק וְתוֹרְךָ נוֹרָאוֹת יְמִינֶךָ׃

6 חִצֶּיךָ שְׁנוּנִים עַמִּים תַּחְתֶּיךָ יִפְּלוּ בְּלֵב אוֹיְבֵי הַמֶּלֶךְ׃

7 כִּסְאֲךָ אֱלֹהִים עוֹלָם וָעֶד שֵׁבֶט מִישֹׁר שֵׁבֶט מַלְכוּתֶךָ׃

8 אָהַבְתָּ צֶּדֶק וַתִּשְׂנָא רֶשַׁע עַל־כֵּן ׀ מְשָׁחֲךָ אֱלֹהִים אֱלֹהֶיךָ שֶׁמֶן שָׂשׂוֹן מֵחֲבֵרֶיךָ׃

9 מֹר וַאֲהָלוֹת קְצִיעוֹת כָּל־בִּגְדֹתֶיךָ מִן־הֵיכְלֵי שֵׁן מִנִּי שִׂמְּחוּךָ׃

10 בְּנוֹת מְלָכִים בְּיִקְּרוֹתֶיךָ נִצְּבָה שֵׁגַל לִימִינְךָ בְּכֶתֶם אוֹפִיר׃

Here and there in the Psalter appear a number of hymns sometimes called "royal" psalms. Their authors, appearing to know nothing of the misery of persecution or the rapturous longing for God that characterize so many other psalms, have kingship on their minds and they write about the reverence due earthly monarchs with great passion and literary skill. The psalmist whose poem we know as the forty-fifth psalm, for example, falls into that category. His poem is an ode to his king, meaning the earthly sovereign who rules in Jerusalem. And so, fabulously, he describes the trappings of majesty that characterize royal life in old Jerusalem: the king, scented with myrrh and aloe, is depicted as seated on what the poet calls his "divinely granted" throne in his ivory palace with the queen, swathed in gold, standing to his right as he dispenses judgment to the people.

But when was this poem written? The poet promises to memorialize the king's name for all generations, but—either paradoxically or ironically—he omits the actual name of the king whose praises he is singing with such intense fervor. During the part of the Second Temple period when the Psalter came into being, no kings ruled over the Jews in the Land of Israel. By then,

45 For the conductor, a wise-song of love by the Korachides to the tune of "Lilies."

[2] My heart is astir with good things as I prepare to report my deeds to the king; my tongue is the pen of a ready scribe.

[3] You are the most handsome of men; grace itself is poured onto your lips as a sign that God has granted you eternal blessing.

[4] Strap your sword onto your thigh, O hero, for it is your glory and your splendor.

[5] Succeed splendidly as you ride forth in the cause of truth and humble justice, and may your right hand teach you awesome things.

[6] Your arrows are sharpened; let nations fall beneath you as those arrows land in the hearts of the king's enemies.

[7] A divinely granted throne is yours for ever and always; your royal scepter is a scepter of fairness.

[8] You love justice and hate evil; therefore has God, your God, anointed you rather than one of your friends with the joyful oil.

[9] All your garments have the scent of myrrh and aloes, even the aroma of cassia; your people come forth from ivory palaces to gladden you.

[10] The daughters of kings vie to honor you; the queen herself stands by your right hand dressed in the gold of Ophir.

Davidic kingship was a distant memory of something that had characterized the happy years before the destruction of Jerusalem by the Babylonians at the beginning of the sixth century B.C.E., but which, for one reason or another, was never restored. Was this an ancient poem taken into the Psalter as a reminder of the days when the Jewish people was ruled by a Jewish king in an independent Jewish kingdom? Or was it composed after the Exile by a bard who wished to awaken in the people the recollection of happier times?

In either case, the question really is not what it may have once meant, but what it can mean to readers today. There is a strong tendency in most people to idealize the past, especially the distant past, but this rarely reflects actual historical reality. Modern readers, therefore, may wish to respond to the poet's words by considering how we in our world relate to the past. The notion, after

[11] שִׁמְעִי־בַת וּרְאִי וְהַטִּי אָזְנֵךְ וְשִׁכְחִי עַמֵּךְ וּבֵית אָבִיךְ׃ [12] וְיִתְאָו הַמֶּלֶךְ יָפְיֵךְ כִּי הוּא אֲדֹנַיִךְ וְהִשְׁתַּחֲוִי־לוֹ׃
[13] וּבַת־צֹר ׀ בְּמִנְחָה פָּנַיִךְ יְחַלּוּ עֲשִׁירֵי עָם׃
[14] כׇּל־כְּבוּדָּה בַת־מֶלֶךְ פְּנִימָה מִמִּשְׁבְּצוֹת זָהָב לְבוּשָׁהּ׃
[15] לִרְקָמוֹת תּוּבַל לַמֶּלֶךְ בְּתוּלוֹת אַחֲרֶיהָ רֵעוֹתֶיהָ מוּבָאוֹת לָךְ׃
[16] תּוּבַלְנָה בִּשְׂמָחֹת וָגִיל תְּבֹאֶינָה בְּהֵיכַל מֶלֶךְ׃
[17] תַּחַת אֲבֹתֶיךָ יִהְיוּ בָנֶיךָ תְּשִׁיתֵמוֹ לְשָׂרִים בְּכׇל־הָאָרֶץ׃ [18] אַזְכִּירָה שִׁמְךָ בְּכׇל־דֹּר וָדֹר עַל־כֵּן עַמִּים יְהוֹדֻךָ לְעֹלָם וָעֶד׃

all, that past centuries were simpler times is not exactly correct (although we seem to feel obliged constantly to refer to them that way), and neither is it true that our ancestors lived lives less fraught with danger and risk than we do. Nor does it make any real sense to imagine that the absence of modern technology must inevitably have made the men and women of previous generations more personally involved in each other's lives than moderns could ever hope to be. Perhaps the almost universal tendency to romanticize the past has more to do with the way moderns feel about personal responsibility than with any specific details about how people of other centuries actually may have lived. By imagining that culture is degenerating rather than evolving, for example, moderns effectively make it sound rational not to move forward, not to progress, and not to develop in ways that will take us even *farther* away from the rosy ideal of past generations. By finding the past to be better in every way than the present, we are suggesting that the logical course to take would be to emulate the past, rather than to attempt to improve on it. As a result, growth—and especially growth in intellectually and spiritually novel directions—sounds suspect, even by its nature counterproductive. Eventually, even the much-discussed concept of standing on the shoulders of the great men and women of the past as we chart our way into

[11] And so might one address one of those princesses: "Listen, lass, and look well and pay attention. Forget your people and your father's house, [12]for the king desires your beauty and, as he is your lord, you must bow down to him.
[13] But even when the wealthiest citizens entreat your favor with gifts, O daughter of Tyre, [14]you must not forget that the true glory of a king's daughter lies in her inner character . . . and this is so even if her outer garment is fashioned of squares of the most precious woven gold.
[15] Such a woman will be brought to the king on gorgeous carpets, escorted to him by a bevy of virgins and followed by all her friends.
[16] All together, they shall come to the king in great joy and gladness. In joy shall they approach the palace of the king."
[17] And to the king, one might say this: "Your sons shall rule as did your ancestors. You shall appoint them princes throughout the land. [18]I shall make your name known in every generation so that nations acknowledge you for all time."

the future acquires a peculiar ring to it: why should we stand on their shoulders at all, when all that we really want to do is to stand precisely where they stood? Even the desire to learn of the past begins to make sense only if the point of all that study is to find our way *back* to the world of our ancestors, not to move *forward* at all. Moderns mostly insist that growth is a positive force in the lives of individuals and peoples. Too often, however, they succumb to the kind of intense nostalgia that leads them to look to the past as an excuse to avoid looking productively and innovatively into the future . . . and to avoid working to improve the world by inventing it anew. In the end, it all comes down to a series of simple questions: Do bygone eras always sound better to us than our own? Do we naturally assume that whatever once was will always be, almost by definition, better than what now is? Do we look to the past for succor, or to the future? Or do we look to God, the Author of History *and* Destiny?

מז

לַמְנַצֵּחַ לִבְנֵי־קֹרַח עַל־עֲלָמוֹת שִׁיר׃
2 אֱלֹהִים לָנוּ מַחֲסֶה וָעֹז עֶזְרָה בְצָרוֹת נִמְצָא מְאֹד׃
3 עַל־כֵּן לֹא־נִירָא בְּהָמִיר אָרֶץ וּבְמוֹט הָרִים בְּלֵב יַמִּים׃
4 יֶהֱמוּ יֶחְמְרוּ מֵימָיו יִרְעֲשׁוּ הָרִים בְּגַאֲוָתוֹ סֶלָה׃
5 נָהָר פְּלָגָיו יְשַׂמְּחוּ עִיר־אֱלֹהִים קְדֹשׁ מִשְׁכְּנֵי עֶלְיוֹן׃ 6 אֱלֹהִים בְּקִרְבָּהּ בַּל־תִּמּוֹט יַעְזְרֶהָ אֱלֹהִים לִפְנוֹת בֹּקֶר׃
7 הָמוּ גוֹיִם מָטוּ מַמְלָכוֹת נָתַן בְּקוֹלוֹ תָּמוּג אָרֶץ׃
8 יְהוָה צְבָאוֹת עִמָּנוּ מִשְׂגָּב־לָנוּ אֱלֹהֵי יַעֲקֹב סֶלָה׃
9 לְכוּ־חֲזוּ מִפְעֲלוֹת יְהוָה אֲשֶׁר־שָׂם שַׁמּוֹת בָּאָרֶץ׃
10 מַשְׁבִּית מִלְחָמוֹת עַד־קְצֵה הָאָרֶץ קֶשֶׁת יְשַׁבֵּר וְקִצֵּץ חֲנִית עֲגָלוֹת יִשְׂרֹף בָּאֵשׁ׃
11 הַרְפּוּ וּדְעוּ כִּי־אָנֹכִי אֱלֹהִים אָרוּם בַּגּוֹיִם אָרוּם בָּאָרֶץ׃
12 יְהוָה צְבָאוֹת עִמָּנוּ מִשְׂגָּב־לָנוּ אֱלֹהֵי יַעֲקֹב סֶלָה׃

The poet begins his poem by contemplating Jerusalem, the Holy City. It is a sacred place of refuge and holiness, but the poet knows that it is only a symbol . . . and that the citadel in which Israel's security may truly be found is fashioned not of stone, but of faith in God. Indeed, the poet knows that war and peace on earth are themselves functions of the degree to which God is revered—or reviled—by the nations of the world and that, at a word, God can stop all wars, destroy all weapons, and disable all chariots. But just as the poet is giving voice to these thoughts, he receives an oracle from God that confirms his theory and takes it one step further by declaring that the way for a nation to live in a world at peace is not to defeat all the other nations in it, but to create a world in which God's sovereignty is acknowledged by all peoples.

Moderns will want to ask themselves if they too believe that God is the

46

For the conductor, a psalm of the Korachides to the tune of "Maidens of Song."

[2] God is our haven and our strength, our help in times of trouble so intensely present [3] that we would not know fear even if the earth were to shake or the mountains topple into the heart of the sea.

[4] Let the waters of the sea rage and foam; let the mountains erupt with pride worthy of God, *selah.*

[5] The city of God, the sacred dwelling of God Most High, is made delightful by being watered amply by a swiftly-flowing river; [6] God is in the midst of that city and so shall it ever remain secure. No matter how dark the night, God will always help towards morning.

[7] Nations can rage and kingdoms topple, but when God speaks, the earth melts away.

[8] יהוה of the celestial legions is with us; the God of Jacob is our refuge, *selah.*

[9] Go forth and gaze on the works of יהוה, the God whose power is sufficient to make desolate the earth.

[10] God can bring war to a halt even at the very ends of the earth by snapping bows, by breaking swords, by burning chariots with fire.

[11] God puts it this way: "Abandon your fantasies and know that I am God. I shall be exalted among the nations; I shall be exalted in all the earth."

[12] יהוה of the celestial legions is with us; the God of Jacob is our refuge, *selah.*

Author of war and peace. Can we work for peace by seeking God? Can the world eliminate war by embracing faith? Is war what occurs when nations seek security in military power rather than by accepting the quest for the love of God as their national mission? Can the divine oracle *arum baggoyim arum ba'aretz* ("I shall be exalted among the nations, I shall be exalted in all the earth") inspire moderns to find in God a source of security more potent even than the mightiest fortress and the best equipped, most sophisticated army?

מז

לַמְנַצֵּחַ ׀ לִבְנֵי־קֹרַח מִזְמוֹר׃
2 כָּל־הָעַמִּים תִּקְעוּ־כָף הָרִיעוּ לֵאלֹהִים בְּקוֹל רִנָּה׃
3 כִּי־יְהוָה עֶלְיוֹן נוֹרָא מֶלֶךְ גָּדוֹל עַל־כָּל־הָאָרֶץ׃
4 יַדְבֵּר עַמִּים תַּחְתֵּינוּ וּלְאֻמִּים תַּחַת רַגְלֵינוּ׃
5 יִבְחַר־לָנוּ אֶת־נַחֲלָתֵנוּ אֶת גְּאוֹן יַעֲקֹב אֲשֶׁר־אָהֵב סֶלָה׃
6 עָלָה אֱלֹהִים בִּתְרוּעָה יְהוָה בְּקוֹל שׁוֹפָר׃
7 זַמְּרוּ אֱלֹהִים זַמֵּרוּ זַמְּרוּ לְמַלְכֵּנוּ זַמֵּרוּ׃ 8 כִּי מֶלֶךְ כָּל־הָאָרֶץ אֱלֹהִים זַמְּרוּ מַשְׂכִּיל׃
9 מָלַךְ אֱלֹהִים עַל־גּוֹיִם אֱלֹהִים יָשַׁב ׀ עַל־כִּסֵּא קָדְשׁוֹ׃
10 נְדִיבֵי עַמִּים ׀ נֶאֱסָפוּ עַם אֱלֹהֵי אַבְרָהָם כִּי לֵאלֹהִים מָגִנֵּי־אֶרֶץ מְאֹד נַעֲלָה׃

Sensitive moderns tend to react with a certain ambivalence even to their own military victories. The ancients, on the other hand, saw nothing wrong with rejoicing at the defeat of their enemies and, although its precise historical context is uncertain, the forty-seventh psalm is just such an ode to success in battle. The enemy nation has been beaten, the poet writes, and made into little more than a footstool for the victors. The sound of the *shofar,* which was used in ancient times as a call to battle, is still ringing in the poet's ears. Indeed, he invites his co-citizens to transform their *shofar* blasts from calls to war into expressions of national gratitude that acknowledge God's function in the military history of Israel both as the source of safety for the nation's armies and of their victories.

Modern readers can profitably use the forty-seventh psalm as an impetus to think about the notion that victory in war is nothing more—but also nothing

47

For the conductor, a psalm of the Korachides.

[2] All you nations, clap your hands; blast your horns to God with joyful sound, [3] for יהוה is most high and awesome, a great Sovereign over the whole earth.

[4] God subdues nations beneath us, peoples beneath our feet. [5] God has chosen our inheritance for us: this land that is the pride of Jacob, beloved of God, *selah.*

[6] God rises up amidst the blasts of the horn; יהוה rises up at the sound of the *shofar.*

[7] Sing to God, sing out; sing to our Sovereign, sing out, [8] for God is Sovereign over all the earth. Sing out a wise-song to God!

[9] God reigns over all the nations; God is seated on the holy divine throne.

[10] Therefore do the nobles of the nations gather to ally themselves with the people of the God of Abraham, for God's are the shields that protect the most exalted land.

less—than a gift from God to the victorious nation. In our world, it is commonplace to assert that all decent people abhor war. That was probably no less true in antiquity, but occasionally wars simply must be fought . . . and in that case, the poet has no difficulty identifying faith in God as the ultimate weapon in the nation's arsenal. Thinking of God in military terms makes most moderns uneasy, so reading the forty-seventh psalm can be a useful opportunity to reflect on this ill ease by exploring our thoughts about the role of God in history. What can it mean, after all, to say that war is tragic at the same time that we acclaim God as the Author of victory?

מח

שִׁיר מִזְמוֹר לִבְנֵי־קֹרַח׃
2 גָּדוֹל יְהוָה וּמְהֻלָּל מְאֹד בְּעִיר אֱלֹהֵינוּ הַר־קָדְשׁוֹ׃
3 יְפֵה נוֹף מְשׂוֹשׂ כָּל־הָאָרֶץ הַר־צִיּוֹן יַרְכְּתֵי צָפוֹן קִרְיַת מֶלֶךְ רָב׃ 4 אֱלֹהִים בְּאַרְמְנוֹתֶיהָ נוֹדַע לְמִשְׂגָּב׃
5 כִּי־הִנֵּה הַמְּלָכִים נוֹעֲדוּ עָבְרוּ יַחְדָּו׃ 6 הֵמָּה רָאוּ כֵּן תָּמָהוּ נִבְהֲלוּ נֶחְפָּזוּ׃
7 רְעָדָה אֲחָזָתַם שָׁם חִיל כַּיּוֹלֵדָה׃ 8 בְּרוּחַ קָדִים תְּשַׁבֵּר אֳנִיּוֹת תַּרְשִׁישׁ׃
9 כַּאֲשֶׁר שָׁמַעְנוּ | כֵּן רָאִינוּ בְּעִיר יְהוָה צְבָאוֹת בְּעִיר אֱלֹהֵינוּ אֱלֹהִים יְכוֹנְנֶהָ עַד־עוֹלָם סֶלָה׃
10 דִּמִּינוּ אֱלֹהִים חַסְדֶּךָ בְּקֶרֶב הֵיכָלֶךָ׃ 11 כְּשִׁמְךָ אֱלֹהִים כֵּן תְּהִלָּתְךָ עַל־קַצְוֵי־אֶרֶץ צֶדֶק מָלְאָה יְמִינֶךָ׃
12 יִשְׂמַח | הַר־צִיּוֹן תָּגֵלְנָה בְּנוֹת יְהוּדָה לְמַעַן מִשְׁפָּטֶיךָ׃
13 סֹבּוּ צִיּוֹן וְהַקִּיפוּהָ סִפְרוּ מִגְדָּלֶיהָ׃ 14 שִׁיתוּ לִבְּכֶם | לְחֵילָה פַּסְּגוּ אַרְמְנוֹתֶיהָ לְמַעַן תְּסַפְּרוּ לְדוֹר אַחֲרוֹן׃
15 כִּי זֶה | אֱלֹהִים אֱלֹהֵינוּ עוֹלָם וָעֶד הוּא יְנַהֲגֵנוּ עַל־מוּת׃

The poet omits the names and dates any modern reader would consider vital background information, but the basic story appears to be that a congress of world leaders—one which did not bode well for Judah at all—took place in Jerusalem. The kings, however, were so awed by the splendor of the Holy City that they lost whatever hostility they may previously have harbored and, in the end, they all slunk off without making any untoward demands. The poet's response to this unexpectedly happy ending to what could surely have been a very sad story is to praise God, whose Temple the poet considered not merely magnificent, but more than sufficiently imposing to have somehow effected the city's deliverance simply by virtue of its presence.

48

A psalm-song of the Korachides.

[2] Great is יהוה and greatly to be praised in the city of our God, home of God's holy mountain.

[3] Its lovely landscape the delight of all the earth, Mount Zion lies at the extreme northern point of the city of our great king; [4] in its palaces, God is known to maintain a stronghold.

[5] For here did kings gather, meeting together in council; [6] once gathered, they looked around and were duly amazed. They were in awe, overwhelmed.

[7] A trembling took hold of them there akin to the shuddering of a woman in labor; [8] with an easterly breeze, You foundered the ships of Tarshish.

[9] And just as we had heard would happen, so did we see things actually unfold in the city of יהוה of the celestial legions, in the city of our God established by God forever, *selah*.

[10] We imagined Your mercy, O God, in the midst of Your palace, [11] for the praise due to You, just as Your name, reaches to the ends of the earth; Your right hand is filled with justice.

[12] Let Mount Zion rejoice; let the daughters of Judah be glad because of Your laws.

[13] Surround Zion and encompass it, then count its towers; [14] turn your heart to its ramparts, then climb up to its palaces so that you can tell of them to the next generation.

[15] For this is God, our God for ever and always whose leadership makes it possible for us to transcend death.

Moderns pondering this joyous psalm will want to ask themselves several questions as they reflect on the role of God in the geopolitics of the modern world. Is God necessarily present *or* absent when world leaders meet? How does God govern the world through earthly leaders? What, precisely, is the relationship between legitimate political leadership and absolute divine sovereignty?

מט

לַמְנַצֵּחַ ׀ לִבְנֵי־קֹרַח מִזְמוֹר׃

2 שִׁמְעוּ־זֹאת כָּל־הָעַמִּים הַאֲזִינוּ כָּל־יֹשְׁבֵי חָלֶד׃

3 גַּם־בְּנֵי אָדָם גַּם־בְּנֵי־אִישׁ יַחַד עָשִׁיר וְאֶבְיוֹן׃

4 פִּי יְדַבֵּר חָכְמוֹת וְהָגוּת לִבִּי תְבוּנוֹת׃

5 אַטֶּה לְמָשָׁל אָזְנִי אֶפְתַּח בְּכִנּוֹר חִידָתִי׃

6 לָמָּה אִירָא בִּימֵי רָע עֲוֺן עֲקֵבַי יְסוּבֵּנִי׃

7 הַבֹּטְחִים עַל־חֵילָם וּבְרֹב עָשְׁרָם יִתְהַלָּלוּ׃

8 אָח לֹא־פָדֹה יִפְדֶּה אִישׁ לֹא־יִתֵּן לֵאלֹהִים כָּפְרוֹ׃

9 וְיֵקַר פִּדְיוֹן נַפְשָׁם וְחָדַל לְעוֹלָם׃

10 וִיחִי־עוֹד לָנֶצַח לֹא יִרְאֶה הַשָּׁחַת׃

11 כִּי יִרְאֶה ׀ חֲכָמִים יָמוּתוּ יַחַד כְּסִיל וָבַעַר יֹאבֵדוּ
וְעָזְבוּ לַאֲחֵרִים חֵילָם׃

Although the forty-ninth psalm contains many difficult expressions, obscure passages, and almost undecipherable turns of phrase, it is nonetheless one of the most recited of all the psalms because of its regular recitation in Jewish houses of mourning. As a result, there is something almost eerily familiar about this psalm, something that makes modern readers (or at least Jewish ones) feel a certain intimacy with its challenging text.

The poet remains silent about his personal circumstances, however, and merely reflects on the nature of life and death by asking some especially unsettling questions. If only a crazy person would anticipate enjoying wealth in the grave, then why is it that human beings put so much stock in the acquisition of material things? If not even the most powerful and rich among us can hope to bribe God into letting them escape the clutches of death forever, then why do people think of the rich as so all-powerful in the first place? And if immortality cannot be bought for any price at all, then why do people spend entire lifetimes in pursuit of money, only to die just like everybody else and go to the same dank, earthen graves that await us all?

When asked so baldly, these questions sound fatuous, perhaps even slightly insolent. But moderns wishing to use the forty-ninth psalm as a kind of meditative springboard from which to jump into an honest investigation of their own beliefs will want to begin by asking themselves precisely the same questions. We all spend our lives in the pursuit of wealth and its handmaidens: power, respect, influence, and authority. We tell ourselves that wealth has no permanence and that true security comes from faith in God, not from money in the bank. Yet, most people live precisely contrary to these obvious principles, spending their lives working not to serve God, but to generate wealth. Perhaps reading this psalm can inspire us to ask why so many moderns live

49

For the conductor, a psalm of the Korachides.

[2] Hear this all nations, give ear all residents of earth, [3]children of Adam, all humanity, wealthy and poor alike.

[4] My mouth shall speak words of wisdom; the thoughts of my heart that I am about to express will be possessed of deep insight.

[5] I shall incline my ear to hear a parable developing in my thoughts; I shall open my riddle-song with a flourish of the lyre.

[6] Why should I know fear on an evil day, merely because the iniquity of my pursuers surrounds me?

[7] They, after all, are the ones who place their trust in their riches, praising themselves because of the extent of their wealth.

[8–9] But no man can redeem a brother from divine punishment. Indeed, it is because the redemption of the souls of sinners is so very precious that one cannot effect it merely by paying a ransom to God; the punishment for sin is that one simply ceases to exist forever.

[10] Shall a human being live forever, then, and never see the grave?

[11] One can see, after all, that even sages die; together with fools and boors they perish and leave their wealth to others.

lives so utterly at odds with the values they profess to hold dear. What is it about money that renders it powerful enough to make people forget God? Do we really think that wealth can save us from the grave? Surely only a fool would think that, yet most people seem incapable of treasuring faith over wealth no matter what they feel they *ought* to believe . . . or insist that they actually *do* think.

Perhaps the real reasons moderns are so obsessed with the pursuit of affluence are rooted in their basic insecurity about the human condition. We are obsessed with the fragility of the world we have constructed—and well aware of the fact that, by seeking our well-being in the construction of ever more complex and intricate machines, we have made our world only *more* vulnerable to disruption than the medieval world, or even the ancient world, ever was. Indeed, most of us are prepared to do anything at all to feel safe in an unsafe world, and death is thus often relegated to the least of our worries: since we know that no one can live forever and that death is the common fate of all humanity, it seems pointless to waste our lives worrying about it. The other

12 קִרְבָּם בָּתֵּימוֹ | לְעוֹלָם מִשְׁכְּנֹתָם לְדֹר וָדֹר קָרְאוּ
בִשְׁמוֹתָם עֲלֵי אֲדָמוֹת׃ 13 וְאָדָם בִּיקָר בַּל־יָלִין
נִמְשַׁל כַּבְּהֵמוֹת נִדְמוּ׃
14 זֶה דַרְכָּם כֵּסֶל לָמוֹ וְאַחֲרֵיהֶם | בְּפִיהֶם יִרְצוּ
סֶלָה׃
15 כַּצֹּאן | לִשְׁאוֹל שַׁתּוּ מָוֶת יִרְעֵם וַיִּרְדּוּ בָם יְשָׁרִים |
לַבֹּקֶר *וְצוּרָם לְבַלּוֹת שְׁאוֹל מִזְּבֻל לוֹ׃
16 אַךְ־אֱלֹהִים יִפְדֶּה נַפְשִׁי מִיַּד־שְׁאוֹל כִּי יִקָּחֵנִי
סֶלָה׃
17 אַל־תִּירָא כִּי־יַעֲשִׁר אִישׁ כִּי־יִרְבֶּה כְּבוֹד בֵּיתוֹ׃
18 כִּי לֹא בְמוֹתוֹ יִקַּח הַכֹּל לֹא־יֵרֵד אַחֲרָיו כְּבוֹדוֹ׃
19 כִּי־נַפְשׁוֹ בְּחַיָּיו יְבָרֵךְ וְיוֹדֻךָ כִּי־תֵיטִיב לָךְ׃
20 תָּבוֹא עַד־דּוֹר אֲבוֹתָיו עַד־נֵצַח לֹא יִרְאוּ־אוֹר׃
21 אָדָם בִּיקָר וְלֹא יָבִין נִמְשַׁל כַּבְּהֵמוֹת נִדְמוּ׃

v. 15 וצירם כתיב

worries and fears we all entertain, on the other hand, can be combated far more effectively with a great deal of wealth to spend on the effort than they can be from a position of modest means and limited funds. It is this kind of thinking that leads people to purchase elaborate security systems for their homes, to engage financial advisors to insulate themselves from unanticipated economic disaster, and even to hire security guards to protect them in especially vulnerable situations. The common reality that binds all these examples together, however, is a simple truth: the more money people have in the bank, the more things they can buy to make themselves feel safe. And that, perhaps is why the desire for wealth is as potent a force as it is in the world we all inhabit. We *say* we want money to buy more and more things, but what we *really* want to buy is freedom from worrying about all the things we already possess. Could it be that what moderns really want from all their money is a good night's sleep?

Yet there is comfort in the psalmist's poem alongside the bleakness. True, no one lives forever. No one takes anything along to Sheol. The common fate of all humanity is precisely as advertised. There are no reprieves, no amnesties, no pardons, and no exceptions. But there *is* one detail the poet knows that can cast all of this grim reality in a different light: the detail that God, the Author of life and death, can and will grant life to the dead by bringing them forth from Sheol when the final redemption comes. The question for moderns is not whether they can admire the poet's attitude, however, but whether they can adopt it for themselves. Fortunately, there is a certain logic to the poet's argu-

[12] Their graves become their permanent homes, their residences from generation to generation and the earthly addresses by which they are known; [13]human beings, similar in this to the beasts whose mortality they share, cannot live forever because of their earthly wealth.

[14] This is the way of all who cannot accept their own mortality: foolishness belongs to them and, afterwards, to those who find their words pleasing, *selah.*

[15] They go down to Sheol like slaughtered sheep, Death serving as their shepherd and the righteous ruling over them in the morning. Indeed, such people so regularly make God, their rock, punish them with death that Sheol can no longer serve as the sole residence of the dead.

[16] Yet God will redeem my soul from the grasp of Sheol by bringing me forth, *selah.*

[17] Be not in awe when an individual waxes wealthy or when the honor of that person's house grows great.

[18] When such a person dies, he will not take it all with him. His glorious possessions will not descend to Sheol after him [19]because he blessed his own soul during his lifetime; instead, he ought to have thanked You when things went well for him.

[20] His soul shall join the ranks of his ancestors who shall never again see light, [21]for human beings, similar in this to the beasts whose mortality they share, are more than capable of loving earthly wealth without understanding its highly transient nature.

ment: if God can decree death for the living, why should it be impossible to imagine that the reverse could also be true?

The poet only touches briefly on the idea and then returns almost immediately to his catalogue of morose observations about human mortality. Still, the assertion that the poet believes that God will redeem him from the grave makes the whole psalm as much about faith as about death. Indeed, it is precisely in the light of the poet's assertion that God will redeem him from the grave that moderns will read the 49th psalm the most profitably . . . and this is no less the case for those reading it in houses of mourning than for those reading it as part of a program of contemplative meditation and prayer.

נ

מִזְמוֹר לְאָסָף

אֵל ׀ אֱלֹהִים יְהוָה דִּבֶּר וַיִּקְרָא־אָרֶץ מִמִּזְרַח־
שֶׁמֶשׁ עַד־מְבֹאוֹ׃ 2 מִצִּיּוֹן מִכְלַל־יֹפִי אֱלֹהִים
הוֹפִיעַ׃

3 יָבֹא אֱלֹהֵינוּ וְאַל־יֶחֱרַשׁ אֵשׁ־לְפָנָיו תֹּאכֵל
וּסְבִיבָיו נִשְׂעֲרָה מְאֹד׃

4 יִקְרָא אֶל־הַשָּׁמַיִם מֵעָל וְאֶל־הָאָרֶץ לָדִין עַמּוֹ׃

5 אִסְפוּ־לִי חֲסִידָי כֹּרְתֵי בְרִיתִי עֲלֵי־זָבַח׃

6 וַיַּגִּידוּ שָׁמַיִם צִדְקוֹ כִּי־אֱלֹהִים ׀ שֹׁפֵט הוּא סֶלָה׃

7 שִׁמְעָה עַמִּי ׀ וַאֲדַבֵּרָה יִשְׂרָאֵל וְאָעִידָה בָּךְ
אֱלֹהִים אֱלֹהֶיךָ אָנֹכִי׃ 8 לֹא עַל־זְבָחֶיךָ אוֹכִיחֶךָ
וְעוֹלֹתֶיךָ לְנֶגְדִּי תָמִיד׃

9 לֹא־אֶקַּח מִבֵּיתְךָ פָר מִמִּכְלְאֹתֶיךָ עַתּוּדִים׃

10 כִּי־לִי כָל־חַיְתוֹ־יָעַר בְּהֵמוֹת בְּהַרְרֵי־אָלֶף׃

11 יָדַעְתִּי כָּל־עוֹף הָרִים וְזִיז שָׂדַי עִמָּדִי׃

12 אִם־אֶרְעַב לֹא־אֹמַר לָךְ כִּי לִי תֵבֵל וּמְלֹאָהּ׃

13 הַאוֹכַל בְּשַׂר אַבִּירִים וְדַם עַתּוּדִים אֶשְׁתֶּה׃

In his mind's eye, the poet imagines God as the supreme Judge coming to court. The defendants are neither those who have divorced themselves totally from the worship of the Divine nor those who know nothing of the homage due the Almighty, however, but rather those rank hypocrites who appear outwardly to be consecrated to God's service but who are really only devoted to the pageantry of the cult and to the splendiferous rituals and rites of Temple worship. Indeed, the poet writes, God is coming precisely to judge those phonies and frauds who appear to be living religious lives, but who really only want to use (or, rather, to abuse) the system so as to campaign most effectively for public approval. And then, what began as the poet's attempt to describe God coming to the world of mankind turns into an extended vision almost before the reader's eyes.

On the judge's bench sits the Almighty girded in fire. In the prisoner's docket stands a wicked priest—a specific choice rooted in the origin of this poem as a Temple hymn, but easily understandable to moderns as symbolic of anyone devoted solely to the formal worship-by-the-book ritual of any religious system. The poet himself sits quietly in the spectators' gallery taking it all in, perhaps jotting down notes for the poem he is already planning

50

A psalm of Asaph.

God, Elohim-יהוה, speaks, calling to the earth from east to west, [2]then appears in Zion, the city of sublime beauty.

[3] May our God, preceded by consuming fire and surrounded by a mightily raging storm, come to us and be not silent.

[4] God calls the heavens on high and the earth to the people's trial: [5]"Bring Me My faithful ones, My partners in a covenant sealed with sacrifice."

[6] Let the heavens declare God's justice, for God is to be their Judge, *selah*.

[7] And thus does God indict the people: "Listen, O My people, when I speak. Pay attention, O Israel, when I give testimony about you. I am God, your God, [8]but I have not come today to rebuke you about deficiencies in your sacrificial service or about any flaws in the wholly burnt offerings you are constantly offering up to Me.

[9] Nor have I come to seize more bulls from your homes or goats from your pens, [10]for all the animals of the forest and the wild oxen that dwell by the thousands in the mountains belong to Me anyway. [11]I know every bird that lives in those mountains, too; indeed, I keep a record with Me of everything that moves in any of My fields.

[12] Nor do I hunger—but even if I did, I would not need to tell you about it, for the world and everything in it are Mine anyway.

[13] Do you really believe that I eat the flesh of bulls? That I drink the blood of goats?

to write. As befits the remarkable situation, God begins the proceedings by swearing in Heaven and Earth as witnesses, then proceeds to read out the specifics of the indictment. The accused, everyone admits, follows all the rules in the book. He presides over the slaughter of thousands of oxen every year, overseeing the incineration of their carcasses on the altar and the sacral disposition of their blood. He is, it is further admitted, scrupulous about wearing the proper outfit for each aspect of the priestly ceremonial and he has no difficulty

14 זְבַח לֵאלֹהִים תּוֹדָה וְשַׁלֵּם לְעֶלְיוֹן נְדָרֶיךָ׃
15 וּקְרָאֵנִי בְּיוֹם צָרָה אֲחַלֶּצְךָ וּתְכַבְּדֵנִי׃
16 וְלָרָשָׁע ׀ אָמַר אֱלֹהִים מַה־לְּךָ לְסַפֵּר חֻקָּי וַתִּשָּׂא
בְרִיתִי עֲלֵי־פִיךָ׃ 17 וְאַתָּה שָׂנֵאתָ מוּסָר וַתַּשְׁלֵךְ
דְּבָרַי אַחֲרֶיךָ׃ 18 אִם־רָאִיתָ גַנָּב וַתִּרֶץ עִמּוֹ וְעִם
מְנָאֲפִים חֶלְקֶךָ׃ 19 פִּיךָ שָׁלַחְתָּ בְרָעָה וּלְשׁוֹנְךָ
תַּצְמִיד מִרְמָה׃ 20 תֵּשֵׁב בְּאָחִיךָ תְדַבֵּר בְּבֶן־אִמְּךָ
תִּתֶּן־דֹּפִי׃
21 אֵלֶּה עָשִׂיתָ ׀ וְהֶחֱרַשְׁתִּי דִּמִּיתָ הֱיוֹת אֶהְיֶה כָמוֹךָ
אוֹכִיחֲךָ וְאֶעֶרְכָה לְעֵינֶיךָ׃ 22 בִּינוּ־נָא זֹאת שֹׁכְחֵי
אֱלוֹהַּ פֶּן־אֶטְרֹף וְאֵין מַצִּיל׃
23 זֹבֵחַ תּוֹדָה יְכַבְּדָנְנִי וְשָׂם דֶּרֶךְ אַרְאֶנּוּ בְּיֵשַׁע
אֱלֹהִים׃

remembering the precise laws that apply to each of the many different varieties and subvarieties of sacrifice. In short, the defendant *appears* to be totally devoted to divine worship, but that is only how things *seem.* The reality, the poet knows, is actually quite different.

The accused, it turns out, may enjoy great stature in the eyes of the world, but he enjoys the company of thieves and adulterers even more when the public isn't present. He is thought of as a man devoted to the worship of God, but he has no difficulty slandering others when the opportunity for calumny presents itself. He enjoys the respect of his peers, but he displays no interest in

[14] Sacrifice instead an offering of thanksgiving to God and fulfill your oaths to the Most High.
[15] Call on Me on a day of trouble, for in so doing, you will honor Me and I will grant you relief."
[16] And to the wicked one, God says: "Who gave you the right to teach My laws or to give forth about the terms of My covenant with Israel, [17]when you hate reproach and freely toss away My words behind you? [18]If you see a thief, you can hardly wait to run with him to steal—and the rest of the time, adulterers are your company. [19]You use your mouth to do evil; your tongue, you join to swindling. [20]You sit with your brother and then speak evil of him, thus slandering your own mother's son."
[21] Shall I remain silent when you have done these things? If I did, you would imagine that I were just like you. Therefore I rebuke and evaluate you openly. [22]Consider that, you who so easily forget God, lest I tear you apart and there be none to save you.
[23] And God says this as well: "Whoever offers Me a thanksgiving offering does Me honor and paves a way towards Me; to that one shall I show divine salvation."

striving for personal communion with the Divine. Now there may be no need for drawn-out deliberation when all-knowing God is the Judge, but neither is the court without mercy and, in the end, the accused is put on notice either to learn his lesson or to risk the death penalty.

Can we, the modern readers of the fiftieth psalm, take that same lesson to heart? Can we accept that only those whose worship is an expression of thanksgiving (rather than the formal discharge of obligation) may hope to be granted the ability to pave a path that will lead them to God, to the salvation *of* God, and to a life *in* God?

נא

לַמְנַצֵּחַ מִזְמוֹר לְדָוִד׃ 2 בְּבוֹא־אֵלָיו נָתָן הַנָּבִיא
כַּאֲשֶׁר־בָּא אֶל־בַּת־שָׁבַע׃
3 חָנֵּנִי אֱלֹהִים כְּחַסְדֶּךָ כְּרֹב רַחֲמֶיךָ מְחֵה פְשָׁעָי׃
4 *הֶרֶב כַּבְּסֵנִי מֵעֲוֺנִי וּמֵחַטָּאתִי טַהֲרֵנִי׃
5 כִּי־פְשָׁעַי אֲנִי אֵדָע וְחַטָּאתִי נֶגְדִּי תָמִיד׃
6 לְךָ לְבַדְּךָ ׀ חָטָאתִי וְהָרַע בְּעֵינֶיךָ עָשִׂיתִי לְמַעַן־
תִּצְדַּק בְּדָבְרֶךָ תִּזְכֶּה בְשָׁפְטֶךָ׃
7 הֵן־בְּעָווֹן חוֹלָלְתִּי וּבְחֵטְא יֶחֱמַתְנִי אִמִּי׃
8 הֵן־אֱמֶת חָפַצְתָּ בַטֻּחוֹת וּבְסָתֻם חָכְמָה תוֹדִיעֵנִי׃
9 תְּחַטְּאֵנִי בְאֵזוֹב וְאֶטְהָר תְּכַבְּסֵנִי וּמִשֶּׁלֶג אַלְבִּין׃
10 תַּשְׁמִיעֵנִי שָׂשׂוֹן וְשִׂמְחָה תָּגֵלְנָה עֲצָמוֹת דִּכִּיתָ׃
11 הַסְתֵּר פָּנֶיךָ מֵחֲטָאָי וְכָל־עֲוֺנֹתַי מְחֵה׃
12 לֵב טָהוֹר בְּרָא־לִי אֱלֹהִים וְרוּחַ נָכוֹן חַדֵּשׁ
בְּקִרְבִּי׃
13 אַל־תַּשְׁלִיכֵנִי מִלְּפָנֶיךָ וְרוּחַ קָדְשְׁךָ אַל־תִּקַּח
מִמֶּנִּי׃

v. 4 הרבה כתיב

Just under half of all the poems in the Book of Psalms (that is, seventy-three psalms) are attributed, one way or another, to King David. Although it is certainly possible that some of them really are that old, it is far more likely that the psalmists whose poems became the hymns of the Psalter were *inspired* by David—by his story, and by the specific details of his life—to the point that they saw themselves, at least in a certain sense, as latter-day Davids. It was neither the mighty warrior nor the successful monarch ruling over a strong kingdom at peace that spoke most directly to the poets, however. Rather, it was the fugitive David running away from Saul (or, later, from his own seditious son, Absalom), the lonely man hiding in caves and wondering when his day would come (or, indeed, *if* it would ever come), and the sinner whose spiritual greatness and intimacy with the Divine failed to grant him the kind of dominion over his own passions and evil inclinations (or rather, that failed to grant him permanent, absolute control over them) that naive people imagine is the corollary of faith in God and its principal earthly reward. And the psalmists' David was also the *ne'im zemirot yisrael*—the sweet singer of Israel—whose career as hymnist granted legitimacy to the psalmists' own quest to use song as the medium through which to seek communion with the divine realm.

But David was an appropriate choice as spiritual ancestor of the psalmists

51

For the conductor, a psalm of David [2]composed when the prophet Nathan came to him after he, David, had seduced Bathsheba.

[3] Take pity on me, O God, in accordance with Your mercy; in the fullness of Your compassion, erase my transgressions.

[4] Cleanse me utterly of my iniquity, purify me from my sin.

[5] For I know my own transgressions; my sin is permanently before me.

[6] On its deepest level, my sin was really against You; I have done that which is evil in Your eyes. I confess this freely so that Your verdict will be just, Your judgment, correct.

[7] Truly, I was born in iniquity and conceived by my mother in sin.

[8] Truly, You desire that I speak only the truth and certainties, and so I must pray: when my wisdom is insufficient to know the truth, make it known to me.

[9] If You cleanse me with hyssop, I shall be purified; if You wash me, I shall be whiter than snow.

[10] Let me hear words of gladness and joy; let these bones You are crushing rejoice instead.

[11] Hide Your face from my sins; erase all my iniquities.

[12] O God, create a pure heart for me; and renew within me a spirit of decency.

[13] Cast me not out from before You and take not Your holy spirit from me.

for another reason as well: he was the very model of the amateur prophet. No member of the prophetic guild he, the holy spirit—the embodiment of prophetic inspiration called the *ruaḥ hakodesh* or the *ruaḥ* יהוה in Hebrew—nonetheless came over him at the very moment Samuel anointed him king: "Samuel took the horn of oil and anointed him in the company of his brothers, whereupon the spirit of the Lord seized him and remained with him permanently (1 Samuel 16:13)."

The Levites whose hymnal became our Book of Psalms must have found this portrait of a musician-king chosen by God, yet despised and persecuted by a world filled with people who failed to perceive his election, quite compelling . . . for they too write of being persecuted, even

14 הָשִׁיבָה לִּי שְׂשׂוֹן יִשְׁעֶךָ וְרוּחַ נְדִיבָה תִסְמְכֵנִי׃
15 אֲלַמְּדָה פֹשְׁעִים דְּרָכֶיךָ וְחַטָּאִים אֵלֶיךָ יָשׁוּבוּ׃
16 הַצִּילֵנִי מִדָּמִים ׀ אֱלֹהִים אֱלֹהֵי תְּשׁוּעָתִי תְּרַנֵּן
לְשׁוֹנִי צִדְקָתֶךָ׃
17 אֲדֹנָי שְׂפָתַי תִּפְתָּח וּפִי יַגִּיד תְּהִלָּתֶךָ׃
18 כִּי ׀ לֹא־תַחְפֹּץ זֶבַח וְאֶתֵּנָה עוֹלָה לֹא תִרְצֶה׃
19 זִבְחֵי אֱלֹהִים רוּחַ נִשְׁבָּרָה לֵב־נִשְׁבָּר וְנִדְכֶּה
אֱלֹהִים לֹא תִבְזֶה׃
20 הֵיטִיבָה בִרְצוֹנְךָ אֶת־צִיּוֹן תִּבְנֶה חוֹמוֹת
יְרוּשָׁלָם׃
21 אָז תַּחְפֹּץ זִבְחֵי־צֶדֶק עוֹלָה וְכָלִיל אָז יַעֲלוּ
עַל־מִזְבַּחֲךָ פָרִים׃

despised, by the citizens of the world in which they lived. Yet, their poems are studded with oracles of prophecy that can only have come to them through the cultivation of that very same divine spirit of prophecy that once came over David.

And so, the fifty-first psalm. The poet writes as David just as he must have felt after his awful encounter with the prophet Nathan. David had sinned grievously, intentionally causing the death of another man so that he, David, could continue to bed the man's wife and perhaps manage to hide the fact that she was already pregnant with his, David's, child. He was thus both an adulterer and a murderer, and the prophet had no difficulty whatsoever accusing him openly of both sins. To his credit, however, David owned up to his sin rather than seeking to excuse himself on whatever flimsy grounds he might otherwise have dreamed up. And indeed, the poet, inspired, imagines David coming to a great truth through his anguish as he admits his sin, begs for forgiveness, and pleads that the *ruaḥ hakodesh* not be taken from him as a consequence of his incredibly callous crime.

From the contemplation of David's experience, the psalmist learns that the

[14] Return to me the gladness of Your salvation, and visit me with a generous spirit.

[15] I will teach transgressors Your ways, whereupon sinners will return unto You.

[16] Save me from a bloody death, O God, the God of my salvation, and my tongue will sing joyously of Your righteousness.

[17] Adonai, part my lips that my mouth might tell Your praise.

[18] For You do not desire sacrifices—although I would certainly offer them to You if You did—and neither do you care for wholly burnt offerings.

[19] The real sacrifice to God is a broken spirit; God will never despise the gift of a broken heart suffused with melancholy.

[20] Be good to Zion in accordance with Your beneficent will; build up the walls of Jerusalem.

[21] Then You will desire sacrifices of righteousness, especially wholly burnt offerings totally consumed; then shall they offer up bulls on Your altar.

God of Israel can never be placated with rituals unless they are invested—and invested totally—with longing for God, contrition for past sins, and the endless power of the broken heart that yearns, not for this or that thing, but for the compassionate forgiveness of God, for the communicative presence of God, and for the boundless love of God. This, the poet is saying, was David's great lesson and it was apparently his as well. Whether it is a lesson moderns can take to heart is an entirely different question, however, and one that will rest in the willingness of any individual to accept that ritual is a path, not a destination . . . and that imagining the destination to which that path leads to be anything other than God is, almost by definition, perverse.

לַמְנַצֵּחַ מַשְׂכִּיל לְדָוִד׃ 2 בְּבוֹא ׀ דּוֹאֵג הָאֲדֹמִי וַיַּגֵּד לְשָׁאוּל וַיֹּאמֶר לוֹ בָּא דָוִד אֶל־בֵּית אֲחִימֶלֶךְ׃
3 מַה־תִּתְהַלֵּל בְּרָעָה הַגִּבּוֹר חֶסֶד אֵל כָּל־הַיּוֹם׃
4 הַוּוֹת תַּחְשֹׁב לְשׁוֹנֶךָ כְּתַעַר מְלֻטָּשׁ עֹשֵׂה רְמִיָּה׃
5 אָהַבְתָּ רָּע מִטּוֹב שֶׁקֶר ׀ מִדַּבֵּר צֶדֶק סֶלָה׃
6 אָהַבְתָּ כָל־דִּבְרֵי־בָלַע לְשׁוֹן מִרְמָה׃
7 גַּם־אֵל יִתָּצְךָ לָנֶצַח יַחְתְּךָ וְיִסָּחֲךָ מֵאֹהֶל וְשֵׁרֶשְׁךָ מֵאֶרֶץ חַיִּים סֶלָה׃
8 וְיִרְאוּ צַדִּיקִים וְיִירָאוּ וְעָלָיו יִשְׂחָקוּ׃ 9 הִנֵּה הַגֶּבֶר לֹא־יָשִׂים אֱלֹהִים מָעוּזּוֹ וַיִּבְטַח בְּרֹב עָשְׁרוֹ יָעֹז בְּהַוָּתוֹ׃
10 וַאֲנִי ׀ כְּזַיִת רַעֲנָן בְּבֵית אֱלֹהִים בָּטַחְתִּי בְחֶסֶד אֱלֹהִים עוֹלָם וָעֶד׃
11 אוֹדְךָ לְעוֹלָם כִּי עָשִׂיתָ וַאֲקַוֶּה שִׁמְךָ כִּי־טוֹב נֶגֶד חֲסִידֶיךָ׃

When David was fleeing from mad King Saul, he stopped by the sanctuary at Nob for some supplies and ended up both with food for his men and with the sword of Goliath (which he himself had used to behead the Philistine giant after vanquishing him with his sling). A certain Doeg of Edom, one of Saul's men, took in the entire encounter at Nob, however, and later reported it to Saul, who responded by sentencing to death not only the priest Ahimelech, but all the other priests of Nob as well. Doeg himself carried out the executions, but the responsibility was neither totally his nor totally Saul's: some of the blame must fall on David himself, who later admitted that he knew that Doeg had been present at Nob on the fateful day, but failed adequately to think through the implications of that fact.

The author of the fifty-second psalm has an enemy whom he thinks of as his personal Doeg. He has, one must assume, been denounced by his enemy.

52

For the conductor, a wise-song of David, [2]composed when Doeg the Edomite went to tell Saul that David had gone to the house of Ahimelech.

[3] How dare you take pride in your evil ways, you who are known as a hero? How dare you spend all day long doing deeds abominable to God?

[4] Your tongue calculates evil schemes; it is like a polished razor that excels at fraud.

[5] You love evil more than good, the telling of a lie more than speaking justly, *selah*.

[6] You love the muttered falsehood, the speech of treachery.

[7] But this too must you know: God will demolish you forever, annihilating you and sweeping you out of your tent, uprooting you from the land of the living, *selah*.

[8] The righteous will look on and be awestruck. They will laugh at such a one and say, [9]"Here is a fellow who did not make God his refuge, but instead trusted in his great wealth and schemed mightily."

[10] I, on the other hand, am like a fresh olive tree in the House of God; I trust in the mercy of God for ever and always.

[11] I am thankful to You forever for what You have done for me and I trust in Your name, for You are good towards your faithful worshipers.

And the poet clearly is unnerved. Yet although Scripture does not report on the original Doeg's fate, the poet has no difficulty saying what he hopes lies ahead for his own libelous adversary.

Is there something ignoble, or even immoral, about praying for the death of one's enemies? Moderns tend to think so, but Scripture's point of view is crystal clear: there is as little wrong with cursing those who hate God as there is in blessing those who love God. Hate is considered a negative emotion by most spiritually adept moderns. The fifty-second psalm suggests that it might be fruitful for moderns to ask themselves why it is exactly that they cannot readily accept that only good can come from hating evil.

נג

לַמְנַצֵּחַ עַל־מָחֲלַת מַשְׂכִּיל לְדָוִד׃
2 אָמַר נָבָל בְּלִבּוֹ אֵין אֱלֹהִים הִשְׁחִיתוּ וְהִתְעִיבוּ
עָוֶל אֵין עֹשֵׂה־טוֹב׃
3 אֱלֹהִים מִשָּׁמַיִם הִשְׁקִיף עַל־בְּנֵי אָדָם לִרְאוֹת
הֲיֵשׁ מַשְׂכִּיל דֹּרֵשׁ אֶת־אֱלֹהִים׃ 4 כֻּלּוֹ סָג יַחְדָּו
נֶאֱלָחוּ אֵין עֹשֵׂה־טוֹב אֵין גַּם אֶחָד׃
5 הֲלֹא יָדְעוּ פֹּעֲלֵי אָוֶן אֹכְלֵי עַמִּי אָכְלוּ לֶחֶם
אֱלֹהִים לֹא קָרָאוּ׃
6 שָׁם פָּחֲדוּ־פַחַד לֹא־הָיָה פָחַד כִּי־אֱלֹהִים פִּזַּר
עַצְמוֹת חֹנָךְ הֱבִשֹׁתָה כִּי־אֱלֹהִים מְאָסָם׃
7 מִי־יִתֵּן מִצִּיּוֹן יְשֻׁעוֹת יִשְׂרָאֵל בְּשׁוּב אֱלֹהִים
שְׁבוּת עַמּוֹ יָגֵל יַעֲקֹב יִשְׂמַח יִשְׂרָאֵל׃

Is God a philosophical construct invented by human beings to explain the world, to impose order and reason on the world, or perhaps even to allow them to dominate the world by making it meaningful? Or is God a real force, one to be reckoned with not because it *ought* to exist, but because it *does* exist—and not in theory or within the rarefied constructs of human consciousness, but even independently of the hopes of those who believe in its reality? The psalmist's enemy declares openly and shamelessly, perhaps even with a bit of pride: *ein elohim,* there is no God. He does not claim that there are other gods or that the God of Israel is one of many gods who rule the world, but that there is no *such thing* as divinity . . . and that for all we may well pay lip-service to the concept if and when it suits us, the truth of the situation is that the world has no master, no judge, no creator.

The poet has given up on rational argument, and neither does the poet's personal experience of God matter to his enemy. Indeed, the poet knows full well that people who refuse to open their hearts to God under most circumstances will feel entirely differently when the going gets rough. We have no foxholes in our world for atheists to reconsider their atheism in, but we have other places for deniers of God to rethink their rejection of faith: oncologists' offices, ICU waiting rooms, bankruptcy courts, mismanaged old age homes, airplane crash sites, and the kind of temporary morgues set up in high school gymnasiums after massive disasters strike. Can anything that leads to faith in God be considered a curse? The poet makes his point, then leaves us to contemplate its various implications on our own.

A version of this poem also appears in the Psalter as the fourteenth psalm.

53 For the conductor, a wise-song of David to the tune of *"Maḥalat."*

[2] The scoundrel says in his heart, "There is no God," and thus do his people behave corruptly and perpetrate abominable crimes; no one does good.

[3] Meanwhile, God surveys humanity from heaven to see if there is anyone on earth wise enough to seek God, but [4] all have retreated together to plot depravity. No one does good, not even one single soul.

[5] Do not sinners know that they court disaster when they devour my people as though they were eating bread, when they fail to cry out to God?

[6] The fears that assail God's people are groundless, for God will scatter the bones of those who camp against you, O Israel, and, loathing them, will make putrid the decaying flesh of your enemies.

[7] Whenever will the salvation of Israel come to us from Zion? When God restores the nation's fortunes, Jacob will rejoice, Israel will exult.

נד

לַמְנַצֵּחַ בִּנְגִינֹת מַשְׂכִּיל לְדָוִד׃ 2 בְּבוֹא הַזִּיפִים
וַיֹּאמְרוּ לְשָׁאוּל הֲלֹא־דָוִד מִסְתַּתֵּר עִמָּנוּ׃
3 אֱלֹהִים בְּשִׁמְךָ הוֹשִׁיעֵנִי וּבִגְבוּרָתְךָ תְדִינֵנִי׃
4 אֱלֹהִים שְׁמַע תְּפִלָּתִי הַאֲזִינָה לְאִמְרֵי־פִי׃ 5 כִּי
זָרִים ׀ קָמוּ עָלַי וְעָרִיצִים בִּקְשׁוּ נַפְשִׁי לֹא שָׂמוּ
אֱלֹהִים לְנֶגְדָּם סֶלָה׃
6 הִנֵּה אֱלֹהִים עֹזֵר לִי אֲדֹנָי בְּסֹמְכֵי נַפְשִׁי׃ 7 *יָשִׁיב
הָרַע לְשֹׁרְרָי בַּאֲמִתְּךָ הַצְמִיתֵם׃
8 בִּנְדָבָה אֶזְבְּחָה־לָּךְ אוֹדֶה שִּׁמְךָ יְהוָה כִּי־טוֹב׃ 9 כִּי
מִכָּל־צָרָה הִצִּילָנִי וּבְאֹיְבַי רָאֲתָה עֵינִי׃

v. 7 ישוב כתיב

Ziph is not a country, just the name of a wilderness region in Judah. The Ziphites, therefore, were not hostile foreigners, but locals doing their civic duty by informing King Saul on two separate occasions that the fugitive David, whom the king was seeking, was hiding out in their neck of the woods.

An ancient poet found David's predicament worth memorializing in an ode to frustration and embittered anger not because the story in the First Book of Samuel is unclear, but because the poet too felt chosen by God for great things in a way that the authorities in his day simply could not, or would not, understand or accept. The emotions on display in the fifty-fourth psalm, at any rate, make for a strange brew: faith in the saving power of God, the ignoble wish for the annihilation of one's enemies (rather than their repentance), a sense of intense, unyielding frustration in the face of implacable hatred, and hope in the goodness of God's holy name. The poet doesn't reveal too many particulars, but modern readers of the poem can still use the devotional recitation of this text as an occasion to contemplate their own situations in a world that pays lip-service to religion, but which actually despises the truly religious spirit, holds spirituality unfettered by convention in contempt,

54 For the choral conductor, a wise-song of David, [2]written when he learned that the Ziphites had come and asked rhetorically of Saul, "Is not David hiding among us?"

[3] God, save me with Your name; avenge me with Your might.

[4] God, hear my prayer. Listen to the words of my mouth, [5]for strangers oppose me and cruel villains who do not hold God in esteem are seeking to take my life, *selah.*

[6] Through it all, God helps me; Adonai, foremost among the supporters of my soul, [7]requites the evil done me by those who habitually spy on me. May You annihilate them totally with Your truth!

[8] With gratitude I shall sacrifice to You; I shall give thanks to Your name, יהוה, for You are good, [9]for You have saved me from every trouble so that my eyes may now gaze at my enemies without worry.

and has no patience —real or often even feigned—for individuals who insist on living lives in God in the context of total spiritual integrity. Indeed, the image of David as a fugitive running away from the blind rage of his king and seeking at the same time comfort in his own private, intensely personal relationship with God must have been *very* comforting to the psalmists.

Most of us are not fugitives from justice blindly or unfairly meted out, nor will any modern readers be people marked for death by a king slipping into madness. But when latter-day readers steeped in the quest for God attempt to free themselves from the web of antipathy and subtle or overt antagonism in which they may have become entangled without feeling foolish or delusional for having placed the worship of God first on their list of daily tasks, they then become latter-day Davids . . . and no less so than the ancient poet.

נה

לַמְנַצֵּ֥חַ בִּנְגִינֹ֗ת מַשְׂכִּ֥יל לְדָוִֽד׃
2 הַאֲזִ֣ינָה אֱ֭לֹהִים תְּפִלָּתִ֑י וְאַל־תִּ֝תְעַלַּ֗ם מִתְּחִנָּתִֽי׃
3 הַקְשִׁ֣יבָה לִּ֣י וַעֲנֵ֑נִי אָרִ֖יד בְּשִׂיחִ֣י וְאָהִֽימָה׃
4 מִקּ֥וֹל אוֹיֵ֗ב מִפְּנֵ֣י עָקַ֣ת רָשָׁ֑ע כִּי־יָמִ֥יטוּ עָלַ֥י אָ֝֗וֶן
וּבְאַ֥ף יִשְׂטְמֽוּנִי׃ 5 לִ֭בִּי יָחִ֣יל בְּקִרְבִּ֑י וְאֵימ֥וֹת מָ֝֗וֶת
נָפְל֥וּ עָלָֽי׃ 6 יִרְאָ֣ה וָ֭רַעַד יָ֣בֹא בִ֑י וַ֝תְּכַסֵּ֗נִי פַּלָּצֽוּת׃
7 וָאֹמַ֗ר מִֽי־יִתֶּן־לִּ֣י אֵ֭בֶר כַּיּוֹנָ֗ה אָע֥וּפָה וְאֶשְׁכֹּֽנָה׃
8 הִ֭נֵּה אַרְחִ֣יק נְדֹ֑ד אָלִ֖ין בַּמִּדְבָּ֣ר סֶֽלָה׃ 9 אָחִ֣ישָׁה
מִפְלָ֣ט לִ֑י מֵר֖וּחַ סֹעָ֣ה מִסָּֽעַר׃
10 בַּלַּ֣ע אֲ֭דֹנָי פַּלַּ֣ג לְשׁוֹנָ֑ם כִּֽי־רָאִ֨יתִי חָמָ֖ס וְרִ֣יב
בָּעִֽיר׃
11 יוֹמָ֤ם וָלַ֗יְלָה יְסוֹבְבֻ֥הָ עַל־חוֹמֹתֶ֑יהָ וְאָ֖וֶן וְעָמָ֣ל
בְּקִרְבָּֽהּ׃
12 הַוּ֥וֹת בְּקִרְבָּ֑הּ וְֽלֹא־יָמִ֥ישׁ מֵ֝רְחֹבָ֗הּ תֹּ֣ךְ וּמִרְמָֽה׃
13 כִּ֤י לֹֽא־אוֹיֵ֥ב יְחָרְפֵ֗נִי וְאֶ֫שָּׂ֥א לֹֽא־מְ֭שַׂנְאִי עָלַ֣י
הִגְדִּ֑יל וְאֶסָּתֵ֥ר מִמֶּֽנּוּ׃
14 וְאַתָּ֣ה אֱנ֣וֹשׁ כְּעֶרְכִּ֑י אַ֝לּוּפִ֗י וּמְיֻדָּעִֽי׃ 15 אֲשֶׁ֣ר יַ֭חְדָּו
נַמְתִּ֣יק ס֑וֹד בְּבֵ֥ית אֱ֝לֹהִ֗ים נְהַלֵּ֥ךְ בְּרָֽגֶשׁ׃

A man is mugged in the street by a hooligan who wants his wallet. Afterwards, the victim is outraged, furious and fuming with dismay at the level of urban mayhem society is prepared to tolerate . . . but his heart, his soul, and his innermost self are left untouched and unaffected. In the end, incidents like this will be remembered as nuisances, but not as crises of identity or faith: they do not affect the codes people use to explain their lives, or alter their basic belief about God, or force them to doubt the strength of the pillars that support their personal philosophical understanding of how the world works. How different is the experience of being betrayed by a confidant, one who (absent the treachery) would have been considered a friend, someone who (under other circumstances) would have been admired, perhaps even considered a worthy role model! The anguish of being betrayed by someone whose values appear to be exemplary, whose behavior seems impeccable, and whose devotion to the service of God strikes even careful observers as passionately real—that experience is the one that rocks the boat and forces people to re-evaluate what they think about the way the world works and, perhaps especially, the way God works in the world. The misery of the poet is almost palpable as he writes his long ode to rejection at the hands of a formerly beloved friend who, before he turned against the poet, had actually inspired him with his spiritual bearing as

55 For the choral conductor, a wise-song of David.
[2] Listen, O God, to my prayer and turn not away from my supplication.
[3] Take note of me and answer me, for my every word is misery and I am in turmoil.
[4] At the sound of the enemy's voice—and because of the threat of the evildoer who wishes me ill and who, enraged, loathes me—[5]my heart is fluttering within me as the fear of death befalls me; [6]fear and trembling have come over me, enveloping me with horror.
[7] I cry out, "Who will give me wings like a dove, that I might fly away and live elsewhere? [8]To that place I would go, even if it were to mean wandering far and sleeping in the desert, *selah,* [9]for there would I find refuge quickly from this whirlwind of terror more violent than a real storm."
[10] Adonai, swallow them up and then make them incapable of understanding each other's speech, for I see violence and strife in the city.
[11] Day and night, they do circuits on her walls while sin and suffering dwell within.
[12] Scheming too dwells in the city; larceny and deceit never leave her plaza.
[13] For it is not an external enemy who is taunting me. (That, I could bear.) Nor is it one of my traditional foes who is lording himself over me. (From such a one, I could hide.)
[14] No, you are a man of my own station who should be my leader, a man well-known to me, [15]whose company I once found so delightful, a man with whom I used to walk about in the House of God with such feeling.

they walked together in the courtyards of the Temple in Jerusalem. What caused the psalmist's former friend to break with him? What brought about the crisis of which the fifty-fifth psalm is the literary echo? We will never be able to know with certainty, but the image of the poet—broken, despondent, dejected, and rejected—retains its force even without the reader knowing the specific background details that led to the composition of the poem. When modern readers contemplate the psalmist praying for the wings of a dove so that he might fly away and leave the horror of his world behind, so that he might be safe from

16 *יַשִּׁיא מָוֶת | עָלֵימוֹ יֵרְדוּ שְׁאוֹל חַיִּים כִּי־רָעוֹת
בִּמְגוּרָם בְּקִרְבָּם׃
17 אֲנִי אֶל־אֱלֹהִים אֶקְרָא וַיהֹוָה יוֹשִׁיעֵנִי׃
18 עֶרֶב וָבֹקֶר וְצָהֳרַיִם אָשִׂיחָה וְאֶהֱמֶה וַיִּשְׁמַע
קוֹלִי׃ 19 פָּדָה בְשָׁלוֹם נַפְשִׁי מִקֲּרָב־לִי כִּי־בְרַבִּים
הָיוּ עִמָּדִי׃
20 יִשְׁמַע | אֵל וְיַעֲנֵם וְיֹשֵׁב קֶדֶם סֶלָה אֲשֶׁר אֵין
חֲלִיפוֹת לָמוֹ וְלֹא יָרְאוּ אֱלֹהִים׃ 21 שָׁלַח יָדָיו
בִּשְׁלֹמָיו חִלֵּל בְּרִיתוֹ׃
22 חָלְקוּ | מַחְמָאֹת פִּיו וּקְרָב־לִבּוֹ רַכּוּ דְבָרָיו מִשֶּׁמֶן
וְהֵמָּה פְתִחוֹת׃
23 הַשְׁלֵךְ עַל־יְהֹוָה | יְהָבְךָ וְהוּא יְכַלְכְּלֶךָ לֹא־יִתֵּן
לְעוֹלָם מוֹט לַצַּדִּיק׃
24 וְאַתָּה אֱלֹהִים | תּוֹרִדֵם לִבְאֵר שַׁחַת אַנְשֵׁי דָמִים
וּמִרְמָה לֹא־יֶחֱצוּ יְמֵיהֶם וַאֲנִי אֶבְטַח־בָּךְ׃

v. 16 ישימות כתיב

the reach of human treachery, and so that he might transcend a friend's disloyalty—that is a picture of misery with which any human being will identify all too easily, even without knowing the poet's particular story of woe.

For most moderns, the poet's take on friendship will be quite resonant. Yet, one might expect just the opposite to be the case, since our society appears to protect family relationships much more fiercely than (mere) friendships. We deem blood relationships, for example, to be so permanent that their actual existence is never seriously questioned or debated merely because the relatives in question are estranged from—or enraged with—each other. In this regard, the relationship of lovers is the exception that proves the rule: the institution of marriage exists *precisely* to grant legally binding stability and durability to relationships that, although lacking the common genetic heritage of a blood relationship, have nevertheless attained the level of emotional involvement that makes lovers wish to be committed to each other absolutely and, at least ideally, irrevocably.

For friendship, however, society has evolved no such protective institutions. Indeed, friends come and go in most people's lives without anyone registering the formal onset of the relationship or scrupling to justify its eventual end. But betrayal by a former friend may cause as much emotional distress as rejection by a blood relative or by a spouse, and in this psalm the poet sounds as though he has reached the nadir of misery by experiencing just that kind of rejection.

[16] May God curse him and his cohorts with death. May they go down to Sheol while still alive, for there is evil in them . . . and in their homes as well.

[17] As I cry out unto God, I feel secure that יהוה will save me.

[18] Evening, morning, and afternoon I beg and moan, whereupon God, hearing my voice, [19] redeems my soul peacefully from the battle being waged against me as though there were mighty minions on my side.

[20] May God listen to the taunts of my enemies and punish them. May the Ancient One, *selah,* identify them and no others as people who fear not God; [21] he—their leader—has set his hands against his former allies and annulled their covenant.

[22] My enemy's speech is smoother than butter, but he is planning war in his heart. His words may be more unguent than oil, but they are all daggers.

[23] Place your hope in יהוה, who will sustain you, who will never let a righteous person stumble.

[24] And You, O God, send my enemies to the bottom of the Well of Oblivion, for they are men of bloodshed and treachery. They will not reach even half their allotted days, but I put my trust in You.

Most moderns, participants in a transient society that deprives most people of the company of extended family and which considers divorce more nuisance than tragedy, will know just what he means.

Read in this light, the poet's words can prompt latter-day readers to ask some interesting questions about friendship. What is it about friendship that makes its bonds so fragile and so powerful at the same time? Why, if friendship so often forms the model for other intimate relationships in life, has society failed to nod to its essential nature in human relations by evolving any specific rituals around its onset and demise? And why, if friendship is the arena in which most of us learn the most basic societal skills—trust, companionability, reliability, and confidence in others—have we created a society in which the basic techniques necessary to establish and maintain friendships are never taught formally to anybody at all . . . and are only rarely even named, let alone analyzed, studied, or discussed in depth?

נו

לַמְנַצֵּחַ עַל־יוֹנַת אֵלֶם רְחֹקִים לְדָוִד מִכְתָּם בֶּאֱחֹז אֹתוֹ פְלִשְׁתִּים בְּגַת׃
2 חָנֵּנִי אֱלֹהִים כִּי־שְׁאָפַנִי אֱנוֹשׁ כָּל־הַיּוֹם לֹחֵם יִלְחָצֵנִי׃
3 שָׁאֲפוּ שׁוֹרְרַי כָּל־הַיּוֹם כִּי־רַבִּים לֹחֲמִים לִי מָרוֹם׃
4 יוֹם אִירָא אֲנִי אֵלֶיךָ אֶבְטָח׃
5 בֵּאלֹהִים אֲהַלֵּל דְּבָרוֹ בֵּאלֹהִים בָּטַחְתִּי לֹא אִירָא מַה־יַּעֲשֶׂה בָשָׂר לִי׃
6 כָּל־הַיּוֹם דְּבָרַי יְעַצֵּבוּ עָלַי כָּל־מַחְשְׁבֹתָם לָרָע׃
7 יָגוּרוּ *יִצְפּוֹנוּ הֵמָּה עֲקֵבַי יִשְׁמֹרוּ כַּאֲשֶׁר קִוּוּ נַפְשִׁי׃
8 עַל־אָוֶן פַּלֶּט־לָמוֹ בְּאַף עַמִּים ׀ הוֹרֵד אֱלֹהִים׃
9 נֹדִי סָפַרְתָּה אָתָּה שִׂימָה דִמְעָתִי בְנֹאדֶךָ הֲלֹא בְּסִפְרָתֶךָ׃
10 אָז ׀ יָשׁוּבוּ אוֹיְבַי אָחוֹר בְּיוֹם אֶקְרָא זֶה־יָדַעְתִּי כִּי־אֱלֹהִים לִי׃
11 בֵּאלֹהִים אֲהַלֵּל דָּבָר בַּיהוָה אֲהַלֵּל דָּבָר׃
12 בֵּאלֹהִים בָּטַחְתִּי לֹא אִירָא מַה־יַּעֲשֶׂה אָדָם לִי׃
13 עָלַי אֱלֹהִים נְדָרֶיךָ אֲשַׁלֵּם תּוֹדֹת לָךְ׃
14 כִּי הִצַּלְתָּ נַפְשִׁי מִמָּוֶת הֲלֹא רַגְלַי מִדֶּחִי לְהִתְהַלֵּךְ לִפְנֵי אֱלֹהִים בְּאוֹר הַחַיִּים׃

v. 7 יצפינו כתיב

In his mind's eye, the poet sees God seated on the Throne of Glory in the celestial throne room. Before the Almighty are the divine minions, but amidst all that celestial splendor, God has room beneath the divine throne for the most humble of all things: an old wineskin in which to collect the tears shed on earth by those who love God, who suffer for that love, and who weep for the pain the quest for that love has brought them and will yet bring them. That old wineskin, the poet realizes, *is* the famous book in which God records the rewards due to the faithful. Are tears, then, the coin in which obligations to heaven are paid? Surely tears are not the only currency God accepts on high, but the poet is telling us that tears shed by those who suffer for their love of God are especially beloved in heaven. Furthermore, as the physical proof that there are those on earth who will endure any torment for the sake of

56

For the conductor, a golden-song of David composed when the Philistines seized him in Gath, a song to be sung to the tune of "O Dove of Distant Elem."

[2] Be gracious unto me, O God, for a certain individual desires ill for me; a warrior oppresses me all day long.

[3] Those who spy on me all day long desire ill for me; the number of those who fight against me is terribly high.

[4] On a day of fear, I trust in You.

[5] In God—I shall praise the divine promise—in God do I trust; I shall not be afraid. What can mere mortals do to me?

[6] Yet my words are worried all day long; all the enemies' thoughts in my regard are for ill.

[7] They plot, they hide, they keep track of my every step . . . and they hope to take my life.

[8] Rid me of them because of their sinful ways. Bring down these aliens in anger, O God.

[9] You count the steps of my wandering; You catch my tears in Your divine wineskin—is that not the same as recording them in Your divine record book?

[10] Then, on the day I cry out to God, my enemies shall fall back; this I know, for God is with me.

[11] In God, I shall praise the divine promise. In יהוה, I shall praise the divine promise.

[12] Because I trust in God, I shall not be afraid; what can mere human beings do to me?

[13] My vows to You, O God, are mine to fulfill; I will pay out all the thanksgiving offerings I have vowed to bring to You, [14]for You have saved my soul from death. Have You not kept my foot from stumbling, so that I might walk before God in the light of the living?

knowing God, hearing God's voice, and yearning for God's love, those tears become God's wealth and, as such, the true coin of the divine realm.

Moderns contemplating the fifty-sixth psalm will want to ask if they think it conceivable that any of their own tears might be in God's wineskin. And if they have never shed a tear in the course of their spiritual journeys, is it because they have had the exceptional good fortune never to have suffered for their faith . . . or is it because their spiritual lives are simply too dull to warrant that kind of emotional investment?

נז

לַמְנַצֵּחַ אַל־תַּשְׁחֵת לְדָוִד מִכְתָּם בְּבָרְחוֹ מִפְּנֵי־
שָׁאוּל בַּמְּעָרָה׃
2 חָנֵּנִי אֱלֹהִים ׀ חָנֵּנִי כִּי בְךָ חָסָיָה נַפְשִׁי וּבְצֵל־
כְּנָפֶיךָ אֶחְסֶה עַד יַעֲבֹר הַוּוֹת׃
3 אֶקְרָא לֵאלֹהִים עֶלְיוֹן לָאֵל גֹּמֵר עָלָי׃
4 יִשְׁלַח מִשָּׁמַיִם ׀ וְיוֹשִׁיעֵנִי חֵרֵף שֹׁאֲפִי סֶלָה יִשְׁלַח
אֱלֹהִים חַסְדּוֹ וַאֲמִתּוֹ׃
5 נַפְשִׁי ׀ בְּתוֹךְ לְבָאִם אֶשְׁכְּבָה לֹהֲטִים בְּנֵי־אָדָם
שִׁנֵּיהֶם חֲנִית וְחִצִּים וּלְשׁוֹנָם חֶרֶב חַדָּה׃
6 רוּמָה עַל־הַשָּׁמַיִם אֱלֹהִים עַל כָּל־הָאָרֶץ כְּבוֹדֶךָ׃
7 רֶשֶׁת ׀ הֵכִינוּ לִפְעָמַי כָּפַף נַפְשִׁי כָּרוּ לְפָנַי שִׁיחָה
נָפְלוּ בְתוֹכָהּ סֶלָה׃
8 נָכוֹן לִבִּי אֱלֹהִים נָכוֹן לִבִּי אָשִׁירָה וַאֲזַמֵּרָה׃
9 עוּרָה כְבוֹדִי עוּרָה הַנֵּבֶל וְכִנּוֹר אָעִירָה שָּׁחַר׃
10 אוֹדְךָ בָעַמִּים ׀ אֲדֹנָי אֲזַמֶּרְךָ בַּלְאֻמִּים׃
11 כִּי־גָדֹל עַד־שָׁמַיִם חַסְדֶּךָ וְעַד־שְׁחָקִים אֲמִתֶּךָ׃
12 רוּמָה עַל־שָׁמַיִם אֱלֹהִים עַל כָּל־הָאָרֶץ כְּבוֹדֶךָ׃

One day as he was fleeing from Saul, David hid in a cave near Ein Gedi, only to have the king himself step into that very cave shortly thereafter to void the royal bowels in a private place. Of course, Saul had no idea David was hiding in the cave when he entered it, which only makes the irony more exquisite: Saul, who has been searching high and low for David, only finds him when he finally stops looking and allows himself to be found *by* him. And Saul doesn't even realize his own success!

The poet's lesson for our own spiritual lives is profound. We spend our lives searching for God, but, in the end, only those who let themselves be found *by* God will be successful in their quests. Of them, some will be Sauls, totally

57 For the conductor, a golden-song of David composed when he fled from Saul into the cave, a song to be sung to "Destroy Not."

[2] Be gracious unto me, O God, be gracious unto me, for my soul has sought refuge in You and thus shall I seek refuge in the shadow of Your wings until the scheming passes.

[3] I call out to God Most High, to the God who is so very kind to me.

[4] Send salvation from heaven and save me, for the one who wishes me ill has blasphemed, *selah;* may God send me godly mercy and divine truth.

[5] My soul dwells among lions and there do I lie down to rest, even though those "lions" are actually enraged people whose teeth are as sharp as sabers and as deadly as arrows. Their tongues are sharpened swords.

[6] Rise up over the heavens, O God, for Your glory is over all the earth.

[7] My soul is depressed, for they set a trap to ensnare my feet; they even dug a pit to capture me, but they themselves fell into it, *selah.*

[8] My heart is ready, O God, my heart is ready; I shall sing and chant hymns of praise.

[9] Awake, my glorious soul. Awake, lute and lyre, for I shall awaken the dawn.

[10] I shall acknowledge You among the nations, Adonai; I shall sing of You among the peoples of the world.

[11] For Your mercy reaches up to the heavens, Your truth, to the highest skies.

[12] Rise up over the heavens, O God, for Your glory is over all the earth.

unaware of the divine presence in the cave into which they've inadvertently stumbled. Others, however, will have spent a lifetime learning to be sensitive to the presence of God, the celestial Sovereign whose majesty parallels the glory of earthly kings. The poet's advice to his readers is to labor intensely to place themselves squarely in the latter category . . . and to be intensely grateful if they succeed.

A version of the last five verses of this psalm appears elsewhere in the Psalter as verses 2–6 of Psalm 108.

לַמְנַצֵּחַ אַל־תַּשְׁחֵת לְדָוִד מִכְתָּם׃

2 הַאֻמְנָם אֵלֶם צֶדֶק תְּדַבֵּרוּן מֵישָׁרִים תִּשְׁפְּטוּ בְּנֵי
אָדָם׃ 3 אַף־בְּלֵב עוֹלֹת תִּפְעָלוּן בָּאָרֶץ חֲמַס
יְדֵיכֶם תְּפַלֵּסוּן׃

4 זֹרוּ רְשָׁעִים מֵרָחֶם תָּעוּ מִבֶּטֶן דֹּבְרֵי כָזָב׃

5 חֲמַת־לָמוֹ כִּדְמוּת חֲמַת־נָחָשׁ כְּמוֹ־פֶתֶן חֵרֵשׁ
יַאְטֵם אָזְנוֹ׃ 6 אֲשֶׁר לֹא־יִשְׁמַע לְקוֹל מְלַחֲשִׁים
חוֹבֵר חֲבָרִים מְחֻכָּם׃

7 אֱלֹהִים הֲרָס־שִׁנֵּימוֹ בְּפִימוֹ מַלְתְּעוֹת כְּפִירִים
נְתֹץ ׀ יְהוָה׃

8 יִמָּאֲסוּ כְמוֹ־מַיִם יִתְהַלְּכוּ־לָמוֹ יִדְרֹךְ *חִצָּיו כְּמוֹ
יִתְמֹלָלוּ׃ 9 כְּמוֹ שַׁבְּלוּל תֶּמֶס יַהֲלֹךְ נֵפֶל אֵשֶׁת
בַּל־חָזוּ שָׁמֶשׁ׃

10 בְּטֶרֶם יָבִינוּ סִּירֹתֵיכֶם אָטָד כְּמוֹ־חַי כְּמוֹ־חָרוֹן
יִשְׂעָרֶנּוּ׃

11 יִשְׂמַח צַדִּיק כִּי־חָזָה נָקָם פְּעָמָיו יִרְחַץ בְּדַם
הָרָשָׁע׃ 12 וְיֹאמַר אָדָם אַךְ־פְּרִי לַצַּדִּיק אַךְ
יֵשׁ־אֱלֹהִים שֹׁפְטִים בָּאָרֶץ׃

v. 8 חצו כתיב

The poet's enemy is so base and so unremittingly evil that the poet can barely find words adequate to describe him and must make do, therefore, with whatever terms of opprobrium he *can* manage to muster. He is a thorn that sinks a canvas boat, a snail that leaves its revolting sludge in its wake, a lion whose response to adversity is to maul and then tear apart its enemies. He is a dead fetus, a deaf snake, a bloody corpse lying in the poet's gutter. He is perverse, corrupt, unfair, prejudiced . . . a crooked judge, a liar, a cheat. What could occasion such hatred? We will, of course, never know, but we can still be inspired by the poet's words to contemplate our own feelings about good and evil in the world. Do we truly hate depravity, or do we make endless excuses for poor behavior, for criminal activity, and for wanton, im-

58 For the conductor, a golden-song of David to be sung to the tune of "Destroy Not."

[2] Do you really think it counts if you speak of righteous things inaudibly? What matters is that you judge people fairly! [3]So far your depraved plans may be only in your heart, but your hands are already laying the groundwork for violence.

[4] The wicked are perverse even before they exit the womb. Liars wander the crooked path even before leaving their mothers' bellies.

[5] Their venom is like a snake's. Indeed, each of them is like a deaf asp that stops up its ear [6]so as not to hear the voice of the snake charmer, that well-trained caster of magical spells.

[7] God, break their teeth in their mouths; יהוה, smash the lions' fangs.

[8] Let them melt like ice that turns to water and then flows away. May God set arrows on the divine bow and shoot at the wicked as though they were targets made of dried out straw, [9]as though they were snails who leak slime as they crawl along, as though they were miscarried embryos who did not live long enough to see the light of the sun.

[10] Before they are old enough to know how much damage a single thorn can do to a canvas boat, may they be swept away like a frail life in a whirlwind of anger.

[11] The righteous will rejoice when they see revenge, when they can wash the soles of their feet with the blood of the wicked, [12]when they can say, "There are just desserts for the righteous. Indeed, there are decent judges who judge justly in the world."

moral acts? Are we outraged—not just irritated, but truly outraged—by deceit, dishonesty, chicanery, and fraud? Have we totally internalized the awful truth that any toleration of injustice in the world is a step away from God, the divine Arbiter of right and wrong in whose court all humanity must stand in judgment? Or are we so busy making excuses, for ourselves and for others, that we never actually have the time to take a stand against the evil that runs rampant in the world?

נט

לַמְנַצֵּחַ אַל־תַּשְׁחֵת לְדָוִד מִכְתָּם בִּשְׁלֹחַ שָׁאוּל וַיִּשְׁמְרוּ אֶת־הַבַּיִת לַהֲמִיתוֹ׃
[2] הַצִּילֵנִי מֵאֹיְבַי ׀ אֱלֹהָי מִמִּתְקוֹמְמַי תְּשַׂגְּבֵנִי׃
[3] הַצִּילֵנִי מִפֹּעֲלֵי אָוֶן וּמֵאַנְשֵׁי דָמִים הוֹשִׁיעֵנִי׃
[4] כִּי הִנֵּה אָרְבוּ לְנַפְשִׁי יָגוּרוּ עָלַי עַזִּים לֹא־פִשְׁעִי וְלֹא־חַטָּאתִי יְהוָה׃
[5] בְּלִי־עָוֺן יְרוּצוּן וְיִכּוֹנָנוּ עוּרָה לִקְרָאתִי וּרְאֵה׃
[6] וְאַתָּה יְהוָה־אֱלֹהִים ׀ צְבָאוֹת אֱלֹהֵי יִשְׂרָאֵל הָקִיצָה לִפְקֹד כָּל־הַגּוֹיִם אַל־תָּחֹן כָּל־בֹּגְדֵי אָוֶן סֶלָה׃
[7] יָשׁוּבוּ לָעֶרֶב יֶהֱמוּ כַכָּלֶב וִיסוֹבְבוּ עִיר׃ [8] הִנֵּה ׀ יַבִּיעוּן בְּפִיהֶם חֲרָבוֹת בְּשִׂפְתוֹתֵיהֶם כִּי מִי שֹׁמֵעַ׃
[9] וְאַתָּה יְהוָה תִּשְׂחַק־לָמוֹ תִּלְעַג לְכָל־גּוֹיִם׃
[10] עֻזּוֹ אֵלֶיךָ אֶשְׁמֹרָה כִּי אֱלֹהִים מִשְׂגַּבִּי׃
[11] אֱלֹהֵי *חַסְדִּי יְקַדְּמֵנִי אֱלֹהִים יַרְאֵנִי בְשֹׁרְרָי׃
[12] אַל־תַּהַרְגֵם ׀ פֶּן־יִשְׁכְּחוּ עַמִּי הֲנִיעֵמוֹ בְחֵילְךָ וְהוֹרִידֵמוֹ מָגִנֵּנוּ אֲדֹנָי׃

v. 11 חסדו כתיב

David's life fell into ever greater danger as King Saul descended into madness. He promised David his daughter's hand in marriage in exchange for the foreskins of one hundred Philistines, then had to gnash his teeth in silence when David gathered not one, but two, hundred specimens (and was not killed—as Saul had hoped and expected—while procuring them). For a while David was safe, but then the paranoia returned and Saul himself tried to murder David, driving his own spear into the wall where David sat playing his lyre. And then Saul sent messengers to sit outside the home David shared with his wife Michal, Saul's daughter, and to kill him when he emerged.

Michal, realizing the mortal danger facing her husband, had to choose: was she going to scheme to save his life or step aside to permit her father to do as he wished to the man she loved? The original story is more about Michal than David, but it was precisely at this juncture in the story that the poet found the David who inspired him. There are many Davids in Scripture, but it was neither the man betrayed by his king nor the man unsure which of his friends to trust that spoke to the poet's soul, nor was it even the man uncertain

59 For the conductor, a golden-song of David composed when Saul sent messengers to stand watch over David's house and kill him, a song to be sung to "Destroy Not."

[2] Save me from my enemies, O my God; exalt me over those who rise up against me.

[3] Save me from those who do evil; deliver me from violent people, [4]for they are out to ambush me. Powerful people are lying in wait for me, to avenge some affront that is neither my sin nor my transgression, O יהוה.

[5] I am without sin, yet they run to plot against me. Wake up and look in my direction! [6]Awaken, O יהוה-Elohim of the celestial legions and God of Israel, to requite the sins of all nations; have no mercy on seditious sinners, *selah.*

[7] They return every evening to encircle the city moaning like dogs, [8]talking with mouths featuring razor-sharp lips, thinking to themselves, "Who is listening?"

[9] But You, O יהוה, shall mock them; You shall scorn all the nations.

[10] Therefore shall I guard my strength for You, for God is my refuge.

[11] My merciful God will go before me and show me the fate of those who spy against me.

[12] Do not kill them, lest my people forget the fate of the wicked; instead, shake them up mightily and bring them down low, Adonai, our shield.

if he could count on the unyielding support of his own brothers (or even of his own father) that inspired the psalmist. All those Davids have their place in the Psalter, but the poet whose psalm is the fifty-ninth in our book seizes on a different David as his model: the man who must decide if the woman he loves—in whose bed he sleeps and to whom he has given himself completely and utterly—if *that* woman is going to be able to find the strength to stand by his side *no matter what.* The end of the story is a happy one, at least for David. Michal does support him, helping him climb out a window and then stuffing their bed and lying to her father's men to make them think that David himself lies ill under the covers. But how did the poet's story end?

Like David, the poet also has powerful enemies—foes he likens to dogs

13 חַטַּאת פִּימוֹ דְּֽבַר־שְׂפָתֵ֫ימוֹ וְיִלָּכְד֥וּ בִגְאוֹנָ֑ם וּמֵאָלָ֖ה וּמִכַּ֣חַשׁ יְסַפֵּֽרוּ׃

14 כַּלֵּ֥ה בְחֵמָה֮ כַּלֵּ֪ה וְֽאֵ֫ינֵ֥מוֹ וְֽיֵדְע֗וּ כִּֽי־אֱ֭לֹהִים מֹשֵׁ֣ל בְּיַעֲקֹ֑ב לְאַפְסֵ֖י הָאָ֣רֶץ סֶֽלָה׃

15 וְיָשֻׁ֣בוּ לָ֭עֶרֶב יֶהֱמ֥וּ כַכָּ֗לֶב וִיס֥וֹבְבוּ עִֽיר׃ 16 הֵ֭מָּה *יְנִיע֣וּן לֶֽאֱכֹ֑ל אִם־לֹ֥א יִ֝שְׂבְּע֗וּ וַיָּלִֽינוּ׃

17 וַאֲנִ֤י ׀ אָשִׁ֬יר עֻזֶּ֗ךָ וַאֲרַנֵּ֣ן לַבֹּ֣קֶר חַ֫סְדֶּ֥ךָ כִּֽי־הָיִ֣יתָ מִשְׂגָּ֣ב לִ֑י וּ֝מָנ֗וֹס בְּי֣וֹם צַר־לִֽי׃

18 עֻ֭זִּי אֵלֶ֣יךָ אֲזַמֵּ֑רָה כִּֽי־אֱלֹהִ֥ים מִ֝שְׂגַּבִּ֗י אֱלֹהֵ֥י חַסְדִּֽי׃

v. 16 ינועון כתיב

growling in the street, rabid curs who mock and hate God and who will stop at nothing to bring the poet down. He has no idea whom to trust. Can he rely on his friends or his relations? Can he count on his colleagues among the poets to stand by his side *no matter what*? Or did the poet, in dedicating his poem to David at home, mean to ask an even more awful question: could he count on his wife for unyielding, absolute, and unwavering support? He may have loved her, he might have felt secure in her love for him, and he probably felt that he had given himself totally to her. In the end, however, his poem suggests he was still David lying in his bed at night *wondering if his wife was going to betray him or stand by him* . . . and suspecting strongly that no man could ever

[13] The sin of their mouths is the word on their lips; may they be ensnared by their pride, by their false oaths, by the lies they tell.

[14] Destroy them in anger, destroy them until they no longer exist . . . then shall the rest of us know that God rules over Jacob and as far as the ends of the earth, *selah.*

[15] As for them, let them return every evening to encircle the city moaning like dogs [16] wandering about looking for something to eat, dogs who only settle down to rest for the night once they no longer expect to be satisfied.

[17] But I shall sing of Your strength and praise Your mercy in song every morning, for You have been my refuge, my hiding place in my day of trouble.

[18] My source of strength, I shall give forth in song to You, for God, my merciful God, is my place of refuge.

know the loneliness and ill ease that he himself felt, lying in the one place men are supposed to feel totally secure but giving himself over instead to worry.

In the end, the only real source of security in the poet's world is faith in God. Even love—even the overwhelming power of romantic love in its most exalted state between husband and wife—can, in the end, fade and ebb. Even a once-loyal spouse can be moved to treachery, the poet knows, but God remains constant, unchanging and devoid of fickleness. Only in God is there permanence, he believes. And only in God, therefore, can there ever be true and absolute certainty—or utterly true and absolutely certain love.

ס

לַמְנַצֵּ֥חַ עַל־שׁוּשַׁ֥ן עֵד֑וּת מִכְתָּ֖ם לְדָוִ֣ד לְלַמֵּֽד׃
2 בְּהַצּוֹת֨וֹ ׀ אֶ֥ת אֲרַ֣ם נַהֲרַיִם֮ וְאֶת־אֲרַ֪ם צ֫וֹבָ֥ה
וַיָּ֤שָׁב יוֹאָ֗ב וַיַּ֣ךְ אֶת־אֱד֣וֹם בְּגֵיא־מֶ֑לַח שְׁנֵ֖ים עָשָׂ֣ר
אָֽלֶף׃
3 אֱ֭לֹהִים זְנַחְתָּ֣נוּ פְרַצְתָּ֑נוּ אָ֝נַ֗פְתָּ תְּשׁ֣וֹבֵֽב לָֽנוּ׃
4 הִרְעַ֣שְׁתָּה אֶ֣רֶץ פְּצַמְתָּ֑הּ רְפָ֖ה שְׁבָרֶ֣יהָ כִי־מָֽטָה׃
5 הִרְאִ֣יתָה עַמְּךָ֣ קָשָׁ֑ה הִ֝שְׁקִיתָ֗נוּ יַ֣יִן תַּרְעֵלָֽה׃
6 נָ֤תַ֥תָּה לִּירֵאֶ֣יךָ נֵּ֭ס לְהִתְנוֹסֵ֑ס מִ֝פְּנֵ֗י קֹ֣שֶׁט סֶֽלָה׃
7 לְ֭מַעַן יֵחָלְצ֣וּן יְדִידֶ֑יךָ הוֹשִׁ֖יעָה יְמִֽינְךָ֣ *וַעֲנֵֽנִי׃
8 אֱלֹהִ֤ים ׀ דִּבֶּ֥ר בְּקָדְשׁ֗וֹ אֶ֫עְלֹ֥זָה אֲחַלְּקָ֥ה שְׁכֶ֑ם וְעֵ֖מֶק
סֻכּ֣וֹת אֲמַדֵּֽד׃ 9 לִ֤י גִלְעָ֨ד ׀ וְלִ֬י מְנַשֶּׁ֗ה וְ֭אֶפְרַיִם
מָע֣וֹז רֹאשִׁ֑י יְ֝הוּדָ֗ה מְחֹֽקְקִֽי׃ 10 מוֹאָ֤ב ׀ סִ֬יר רַחְצִ֗י
עַל־אֱ֭דוֹם אַשְׁלִ֣יךְ נַעֲלִ֑י עָ֝לַ֗י פְּלֶ֣שֶׁת הִתְרֹעָֽעִי׃
11 מִ֣י יֹ֭בִלֵנִי עִ֣יר מָצ֑וֹר מִ֖י נָחַ֣נִי עַד־אֱדֽוֹם׃
12 הֲלֹֽא־אַתָּ֣ה אֱ֭לֹהִים זְנַחְתָּ֑נוּ וְלֹֽא־תֵצֵ֥א אֱ֝לֹהִ֗ים
בְּצִבְאוֹתֵֽינוּ׃
13 הָֽבָה־לָּ֣נוּ עֶזְרָ֣ת מִצָּ֑ר וְ֝שָׁ֗וְא תְּשׁוּעַ֥ת אָדָֽם׃
14 בֵּֽאלֹהִ֥ים נַעֲשֶׂה־חָ֑יִל וְ֝ה֗וּא יָב֥וּס צָרֵֽינוּ׃

v. 7 ועננו כתיב

The Psalter is studded with vague (and occasionally explicit) references to people gathering in the Temple in Jerusalem in the middle of the night to cultivate the experience of hearing God speak to them. Indeed, the sixtieth psalm is a worthy addition to the Psalter not because it reports on an ancient battle, but precisely because it reports on an actual oracle of God. Although the poet omits mention of the precise method he used to provoke divine speech, he nonetheless proves his point by revealing to us the substance of the words he heard. What they mean, who can say? It is the nature of oracles to be gnomic and obscure, but whether even the poet himself knew what it meant for Moab to be God's washing-tub, or what the precise importance was of the Almighty's promise to survey the Vale of Sukkot anew, is not something modern readers can know with any degree of certainty. Far more important for us, however, should be the fact that God spoke to the faithful once and would, one can only presume, speak to us too,

60

For the conductor, an instructive golden-song of David to be sung to "A Lily of Testimony," [2]composed when he fought a war against Aram Naharaim and Aram Tzoba, and Joab returned and smote twelve thousand Edomites in Gei-Melach.

[3] You have abandoned us, O God. You have made a breach in our defenses. You have been angry with us; now restore us.

[4] You have made the earth tremble and split open; now heal its wounds for it is close to collapse.

[5] You have shown Your people toughness and given them poisoned wine to drink; [6]now give a banner to those who fear You so that they may wave it as their insignia, *selah.*

[7] Let Your right hand effect salvation as You answer me, so that those who love You might find relief.

[8] I rejoice that God has spoken in the divine sanctuary. "I shall divide Shechem," God said. "I shall survey the Valley of Sukkot, [9]for Mine is Gilead and Mine are Manasseh and Ephraim, my main strongholds. Mine is Judah, My terrestrial legislator; [10]Mine is Moab, My washing-tub. I shall stamp My shoe down on Edom; quake, Philistia, on My account."

[11] Who will bring me to the besieged city? Who will lead me to Edom?

[12] Is it not You, O God, who has abandoned us? Will You not go forth with our armies, O God?

[13] Grant us help against our enemies, since hoping for salvation from human beings is folly. [14]With God, we shall prevail; the Almighty will trample our enemies.

if only we merited that same kind of intimate communion with the divine realm so ardently (and apparently successfully) cultivated by the ancients. The sixtieth psalm, therefore, is as much a challenge to the faithful as it is a report of something obscure that God once said. Treating it dismissively because of the obscurity of its most formal, and least important, message, therefore, would be to miss the point almost entirely.

A version of the last eight verses of this psalm appears elsewhere in the Psalter as the last eight verses of Psalm 108.

סא

לַמְנַצֵּחַ עַל־נְגִינַת לְדָוִד׃
2 שִׁמְעָה אֱלֹהִים רִנָּתִי הַקְשִׁיבָה תְּפִלָּתִי׃
3 מִקְצֵה הָאָרֶץ ׀ אֵלֶיךָ אֶקְרָא בַּעֲטֹף לִבִּי בְּצוּר־יָרוּם
מִמֶּנִּי תַנְחֵנִי׃ 4 כִּי־הָיִיתָ מַחְסֶה לִי מִגְדַּל־עֹז מִפְּנֵי
אוֹיֵב׃
5 אָגוּרָה בְאָהָלְךָ עוֹלָמִים אֶחֱסֶה בְסֵתֶר כְּנָפֶיךָ
סֶּלָה׃
6 כִּי־אַתָּה אֱלֹהִים שָׁמַעְתָּ לִנְדָרָי נָתַתָּ יְרֻשַּׁת יִרְאֵי
שְׁמֶךָ׃
7 יָמִים עַל־יְמֵי־מֶלֶךְ תּוֹסִיף שְׁנוֹתָיו כְּמוֹ־דֹר וָדֹר׃
8 יֵשֵׁב עוֹלָם לִפְנֵי אֱלֹהִים חֶסֶד וֶאֱמֶת מַן יִנְצְרֻהוּ׃
9 כֵּן אֲזַמְּרָה שִׁמְךָ לָעַד לְשַׁלְּמִי נְדָרַי יוֹם ׀ יוֹם׃

The Book of Psalms came into existence in an age when Israel no longer had a reigning monarch, but its final editors accepted several hymns into the anthology that speak of their authors' hopes and prayers for a king. Were these even then old poems composed in earlier days when a regent sat on the throne of Israel? Or were they contemporary songs designed to evoke memories of a happier age when a scion of David once sat on the throne in Jerusalem and ruled over the people as the living emblem of God's personal interest in them? Was their inclusion meant to encourage the belief that a descendant of David might yet again rule over Israel? Or were these hymns merely designed, slightly obliquely, to remind the people that God is the only Sovereign left for Israel and that they should conduct themselves, therefore, in a way that will guarantee that they remain in that Sovereign's royal favor? The answers to these questions can no longer be known. Yet reading the sixty-first psalm will still be a profitable experience if it provokes modern readers to ask themselves if sovereignty remains a reasonable model for moderns seeking to imagine God—in a world in which the notion that true kings and queens rule by divine right holds no sway whatsoever.

61

For the conductor, a psalm of David to be sung to *"Neginat."*

[2] Hear my joyous song, O God; give ear to my prayer.

[3] Even from the edge of the earth, I would cry out to You when my heart is enshrouded in sadness. Lead me to a rocky crag that towers over me, [4]for You have always been my haven, my tower of strength in the face of the enemy.

[5] I shall dwell in Your tent forever; in the secret space beneath Your wings I shall seek refuge, *selah.*

[6] For You, O God, have listened to my oaths and have endorsed the bequests of those who fear Your name.

[7] Add many days to the days already allotted the king; make his years almost everlasting.

[8] May he reign forever before God and may You appoint mercy and truth to guard him.

[9] And so shall I sing the praises of Your name forever; thus shall I fulfill my oaths every single day.

The notion that God is an absolute monarch who rules over subjects who nevertheless remain entirely free to chart their own courses in life appears, at any rate, to be almost meaningless. Yet that is precisely how our liturgy prompts us to think about the way God functions in our world. To turn in prayer to God using the language of royalty in a world without absolute monarchs, to sing hymns that acknowledge God as the King of the kings of kings when there simply are no all-powerful kings for God to rule over as their celestial Sovereign, to feel called upon to approach Sovereign God as willing and obedient subjects somehow nevertheless possessed of free will . . . these are all paradoxes with which any modern imbued with faith must live. In turn, the resolve to spend a lifetime struggling to invest the notion of divine sovereignty with profundity and meaning is the modern-day equivalent of the poet's promise to spend the hours of his life praising God.

סב

לַמְנַצֵּחַ עַל־יְדוּתוּן מִזְמוֹר לְדָוִד׃
2 אַךְ אֶל־אֱלֹהִים דּוּמִיָּה נַפְשִׁי מִמֶּנּוּ יְשׁוּעָתִי׃
3 אַךְ־הוּא צוּרִי וִישׁוּעָתִי מִשְׂגַּבִּי לֹא־אֶמּוֹט רַבָּה׃
4 עַד־אָנָה ׀ תְּהוֹתְתוּ עַל־אִישׁ תְּרָצְּחוּ כֻלְּכֶם כְּקִיר
נָטוּי גָּדֵר הַדְּחוּיָה׃
5 אַךְ מִשְּׂאֵתוֹ ׀ יָעֲצוּ לְהַדִּיחַ יִרְצוּ כָזָב בְּפִיו יְבָרֵכוּ
וּבְקִרְבָּם יְקַלְלוּ־סֶלָה׃
6 אַךְ לֵאלֹהִים דּוֹמִּי נַפְשִׁי כִּי־מִמֶּנּוּ תִּקְוָתִי׃
7 אַךְ־הוּא צוּרִי וִישׁוּעָתִי מִשְׂגַּבִּי לֹא אֶמּוֹט׃
8 עַל־אֱלֹהִים יִשְׁעִי וּכְבוֹדִי צוּר־עֻזִּי מַחְסִי
בֵּאלֹהִים׃ 9 בִּטְחוּ בוֹ בְכָל־עֵת ׀ עָם שִׁפְכוּ לְפָנָיו
לְבַבְכֶם אֱלֹהִים מַחֲסֶה־לָּנוּ סֶלָה׃
10 אַךְ הֶבֶל בְּנֵי־אָדָם כָּזָב בְּנֵי אִישׁ בְּמֹאזְנַיִם
לַעֲלוֹת הֵמָּה מֵהֶבֶל יָחַד׃
11 אַל־תִּבְטְחוּ בְעֹשֶׁק וּבְגָזֵל אַל־תֶּהְבָּלוּ חַיִל ׀ כִּי
יָנוּב אַל־תָּשִׁיתוּ לֵב׃
12 אַחַת ׀ דִּבֶּר אֱלֹהִים שְׁתַּיִם־זוּ שָׁמָעְתִּי כִּי עֹז
לֵאלֹהִים׃ 13 וּלְךָ־אֲדֹנָי חָסֶד כִּי־אַתָּה תְשַׁלֵּם
לְאִישׁ כְּמַעֲשֵׂהוּ׃

The poet is waiting. He does not note where precisely he sits and waits for God, but we may set the scene ourselves based on analogous passages in other psalms: it is midnight and the poet is lingering in the Temple forecourt, waiting for the experience either of hearing the sound of God's voice or of seeing the light of God's face. Possibly, he is hoping to experience both. He may even have been preparing to undertake some mysterious rituals designed to provoke that kind of mystic experience when he was suddenly seized by fear. What precisely it was that the poet feared—whether he was unnerved by the possibility of his own success or perhaps only terrified of discovery by enemies who, taking a dim view of that kind of spiritual endeavor, would shrink back neither from libel nor from murder—is unclear. Nevertheless, the poet comforts himself with the recollection that, in the vast scheme of things, human beings are less consequential than an

62

For the conductor, a psalm of David to be sung to "Jeduthun."

[2] Although my soul is silent before God, it is nevertheless from the Almighty that my salvation will come, [3]for God is my rock and the source of my salvation, my great place of refuge from which I shall not be banished.

[4] How long will all of you plot to slay a man as though he were naught but a tottering wall or a fence you could easily push down?

[5] Truly, they scheme to depose him from his position; they wish for nothing more than to catch him with a lie in his mouth. They bless him in public, then curse him when they are in their own company, *selah.*

[6] Be silent, my soul, before God, for it is in the Almighty that I place my hope, [7]for God is my Rock and the source of my salvation, my place of refuge from which I shall not be banished.

[8] My honor and my hope for salvation rest in God; indeed, in God have I found my rocky haven. [9]Therefore, you too should trust in God at all times, O people who pour out your hearts before God, for God is our haven, *selah.*

[10] In the end, people are just breath, human existence, naught but delusion; taken all together as things truly are, all humanity would not outweigh a single breath on a scale.

[11] Trust not in swindling; do not place false value in theft. You must learn not to care even if violence occasionally does bear fruit.

[12] God has said one thing, but I heard two: that true strength belongs to God [13]and that mercy is Yours, Adonai, for You will requite every individual according to that person's deeds.

exhaled breath and that true security comes only from faith in God, the refuge and haven of all who seek comfort in the world. We are expecting a hymn to waiting . . . but then God actually does speak. What precisely the poet hears is left untold, but there was something peculiar about the experience: the poet is certain he only heard one word, but it later seemed to him that God actually had said two different things, that both true strength and real mercy are God's alone. Could the point of the revelation be that, in the end, the two ideas are synonymous?

סג

מִזְמ֥וֹר לְדָוִ֑ד בִּ֝הְיוֹת֗וֹ בְּמִדְבַּ֥ר יְהוּדָֽה׃
2 אֱלֹהִ֤ים ׀ אֵלִ֥י אַתָּ֗ה אֲֽשַׁ֫חֲרֶ֥ךָּ צָמְאָ֬ה לְךָ֨ ׀ נַפְשִׁ֗י
כָּמַ֣הּ לְךָ֣ בְשָׂרִ֑י בְּאֶֽרֶץ־צִיָּ֖ה וְעָיֵ֣ף בְּלִי־מָֽיִם׃
3 כֵּ֭ן בַּקֹּ֣דֶשׁ חֲזִיתִ֑יךָ לִרְא֥וֹת עֻ֝זְּךָ֗ וּכְבוֹדֶֽךָ׃
4 כִּי־ט֣וֹב חַ֭סְדְּךָ מֵֽחַיִּ֗ים שְׂפָתַ֥י יְשַׁבְּחֽוּנְךָ׃
5 כֵּ֣ן אֲבָרֶכְךָ֣ בְחַיָּ֑י בְּ֝שִׁמְךָ֗ אֶשָּׂ֥א כַפָּֽי׃
6 כְּמ֤וֹ חֵ֣לֶב וָ֭דֶשֶׁן תִּשְׂבַּ֣ע נַפְשִׁ֑י וְשִׂפְתֵ֥י רְ֝נָנ֗וֹת
יְהַלֶּל־פִּֽי׃
7 אִם־זְכַרְתִּ֥יךָ עַל־יְצוּעָ֑י בְּ֝אַשְׁמֻר֗וֹת אֶהְגֶּה־בָּֽךְ׃
8 כִּֽי־הָיִ֣יתָ עֶזְרָ֣תָה לִּ֑י וּבְצֵ֖ל כְּנָפֶ֣יךָ אֲרַנֵּֽן׃
9 דָּבְקָ֣ה נַפְשִׁ֣י אַחֲרֶ֑יךָ בִּ֝֗י תָּמְכָ֥ה יְמִינֶֽךָ׃
10 וְהֵ֗מָּה לְ֭שׁוֹאָה יְבַקְשׁ֣וּ נַפְשִׁ֑י יָ֝בֹ֗אוּ בְּֽתַחְתִּיּ֥וֹת
הָאָֽרֶץ׃
11 יַגִּירֻ֥הוּ עַל־יְדֵי־חָ֑רֶב מְנָ֖ת שֻׁעָלִ֣ים יִהְיֽוּ׃
12 וְהַמֶּ֗לֶךְ יִשְׂמַ֬ח בֵּאלֹהִ֗ים יִ֭תְהַלֵּל כָּל־הַנִּשְׁבָּ֣ע בּ֑וֹ
כִּ֥י יִ֝סָּכֵ֗ר פִּ֣י דֽוֹבְרֵי־שָֽׁקֶר׃

The goal, the poet teaches, is to long for God and to *want* God—not in the vague, polite way decent people *want* good weather on the day of an outdoor wedding or *want* children to be pleased with their birthday gifts, but in the overpowering way people *want* their lives to be filled with joy and meaning, and *want* their lives to be characterized by the deep satisfaction that most people only know as the result of mature, physical love. The poet likens his need for God to the way parched soil needs water and he presents that image for us to ponder and, perhaps, for it to provoke some productive introspection. Are we customers in God's store who hope to pay as little as possible for the blessings we yearn to acquire? Or are we lovers overwhelmed with desire for God who are as little capable of controlling our longing for the physically perceptible presence of the Divine as anyone who senses the nearness of his or her beloved would be for that person's actual physical presence? The poet, it appears, has experienced the visible presence of the Divine and his personal answer, therefore, is perfectly clear to him: he knows the Almighty to be near, always, to the pious few who seek communion with God in the context of absolute intellectual and spiritual integrity, and he wishes always to be among their number.

63

A psalm of David, composed when he was in the Wilderness of Judah.

[2] O God, You are my God and thus shall I be first every morning to seek You out. My soul thirsts for You; my flesh longs for You as though I were parched in an arid land, as though I were exhausted in a land without water.

[3] Surely I have seen You in the sanctuary; I have merited to see Your power and glory.

[4] And, as Your mercy is better than life itself, my lips shall always praise You.

[5] Surely I shall bless You during my lifetime; in Your name shall I lift up my hands in blessing.

[6] You satisfy my soul no less than do fat and marrow; therefore shall my mouth sing songs of Your praise with joyful lips.

[7] If I invoke You as I lay on my bed, then I shall just as surely meditate upon You during my hours on the nighttime watch.

[8] For You have been my help, and it is in the shadow of Your wings that I rejoice.

[9] My soul cleaves unto You; Your right hand ever supports me.

[10] And as for those who seek disaster for my soul, may they descend into the depths of the earth.

[11] May my supporters defeat my foe with a sword. May the carcasses of my foes end up as so much fox food.

[12] May the king rejoice in God. May those who swear in God's name be praised, even as the mouths of those who speak lies are dammed up.

סד

לַמְנַצֵּחַ מִזְמוֹר לְדָוִד:
2 שְׁמַע אֱלֹהִים קוֹלִי בְשִׂיחִי מִפַּחַד אוֹיֵב תִּצֹּר חַיָּי:
3 תַּסְתִּירֵנִי מִסּוֹד מְרֵעִים מֵרִגְשַׁת פֹּעֲלֵי אָוֶן: 4 אֲשֶׁר
שָׁנְנוּ כַחֶרֶב לְשׁוֹנָם דָּרְכוּ חִצָּם דָּבָר מָר: 5 לִירוֹת
בַּמִּסְתָּרִים תָּם פִּתְאֹם יֹרֻהוּ וְלֹא יִירָאוּ:
6 יְחַזְּקוּ־לָמוֹ ׀ דָּבָר רָע יְסַפְּרוּ לִטְמוֹן מוֹקְשִׁים אָמְרוּ
מִי יִרְאֶה־לָּמוֹ:
7 יַחְפְּשׂוּ עוֹלֹת תַּמְנוּ חֵפֶשׂ מְחֻפָּשׂ וְקֶרֶב אִישׁ וְלֵב
עָמֹק:
8 וַיֹּרֵם אֱלֹהִים חֵץ פִּתְאוֹם הָיוּ מַכּוֹתָם:
9 וַיַּכְשִׁילוּהוּ עָלֵימוֹ לְשׁוֹנָם יִתְנֹדְדוּ כָּל־רֹאֵה בָם:
10 וַיִּירְאוּ כָּל־אָדָם וַיַּגִּידוּ פֹּעַל אֱלֹהִים וּמַעֲשֵׂהוּ
הִשְׂכִּילוּ:
11 יִשְׂמַח צַדִּיק בַּיהוָה וְחָסָה בוֹ וְיִתְהַלְלוּ כָּל־
יִשְׁרֵי־לֵב:

Can something that brings an individual closer to God be anything but a blessing? It hardly takes any courage to feel that way about instances of fabulous good fortune: winning enormous lottery prizes, being unexpectedly cured of potentially terminal illnesses, being selected out of huge pools of applicants to get desirable jobs, winning difficult races, or waking up in time to save the children when one's home accidentally catches on fire in the middle of the night. But how many of us feel that way *absolutely*? Are we grateful for *anything* at all that makes us more aware of the presence of God in the world—or, more specifically, in our personal lives? The psalmist whose poem is our sixty-fourth psalm has had a very rough ride. His enemies have slandered him in public. They have attempted to ambush him, perhaps even to kidnap him, certainly to harm him grievously. He has survived, but he is terrified, horrified, and panicked. Yet, at the same time, he has the insight to realize that the very terror that so unnerved him has brought

64

For the conductor, a psalm of David.

[2] O God, hear my voice when I speak; protect my life from the enemy's fearful ways.

[3] Hide me from a gang of evildoers, from a mob of sinners [4]who have made their tongues as sharp as swords, whose arrows are bitter words, [5]who bend their bows to shoot at an innocent person from secret places, then shoot suddenly and fearlessly.

[6] An evil word gives them strength; as they conspire to lay snares, they ask, "Who will see our victims?"

[7] Let them look to their own sins instead, saying to themselves, "We have completed a vigorous inquiry into our interior beings, looking deep into our hearts."

[8] May God shoot at them suddenly, so that the arrow that strikes them comes as an unexpected blow.

[9] May their tongues trip them up, so that all who see them recoil in horror.

[10] May all those people be terrified, so that they become inspired to tell what God has wrought and so that they understand how God works in the world.

[11] A righteous person will always rejoice in יהוה and take refuge in God; the decent of heart will ever sing songs of praise.

him closer to God. It has made him more sensitive to God's saving power and has turned him more profoundly to faith. His predicament may have been horrific, but it helped him to acknowledge that having the will and the desire to seek refuge in God is a blessing, no matter how depraved or horrifying the circumstances that prompted an individual's need for haven in the first place may have been. The question for moderns is simple: can we truly embrace that kind of surrender to God as a worthy spiritual goal? Or are we doomed by our own intransigence to move further and further away from God with every instance of unhappiness that comes our way?

סה

לַמְנַצֵּ֥חַ מִזְמ֗וֹר לְדָוִ֥ד שִֽׁיר׃
2 לְךָ֤ דֻֽמִיָּ֨ה תְהִלָּ֓ה אֱלֹהִ֣ים בְּצִיּ֑וֹן וּ֝לְךָ֗ יְשֻׁלַּם־נֶֽדֶר׃
3 שֹׁמֵ֥עַ תְּפִלָּ֑ה עָ֝דֶ֗יךָ כָּל־בָּשָׂ֥ר יָבֹֽאוּ׃
4 דִּבְרֵ֣י עֲ֭וֺנֹת גָּ֣בְרוּ מֶ֑נִּי פְּ֝שָׁעֵ֗ינוּ אַתָּ֥ה תְכַפְּרֵֽם׃
5 אַשְׁרֵ֤י ׀ תִּֽבְחַ֣ר וּתְקָרֵב֮ יִשְׁכֹּ֪ן חֲצֵ֫רֶ֥יךָ נִ֭שְׂבְּעָה בְּט֣וּב בֵּיתֶ֑ךָ קְ֝דֹ֗שׁ הֵיכָלֶֽךָ׃
6 נ֤וֹרָא֨וֹת ׀ בְּצֶ֣דֶק תַּ֭עֲנֵנוּ אֱלֹהֵ֣י יִשְׁעֵ֑נוּ מִבְטָ֥ח כָּל־קַצְוֵי־אֶ֝֗רֶץ וְיָ֣ם רְחֹקִֽים׃ 7 מֵכִ֣ין הָרִ֣ים בְּכֹח֑וֹ נֶ֝אְזָ֗ר בִּגְבוּרָֽה׃ 8 מַשְׁבִּ֤יחַ ׀ שְׁא֣וֹן יַ֭מִּים שְׁא֣וֹן גַּלֵּיהֶ֑ם וַ֝הֲמ֗וֹן לְאֻמִּֽים׃
9 וַיִּֽירְא֨וּ ׀ יֹשְׁבֵ֣י קְ֭צָוֺת מֵאוֹתֹתֶ֑יךָ מֽוֹצָאֵי־בֹ֖קֶר וָעֶ֣רֶב תַּרְנִֽין׃
10 פָּקַ֥דְתָּ הָאָ֨רֶץ ׀ וַתְּשֹׁ֪קְקֶ֡הָ רַבַּ֬ת תַּעְשְׁרֶ֗נָּה פֶּ֣לֶג אֱ֭לֹהִים מָ֣לֵא מָ֑יִם תָּכִ֥ין דְּ֝גָנָ֗ם כִּי־כֵ֥ן תְּכִינֶֽהָ׃

The poet stands on Mount Zion and sees evidence of the splendor of God's creation in every direction: the distant horizons to the east and west, the green rolling fields made fertile through God's gentle rain, the endless flocks of sheep grazing in innumerable fields of green grass in a world overflowing with divine bounty. In his mind's eye, the poet imagines he can see the sea in the distance, its breakers roaring up against the shore and suggesting with their raging power the even more impressive might of their Creator, the Maker of Seas. He looks to the mountains and finds evidence there too of God's greatness: their majesty, immensity, and incredible immobility all remind the poet of the overwhelming power of a God who does not change or grow old or weak, but who merely exists as the quintessence of immutable Being. The poet turns to the meadows, to the fields, to the farmer's furrows filled with seed, to the endless stalks of grain he imagines he can hear singing God's praises as they wave gently to and fro in the soft wind of a gentle summer's day, and he is overwhelmed by the depth of his gratitude to God.

Who can fail to be moved by the poet's surrender to the goodness of the earth and to its Maker—or by his ability to utilize the wonders of nature as a kind of bridge capable of spanning the otherwise untraversable chasm between the world and its God? But which of the poet's admirers would have opened such a paean to the abundant world with the slightly unsettling thought that the only true praise of God is silence itself? Without that notion in place, the sixty-fifth psalm would simply be a lovely poem about nature. By

65

For the conductor, a psalm-song of David.
[2] To You, silence alone is praise, O God in Zion, and to You shall my vow be fulfilled.
[3] Unto You, the God who listens to prayer, shall all flesh come.
[4] The words telling our iniquities are too many for me to count, but You will still forgive our sins.
[5] Happy is the one You choose to come close to You—that one will dwell in the forecourt of Your Temple, that one will be sated with the goodness of Your house, with the holiness of Your Temple.
[6] With wonders will You rightly answer us, O God of our salvation, You who are the stronghold of the nations found in every distant corner of the earth and across every sea, [7] You who make the mountains stand by Your might, You who are girded with power, [8] You who calm the raging seas and their raging waves, You who calm the tumult of nations.
[9] Even those who live at the edges of the world will hold You in awe because of Your great signs; You make joyous those who live in the distant east and west.
[10] You look after the world and water it, thus enriching it greatly and making it into a well-irrigated precinct of God; indeed, You prepare, You surely do prepare, grain for the world's inhabitants.

beginning his poem with those provocative words, however, the poet has transformed his ode to nature into a deep theological statement.

We all know that words have no meaning other than whatever a given speaker invests in them. There is no organic connection, for example, between the word "apple" and the piece of fruit we English-speakers designate with that word. Furthermore, we all know that language is such a poor tool for communication that words can never describe adequately how someone looks, how a plum tastes, how lilacs smell, how green is different from blue, how love feels, or even how hot soup feels in one's throat on a wintery day. Language is indeed our primary medium of communication—but it fails utterly when we wish to express ideas rooted in feeling and perception. The poet begins his poem by translating that thought into the sphere of hymn and prayer.

11 תְּלָמֶיהָ רַוֵּה נַחֵת גְּדוּדֶיהָ בִּרְבִיבִים תְּמֹגְגֶנָּה
צִמְחָהּ תְּבָרֵךְ׃
12 עִטַּרְתָּ שְׁנַת טוֹבָתֶךָ וּמַעְגָּלֶיךָ יִרְעֲפוּן דָּשֶׁן׃
13 יִרְעֲפוּ נְאוֹת מִדְבָּר וְגִיל גְּבָעוֹת תַּחְגֹּרְנָה׃
14 לָבְשׁוּ כָרִים ׀ הַצֹּאן וַעֲמָקִים יַעַטְפוּ־בָר יִתְרוֹעֲעוּ
אַף־יָשִׁירוּ׃

To God, he writes, only silence is praise. Any word a human being utters is, by definition, rooted in his or her own consciousness. Moreover, since spoken words can only bear the meaning their speakers invest in them, they can have no meaning at all beyond the sphere of human experience. But God is above, beyond, and behind all human experience. The idea that one can express anything at all about God through the medium of language is, therefore, an absurdity only rendered more pathetic by the fact that language is the most, not the least, effective method most of us have of expressing ourselves to others. And so the poet, overwhelmed with the grandeur of God's world, begins by admitting this simple truth and leaving his readers to ponder its implications and slightly upsetting ramifications. To God, silence alone is praise. The most honest way human beings can speak about God is to say nothing at all. Silence is the only reliable medium in which honest faith can take root and grow. Saying more is saying less. One spoken word about God is one lie about God. Nothing truly honest can be said about the

[11] You irrigate the furrows of the earth. You make level its fields; You soften them with Your rain and bless its produce.

[12] You crown the year with such goodness that the world's highways are overflowing with its bounty. [13]Desert oases overflow with plenty; the hills themselves are girded with happiness.

[14] The pastures are covered with sheep; the valleys are covered with grain that almost sings as it waves in the wind.

Almighty. We speak because we must . . . but the only way to make reasonable the act of speaking even a single word in the praise of the Divine is to admit from the very onset—as the psalmist does with humility and candor—that the only true praise of God is fashioned of human will free of the suffocating strictures of human language. Indeed, by beginning his poem with such a bold statement about the nature of prayer—and of all talk to God and about God— and then continuing with a paean to the bounty of God's world, the poet is saying something both profound and slightly unsettling. To seek the Creator in Creation, he is suggesting, one must first learn to look out at the world deeply and meaningfully without talking endlessly—or, if one has the inner strength necessary, without talking at all—about what one sees of God in one's field of vision. The "naming reflex" that makes the name of an object pop into our minds almost as soon as we perceive it is so powerful that the interval between the two experiences feels almost non-existent. But, of course, the interval must (and does) exist—and in that indescribably brief moment between identifying an object and naming it, *that* is where, the poet suggests, human beings searching for the Creator in the splendor of Creation might best begin their quest.

סו

לַמְנַצֵּחַ שִׁיר מִזְמוֹר
הָרִיעוּ לֵאלֹהִים כָּל־הָאָרֶץ׃
2 זַמְּרוּ כְבוֹד־שְׁמוֹ שִׂימוּ כָבוֹד תְּהִלָּתוֹ׃
3 אִמְרוּ לֵאלֹהִים מַה־נּוֹרָא מַעֲשֶׂיךָ בְּרֹב עֻזְּךָ
יְכַחֲשׁוּ לְךָ אֹיְבֶיךָ׃
4 כָּל־הָאָרֶץ ׀ יִשְׁתַּחֲווּ לְךָ וִיזַמְּרוּ־לָךְ יְזַמְּרוּ שִׁמְךָ
סֶלָה׃
5 לְכוּ וּרְאוּ מִפְעֲלוֹת אֱלֹהִים נוֹרָא עֲלִילָה עַל־בְּנֵי
אָדָם׃ 6 הָפַךְ יָם ׀ לְיַבָּשָׁה בַּנָּהָר יַעַבְרוּ בְרָגֶל שָׁם
נִשְׂמְחָה־בּוֹ׃
7 מֹשֵׁל בִּגְבוּרָתוֹ ׀ עוֹלָם עֵינָיו בַּגּוֹיִם תִּצְפֶּינָה
הַסּוֹרְרִים ׀ אַל־*יָרוּמוּ לָמוֹ סֶלָה׃
8 בָּרְכוּ עַמִּים ׀ אֱלֹהֵינוּ וְהַשְׁמִיעוּ קוֹל תְּהִלָּתוֹ׃
9 הַשָּׂם נַפְשֵׁנוּ בַּחַיִּים וְלֹא־נָתַן לַמּוֹט רַגְלֵנוּ׃
10 כִּי־בְחַנְתָּנוּ אֱלֹהִים צְרַפְתָּנוּ כִּצְרָף־כָּסֶף׃
11 הֲבֵאתָנוּ בַמְּצוּדָה שַׂמְתָּ מוּעָקָה בְמָתְנֵינוּ׃
12 הִרְכַּבְתָּ אֱנוֹשׁ לְרֹאשֵׁנוּ בָּאנוּ־בָאֵשׁ וּבַמַּיִם
וַתּוֹצִיאֵנוּ לָרְוָיָה׃

v. 7 ירימו כתיב

The poet enters the courtyard of the Jerusalem Temple and contemplates the scene before him. The great bronze altar is overflowing with burnt offerings—with the smoldering carcasses of oxen, goats, and rams—and symbolizes the blessings of prosperity and peace God has bestowed upon the people. But, as the poet knows all too well, these happy times for his nation are not merely the natural, inevitable consequence of being God's treasured people. Rather, there has been a severe political crisis in which a tyrant imposed his self-serving will on the people and forced them to walk (in the poet's own words) through fire and water before God finally intervened in the political affairs of the Holy City to undo a situation that had clearly gotten out of hand.

Who was this tyrant? Was he an alien prince who briefly—or not so briefly—held sway over the Jews of Jerusalem? Or was he a home-grown gangster of some sort who managed to seize control of the city's administration and bend it to his own will while remaining totally oblivious to the needs and wishes of the city's inhabitants? The poet gives us no useful clues, but the sixty-sixth psalm is an ode to faith and the hope born of confidence in God's saving power, not an essay of political analysis. It can therefore be read

66 For the conductor, a psalm-song.
Raise up a great noise unto God, all people on earth.

2 Sing of the glory due God's name; make glorious the praise due God.

3 Say unto God, "How awesome are Your works! Because of Your great strength have Your enemies vanished before You.

4 All the earth shall bow down before You and sing to You; they shall sing hymns of praise to Your name, *selah*."

5 Go and see the accomplishments of God so celebrated as awesome of deed by humanity, 6 that same God who turned the sea to dry land so that the Israelites could cross the river on foot; let us therefore rejoice in our God.

7 God rules by divine might over the world; the eyes of God keep watch over the nations. May the violent not succeed at vaunting themselves over the meek, *selah*.

8 Bless our God, O nations; make audible the sound of the praise due the One 9 who grants life to our souls, that One who does not suffer our feet to stumble.

10 For You have tried us, O God; You have tested us as a smith might test silver.

11 You brought us into a trap; You applied pressure to our loins.

12 You placed a human master over us; we went through fire and water; yet, in the end, You brought us to comfort.

profitably by moderns even without any precise information about the specific circumstances that inspired the poet to compose his psalm.

Indeed, the poet's ideas will challenge moderns to rethink some of their most basic assumptions about the role of religious faith in the affairs of the world. The poet, after all, does not explain God's willingness to act on the people's behalf as a function of divine obligation, but rather as the Almighty's response to the prayers of those who have no iniquity in their hearts. The world, the poet knows, is not filled to overflowing with such people. But, when those pure souls who live sinless lives of fealty and obedience to God's word *do* raise up their holy voices in prayer, the response normally is positive. And that, the poet suggests, is how God governs

13 אָבוֹא בֵיתְךָ בְעוֹלוֹת אֲשַׁלֵּם לְךָ נְדָרָי׃ 14 אֲשֶׁר־פָּצוּ שְׂפָתָי וְדִבֶּר־פִּי בַּצַּר־לִי׃
15 עֹלוֹת מֵחִים אַעֲלֶה־לָּךְ עִם־קְטֹרֶת אֵילִים אֶעֱשֶׂה בָקָר עִם־עַתּוּדִים סֶלָה׃
16 לְכוּ שִׁמְעוּ וַאֲסַפְּרָה כָּל־יִרְאֵי אֱלֹהִים אֲשֶׁר עָשָׂה לְנַפְשִׁי׃
17 אֵלָיו פִּי־קָרָאתִי וְרוֹמַם תַּחַת לְשׁוֹנִי׃
18 אָוֶן אִם־רָאִיתִי בְלִבִּי לֹא יִשְׁמַע ׀ אֲדֹנָי׃
19 אָכֵן שָׁמַע אֱלֹהִים הִקְשִׁיב בְּקוֹל תְּפִלָּתִי׃
20 בָּרוּךְ אֱלֹהִים אֲשֶׁר לֹא־הֵסִיר תְּפִלָּתִי וְחַסְדּוֹ מֵאִתִּי׃

the world: not by imposing some preconceived string of events on unsuspecting humanity, but by responding faithfully to the prayers of decent and good citizens.

Moderns reading the sixty-sixth psalm may be prompted to ask themselves if they have the psalmist's kind of faith in the efficacy of prayer. Perhaps even more importantly, they may wish to ponder whether they believe (even theoretically) in the unavoidable corollary of the poet's notion: that those whose prayers can inspire God to intervene in human affairs bear profound and permanent responsibility for the safety and well-being of the world. For all who take the trappings of modern religious life seriously, then, the psalm poses the slightly

[13] I shall come to Your House with offerings to be wholly burnt; I shall honor my vows to You, [14]those vows which my lips uttered, which my mouth spoke when I was in trouble.

[15] I shall offer up especially fatty wholly burnt offerings along with the sweet savor of roasting rams; I shall provide sacrifices of cattle and goats, *selah*.

[16] Come and hear, all you who fear God, and I shall speak about all that God has done for my soul.

[17] It was to God that my mouth cried out, high praise issuing forth from beneath my tongue.

[18] Had I seen any iniquity in my heart, surely Adonai would not have heard my plea.

[19] But God did indeed hear, listening carefully to the sound of my prayer.

[20] Blessed be God, who neither turned my prayer away nor withheld divine mercy from me.

unnerving question of precisely how rational it is to attribute that kind of power to earnest prayer. The poet seems to consider his view on the relationship between prayer and divine governance of the world to be self-evident. But can moderns be similarly uplifted and inspired by that notion? Or are we doomed by the frailty of our faith merely to be *theoretically* terrified by the implications this poet's worldview *would* hold for us and for the world . . . if we could somehow bring ourselves to believe it actually reflects how things truly are in this world we inhabit?

סז

לַמְנַצֵּ֥חַ בִּנְגִינֹ֗ת מִזְמ֥וֹר שִֽׁיר׃
2 אֱלֹהִ֗ים יְחָנֵּ֥נוּ וִיבָרְכֵ֑נוּ יָ֤אֵ֥ר פָּנָ֖יו אִתָּ֣נוּ סֶֽלָה׃
3 לָדַ֣עַת בָּאָ֣רֶץ דַּרְכֶּ֑ךָ בְּכָל־ג֝וֹיִ֗ם יְשׁוּעָתֶֽךָ׃
4 יוֹד֖וּךָ עַמִּ֥ים ׀ אֱלֹהִ֑ים י֝וֹד֗וּךָ עַמִּ֥ים כֻּלָּֽם׃
5 יִ֥שְׂמְח֥וּ וִירַנְּנ֗וּ לְאֻ֫מִּ֥ים כִּֽי־תִשְׁפֹּ֣ט עַמִּ֣ים מִישֹׁ֑ור
וּלְאֻמִּ֓ים ׀ בָּאָ֖רֶץ תַּנְחֵ֣ם סֶֽלָה׃
6 יוֹד֖וּךָ עַמִּ֥ים ׀ אֱלֹהִ֑ים י֝וֹד֗וּךָ עַמִּ֥ים כֻּלָּֽם׃
7 אֶ֭רֶץ נָתְנָ֣ה יְבוּלָ֑הּ יְ֝בָרְכֵ֗נוּ אֱלֹהִ֥ים אֱלֹהֵֽינוּ׃
8 יְבָרְכֵ֥נוּ אֱלֹהִ֑ים וְיִֽירְא֥וּ א֝וֹת֗וֹ כָּל־אַפְסֵי־אָֽרֶץ׃

The author of the sixty-seventh psalm has written a short, slightly disjointed hymn with a refrain: *yodukha amim, Elohim / yodukha amim kulam* ("the nations will give thanks to You, O God / the nations, all of them, will give thanks to You"). Modern readers seeking to incorporate the sixty-seventh psalm into their devotional lives will want to use its recitation as an opportunity to consider the precise relationship between God, the Jewish people, and the nations of the world. The poet begins with a prayer for his nation, hoping aloud that God will be gracious to Israel, bless them, and cause the light of the divine countenance to shine down upon them. But then he switches gears and implies that it will be through contemplating God's caring governance of Israel that the nations of the world will come to believe in God's awesome power and will be moved to feelings of deep, permanent gratitude.

The poet appears to imply that Israel's mission is to be the happy recipient of divine beneficence so that the nations of the world can see what comes

67

For the choral conductor, a psalm-song.

[2] God shall be gracious unto us and bless us,
then illuminate the divine face for us, *selah.*

[3] And so shall Your way become known in the world, Your salvation among the world's peoples.

[4] The nations will give thanks to You, O God;
the nations, all of them, will give thanks to You.

[5] The countries of the world will rejoice and be glad, for You judge nations fairly and lead the countries of the world to justice, *selah.*

[6] The nations will give thanks to You, O God;
the nations, all of them, will give thanks to You.

[7] The world has yielded its bounty; may God, our God, bless us. [8]May God bless us and may even the peoples at the very ends of the earth hold God in awe as a result.

of being devoted to the service of God. Moderns uncertain if the world still works in precisely that way can still profit from a careful reading of the sixty-seventh psalm, however, by allowing its confident cadences to provoke them into asking what role they perceive for Israel among the nations of today's world. It is one thing, after all, to refer vaguely to the mission of Israel, but quite another to say specifically what that mission actually is. Does the place of the Jewish people in the world provide sufficient proof of God's caring governance to inspire nations without a history of monotheism to adopt faith in the one God? Any nation devoted to the service of God would, understandably, like to think that of itself. But whether it is entirely or just partially true—or whether it is nothing more than the most self-serving of flattering fantasies—is another question entirely.

סח

לַמְנַצֵּחַ לְדָוִד מִזְמוֹר שִׁיר:
2 יָקוּם אֱלֹהִים יָפוּצוּ אוֹיְבָיו וְיָנוּסוּ מְשַׂנְאָיו מִפָּנָיו:
3 כְּהִנְדֹּף עָשָׁן תִּנְדֹּף כְּהִמֵּס דּוֹנַג מִפְּנֵי־אֵשׁ יֹאבְדוּ
רְשָׁעִים מִפְּנֵי אֱלֹהִים: 4 וְצַדִּיקִים יִשְׂמְחוּ יַעַלְצוּ
לִפְנֵי אֱלֹהִים וְיָשִׂישׂוּ בְשִׂמְחָה:
5 שִׁירוּ | לֵאלֹהִים זַמְּרוּ שְׁמוֹ סֹלּוּ לָרֹכֵב בָּעֲרָבוֹת
בְּיָהּ שְׁמוֹ וְעִלְזוּ לְפָנָיו: 6 אֲבִי יְתוֹמִים וְדַיַּן
אַלְמָנוֹת אֱלֹהִים בִּמְעוֹן קָדְשׁוֹ: 7 אֱלֹהִים | מוֹשִׁיב
יְחִידִים | בַּיְתָה מוֹצִיא אֲסִירִים בַּכּוֹשָׁרוֹת
אַךְ־סוֹרְרִים שָׁכְנוּ צְחִיחָה:
8 אֱלֹהִים בְּצֵאתְךָ לִפְנֵי עַמֶּךָ בְּצַעְדְּךָ בִישִׁימוֹן
סֶלָה: 9 אֶרֶץ רָעָשָׁה | אַף־שָׁמַיִם נָטְפוּ מִפְּנֵי
אֱלֹהִים זֶה סִינַי מִפְּנֵי אֱלֹהִים אֱלֹהֵי יִשְׂרָאֵל:
10 גֶּשֶׁם נְדָבוֹת תָּנִיף אֱלֹהִים נַחֲלָתְךָ וְנִלְאָה אַתָּה
כוֹנַנְתָּהּ:
11 חַיָּתְךָ יָשְׁבוּ־בָהּ תָּכִין בְּטוֹבָתְךָ לֶעָנִי אֱלֹהִים:
12 אֲדֹנָי יִתֶּן־אֹמֶר הַמְבַשְּׂרוֹת צָבָא רָב: 13 מַלְכֵי
צְבָאוֹת יִדֹּדוּן יִדֹּדוּן וּנְוַת בַּיִת תְּחַלֵּק שָׁלָל:

In spite of its majestic use of language, the sixty-eighth psalm is relentlessly obscure in dozens of passages. Yet, for all its thorny riddles of word and phrase, a certain idea comes through from beginning to end: the history of the natural world and the course of human (and especially Jewish) events are two aspects of the same phenomenon of divine governance in the world. Thus, the liberation of Israel from Egyptian bondage was not only a historical event in the life of a specific people, but also a cosmic event with specific repercussions in heaven and on earth. Indeed, the people's emancipation from slavery effected all sorts of responses in nature: the earth quaked, Sinai trembled, and the sky drizzled down a refreshing rain on the newly-freed people. Similarly, the devotion Israel shows to the worship of God has potentially profound ramifications for others in God's world: if Israel's worship is sufficiently pure and intense, the nations of the world will be inspired to compose their own hymns of praise to God. And even the animals will be moved, despite their obvious intellectual and spiritual limitations, to whatever level of piety they are capable of attaining.

Moderns reading the sixty-eighth psalm in English will find it difficult to seize in parts, but the original Hebrew is no less hard to work through with any sort of precision or security. Still, the language has a grand, deeply moving quality in the original, and there is undeniable majesty to the idea that the

68

For the conductor, a psalm-song of David.
[2] May God rise up and let the enemies of the Almighty be scattered; let those who hate God flee from before the divine face.
[3] May the wicked vanish before God like smoke that drifts away, like wax that melts when exposed to flame. [4]But may the righteous rejoice and exult before God; may they experience pure joy.
[5] Sing to God, chant hymns to God's name; sing melodies to the Rider upon the Heavens using the divine name יה and exult before our God, [6]before that God who is a parent to orphans and the just judge of widows, God who dwells in the holy, divine residence, [7]God who provides a home for the lonely, who brings forth those imprisoned in chains, who grants relief even to those brigands who dwell in the parched desert.
[8] God, when You went out before Your people, when You strode into the wilderness, *selah,* [9]the earth shook and the heavens began to melt in the presence of God; even Sinai trembled in the presence of God, the God of Israel.
[10] With generous rainfall did You shower Your inheritance, O God; when the people of Your inheritance wearied, You sustained them.
[11] When Your clan settled there, You readied the land with Your goodness for the poor, O God.
[12] Adonai would give the word and a mighty host of women would proclaim it; [13]the kings of armies wandered the earth endlessly, while the home front shared out the spoil.

quest for personal deliverance is paralleled both on a national level, by a people's search for security, and also on a cosmic level, by the various phenomena of the natural world yearning to come to their own state of equilibrium. The integration of an individual's quest for personal salvation, a nation's desire to live in peace, and the growth of all natural things towards balance and graceful symmetry is at the heart of the poet's message. Moderns, however, will want to ask themselves how to translate that kind of poetic vision into the stuff of useful spirituality. We tend to make a fairly absolute distinction in our thinking between the animate beings of the world and its inanimate things. The poet is suggesting, however, that the quality of createdness by God unites the things and the beings of the

14 אִם־תִּשְׁכְּבוּן בֵּין שְׁפַתָּיִם כַּנְפֵי יוֹנָה נֶחְפָּה בַכֶּסֶף וְאֶבְרוֹתֶיהָ בִּירַקְרַק חָרוּץ׃
15 בְּפָרֵשׂ שַׁדַּי מְלָכִים בָּהּ תַּשְׁלֵג בְּצַלְמוֹן׃
16 הַר־אֱלֹהִים הַר־בָּשָׁן הַר־גַּבְנֻנִּים הַר־בָּשָׁן׃
17 לָמָּה ׀ תְּרַצְּדוּן הָרִים גַּבְנֻנִּים הָהָר חָמַד אֱלֹהִים לְשִׁבְתּוֹ אַף־יְהֹוָה יִשְׁכֹּן לָנֶצַח׃
18 רֶכֶב אֱלֹהִים רִבֹּתַיִם אַלְפֵי שִׁנְאָן אֲדֹנָי בָם סִינַי בַּקֹּדֶשׁ׃
19 עָלִיתָ לַמָּרוֹם ׀ שָׁבִיתָ שֶּׁבִי לָקַחְתָּ מַתָּנוֹת בָּאָדָם וְאַף סוֹרְרִים לִשְׁכֹּן ׀ יָהּ אֱלֹהִים׃
20 בָּרוּךְ אֲדֹנָי יוֹם ׀ יוֹם יַעֲמָס־לָנוּ הָאֵל יְשׁוּעָתֵנוּ סֶלָה׃
21 הָאֵל ׀ לָנוּ אֵל לְמוֹשָׁעוֹת וְלֵיהוִֹה אֲדֹנָי לַמָּוֶת תּוֹצָאוֹת׃
22 אַךְ־אֱלֹהִים יִמְחַץ רֹאשׁ אֹיְבָיו קָדְקֹד שֵׂעָר מִתְהַלֵּךְ בַּאֲשָׁמָיו׃
23 אָמַר אֲדֹנָי מִבָּשָׁן אָשִׁיב אָשִׁיב מִמְּצֻלוֹת יָם׃
24 לְמַעַן ׀ תִּמְחַץ רַגְלְךָ בְּדָם לְשׁוֹן כְּלָבֶיךָ מֵאוֹיְבִים מִנֵּהוּ׃

world far more potently than the absence of consciousness separates some of those creations from some others. When the kings of evil kingdoms are defeated, it is not, after all, only the living creatures in those kingdoms whose lots in life are altered: the doves taken home by the victors as booty may end up with silvered wings, but the trembling of distant mountaintops also attests to the triumph of good. Can moderns imagine a universe so in rhythm with itself that it functions totally around the effort to make decency prevail? Can we moderns learn to feel true kinship with the other created things of the world? Belief in God the Creator, the poet implies, seems to require no less. But what will moderns make of the notion of an ecology of faith that links *all* existent things, living and inanimate, in God?

In order best to profit from a contemplative perusal of the 68th psalm, then, modern readers will have to consider carefully how they view the physical universe itself. Must the universe be seen as a collection of things linked solely by their common existence within a set of shared spatial and temporal coordinates, or can it reasonably be interpreted as a divine symphony of complex creative endeavor? If the latter is the case, then what is the relationship between moral values and the physical existence of things: do the inanimate parts of the world exist to serve God in any way analogous to the manner in

[14] And so did they proclaim: "Even if you lie down between the sheepfolds, you will still go home with treasures: doves' wings overlaid with silver, doves' pinions plated with pale green gold.

[15] When Shaddai scattered the kings in the land, it was like a Zalmon snowstorm of defeated monarchs.

[16] O godlike mountain, Mount Bashan; O mountain of jagged peaks, Mount Bashan, [17]why are you trembling? O range of jagged mountain peaks, is it out of envy of the mountain God has desired to inhabit that you tremble, that place where יהוה will dwell forever?

[18] The chariots of God ran to the tens of thousands driven by thousands of angels; Adonai was in them all, as God was later on Sinai and is in the Sanctuary.

[19] It was as though You went up to the heights and took captives there; You took gifts from humankind, even from brigands, that יה-Elohim might dwell there.

[20] Blessed be Adonai, who day by day bears our burden and who is the God of our salvation, *selah*.

[21] Our God is a God of saving acts; יהוה-Adonai is the provider of rescue from death.

[22] For the Almighty shall crush the heads of God's enemies, the hirsute skulls of all who walk about with no thought of hiding their guilty acts.

[23] Adonai says, "I will bring My enemies back from Bashan, I shall bring them back from the depths of the sea, [24]so that you may stamp down your foot in their blood, so that the tongues of your dogs may have a meal out of those enemies."

which human beings (and possibly even animals) do?

Leaving his readers to ponder what exactly it would mean, for example, for a mountain range to tremble out of frustration when God chooses to settle the divine glory on a different peak, the poet imagines the nations of the world taking their places among the other things of God's Creation and responding, both positively and negatively, to the election of Israel. Are nations more like inanimate created things than they are like individual people? The poet seems to think so, and his sense of the spiritual geopolitics of his world flows directly from that insight. The countries of the world—the nations that choose either to treat

25 רָאוּ הֲלִיכוֹתֶיךָ אֱלֹהִים הֲלִיכוֹת אֵלִי מַלְכִּי
בַקֹּדֶשׁ׃ 26 קִדְּמוּ שָׁרִים אַחַר נֹגְנִים בְּתוֹךְ עֲלָמוֹת
תּוֹפֵפוֹת׃ 27 בְּמַקְהֵלוֹת בָּרְכוּ אֱלֹהִים יְהוָה
מִמְּקוֹר יִשְׂרָאֵל׃
28 שָׁם בִּנְיָמִן ׀ צָעִיר רֹדֵם שָׂרֵי יְהוּדָה רִגְמָתָם שָׂרֵי
זְבֻלוּן שָׂרֵי נַפְתָּלִי׃
29 צִוָּה אֱלֹהֶיךָ עֻזֶּךָ עוּזָּה אֱלֹהִים זוּ פָּעַלְתָּ לָּנוּ׃
30 מֵהֵיכָלֶךָ עַל־יְרוּשָׁלָםִ לְךָ יוֹבִילוּ מְלָכִים שָׁי׃
31 גְּעַר חַיַּת קָנֶה עֲדַת אַבִּירִים ׀ בְּעֶגְלֵי עַמִּים
מִתְרַפֵּס בְּרַצֵּי־כָסֶף בִּזַּר עַמִּים קְרָבוֹת יֶחְפָּצוּ׃
32 יֶאֱתָיוּ חַשְׁמַנִּים מִנִּי מִצְרָיִם כּוּשׁ תָּרִיץ יָדָיו
לֵאלֹהִים׃
33 מַמְלְכוֹת הָאָרֶץ שִׁירוּ לֵאלֹהִים זַמְּרוּ אֲדֹנָי סֶלָה׃
34 לָרֹכֵב בִּשְׁמֵי שְׁמֵי־קֶדֶם הֵן־יִתֵּן בְּקוֹלוֹ קוֹל עֹז׃
35 תְּנוּ עֹז לֵאלֹהִים עַל־יִשְׂרָאֵל גַּאֲוָתוֹ וְעֻזּוֹ
בַּשְּׁחָקִים׃
36 נוֹרָא אֱלֹהִים מִמִּקְדָּשֶׁיךָ אֵל יִשְׂרָאֵל הוּא נֹתֵן ׀ עֹז
וְתַעֲצֻמוֹת לָעָם בָּרוּךְ אֱלֹהִים׃

Israel with respect and deference or to make themselves into Israel's enemies—are, in the poet's conception, a reflection of the physical universe. Like human beings able to live in obedience to God's word, and like the things of the universe that are able to flourish harmoniously in conformity with the natural laws imposed by God on Creation, the nations of the world have a deep and profoundly meaningful decision to make as they chart their national policies towards the Jewish people. Will they be responsive to the fate of Israel in a way that will grant them some sort of ancillary role in the unfolding relationship between God and God's people? Will they seek to find balance and purpose in their own national lives by attempting to live in harmony not solely with the people Israel itself, but also with the set of divine promises and guarantees bestowed by God on Israel? Will the nations of the world unwittingly use hostility towards Israel to estrange themselves from God? Or will they utilize their national policy towards Israel to come ever closer to embracing their own destinies in God through their acceptance of God's plan for the Jewish people?

Modern readers may find the poet's fundamental assumption that the nations of the world exist in a kind of delicate counterpoint with the divine design for Israel more than a bit dismissive of the natural rights of those nations to chart their own national courses. For citizens of democratic states schooled

[25] When they saw Your deeds, O God—the deeds of my God, my Sovereign of the Sanctuary—[26] the singers came along right after the musicians, all of them amidst the maiden drummers; [27] in choirs did they bless Elohim, Adonai from the wellsprings of Israel.

[28] There is young Benjamin ruling over the princes of Judah gathered together with their allies, the princes of Zebulun and the princes of Naftali.

[29] Your God has bequeathed us strength, the divine strength that you have procured for us. [30] From your palace overlooking Jerusalem to which the kings of the world bring You tribute, [31] from that place, scold that beast of the reeds, the congregation of oxen among the calves of the nations that submits for a few pieces of silver. Scatter the nations that delight in war.

[32] The most impressive gifts shall come from Egypt; even Ethiopia will stretch out her hand to God.

[33] Sing unto God, O kingdoms of the earth; chant hymns to Adonai, *selah*, [34] to the One who rides on the most exalted layer of primeval heaven, to the One who gives forth with a mighty voice, the voice of God.

[35] Ascribe strength to God, whose pride is in Israel and whose strength is manifest in the heavens.

[36] God, You are awe-inspiring when You come forth from Your sanctuaries; it is the God of Israel who grants strength and power to the people. Blessed be God.

in the principle that nations have a basic and inalienable right to pursue their national fortunes according to their own lights, the concept that those nations' success will inevitably be a function of the degree to which they exist in harmony with (or in opposition to) God's plan for Israel will always be offensive. For the poet, the idea rang true and fit in nicely with his sense of all Creation acting in concert to affirm God's rule on earth. Moderns who feel certain that the fate of Israel is a matter of cosmic significance, but who find the poet's assumptions about the other nations troublesome, will therefore have to find their own way to answer the question the poet leaves for his readers to ponder: if the destiny of other peoples does *not* actually depend on their relationship to Israel, then what exactly does it mean for Israel to exist in its special relationship with the God of all nations?

סט

לַמְנַצֵּחַ עַל־שׁוֹשַׁנִּים לְדָוִד׃
2 הוֹשִׁיעֵנִי אֱלֹהִים כִּי בָאוּ מַיִם עַד־נָפֶשׁ׃
3 טָבַעְתִּי בִּיוֵן מְצוּלָה וְאֵין מָעֳמָד בָּאתִי בְמַעֲמַקֵּי־מַיִם וְשִׁבֹּלֶת שְׁטָפָתְנִי׃
4 יָגַעְתִּי בְקָרְאִי נִחַר גְּרוֹנִי כָּלוּ עֵינַי מְיַחֵל לֵאלֹהָי׃
5 רַבּוּ ׀ מִשַּׂעֲרוֹת רֹאשִׁי שֹׂנְאַי חִנָּם עָצְמוּ מַצְמִיתַי אֹיְבַי שֶׁקֶר אֲשֶׁר לֹא־גָזַלְתִּי אָז אָשִׁיב׃
6 אֱלֹהִים אַתָּה יָדַעְתָּ לְאִוַּלְתִּי וְאַשְׁמוֹתַי מִמְּךָ לֹא־נִכְחָדוּ׃
7 אַל־יֵבֹשׁוּ בִי ׀ קֹוֶיךָ אֲדֹנָי יְהוִה צְבָאוֹת אַל־יִכָּלְמוּ בִי מְבַקְשֶׁיךָ אֱלֹהֵי יִשְׂרָאֵל׃
8 כִּי־עָלֶיךָ נָשָׂאתִי חֶרְפָּה כִּסְּתָה כְלִמָּה פָנָי׃
9 מוּזָר הָיִיתִי לְאֶחָי וְנָכְרִי לִבְנֵי אִמִּי׃ 10 כִּי־קִנְאַת בֵּיתְךָ אֲכָלָתְנִי וְחֶרְפּוֹת חוֹרְפֶיךָ נָפְלוּ עָלָי׃
11 וָאֶבְכֶּה בַצּוֹם נַפְשִׁי וַתְּהִי לַחֲרָפוֹת לִי׃ 12 וָאֶתְּנָה לְבוּשִׁי שָׂק וָאֱהִי לָהֶם לְמָשָׁל׃ 13 יָשִׂיחוּ בִי יֹשְׁבֵי שָׁעַר וּנְגִינוֹת שׁוֹתֵי שֵׁכָר׃

Many of the psalmists write about being afraid for their personal security, about being worried about the plots their enemies may be hatching against them, and about feeling bereft and abandoned by the very people to whom they once looked confidently for succor and support. Still, only a few of the ancient authors whose works became the poetry of the Book of Psalms approach the depths of pathos and misery—or the spiritual audacity and insight—attained by the author of the sixty-ninth psalm. The poet imagines himself to be a drowning man slowly watching the level of the water rising around him and knowing that he is experiencing the last few moments of his life. As would befit a man in the throes of death, the images that crowd his consciousness switch rapidly from one to the next as though he were having a terrifying dream. First he is drowning, but a moment later he is sinking into a pit of bottomless mud. Then he is facing death by water again, only this time he is not watching the water level rise, but trying to maintain his balance in a current so swift that he knows with awful certainty it will wash him away momentarily.

The poet's horrifying fantasies mirror the awfulness of his actual situation. He has been totally abandoned, not merely by fair-weather friends but even by his own family, and he writes with acidulous bitterness of his almost total estrangement from his own brothers. Yet it is the reason he gives for that es-

69

For the conductor, a psalm of David to the tune of "Lilies."

[2] Save me, O God, for the water level is rising to the point of mortal danger.

[3] I am drowning in mud so deep I cannot stand up in it; I am in the deepest water and a strong current is threatening to wash me away.

[4] I am weary with crying out and my throat is sore; my eyes have run out of tears as I hope for my God.

[5] Those who hate me without cause outnumber the hairs on my head; those who would destroy me, enemies for no real reason, are many. Shall I give back what I have not stolen in the first place?

[6] God, You know my wickedness and my guilty offenses are not hidden from You.

[7] Let not those who trust in You be shamed by what happens to me, O Adonai-יהוה of the celestial legions; let people who seek You not be embarrassed by my fate, O God of Israel.

[8] For because of my faith in You, I am suffering this degradation and embarrassment covers my face.

[9] I am estranged from my own brothers; the children of my own mother think of me as a foreigner [10] because zeal for Your house has consumed me and degradation by those seeking to degrade You has befallen me.

[11] I weep as my soul fasts, becoming a source of degradation even to me myself; [12] I only give myself sackcloth to wear that I might be an example to others, [13] so that those who sit in the city gate can discuss me and drunkards can sing of my wretched fate.

trangement that is the most shocking: he has been shut out by his own kinsmen not because of his sinful or criminal ways, but because of their embarrassment over the depth of his religious zeal and, especially, the degree of his devotion to the Temple. And it is not only members of the poet's own family that oppose him. Indeed, he writes that the number of people in Jerusalem who loathe him outnumber the hairs on his weary head.

We will never know the specific circumstances that led the poet to attribute his horrific degradation to his allegiance to God, but moderns reading the sixty-ninth psalm may

14 וַאֲנִי תְפִלָּתִי־לְךָ ׀ יְהוָה עֵת רָצוֹן אֱלֹהִים בְּרָב־
חַסְדֶּךָ עֲנֵנִי בֶּאֱמֶת יִשְׁעֶךָ׃
15 הַצִּילֵנִי מִטִּיט וְאַל־אֶטְבָּעָה אִנָּצְלָה מִשֹּׂנְאַי
וּמִמַּעֲמַקֵּי־מָיִם׃
16 אַל־תִּשְׁטְפֵנִי ׀ שִׁבֹּלֶת מַיִם וְאַל־תִּבְלָעֵנִי מְצוּלָה
וְאַל־תֶּאְטַר עָלַי בְּאֵר פִּיהָ׃
17 עֲנֵנִי יְהוָה כִּי־טוֹב חַסְדֶּךָ כְּרֹב רַחֲמֶיךָ פְּנֵה אֵלָי׃
18 וְאַל־תַּסְתֵּר פָּנֶיךָ מֵעַבְדֶּךָ כִּי־צַר־לִי מַהֵר עֲנֵנִי׃
19 קָרְבָה אֶל־נַפְשִׁי גְאָלָהּ לְמַעַן אֹיְבַי פְּדֵנִי׃
20 אַתָּה יָדַעְתָּ חֶרְפָּתִי וּבָשְׁתִּי וּכְלִמָּתִי נֶגְדְּךָ
כָּל־צוֹרְרָי׃
21 חֶרְפָּה ׀ שָׁבְרָה לִבִּי וָאָנוּשָׁה וָאֲקַוֶּה לָנוּד וָאַיִן
וְלַמְנַחֲמִים וְלֹא מָצָאתִי׃
22 וַיִּתְּנוּ בְּבָרוּתִי רֹאשׁ וְלִצְמָאִי יַשְׁקוּנִי חֹמֶץ׃
23 יְהִי שֻׁלְחָנָם לִפְנֵיהֶם לְפָח וְלִשְׁלוֹמִים לְמוֹקֵשׁ׃
24 תֶּחְשַׁכְנָה עֵינֵיהֶם מֵרְאוֹת וּמָתְנֵיהֶם תָּמִיד
הַמְעַד׃
25 שְׁפָךְ־עֲלֵיהֶם זַעְמֶךָ וַחֲרוֹן אַפְּךָ יַשִּׂיגֵם׃
26 תְּהִי־טִירָתָם נְשַׁמָּה בְּאָהֳלֵיהֶם אַל־יְהִי יֹשֵׁב׃

well wish to respond to the poet's plight by asking themselves if they are annoyed or inspired by people whose faith is deeper and more secure than their own. The definition of "religious maniac" as someone more devout than oneself is not quite as funny as it ought to be and, indeed, there are many people who are intensely irritated, or even angered, to find themselves in the company of people of stricter observance than their own. Must the pious lie about the depth of their faith if they are to survive in a world filled with people who claim to esteem religious commitment, but who are actually unnerved and put off by strict adherence to dogma and ritual? (Is that what the poet means when he asks sarcastically if he must indeed give back that which he had not stolen?) Moderns will also want to ponder the question that lies at the heart of the matter: does faith originate in the heart or in the mind? Or does it have its true origins in the uncontrollable, and so quintessentially human, need to love and to be loved by God? But if that were the case, then how could people of faith ever know whether they have embraced a higher reality or have merely fallen prey to a very satisfying delusion? The answer to that question, obviously, will vary from person to person, but the best model for understanding the love of God will always be

[14] But my prayer is directed to You, יהוה; let this be a propitious time for supplication. God, in the abundance of Your mercy, answer me with the truth of Your salvation.

[15] Save me from the mud so that I do not drown, so that I may be saved both from those who hate me and from the depths of the waters.

[16] Let not the swift current of water wash me away nor let the depths swallow me up; let not the well close its mouth over me.

[17] Answer me, יהוה, for Your mercy is good; turn to me in accordance with Your great compassion.

[18] Turn not Your face away from Your servant, for I am in distress; answer me speedily!

[19] May my soul's redemption draw close; rescue me from the grasp of my enemies.

[20] You know my degradation and my shame and my embarrassment; all of my foes stand out before You.

[21] Degradation has broken my heart to the point of making me ill; I hoped to flee, but there was no possibility of escape. I hoped for someone to comfort me, but I found no one at all.

[22] They put gall in my food; when I am thirsty, they give me vinegar to drink.

[23] Let their table become a trap for them, a snare for their allies.

[24] May their eyesight become too dim for them to see; may their hips constantly dislocate.

[25] Pour out Your wrath on them and may Your fury overtake them.

[26] May their castle be destroyed; let there not be even a single inhabitant in their tents.

the love between human lovers. There is, after all, a certain basic blindness that all affects all lovers at the beginning of any relationship's trajectory, as the parties involved struggle to determine whether they have found true love or have merely given themselves over to the fantasy that they have. Eventually though, as weeks and months pass and love sets down roots in both lovers' psyches and grows into every corner of their consciousnesses, the insecurity passes. And, as months turn into years and decades, lovers eventually do accept the reality of love in their lives, even though that love can neither be

27 כִּֽי־אַתָּ֣ה אֲשֶׁר־הִכִּ֣יתָ רָדָ֑פוּ וְאֶל־מַכְא֖וֹב חֲלָלֶ֣יךָ יְסַפֵּֽרוּ׃
28 תְּֽנָה־עָ֭וֺן עַל־עֲוֺנָ֑ם וְאַל־יָ֝בֹ֗אוּ בְּצִדְקָתֶֽךָ׃
29 יִ֭מָּחוּ מִסֵּ֣פֶר חַיִּ֑ים וְעִ֥ם צַ֝דִּיקִ֗ים אַל־יִכָּתֵֽבוּ׃
30 וַ֭אֲנִי עָנִ֣י וְכוֹאֵ֑ב יְשׁוּעָתְךָ֖ אֱלֹהִ֣ים תְּשַׂגְּבֵֽנִי׃
31 אֲהַֽלְלָ֣ה שֵׁם־אֱלֹהִ֣ים בְּשִׁ֑יר וַאֲגַדְּלֶ֥נּוּ בְתוֹדָֽה׃
32 וְתִיטַ֣ב לַ֭יהוָה מִשּׁ֥וֹר פָּ֗ר מַקְרִ֥ן מַפְרִֽיס׃
33 רָא֣וּ עֲנָוִ֣ים יִשְׂמָ֑חוּ דֹּרְשֵׁ֥י אֱ֝לֹהִ֗ים וִיחִ֥י לְבַבְכֶֽם׃
34 כִּֽי־שֹׁמֵ֣עַ אֶל־אֶבְיוֹנִ֣ים יְהוָ֑ה וְאֶת־אֲ֝סִירָ֗יו לֹ֣א בָזָֽה׃
35 יְ֭הַלְלוּהוּ שָׁמַ֣יִם וָאָ֑רֶץ יַ֝מִּ֗ים וְכָל־רֹמֵ֥שׂ בָּֽם׃
36 כִּ֤י אֱלֹהִ֨ים ׀ י֘וֹשִׁ֤יעַ צִיּ֗וֹן וְ֭יִבְנֶה עָרֵ֣י יְהוּדָ֑ה וְיָ֥שְׁבוּ שָׁ֝֗ם וִירֵשֽׁוּהָ׃ 37 וְזֶ֣רַע עֲ֭בָדָיו יִנְחָל֑וּהָ וְאֹהֲבֵ֥י שְׁ֝מ֗וֹ יִשְׁכְּנוּ־בָֽהּ׃

proven scientifically nor demonstrated unconditionally to exist. Indeed, love can only be perceived because it is experienced by the parties involved as a blending of human connectedness, emotional involvement, and sensual intimacy so totally real for its existence to feel axiomatic. Can that model also hold true for people seeking to embrace faith in God? It can, surely, for people like the poet whose poem became our 69th psalm, people for whom the reality of God's love is so overpowering—and so totally, completely present in every aspect of their lives—for its existence to be absolutely self-evident in the same way that lovers feel the existence of their love to be indisputable and undeniable. But what of the rest of the world?

Modern readers may wish to use the anguished lines of the 69th psalm as a kind of impetus to compare the kind of belief that passes for faith in God in our world with the passion of lovers. We talk, for example, about having faith in God, about believing in God, about embracing God's reality in our daily lives . . . but how many of us would find it as preposterous to debate God's existence as lovers would find it absurd to discuss whether or not their emotions are genuine? How many of us believe in God with the same absolute conviction that we believe that the furniture in our living rooms exists? Or, for that matter, that we ourselves do? The poet's kind of bedrock faith in divine reality makes people no less nervous in our spiritually ambivalent world than it apparently did in his day, but the poet does not appear to be even slightly unnerved by the firmness of his faith. Just to the contrary, his faith in God was the balm that made the poet's misery bearable, and the only effective

[27] Do this so that those whom You smite will flee and tell of the pain suffered by those who will have already died.

[28] Add sins on top of the sins they have already perpetrated; let them never atone sufficiently for You to consider them righteous.

[29] May they be erased from the book of the living and not written up with the righteous.

[30] For I am poor and in pain; only Your salvation, O God, will lift me up.

[31] I shall praise God's name with song; I shall magnify God with hymns of thanksgiving [32]that will please יהוה more than an ox or a bull or any beast of horn and hoof.

[33] The humble shall see and rejoice; you who seek God, may your hearts revive, [34]for יהוה listens to the prayers of the poverty-stricken and will never despise those who suffer imprisonment because of their faith.

[35] Let heaven and earth, the seas and all that swims in them, praise God.

[36–37] For God will save Zion and rebuild the cities of Judah; the descendants of God's servants will live there and inherit it, even acquire it finally as an inheritance, for those who love God's name shall dwell there.

antidote to the insults and physical tortures he was obliged to undergo because of the depth of his passion for God and for the service of God.

But how *will* moderns respond to that kind of spiritual model? The poet's faith must have struck him as no less real than anything else he deemed truly to exist in his world, and it was that spiritual bearing that gave him the strength to harness his unhappiness and to find within it the creative literary energy necessary to produce a work of the depth and pathos of the 69th psalm. Moderns will be easily moved by the poet's words, but may not find it entirely pleasant to let those same words challenge them and goad them into analyzing and evaluating their own relationship to faith, hence to God. Can moderns aspire to the psalmist's kind of belief? Surely they can . . . and there does not seem to be any obvious reason why they could not attain it as well. Why, then, does the kind of faith in God of which the poet wrote *feel* so elusive to moderns . . . and often no less so to those devoted to the rituals of faith than to those distant from observance?

ע

לַמְנַצֵּחַ לְדָוִד לְהַזְכִּיר׃
2 אֱלֹהִים לְהַצִּילֵנִי יְהוָה לְעֶזְרָתִי חוּשָׁה׃
3 יֵבֹשׁוּ וְיַחְפְּרוּ מְבַקְשֵׁי נַפְשִׁי יִסֹּגוּ אָחוֹר וְיִכָּלְמוּ חֲפֵצֵי רָעָתִי׃ 4 יָשׁוּבוּ עַל־עֵקֶב בָּשְׁתָּם הָאֹמְרִים הֶאָח ׀ הֶאָח׃
5 יָשִׂישׂוּ וְיִשְׂמְחוּ ׀ בְּךָ כָּל־מְבַקְשֶׁיךָ וְיֹאמְרוּ תָמִיד יִגְדַּל אֱלֹהִים אֹהֲבֵי יְשׁוּעָתֶךָ׃
6 וַאֲנִי ׀ עָנִי וְאֶבְיוֹן אֱלֹהִים חוּשָׁה־לִּי עֶזְרִי וּמְפַלְטִי אַתָּה יְהוָה אַל־תְּאַחַר׃

The body of the seventieth psalm is essentially identical to the last five verses of the fortieth, but it has been preserved in our Psalter as a poem in its own right. The background furnished by the original setting is not essential to appreciating this version of the poet's words, however. To be sure, knowing whether the poet's description of himself as poor and indigent was meant literally or figuratively could help the reader appreciate the reasons he came to feel the way he did about the world. Yet, the poem stands well on its own even absent the larger picture as a kind of hymn to resignation born of pain and suffering. The poet contrasts two groups of citizens: the good and the evil, the righteous and the wicked. Of the righteous, he notes several defining characteristics: they seek God, they constantly say *yigdal Elohim* ("God be great"), and they love the prospect of deliverance in God. And the wicked, here exemplified by the poet's own enemies, also have their own defining characteristics: they hate the poet and wish him nothing but ill—presumably on account of his piety and the freedom with which he proclaims the word of God. Moreover, they are prepared to back up their loathing with acts of real physical violence, even to the point of murder. Worse

70 For the conductor, a memorial-psalm of David.
[2] Hurry, O God, to save me; יהוה, hasten to my aid.
[3] Let those who are seeking to kill me be ashamed, even humiliated; may those whose only desire is to do me evil retreat and be mortified. [4] May those who greet my misery with calls of "Hurrah! Hurrah!" be shamed, then destroyed altogether.
[5] But may all who seek You rejoice and be glad; may those who love the prospect of Your deliverance always say, "God be great."
[6] And as for poor, indigent me—O God, hurry to me, for You are my help and my refuge; O יהוה, do not delay!

still, they eschew any attempt to make peace through dialogue, preferring to jeer openly at the poet in his misery in the manner of sports fans cheering a favorite athlete on to victory.

In between these two groups stands the poet, poor and lonely, driven to proclaim the word of God and willing to suffer the indignities that come with such freedom of speech, but also afraid and deeply worried about what might actually befall him as a consequence of his own eloquence. His solution—to call on God to save him—is moving in its own right, but can also serve as a springboard for modern readers considering the world in which they live. Does the poet's notion of a world divided into camps of good and evil apply to our world as well? Are people in our world either individuals of violence and hate *or* seekers of God whose only hope is for divine deliverance? If we consider our world to be far more complex than the poet's simple model of two opposing camps, then how, precisely, do we think our world is structured? Can a person be in both camps at the same time? Can one embrace both good and evil? Can one search for God sometimes and seek to murder poets at others?

עא

בְּךָ־יְהוָה חָסִיתִי אַל־אֵבוֹשָׁה לְעוֹלָם׃

2 בְּצִדְקָתְךָ תַּצִּילֵנִי וּתְפַלְּטֵנִי הַטֵּה־אֵלַי אָזְנְךָ וְהוֹשִׁיעֵנִי׃

3 הֱיֵה לִי ׀ לְצוּר מָעוֹן לָבוֹא תָּמִיד צִוִּיתָ לְהוֹשִׁיעֵנִי כִּי־סַלְעִי וּמְצוּדָתִי אָתָּה׃

4 אֱלֹהַי פַּלְּטֵנִי מִיַּד רָשָׁע מִכַּף מְעַוֵּל וְחוֹמֵץ׃

5 כִּי־אַתָּה תִקְוָתִי אֲדֹנָי יֱהוִה מִבְטַחִי מִנְּעוּרָי׃

6 עָלֶיךָ ׀ נִסְמַכְתִּי מִבֶּטֶן מִמְּעֵי אִמִּי אַתָּה גוֹזִי בְּךָ תְהִלָּתִי תָמִיד׃

7 כְּמוֹפֵת הָיִיתִי לְרַבִּים וְאַתָּה מַחֲסִי־עֹז׃

8 יִמָּלֵא פִי תְּהִלָּתֶךָ כָּל־הַיּוֹם תִּפְאַרְתֶּךָ׃

9 אַל־תַּשְׁלִיכֵנִי לְעֵת זִקְנָה כִּכְלוֹת כֹּחִי אַל־תַּעַזְבֵנִי׃

10 כִּי־אָמְרוּ אוֹיְבַי לִי וְשֹׁמְרֵי נַפְשִׁי נוֹעֲצוּ יַחְדָּו׃

11 לֵאמֹר אֱלֹהִים עֲזָבוֹ רִדְפוּ וְתִפְשׂוּהוּ כִּי אֵין מַצִּיל׃

12 אֱלֹהִים אַל־תִּרְחַק מִמֶּנִּי אֱלֹהַי לְעֶזְרָתִי *חוּשָׁה׃

13 יֵבֹשׁוּ יִכְלוּ שֹׂטְנֵי נַפְשִׁי יַעֲטוּ חֶרְפָּה וּכְלִמָּה מְבַקְשֵׁי רָעָתִי׃

v. 12 חישה כתיב

Although the seventy-first psalm echoes themes that are developed in many different places in the Book of Psalms, and although the first few verses seem almost to be an alternate version of the opening verses of the thirty-first psalm, the poem presents its own cogent message of faith in the face of adversity and sadness. The poet writes as an older man looking back on his youth as he faces implacable hostility on the part of violent enemies in his later years. Considering his situation carefully, the poet attributes his faith in God's saving power to his having been taught to trust absolutely in the beneficence of the Divine as a very young child—even (the poet notes with a bit of hyperbole) while he was still an embryo in his mother's womb—and not from some sort of unanticipated latter-day conversion to religion. And the lesson was well learned: the poet feels perfectly certain that God will save him from his foes and cause those who would do him ill to suffer shame, embarrassment, and disgrace.

Moderns reading the seventy-first psalm will want to ask themselves if that kind of certainty in the benevolent governance of God can *ever* come to people whose faith was not inculcated in early childhood. Is it possible for people who grow up uncertain about God's role in the world ever to come to think of

71

In You, יהוה, have I sought refuge; may I never be ashamed.

[2] Save me, rescue me with Your righteousness; incline Your ear towards me and deliver me.

[3] Become my stone-fortified residence, the place to which I can always come, the place You have willed to be the site of my deliverance—for You are my Rock and my Fortress.

[4] O my God, rescue me from the hand of the wicked individual, from the grasp of the doer of iniquity, from the violent churl.

[5] For You are my hope, Adonai-יהוה, my stronghold since the days of my youth.

[6] I have leaned on You since the womb; You have been my support since you brought me forth from my mother's belly; my words of praise have always been about You.

[7] I have been a wonder in the eyes of many, but You are my secure haven.

[8] Let my mouth be filled with Your praise, with the telling of Your splendor all day long.

[9] Do not cast me away in old age; when my strength ebbs, do not abandon me.

[10] For my enemies are speaking about me. Those who stake out my soul are taking counsel together [11] and saying, "God has forsaken him. Pursue and grab him, for there is no one to save him."

[12] O God, do not distance Yourself from me; my God, hurry to my assistance.

[13] Let those who loathe my soul vanish in embarrassment; let those who seek to do me evil be enshrouded with shame and ignominy.

God as their personal fortress and place of ultimate refuge? The poet knows of no such difficulties, but most moderns will have to face them eventually if they wish to become (or remain) people of faith. Most moderns accept that doubting and questioning are part of any thinking person's spiritual life and may be, therefore, not quite sure how to categorize the kind of bedrock faith of which the psalmist writes so openly. Surely, certainty about God is a positive goal towards which thinking people who embrace religion will wish to work . . . but even holding out that kind of faith as a *theoretically* attainable goal leads almost inevitably to some provocative questions. Can moderns *actually* hope to attain it? Does that kind of

14 וַאֲנִי תָּמִיד אֲיַחֵל וְהוֹסַפְתִּי עַל־כָּל־תְּהִלָּתֶךָ׃
15 פִּי ׀ יְסַפֵּר צִדְקָתֶךָ כָּל־הַיּוֹם תְּשׁוּעָתֶךָ כִּי לֹא
יָדַעְתִּי סְפֹרוֹת׃
16 אָבוֹא בִּגְבֻרוֹת אֲדֹנָי יְהוִה אַזְכִּיר צִדְקָתְךָ לְבַדֶּךָ׃
17 אֱלֹהִים לִמַּדְתַּנִי מִנְּעוּרָי וְעַד־הֵנָּה אַגִּיד
נִפְלְאוֹתֶיךָ׃
18 וְגַם עַד־זִקְנָה ׀ וְשֵׂיבָה אֱלֹהִים אַל־תַּעַזְבֵנִי
עַד־אַגִּיד זְרוֹעֲךָ לְדוֹר לְכָל־יָבוֹא גְּבוּרָתֶךָ׃
19 וְצִדְקָתְךָ אֱלֹהִים עַד־מָרוֹם אֲשֶׁר־עָשִׂיתָ גְדֹלוֹת
אֱלֹהִים מִי כָמוֹךָ׃
20 אֲשֶׁר *הִרְאִיתַנִי ׀ צָרוֹת רַבּוֹת וְרָעוֹת תָּשׁוּב
*תְּחַיֵּינִי וּמִתְּהֹמוֹת הָאָרֶץ תָּשׁוּב *תַּעֲלֵנִי׃
21 תֶּרֶב ׀ גְּדֻלָּתִי וְתִסֹּב תְּנַחֲמֵנִי׃
22 גַּם־אֲנִי ׀ אוֹדְךָ בִכְלִי־נֶבֶל אֲמִתְּךָ אֱלֹהָי אֲזַמְּרָה
לְךָ בְכִנּוֹר קְדוֹשׁ יִשְׂרָאֵל׃
23 תְּרַנֵּנָּה שְׂפָתַי כִּי אֲזַמְּרָה־לָּךְ וְנַפְשִׁי אֲשֶׁר פָּדִיתָ׃
24 גַּם־לְשׁוֹנִי כָּל־הַיּוֹם תֶּהְגֶּה צִדְקָתֶךָ כִּי־בֹשׁוּ
כִי־חָפְרוּ מְבַקְשֵׁי רָעָתִי׃

v. 20 ראיתנו כתיב, תחיינו כתיב, תעלנו כתיב

serene faith come *as a result* of a lifetime of speculative questioning or *despite* it? And how, precisely, *does* someone coming to religion as a thoughtful, intelligent adult come to believe in God as part of immutable, self-evident reality?

The author of the thirty-first psalm, a poem with close ties to the seventy-first, refers to the Almighty as *El emet,* as the God of truth. For most moderns, however, the notion that God exists in the world as the quintessence of truth will point unavoidably to the idea, almost a corollary, that the telling of lies about God—even pious ones—can only lead one further away from real spiritual fulfillment. And, indeed, basic to the Jewish worldview is the concept that debate and argument for the sake of heaven (that is: when neither party resorts to falsehoods to win the argument) can only lead the debaters upwards to a level of spiritual integrity they may not otherwise have attained. Still, it is also the case that, for most moderns coming to faith, participation in endless discussion about the nature of God weakens (rather than strengthens) that faith, because the prolonged public dissection of *anything* that cannot be proven scientifically to exist is bound to sow seeds of doubt where uncertainty might otherwise have not taken root at all. Thankfully, though, this is only true in the short run. As years pass and the faithful do not desist from asking even the most difficult questions about God and do not hold back from discussing and debating them candidly and openly,

[14] As for me, I shall always hope in You and shall add even more onto all of Your praises; [15]my mouth shall tell of Your righteousness and all day long I shall speak of Your salvation, for I will never know how to recount all there is to tell.

[16] I shall come with tales of Your might, Adonai-יהוה; I shall recall Your righteousness and no one else's.

[17] God, You have trained me since my youth and I still tell of Your wonders.

[18] Even when I reach hoary old age, do not abandon me, O God, until I tell of Your mighty arm to the next generation, until I tell of Your might to all those who are to come.

[19] You have done great things, O God; Your righteousness reaches up to the heights. God, who is like unto You?

[20] For although You have shown me many horrific troubles, You always return to grant me life; You always raise me up from the depths of the earth.

[21] You maximize my claim to greatness; You turn to me and grant me comfort.

[22] And so shall I give thanks to You, declaring Your truth, O my God, while accompanying myself on the *nevel;* I shall sing hymns to You while accompanying myself on the lyre, O Holy One of Israel.

[23] My lips shall rejoice when I sing hymns unto You, as shall my soul which You have redeemed.

[24] My tongue as well shall speak of Your righteousness all day long, for those who sought to do me ill have been embarrassed, even disgraced.

different seeds are planted . . . and those seeds, rooted as they are in the soil of absolute spiritual integrity and scrupulous intellectual honesty, do have the capacity of blossoming into faith.

In the end, we come to believe in God by seeking evidence of divine reality in the warp and woof of the lives we live and the world we inhabit. That believing is not the same as wishing to believe or feeling obliged to believe, most moderns would grant. But the plausibility of coming to faith in some context *other* than the framework of total commitment to rigorous intellectual honesty will never ring true to those who hope wholeheartedly to embrace faith in the God of truth.

עב

לִשְׁלֹמֹה ׀
אֱלֹהִים מִשְׁפָּטֶיךָ לְמֶלֶךְ תֵּן וְצִדְקָתְךָ לְבֶן־מֶלֶךְ׃
2 יָדִין עַמְּךָ בְצֶדֶק וַעֲנִיֶּיךָ בְמִשְׁפָּט׃
3 יִשְׂאוּ הָרִים שָׁלוֹם לָעָם וּגְבָעוֹת בִּצְדָקָה׃
4 יִשְׁפֹּט ׀ עֲנִיֵּי־עָם יוֹשִׁיעַ לִבְנֵי אֶבְיוֹן וִידַכֵּא עוֹשֵׁק׃
5 יִירָאוּךָ עִם־שָׁמֶשׁ וְלִפְנֵי יָרֵחַ דּוֹר דּוֹרִים׃
6 יֵרֵד כְּמָטָר עַל־גֵּז כִּרְבִיבִים זַרְזִיף אָרֶץ׃
7 יִפְרַח־בְּיָמָיו צַדִּיק וְרֹב שָׁלוֹם עַד־בְּלִי יָרֵחַ׃
8 וְיֵרְדְּ מִיָּם עַד־יָם וּמִנָּהָר עַד־אַפְסֵי־אָרֶץ׃
9 לְפָנָיו יִכְרְעוּ צִיִּים וְאֹיְבָיו עָפָר יְלַחֵכוּ׃
10 מַלְכֵי תַרְשִׁישׁ וְאִיִּים מִנְחָה יָשִׁיבוּ מַלְכֵי שְׁבָא
וּסְבָא אֶשְׁכָּר יַקְרִיבוּ׃
11 וְיִשְׁתַּחֲווּ־לוֹ כָל־מְלָכִים כָּל־גּוֹיִם יַעַבְדוּהוּ׃
12 כִּי־יַצִּיל אֶבְיוֹן מְשַׁוֵּעַ וְעָנִי וְאֵין־עֹזֵר לוֹ׃

Whether the author of the seventy-second psalm was a Temple Levite named Solomon, or whether the superscription of the poem means that the poet meant to attribute his poem to King Solomon (or perhaps even simply to dedicate it to the king's memory), or whether the poem actually dates back to the time of Solomon himself cannot be known with certainty. Nor does the fact that the third book of the Psalter concludes with an editorial note that with it "end the prayers of David, son of Jesse" rule out any of the above possibilities, since we cannot say with certainty what the editors meant by the expression "prayers of David." (Many psalms attributed to David follow the seventy-second psalm in the Psalter as it has come down to us. Possibly the note survives from an earlier collection of psalms in which this was the final poem. Or perhaps certain psalms were known technically as "prayers" and the seventy-second psalm was their last example in the Psalter at some stage of its editorial history. In our Book of Psalms, however, Psalms 17, 86, and 142—which is also called a *maskil,* a "wise-song"—are formally called "prayers of David.")

The seventy-second psalm considered in its own right, however, is a stirring ode to kingship. No avenue of literary expression—realistic, symbolic, or metaphoric—is avoided in the poet's effort to sing the praises of his king as loudly and clearly as possible. Not only are the oceans and the rivers pressed into service, for example, but even the sun and the moon are called upon to provide an exalted context in which the poet's king can have his praises ade-

72

(A psalm) of Solomon.

O God, grant Your legal acumen to a king
and Your righteousness to the son of a king.
[2] May he judge Your people justly, Your humble folk fairly.
[3] May the mountains, even the hills, bear peace to the people through royal righteousness.
[4] May he judge the poor of the people, save the needy, and crush the oppressor.
[5] People shall fear You as long as there will be a sun, as will every generation for as long as there will be a moon.
[6] May he be as welcomed by the people as rain that falls gently on mown grass, as soft rain that falls on the fields of the earth.
[7] May the righteous flower in his day and may there be great peace in the land, a peace so permanent that it risks outlasting the moon.
[8] May he reign from sea to sea, from the river to the ends of the earth.
[9] His platoons kneel before him, but his enemies shall lick up his dust.
[10] The kings of Tarshish and the islands shall bring him gifts; the kings of Sheba and Seba shall offer him tribute.
[11] Indeed, all kings shall bow down to him and all nations serve him, [12]for he saves the needy individual who cries out, the poor person who has none to help.

quately declaimed. Moderns reading the seventy-second psalm, especially in a devotional context, will want to ask what such accolades to majesty can mean to people who live in countries with no sovereigns at all, or else with kings or queens who are mere figureheads and who wield no real political power. Surely no modern would write a psalm comparing the majesty of the Divine to the pomp that attends the offices of our presidents or prime ministers!

Yet modern readers will do well to take the poet's point seriously. Those who govern in this world can indeed be judged with respect to how well they garner the respect of the people they govern and how successfully they care for their country's poor. Although no one would suggest that democracy is inevitably a sham because God personally arranges for

13 יָחֹס עַל-דַּל וְאֶבְיוֹן וְנַפְשׁוֹת אֶבְיוֹנִים יוֹשִׁיעַ:

14 מִתּוֹךְ וּמֵחָמָס יִגְאַל נַפְשָׁם וְיֵיקַר דָּמָם בְּעֵינָיו:

15 וִיחִי וְיִתֶּן-לוֹ מִזְּהַב שְׁבָא וְיִתְפַּלֵּל בַּעֲדוֹ תָמִיד
כָּל-הַיּוֹם יְבָרֲכֶנְהוּ:

16 יְהִי פִסַּת-בַּר ׀ בָּאָרֶץ בְּרֹאשׁ הָרִים יִרְעַשׁ כַּלְּבָנוֹן
פִּרְיוֹ וְיָצִיצוּ מֵעִיר כְּעֵשֶׂב הָאָרֶץ:

17 יְהִי שְׁמוֹ לְעוֹלָם לִפְנֵי שֶׁמֶשׁ *יִנּוֹן שְׁמוֹ וְיִתְבָּרְכוּ
בוֹ כָּל-גּוֹיִם יְאַשְּׁרוּהוּ:

18 בָּרוּךְ ׀ יְהוָה אֱלֹהִים אֱלֹהֵי יִשְׂרָאֵל עֹשֵׂה נִפְלָאוֹת
לְבַדּוֹ: 19 וּבָרוּךְ ׀ שֵׁם כְּבוֹדוֹ לְעוֹלָם וְיִמָּלֵא כְבוֹדוֹ
אֶת-כָּל-הָאָרֶץ אָמֵן ׀ וְאָמֵן:

20 כָּלּוּ תְפִלּוֹת דָּוִד בֶּן-יִשָׁי:

v. 17 ינין כתיב

specific candidates to win national elections, the notion that the rule of law, justice, and decency is a blessing from God is an idea that can be as resonant today as it was thousands of years ago.

Moderns contemplating the seventy-second psalm may use its ancient strophes as an effective jumping-off point for the consideration of some very difficult questions. How precisely does God go about governing a world of people endowed with freedom of will? Does evil triumph in our world because God fails to intervene in the

[13] He takes pity on the poverty-stricken and needy, and he delivers the souls of the needy from want.

[14] He redeems their souls from strife and violence; their blood is precious in his eyes.

[15] May he live and may others give him of the gold of Sheba and always pray for him and bless him all day long.

[16] May there be an abundance of grain in the land and on the mountain-tops. May the fruit in his orchards tremble on the bough like on bounteous Mount Lebanon; may the king's produce sprout up in the cities like the grass of the countryside.

[17] May his name endure forever. May his name outlast the sun; may all the nations of the earth be blessed because of their association with him and may they all declare him happy.

[18] Blessed be יהוה-Elohim, God of Israel, unique Doer of wonders, [19]and blessed be the glorious name of God forever. May the glory of God fill all the earth, amen and amen.

[20] Here end the prayers of David, son of Jesse.

politics of terrestrial life? What does it mean to acclaim God as "the Sovereign of the World," as we do so regularly in our prayers? If God is our perfect, all-powerful Sovereign, are we then subjects of an absolute Monarch? Could God be any less? But how can the subjects of an absolute Monarch possibly have the ability to choose either to walk in their Sovereign's ways or to turn their back at will on whatever royal decrees they find uninspiring or unpalatable, without that sense of personal freedom being anything other than a self-serving delusion? Are our human rights inherent in our humanity . . . or are they blessings from a benevolent God that will be acknowledged as such by honest people of faith?

עג

מִזְמוֹר לְאָסָף
אַךְ טוֹב לְיִשְׂרָאֵל אֱלֹהִים לְבָרֵי לֵבָב׃
2 וַאֲנִי כִּמְעַט *נָטָיוּ רַגְלָי כְּאַיִן *שֻׁפְּכוּ אֲשֻׁרָי׃
3 כִּי־קִנֵּאתִי בַּהוֹלְלִים שְׁלוֹם רְשָׁעִים אֶרְאֶה׃ 4 כִּי
אֵין חַרְצֻבּוֹת לְמוֹתָם וּבָרִיא אוּלָם׃
5 בַּעֲמַל אֱנוֹשׁ אֵינֵמוֹ וְעִם־אָדָם לֹא יְנֻגָּעוּ׃ 6 לָכֵן
עֲנָקַתְמוֹ גַאֲוָה יַעֲטָף־שִׁית חָמָס לָמוֹ׃
7 יָצָא מֵחֵלֶב עֵינֵמוֹ עָבְרוּ מַשְׂכִּיּוֹת לֵבָב׃
8 יָמִיקוּ ׀ וִידַבְּרוּ בְרָע עֹשֶׁק מִמָּרוֹם יְדַבֵּרוּ׃
9 שַׁתּוּ בַשָּׁמַיִם פִּיהֶם וּלְשׁוֹנָם תִּהֲלַךְ בָּאָרֶץ׃ 10 לָכֵן
*יָשׁוּב עַמּוֹ הֲלֹם וּמֵי מָלֵא יִמָּצוּ לָמוֹ׃
11 וְאָמְרוּ אֵיכָה יָדַע־אֵל וְיֵשׁ דֵּעָה בְעֶלְיוֹן׃
12 הִנֵּה־אֵלֶּה רְשָׁעִים וְשַׁלְוֵי עוֹלָם הִשְׂגּוּ־חָיִל׃
13 אַךְ־רִיק זִכִּיתִי לְבָבִי וָאֶרְחַץ בְּנִקָּיוֹן כַּפָּי׃ 14 וָאֱהִי
נָגוּעַ כָּל־הַיּוֹם וְתוֹכַחְתִּי לַבְּקָרִים׃
15 אִם־אָמַרְתִּי אֲסַפְּרָה כְמוֹ הִנֵּה דוֹר בָּנֶיךָ בָגָדְתִּי׃

v. 2 נטוי כתיב, שפכה כתיב
v. 10 ישיב כתיב

Like all people occasionally do, the poet looks around in the world and finds himself puzzled by the good fortune enjoyed by so many evildoers. Indeed, the seventy-third psalm chronicles the poet's increasing attraction to the notion that the wealth and success of villains indicate the lack of divine governance in the world . . . only to then find himself visited by the truth about the way God works in the world as a result of an unexpected epiphany in the Temple.

The poet's milieu may be ancient, but moderns will find nothing antique or archaic in the poet's fabulously trenchant description of the wicked as obese, arrogant scoffers who stop stuffing their mouths only long enough to hatch more and more villainy against the pure of heart and the defenseless . . . or to mock God. But how will modern readers react to the poet's discovery that God governs the world by embodying faith in the hearts of people who seek refuge in the Almighty, and whose ultimate happiness derives from the deep, unshakable sense they possess of God's interest in their personal destinies?

The poet's self-deprecating remarks ("I was a boor who knew nothing . . .") will strike a chord with those readers who have experienced similar unanticipated instances of spiritual intelligence. Indeed, after having a sudden burst of belief in the nearness of God, who would *not* describe the experience as a kind of sudden investiture of vision and unanticipated insight?

BOOK THREE

73

A psalm of Asaph.

Truly God is good to the pure-hearted of Israel.

[2] As for me, my feet almost swerved from the right path; my legs practically ran away on their own, [3]for I was jealous of the debauched. I looked longingly on the peace of the wicked, [4]people for whom death is no constraint and whose bodies somehow still remain healthy.

[5] They appear to have no part in the troubles of humanity; neither do they become ill like other people, [6]and so pride is their necklace. They don violence as though it were a pleasant garment.

[7] Their eyes bulge from all the fat they eat; their deeds surpass even the fantasies of their hearts.

[8] They devise putrid and wicked plans, planning oppression as though they were God speaking on high.

[9] They have set their mouths against heaven, while their tongues spread calumnies on earth. [10]In this way do they return to oppress God's people again and again, not stopping until the life-fluids are squeezed out of them totally.

[11] They say, "How will God know of this? Does God Most High possess real knowledge?"

[12] These are the wicked, the tranquil of the earth who amass great wealth.

[13] As for me, I purified my heart and washed clean my hands for nothing, [14]for I was smitten all day long anyway, enduring rebuke every morning.

[15] Had I said, "I will tell of things as they really are . . . ," then I would have betrayed the circle of Your disciples.

The seventy-third psalm can play a deep role in the devotional life of anyone who has ever envied the prosperity of people who live comfortable, luxury-driven lives devoid of faith. That people can live without God seems obvious, but what of those among us incapable of conceiving of a meaningful, happy life without faith? They too are surely entitled to live as they see fit, but how exactly are such people to go about acquiring the kind of faith they so ardently desire? Can they hope for epiphanies similar to the psalmist's? Or is the challenge for the would-be pious to engender faith within themselves by learning to translate yearning for God into the ritualized language of day-to-day worship, so that human life

16 וָאֲחַשְּׁבָה לָדַעַת זֹאת עָמָל *הוּא בְעֵינָי׃
17 עַד־אָבוֹא אֶל־מִקְדְּשֵׁי־אֵל אָבִינָה לְאַחֲרִיתָם׃
18 אַךְ בַּחֲלָקוֹת תָּשִׁית לָמוֹ הִפַּלְתָּם לְמַשּׁוּאוֹת׃
19 אֵיךְ הָיוּ לְשַׁמָּה כְרָגַע סָפוּ תַמּוּ מִן־בַּלָּהוֹת׃
20 כַּחֲלוֹם מֵהָקִיץ אֲדֹנָי בָּעִיר ׀ צַלְמָם תִּבְזֶה׃
21 כִּי יִתְחַמֵּץ לְבָבִי וְכִלְיוֹתַי אֶשְׁתּוֹנָן׃
22 וַאֲנִי־בַעַר וְלֹא אֵדָע בְּהֵמוֹת הָיִיתִי עִמָּךְ׃ 23 וַאֲנִי תָמִיד עִמָּךְ אָחַזְתָּ בְּיַד־יְמִינִי׃
24 בַּעֲצָתְךָ תַנְחֵנִי וְאַחַר כָּבוֹד תִּקָּחֵנִי׃ 25 מִי־לִי בַשָּׁמָיִם וְעִמְּךָ לֹא־חָפַצְתִּי בָאָרֶץ׃
26 כָּלָה שְׁאֵרִי וּלְבָבִי צוּר־לְבָבִי וְחֶלְקִי אֱלֹהִים לְעוֹלָם׃ 27 כִּי־הִנֵּה רְחֵקֶיךָ יֹאבֵדוּ הִצְמַתָּה כָּל־זוֹנֶה מִמֶּךָּ׃
28 וַאֲנִי ׀ קִרֲבַת אֱלֹהִים לִי־טוֹב שַׁתִּי ׀ בַּאדֹנָי יְהוִה מַחְסִי לְסַפֵּר כָּל־מַלְאֲכוֹתֶיךָ׃

v. 16 היא כתיב

itself becomes the medium of divine self-revelation in the world of ordinary men and women?

In the end, no one struggling to know God will enjoy contemplating the tranquility and untroubled lifestyles of people who live without faith. And when those people are prosperous, perhaps even truly wealthy, the experience will be even less pleasant to ponder, since we are taught by society (and common sense) to consider prosperity to be one of God's greatest blessings. But perhaps the solution rests precisely in the very ill ease we feel when we consider the apparent lack of balance between faith and material reward in our world. The problem, after all, only exists if one actually does equate money with divine favor. But what if the contemplation of, say, a neighbor possessed of every creature comfort imaginable, but totally devoid of faith in God, were to occasion the latter-day equivalent of the poet's Temple epiphany? What if the someone striving to come to faith were to look on such a privileged, yet faithless, person and—suddenly and unexpectedly—be visited with the realization (and the absolute, unswerving conviction) that the person under observation is wealthy only in

[16] Yet when I tried to think all this through, it was torture in my eyes, [17]until I came into the sacred precincts of God and suddenly understood the end that awaits the wicked: [18]You will set them on a slippery slope and hurl them down to disaster.

[19] How they shall all at once become a ruin! How they shall vanish! How they shall be destroyed by horrors, [20]annihilated to the point at which they vanish like characters in a dream who disappear when the dreamer awakens; Adonai will show nothing but scorn to their image in the city.

[21] But as for me, the blood in my heart feels as though it has turned to vinegar and I feel as though my kidneys have been stabbed.

[22] I was a boor who knew nothing; I behaved like an animal before You. [23]However, I am always with You now; grasp me in Your right hand.

[24] Guide me with Your counsel and bring me to search for honor. [25]Whom else do I have in heaven? Do I desire anything but to be with You on earth?

[26] My flesh and my heart are weak, but You are the rock of my heart and my portion forever, O God. [27]For surely those who distance themselves from You will perish; You destroy those who stray from You.

[28] But as for me, the nearness of God is my ultimate happiness; I have made Adonai-יהוה my place of haven so that I may tell of all Your works.

the most crass, least important, sense possible of the word conceivable? That the person of whose fortune one was jealous only moments earlier has no real fortune to be envious of, no riches to covet, and nothing of true value for others to yearn to possess? What if faith itself were to be the ultimate wealth . . . and what if the contemplation of faithless people could provide precisely the context for average people to come to terms, finally, with the fact that faith must, almost by definition, serve the faithful as its own greatest reward?

עד

מַשְׂכִּיל לְאָסָף
לָמָה אֱלֹהִים זָנַחְתָּ לָנֶצַח יֶעְשַׁן אַפְּךָ בְּצֹאן
מַרְעִיתֶךָ׃
2 זְכֹר עֲדָתְךָ ׀ קָּנִיתָ קֶּדֶם גָּאַלְתָּ שֵׁבֶט נַחֲלָתֶךָ
הַר־צִיּוֹן זֶה ׀ שָׁכַנְתָּ בּוֹ׃
3 הָרִימָה פְעָמֶיךָ לְמַשֻּׁאוֹת נֶצַח כָּל־הֵרַע אוֹיֵב
בַּקֹּדֶשׁ׃
4 שָׁאֲגוּ צֹרְרֶיךָ בְּקֶרֶב מוֹעֲדֶךָ שָׂמוּ אוֹתֹתָם אֹתוֹת׃
5 יִוָּדַע כְּמֵבִיא לְמָעְלָה בִּסֲבָךְ־עֵץ קַרְדֻּמּוֹת׃
6 *וְעַתָּה פִּתּוּחֶיהָ יָּחַד בְּכַשִּׁיל וְכֵילַפֹּת יַהֲלֹמוּן׃
7 שִׁלְחוּ בָאֵשׁ מִקְדָּשֶׁךָ לָאָרֶץ חִלְּלוּ מִשְׁכַּן־שְׁמֶךָ׃
8 אָמְרוּ בְלִבָּם נִינָם יָחַד שָׂרְפוּ כָל־מוֹעֲדֵי־אֵל
בָּאָרֶץ׃
9 אוֹתֹתֵינוּ לֹא־רָאִינוּ אֵין־עוֹד נָבִיא וְלֹא־אִתָּנוּ יֹדֵעַ
עַד־מָה׃
10 עַד־מָתַי אֱלֹהִים יְחָרֶף צָר יְנָאֵץ אוֹיֵב שִׁמְךָ
לָנֶצַח׃
11 לָמָּה תָשִׁיב יָדְךָ וִימִינֶךָ מִקֶּרֶב *חֵיקְךָ כַלֵּה׃
12 וֵאלֹהִים מַלְכִּי מִקֶּדֶם פֹּעֵל יְשׁוּעוֹת בְּקֶרֶב
הָאָרֶץ׃

v. 6 ועת כתיב
v. 11 חוקך כתיב

As far as anyone knows, the First Temple was only razed once in its long history, by the Babylonians at the beginning of the sixth century B.C.E. (Later, the Second Temple was burnt down by the Romans at the end of the first century C.E.) That being the case, the poet, who lived while the Second Temple stood, can only have been thinking of the razing of Jerusalem by Babylon. When he lived and what the precise perspective was from which he wrote, however, cannot be known. The psalmist does add some details to other biblical accounts of the debacle, however, such as the image of enemy soldiers methodically working their way through the Temple with axes and chopping down its sacred appurtenances as though they were lumberjacks working their way through a virgin forest. Yet, it is his theological insight that is the most startling. Although there is something rational and reasonable about taking the destruction of Jerusalem as the catastrophic outcome of an alien nation's attempt to dominate the Jews of ancient Judah, it is the poet's point that it can (and probably should) also be described as an act of sacrilege against God. This notion—that enmity to-

74 A wise-song of Asaph.

O God, why does it seem as though You have abandoned us for good? Why does Your anger smolder against the sheep of Your own pastureland?

[2] Remember the congregation that You created in ancient times; recall how You redeemed the tribe of Your inheritance and Mount Zion, the place in which You chose to reside.

[3] Lift up Your feet to avenge this never-ending debacle, to avenge all the evil that the enemy has perpetrated in the Sanctuary.

[4] Your foes have roared in the midst of Your assembly-places, taking the portents of their own seers seriously.

[5] They became noticeable as they ascended towards the Temple like men working their way through a thicket of trees with axes, [6] now coming together to smash the carved woodwork with hatchet and adze.

[7] They burnt Your Temple to the ground, thus profaning the dwelling-place of Your name.

[8] They said in their hearts, "Let us destroy it all." Indeed, they burnt down all the assembly-places of God in the land.

[9] We see no signs. There are no more prophets. None among us knows how long this horror will last.

[10] How long, O God, will the foe blaspheme? Will the enemy incessantly insult Your name?

[11] Why do you keep back Your hand, Your right arm? Draw it forth from Your bosom and destroy them!

[12] For God is my Sovereign of old, the One who effects salvation in the midst of the earth.

wards Israel constitutes, almost by definition, blasphemy against God—is an idea that appears to have struck the poet as self-evident, but it will especially challenge moderns attempting to use the seventy-fourth psalm as a framework for constructive reflection. Is it just bad luck for the Jews that anti-Semitism exists in the world, or is there a cosmic dimension to the prejudice and hatred that Jews have, it seems, always encountered? And what are the theological and spiritual implications for Jews living after the Shoah when the poet declares that the foe's war was only for-

13 אַתָּה פוֹרַרְתָּ בְעָזְּךָ יָם שִׁבַּרְתָּ רָאשֵׁי תַנִּינִים עַל־הַמָּיִם׃

14 אַתָּה רִצַּצְתָּ רָאשֵׁי לִוְיָתָן תִּתְּנֶנּוּ מַאֲכָל לְעָם לְצִיִּים׃

15 אַתָּה בָקַעְתָּ מַעְיָן וָנָחַל אַתָּה הוֹבַשְׁתָּ נַהֲרוֹת אֵיתָן׃

16 לְךָ יוֹם אַף־לְךָ לָיְלָה אַתָּה הֲכִינוֹתָ מָאוֹר וָשָׁמֶשׁ׃

17 אַתָּה הִצַּבְתָּ כָּל־גְּבוּלוֹת אָרֶץ קַיִץ וָחֹרֶף אַתָּה יְצַרְתָּם׃

18 זְכָר־זֹאת אוֹיֵב חֵרֵף ׀ יְהוָה וְעַם־נָבָל נִאֲצוּ שְׁמֶךָ׃

19 אַל־תִּתֵּן לְחַיַּת נֶפֶשׁ תּוֹרֶךָ חַיַּת עֲנִיֶּיךָ אַל־תִּשְׁכַּח לָנֶצַח׃

20 הַבֵּט־לַבְּרִית כִּי־מָלְאוּ מַחֲשַׁכֵּי־אֶרֶץ נְאוֹת חָמָס׃

21 אַל־יָשֹׁב דַּךְ נִכְלָם עָנִי וְאֶבְיוֹן יְהַלְלוּ שְׁמֶךָ׃

22 קוּמָה אֱלֹהִים רִיבָה רִיבֶךָ זְכֹר חֶרְפָּתְךָ מִנִּי־נָבָל כָּל־הַיּוֹם׃

23 אַל־תִּשְׁכַּח קוֹל צֹרְרֶיךָ שְׁאוֹן קָמֶיךָ עֹלֶה תָמִיד׃

mally an attack against Israel, but was actually an act of sustained aggression against God?

Moreover, the notion that making war against Israel constitutes, almost by definition, making war against God brings a whole set of different questions in its wake for post-Holocaust moderns to ponder. Is the fact that the enemy lost the war a result of divine intervention in the history of humanity? Is it more amazing that the Shoah happened at all, or that, despite the best efforts of the most powerful, most mechanized, most heartless enemy the Jewish people ever encountered, two-thirds of world Jewry survived the onslaught? Even saying that out loud sounds like a pathetic attempt to rescue the notion of a permanently effective covenant between Israel and God from being overwhelmed by the tides of historical reality. Yet, denying it feels just a step or two short of admitting that the concept of such a covenant ought finally to fall into desuetude and be recalled merely as a feature of the religious philosophy of ancient times. Fortunately, the 74th psalm suggests an alternate approach.

The poet whose poem became our psalm lived *after* the destruction of the most sacred of shrines imaginable. The other prayer houses and worship centers of his land had similarly been burnt down. There were no signs, no portents, and no prophets bearing encouraging oracles about the future. The king was in exile; the priesthood was decimated. The poet lived in a world that had experienced what must have widely been considered the ultimate horror *and*

[13] You shattered the sea with Your strength; You smashed the heads of the sea monsters on its waters.

[14] You crushed the heads of Leviathan, giving them as food to citizen and soldier.

[15] You split fountain and river; You dried up mighty rivers.

[16] Day is Yours, as is night; You invented star and sun.

[17] You set up the boundaries of the earth's nations; You created summer and winter.

[18] Remember how the enemy cursed יהוה, how a debauched people insulted Your name.

[19] Give not Your turtledove to a wild creature; indeed, never forget Your pathetic creature.

[20] Look to the covenant, for the dark places of the earth are filled with dens of violence.

[21] Let not the oppressed turn back ashamed; let instead the poor and impoverished of the earth praise Your name.

[22] Rise up, O God, and defend Yourself; remember the insults hurled at You all day long by the debauched foe.

[23] Do not forget to take note of the voice of Your adversaries, to the endlessly reverberating din of those who would rise up against You.

the most monstrous crime conceivable, yet the silence of God in the wake of the debacle appears not to have inspired the poet to abandon his faith. Just to the contrary, the catastrophe appears to have energized him and given him the strength to call out to God in prayer and supplication. When he calls out to God with the words *habet laberit* ("Look to the covenant!"), he does not sound at all like someone who is riddled with doubt about the reality of God's ongoing relationship with the Jewish people. Rather, he sounds like someone certain that even the silence of God must surely be part of the larger picture of an ongoing, intact covenantal relationship. In the depths of his despair, the poet found courage and faith. Moderns will surely admire his fortitude, but the real question for moderns to answer is not really whether spiritual stamina like the poet's can reasonably be praised, but whether it can be effectively imitated. And this one as well: can Israel accept its place in God's plan for history graciously and humbly, without falling prey to self-centered, self-serving, self-referential chauvinism?

עה

לַמְנַצֵּחַ אַל־תַּשְׁחֵת מִזְמוֹר לְאָסָף שִׁיר׃
2 הוֹדִינוּ לְּךָ ׀ אֱלֹהִים הוֹדִינוּ וְקָרוֹב שְׁמֶךָ סִפְּרוּ
נִפְלְאוֹתֶיךָ׃
3 כִּי־אֶקַּח מוֹעֵד אֲנִי מֵישָׁרִים אֶשְׁפֹּט׃ 4 נְמוֹגִים־
אֶרֶץ וְכָל־יֹשְׁבֶיהָ אָנֹכִי תִּכַּנְתִּי עַמּוּדֶיהָ סֶּלָה׃
5 אָמַרְתִּי לַהוֹלְלִים אַל־תָּהֹלּוּ וְלָרְשָׁעִים אַל־
תָּרִימוּ קָרֶן׃ 6 אַל־תָּרִימוּ לַמָּרוֹם קַרְנְכֶם תְּדַבְּרוּ
בְצַוָּאר עָתָק׃
7 כִּי לֹא מִמּוֹצָא וּמִמַּעֲרָב וְלֹא מִמִּדְבַּר הָרִים׃
8 כִּי־אֱלֹהִים שֹׁפֵט זֶה יַשְׁפִּיל וְזֶה יָרִים׃
9 כִּי כוֹס בְּיַד־יְהוָה וְיַיִן חָמַר ׀ מָלֵא מֶסֶךְ וַיַּגֵּר מִזֶּה
אַךְ־שְׁמָרֶיהָ יִמְצוּ יִשְׁתּוּ כֹּל רִשְׁעֵי־אָרֶץ׃
10 וַאֲנִי אַגִּיד לְעֹלָם אֲזַמְּרָה לֵאלֹהֵי יַעֲקֹב׃
11 וְכָל־קַרְנֵי רְשָׁעִים אֲגַדֵּעַ תְּרוֹמַמְנָה קַרְנוֹת צַדִּיק׃

As befits a book that suggests in dozens of places that it is perfectly reasonable for human beings to experience auditory (and occasionally even visual) communion with God, the Psalter is studded with many oracular passages recounting what God was heard to say during the poets' mystic encounters with the Divine. The author of the seventy-fifth psalm, for example, reports that some of his colleagues experienced the overwhelming presence of God's name somehow transformed into the stuff of human language, and the poet has no compunction about telling us what they heard God say.

It's hard to decide what, if anything, the poet meant by structuring his poem as he did, but moderns contemplating the seventy-fifth psalm will find the actual oracular message—that God is a just judge to whose judgment all must accede with humility and a renunciation of debauchery—inspiring in its own right. Still, for most modern readers, the real power of the psalm

75

For the conductor, a psalm-song of Asaph to be sung to the tune of "Destroy Not."

[2] We give thanks to You, O God, we give thanks to You; feeling Your name to dwell close by, we shall tell of Your wonders.

[3]"When I determine the time to be right, I shall render just judgment," says God. [4]"The earth and all its inhabitants may melt away, but that will not matter, for it was I who first established the pillars of the earth, *selah*.

[5] To the debauched I say, 'Do not be debauched.' To the wicked, I say, 'Do not raise up your horns to do evil. [6]Do not raise up high your horns, lest you speak arrogantly with an outstretched neck.'"

[7] For vindication comes from neither east nor west, nor does it come from the mountainous desert, [8]for God is the ultimate Judge, casting down one party to a dispute and raising up the other.

[9] Indeed, there is a cup in the hand of יהוה; it is full of fermented wine fully mixed that God pours for the vindicated. The wicked of the land, on the other hand, will be obliged to strain out the dregs and drink them.

[10] As for me, I will always tell of God; I will chant hymns to the God of Jacob.

[11] And God says this as well: "I shall lop off the horns of the wicked, but the horns of the righteous shall be raised up."

will come from the questions it prompts us to ask. If we find it so acceptable and reasonable to describe God as all-powerful, why do we remain blissfully content for our once-verbal God no longer to speak to anyone directly or personally? Why do even the faithful routinely label any who claim to hear the voice of God as demented dreamers . . . or worse? Why do moderns so often appear to fear the concept of hearing God's voice even more than their behavior suggests they fear God's judgment?

עו

לַמְנַצֵּ֥חַ בִּנְגִינֹ֑ת מִזְמ֖וֹר לְאָסָ֣ף שִֽׁיר׃
2 נוֹדָ֣ע בִּֽיהוּדָ֣ה אֱלֹהִ֑ים בְּ֝יִשְׂרָאֵ֗ל גָּד֥וֹל שְׁמֽוֹ׃
3 וַיְהִ֣י בְשָׁלֵ֣ם סֻכּ֑וֹ וּמְעוֹנָת֥וֹ בְצִיּֽוֹן׃
4 שָׁ֭מָּה שִׁבַּ֣ר רִשְׁפֵי־קָ֑שֶׁת מָגֵ֖ן וְחֶ֖רֶב וּמִלְחָמָ֣ה
סֶֽלָה׃
5 נָ֭אוֹר אַתָּ֣ה אַדִּ֗יר מֵֽהַרְרֵי־טָֽרֶף׃
6 אֶשְׁתּוֹלְל֨וּ ׀ אַבִּ֣ירֵי לֵ֭ב נָמ֣וּ שְׁנָתָ֑ם וְלֹא־מָצְא֖וּ
כָל־אַנְשֵׁי־חַ֣יִל יְדֵיהֶֽם׃ 7 מִ֭גַּעֲרָתְךָ אֱלֹהֵ֣י יַעֲקֹ֑ב
נִ֝רְדָּ֗ם וְרֶ֣כֶב וָסֽוּס׃
8 אַתָּ֤ה ׀ נ֘וֹרָ֤א אַ֗תָּה וּמִֽי־יַעֲמֹ֥ד לְ֝פָנֶ֗יךָ מֵאָ֥ז אַפֶּֽךָ׃
9 מִ֭שָּׁמַיִם הִשְׁמַ֣עְתָּ דִּ֑ין אֶ֖רֶץ יָֽרְאָ֣ה וְשָׁקָֽטָה׃
10 בְּקוּם־לַמִּשְׁפָּ֣ט אֱלֹהִ֑ים לְהוֹשִׁ֖יעַ כָּל־עַנְוֵי־אֶ֣רֶץ
סֶֽלָה׃
11 כִּֽי־חֲמַ֣ת אָדָ֣ם תּוֹדֶ֑ךָּ שְׁאֵרִ֖ית חֵמֹ֣ת תַּחְגֹּֽר׃
12 נְדָר֣וּ וְשַׁלְּמ֡וּ לַיהוָ֣ה אֱלֹהֵיכֶ֑ם כָּל־סְבִיבָ֥יו יֹבִ֥ילוּ
שַׁ֝֗י לַמּוֹרָֽא׃
13 יִ֭בְצֹר ר֣וּחַ נְגִידִ֑ים נ֝וֹרָ֗א לְמַלְכֵי־אָֽרֶץ׃

Scholars have long debated what precise incident might have inspired the author of the seventy-sixth psalm to compose his ode of gratitude to God's role in the miraculous deliverance of the Holy City from a fierce foe who threatened to seize (or perhaps even destroy) it. Moderns seeking to incorporate the recitation of this psalm into their devotional lives will be less interested in wondering what *specific* event inspired the poet, however, than in pondering the very challenging idea that human beings can provoke God to act in history through their personal acts of piety and charity. We speak regularly, especially

76

For the choral conductor, a psalm-song of Asaph.
[2] God is known in Judah; God's name is great in Israel.
[3] In Salem is God's dwelling, God's domicile in Zion.
[4] It was there that God broke the fire-bows of the enemy, their shields and swords and other weapons of war, *selah.*
[5] You were resplendent, O God, even more impressively mighty than the mountains of slaughter on which the enemy fell.
[6] The enemy, once so courageous of heart, was stupefied and sleepy; the formerly mighty could not even locate their own hands. [7]At Your rebuke, O God of Jacob, both charioteer and horse fell asleep.
[8] You are awesome, O God. Who can stand before You or Your ancient anger?
[9] From heaven, You decreed judgment; the earth became terrified and fell still [10]when God rose up to pronounce the verdict that would save all the afflicted of the earth, *selah.*
[11] For indeed, even the rage of the downtrodden is a way of acknowledging You; indeed, You gird Yourself with the residue of that anger.
[12] Make vows to יהוה, your God, and honor them; let all who surround God's Temple bring gifts to the Awesome One.
[13] For God fashions the princely spirit and is consequently held in awe by the kings of the earth.

in our prayers, of a God whose power to govern the world is absolute. Yet we seem to find it morally questionable, sometimes even troubling, actually to beseech God to intervene forcefully in the affairs of humanity. Is this because we prefer not asking the question to not receiving a clear answer to it? Or is it because the corollary of the idea that God governs the world in goodness—that evil is what happens when God is *not* provoked to govern the world directly—is so upsetting?

עז

לַמְנַצֵּחַ עַל־*יְדוּתוּן לְאָסָף מִזְמוֹר׃
2 קוֹלִי אֶל־אֱלֹהִים וְאֶצְעָקָה קוֹלִי אֶל־אֱלֹהִים וְהַאֲזִין אֵלָי׃
3 בְּיוֹם צָרָתִי אֲדֹנָי דָּרָשְׁתִּי יָדִי | לַיְלָה נִגְּרָה וְלֹא תָפוּג מֵאֲנָה הִנָּחֵם נַפְשִׁי׃
4 אֶזְכְּרָה אֱלֹהִים וְאֶהֱמָיָה אָשִׂיחָה | וְתִתְעַטֵּף רוּחִי סֶלָה׃
5 אָחַזְתָּ שְׁמֻרוֹת עֵינָי נִפְעַמְתִּי וְלֹא אֲדַבֵּר׃
6 חִשַּׁבְתִּי יָמִים מִקֶּדֶם שְׁנוֹת עוֹלָמִים׃ 7 אֶזְכְּרָה נְגִינָתִי בַּלָּיְלָה עִם־לְבָבִי אָשִׂיחָה וַיְחַפֵּשׂ רוּחִי׃
8 הַלְעוֹלָמִים יִזְנַח | אֲדֹנָי וְלֹא־יֹסִיף לִרְצוֹת עוֹד׃
9 הֶאָפֵס לָנֶצַח חַסְדּוֹ גָּמַר אֹמֶר לְדֹר וָדֹר׃
10 הֲשָׁכַח חַנּוֹת אֵל אִם־קָפַץ בְּאַף רַחֲמָיו סֶלָה׃
11 וָאֹמַר חַלּוֹתִי הִיא שְׁנוֹת יְמִין עֶלְיוֹן׃ 12 *אֶזְכּוֹר מַעַלְלֵי־יָהּ כִּי־אֶזְכְּרָה מִקֶּדֶם פִּלְאֶךָ׃ 13 וְהָגִיתִי בְכָל־פָּעֳלֶךָ וּבַעֲלִילוֹתֶיךָ אָשִׂיחָה׃
14 אֱלֹהִים בַּקֹּדֶשׁ דַּרְכֶּךָ מִי־אֵל גָּדוֹל כֵּאלֹהִים׃
15 אַתָּה הָאֵל עֹשֵׂה פֶלֶא הוֹדַעְתָּ בָעַמִּים עֻזֶּךָ׃

v. 1 ידיתון כתיב
v. 12 אזכיר כתיב

Although almost all of its themes appear in other psalms, there is something uncannily haunting about the seventy-seventh psalm, something that sets it apart from every other poem in the Psalter and makes it unique. Under siege from every corner, the poet yearns for communion with God. In so doing, he recalls a night years earlier when he managed to find the succor of divine proximity he now so ardently hopes to experience once more. Will he succeed again in calling up the presence of God? He has no way to know, but as he sits and waits for God, he is assailed by questions not so different from those any modern would ask in a similar situation. Are his recollections real or illusionary? Is it just possible that God has finished communing with humankind for all time, that the words of God preserved in Scripture are the sum total of everything God wishes to say to humanity? Is it reasonable to expect God to relate to him again on a personal level, or is the image of a gracious, caring God presented in the pages of Scripture simply a relic of hoary antiquity he was once able to mimic successfully? Does the same God who once cared so deeply about the pious still exist in the modern world, but in a state of blissful unconcern with their troubles and worries? Can real

77

For the conductor, a psalm of Asaph to be sung to the tune of *Yedutun*.

[2] When I cry out, my voice calls to God; God listens to me when my voice calls out.

[3] In my day of trouble, I reached out to Adonai; by nighttime my soul suffered without respite, then refused to be comforted.

[4] I groan when I recall that night, O God; when I ponder it, my soul becomes faint, *selah*.

[5] When You seized control of my eyesight, I became too agitated to speak.

[6] In my trance, I recalled ancient days and years long gone; [7] I recall now my song of that evening, how I spoke directly to my heart, how my spirit sought God.

[8] "Has Adonai abandoned me permanently?" I asked myself. "Will God never again find favor in me?

[9] Is God's mercy gone forever? Has God finished speaking for all generations?

[10] Has God forgotten how to be gracious? Has God used anger to overwhelm divine compassion, *selah*?"

[11] I said, "This is my hope for as long as the right arm of God Most High should endure: [12] that I should always remember the deeds of יה, that I should forever recall Your wonders of olden times, [13] that I should always meditate on all Your acts and speak constantly about Your great accomplishments."

[14] O God, Your way leads to the Sanctuary; which nation considers its god to be as great as the true God actually is?

[15] You are the God who does wonders; You have made known Your strength to the nations.

people hope for real help from God or has God, fed up with the insincerity and hypocrisy of humankind, finally allowed the quality of divine anger to overwhelm the compassion that might otherwise have been the decisive factor in the way the world is judged?

In the end, the poet finds the strength to hope for God in the contemplation of the various saving acts the Almighty performed in ancient times—acts that themselves demonstrate the reality of God's governance of the world. Whether or not moderns can find similar traces of divine intervention in the study of Israel's past is a

16 גָּאַלְתָּ בִּזְרוֹעַ עַמֶּךָ בְּנֵי־יַעֲקֹב וְיוֹסֵף סֶלָה׃

17 רָאוּךָ מַּיִם | אֱלֹהִים רָאוּךָ מַּיִם יָחִילוּ אַף יִרְגְּזוּ תְהֹמוֹת׃

18 זֹרְמוּ מַיִם | עָבוֹת קוֹל נָתְנוּ שְׁחָקִים אַף־חֲצָצֶיךָ יִתְהַלָּכוּ׃

19 קוֹל רַעַמְךָ | בַּגַּלְגַּל הֵאִירוּ בְרָקִים תֵּבֵל רָגְזָה וַתִּרְעַשׁ הָאָרֶץ׃

20 בַּיָּם דַּרְכֶּךָ *וּשְׁבִילְךָ בְּמַיִם רַבִּים וְעִקְּבוֹתֶיךָ לֹא נֹדָעוּ׃

21 נָחִיתָ כַצֹּאן עַמֶּךָ בְּיַד־מֹשֶׁה וְאַהֲרֹן׃

v. 20 ושבילך כתיב

question we must all answer on our own, based on our understanding of God's relationship to history. The poet does offer his audience some bittersweet advance solace, however, by noting that even the ancient Israelites—who had personally experienced the saving might of God as the waters of the sea parted before them—did not *actually* see any divinely-made footprints in the mud as physical evidence of God's saving presence.

Moderns, of course, are trained from childhood on never to expect any trace of God's presence as simply real and as easily discernable as footprints in the mud of a riverbed to present itself for their thoughtful consideration. Just to the contrary, we are taught as children to think of God—to the extent that we are encouraged to think of God at all—as a kind of intangible force for order and good in the universe that, by the very nature of divine existence, cannot be perceived in the normal, pedestrian way people see and touch and smell the things they feel absolutely certain exist in their world. Indeed, we are taught that the various metaphors we use when speaking of God—calling God a celestial Sovereign or a divine Parent or scrupulously fair Judge—are reasonable *precisely* because without the supportive scaffolding of symbol, myth, and

[16] You redeemed Your people, the children of Jacob and Joseph, with Your great arm, *selah.*

[17] The waters saw You, O God. They saw You and trembled; even the deeps became agitated.

[18] The water of the clouds poured out; the heavens resounded with sound as Your arrows flew all about.

[19] The sound of Your thunder was heard in the heavens; Your lightning bolts illuminated the world as the earth quivered and quaked.

[20] Your highway led through the sea and Your path through mighty waters, yet Your footsteps were imperceptible.

[21] You led Your people like a flock of sheep as they were guided by Moses and Aaron.

metaphor, we would be entirely incapable of talking about God at all.

The 77th psalm can thus be read as a kind of challenge to moderns used to relying on the reassuring frailty of their own intellects to avoid having to encounter God. The ancients didn't see any actual footprints either, the poet notes, but neither were they content to perceive the reality of God solely through the prism of symbolic language. Just to the contrary, their faith was unshakable precisely because their perception of God's saving role in their lives was so apparent as to be unquestionable. The thunder, the lightning, the quivering earth, the parted sea itself . . . all these granted "the children of Jacob and Joseph" a kind of immutable, unchallengeable, unassailable understanding that God's role in their lives was undeniably real, not merely theoretically likely.

God's role in our lives is no less real or profound than it was in the lives of the Israelites whom the poet is describing, only it is less dramatically overt and thus distinctly more challenging to detect. Can moderns ever hope to find God's existence as self-evident as the ancients who stood at the sea and watched its waters part? The poet seems to have overcome the hurdle himself, so perhaps moderns would do best merely to contemplate his faith and try to learn from it . . . just as the poet himself contemplated the faith of his ancestors at the sea and thus learned to know God.

עח

מַשְׂכִּיל לְאָסָף
הַאֲזִינָה עַמִּי תּוֹרָתִי הַטּוּ אָזְנְכֶם לְאִמְרֵי־פִי׃
2 אֶפְתְּחָה בְמָשָׁל פִּי אַבִּיעָה חִידוֹת מִנִּי־קֶדֶם׃
3 אֲשֶׁר שָׁמַעְנוּ וַנֵּדָעֵם וַאֲבוֹתֵינוּ סִפְּרוּ־לָנוּ׃
4 לֹא נְכַחֵד ׀ מִבְּנֵיהֶם לְדוֹר אַחֲרוֹן מְסַפְּרִים תְּהִלּוֹת
יְהוָה וֶעֱזוּזוֹ וְנִפְלְאוֹתָיו אֲשֶׁר עָשָׂה׃
5 וַיָּקֶם עֵדוּת ׀ בְּיַעֲקֹב וְתוֹרָה שָׂם בְּיִשְׂרָאֵל אֲשֶׁר־
צִוָּה אֶת־אֲבוֹתֵינוּ לְהוֹדִיעָם לִבְנֵיהֶם׃ 6 לְמַעַן
יֵדְעוּ ׀ דּוֹר אַחֲרוֹן בָּנִים יִוָּלֵדוּ יָקֻמוּ וִיסַפְּרוּ
לִבְנֵיהֶם׃ 7 וְיָשִׂימוּ בֵאלֹהִים כִּסְלָם וְלֹא יִשְׁכְּחוּ
מַעַלְלֵי־אֵל וּמִצְוֹתָיו יִנְצֹרוּ׃ 8 וְלֹא יִהְיוּ ׀ כַּאֲבוֹתָם
דּוֹר סוֹרֵר וּמֹרֶה דּוֹר לֹא־הֵכִין לִבּוֹ וְלֹא־נֶאֶמְנָה
אֶת־אֵל רוּחוֹ׃
9 בְּנֵי־אֶפְרַיִם נוֹשְׁקֵי רוֹמֵי־קָשֶׁת הָפְכוּ בְּיוֹם קְרָב׃
10 לֹא שָׁמְרוּ בְּרִית אֱלֹהִים וּבְתוֹרָתוֹ מֵאֲנוּ לָלֶכֶת׃
11 וַיִּשְׁכְּחוּ עֲלִילוֹתָיו וְנִפְלְאוֹתָיו אֲשֶׁר הֶרְאָם׃
12 נֶגֶד אֲבוֹתָם עָשָׂה פֶלֶא בְּאֶרֶץ מִצְרַיִם שְׂדֵה־צֹעַן׃
13 בָּקַע יָם וַיַּעֲבִירֵם וַיַּצֶּב־מַיִם כְּמוֹ־נֵד׃ 14 וַיַּנְחֵם
בֶּעָנָן יוֹמָם וְכָל־הַלַּיְלָה בְּאוֹר אֵשׁ׃
15 יְבַקַּע צֻרִים בַּמִּדְבָּר וַיַּשְׁקְ כִּתְהֹמוֹת רַבָּה׃

The ancients took the tales of Israelite history as lessons in didactic spirituality (rather than as mere records to be preserved and studied because of their intrinsic historical importance or literary interest) and it was probably for that reason that the editors of the various books of the Bible did not feel troubled about presenting multiple versions of certain stories even when those versions failed to match each other in every last detail. Still, given the fact that these tales were preserved not over centuries, but—at least eventually—over millennia, it is striking how very similar all these various retellings of the stories of God's involvement in the history of Israel are. A careful reading of the seventy-eighth psalm is a good example: although the poet clearly knew at least some stories unrecorded elsewhere in the biblical narrative (as well as some unfamiliar versions of some stories that do appear elsewhere), it is equally obvious that he knew the same basic outline of his people's past as is found in the other biblical accounts of Israelite history.

But the so-called historical psalms are works of spiritual philosophy as much as retellings of ancient events. And for the poet who produced the poem we know as the seventy-eighth psalm, the long, drawn-out story of Israel's alternating periods of devotion and alienation from their God was the ideal

78

A wise-song of Asaph.

Give ear to my teaching, O my people; incline your ear to the words of my mouth.

[2] I shall open my mouth with a parable; I shall declaim ancient riddle-songs [3]we heard and solved when our parents told them to us.

[4] Having learnt them ourselves, we will not deny them to their descendants, telling the next generation the praises of יהוה and also telling of God's power and the wonders God has wrought.

[5] God established testimony in Jacob and bestowed teaching upon Israel, a *torah* bequeathed to our ancestors so that they might make it known to their children, [6]so that even the children born to the latest generation will rise up and tell of it to their own children, [7]so that they will put their faith in God and not forget the deeds of God, so that they will keep the commandments of God, [8]so that they not become a stubborn and rebellious generation like their ancestors, a generation that did not make its heart right and whose spirit was not faithful to God.

[9] The Ephraimites were warriors and archers, but they turned and ran away on the day of battle; [10]they did not keep the covenant of God and refused to follow God's teaching; [11]they forgot God's deeds and the wonders that had been shown them.

[12] In the presence of their ancestors, God wrought wonders in the land of Egypt, the field of Zoan, [13]dividing the sea and letting the people travel across, making the water to stand up like a wall, [14]then leading them in a cloud by day and all night long with luminescent fire.

[15] God split rocks in the desert and gave the people to drink so bounteously that it was

framework for just the poetic disquisition on the way God lives in history the poet hoped to pen. Indeed, the poet starts with a detail unfamiliar to us from other biblical accounts—that the tribe of Ephraim fled from the battlefield at a certain specific moment in Israelite history—and uses that act of military cowardice as his jumping-off point for a long review of Israelite history, which, in turn, allows him to learn something profound from the way Israel alternately cleaves unto its God and then capriciously rebels against divine governance. (Some commentators find a vague second biblical reference to the flight of the

16 וַיּוֹצִא נוֹזְלִים מִסָּלַע וַיּוֹרֶד כַּנְּהָרוֹת מָיִם׃
17 וַיּוֹסִיפוּ עוֹד לַחֲטֹא־לוֹ לַמְרוֹת עֶלְיוֹן בַּצִּיָּה׃
18 וַיְנַסּוּ־אֵל בִּלְבָבָם לִשְׁאָל־אֹכֶל לְנַפְשָׁם׃
19 וַיְדַבְּרוּ בֵּאלֹהִים אָמְרוּ הֲיוּכַל אֵל לַעֲרֹךְ שֻׁלְחָן בַּמִּדְבָּר׃ 20 הֵן הִכָּה־צוּר ׀ וַיָּזוּבוּ מַיִם וּנְחָלִים יִשְׁטֹפוּ הֲגַם־לֶחֶם יוּכַל תֵּת אִם־יָכִין שְׁאֵר לְעַמּוֹ׃
21 לָכֵן ׀ שָׁמַע יְהוָה וַיִּתְעַבָּר וְאֵשׁ נִשְּׂקָה בְיַעֲקֹב וְגַם־אַף עָלָה בְיִשְׂרָאֵל׃ 22 כִּי לֹא הֶאֱמִינוּ בֵּאלֹהִים וְלֹא בָטְחוּ בִּישׁוּעָתוֹ׃
23 וַיְצַו שְׁחָקִים מִמָּעַל וְדַלְתֵי שָׁמַיִם פָּתָח׃ 24 וַיַּמְטֵר עֲלֵיהֶם מָן לֶאֱכֹל וּדְגַן שָׁמַיִם נָתַן לָמוֹ׃
25 לֶחֶם אַבִּירִים אָכַל אִישׁ צֵידָה שָׁלַח לָהֶם לָשֹׂבַע׃
26 יַסַּע קָדִים בַּשָּׁמָיִם וַיְנַהֵג בְּעֻזּוֹ תֵימָן׃ 27 וַיַּמְטֵר עֲלֵיהֶם כֶּעָפָר שְׁאֵר וּכְחוֹל יַמִּים עוֹף כָּנָף׃
28 וַיַּפֵּל בְּקֶרֶב מַחֲנֵהוּ סָבִיב לְמִשְׁכְּנֹתָיו׃ 29 וַיֹּאכְלוּ וַיִּשְׂבְּעוּ מְאֹד וְתַאֲוָתָם יָבִא לָהֶם׃

Ephraimites in 1 Chronicles 7:21.)

The whole psalm follows this pattern of telling one story of divine beneficence followed by one about Israelite rebelliousness. God led Israel through the sea and provided ample potable water for them to drink in the desert, but Israel nevertheless refused to submit to God's rule and brought divine wrath against themselves by defying God to abandon them. God made manna fall from heaven and arranged for an endless supply of fowl for the Israelites to eat, but it still was not impressive enough to move Israel to become the nation of grateful servants of God it was, the poet clearly believes, more than reasonable to expect it to become. In the desert, the people even forgot the various plagues God had sent against the Egyptians . . . and although the poet's list of plagues is not given in precisely the same order as in the Book of Exodus, the idea is still easily accessible: God wrought mighty wonders unparalleled in the history of Israel, but the people were too obstinate to acknowledge God's responsibility for their survival in a hostile, alien climate that easily could have swallowed them up without leaving even a trace of their existence behind.

Nor did the situation improve after the people became settled in their land. Indeed, it worsened: God banished the indigenous nations of Canaan to make room for the conquering Israelites, but the latter's endless disobedience and disloyalty eventually resulted in the destruction of the famous sanctuary at Shiloh. (Although it seems to be a given in other biblical passages, this particular incident is not specifically mentioned or described elsewhere in the Bible.) Israel was still obstinate and difficult, however, refusing to respond with allegiance and fidelity to what by then had become an almost endless series of acts of divine goodness and caring. In the end, Ephraim—now used as a poetic name for the northern kingdom of Israel—was swept away into exile and, at least in

as though the water were coming to them from deep underground springs; [16]God brought forth streams of water from a rock, and caused the water to flow like a river.

[17] But still they continued to sin against God, defying the Most High in the wilderness [18]and testing God in their hearts by demanding food for their sustenance.

[19] They spoke against God saying, "Can God set a table for us in the desert? [20]To be sure, God struck a rock and water flowed out in gushing streams, but will the Almighty be able to provide bread for us as well . . . or meat for God's people?"

[21] Upon hearing this, יהוה became enraged and a fire was kindled against Jacob; divine anger too rose up against Israel [22]because the people neither believed in God nor put their trust in divine salvation.

[23] But, nevertheless, God gave a command to the heavens on high and opened the portals of heaven; [24]God caused manna to rain down on them, thus giving them heavenly grain to eat.

[25] The bread of the mighty did each person eat; God sent them more than enough provisions for their journey.

[26] God made the east wind blow in the heavens and with divine strength made bluster the wind from the south, [27]then caused meat to rain down on them like dust, sending winged fowl as many as the grains of sand at the beach.

[28] God made it fall in the midst of their camp all around their dwellings, [29]whereupon they ate and were very satisfied. God gave them what they craved.

30 לֹא־זָרוּ מִתַּאֲוָתָם עוֹד אָכְלָם בְּפִיהֶם׃ 31 וְאַף אֱלֹהִים | עָלָה בָהֶם וַיַּהֲרֹג בְּמִשְׁמַנֵּיהֶם וּבַחוּרֵי יִשְׂרָאֵל הִכְרִיעַ׃
32 בְּכָל־זֹאת חָטְאוּ־עוֹד וְלֹא הֶאֱמִינוּ בְּנִפְלְאוֹתָיו׃
33 וַיְכַל־בַּהֶבֶל יְמֵיהֶם וּשְׁנוֹתָם בַּבֶּהָלָה׃
34 אִם־הֲרָגָם וּדְרָשׁוּהוּ וְשָׁבוּ וְשִׁחֲרוּ־אֵל׃ 35 וַיִּזְכְּרוּ כִּי־אֱלֹהִים צוּרָם וְאֵל עֶלְיוֹן גֹּאֲלָם׃
36*וַיְפַתּוּהוּ בְּפִיהֶם וּבִלְשׁוֹנָם יְכַזְּבוּ־לוֹ׃ 37 וְלִבָּם לֹא־נָכוֹן עִמּוֹ וְלֹא נֶאֶמְנוּ בִּבְרִיתוֹ׃ 38 וְהוּא רַחוּם | יְכַפֵּר עָוֹן וְלֹא־יַשְׁחִית וְהִרְבָּה לְהָשִׁיב אַפּוֹ וְלֹא־יָעִיר כָּל־חֲמָתוֹ׃ 39 וַיִּזְכֹּר כִּי־בָשָׂר הֵמָּה רוּחַ הוֹלֵךְ וְלֹא יָשׁוּב׃
40 כַּמָּה יַמְרוּהוּ בַמִּדְבָּר יַעֲצִיבוּהוּ בִּישִׁימוֹן׃
41 וַיָּשׁוּבוּ וַיְנַסּוּ אֵל וּקְדוֹשׁ יִשְׂרָאֵל הִתְווּ׃
42 לֹא־זָכְרוּ אֶת־יָדוֹ יוֹם אֲשֶׁר־פָּדָם מִנִּי־צָר׃
43 אֲשֶׁר־שָׂם בְּמִצְרַיִם אֹתוֹתָיו וּמוֹפְתָיו בִּשְׂדֵה־צֹעַן׃ 44 וַיַּהֲפֹךְ לְדָם יְאֹרֵיהֶם וְנֹזְלֵיהֶם בַּל־

v. 36 חצי הספר בפסוקים

the poet's conception, God's favor was focused solely on the southern kingdom of Judah.

We cannot know whether the poet lived in pre-exilic Jerusalem and hoped that the people would never provoke God to punish his people with devastation and exile, or whether he lived after the destruction and subsequent exile and therefore knew all too well what was to come. In either case, the point is that God's covenant with Israel does not preclude even the most horrible kind of disaster, and that the Jewish people can bring upon itself untold suffering and misery *despite* its covenantal relationship with God. The ebb and flow of grace, the alternating periods of sunlight and shadow, of peace and war, of favor and divine disfavor—these are not the arbitrary details of unalterably foreordained history, but the consequence of a people's apparently endemic inability to turn wholeheartedly unto God. Moderns will want to add in the disasters and triumphs of Jewish history in the twenty-odd centuries that have unfolded since the psalmist's day and ask how things have changed in all that time between God and Israel . . . if, indeed, they have changed at all. And they will want to ask themselves an even more disturbing question as well: if Israel is doomed to continue its age-old pattern of accepting and then rejecting divine guidance, then who exactly has issued the unalterable decree . . . and on what authority?

[30–31] They had not tired of those cravings—indeed, the food was still in their mouths—when the anger of God rose up against them as the Almighty subdued the youths of Israel, killing even the most robust among them.

[32] For all that, they continued to sin and did not believe in God's wonders.

[33] God ended their days in futility, their years in panic; [34]when God moved to slay them, they finally sought out the Almighty, turning back and searching for God, [35]for once remembering that God was their Rock, God Most High, their Redeemer.

[36] They tried to mislead God with their mouths, to lie to the Almighty with their tongues, [37]for neither were their hearts right with God nor were they faithful to God's covenant—and this, despite the fact that [38]God is compassionate, forgiving of iniquity, forbearing to destroy, vastly preferring to hold back divine rage and never doing anything to stir up divine wrath; [39]God was nonetheless moved by pity, remembering that they were just flesh animated by a soul that eventually departs never to return.

[40] How often did they rebel against God in the wilderness and sadden the Almighty in the wasteland! [41]Yet they chose to test God again and again, demanding a sign that the Holy One of Israel was in their midst.

[42] They remembered neither God's hand nor the day the Almighty redeemed them from the enemy; [43]for God did indeed send divine signs against Egypt and divine wonders in the field of Zoan, [44]turning their rivers to blood so that they could not drink from their streams,

Surely, after all, the free will granted by God to all humanity applies to the Jewish people as well. But if that is the case, then why should Israel be doomed to behave in any particular way, merely because that was the pattern of behavior the nation followed in the past?

There is something satisfying and reassuring about the notion that nations are not entirely free to chart their own destinies, that some supernatural force is invariably guiding them along. Indeed, it is *very* comforting to feel that nations do not bear ultimate responsibility for their own acts because they are not entirely free to act as they choose.

יִשְׁתָּיוּן׃ 45 יְשַׁלַּח בָּהֶם עָרֹב וַיֹּאכְלֵם וּצְפַרְדֵּעַ
וַתַּשְׁחִיתֵם׃
46 וַיִּתֵּן לֶחָסִיל יְבוּלָם וִיגִיעָם לָאַרְבֶּה׃ 47 יַהֲרֹג
בַּבָּרָד גַּפְנָם וְשִׁקְמוֹתָם בַּחֲנָמַל׃ 48 וַיַּסְגֵּר לַבָּרָד
בְּעִירָם וּמִקְנֵיהֶם לָרְשָׁפִים׃
49 יְשַׁלַּח־בָּם ׀ חֲרוֹן אַפּוֹ עֶבְרָה וָזַעַם וְצָרָה מִשְׁלַחַת
מַלְאֲכֵי רָעִים׃
50 יְפַלֵּס נָתִיב לְאַפּוֹ לֹא־חָשַׂךְ מִמָּוֶת נַפְשָׁם וְחַיָּתָם
לַדֶּבֶר הִסְגִּיר׃ 51 וַיַּךְ כָּל־בְּכוֹר בְּמִצְרָיִם רֵאשִׁית
אוֹנִים בְּאָהֳלֵי־חָם׃
52 וַיַּסַּע כַּצֹּאן עַמּוֹ וַיְנַהֲגֵם כַּעֵדֶר בַּמִּדְבָּר׃ 53 וַיַּנְחֵם
לָבֶטַח וְלֹא פָחָדוּ וְאֶת־אוֹיְבֵיהֶם כִּסָּה הַיָּם׃
54 וַיְבִיאֵם אֶל־גְּבוּל קָדְשׁוֹ הַר־זֶה קָנְתָה יְמִינוֹ׃
55 וַיְגָרֶשׁ מִפְּנֵיהֶם ׀ גּוֹיִם וַיַּפִּילֵם בְּחֶבֶל נַחֲלָה וַיַּשְׁכֵּן
בְּאָהֳלֵיהֶם שִׁבְטֵי יִשְׂרָאֵל׃
56 וַיְנַסּוּ וַיַּמְרוּ אֶת־אֱלֹהִים עֶלְיוֹן וְעֵדוֹתָיו לֹא
שָׁמָרוּ׃ 57 וַיִּסֹּגוּ וַיִּבְגְּדוּ כַּאֲבוֹתָם נֶהְפְּכוּ כְּקֶשֶׁת

Whether one explains this as a result of being cursed with a national ethos that cannot be thwarted, or whether one imagines nations being subject to the tyranny of some sort of national genetic heritage, the notion that a nation's flaws are somehow inherent in its national character is an idea many will be all too happy to embrace. Regretfully, this line of thinking is far more self-serving than it is reasonable or demonstrable. Nations do *not* possess genes. The national character of a country is simply another name for the collective will of its citizenry. The perceived inclination of a country to follow a certain course in history, again and again, merely mirrors the fact that people of that country have chosen, time and time again, to travel down the same path. Nations, therefore, are not doomed to behave in specific ways any more than their citizens are. As unpleasant a reality it is to face, reading the 78th psalm can prompt us to accept that nations do not have to behave in *any* particular way because of history—not the history of other countries and certainly not their own history.

The poet is, therefore, not writing to reflect on the ineluctable obligation of Israel to abandon God at regular intervals throughout history. Rather, he is writing to teach a lesson to his audience, a lesson that he feels they should take seriously to heart. God, he notes, has been endlessly patient with Israel. No matter how many times the people turned away from the path of the covenant, God forgave them and protected them from their enemies. No matter how often Israel showed itself to be stubborn and willful, God did not respond by unilaterally annulling the covenant, but rather by hewing all the more carefully to the divine end of the bargain and protecting Israel until the people came to their senses and turned back to God. But, the poet is also hinting, God cannot be presumed to be bound to future action by past history any more than can Israel. In other words, just as Israel can return

[45]sending wild beasts to eat them and frogs to destroy them.

[46] Nor did they remember the Almighty when God gave their produce to the grasshopper and the fruit of their labor to the locust, [47]then killed their vines with hail and their sycamores with frozen rain, [48]then made their cattle prisoners of the hail, and their herds, prisoners of lightning bolts.

[49] God sent wrathful anger against them, dispatching Rage, Fury, and Trouble as a delegation of evil angels.

[50] God made a pathway for those messengers of divine anger, neither sparing the souls of the Egyptians from death nor refraining from making their animals victims of pestilence; [51]God slew every firstborn son of Egypt, those foremost in strength in the tents of Ham.

[52] But God's own people, the Almighty sent off like sheep, guiding them in the desert like a flock, [53]leading them to safety so that they did not fear while the sea covered up their enemies, [54]taking them to the holy precinct, to the mountain God's own right hand had once made.

[55] God banished nations from before them, apportioning out for them their inheritance with a plumb line and settling the tribes of Israel into their tents.

[56] And yet they continued to test and to rebel against God Most High, whose testimonies they did not keep; [57]they retreated and behaved treacherously like their ancestors, turning away from God like a bow strung in the wrong direc-

רְמִיָּֽה׃ [58] וַיַּכְעִיסֽוּהוּ בְּבָמוֹתָם וּבִפְסִילֵיהֶם
יַקְנִיאֽוּהוּ׃
[59] שָׁמַע אֱלֹהִים וַיִּתְעַבָּר וַיִּמְאַס מְאֹד בְּיִשְׂרָאֵֽל׃
[60] וַיִּטֹּשׁ מִשְׁכַּן שִׁלוֹ אֹהֶל שִׁכֵּן בָּאָדָֽם׃ [61] וַיִּתֵּן
לַשְּׁבִי עֻזּוֹ וְתִפְאַרְתּוֹ בְיַד־צָֽר׃ [62] וַיַּסְגֵּר לַחֶרֶב עַמּוֹ
וּבְנַחֲלָתוֹ הִתְעַבָּֽר׃
[63] בַּחוּרָיו אָֽכְלָה־אֵשׁ וּבְתוּלֹתָיו לֹא הוּלָּֽלוּ׃
[64] כֹּהֲנָיו בַּחֶרֶב נָפָלוּ וְאַלְמְנֹתָיו לֹא תִבְכֶּֽינָה׃
[65] וַיִּקַץ כְּיָשֵׁן ׀ אֲדֹנָי כְּגִבּוֹר מִתְרוֹנֵן מִיָּֽיִן׃ [66] וַיַּךְ־צָרָיו
אָחוֹר חֶרְפַּת עוֹלָם נָתַן לָֽמוֹ׃
[67] וַיִּמְאַס בְּאֹהֶל יוֹסֵף וּבְשֵׁבֶט אֶפְרַיִם לֹא בָחָֽר׃
[68] וַיִּבְחַר אֶת־שֵׁבֶט יְהוּדָה אֶת־הַר צִיּוֹן אֲשֶׁר אָהֵֽב׃
[69] וַיִּבֶן כְּמוֹ־רָמִים מִקְדָּשׁוֹ כְּאֶרֶץ יְסָדָהּ לְעוֹלָֽם׃
[70] וַיִּבְחַר בְּדָוִד עַבְדּוֹ וַיִּקָּחֵהוּ מִֽמִּכְלְאֹת צֹֽאן׃
[71] מֵאַחַר עָלוֹת הֱבִיאוֹ לִרְעוֹת בְּיַעֲקֹב עַמּוֹ
וּבְיִשְׂרָאֵל נַחֲלָתֽוֹ׃
[72] וַיִּרְעֵם כְּתֹם לְבָבוֹ וּבִתְבוּנוֹת כַּפָּיו יַנְחֵֽם׃

wholeheartedly and permanently to the service of God without reference to past instances of rebelliousness or disobedience, so can God also act in history without reference to the past. So far, the poet assures his readers and listeners, God has been endlessly merciful. The people rebelled repeatedly in the wilderness and God punished them, but then brought them to the Promised Land anyway. The nation was disobedient, but God nevertheless granted that they conquer the land. When the Israelites built forbidden high places and worshiped idols, God responded by allowing the shrine at Shiloh to be destroyed; but God then relented, choosing David to establish a new national shrine and subsequently loving the Jerusalem Temple more than any other sanctuary. But to assume that the future will always be as the past has been—

tion, [58]angering the Almighty with their high places and provoking God to jealousy with their idols.

[59] God heard and became enraged, abhorring Israel greatly, [60]abandoning the shrine at Shiloh—the very sanctuary the Almighty had set in the midst of humanity—[61]thus at once letting the symbols of divine strength go into captivity, allowing the emblems of divine splendor to pass into the hands of the foe, [62]consigning the people of God to the sword and expressing divine outrage at God's own inheritance.

[63] Fire consumed God's young men; the virgins of God's people were doomed never to wed.

[64] God's priests fell to the sword, but their widows did not weep for them.

[65] Then Adonai awakened as one who had been asleep, as a hero sobering up from too much wine, [66]and beat back the enemy, giving them permanent shame.

[67] Thus did God come to abhor the tent of Joseph, no longer to consider the tribe of Ephraim to be the chosen clan of God.

[68] Instead, the Almighty chose the tribe of Judah and Mount Zion, beloved of God, [69]then built the divine sanctuary as an elevated fortress, like a world unto itself established with permanence, [70]and chose God's servant David by taking him from the sheepfolds [71]and bringing him from among the ewes to be shepherd over Jacob, God's people, and over Israel, God's inheritance.

[72] And he did indeed shepherd them, acting in accordance with his guileless heart, leading them forward with his wise hands.

that God may or may not punish Israel for individual acts of disobedience, but will never actually cancel the covenant itself—that, the poet is saying, is something logical, thoughtful, realistic students of history should never presume. Moderns can indeed learn from history, he suggests, but for the lesson truly to be meaningful, it must be rooted in the conviction that the past can only *suggest* what the future might bring, never *guarantee* that anything in particular that happened once must unavoidably happen again.

עט

מִזְמוֹר לְאָסָף
אֱלֹהִים בָּאוּ גוֹיִם ׀ בְּנַחֲלָתֶךָ טִמְּאוּ אֶת־הֵיכַל
קָדְשֶׁךָ שָׂמוּ אֶת־יְרוּשָׁלִַם לְעִיִּים׃
2 נָתְנוּ אֶת־נִבְלַת עֲבָדֶיךָ מַאֲכָל לְעוֹף הַשָּׁמָיִם בְּשַׂר
חֲסִידֶיךָ לְחַיְתוֹ־אָרֶץ׃
3 שָׁפְכוּ דָמָם ׀ כַּמַּיִם סְבִיבוֹת יְרוּשָׁלִָם וְאֵין קוֹבֵר׃
4 הָיִינוּ חֶרְפָּה לִשְׁכֵנֵינוּ לַעַג וָקֶלֶס לִסְבִיבוֹתֵינוּ׃
5 עַד־מָה יְהוָה תֶּאֱנַף לָנֶצַח תִּבְעַר כְּמוֹ־אֵשׁ
קִנְאָתֶךָ׃
6 שְׁפֹךְ חֲמָתְךָ אֶל־הַגּוֹיִם אֲשֶׁר לֹא־יְדָעוּךָ וְעַל
מַמְלָכוֹת אֲשֶׁר בְּשִׁמְךָ לֹא קָרָאוּ׃ 7 כִּי־אָכַל
אֶת־יַעֲקֹב וְאֶת־נָוֵהוּ הֵשַׁמּוּ׃
8 אַל־תִּזְכָּר־לָנוּ עֲוֺנֹת רִאשֹׁנִים מַהֵר יְקַדְּמוּנוּ
רַחֲמֶיךָ כִּי דַלּוֹנוּ מְאֹד׃
9 עָזְרֵנוּ ׀ אֱלֹהֵי יִשְׁעֵנוּ עַל־דְּבַר כְּבוֹד־שְׁמֶךָ וְהַצִּילֵנוּ
וְכַפֵּר עַל־חַטֹּאתֵינוּ לְמַעַן שְׁמֶךָ׃

Jewish readers of the seventy-ninth psalm will recognize the psalmist's prayer that God pour out a full measure of divine wrath on godless alien nations from the liturgy recited during the Passover *seder* meal. No one who reads the psalmist's description of Jerusalem in ruins, however, can possibly fail to recognize—and to be shaken by—the terror that suffuses its horrifying cadences. Indeed, even after decades of watching television reports of terror attacks aimed at the citizens of the Holy City, modern readers will still find it difficult to imagine Jerusalem absolutely and utterly devastated, its alleyways littered with rotting cadavers of priests and Levites too numerous for the handful of survivors to bury, even though animals are already wandering through the city and picking at them. Still, reading and rereading the psalmist's work can allow us some degree of insight into the utter hopelessness the survivors must have felt as they contemplated Zion in ruins. And even readers who find it impossible to develop of clear mental image of the city's drainage ditches flowing and overflowing with blood should still be able to conjure up a picture of stunned survivors sitting dumbfounded and overwhelmed as they listen to the derisive laughter of the enemy hordes asking what good, after all, the God of Israel was for the people that so ardently trusted in the protective goodness of the Divine.

But the seventy-ninth psalm need not function solely as a testimony to the misery inflicted on ancient Jerusalem by phalanxes of arrogant enemy

79

A psalm of Asaph.

O God, the nations came into Your estate; they profaned Your holy Temple and made Jerusalem a ruin.

[2] They gave the corpses of Your servants to the birds of heaven as food, the flesh of Your pious to the beasts of the land.

[3] They spilled their blood like water; there were cadavers all around Jerusalem, but no one to bury them.

[4] We were the embodiment of shame in the eyes of our neighbors, the essence of scorn and derision to the peoples all around.

[5] To what point, יהוה, will You appear to remain permanently angry? How long will Your jealousy burn like fire?

[6] Pour out Your wrath instead on the nations who do not know You, on the kingdoms that do not call out in Your name, [7] for they are the ones who have consumed Jacob and destroyed his people's Temple.

[8] Recall not the sins of our ancestors. May Your compassion come quickly to the fore, for we are fallen very low indeed.

[9] O God of our salvation, help us for the sake of the glory due Your name and save us and forgive our sins for the sake of Your name.

soldiers. Indeed, moderns may well want to respond to the challenge of this psalm by asking themselves an entirely different set of questions. The ancients who witnessed the destruction of Jerusalem had, after all, not only a geopolitical and military catastrophe on their hands, but also a theological one. Could God be worshiped in the absence of a Holy Temple? Could there be any acceptable substitute for the animal sacrifices ordained by Scripture, but not doable in the absence of sanctuary and altar? Is it conceivable that God could totally abandon the Holy City, the one place on earth where, according to Jewish tradition, the indwelling of the divine presence was so intensely and palpably concentrated that pilgrims and visitors could actually feel that presence merely by entering the city's walls?

At least for the most part, we moderns are not too seriously worried about the absence of animal sacrifices in modern Judaism. We will certainly want

10 לָמָּה ׀ יֹאמְר֣וּ הַגּוֹיִם֮ אַיֵּ֪ה אֱלֹהֵ֫יהֶ֥ם יִוָּדַ֣ע *בַּגּוֹיִ֣ם
לְעֵינֵ֑ינוּ נִ֝קְמַ֗ת דַּם־עֲבָדֶ֥יךָ הַשָּׁפֽוּךְ׃
11 תָּב֤וֹא לְפָנֶ֗יךָ אֶ֫נְקַ֥ת אָ֫סִ֥יר כְּגֹ֥דֶל זְרוֹעֲךָ֑ ה֝וֹתֵ֗ר בְּנֵ֣י
תְמוּתָֽה׃ 12 וְהָשֵׁ֬ב לִשְׁכֵנֵ֣ינוּ שִׁ֭בְעָתַיִם אֶל־חֵיקָ֑ם
חֶ֝רְפָּתָ֗ם אֲשֶׁ֣ר חֵרְפ֣וּךָ אֲדֹנָֽי׃
13 וַאֲנַ֤חְנוּ עַמְּךָ֨ ׀ וְצֹ֤אן מַרְעִיתֶ֗ךָ נ֤וֹדֶה לְּךָ֗ לְע֫וֹלָ֥ם
לְדֹ֣ר וָדֹ֑ר נְ֝סַפֵּ֗ר תְּהִלָּתֶֽךָ׃

v. 10 בגיים כתיב

to ask ourselves, however, if we believe the covenant between God and the Jewish people to be absolutely inviolate, or whether we believe that its terms could be annulled by a display of sufficient disloyalty to its codicils by the human parties to the accord.

And there is the question of the Shoah to consider as well. For most of us, the Holocaust provides the same impetus to re-evaluate the nature of the covenant between God and Israel that the destruction of Jerusalem provided for the ancients. Neither event, after all, feels like merely another disastrous event in the history of the Jewish people. On the contrary, both events feel so absolutely different from other horrors that have befallen Israel (in quality as well as in intensity) that it seems inappropriate to respond simply by quoting

[10] Why should the nations ask, "Where is their God?" May our eyes see it become known among the nations how the spilt blood of Your servants is to be avenged.

[11] Let the groaning of a prisoner come before You. Let the might of Your arm release the condemned [12] and return to our neighbors' midst sevenfold the shame they have inflicted upon You, Adonai.

[13] For it is we who are Your people and the sheep of Your flock, we who will give thanks to You forever, we who will tell of the praise due You from generation to generation.

verses from Scripture or blithely asserting our ongoing faith in God's eternal commitment to our protection. Indeed even a cursory study of both events will make it obvious that there is no degree of depravity or suffering from which God will inevitably and unconditionally shield the Jewish people. Yet, the contemplation of God's role in the history of Israel does not have to be unremittingly dour or depressing. Instead, reading the seventy-ninth psalm can serve as a spur to pondering the nature of the *berit*—its terms, its theoretical inviolability and unchangeability, its permanence, and its uniqueness—and for making some firm decisions about the way we understand our own relationship with God. It is one thing, after all, to speak in lofty covenantal terms when we talk about God and Israel . . . but quite another to say what we mean exactly.

פ

לַמְנַצֵּחַ אֶל־שֹׁשַׁנִּים עֵדוּת לְאָסָף מִזְמוֹר׃
2 רֹעֵה יִשְׂרָאֵל | הַאֲזִינָה נֹהֵג כַּצֹּאן יוֹסֵף יֹשֵׁב הַכְּרוּבִים הוֹפִיעָה׃
3 לִפְנֵי אֶפְרַיִם | וּבִנְיָמִן וּמְנַשֶּׁה עוֹרְרָה אֶת־גְּבוּרָתֶךָ וּלְכָה לִישֻׁעָתָה לָּנוּ׃
4 אֱלֹהִים הֲשִׁיבֵנוּ וְהָאֵר פָּנֶיךָ וְנִוָּשֵׁעָה׃
5 יְהוָה אֱלֹהִים צְבָאוֹת עַד־מָתַי עָשַׁנְתָּ בִּתְפִלַּת עַמֶּךָ׃
6 הֶאֱכַלְתָּם לֶחֶם דִּמְעָה וַתַּשְׁקֵמוֹ בִּדְמָעוֹת שָׁלִישׁ׃
7 תְּשִׂימֵנוּ מָדוֹן לִשְׁכֵנֵינוּ וְאֹיְבֵינוּ יִלְעֲגוּ־לָמוֹ׃
8 אֱלֹהִים צְבָאוֹת הֲשִׁיבֵנוּ וְהָאֵר פָּנֶיךָ וְנִוָּשֵׁעָה׃
9 גֶּפֶן מִמִּצְרַיִם תַּסִּיעַ תְּגָרֵשׁ גּוֹיִם וַתִּטָּעֶהָ׃
10 פִּנִּיתָ לְפָנֶיהָ וַתַּשְׁרֵשׁ שָׁרָשֶׁיהָ וַתְּמַלֵּא־אָרֶץ׃
11 כָּסּוּ הָרִים צִלָּהּ וַעֲנָפֶיהָ אַרְזֵי־אֵל׃
12 תְּשַׁלַּח קְצִירֶהָ עַד־יָם וְאֶל־נָהָר יוֹנְקוֹתֶיהָ׃

The image of Israel as the vine of God is not unique to the eightieth psalm, but no poet developed that image as seriously as did the author of this ancient poem. He imagines the vine as beginning in Egypt, but he can see God, the cosmic Vintner, personally endeavoring to train it away from its original setting and guide it across the wilderness to the Land of Israel. Just as any decent vintner would first get rid of weeds before introducing the specific vine he wants to cultivate into the setting in which he hopes it will flourish, so did God banish the aboriginal peoples of Canaan to set the stage for Israel's growth to secure nationhood in its own land. What happened next, however, was nothing short of miraculous, both in viticultural and geopolitical terms: not only did the vine take root in its new setting, but it began to grow to amazing, almost unbelievable, proportions. Its roots sank deep into the ground as its runners grew into every corner of the land. It became so immensely large—as thick as a cedar trunk, the poet writes—that it was able to cast its shadow on mighty mountains. And it grew in every direction at once, stopping in the west only at the shores of the Mediterranean and growing in the east as far as the distant Euphrates.

But now, the poet writes, an unanticipated disaster has befallen the sacred vine of Israel. The fence that guards it—the nation's defenses—have been knocked down. Wild boars gnaw on its runners without the slightest hindrance. Human foes treat it with a similar lack of respect, chopping it down

80

For the conductor, a testimony-psalm of Asaph, to be sung to the tune of "Lilies."

[2] O Shepherd of Israel, give ear! O God enthroned upon the cherubim, who leads forth Joseph like a shepherd might lead a flock of sheep, appear!

[3] Awaken Your might before Ephraim and Benjamin and Manasseh, and go forth to effect salvation for us.

[4] O God, return us to You; illuminate Your face that we may be saved.

[5] O יהוה-Elohim of the celestial legions, how long will You smolder in rage and spurn the prayers of Your people?

[6] You have fed them bread kneaded with tears; indeed, a third of what You give them to drink is tears.

[7] You have made us a source of contention with our neighbors and our enemies mock us freely.

[8] O God of the celestial legions, return us to You; illuminate Your face that we may be saved.

[9] You trained a vine to grow from Egypt, then banished nations and planted it in their place.

[10] You cleared a place before it and sunk its roots deep in the soil, so that it grew to fill up the land.

[11] Its shadow covered mountains and its branches were as thick as mighty cedars.

[12] You sent its offshoots as far as the Sea, its runners as far as the River.

or burning it as kindling. And so the poet turns to God to plead for the restoration of the vine's fortunes. Mixing his metaphor for the sake of heightened effect, the poet reminds the Almighty that the vine is not just a plant, after all, but also the very child that considers itself to be God's own adopted offspring. If God-as-Vintner fails to respond with sufficient sympathy to the travails of a vine, then surely God-as-Parent will respond to the notion that a child is calling out in pain!

What precise political crisis prompted the composition of the eightieth psalm cannot be known, but moderns who wish to use this poem as a focus for devotional meditation will wish to consider whether the relationship between Israel and God is as parallel to the one that exists between vintner and vine as the ancient poet appears to

13 לָ֭מָּה פָּרַ֣צְתָּ גְדֵרֶ֑יהָ וְ֝אָר֗וּהָ כָּל־עֹ֥בְרֵי דָֽרֶךְ׃
14 יְכַרְסְמֶ֣נָּה חֲזִ֣יר *מִיָּ֑עַר וְזִ֖יז שָׂדַ֣י יִרְעֶֽנָּה׃
15 אֱלֹהִ֣ים צְבָאוֹת֮ שֽׁוּב־נָ֥א הַבֵּ֣ט מִשָּׁמַ֣יִם וּרְאֵ֑ה
וּ֝פְקֹ֗ד גֶּ֣פֶן זֹֽאת׃ 16 *וְ֭כַנָּה אֲשֶׁר־נָ֣טְעָ֣ה יְמִינֶ֑ךָ
וְעַל־בֵּ֝֗ן אִמַּ֥צְתָּה לָּֽךְ׃
17 שְׂרֻפָ֣ה בָ֭אֵשׁ כְּסוּחָ֑ה מִגַּעֲרַ֖ת פָּנֶ֣יךָ יֹאבֵֽדוּ׃
18 תְּהִי־יָ֭דְךָ עַל־אִ֣ישׁ יְמִינֶ֑ךָ עַל־בֶּן־אָ֝דָ֗ם אִמַּ֥צְתָּ
לָּֽךְ׃
19 וְלֹא־נָס֥וֹג מִמֶּ֑ךָּ תְּ֝חַיֵּ֗נוּ וּבְשִׁמְךָ֥ נִקְרָֽא׃
20 יְהוָ֘ה אֱלֹהִ֥ים צְבָא֗וֹת הֲשִׁיבֵ֑נוּ הָ֥אֵ֥ר פָּ֝נֶ֗יךָ
וְנִוָּשֵֽׁעָה׃

v. 14 עין תלויה
v. 16 כ׳ רבתי

have thought. That relationship, after all, is hardly one of equals: the vine responds to the vintner's care by growing mature, sweet grapes, but its role consists solely of responding to outside stimuli and little else. More to the point, the vine lacks all capacity to decide for itself whether to accept or reject the vintner's ministrations; it must therefore always (and only) act in a way foreordained by its very nature and further determined by the vintner's skill. And then there are outside factors like weather to consider as well, influences over which neither vine nor vintner can exert any influence at all.

For our part, we tend to think of Israel's relationship with God differently: as partners-in-dialogue, as willing participants in an ancient covenant, or as independent, self-directed lovers in a successful, if occasionally rocky,

[13] Why, then, have You broken down fences that protected it so that all who pass by now curse it, [14] so that wild boars trample it and wild beasts feed off it?

[15] O God of the celestial legions, I beseech You to return to us; look down from heaven and see and take note of what has happened to this vine, [16] to the stock that Your right hand planted, to the child You adopted as Your own.

[17] The vine is burnt with fire and chopped down; it is lost because of the rebuke of Your face.

[18] May Your hand be upon the people who are that vine planted by Your right hand, and upon the nation You think of as the child You adopted as Your own.

[19] We shall not retreat from You; therefore, grant us life and we shall be called by Your name.

[20] O יהוה-Elohim of the celestial legions, return us to You; illuminate Your face that we may be saved.

marriage. Did the psalmist think of that relationship differently than we do? Or did he merely choose to emphasize a different part of it, one most moderns find at least slightly unpalatable to consider? Was his point that, for all human beings are endowed with the freedom to turn their back on God, they can only do so by perverting their inmost nature, by suppressing the most (not the least) basic needs of their own souls? The poet was attempting to assert that, in the end, it is as natural and easy for people to embrace faith as it is for a vine to respond with growth and robust health when it is adequately fed and watered. But how will moderns, trained to accept as rational the faithlessness of non-believers, respond to his metaphor?

פא

לַמְנַצֵּחַ ׀ עַל־הַגִּתִּית לְאָסָף׃
2 הַרְנִינוּ לֵאלֹהִים עוּזֵּנוּ הָרִיעוּ לֵאלֹהֵי יַעֲקֹב׃
3 שְׂאוּ־זִמְרָה וּתְנוּ־תֹף כִּנּוֹר נָעִים עִם־נָבֶל׃
4 תִּקְעוּ בַחֹדֶשׁ שׁוֹפָר בַּכֵּסֶה לְיוֹם חַגֵּנוּ׃ 5 כִּי חֹק
לְיִשְׂרָאֵל הוּא מִשְׁפָּט לֵאלֹהֵי יַעֲקֹב׃ 6 עֵדוּת ׀
בִּיהוֹסֵף שָׂמוֹ בְּצֵאתוֹ עַל־אֶרֶץ מִצְרָיִם שְׂפַת
לֹא־יָדַעְתִּי אֶשְׁמָע׃
7 הֲסִירוֹתִי מִסֵּבֶל שִׁכְמוֹ כַּפָּיו מִדּוּד תַּעֲבֹרְנָה׃
8 בַּצָּרָה קָרָאתָ וָאֲחַלְּצֶךָּ אֶעֶנְךָ בְּסֵתֶר רַעַם אֶבְחָנְךָ
עַל־מֵי מְרִיבָה סֶלָה׃
9 שְׁמַע עַמִּי וְאָעִידָה בָּךְ יִשְׂרָאֵל אִם־תִּשְׁמַע־לִי׃
10 לֹא־יִהְיֶה בְךָ אֵל זָר וְלֹא תִשְׁתַּחֲוֶה לְאֵל נֵכָר׃
11 אָנֹכִי ׀ יְהוָה אֱלֹהֶיךָ הַמַּעַלְךָ מֵאֶרֶץ מִצְרָיִם
הַרְחֶב־פִּיךָ וַאֲמַלְאֵהוּ׃

Careful not to reveal too much and daring to refer only obliquely to esoteric rituals of the greatest obscurity, the psalmist whose poem became our eighty-first psalm paints a dark, mysterious picture for us to ponder.

We are gathered in the Temple courtyard late at night on the eve of the New Moon. Except for the most slender sliver of silvery moon, the sky is pitch black; the only sound to be heard is the poet inviting his colleagues to sing a specific hymn to the accompaniment of lyre and drum. The rituals designed to provoke the visual and auditory experience of God's presence begin, and begin to work almost at once. Just as at Sinai, God's immanent presence is heralded by a *shofar* blast. But the poet and his friends cannot know precisely who has responded to their mystic call by sounding the *shofar* . . . or even if the blast was real or only imagined as part of some sort of shared, yet physically unreal, experience. The ritual continues. There is some sort of dramatic unburdening of either real or symbolic loads from each other's shoulders, perhaps dramatizing the need to set down the preconceptions and prejudices people so often carry around with them before becoming able to hear the voice of the Divine. There is also a ritual of some sort involving the removal of one's hands from a pot. The rituals to which the poet refers are obscure in the extreme, but they appear—at least in the context of the poet's psalm—to be successful and, eventually, God speaks.

It seems clear that the purpose of this secret nighttime conclave is to create a ritual framework for provoking the experience of communicative communion with God, and so the poet has no choice but to use metaphors to express

81

For the conductor, a song of Asaph to be accompanied on the *gittit*.

[2] Sing joyously to the God of our strength; make joyous noise unto the God of Jacob.

[3] Take up a song, accompany it on the drum, on the delightful lyre, on the *nevel*.

[4] Blow the *shofar* on the New Moon, on the eve of our festival day, [5] for doing so is a law for Israel, a statute of the God of Jacob, [6] who vouchsafed divine testimony to Jehoseph while going forth against the land of Egypt. I hear words now, although I do not know fully what they mean.

[7] Then, as I removed some of the burden from another's back and his hands passed away from the pot, God spoke:

[8] "In distress you call out and I shall grant you relief; I shall answer you with mysterious thunder. I shall test you at the waters of Meribah, *selah*.

[9] Hear, O My people, and I shall vouchsafe testimony to you—even to you, O Israel, if you will only listen. [10] There shall be no alien god among you, nor shall you bow down to a foreign god.

[11] I am יהוה your God, who took you out of the land of Egypt, saying, 'Open wide your mouth and I shall fill it up.'

what is essentially beyond the framework of human language. He hears speech he can somehow understand intuitively, despite the fact that it is not in any language he can actually speak. The voice comes in a clap of thunder, but even that thunder is a *seter ra'am*—some sort of secret, mysterious sound from the sky that the poet hears and doesn't recognize, just as he understood, but could not identify, the language heralded by that thunder. Still, obscure or not, the poet somehow does manage to seize the gist of the divine message he is receiving . . . and it is as unexpected as it is self-validating: when God took Israel forth from Egypt—the ultimate paradigm for being released from the confines of human disability—the essential part of the experience was hearing God say to each individual Israelite *harḥev pikha va'amalehu* ("Open wide your mouth and I shall fill it up"). These words appear only here, not in any biblical narrative describing the Israelites camped at Mount Sinai. They are, therefore, part of the poet's experience of

12 וְלֹא־שָׁמַע עַמִּי לְקוֹלִי וְיִשְׂרָאֵל לֹא־אָבָה לִי׃
13 וָאֲשַׁלְּחֵהוּ בִּשְׁרִירוּת לִבָּם יֵלְכוּ בְּמוֹעֲצוֹתֵיהֶם׃
14 לוּ עַמִּי שֹׁמֵעַ לִי יִשְׂרָאֵל בִּדְרָכַי יְהַלֵּכוּ׃ 15 כִּמְעַט
אוֹיְבֵיהֶם אַכְנִיעַ וְעַל־צָרֵיהֶם אָשִׁיב יָדִי׃
16 מְשַׂנְאֵי יְהוָה יְכַחֲשׁוּ־לוֹ וִיהִי עִתָּם לְעוֹלָם׃
17 וַיַּאֲכִילֵהוּ מֵחֵלֶב חִטָּה וּמִצּוּר דְּבַשׁ אַשְׂבִּיעֶךָ׃

God and, as such, their message is as profound as it is challenging: the real point, the poet perceives God to be telling him, of being freed from bondage was that the nation become a kingdom of prophets, a nation of divine intimates who have only to step into God's presence, remove the burden from their backs, open their mouths wide, and then allow God to fill them with words of divine wisdom.

Alas, it was not to be—or rather, it was not to be then. The poet reports that the Israelites did not respond to the call, choosing instead to pay lip service to the institution of prophecy without actually taking to heart the fact that they were henceforth all personally entitled to participate in personalized, auditory communion with God. All was not lost, however, and now the poet's group has set itself to traveling the road not taken as part of a serious latter-day quest for ecstatic communion with God. And, at least in the context of the eighty-first

[12] But My people did not listen to My voice;
indeed, Israel had no desire for Me.

[13] And so did I send them forth in the stubbornness of their heart, letting them go forward according to their own counsel.

[14] If My people would only listen to Me, if Israel would only walk in My ways, [15]then would I soon overwhelm their enemies and turn My hand against their foes."

[16] Those who hate יהוה will always deny the reality of God, but will their time last forever?

[17] But as for the pious, God will feed them of the choicest wheat germ, saying, "I will satisfy you with honey from a rock."

psalm, their efforts have yielded fruit and God has spoken.

Moderns will want to ask themselves how they feel about Judaism having distanced itself from the great goal of seeking to stimulate communicative communion with God. Could moderns become prophets today if they only sought to hear God's voice with sufficient assiduity? Can *anyone* today hear the voice of God? When we insist that people who claim to hear God's voice are, almost by definition, crazy and delusional, are we being stubborn . . . or simply honest, candid realists? Can we moderns cast the burdens *we* carry around from *our* shoulders long enough to hear the voice of God?

פב

מִזְמוֹר לְאָסָף
אֱלֹהִים נִצָּב בַּעֲדַת־אֵל בְּקֶרֶב אֱלֹהִים יִשְׁפֹּט׃
2 עַד־מָתַי תִּשְׁפְּטוּ־עָוֶל וּפְנֵי רְשָׁעִים תִּשְׂאוּ־סֶלָה׃
3 שִׁפְטוּ־דַל וְיָתוֹם עָנִי וָרָשׁ הַצְדִּיקוּ׃ 4 פַּלְּטוּ־דַל
וְאֶבְיוֹן מִיַּד רְשָׁעִים הַצִּילוּ׃
5 לֹא יָדְעוּ ׀ וְלֹא יָבִינוּ בַּחֲשֵׁכָה יִתְהַלָּכוּ יִמּוֹטוּ
כָּל־מוֹסְדֵי אָרֶץ׃
6 אֲנִי אָמַרְתִּי אֱלֹהִים אַתֶּם וּבְנֵי עֶלְיוֹן כֻּלְּכֶם׃
7 אָכֵן כְּאָדָם תְּמוּתוּן וּכְאַחַד הַשָּׂרִים תִּפֹּלוּ׃
8 קוּמָה אֱלֹהִים שָׁפְטָה הָאָרֶץ כִּי־אַתָּה תִנְחַל
בְּכָל־הַגּוֹיִם׃

The psalmist, disgusted with the corruption of the judicial system in his time and place, has a vision of God feeling equally repulsed by the lack of fairness among the celestial beings who judge the earth. In the poet's vision, God rules over a council of heavenly magistrates whose job, it appears, is to execute fair and equitable judgment upon the various nations of the world. Only God, similar to how the poet feels about earthly judges, is totally enraged by the quality of the verdicts the celestial judges have been reaching. Indeed, they have fallen prey to the same weaknesses and errors of judgment that ruin the quality of judgment among human judges. They favor the wealthy. They either render cursory, unsympathetic judgment to the poor and the destitute or else they ignore them entirely. The earth is tottering beneath their inadequacy, but they barely take time away from favoring the powerful over the weak to take notice. And so the poet imagines God rebuking his celestial underlings, then punishing them by depriving them of their immortality—and, at the same time, promising them that it is not too late to learn to judge justly and bring at least belated justice to the nations of the world.

Modern readers of the eighty-second psalm may be a bit put off by the poem's unfamiliar mythological framework, but the more profound aspect of

82 A psalm of Asaph.

God stands up in the divine council, speaking words of judgment in the midst of the celestial assembly:

[2] "How long will you render false judgment, favoring the faces of the wicked, *selah*?

[3] Judge the poor person and the orphan fairly, deal justly with the poverty-stricken and the destitute; [4] rescue the wretched and save the miserable from the wicked."

[5] They know nothing, understand nothing; they walk around in darkness while the very foundations of the world totter.

[6] "I say," God continues, "You may well be members of the celestial assembly, all of you supernal beings—[7] but you will henceforth die like human beings and fall down dead like earthly princes."

[8] Rise up, O God, and judge the earth Yourself, for the nations of the world are Yours to possess.

the poem should not be overlooked merely because of the strangeness of its setting. There are complex judicial systems in all of the world's countries served by countless thousands of judges of various types, but the psalmist is encouraging us to look past those man-made juridical structures to the image of God as Judge of all the earth. In so doing, however, we are challenged to respond to some especially deep questions about our own faith. What does it mean for moderns to declare God to be the personal Judge of every individual man and woman on earth? How are we to understand the notion that God is the Judge of our land and, perhaps even more unsettlingly, the Judge of our judges? In a world riddled with injustice and unfairness, how are we to embrace the concept of God as the ultimate Dispenser of fairness in judgment, as the cosmic Defender of those treated unjustly by the world? Can moderns come to faith by thinking of the earth as a courtroom . . . and of themselves as defendants obliged to stand in judgment before an all-knowing Judge?

פג

שִׁיר מִזְמוֹר לְאָסָף׃
2 אֱלֹהִים אַל־דֳּמִי־לָךְ אַל־תֶּחֱרַשׁ וְאַל־תִּשְׁקֹט אֵל׃
3 כִּי־הִנֵּה אוֹיְבֶיךָ יֶהֱמָיוּן וּמְשַׂנְאֶיךָ נָשְׂאוּ רֹאשׁ׃
4 עַל־עַמְּךָ יַעֲרִימוּ סוֹד וְיִתְיָעֲצוּ עַל־צְפוּנֶיךָ׃
5 אָמְרוּ לְכוּ וְנַכְחִידֵם מִגּוֹי וְלֹא־יִזָּכֵר שֵׁם־יִשְׂרָאֵל עוֹד׃
6 כִּי נוֹעֲצוּ לֵב יַחְדָּו עָלֶיךָ בְּרִית יִכְרֹתוּ׃
7 אָהֳלֵי אֱדוֹם וְיִשְׁמְעֵאלִים מוֹאָב וְהַגְרִים׃ 8 גְּבָל וְעַמּוֹן וַעֲמָלֵק פְּלֶשֶׁת עִם־יֹשְׁבֵי צוֹר׃ 9 גַּם־אַשּׁוּר נִלְוָה עִמָּם הָיוּ זְרוֹעַ לִבְנֵי־לוֹט סֶלָה׃
10 עֲשֵׂה־לָהֶם כְּמִדְיָן כְּסִיסְרָא כְיָבִין בְּנַחַל קִישׁוֹן׃
11 נִשְׁמְדוּ בְעֵין־דֹּאר הָיוּ דֹּמֶן לָאֲדָמָה׃
12 שִׁיתֵמוֹ נְדִיבֵמוֹ כְּעֹרֵב וְכִזְאֵב וּכְזֶבַח וּכְצַלְמֻנָּע כָּל־נְסִיכֵמוֹ׃ 13 אֲשֶׁר אָמְרוּ נִירְשָׁה לָּנוּ אֵת נְאוֹת אֱלֹהִים׃

Over the generations, the Jewish people has faced a host of enemies, some possessed of such devastating power and might that the total annihilation of Israel might certainly have been one possible outcome. Fortunately, these enemies have usually been faced serially, one after another of them appearing on the stage of history as representatives of humanity gone berserk . . . and of a world so overcome by loathing for the people of God that no form of persecution seems so extreme as to be unthinkable.

The psalmist whose poem became our eighty-third psalm has his own take on Jewish history. In a horrific vision, he imagines the enemies of Israel not appearing one by one in the pageant of passing centuries, but gathered together as allies preparing to mount one final assault on Israel in a unified fighting force—one that will bring together the various strengths of all their armies, the combined insight of all their intelligence forces, and the cunning of all their generals at once. Against such an array of military power, there can only be one answer for Israel, only one potential avenue of escape from the doom that would certainly appear inevitable if such an alliance were ever actually to come into existence.

The poet knows that this kind of potential calamity is something no sane person could ever wish to encounter. He is prepared, however, to imagine that the experience of feeling totally isolated with the entire world arrayed against one tiny people might perhaps have worth within the larger scheme of human

83 A psalm-song of Asaph.

[2] God, be neither silent nor speechless; God, do not be still, [3]for Your enemies are in a state of agitation and those who hate You are rearing their heads.

[4] They are plotting in crafty council against Your people, taking counsel against Your treasured people.

[5] They are saying, "Come, let us destroy them so totally that they are no longer a nation, so that the name of Israel no longer be recalled."

[6] Indeed, they are of one mind in this regard: they are making an alliance against You.

[7] The tents of Edom and the Ishmaelites, Moab and the Hagrites, [8]Gebal and Ammon and Amalek, Philistia and the inhabitants of Tyre, [9]even Assyria—they have all joined together as allies of the descendants of Lot, *selah.*

[10] Do unto them as with Midian, as You did at the Wadi Kishon unto Sisera and Jabin, [11]who were destroyed at Ein-Dor and whose remains were spread over the earth like dung.

[12] Make their nobles like Oreb and Zeeb, their princes like Zebah and Zalmunna, [13]who said, "Let us take the pastures of God as our inheritance."

spiritual history. If, he suggests, the fear of annihilation will bring Israel closer to its God, then surely that experience must have some element of blessing in it, just as must every experience that brings people closer to faith. Furthermore, if the combined forces of the enemy are defeated and if that experience brings the nations of the world to recognize that God alone is supreme in majesty over the entire earth, then there would certainly be some element of blessing in that experience for those nations as well.

Moderns will probably find it simpler to seize the poet's point if they first take a moment to update its references. The story of King Zebah and King Zalmunna of Midian is told in the eighth chapter of the Book of Judges, for example, and most of the poet's other references also derive from biblical accounts we may locate and profitably study. Modern readers, however, will get closer to the poet's intention by thinking of an unholy alliance of taskmasters, legionnaires, inquisitors, cossacks, and stormtroopers gathering

14 אֱלֹהַי שִׁיתֵמוֹ כַגַּלְגַּל כְּקַשׁ לִפְנֵי־רוּחַ׃ 15 כְּאֵשׁ
תִּבְעַר־יָעַר וּכְלֶהָבָה תְּלַהֵט הָרִים׃ 16 כֵּן תִּרְדְּפֵם
בְּסַעֲרֶךָ וּבְסוּפָתְךָ תְבַהֲלֵם׃
17 מַלֵּא פְנֵיהֶם קָלוֹן וִיבַקְשׁוּ שִׁמְךָ יְהוָה׃
18 יֵבֹשׁוּ וְיִבָּהֲלוּ עֲדֵי־עַד וְיַחְפְּרוּ וְיֹאבֵדוּ׃
19 וְיֵדְעוּ כִּי־אַתָּה שִׁמְךָ יְהוָה לְבַדֶּךָ עֶלְיוֹן עַל־כָּל־
הָאָרֶץ׃

together to transcend the boundaries of history to make war on the Jewish people. The fear engendered by an alliance featuring the combined might of all the enemies of Israel from all historical periods at once would be immense, but would it lead us closer to God or further away from faith? Would the fear of annihilation inspire us to cling even more closely to God or would it make us wonder if there even *is* a God in heaven, let alone one whose

[14] O my God, make them like tumbleweed, like straw blowing in the wind. [15]Like fire that burns down the forest or like a flame that ignites mountains, pursue them with Your storm, [16]terrify them with Your whirlwind.

[17] Fill their faces with shame, that they might be moved to seek Your name, יהוה.

[18] May they be embarrassed and intensely terrified, both ashamed and lost.

[19] And may they come to know that You alone bear the name יהוה, that You alone are supreme over the whole earth.

covenant with Israel is eternal? Would our faith be the last or the first thing to go in the face of what would appear as certain destruction? We moderns can use this psalm as a springboard to contemplate our own feelings about the role of God in history, and especially in Jewish history. Is the notion that all true security comes from faith in God something we can reasonably embrace? And, more to the point: what—if anything—would be the alternative?

פד

לַמְנַצֵּחַ עַל־הַגִּתִּית לִבְנֵי־קֹרַח מִזְמוֹר׃
2 מַה־יְּדִידוֹת מִשְׁכְּנוֹתֶיךָ יְהוָה צְבָאוֹת׃
3 נִכְסְפָה וְגַם־כָּלְתָה ׀ נַפְשִׁי לְחַצְרוֹת יְהוָה לִבִּי
וּבְשָׂרִי יְרַנְּנוּ אֶל־אֵל חָי׃
4 גַּם־צִפּוֹר ׀ מָצְאָה בַיִת וּדְרוֹר ׀ *קֵן לָהּ אֲשֶׁר־שָׁתָה
אֶפְרֹחֶיהָ אֶת־מִזְבְּחוֹתֶיךָ יְהוָה צְבָאוֹת מַלְכִּי
וֵאלֹהָי׃
5 אַשְׁרֵי יוֹשְׁבֵי בֵיתֶךָ עוֹד יְהַלְלוּךָ סֶּלָה׃
6 אַשְׁרֵי אָדָם עוֹז לוֹ־בָךְ מְסִלּוֹת בִּלְבָבָם׃
7 עֹבְרֵי ׀ בְּעֵמֶק הַבָּכָא מַעְיָן יְשִׁיתוּהוּ גַּם־בְּרָכוֹת
יַעְטֶה מוֹרֶה׃ 8 יֵלְכוּ מֵחַיִל אֶל־חָיִל יֵרָאֶה
אֶל־אֱלֹהִים בְּצִיּוֹן׃
9 יְהוָה אֱלֹהִים צְבָאוֹת שִׁמְעָה תְפִלָּתִי הַאֲזִינָה
אֱלֹהֵי יַעֲקֹב סֶלָה׃
10 מָגִנֵּנוּ רְאֵה אֱלֹהִים וְהַבֵּט פְּנֵי מְשִׁיחֶךָ׃
11 כִּי טוֹב־יוֹם בַּחֲצֵרֶיךָ מֵאָלֶף בָּחַרְתִּי הִסְתּוֹפֵף
בְּבֵית אֱלֹהַי מִדּוּר בְּאָהֳלֵי־רֶשַׁע׃
12 כִּי שֶׁמֶשׁ ׀ וּמָגֵן יְהוָה אֱלֹהִים חֵן וְכָבוֹד יִתֵּן יְהוָה
לֹא־יִמְנַע טוֹב לַהֹלְכִים בְּתָמִים׃
13 יְהוָה צְבָאוֹת אַשְׁרֵי אָדָם בֹּטֵחַ בָּךְ׃

v. 4 ק׳ רבתי

For the poet, the great Temple in Jerusalem is not merely a shrine worthy of veneration or a curiosity worth a tourist's visit, but the very presence of God on earth sculpted not in myth or metaphor, but in stone. Given that starting point, it is logical that the poet does not merely wish to spend time there or even to participate in the worship service there, but actually to dwell there and to live there always—or, more precisely, to live in God *by means of* living there. The poet needs a model, though, adequate to express his desire to live a life of ongoing communion with God. He expresses himself, therefore, by comparing his situation to that of a swallow who builds a nest and then, content, wants nothing more than to lay her eggs in it and raise her young there in its safe, familiar confines.

84

For the conductor, a psalm of the Korachides to be accompanied on the *gittit*.

[2] How lovely are Your dwellings, O יהוה of the celestial legions.

[3] Even to the point of becoming faint, my soul yearns for the courtyards of יהוה; my heart and my flesh sing in gladness to the living God.

[4] Even a bird can find a home, and a swallow, a nest where she may set her young, amidst Your altars, O יהוה of the celestial legions, my Sovereign, my God.

[5] Happy are those who dwell in Your House, for, in so doing, they praise You endlessly, *selah*.

[6] Happy is the individual whose strength is in You; happy are those in whose hearts lie paths leading to You.

[7] When they pass through the Bacha Valley, they are able to make it into a place of flowing waters, for the early rain covers the place with blessings on their account; [8]they go from strength to strength on their way to appear before God in Zion.

[9] O יהוה-Elohim of the celestial legions, hear my prayer; listen, O God of Jacob, *selah*.

[10] Look, O God, our Shield, and see the face of Your anointed one.

[11] For one day in Your courtyards is better than a thousand days elsewhere; I would easily choose an opportunity to tarry at the threshold of the House of my God over a chance to dwell permanently in the tents of the wicked.

[12] For יהוה-Elohim is sun and shield; יהוה grants us grace and honor and will never withhold goodness from those who pursue the path of guilelessness.

[13] O יהוה of the celestial legions, happy is the individual who trusts in You.

Moderns will want to contemplate the idea of living a life totally and always in God. The Temple stands no longer, but God lives on—and so, at least briefly, do we. That being the case, what do *we* do to express our yearning for a life in God? What words could we use to express the kind of deep love for God that so inspired the ancient poet? Where can we, in our Temple-less world, contemplate going to live with and in God?

פה

לַמְנַצֵּחַ ׀ לִבְנֵי־קֹרַח מִזְמוֹר:
2 רָצִיתָ יְהֹוָה אַרְצֶךָ שַׁבְתָּ *שְׁבִית יַעֲקֹב:
3 נָשָׂאתָ עֲוֺן עַמֶּךָ כִּסִּיתָ כָל־חַטָּאתָם סֶלָה:
4 אָסַפְתָּ כָל־עֶבְרָתֶךָ הֱשִׁיבוֹתָ מֵחֲרוֹן אַפֶּךָ: 5 שׁוּבֵנוּ
אֱלֹהֵי יִשְׁעֵנוּ וְהָפֵר כַּעַסְךָ עִמָּנוּ:
6 הַלְעוֹלָם תֶּאֱנַף־בָּנוּ תִּמְשֹׁךְ אַפְּךָ לְדֹר וָדֹר:
7 הֲלֹא־אַתָּה תָּשׁוּב תְּחַיֵּנוּ וְעַמְּךָ יִשְׂמְחוּ־בָךְ:
8 הַרְאֵנוּ יְהֹוָה חַסְדֶּךָ וְיֶשְׁעֲךָ תִּתֶּן־לָנוּ:
9 אֶשְׁמְעָה מַה־יְדַבֵּר הָאֵל ׀ יְהֹוָה כִּי יְדַבֵּר שָׁלוֹם
אֶל־עַמּוֹ וְאֶל־חֲסִידָיו וְאַל־יָשׁוּבוּ לְכִסְלָה:
10 אַךְ ׀ קָרוֹב לִירֵאָיו יִשְׁעוֹ לִשְׁכֹּן כָּבוֹד בְּאַרְצֵנוּ:
11 חֶסֶד־וֶאֱמֶת נִפְגָּשׁוּ צֶדֶק וְשָׁלוֹם נָשָׁקוּ: 12 אֱמֶת
מֵאֶרֶץ תִּצְמָח וְצֶדֶק מִשָּׁמַיִם נִשְׁקָף:
13 גַּם־יְהֹוָה יִתֵּן הַטּוֹב וְאַרְצֵנוּ תִּתֵּן יְבוּלָהּ:
14 צֶדֶק לְפָנָיו יְהַלֵּךְ וְיָשֵׂם לְדֶרֶךְ פְּעָמָיו:

v. 2 שבות כתיב

The poet begins by noting that God once forgave the sins of the people and restored them to Zion. But the poet's reality is different. His people may well have been restored to their homeland once, but he and his contemporaries feel persecuted and attribute their lack of standing in society to the unabated anger of God. Modern readers may find it moving, even inspiring, to observe the poet, guileless almost to the point of naivete, turning to the Almighty to ask politely how long God will remain enraged. We will, however, derive more benefit from the psalm if we allow ourselves to feel prompted by its words to consider how we respond to unhappiness and distress in our own lives. Do we turn to God in prayer, declaring ourselves ready

85

For the conductor, a psalm of the Korachides.

[2] יהוה, You once looked with favor on Your land and ended the captivity of Jacob.

[3] You forgave the sin of Your people and covered over all their sins, *selah*.

[4] You once gathered up Your anger and turned away from Your fury; [5] now turn again back to us, O God of our salvation, and annul Your anger against us.

[6] Will You forever be enraged with us? Will Your fury continue from generation to generation?

[7] Will You not change Your mind and grant us life, so that Your people might rejoice in You?

[8] Show us Your mercy, יהוה, and grant us Your salvation.

[9] I will listen to whatever God, יהוה, should say—for God will speak words of peace to the people of God, and especially to the pious, so that they may not turn back to folly.

[10] For surely salvation in God is so close to those who fear God that divine glory shall dwell in our land through their efforts.

[11] Then shall mercy and truth coincide, justice and peace join in a kiss; [12] then shall truth sprout up from the earth and justice look down from heaven.

[13] As well, יהוה will bestow goodness upon us and our land will give forth its produce.

[14] Justice will go forth before God, making a path for the soles of the divine feet.

and able to hear the words God might speak to us no matter what they may be? Or do we respond to distress and anguish by turning away from God, by blaming God for our misfortune, and by refusing even to consider that human misery is, almost by definition, always a function of alienation from faith?

פו

תְּפִלָּה לְדָוִד
הַטֵּה יְהוָה אָזְנְךָ עֲנֵנִי כִּי־עָנִי וְאֶבְיוֹן אָנִי׃
2 שָׁמְרָה נַפְשִׁי כִּי־חָסִיד אָנִי הוֹשַׁע עַבְדְּךָ אַתָּה
אֱלֹהַי הַבּוֹטֵחַ אֵלֶיךָ׃
3 חָנֵּנִי אֲדֹנָי כִּי־אֵלֶיךָ אֶקְרָא כָּל־הַיּוֹם׃
4 שַׂמֵּחַ נֶפֶשׁ עַבְדֶּךָ כִּי אֵלֶיךָ אֲדֹנָי נַפְשִׁי אֶשָּׂא׃ 5 כִּי־
אַתָּה אֲדֹנָי טוֹב וְסַלָּח וְרַב־חֶסֶד לְכָל־קֹרְאֶיךָ׃
6 הַאֲזִינָה יְהוָה תְּפִלָּתִי וְהַקְשִׁיבָה בְּקוֹל תַּחֲנוּנוֹתָי׃
7 בְּיוֹם צָרָתִי אֶקְרָאֶךָּ כִּי תַעֲנֵנִי׃
8 אֵין־כָּמוֹךָ בָאֱלֹהִים ׀ אֲדֹנָי וְאֵין כְּמַעֲשֶׂיךָ׃
9 כָּל־גּוֹיִם ׀ אֲשֶׁר עָשִׂיתָ יָבוֹאוּ וְיִשְׁתַּחֲווּ לְפָנֶיךָ
אֲדֹנָי וִיכַבְּדוּ לִשְׁמֶךָ׃ 10 כִּי־גָדוֹל אַתָּה וְעֹשֵׂה
נִפְלָאוֹת אַתָּה אֱלֹהִים לְבַדֶּךָ׃
11 הוֹרֵנִי יְהוָה דַּרְכֶּךָ אֲהַלֵּךְ בַּאֲמִתֶּךָ יַחֵד לְבָבִי
לְיִרְאָה שְׁמֶךָ׃

The poet describes himself using the language of poverty. He declares himself to be an *ani* and an *evyon,* however, not because he lacks funds, but because he is terrified for his life and deeply worried. But then the poet, reminding himself that true wealth in this world can only be a function of the security that comes from faith in God, makes no further reference to himself as being destitute as he calls out to God, places his faith in the saving power of the Almighty, and promises to acknowledge God as the source of his deliverance when he is finally safe from his adversaries.

Like so many of the other poets whose poems are in our Psalter, the poet writes about having violent and bloodthirsty enemies he fears would not hold back, even, from murdering him outright were the chance only to present itself. The poet calls these enemies *zedim* ("arrogant people") and *aritzim* ("cruel villains"), then explains that the source of their arrogance and villainy lies not in some genetic propensity to do others harm, but in the simple fact that they have not taken God into account in their lives . . . and, as a result, have completely failed to build lives for themselves rooted in the morality that inevitably comes as a result of embracing faith in the God of goodness and decency.

The poet thus leaves us with an interesting take on the values of the world. People are destitute and indigent not because they lack money, but because they lack a sense of absolute faith in God's caring presence in their lives. And

86

A prayer of David.
Incline Your ear, O יהוה, and answer me
for I am poor and destitute.
[2] Guard my soul, for I am a pious person; grant salvation to Your servant who trusts in You, for You alone are my God.
[3] Show mercy to me, Adonai, for it is to You that I cry out all day long.
[4] Make the soul of Your servant joyous, for it is to You, Adonai, that I lift up my soul; [5]for You, Adonai, are good and forgiving and so very merciful to those who call upon You.
[6] Give ear to my prayer, O יהוה, and listen to the voice of my supplications.
[7] In my day of trouble I call to You, for You shall answer me.
[8] There is none like You among the gods of the pagan nations, Adonai, and there are no works like Yours.
[9] All the nations that You have made will come and bow down before You, Adonai, and give honor to Your name, [10]for You are great and a Doer of wonders; You are the sole God.
[11] O יהוה, teach me Your way that I might walk in Your truth; unite the chambers of my heart in the awe due to Your name.

their enemies are arrogant fiends not because they were raised poorly by their wicked parents or because they harbor some congenital criminal drive, but simply because they have failed to accept God into their lives and must, therefore, bear the consequences of living without faith.

Modern readers of the eighty-sixth psalm will want to ask themselves if they would describe the world in the same way as the ancient poet and, if not, why precisely they see things differently. The pursuit of affluence is so basic to our society that it is disorienting, perhaps even slightly disturbing, to ask what the world would be like if we were to consider wealth to be what is possessed by people of faith, not what is possessed by people who own big houses or drive expensive cars . . . or if we were to label as prosperous not people lucky enough to earn huge incomes, but people who are guided throughout their days by a strong sense of the saving presence of God in their lives. We can also ask

[12] אוֹדְךָ֤ ׀ אֲדֹנָ֣י אֱ֭לֹהַי בְּכָל־לְבָבִ֑י וַאֲכַבְּדָ֖ה שִׁמְךָ֣
לְעוֹלָֽם׃ [13] כִּֽי־חַ֭סְדְּךָ גָּד֣וֹל עָלָ֑י וְהִצַּ֥לְתָּ נַ֝פְשִׁ֗י
מִשְּׁא֥וֹל תַּחְתִּיָּֽה׃
[14] אֱלֹהִ֤ים ׀ זֵדִ֪ים קָֽמוּ עָלַ֡י וַעֲדַ֣ת עָ֭רִיצִים בִּקְשׁ֣וּ
נַפְשִׁ֑י וְלֹ֖א שָׂמ֣וּךָ לְנֶגְדָּֽם׃
[15] וְאַתָּ֣ה אֲ֭דֹנָי אֵל־רַח֣וּם וְחַנּ֑וּן אֶ֥רֶךְ אַ֝פַּ֗יִם וְרַב־
חֶ֥סֶד וֶאֱמֶֽת׃
[16] פְּנֵ֥ה אֵלַ֗י וְחָ֫נֵּ֥נִי תְּנָֽה־עֻזְּךָ֥ לְעַבְדֶּ֑ךָ וְ֝הוֹשִׁ֗יעָה
לְבֶן־אֲמָתֶֽךָ׃
[17] עֲשֵֽׂה־עִמִּ֥י א֗וֹת לְט֫וֹבָ֥ה וְיִרְא֣וּ שֹׂנְאַ֣י וְיֵבֹ֑שׁוּ
כִּֽי־אַתָּ֥ה יְ֝הֹוָ֗ה עֲזַרְתַּ֥נִי וְנִחַמְתָּֽנִי׃

what the world would be like if criminality, villainy, and violence were considered functions of failing to hold faith in God, rather than simply being some of the bad things to which people turn as a result of some flaw in their upbringing or some defect in their moral character. We moderns can use the careful, considered recitation of this psalm as an opportunity to consider the impact it would have on our lives if the pursuit of wealth were to stop meaning what it always has meant in the secular world and were instead to refer to the acquisition of knowledge and wisdom, of skill at prayer and devotion to the performance of the commandments . . . and of faith in God.

[12] I thank You, Adonai, my God, with all my heart; I shall always show honor to Your name, [13]for Your mercy towards me is great and You have saved my soul from the nethermost reaches of Sheol.

[14] O God, arrogant people have come up against me. A council of cruel villains is seeking to kill me, having failed to take You into account in their lives.

[15] But You, Adonai, are a compassionate and gracious God, long-suffering, intensely merciful and truthful.

[16] Turn to me and be gracious unto me; grant strength to Your servant, salvation to the son of your handmaid.

[17] Offer me a good sign, one that my enemies will see and that will make them ashamed, for You, יהוה, are my source of help and my source of comfort.

פז

לִבְנֵי־קֹרַח מִזְמוֹר שִׁיר
יְסוּדָתוֹ בְּהַרְרֵי־קֹדֶשׁ׃
2 אֹהֵב יְהוָה שַׁעֲרֵי צִיּוֹן מִכֹּל מִשְׁכְּנוֹת יַעֲקֹב׃
3 נִכְבָּדוֹת מְדֻבָּר בָּךְ עִיר הָאֱלֹהִים סֶלָה׃
4 אַזְכִּיר ׀ רַהַב וּבָבֶל לְיֹדְעָי הִנֵּה פְלֶשֶׁת וְצוֹר
עִם־כּוּשׁ זֶה יֻלַּד־שָׁם׃
5 וּלְצִיּוֹן יֵאָמַר אִישׁ וְאִישׁ יֻלַּד־בָּהּ וְהוּא יְכוֹנְנֶהָ
עֶלְיוֹן׃
6 יְהוָה יִסְפֹּר בִּכְתוֹב עַמִּים זֶה יֻלַּד־שָׁם סֶלָה׃
7 וְשָׁרִים כְּחֹלְלִים כָּל־מַעְיָנַי בָּךְ׃

Just as Jews today might contemplate the place of the modern State of Israel among the nations of the world, the poet contemplates the geopolitics of his own world and notes that there is a fundamental difference between the inhabitants of the Holy Land and those of other countries. Other lands are inhabited primarily by indigenous peoples who have no national consciousness of having come from elsewhere to settle in that place. Israel, on the other hand, has a memory of having once been a nomadic tribe of wanderers whom God invited to settle in the land that was to become theirs.

The poet is obliquely asking a question that even today retains its critical importance: does the fact that the most ancient ancestors of Israel came from outside the land make the Jewish claim to the Land of Israel less profound or legally significant than it would be if the Jews were aboriginal to the Holy Land? Citizens of modern immigrant nations struggling to come to terms

87

[1–2]A psalm-song of the Korachides.
יהוה loves the gates of Zion, set among the holy mountains, more than all the other dwellings of Jacob; [3]honored words are spoken about you, O City of God, *selah*.

[4]To my acquaintances, I speak of Rahab and Babylon, even of Philistia and Tyre along with Cush, saying, "The people of these countries were born there."

[5]And of Zion, too, it can be said, "These people were born there and God will guarantee its exalted existence."

[6]יהוה will even enter it in the registry of nations: "These people were all born there, *selah*."

[7]And singers and dancers alike will echo the same sentiment, declaring, "All of my wellsprings are in you, O Zion."

with their own native populations will find this a complex issue, but the poet's answer is as rational as it is reasonable: wherever their ancestors may have originated, the inhabitants of Zion in his day were all born there and, in the end, that is the fact that matters. Moreover, this is the real sense in which the other nations can claim to possess their lands as well. It is not, for example, because the ancestors of the Tyrians lived in Tyre that they have a claim to that land, but because the Tyrians alive in the poet's day were born there. Furthermore, the spiritual roots of the Jewish people in the psalmist's day were not in Abraham's Mesopotamia or Moses' Egypt, but in the Land of Israel—the country that was theirs both because they were born there *and* because they found the deep, abiding wellsprings of their spirituality and their faith along its rugged landscape and deep within its sacred soil.

פח

שִׁ֥יר מִזְמ֗וֹר לִבְנֵ֫י קֹ֥רַח לַמְנַצֵּ֣חַ עַֽל־מַחֲלַ֣ת לְעַנּ֑וֹת
מַ֝שְׂכִּ֗יל לְהֵימָ֥ן הָאֶזְרָחִֽי׃
2 יְהֹוָ֗ה אֱלֹהֵ֥י יְשׁוּעָתִ֑י י֥וֹם צָעַ֖קְתִּי בַלַּ֣יְלָה נֶגְדֶּֽךָ׃
3 תָּב֣וֹא לְ֭פָנֶיךָ תְּפִלָּתִ֑י הַטֵּֽה־אָ֝זְנְךָ֗ לְרִנָּתִֽי׃
4 כִּֽי־שָׂבְעָ֣ה בְרָע֣וֹת נַפְשִׁ֑י וְ֝חַיַּ֗י לִשְׁא֥וֹל הִגִּֽיעוּ׃
5 נֶ֭חְשַׁבְתִּי עִם־י֣וֹרְדֵי ב֑וֹר הָ֝יִ֗יתִי כְּגֶ֣בֶר אֵֽין־אֱיָֽל׃
6 בַּמֵּתִ֗ים חָ֫פְשִׁ֥י כְּמ֤וֹ חֲלָלִ֨ים ׀ שֹׁ֘כְבֵ֤י קֶ֗בֶר אֲשֶׁ֤ר
לֹ֣א זְכַרְתָּ֣ם ע֑וֹד וְ֝הֵ֗מָּה מִיָּדְךָ֥ נִגְזָֽרוּ׃
7 שַׁ֭תַּנִי בְּב֣וֹר תַּחְתִּיּ֑וֹת בְּ֝מַחֲשַׁכִּ֗ים בִּמְצֹלֽוֹת׃
8 עָ֭לַי סָמְכָ֣ה חֲמָתֶ֑ךָ וְכָל־מִ֝שְׁבָּרֶ֗יךָ עִנִּ֥יתָ סֶּֽלָה׃
9 הִרְחַ֥קְתָּ מְיֻדָּעַ֗י מִ֫מֶּ֥נִּי שַׁתַּ֣נִי תוֹעֵב֣וֹת לָ֑מוֹ כָּ֝לֻ֗א
וְלֹ֣א אֵצֵֽא׃ 10 עֵינִ֥י דָאֲבָ֗ה מִנִּ֫י עֹ֥נִי קְרָאתִ֣יךָ יְהֹוָ֣ה
בְּכָל־י֑וֹם שִׁטַּ֖חְתִּי אֵלֶ֣יךָ כַפָּֽי׃
11 הֲלַמֵּתִ֥ים תַּעֲשֶׂה־פֶּ֑לֶא אִם־רְ֝פָאִ֗ים יָ֝ק֤וּמוּ יוֹד֬וּךָ
סֶּֽלָה׃
12 הַיְסֻפַּ֣ר בַּקֶּ֣בֶר חַסְדֶּ֑ךָ אֱ֝מ֥וּנָתְךָ֗ בָּאֲבַדּֽוֹן׃
13 הֲיִוָּדַ֣ע בַּחֹ֣שֶׁךְ פִּלְאֶ֑ךָ וְ֝צִדְקָתְךָ֗ בְּאֶ֣רֶץ נְשִׁיָּֽה׃

The misery of the poet who wrote the poem we know as the eighty-eighth psalm is so deeply felt that it is almost palpable. Yet, it is also so eloquently expressed that the psalm has the odd quality of being both incredibly uplifting and almost unutterably depressing at the same time.

The poet, bereft, abandoned, alone, and lonely, numbers himself among the living dead. His friends have abandoned him. Even casual acquaintances shun him, treating him as an infectious horror to be avoided at all costs. His eyesight is failing. And, as he becomes less and less able to function in the world, he feels his strength failing as well. Indeed, he feels his very humanity ebbing as his health vanishes almost before his eyes and he enters some sort of no-man's-land between life and death. It strikes the poet that his life has been one slow slide into the grave; he now perceives himself to have been already dying even as a youth.

As waves of misery wash over the poet, he begins to conceive of himself not so much as a zombie among the living, but as an actual dead person interred in a narrow tomb from which he cannot escape. He feels the earthen walls of his grave pressing in on either side of his lifeless corpse and, as a living, sentient cadaver, he feels the presence of the other dead people in the cemetery welcoming him into their eerie midst. Most of all, he feels himself cut off from

88

For the conductor, an antiphonal psalm-song of the Korachides and a wise-song of Heman the Ezrahite to be sung to the tune of *"Maḥalat."*

[2] יהוה, God of my salvation, I cry out daily at nighttime before You; [3]may my prayer come before You. Incline Your ear to my joyless song, [4]for my soul is suffused with trouble and my life is so close to being over that I can practically feel myself descending into Sheol.

[5] Indeed, I already think of myself as among those who have gone to their tombs; it is as though I am a man totally devoid of strength. [6]It is as though I were able to wander freely among the dead, among the cadavers, among those who sleep in the grave whom You recall no longer, who are cut off from Your caring hand.

[7] I feel as though You have already laid me down in the deepest tomb, in the utter darkness of the depths of the earth.

[8] Your rage presses down on me; Your tortures come over me like waves, *selah.*

[9] You have distanced my friends from me, making me repulsive to them; I am imprisoned and cannot escape. [10]My eyesight is becoming weak because of my suffering. I call upon You every day, O יהוה; I stretch out my hands to You constantly.

[11] Will You do wonders for dead people? Will ghosts rise to give thanks to You, *selah*?

[12] Will Your mercy be spoken of in the grave, or Your faithfulness in Abadon?

[13] Will Your wondrous nature be known in the darkness, or Your righteousness in the Land of Oblivion?

God. Surely, he observes, the dead do not talk of God's mercies. Surely, they sing no hymns of thanksgiving to the Almighty. Surely, if God wishes to be praised for the divine blessings from which the earth benefits every single day, it would behoove the Eternal One to leave death to the dead and to rescue the poet from his living hell.

The poet's logic is impeccable, but modern readers will want to focus on his incredibly moving description of the despair he feels in his soul, and then ask themselves how they would respond to that kind of agonized desperation in their own lives. The poet is miser-

14 וַאֲנִי | אֵלֶיךָ יְהוָה שִׁוַּעְתִּי וּבַבֹּקֶר תְּפִלָּתִי תְקַדְּמֶךָּ׃
15 לָמָה יְהוָה תִּזְנַח נַפְשִׁי תַּסְתִּיר פָּנֶיךָ מִמֶּנִּי׃
16 עָנִי אֲנִי וְגוֵֹעַ מִנֹּעַר נָשָׂאתִי אֵמֶיךָ אָפוּנָה׃
17 עָלַי עָבְרוּ חֲרוֹנֶיךָ בִּעוּתֶיךָ צִמְּתוּתֻנִי׃ 18 סַבּוּנִי כַמַּיִם כָּל־הַיּוֹם הִקִּיפוּ עָלַי יָחַד׃
19 הִרְחַקְתָּ מִמֶּנִּי אֹהֵב וָרֵעַ מְיֻדָּעַי מַחְשָׁךְ׃

able. He feels cut off from God, despised by God. He has the deep sense that his alienation and misery are punishments from God, and his poem reflects his conviction that suffering on the order that he knows must be divinely imposed. The poet does not, however, respond with blasphemy or arrogance, much less by denying the reality or even the goodness of God. He responds, as any person of faith must, by crying out to God not as a philosophical dogma or as the ordering principle in the universe, but as his personal Redeemer and as the potential source of his salvation from the very suffering

[14] But as for me, I cry out to You, O יהוה; my prayer greets You in the morning before anyone else's.

[15] But then why have You abandoned my soul, יהוה? Why do You hide Your face from me?

[16] I am poor and I have been dying since my youth; I have borne the horrors You have imposed on me since then, yet I am still afraid.

[17] Waves of Your wrath have come over me; Your terrors are destroying me. [18] They surround me all day as though they really were made of water; acting in concert, they encircle me.

[19] You have distanced from me both lover and friend; if my acquaintances actually are somewhere present, then they are hidden in the darkness.

he believes to have come from God in the first place. We might well ask what it would take to engender that kind of bedrock faith in the soul of a citizen of today's world. We tend to respond to agony by searching for someone—*anyone*—to blame for our unhappiness. What kind of spiritual discipline would it take for us to respond to despair by affirming our faith in God—in God's goodness, in the truth inherent in God's judgment, in God's enduring ability to save?

פט

מַשְׂכִּיל לְאֵיתָן הָאֶזְרָחִי׃

2 חַסְדֵי יְהוָה עוֹלָם אָשִׁירָה לְדֹר וָדֹר ׀ אוֹדִיעַ אֱמוּנָתְךָ בְּפִי׃

3 כִּי־אָמַרְתִּי עוֹלָם חֶסֶד יִבָּנֶה שָׁמַיִם ׀ תָּכִן אֱמוּנָתְךָ בָהֶם׃

4 כָּרַתִּי בְרִית לִבְחִירִי נִשְׁבַּעְתִּי לְדָוִד עַבְדִּי׃

5 עַד־עוֹלָם אָכִין זַרְעֶךָ וּבָנִיתִי לְדֹר־וָדוֹר כִּסְאֲךָ סֶלָה׃

6 וְיוֹדוּ שָׁמַיִם פִּלְאֲךָ יְהוָה אַף־אֱמוּנָתְךָ בִּקְהַל קְדֹשִׁים׃

7 כִּי מִי בַשַּׁחַק יַעֲרֹךְ לַיהוָה יִדְמֶה לַיהוָה בִּבְנֵי אֵלִים׃ 8 אֵל נַעֲרָץ בְּסוֹד־קְדֹשִׁים רַבָּה וְנוֹרָא עַל־כָּל־סְבִיבָיו׃ 9 יְהוָה ׀ אֱלֹהֵי צְבָאוֹת מִי־כָמוֹךָ חֲסִין ׀ יָהּ וֶאֱמוּנָתְךָ סְבִיבוֹתֶיךָ׃

10 אַתָּה מוֹשֵׁל בְּגֵאוּת הַיָּם בְּשׂוֹא גַלָּיו אַתָּה תְשַׁבְּחֵם׃

11 אַתָּה דִכִּאתָ כֶחָלָל רָהַב בִּזְרוֹעַ עֻזְּךָ פִּזַּרְתָּ אוֹיְבֶיךָ׃

12 לְךָ שָׁמַיִם אַף־לְךָ אָרֶץ תֵּבֵל וּמְלֹאָהּ אַתָּה יְסַדְתָּם׃

13 צָפוֹן וְיָמִין אַתָּה בְרָאתָם תָּבוֹר וְחֶרְמוֹן בְּשִׁמְךָ יְרַנֵּנוּ׃

The third book of the Psalter ends with a very long poem that has at its center the question of the relationship between faith drawn from the wellsprings of history and faith rooted in the circumstances of any individual's actual daily life.

The poet begins by describing the incredible power of God, bringing up some ancient mythological references that must have sounded archaic even in the poet's own day. His real interest, however, has nothing to do with ancient monsters, but with God's hoary promise to David, an idea best known from the text preserved in the seventh chapter of the Second Book of Samuel. But the poet's version of the divine promise to David is not simply a longer and more detailed literary elaboration of the earlier one. Indeed, the poet emphasizes that the version he presents in his psalm was revealed to him in a group prophetic experience during which God actually spoke the words the poet has recorded for posterity.

Most of what the poet reports he heard God say is not too different from the material preserved in the Book of Samuel. The theme of the divine oracle

89

A wise-song of Ethan the Ezrahite.

[2] Forever shall I sing of the mercies of יהוה; to every generation shall I make Your faithfulness known with my mouth.

[3] And so shall I declare, "The world shall be sustained with mercy, just as You order the heavens with Your faithfulness."

[4] And God responds, "I have made a covenant with My chosen one and an oath to My servant David, saying: [5]'I shall establish Your dynasty forever and sustain Your throne throughout every generation, *selah*.'"

[6] The heavens shall acknowledge Your wondrousness, יהוה, as surely as Your faithfulness shall be acclaimed in the congregation of the holy.

[7] For who in the heavens can be compared to יהוה? Which other divine beings can be likened unto יהוה, [8]a God venerated in the great council of the holy and held in awe by all celestial creatures on every side? [9]יהוה, God of the celestial legions, who is like unto You, mighty יה, with Your faithfulness all around You?

[10] You rule over the proud sea, praising the waves as they crest.

[11] You crushed Rahab like a corpse; with the strength of Your arm, You scattered Your enemies.

[12] The heavens, even the earth, are Yours; You laid the foundation of the earth and all that is in it.

[13] You created North and South, and thus do Mount Tabor and Mount Hermon sing songs of joy in Your name.

that engaged the poet the most profoundly, however, is the idea that no matter how grievous the sins of any of David's descendants, the sustaining mercy of God—and the divine promise made to David—will never be totally withdrawn. Latter-day Davidide kings may be chastised with the rod or be punished with illness—like King Uzziah, for example, whom Scripture reports was made sick with leprosy as punishment for his arrogance and disrespect for God's law. David's line, however, will continue forever. Indeed, God's covenant with David, the poet asserts over and over, cannot be undone, *no matter what.* It is intact, and permanently so.

14 לְךָ זְרוֹעַ עִם־גְּבוּרָה תָּעֹז יָדְךָ תָּרוּם יְמִינֶךָ׃
15 צֶדֶק וּמִשְׁפָּט מְכוֹן כִּסְאֶךָ חֶסֶד וֶאֱמֶת יְקַדְּמוּ
פָנֶיךָ׃
16 אַשְׁרֵי הָעָם יוֹדְעֵי תְרוּעָה יְהֹוָה בְּאוֹר־פָּנֶיךָ
יְהַלֵּכוּן׃
17 בְּשִׁמְךָ יְגִילוּן כָּל־הַיּוֹם וּבְצִדְקָתְךָ יָרוּמוּ׃
18 כִּי־תִפְאֶרֶת עֻזָּמוֹ אָתָּה וּבִרְצֹנְךָ *תָּרוּם קַרְנֵנוּ׃
19 כִּי לַיהֹוָה מָגִנֵּנוּ וְלִקְדוֹשׁ יִשְׂרָאֵל מַלְכֵּנוּ׃
20 אָז דִּבַּרְתָּ־בְחָזוֹן לַחֲסִידֶיךָ וַתֹּאמֶר שִׁוִּיתִי עֵזֶר
עַל־גִּבּוֹר הֲרִימוֹתִי בָחוּר מֵעָם׃ 21 מָצָאתִי דָּוִד
עַבְדִּי בְּשֶׁמֶן קָדְשִׁי מְשַׁחְתִּיו׃ 22 אֲשֶׁר יָדִי תִּכּוֹן
עִמּוֹ אַף־זְרוֹעִי תְאַמְּצֶנּוּ׃ 23 לֹא־יַשִּׁא אוֹיֵב בּוֹ
וּבֶן־עַוְלָה לֹא יְעַנֶּנּוּ׃ 24 וְכַתּוֹתִי מִפָּנָיו צָרָיו
וּמְשַׂנְאָיו אֶגּוֹף׃
25 וֶאֱמוּנָתִי וְחַסְדִּי עִמּוֹ וּבִשְׁמִי תָּרוּם קַרְנוֹ׃
26 וְשַׂמְתִּי בַיָּם יָדוֹ וּבַנְּהָרוֹת יְמִינוֹ׃ 27 הוּא יִקְרָאֵנִי
אָבִי אָתָּה אֵלִי וְצוּר יְשׁוּעָתִי׃ 28 אַף־אָנִי בְּכוֹר
אֶתְּנֵהוּ עֶלְיוֹן לְמַלְכֵי־אָרֶץ׃ 29 לְעוֹלָם *אֶשְׁמָור־לוֹ
חַסְדִּי וּבְרִיתִי נֶאֱמֶנֶת לוֹ׃

v. 18 תרים כתיב
v. 29 יתיר וו

The second part of the poet's psalm, however, tells an entirely different story. Despite the reassuring oracle about Davidic kingship the poet received, he personally felt abandoned, spurned, and rejected by God . . . and his personal experience of the covenant was that it was anything but intact. Indeed, his sense was that the nations of the world were entirely free to deal as they wished with the anointed one of Israel. His splendor, the poet writes, was clearly a thing of the past; it was as though the Almighty took the crown from his head and pitched it into the trash.

Who is our poet? At certain junctures in his poem, he writes as though he himself were the disgraced scion of the House of David. The larger context, however, suggests that he merely identified himself with the image of a king promised permanent divine protection, yet nonetheless obliged to struggle with the reality of God's apparent lack of interest in his security and prosperity. The poet calls out to God *as though* he were the disgraced king—not because he suffers from any delusion that he really is the rejected regent, but because he feels that his situation mirrors that of a king grappling with divine

[14] You possess a mighty arm; indeed, might itself is Yours. Your hand is strong, Your right arm, exalted.

[15] Justice and law are the base of Your throne; mercy and truth precede Your face.

[16] Happy is the people that knows the blast of the *shofar;* יהוה, they shall walk in the light of Your face.

[17] In Your name shall they be glad all the day; indeed, they shall be exalted in Your righteousness, [18]for You are the splendor of their strength and by Your will is our horn raised up.

[19] For such is the authority of יהוה, our Shield, of the Holy One of Israel, our Sovereign.

[20] Then You spoke in a vision to Your pious worshipers, saying, "I have granted My help to a hero, selecting a lad from a whole nation. [21–22]I found my servant, David—the one through whom My hand will be established, even as My arm grants him strength—and then anointed him with My holy oil. [23]The enemy shall not best him, nor shall any lout cause him pain. [24]Instead, I shall personally dash his enemies to pieces before him and smite any who hate him.

[25] My faithfulness and mercy shall abide with him and his horn shall be raised up in My name.

[26] I shall place his hand on the sea, his right hand on the rivers. [27]He shall say to me, 'You are my Progenitor, my God, and the Rock of my salvation.' [28]And I, for My part, shall treat him as a firstborn son and make him supreme over the kings of the earth. [29]I shall forever preserve My mercy for him, and My covenant with him shall remain permanently in force.

promises that appear unkept, while his faith assures him that such a thing simply cannot be.

Modern readers who wish to incorporate the recitation of the eighty-ninth psalm into their spiritual lives will want to ask themselves how they personally believe the covenant between God and Israel operates today. Is it inviolate and permanent? Or is it merely a poetic framework bequeathed to us by inventive ancients to assist us in thinking about the relationship between God and the Jewish people? Most modern Jews will probably find it impossible to ponder these issues without reference to

30 וְשַׂמְתִּי לָעַד זַרְעוֹ וְכִסְאוֹ כִּימֵי שָׁמָיִם׃
31 אִם־יַעַזְבוּ בָנָיו תּוֹרָתִי וּבְמִשְׁפָּטַי לֹא יֵלֵכוּן׃
32 אִם־חֻקֹּתַי יְחַלֵּלוּ וּמִצְוֹתַי לֹא יִשְׁמֹרוּ׃
33 וּפָקַדְתִּי בְשֵׁבֶט פִּשְׁעָם וּבִנְגָעִים עֲוֺנָם׃
34 וְחַסְדִּי לֹא־אָפִיר מֵעִמּוֹ וְלֹא אֲשַׁקֵּר בֶּאֱמוּנָתִי׃
35 לֹא־אֲחַלֵּל בְּרִיתִי וּמוֹצָא שְׂפָתַי לֹא אֲשַׁנֶּה׃
36 אַחַת נִשְׁבַּעְתִּי בְקָדְשִׁי אִם־לְדָוִד אֲכַזֵּב׃ 37 זַרְעוֹ
לְעוֹלָם יִהְיֶה וְכִסְאוֹ כַשֶּׁמֶשׁ נֶגְדִּי׃ 38 כְּיָרֵחַ יִכּוֹן
עוֹלָם וְעֵד בַּשַּׁחַק נֶאֱמָן סֶלָה׃
39 וְאַתָּה זָנַחְתָּ וַתִּמְאָס הִתְעַבַּרְתָּ עִם־מְשִׁיחֶךָ׃
40 נֵאַרְתָּה בְּרִית עַבְדֶּךָ חִלַּלְתָּ לָאָרֶץ נִזְרוֹ׃
41 פָּרַצְתָּ כָל־גְּדֵרֹתָיו שַׂמְתָּ מִבְצָרָיו מְחִתָּה׃
42 שַׁסֻּהוּ כָּל־עֹבְרֵי דָרֶךְ הָיָה חֶרְפָּה לִשְׁכֵנָיו׃
43 הֲרִימוֹתָ יְמִין צָרָיו הִשְׂמַחְתָּ כָּל־אוֹיְבָיו׃
44 אַף־תָּשִׁיב צוּר חַרְבּוֹ וְלֹא הֲקֵימֹתוֹ בַּמִּלְחָמָה׃

the Shoah. That being the case, the recitation of the eighty-ninth psalm can also serve as a useful springboard for asking what the whole idea of a covenant between God and Israel can mean to Jewish people living after the Holocaust.

There is, after all, no more vexing prism through which to look at the horrors of the Shoah than the biblical texts describing the eternal covenant binding God and Israel. (The texts all omit or include different details, but the notion that the covenant is eternal appears basic to them all.) That being the case, moderns seeking to anchor their own spiritual lives in biblical thought may find themselves thinking of the Shoah as an almost impenetrable wall between them and the God described in those ancient texts as merciful, kind, just . . . and endlessly solicitous of the welfare of the Jewish people. Can an omnipotent God have been unable to act to save the innocents? Can an omniscient God not have known of the slaughter? Can the reason God failed to intervene to end the killing simply be too recondite or too impossibly obscure for human beings to seize? And what of other nations that have experienced total or partial genocide? Does the biblical concept of a covenant between God and Israel suggest that those peoples, living without the benefit of a covenantal relationship with God, therefore, have no choice but to *endure* history—without the protective intimacy and commitment that binds Israel to God and protects it from the world? None of these questions has a simple answer, of course, but, merely by enunciating them, modern readers can join the effort to find a reasonable sense

[30] Moreover, I shall grant him a permanent line of descendants; even his throne shall endure for as long as the days of heaven.

[31] If, however, his descendants abandon My teaching and do not follow My laws, [32] if they profane My statutes and do not keep My commandments, [33] then I shall punish their sins with a rod, their iniquity with disease.

[34] But, even under such circumstances, I will not withdraw My mercy from him entirely, nor shall I renounce My promise of faithfulness. [35–36] Having taken an oath in My own sanctuary not to betray My promise to David, I shall neither cancel My covenant nor change the utterance of My mouth, to the effect [37] that he would have a permanent line of descendants and that his throne would be just as enduring as the sun itself exists before Me. [38] It shall always be established, just as the moon is a faithful witness in the sky, *selah*."

[39] But You have abandoned Your anointed one, finding him repulsive and becoming enraged at him.

[40] You have forsaken Your covenant with Your servant and profaned his crown, casting it contemptuously to the ground.

[41] You have breached all his fences and turned his fortresses into rubble. [42] Every passerby scorns him, such that he has become an object of derision to his neighbors.

[43] You have raised up the right hand of his foes, giving his enemies cause to rejoice.

[44] Worse, You have turned back the blade of his sword and have not supported him in battle.

of what the covenant between Israel and God can mean after the Shoah.

Reading the 89th psalm can provide a framework for asking just the right kind of questions to usher us into the fray. The poet writes as a king, certain that God's promise to David is absolutely operative but at the same time overwhelmed by the degree to which he personally feels totally and utterly abandoned. *Ne'arta berit avdekha,* he says bitterly to God: "You have forsaken Your covenant with Your servant." But he also knows that his own words make no sense—not in the context of his faith in God's promise to David and not in

45 הִשְׁבַּתָּ מִטְּהָרוֹ וְכִסְאוֹ לָאָרֶץ מִגַּרְתָּה׃
46 הִקְצַרְתָּ יְמֵי עֲלוּמָיו הֶעֱטִיתָ עָלָיו בּוּשָׁה סֶלָה׃
47 עַד־מָה יְהוָה תִּסָּתֵר לָנֶצַח תִּבְעַר כְּמוֹ־אֵשׁ חֲמָתֶךָ׃
48 זְכָר־אֲנִי מֶה־חָלֶד עַל־מַה־שָּׁוְא בָּרָאתָ כָל־בְּנֵי־אָדָם׃
49 מִי גֶבֶר יִחְיֶה וְלֹא יִרְאֶה־מָּוֶת יְמַלֵּט נַפְשׁוֹ מִיַּד־שְׁאוֹל סֶלָה׃
50 אַיֵּה חֲסָדֶיךָ הָרִאשֹׁנִים ׀ אֲדֹנָי נִשְׁבַּעְתָּ לְדָוִד בֶּאֱמוּנָתֶךָ׃
51 זְכֹר אֲדֹנָי חֶרְפַּת עֲבָדֶיךָ שְׂאֵתִי בְחֵיקִי כָּל־רַבִּים עַמִּים׃ 52 אֲשֶׁר חֵרְפוּ אוֹיְבֶיךָ ׀ יְהוָה אֲשֶׁר חֵרְפוּ עִקְּבוֹת מְשִׁיחֶךָ׃
53 בָּרוּךְ יְהוָה לְעוֹלָם אָמֵן ׀ וְאָמֵן׃

terms of the inner workings of his own heart—and that he is, paradoxically, certain God will continue to care for him and watch over him. He feels both abandoned and not abandoned at the same time, alive to his personal destiny in God at the same time that he feels God taking the crown from his head and pitching it contemptuously to the ground. Under most circumstances, moderns would describe someone in this situation as seriously confused, at best, but the poet—also paradoxically—sounds neither confused nor paralyzed or overwhelmed by his situation. Instead, he seems willing simply to accept how

[45]You have brought an end to his purity and cast his throne down to the earth. [46]You have shortened the days of his youth, enshrouding him in shame, *selah.*

[47] How long, יהוה, will You hide? Will Your rage forever burn like fire?

[48] Remember that I am just a mortal human being; recall how tenuously You created all human life.

[49] What individual can live without seeing death? Will that person's soul escape from the clutches of Sheol, *selah*?

[50] Where are Your traditional mercies, Adonai, the ones that You swore in Your faithfulness to David would always remain intact?

[51] Recall the shame of Your servants, Adonai, how I carry in my bosom the shameful taunts of those many nations, [52]how Your enemies, יהוה, taunted us, how they dogged the footsteps of Your anointed one with taunts.

[53] Blessed be יהוה forever, amen and again amen.

things are and leave the contradictions unresolved, thereby affirming his faith without letting extraneous details destroy the confidence he seems intuitively to understand will be his final bulwark against the onslaught of the world. Can moderns adopt a similar theological stance as they approach the Shoah? By refusing to condemn their own faith in God as irrational or absurd at the same time they decline to look away from even the most horrible of images of human suffering, can moderns learn to live with the paradox of an intact covenant with a merciful God in a world that also knows of genocide?

צ

תְּפִלָּה לְמֹשֶׁה אִישׁ־הָאֱלֹהִים
אֲדֹנָי מָעוֹן אַתָּה הָיִיתָ לָּנוּ בְּדֹר וָדֹר:
2 בְּטֶרֶם ׀ הָרִים יֻלָּדוּ וַתְּחוֹלֵל אֶרֶץ וְתֵבֵל וּמֵעוֹלָם
עַד־עוֹלָם אַתָּה אֵל:
3 תָּשֵׁב אֱנוֹשׁ עַד־דַּכָּא וַתֹּאמֶר שׁוּבוּ בְנֵי־אָדָם:
4 כִּי אֶלֶף שָׁנִים בְּעֵינֶיךָ כְּיוֹם אֶתְמוֹל כִּי יַעֲבֹר
וְאַשְׁמוּרָה בַלָּיְלָה:
5 זְרַמְתָּם שֵׁנָה יִהְיוּ בַּבֹּקֶר כֶּחָצִיר יַחֲלֹף: 6 בַּבֹּקֶר
יָצִיץ וְחָלָף לָעֶרֶב יְמוֹלֵל וְיָבֵשׁ:
7 כִּי־כָלִינוּ בְאַפֶּךָ וּבַחֲמָתְךָ נִבְהָלְנוּ:
8 *שַׁתָּה עֲוֺנֹתֵינוּ לְנֶגְדֶּךָ עֲלֻמֵנוּ לִמְאוֹר פָּנֶיךָ:
9 כִּי כָל־יָמֵינוּ פָּנוּ בְעֶבְרָתֶךָ כִּלִּינוּ שָׁנֵינוּ כְמוֹ־הֶגֶה:
10 יְמֵי שְׁנוֹתֵינוּ ׀ בָהֶם שִׁבְעִים שָׁנָה וְאִם בִּגְבוּרֹת ׀
שְׁמוֹנִים שָׁנָה וְרָהְבָּם עָמָל וָאָוֶן כִּי־גָז חִישׁ
וַנָּעֻפָה:

v. 8 שת כתיב

The notion of God existing outside of time, with its odd combination of simplicity and inscrutability, appears to have beckoned to the ancients no less successfully than it intrigues modern readers. It is, after all, one thing to pay lip service to the idea that God exists outside the constraints of time, but quite another even to begin to explain what such an idea could possibly mean. And, even though it is relatively easy to understand at least some of the ramifications of the basic idea (for example, that millennia of human history are mere moments in the incredibly long existence of God), it will challenge even the most insightful among us to try to fathom what it would mean for anyone or anything, let alone God, to exist outside the framework of time entirely. Such a theology would posit, after all, not simply that God has existed for a very long time and will continue to exist for a very long time, but also that divine existence is not even framed by the concepts of time past and time yet to come . . . and that the state of being in which God exists neither began at a certain moment nor will come to an end at a certain moment. Perhaps most daunting of all, it would imply that the concept of time itself does not apply to God because time is limit and boundary—perhaps the *ultimate* limit or boundary—and God, as faith teaches and reason dictates, exists totally without either.

To profess belief in this aspect of our conception of God is easy, but our human minds balk at going even one step further. What would it mean to exist

BOOK FOUR

90

A prayer of Moses, the man of God.
Adonai, You have been our refuge from generation to generation.
[2] Before the mountains were born and the earth and its land mass conceived, You were already God, just as You always shall be.
[3] You endure humanity until You become too depressed to suffer its foibles, and then You say, "Be gone, O children of Adam." [4] Indeed, a thousand years in Your eyes are as little permanent as a day gone by or as a watch in the night.
[5] The years flow by like dreams through sleep. In the morning heat, people wither like blades of grass; [6] they shoot up in the morning only to wither. And, indeed, by evening, they are faded and dried out.
[7] Indeed, we face annihilation because of Your anger; consequently, we are terrified by Your rage.
[8] You have set our sins before You, the indiscretions of our youth illuminated by the light of Your face.
[9] For all our days vanish when considered by You in anger; we are lost, our years gone in the time it takes to clear one's throat.
[10] The days of our years amount to seventy years or, if we are particularly robust, then perhaps to eighty years—but no matter how many years we are allotted, the mighty deeds of those years are only labor and sin and then, in a twinkling, we fly off and are no more.

outside of time? How can such a timeless God ever manage to *do* anything at all, for would not any action undertaken immediately—and unavoidably—pass from the present into the past, thereby imputing a distinction between the two to a Being we wish to insist exists with reference to neither?

The author of the ninetieth psalm is no more adept at conceptualizing a God outside of time than any of us, but he did have sufficient insight to seek a kind of solution within the sphere of language rather than physical reality. Indeed, when the poet writes that God already existed even "before the mountains were born and the earth and its land mass conceived" and that God, immutable, will always exist in precisely that same way, he is suggesting that God exists *be-*

11 מִֽי־י֭וֹדֵעַ עֹ֣ז אַפֶּ֑ךָ וּ֝כְיִרְאָתְךָ֗ עֶבְרָתֶֽךָ׃
12 לִמְנ֣וֹת יָ֭מֵינוּ כֵּ֣ן הוֹדַ֑ע וְ֝נָבִ֗א לְבַ֣ב חָכְמָֽה׃
13 שׁוּבָ֣ה יְ֭הוָה עַד־מָתָ֑י וְ֝הִנָּחֵ֗ם עַל־עֲבָדֶֽיךָ׃
14 שַׂבְּעֵ֣נוּ בַבֹּ֣קֶר חַסְדֶּ֑ךָ וּֽנְרַנְּנָ֥ה וְ֝נִשְׂמְחָ֗ה בְּכָל־יָמֵֽינוּ׃
15 שַׂ֭מְּחֵנוּ כִּימ֣וֹת עִנִּיתָ֑נוּ שְׁ֝נ֗וֹת רָאִ֥ינוּ רָעָֽה׃
16 יֵרָאֶ֣ה אֶל־עֲבָדֶ֣יךָ פָעֳלֶ֑ךָ וַ֝הֲדָרְךָ֗ עַל־בְּנֵיהֶֽם׃
17 וִיהִ֤י ׀ נֹ֤עַם אֲדֹנָ֥י אֱלֹהֵ֗ינוּ עָ֫לֵ֥ינוּ וּמַעֲשֵׂ֣ה יָ֭דֵינוּ כּוֹנְנָ֣ה עָלֵ֑ינוּ וּֽמַעֲשֵׂ֥ה יָ֝דֵ֗ינוּ כּוֹנְנֵֽהוּ׃

tween spheres of eternity, between the concepts of always-was and always-shall-be.

Time itself is thus a kind of *midrash* on reality that bears meaning in the very same way any adjective spoken of God needs to be taken: as a kind of vague if-God-were-human-we-could-describe-God-as-being-something-like-this remark. When the poet turns to the brevity of human life and contrasts the few, short years of our lives with the endlessness of God, he is essentially making the same point: that speaking of divine timelessness is only meaningful when compared to the span of our own brief lives . . . and that time itself is just a word we use to speak about the world that simply cannot mean anything at all when used of a God who, by definition, cannot be described with reference to the physical universe.

[11] Who knows the force of Your anger or Your rage, just as unmeasurable as the awe in which You are to be held?

[12] Make known to us the best way to count our days so that we may develop hearts of wisdom.

[13] Return, יהוה! How long until You take pity on your servants.

[14] Satisfy us in the morning with Your mercy that we may rejoice and be glad all our days.

[15] Make the number of days we rejoice equal to the number of days You have made us suffer, equal to the years during which we have seen naught but evil.

[16] May Your work be shown to Your servants so that Your splendor be upon their children [17]and the beauty of Adonai, our God, be upon us. May God establish for us the work of our hands; the work of our hands, may God establish it.

Reading the ninetieth psalm can prompt us to ponder the idea of time as a *midrash* on existence, and to ask some of the extremely provocative questions that flow from this idea. What are the implications of the notion of time as mere *midrash* for our sense of personal history? How must the poet's insight into the nature of existence affect our general sense of aging as a kind of ineluctable curse? And how can it alter our fear of death . . . and our yearning to grow towards God over the course of a lifetime of ever passing moments?

צא

יֹשֵׁב בְּסֵתֶר עֶלְיוֹן בְּצֵל שַׁדַּי יִתְלוֹנָן׃
2 אֹמַר לַיהוָה מַחְסִי וּמְצוּדָתִי אֱלֹהַי אֶבְטַח־בּוֹ׃
3 כִּי הוּא יַצִּילְךָ מִפַּח יָקוּשׁ מִדֶּבֶר הַוּוֹת׃
4 בְּאֶבְרָתוֹ ׀ יָסֶךְ לָךְ וְתַחַת כְּנָפָיו תֶּחְסֶה צִנָּה
וְסֹחֵרָה אֲמִתּוֹ׃
5 לֹא־תִירָא מִפַּחַד לָיְלָה מֵחֵץ יָעוּף יוֹמָם׃ 6 מִדֶּבֶר
בָּאֹפֶל יַהֲלֹךְ מִקֶּטֶב יָשׁוּד צָהֳרָיִם׃ 7 יִפֹּל מִצִּדְּךָ ׀
אֶלֶף וּרְבָבָה מִימִינֶךָ אֵלֶיךָ לֹא יִגָּשׁ׃ 8 רַק בְּעֵינֶיךָ
תַבִּיט וְשִׁלֻּמַת רְשָׁעִים תִּרְאֶה׃
9 כִּי־אַתָּה יְהוָה מַחְסִי עֶלְיוֹן שַׂמְתָּ מְעוֹנֶךָ׃
10 לֹא־תְאֻנֶּה אֵלֶיךָ רָעָה וְנֶגַע לֹא־יִקְרַב בְּאָהֳלֶךָ׃
11 כִּי מַלְאָכָיו יְצַוֶּה־לָּךְ לִשְׁמָרְךָ בְּכָל־דְּרָכֶיךָ׃
12 עַל־כַּפַּיִם יִשָּׂאוּנְךָ פֶּן־תִּגֹּף בָּאֶבֶן רַגְלֶךָ׃ 13 עַל־
שַׁחַל וָפֶתֶן תִּדְרֹךְ תִּרְמֹס כְּפִיר וְתַנִּין׃ 14 כִּי בִי
חָשַׁק וַאֲפַלְּטֵהוּ אֲשַׂגְּבֵהוּ כִּי־יָדַע שְׁמִי׃ 15 יִקְרָאֵנִי ׀
וְאֶעֱנֵהוּ עִמּוֹ אָנֹכִי בְצָרָה אֲחַלְּצֵהוּ וַאֲכַבְּדֵהוּ׃
16 אֹרֶךְ יָמִים אַשְׂבִּיעֵהוּ וְאַרְאֵהוּ בִּישׁוּעָתִי׃

By imagining God as a great bird with enormous protective wings beneath which the faithful may seek refuge from the brutality of the world, the author of the ninety-first psalm prompts us to consider where it is that we ourselves seek security in our world. Is it by accumulating wealth? Or do we make ourselves feel secure by having valid passports, by keeping our bags packed, and by knowing that, come what may, we will have some place to hide if it becomes impossible to live safely out in the open wherever it is we are currently located? Moderns may find the snug fit of a bulletproof vest reassuring, but the poet's answer is simpler and more within the reach of most people: he finds his ultimate security in his faith in God, in the belief that the Almighty functions as an unassailable and impregnable fortress to those who fear and love God, and whose lives are in God and of God. But the ultimate shield against the evils

91

Whosoever resides in the secret place of the Most High, abides in the shadow of Shaddai, Almighty God.

[2] This I say to יהוה: "You are my haven and my fortress, My God in whom I trust, [3]the God who saves people from traps before they spring and from infectious scheming, [4]the God who grants people refuge beneath the divine wings by covering them with a divine pinion, the God whose truth is both shield and armor."

[5] And this I say to the faithful: "Fear neither nighttime terror nor arrows that fly freely in the daytime, [6]neither contagion that creeps along in the darkness nor pestilence that prowls forward in the afternoon light. [7]A thousand will fall by your side, perhaps even ten thousand at your right side, but the plague shall not touch you at all. [8]Indeed, this is precisely what you shall see when you inspect the situation carefully: the wicked getting their due."

[9] For You, O יהוה, are my haven; You have fashioned Your residence on high.

[10] And I say this to the faithful as well: "Evil shall not harm you, nor shall sickness approach your tent, [11]for God will appoint angels to guard you in all your paths; [12]they, the angels of God, shall carry you on their hands lest your feet be smitten by stones. [13]You shall tread on lions and asps with impunity, on lion cubs and serpents with no fear of harm, [14]for thus says God: 'I shall save whoever desires Me; I shall exalt whoever knows My name. [15]When that person calls upon Me, I shall answer him; I shall be with him in times of trouble. I shall grant him relief and honor him. [16]I shall satisfy him with length of days and I shall show him salvation in Me.'"

of the world, the poet suggests, lies not merely in possessing faith, but in constructing a belief system on a bedrock foundation of absolute truthfulness, of total intellectual honesty, and of complete and unwavering spiritual integrity. That, the poet is suggesting, is how the truly savvy among the faithful—those who desire God *and* who know God's name—will make themselves safe and secure. But is his model one moderns can actually adopt without falling prey to their own cynicism?

צב

מִזְמוֹר שִׁיר לְיוֹם הַשַּׁבָּת׃
2 טוֹב לְהֹדוֹת לַיהוָה וּלְזַמֵּר לְשִׁמְךָ עֶלְיוֹן׃ 3 לְהַגִּיד
בַּבֹּקֶר חַסְדֶּךָ וֶאֱמוּנָתְךָ בַּלֵּילוֹת׃ 4 עֲלֵי־עָשׂוֹר
וַעֲלֵי־נָבֶל עֲלֵי הִגָּיוֹן בְּכִנּוֹר׃
5 כִּי שִׂמַּחְתַּנִי יְהוָה בְּפָעֳלֶךָ בְּמַעֲשֵׂי יָדֶיךָ אֲרַנֵּן׃
6 מַה־גָּדְלוּ מַעֲשֶׂיךָ יְהוָה מְאֹד עָמְקוּ מַחְשְׁבֹתֶיךָ׃
7 אִישׁ בַּעַר לֹא יֵדָע וּכְסִיל לֹא־יָבִין אֶת־זֹאת׃
8 בִּפְרֹחַ רְשָׁעִים | כְּמוֹ עֵשֶׂב וַיָּצִיצוּ כָּל־פֹּעֲלֵי אָוֶן
לְהִשָּׁמְדָם עֲדֵי־עַד׃ 9 וְאַתָּה מָרוֹם לְעֹלָם יְהוָה׃
10 כִּי הִנֵּה אֹיְבֶיךָ | יְהוָה כִּי־הִנֵּה אֹיְבֶיךָ יֹאבֵדוּ
יִתְפָּרְדוּ כָּל־פֹּעֲלֵי אָוֶן׃ 11 וַתָּרֶם כִּרְאֵים קַרְנִי
בַּלֹּתִי בְּשֶׁמֶן רַעֲנָן׃
12 וַתַּבֵּט עֵינִי בְּשׁוּרָי בַּקָּמִים עָלַי מְרֵעִים תִּשְׁמַעְנָה
אָזְנָי׃
13 צַדִּיק כַּתָּמָר יִפְרָח כְּאֶרֶז בַּלְּבָנוֹן יִשְׂגֶּה׃
14 שְׁתוּלִים בְּבֵית יְהוָה בְּחַצְרוֹת אֱלֹהֵינוּ יַפְרִיחוּ׃
15 עוֹד יְנוּבוּן בְּשֵׂיבָה דְּשֵׁנִים וְרַעֲנַנִּים יִהְיוּ׃
16 לְהַגִּיד כִּי־יָשָׁר יְהוָה צוּרִי וְלֹא־*עַוְלָתָה בּוֹ׃

v. 16 עלתה כתיב

Only one psalm, the ninety-second, is connected formally to a particular day of the week by the biblical text itself. But although the relationship of this psalm to the Sabbath day is explicitly stated in its opening verse, the rest of the poem makes no mention of the Sabbath at all. Instead, the poet follows his opening strophe with a hybrid psalm that promises a happy future to the righteous, exile and death to their enemies, and no relief from the dullness with which brutes attempt (and fail) to understand how God deals with evil people and their evil deeds in the world. Any number of explanations suggest themselves for the mention of the Sabbath, but the simplest is that these are the thoughts that the poet associates with his day of rest: when he has the time to contemplate the world, he always seems to come back to the notion that the righteous will endure, the wicked will perish, the foolish will remain blind, and God will triumph. We are often dis-

92

A psalm-song for the Sabbath day.
[2] It is good to give thanks to יהוה and to sing to Your name, O God on high, [3]to tell in the morning of Your mercy and of Your trustworthiness during the night [4]to the accompaniment of the ten-stringed harp and the *nevel,* of the *higayon* among the lyres.
[5] For You have brought me happiness through Your deeds, יהוה; in the work of Your hands, I rejoice.
[6] How grand are Your works, יהוה; Your thoughts are very deep.
[7] Now a boor will not know this nor will a fool understand: [8–9]when the wicked sprout up like blades of grass and doers of iniquity blossom like flowers, You are sufficiently exalted, יהוה, to destroy them permanently.
[10] For behold, יהוה, behold Your enemies perish and whole gangs of evildoers disband [11]while You raise up my horn like that of an ox and soak me through with fresh oil.
[12] My eye sees those who are watching me; when evildoers rise up against me, my ears hear of it.
[13] A righteous person will blossom like a palm tree and will grow as tall as a cedar on Mount Lebanon; [14]indeed, those who are planted in the House of יהוה will blossom in the courtyards of our God.
[15] In old age, they will still be alive; they will remain more than full enough of sap and freshness [16]to demonstrate that יהוה is just—my rock in whom there is no flaw.

tracted from these truths, but might they not surface and successfully insinuate themselves into our spiritual consciousnesses when, at the end of six long days of frenzied activity, we finally have time for leisurely reflection in the course of a weekly day of rest? And this as well: might not the poet be hinting that having the time to contemplate, and perhaps even to embrace, those core concepts could, in the end, be the greatest and most sacred goal of our hours of Sabbath leisure?

צג

יְהוָ֣ה מָלָךְ֮ גֵּא֪וּת לָ֫בֵ֥שׁ לָבֵ֣שׁ יְ֭הוָה עֹ֣ז הִתְאַזָּ֑ר
אַף־תִּכּ֥וֹן תֵּ֝בֵ֗ל בַּל־תִּמּֽוֹט׃
2 נָכ֣וֹן כִּסְאֲךָ֣ מֵאָ֑ז מֵעוֹלָ֣ם אָֽתָּה׃
3 נָשְׂא֤וּ נְהָר֨וֹת ׀ יְהוָ֗ה נָשְׂא֣וּ נְהָר֣וֹת קוֹלָ֑ם יִשְׂא֖וּ
נְהָר֣וֹת דָּכְיָֽם׃ 4 מִקֹּל֨וֹת ׀ מַ֤יִם רַבִּ֗ים אַדִּירִ֣ים
מִשְׁבְּרֵי־יָ֑ם אַדִּ֖יר בַּמָּר֣וֹם יְהוָֽה׃
5 עֵֽדֹתֶ֨יךָ ׀ נֶאֶמְנ֬וּ מְאֹ֗ד לְבֵיתְךָ֥ נַאֲוָה־קֹ֑דֶשׁ יְ֝הוָ֗ה
לְאֹ֣רֶךְ יָמִֽים׃

By their very nature, metaphors defy any attempt to evaluate their inherent worth. For example, one poet describes the sea as blue and another as green, but although—or perhaps because—water itself has no color at all, neither metaphor ends up being any less true than the other. Nonetheless, certain metaphoric ideas do manage to establish themselves in people's consciousnesses and to become, if not quite more "correct" than their alternatives, then at least more normative. And they eventually do start to sound like basic truths that only pedantic, contrary people challenge.

As an example, we can consider the idea—totally, impossibly false in any but the most extended poetic sense—that God dwells in heaven, that somewhere up in the immeasurable sky is a celestial throne room of some sort in which the King of the kings of kings rules over a dominion so vast as to be almost unchartable. The idea is poetry, not science, but it sounds vaguely right after so much repetition.

It comes, therefore, as a bit of surprise when the poet of the ninety-third psalm proposes a different metaphoric range along which to locate a sense of

93

יהוה reigns wearing robes of majesty. יהוה wears—or rather, girds the divine loins with—that very might once used to create the world and make it sturdy and permanent.

[2] Your throne too stands eternally firm; You Yourself, of course, exist forever.

[3] The rivers, O יהוה, the rivers lift up their voice; the rivers lift up their flood. [4] But יהוה is mighty on high, mightier even than the sound of the great waters, even than the roar of the sea's mightiest breakers.

[5] Your testimonies regarding Your House, the most beautiful of holy places, are entirely true, יהוה, and permanently so.

God's presence. His God is also a supreme Monarch who sits upon a throne more mighty than any earthly regent's, but the ultimate heights here are not the (mere) vault of air and sky. As the story in Genesis makes explicit, the vault of heaven—the sky—is merely the protective barrier that separates the earth from the endless sea of water that exists over it. And so the poet imagines God on the divine throne surrounded not by air but by water. And he does not posit a stagnant sea either, but rather an ocean of immensely powerful breaking waves crashing endlessly around the base of the divine aqua-throne with almost indescribable violence. Moderns who have sailed on the open seas or who have even just stood on the shore and looked out to sea will easily seize how the terrifying power of the ocean's waves provided the poet with the context for developing an image of God as a divine sovereign so powerful as to rule *even* over the celestial sea. How they will translate such an unfamiliar image into the stuff of profitable spiritual contemplation, of course, is another question entirely.

צד

אֵל־נְקָמוֹת יְהוָה אֵל נְקָמוֹת הוֹפִיַע:
2 הִנָּשֵׂא שֹׁפֵט הָאָרֶץ הָשֵׁב גְּמוּל עַל־גֵּאִים:
3 עַד־מָתַי רְשָׁעִים ׀ יְהוָה עַד־מָתַי רְשָׁעִים יַעֲלֹזוּ:
4 יַבִּיעוּ יְדַבְּרוּ עָתָק יִתְאַמְּרוּ כָּל־פֹּעֲלֵי אָוֶן:
5 עַמְּךָ יְהוָה יְדַכְּאוּ וְנַחֲלָתְךָ יְעַנּוּ: 6 אַלְמָנָה וְגֵר יַהֲרֹגוּ וִיתוֹמִים יְרַצֵּחוּ:
7 וַיֹּאמְרוּ לֹא יִרְאֶה־יָּהּ וְלֹא־יָבִין אֱלֹהֵי יַעֲקֹב:
8 בִּינוּ בֹּעֲרִים בָּעָם וּכְסִילִים מָתַי תַּשְׂכִּילוּ: 9 הֲנֹטַע אֹזֶן הֲלֹא יִשְׁמָע אִם־יֹצֵר עַיִן הֲלֹא יַבִּיט: 10 הֲיֹסֵר גּוֹיִם הֲלֹא יוֹכִיחַ הַמְלַמֵּד אָדָם דָּעַת:
11 יְהוָה יֹדֵעַ מַחְשְׁבוֹת אָדָם כִּי הֵמָּה הָבֶל:
12 אַשְׁרֵי הַגֶּבֶר אֲשֶׁר־תְּיַסְּרֶנּוּ יָּהּ וּמִתּוֹרָתְךָ תְלַמְּדֶנּוּ: 13 לְהַשְׁקִיט לוֹ מִימֵי רָע עַד יִכָּרֶה לָרָשָׁע שָׁחַת:
14 כִּי ׀ לֹא־יִטֹּשׁ יְהוָה עַמּוֹ וְנַחֲלָתוֹ לֹא יַעֲזֹב:
15 כִּי־עַד־צֶדֶק יָשׁוּב מִשְׁפָּט וְאַחֲרָיו כָּל־יִשְׁרֵי־לֵב:

The poet whose psalm is our ninety-fourth is an angry man with no compunctions about expressing his rage as forcefully as possible. He lives in a sick, heartless world in which villains routinely murder widows, orphans, and strangers, a world in which the wicked oppress the poor, denounce their enemies falsely in court, torture the pious . . . and yet live happy, contented lives of luxury in lovely homes surrounded by the trappings of wealth and prosperity. In our day, we tend to accept as inevitable that there will always be criminals and rogues in the world who prosper—some to a far greater extent than the pious among us, who spend their lives seeking not wealth or power but God. The poet sees the same phenomenon in his world, but lacking the modern liberal inclination to accept as reasonable whatever about the world appears to be unchangeable, the poet is outraged. He surely knows the ominous words in the Torah's famous Haazinu song *li nakam veshilem* ("Vengeance, yea payback, is Mine," spoken by Moses in the name of God at Deuteronomy 32:35) and he wants some action. If God is truly the all-powerful Judge of the world and if outlaws and gangsters do indeed wander the earth freely, then the poet wants the God of Vengeance to appear on earth, to champion the victims of evildoers, to right their wrongs, and to pay back onto their heads some small part of the misery and suffering they have brought to others. His reference to God as *El nekamot* ("God of Vengeance")

94 יהוה is a God of vengeance; O God of Vengeance, appear!
[2] Rouse Yourself, O Judge of the earth, and pay back the arrogant in kind.
[3] How long, יהוה, how long shall evil people exult? [4]How long shall the wicked express themselves by speaking words of defiance, shall doers of iniquity boast about themselves?
[5] They oppress Your people, יהוה, and torture Your inheritance; [6]they kill widows and strangers, even daring to murder orphans.
[7] They say, "יה will not see; the God of Jacob will not understand."
[8] Understand this, you destroyers of the people, you fools. When will you gain some insight? [9]Does the One who designed the ear not hear? Does the Creator of the eye not see? [10]Shall the One who chastises nations, who endows humanity with intelligence—shall that One not rebuke people like you?
[11] יהוה knows the thoughts of human beings, though they be no more substantive than breath.
[12] Happy is the individual whom You allow to suffer, יה, for thus do You instruct him from Your teaching, [13]keeping him calm on a day of evil . . . until a pit can be dug for the wicked.
[14] For יהוה will neither abandon the people of God nor forsake the very people who constitute the divine inheritance, [15]but, setting an example for the honest to follow, will return a just verdict.

will probably shock modern readers, sounding (as it clearly does) as though the prism through which the poet perceives his God is fashioned of recompense and quid pro quo justice. But when he calls on *El nekamot* actually to appear and bring justice to the world and, especially, suffering and misery to the arrogant scoundrels who are the source of so much unhappiness on earth, the poet's plea sounds quite reasonable.

Does the poet really mean it when he writes that those who suffer are the lucky ones? Does he truly believe that, in the end, those who suffer at the hands of the wicked will eventually see their suffering requited by a just God, and will be sufficiently moved by the experience to embrace faith and live lives in and of God? Is it possible that

16 מִי־יָקוּם לִי עִם־מְרֵעִים מִי־יִתְיַצֵּב לִי עִם־פֹּעֲלֵי אָוֶן:
17 לוּלֵי יְהוָה עֶזְרָתָה לִּי כִּמְעַט ׀ שָׁכְנָה דוּמָה נַפְשִׁי:
18 אִם־אָמַרְתִּי מָטָה רַגְלִי חַסְדְּךָ יְהוָה יִסְעָדֵנִי:
19 בְּרֹב שַׂרְעַפַּי בְּקִרְבִּי תַּנְחוּמֶיךָ יְשַׁעַשְׁעוּ נַפְשִׁי:
20 הַיְחָבְרְךָ כִּסֵּא הַוּוֹת יֹצֵר עָמָל עֲלֵי־חֹק:
21 יָגוֹדּוּ עַל־נֶפֶשׁ צַדִּיק וְדָם נָקִי יַרְשִׁיעוּ: 22 וַיְהִי יְהוָה לִי לְמִשְׂגָּב וֵאלֹהַי לְצוּר מַחְסִי: 23 וַיָּשֶׁב עֲלֵיהֶם ׀ אֶת־אוֹנָם וּבְרָעָתָם יַצְמִיתֵם יַצְמִיתֵם יְהוָה אֱלֹהֵינוּ:

those hoodlums who inflict so much misery on the world, no matter how prosperous they *appear* to be, are actually the unlucky ones whose wrongdoing God is ignoring expressly so as to deny them the impetus to atone for their sins in the course of their natural lifetimes? The poet doesn't say that in so many words, but the idea comes through his entire poem, and it

[16] Who will side with me against evildoers?
Who will stand up for me against the doers of iniquity?

[17] If יהוה were not my help, my soul would almost certainly endure its existence in silence.

[18] If I were to say that my leg is slipping, Your mercy, יהוה, would help me.

[19] Despite the multitude of dour thoughts within me, Your words of comfort delight my soul.

[20] Will You associate Yourself with those who sit on the seat of scheming, who create havoc by promulgating unjust laws?

[21] They may gang up on the righteous soul and do evil to innocent blood, [22]but יהוה is my citadel; my God is my rocky haven, [23]who turns wickedness against the wicked and destroys them with their own evil. Most assuredly, יהוה our God will destroy them.

is that idea more than any other that presents moderns with a profound, slightly disturbing set of questions well worth pondering . . . and at least attempting to answer honestly. The experience, however, will not be a pleasant one for those who find the reality—and the inevitability—of divine justice in our world less than self-evident. Perhaps, though, that is the poet's *real* point: that professing belief in a just God while feeling uncertain about divine justice is, at best, a precarious place in which to seek faith untroubled by crippling paradox.

צה

לְכוּ נְרַנְּנָה לַיהוָה נָרִיעָה לְצוּר יִשְׁעֵנוּ׃
2 נְקַדְּמָה פָנָיו בְּתוֹדָה בִּזְמִרוֹת נָרִיעַ לוֹ׃
3 כִּי אֵל גָּדוֹל יְהוָה וּמֶלֶךְ גָּדוֹל עַל־כָּל־אֱלֹהִים׃
4 אֲשֶׁר בְּיָדוֹ מֶחְקְרֵי־אָרֶץ וְתוֹעֲפוֹת הָרִים לוֹ׃
5 אֲשֶׁר־לוֹ הַיָּם וְהוּא עָשָׂהוּ וְיַבֶּשֶׁת יָדָיו יָצָרוּ׃
6 בֹּאוּ נִשְׁתַּחֲוֶה וְנִכְרָעָה נִבְרְכָה לִפְנֵי־יְהוָה עֹשֵׂנוּ׃
7 כִּי הוּא אֱלֹהֵינוּ וַאֲנַחְנוּ עַם מַרְעִיתוֹ וְצֹאן יָדוֹ
הַיּוֹם אִם־בְּקֹלוֹ תִשְׁמָעוּ׃
8 אַל־תַּקְשׁוּ לְבַבְכֶם כִּמְרִיבָה כְּיוֹם מַסָּה בַּמִּדְבָּר׃
9 אֲשֶׁר נִסּוּנִי אֲבוֹתֵיכֶם בְּחָנוּנִי גַּם־רָאוּ פָעֳלִי׃
10 אַרְבָּעִים שָׁנָה ׀ אָקוּט בְּדוֹר וָאֹמַר עַם תֹּעֵי לֵבָב
הֵם וְהֵם לֹא־יָדְעוּ דְרָכָי׃ 11 אֲשֶׁר־נִשְׁבַּעְתִּי בְאַפִּי
אִם־יְבֹאוּן אֶל־מְנוּחָתִי׃

Since one could say that the Book of Psalms is almost wholly dedicated to the proposition that the prophetic experience of God's voice may be cultivated by average people seeking to know God, those passages within the Psalter in which God's spoken words are recorded are bound to be of special interest to latter-day readers. Indeed, the author of the ninety-fifth psalm, having had just that experience of divine speech, invites us to join him, *even now, even today,* in encountering the communicative God of Israel . . . and he then tells us what he has personally learned from God by hearing the divine voice. God, he has learned, may be Sovereign of the universe, but is also a parent to every human being. Like any loving parent, God punishes when necessary—but hates being forced by the poor behavior of people who really ought to know better into taking action against them. The generation of slaves that left Egypt was duly punished for its rebelliousness with death in the lonely desert. They would not enter the Promised Land, but God was filled

95

Come let us sing hymns of joy to יהוה; let us raise up a joyous noise to the rock of our salvation.

[2] Let us come before the divine face bringing a thanksgiving sacrifice; with songs, let us revel before our God.

[3] For יהוה is a great God, the great Sovereign over all other divinities, [4]the One in whose hand are the farthest reaches of the earth and to whom the great heights of its mountains belong, [5]the One to whom the sea belongs as well—that sea made by God—and also the dry land fashioned by divine hands.

[6] Come let us prostrate ourselves and bow down, let us kneel before יהוה our Maker, [7]for this is our God and thus are we our God's people, the flock of sheep led forward by the divine hand even today, if you would only obey.

[8] And what is God's holy voice saying? "Do not make your hearts hard as you did at Meribah, on that day at Massah [9]when your ancestors tested Me. For although they tried Me, they also saw the power with which I can act.

[10] I spent forty years being irritated with that generation. I said that they were naught but a people of fickle hearts who knew not My ways, [11]and about whom I actually swore in My anger that they should never arrive at the resting place I intended for them."

with regret and ill ease. Should God respond to human disobedience less strictly? How will the children ever learn to behave? Should God be more loving, more patient, and more willing to forgive? "Children," the divine Parent says wistfully, "just don't let your insolence force My great hand again . . ."

The story of Israel's rebelliousness at Massah-and-Meribah can be found at Exodus 17:1–7.

צו

שִׁירוּ לַיהוָה שִׁיר חָדָשׁ שִׁירוּ לַיהוָה כָּל־הָאָרֶץ׃
2 שִׁירוּ לַיהוָה בָּרְכוּ שְׁמוֹ בַּשְּׂרוּ מִיּוֹם־לְיוֹם יְשׁוּעָתוֹ׃
3 סַפְּרוּ בַגּוֹיִם כְּבוֹדוֹ בְּכָל־הָעַמִּים נִפְלְאוֹתָיו׃
4 כִּי גָדוֹל יְהוָה וּמְהֻלָּל מְאֹד נוֹרָא הוּא עַל־כָּל־אֱלֹהִים׃
5 כִּי ׀ כָּל־אֱלֹהֵי הָעַמִּים אֱלִילִים וַיהוָה שָׁמַיִם עָשָׂה׃
6 הוֹד־וְהָדָר לְפָנָיו עֹז וְתִפְאֶרֶת בְּמִקְדָּשׁוֹ׃
7 הָבוּ לַיהוָה מִשְׁפְּחוֹת עַמִּים הָבוּ לַיהוָה כָּבוֹד וָעֹז׃
8 הָבוּ לַיהוָה כְּבוֹד שְׁמוֹ שְׂאוּ־מִנְחָה וּבֹאוּ לְחַצְרוֹתָיו׃
9 הִשְׁתַּחֲווּ לַיהוָה בְּהַדְרַת־קֹדֶשׁ חִילוּ מִפָּנָיו כָּל־הָאָרֶץ׃
10 אִמְרוּ בַגּוֹיִם ׀ יְהוָה מָלָךְ אַף־תִּכּוֹן תֵּבֵל בַּל־תִּמּוֹט יָדִין עַמִּים בְּמֵישָׁרִים׃
11 יִשְׂמְחוּ הַשָּׁמַיִם וְתָגֵל הָאָרֶץ יִרְעַם הַיָּם וּמְלֹאוֹ׃
12 יַעֲלֹז שָׂדַי וְכָל־אֲשֶׁר־בּוֹ אָז יְרַנְּנוּ כָּל־עֲצֵי־יָעַר׃
13 לִפְנֵי יְהוָה ׀ כִּי בָא כִּי בָא לִשְׁפֹּט הָאָרֶץ יִשְׁפֹּט־תֵּבֵל בְּצֶדֶק וְעַמִּים בֶּאֱמוּנָתוֹ׃

As defendants sit in court and wait for their trials to begin, their emotions are a tangled jumble of anxiety, hope, fear, and deep worry. The natural world waits for its Judge, however, in a different frame of mind completely. The fields exult. The trees forget they are made of wood and open their mouths in song. The very heavens roar with gladness. The seas roil and churn with excitement as they proclaim that God is come, come to judge the earth. And what of the people of the earth, those whom God has come, come to judge? For them the psalmist has a word as well, or rather several words. *Shiru, shiru, shiru,* he writes: sing a

96

Sing a new song unto יהוה; sing to יהוה, all the earth.

[2] Sing to יהוה, bless God's holy name; proclaim salvation in God from one day to the next.

[3] Tell of God's glory among the peoples of the earth, of God's wonders among the nations, [4]for יהוה is great and greatly praiseworthy, awesome and supreme over all other forms of divinity.

[5] Indeed, all the gods of the other nations are mere idols, but יהוה made the heavens.

[6] Resplendence and magnificence flourish in God's presence; strength and splendor co-exist in the Temple of God.

[7] Render unto יהוה, O families of the nations, render unto יהוה glory and strength.

[8] Render unto יהוה the honor due God's holy name; take up a grain offering and come to the courtyards of God.

[9] Bow down to יהוה in the magnificence of the Sanctuary; tremble before God all the earth.

[10] Say among the nations, "יהוה reigns over an earth that is firmly established and never totters . . . and will judge the nations in absolute fairness."

[11] Let the heavens rejoice; let the earth be glad. Let the sea and its fullness roar out loud.

[12] Let my fields and all that is in them exult—and then all the trees of the forest—[13]before יהוה our God, the God who is coming, who is actually coming at this very moment, to judge the earth. God will judge the world in righteousness and the nations in good faith.

new song to God, sing out to God all the earth, sing out and bless God's sacred name. Fear nothing, for the Judge is a righteous magistrate. Quell your anxieties, for God is supremely fair, the very Source of fairness and reasonableness in the world. To be indicted of a terrible crime and tried in an earthly court would be a terrifying experience for anyone. To be judged by God, on the other hand, should be exhilarating . . . if one's life has been blameless.

צז

יְהוָה מָלָךְ תָּגֵל הָאָרֶץ יִשְׂמְחוּ אִיִּים רַבִּים׃
2 עָנָן וַעֲרָפֶל סְבִיבָיו צֶדֶק וּמִשְׁפָּט מְכוֹן כִּסְאוֹ׃
3 אֵשׁ לְפָנָיו תֵּלֵךְ וּתְלַהֵט סָבִיב צָרָיו׃
4 הֵאִירוּ בְרָקָיו תֵּבֵל רָאֲתָה וַתָּחֵל הָאָרֶץ׃
5 הָרִים כַּדּוֹנַג נָמַסּוּ מִלִּפְנֵי יְהוָה מִלִּפְנֵי אֲדוֹן
כָּל־הָאָרֶץ׃
6 הִגִּידוּ הַשָּׁמַיִם צִדְקוֹ וְרָאוּ כָל־הָעַמִּים כְּבוֹדוֹ׃
7 יֵבֹשׁוּ ׀ כָּל־עֹבְדֵי פֶסֶל הַמִּתְהַלְלִים בָּאֱלִילִים
הִשְׁתַּחֲווּ־לוֹ כָּל־אֱלֹהִים׃
8 שָׁמְעָה וַתִּשְׂמַח ׀ צִיּוֹן וַתָּגֵלְנָה בְּנוֹת יְהוּדָה לְמַעַן
מִשְׁפָּטֶיךָ יְהוָה׃
9 כִּי־אַתָּה יְהוָה עֶלְיוֹן עַל־כָּל־הָאָרֶץ מְאֹד נַעֲלֵיתָ
עַל־כָּל־אֱלֹהִים׃
10 אֹהֲבֵי יְהוָה שִׂנְאוּ רָע שֹׁמֵר נַפְשׁוֹת חֲסִידָיו מִיַּד
רְשָׁעִים יַצִּילֵם׃
11 אוֹר זָרֻעַ לַצַּדִּיק וּלְיִשְׁרֵי־לֵב שִׂמְחָה׃
12 שִׂמְחוּ צַדִּיקִים בַּיהוָה וְהוֹדוּ לְזֵכֶר קָדְשׁוֹ׃

The poet thinks of his God as light, fire, and heat—or perhaps, more precisely, as the divine analogue of a flame that exists, somehow, with neither weight nor real physical substance, yet which can either destroy an individual or save his life. The ancients who cultivated the sensual experience of God certainly knew to expect light, for God was their "redeeming light." And that the light connected with divine communion would engender a feeling of cozy, comfortable warmth also seemed obvious. But whether that pleasant feeling of warmth could somehow turn to overwhelming, destructive, blazing heat seems to have been something about which the poet was a bit uncertain, perhaps even a bit nervous. If, he theorizes, the heat generated by divine communion was hot enough when experienced by the greatest of all prophets, Moses, to affect and alter his face permanently, then surely the full force of God's presence would melt mountains of granite, thus making the earth itself tremble and quake as it melted into molten ore. To experience the meltdown

97

When יהוה reigns, the earth is glad and its many islands rejoice, [2]cloud and fog come together to surround our God, as do righteousness and justice—the foundation elements of the divine throne.

[3] Fire goes forth before God, consuming enemies on every side.

[4] When bolts of divine lightning illuminate the world, the earth sees and trembles.

[5] Mountains melt like wax before יהוה, before the Ruler of the whole earth.

[6] When the heavens tell of God's righteousness and the nations see God's glory, [7]then all those idolaters who vaunt themselves on account of their gods become ashamed; even their divinities all bow down before God.

[8] Zion will hear this and rejoice, the daughters of Judah will be glad for the sake of Your justice, O יהוה.

[9] For You, יהוה, are supreme above the entire earth; You have made Yourself supreme over every other form of divinity.

[10] Those who love יהוה, hate evil—for the God who watches over the souls of pious followers will surely save them from the wicked.

[11] Indeed, light is sown for the righteous individual and joy for the upright of heart.

[12] Rejoice, O righteous folk, in יהוה and give thanks to God's holy name.

of the world is something no sane person would wish to experience. But to know the warmth of God's saving presence personally, physically, sensually—this is not only *not* something to avoid, but something to work towards . . . ardently. The challenge, of course, is to experience the warmth of God's saving presence without crossing the line to the kind of excessive intimacy with the Divine that can yield unexpected, potentially destructive results.

צח

מִזְמוֹר
שִׁירוּ לַיהוָה ׀ שִׁיר חָדָשׁ כִּי־נִפְלָאוֹת עָשָׂה
הוֹשִׁיעָה־לּוֹ יְמִינוֹ וּזְרוֹעַ קָדְשׁוֹ׃
2 הוֹדִיעַ יְהוָה יְשׁוּעָתוֹ לְעֵינֵי הַגּוֹיִם גִּלָּה צִדְקָתוֹ׃
3 זָכַר חַסְדּוֹ ׀ וֶאֱמוּנָתוֹ לְבֵית יִשְׂרָאֵל רָאוּ כָל־
אַפְסֵי־אָרֶץ אֵת יְשׁוּעַת אֱלֹהֵינוּ׃
4 הָרִיעוּ לַיהוָה כָּל־הָאָרֶץ פִּצְחוּ וְרַנְּנוּ וְזַמֵּרוּ׃
5 זַמְּרוּ לַיהוָה בְּכִנּוֹר בְּכִנּוֹר וְקוֹל זִמְרָה׃
6 בַּחֲצֹצְרוֹת וְקוֹל שׁוֹפָר הָרִיעוּ לִפְנֵי ׀ הַמֶּלֶךְ יְהוָה׃
7 יִרְעַם הַיָּם וּמְלֹאוֹ תֵּבֵל וְיֹשְׁבֵי בָהּ׃
8 נְהָרוֹת יִמְחֲאוּ־כָף יַחַד הָרִים יְרַנֵּנוּ׃ 9 לִפְנֵי־יְהוָה
כִּי בָא לִשְׁפֹּט הָאָרֶץ יִשְׁפֹּט־תֵּבֵל בְּצֶדֶק וְעַמִּים
בְּמֵישָׁרִים׃

One could argue that the ninety-eighth psalm does not really exist, since it seems to be merely an alternate version of the ninety-sixth (or perhaps the latter psalm is an alternate version of this one). The flow of ideas is remarkably similar, at any rate, as are the imagery and the various metaphors used to describe the exultation of the world at the prospect of God coming in judgment. Yet, the ideas remain potent and quite compelling in both settings.

In our world, we tend to think of music as a hobby, or perhaps as something useful for creating a pleasant atmosphere for work or play—a vocation for some lucky, talented few and an avocation for the rest of us. But our psalmists thought of music as something else, as something essentially divine: as something not merely conducive to the cultivation of a sense of the presence of God, but something totally *essential* to the religious quest for intimacy with the Divine. The psalms themselves are testimony to that idea, as the many references to musical instruments, melody, meter, and accompaniment throughout the Psalter make obvious. All those references indicate that the poems of the Psalter were meant to be sung out, not merely read quietly or declaimed.
The real question, therefore, is why so many moderns feel they can do per-

98

A psalm.

Sing a new song unto יהוה, for our God has done wondrous things, bringing salvation with the divine right hand, with that holiest of arms.

[2] יהוה has demonstrated the extent of the saving power of the divine and revealed to the nations the meaning of divine righteousness.

[3] God remembered the mercy and faithfulness once shown to the House of Israel; the very ends of the earth can see the salvation of our God.

[4] Make a joyous noise unto יהוה, all the earth; open your mouth, exult, sing out!

[5] Accompany your song to יהוה on a lyre; play a lyre and sing out with melodious voice.

[6] With trumpets too, and with a blast of the *shofar,* make joyous noise before the divine Sovereign, יהוה.

[7] Let the sea and its fullness roar, the world and its inhabitants.

[8] Let the rivers clap their hands, let all the mountains come together to be glad [9] before יהוה, who is coming to judge the earth . . . for God will surely judge the world with justice and its nations with honesty.

fectly well without music playing much of a role in their private devotional lives at all.

When the poet writes that the mountains sing and the rivers clap their hands when they sense God's nearness, he is merely attributing to the physical features of the earth a reality that he knew from his own personal spiritual life. The poet's most basic response to God was, therefore, not fear or terror or anxiety, but song, rhythm, melody, and harmony—the exquisitely expressive language of music that enables human beings to praise God without becoming mired in the convoluted logic of words and their multivalent levels of meaning. It is interesting to speculate regarding the way the ancient poet came to realize that particular set of truths. Even more compelling, though, should be the question his psalm prompts: why do so many moderns find the concept of prayer outside of language unnerving, even slightly threatening?

צט

יְהוָה מָלָךְ יִרְגְּזוּ עַמִּים יֹשֵׁב כְּרוּבִים תָּנוּט הָאָרֶץ׃
2 יְהוָה בְּצִיּוֹן גָּדוֹל וְרָם הוּא עַל־כָּל־הָעַמִּים׃ 3 יוֹדוּ שִׁמְךָ גָּדוֹל וְנוֹרָא קָדוֹשׁ הוּא׃
4 וְעֹז מֶלֶךְ מִשְׁפָּט אָהֵב אַתָּה כּוֹנַנְתָּ מֵישָׁרִים מִשְׁפָּט וּצְדָקָה בְּיַעֲקֹב ׀ אַתָּה עָשִׂיתָ׃
5 רוֹמְמוּ יְהוָה אֱלֹהֵינוּ וְהִשְׁתַּחֲווּ לַהֲדֹם רַגְלָיו קָדוֹשׁ הוּא׃
6 מֹשֶׁה וְאַהֲרֹן ׀ בְּכֹהֲנָיו וּשְׁמוּאֵל בְּקֹרְאֵי שְׁמוֹ קֹרְאִים אֶל־יְהוָה וְהוּא יַעֲנֵם׃
7 בְּעַמּוּד עָנָן יְדַבֵּר אֲלֵיהֶם שָׁמְרוּ עֵדֹתָיו וְחֹק נָתַן־לָמוֹ׃
8 יְהוָה אֱלֹהֵינוּ אַתָּה עֲנִיתָם אֵל נֹשֵׂא הָיִיתָ לָהֶם וְנֹקֵם עַל־עֲלִילוֹתָם׃
9 רוֹמְמוּ יְהוָה אֱלֹהֵינוּ וְהִשְׁתַּחֲווּ לְהַר קָדְשׁוֹ כִּי־קָדוֹשׁ יְהוָה אֱלֹהֵינוּ׃

The world, at least in the poet's day, was quite adamant that prophets and priests belonged to different realms of spiritual experience. Indeed, it was taken almost as axiomatic that one could satisfactorily devote a life to the service of God according to the norms and practices of priestly tradition without ever experiencing the physical proof of divine nearness that was the sine qua non of prophetic piety. The Levites, whose ancient hymnal became our Book of Psalms, knew better than to insist on this dichotomous way of organizing the world of spiritual endeavor, and they revered especially those personalities from earlier times who intuited that worshiping God and knowing God through personal experience were merely two sides of the same coin. There are not many references in the Psalter to the heroes of earlier Israelite history, but the poet whose poem became our ninety-ninth psalm pauses to laud Moses, Aaron, and Samuel, the three ancients whose scriptural portraits spoke to him the most eloquently.

99

When יהוה reigns, nations tremble. But when God actually sits upon the cherub-throne, the earth itself quakes.

[2] יהוה is great in Zion, exalted over all nations; [3] its inhabitants, therefore, will acclaim Your great and awesome name, for it is holy.

[4] The might of the divine Sovereign derives from loving justice; indeed, You invented fairness, granting both justice and righteousness to Jacob.

[5] Exalt יהוה, our God, and bow down to the divine footstool . . . for God is holy.

[6] As Moses and Aaron were among God's priests, so was Samuel among those who called out in God's name: when they cried out to יהוה, God answered them.

[7] God spoke to them in a pillar of cloud; they kept the sacred testimonies and God gave them law.

[8] יהוה, our God, You answered them. You were their patient God, the One who avenged plots hatched against them.

[9] Exalt יהוה our God and bow down to the holy mountain of God, for יהוה our God is holy.

Generally speaking, tradition presents Aaron as a priest and Moses and Samuel as prophets . . . but the situation is actually quite a bit more complicated. Moses was indeed a prophet, but he was also a priest whom Scripture recalls offering sacrifices and entering the Holy of Holies to encounter the divine personally and experientially. Aaron, revered as the first High Priest of Israel, is also called a prophet . . . and by no less an authority than God, who describes him that way to his brother, Moses. Samuel was, of course, primarily a prophet, but he is also portrayed as a priest in Scripture in a way that suggests that this was an entirely normal role for him to assume. The poet's moral, therefore, is this: be both or be neither! Serve God *and* know God . . . or be content to do neither fully.

ק

מִזְמוֹר לְתוֹדָה
הָרִיעוּ לַיהוָה כָּל־הָאָרֶץ:

2 עִבְדוּ אֶת־יְהוָה בְּשִׂמְחָה בֹּאוּ לְפָנָיו בִּרְנָנָה:

3 דְּעוּ כִּי יְהוָה הוּא אֱלֹהִים הוּא עָשָׂנוּ *וְלוֹ אֲנַחְנוּ
עַמּוֹ וְצֹאן מַרְעִיתוֹ:

4 בֹּאוּ שְׁעָרָיו | בְּתוֹדָה חֲצֵרֹתָיו בִּתְהִלָּה הוֹדוּ לוֹ
בָּרְכוּ שְׁמוֹ:

5 כִּי־טוֹב יְהוָה לְעוֹלָם חַסְדּוֹ וְעַד־דֹּר וָדֹר אֱמוּנָתוֹ:

v. 3 ולא כתיב

I*vdu et* יהוה *besimḥah,* the poet writes, his injunction to worship God with joy phrased neither as a suggestion nor an invitation, but rather as a command no less stark than uncompromising. Then, in the event that the reader has still not quite seized the poet's point, he repeats it: *bo'u lefanav birnanah,* come before God in gladness. Not "It would be optimal to enter the divine precincts in gladness," or "Surely better than facing the service of God as an irritating burden would be engaging worship in joy," but rather the stark command form, "Come!", the unmistakable counterpart to "Worship!" And how, precisely, is one to go about doing that? Moderns tend to view God either as a celestial Sovereign governing the world or as a vague, inchoate force that provides order and meaning to the universe. In the former case, logic makes it only reasonable for us to placate God with whatever it takes—prayer, *mitzvot,* deeds of charity, and the like—to discourage the divine Judge from punishing us for our disobedience by sending plagues or withholding rain. In the latter case, divine worship is worth undertaking for the sake of entering into some kind of harmony with existence itself by embracing

100

A psalm for the thanksgiving sacrifice.
Make joyous noise before יהוה, all the earth.
[2] Worship יהוה in joy; come before God in gladness.
[3] Know that יהוה is God, the God who made us, and that we ourselves are God's people, the nation of God and the sheep of the divine flock.
[4] Come to God's gates with a thanksgiving sacrifice, to the Temple courtyards with songs of praise. Give thanks to God by blessing the divine name.
[5] For יהוה is good and God's mercy, everlasting; God's faithfulness will endure through every generation.

its ordering principle and its interior essence. Both concepts have biblical precedent and neither is sufficiently untrue to make it a foolish choice for moderns to adopt as a metaphoric range along which to seek God, but the author of the one hundredth psalm has another idea in mind. He proposes God neither as potentate nor principle, but as the source of joy in the world.

Can moderns adopt such a model profitably? Joy, cheerfulness, and gladness, after all, are slightly discredited emotions in a world far more fixated on personal gratification, sensual release, and intellectual satisfaction than on simple happiness. But the poet is adamant that the essence of worship is to find in God the source of joy, that most uplifting and challenging of all emotions. Could moderns ever give themselves totally to God not out of obligation but out of sheer exuberance, out of the unrestrained—and unrestrainable—sense of exhilaration they might come to experience as children of God? That, the poet is suggesting, is a far more profound question than it will seem at first to most people.

קא

לְדָוִד מִזְמוֹר
חֶסֶד־וּמִשְׁפָּט אָשִׁירָה לְךָ יְהֹוָה אֲזַמֵּרָה:
2 אַשְׂכִּילָה ׀ בְּדֶרֶךְ תָּמִים מָתַי תָּבוֹא אֵלָי אֶתְהַלֵּךְ
בְּתָם־לְבָבִי בְּקֶרֶב בֵּיתִי:
3 לֹא־אָשִׁית ׀ לְנֶגֶד עֵינַי דְּבַר־בְּלִיָּעַל עֲשֹׂה־סֵטִים
שָׂנֵאתִי לֹא יִדְבַּק בִּי:
4 לֵבָב עִקֵּשׁ יָסוּר מִמֶּנִּי רָע לֹא אֵדָע:
5* מְלָשְׁנִי בַסֵּתֶר ׀ רֵעֵהוּ אוֹתוֹ אַצְמִית גְּבַהּ־עֵינַיִם
וּרְחַב לֵבָב אֹתוֹ לֹא אוּכָל:
6 עֵינַי ׀ בְּנֶאֶמְנֵי־אֶרֶץ לָשֶׁבֶת עִמָּדִי הֹלֵךְ בְּדֶרֶךְ
תָּמִים הוּא יְשָׁרְתֵנִי:
7 לֹא־יֵשֵׁב ׀ בְּקֶרֶב בֵּיתִי עֹשֵׂה רְמִיָּה דֹּבֵר שְׁקָרִים
לֹא־יִכּוֹן לְנֶגֶד עֵינָי:
8 לַבְּקָרִים אַצְמִית כָּל־רִשְׁעֵי־אָרֶץ לְהַכְרִית
מֵעִיר־יְהֹוָה כָּל־פֹּעֲלֵי אָוֶן:

v. 5 מלושני כתיב

The poet asks the simplest of all questions ever posed to God, *matai tavo elai*? ("When will You come to me?"), then proceeds to count off the reasons he feels he has earned the right to feel the palpable presence of God in his personal life. He conducts himself blamelessly. He abhors slander. He refuses to have swindlers or liars in his company, let alone as guests in his house. As a Jerusalemite, not only does he find the presence of evildoers in the vicinity intolerable, but he actively works to banish them from the City of God and to remove their iniquity from its precincts. Indeed, it is in

101

A psalm of David.

I shall sing of mercy and justice; to You, יהוה, shall I chant.

[2] I shall compose a wisdom-song to ask guilelessly, "When will You come to me?", then wander about my house with a guileless heart while waiting for an answer.

[3] I shall not place any corrupt thing before my eyes, for I loathe the doing of perverse deeds and therefore such desires do not cling to me.

[4] My obstreperous heart shall vanish; I shall not know evil.

[5] I shall destroy any individual who slanders another in secret; I shall find unbearable any individual with haughty eyes or a heart wide open to evil.

[6] My eyes are fixed on the faithful of our land in the hope that they will dwell with me; the individual who travels a guileless path shall be my servant.

[7] Swindlers and liars shall not dwell in my house; such people shall not establish themselves before my eyes.

[8] Every morning I shall destroy the evil of the earth so that I thus, eventually, remove all purveyors of iniquity from the city of יהוה.

this context that he has come to loathe haughtiness and wideheartedness (by which he presumably means the all-too-human willingness to tolerate the intolerable).

Reading this psalm can prompt a fascinating exercise in self-analysis. In our multifaceted democratic states, we vaunt tolerance above almost every other civic virtue. But how many of us are certain where to draw the line? Do we always know when, precisely, we are no longer merely enduring some unpleasant features of the world with reasonable (and therefore acceptable) stoicism, but are actually becoming partners with villains in villainy by refusing to work to eradicate evil?

קב

תְּפִלָּה לְעָנִי כִֽי־יַעֲטֹף וְלִפְנֵי יְהֹוָה יִשְׁפֹּךְ שִׂיחוֹ׃
2 יְהֹוָה שִׁמְעָה תְפִלָּתִי וְשַׁוְעָתִי אֵלֶיךָ תָבוֹא׃
3 אַל־תַּסְתֵּר פָּנֶיךָ ׀ מִמֶּנִּי בְּיוֹם צַר לִי הַטֵּה־אֵלַי
אָזְנֶךָ בְּיוֹם אֶקְרָא מַהֵר עֲנֵנִי׃ 4 כִּֽי־כָלוּ בְעָשָׁן יָמָי
וְעַצְמוֹתַי כְּמוֹקֵד נִחָרוּ׃ 5 הוּכָּה־כָעֵשֶׂב וַיִּבַשׁ לִבִּי
כִּֽי־שָׁכַחְתִּי מֵאֲכֹל לַחְמִי׃ 6 מִקּוֹל אַנְחָתִי דָּבְקָה
עַצְמִי לִבְשָׂרִי׃
7 דָּמִיתִי לִקְאַת מִדְבָּר הָיִיתִי כְּכוֹס חֳרָבוֹת׃
8 שָׁקַדְתִּי וָאֶהְיֶה כְּצִפּוֹר בּוֹדֵד עַל־גָּג׃
9 כָּל־הַיּוֹם חֵרְפוּנִי אוֹיְבָי מְהוֹלָלַי בִּי נִשְׁבָּעוּ׃
10 כִּי אֵפֶר כַּלֶּחֶם אָכָלְתִּי וְשִׁקֻּוַי בִּבְכִי מָסָכְתִּי׃
11 מִפְּנֵי־זַעַמְךָ וְקִצְפֶּךָ כִּי נְשָׂאתַנִי וַתַּשְׁלִיכֵנִי׃
12 יָמַי כְּצֵל נָטוּי וַאֲנִי כָּעֵשֶׂב אִיבָשׁ׃
13 וְאַתָּה יְהֹוָה לְעוֹלָם תֵּשֵׁב וְזִכְרְךָ לְדֹר וָדֹר׃
14 אַתָּה תָקוּם תְּרַחֵם צִיּוֹן כִּי עֵת לְחֶנְנָהּ כִּי בָא
מוֹעֵד׃
15 כִּֽי־רָצוּ עֲבָדֶיךָ אֶת־אֲבָנֶיהָ וְאֶת־עֲפָרָהּ יְחֹנֵנוּ׃
16 וְיִירְאוּ גוֹיִם אֶת־שֵׁם יְהֹוָה וְכָל־מַלְכֵי הָאָרֶץ

An ancient poet looks at himself in the mirror and, for once, sees himself perfectly clearly. He is poor, perhaps even destitute. He sees himself as a lonely bird hopping around on somebody else's cold rooftop, as a scavenger rooting around in the rotting remains of some ruined city or pecking its way across the wilderness in search of a dead mouse or some other putrefying rodent. He contemplates his emaciated, broken body and the way his brittle bones are poking through his sallow skin and he not only knows himself to be ill, but he understands his illness to be terminal. When he writes that his life is drawing to a close after only half its natural course, his comment reads like the self-diagnoses of so many terminally ill patients who are almost preternaturally able to understand what is happening to them with perfect clarity no matter who tells them what lies. Yet the poet, for all the precision with which he seizes the gravity of his situation, has not lost his faith. He calls out to God not in bitterness or in resignation, but in hope—in abiding, real hope in God's ability to heal. And that is the real point the poet is writing to convey: that the only secure hope for healing rests in faith in the beneficence of the Almighty.

Modern readers will admire the poet's steadfast piety, but his psalm challenges readers to ask some hard questions as well. How many of us are prompted by illness or weakness to become angry with God or, worse, to

102

The prayer of a poor man who, on the verge of fainting, finds the strength to pour out his entreaty before יהוה.

[2] יהוה, hear my prayer; let my supplication come before You.

[3] Hide not Your face from me; on my day of woe, incline Your ear towards me. On the day I call out, answer me quickly—[4]for my days are vanished like smoke, my bones are burning like twigs in a hearth; [5]my heart is as dried out as stomped-upon grass, for I have neglected to eat my bread and [6]my bones cling to my flesh at the sound of my groaning.

[7] I am become like a great desert *kat,* like a *kos* that lives in ruins. [8]I can practically see myself like a solitary bird sitting alone on a roof.

[9] My enemies taunt me all day long. People who despise me actually take oaths using me as an example of what they curse their enemies that they become, [10]for I eat dust as my bread and dilute whatever I drink with my own tears. [11]All this I suffer because of Your anger, because of Your rage, because You lifted me up and cast me off, [12]thus making my days feel like an ebbing shadow and me myself like so much dried out grass.

[13] But You, יהוה, shall reign forever; Your name shall endure throughout every generation.

[14] You shall rise up and show compassion to Zion when the time is right to deal mercifully with her, when the right moment comes.

[15] For when Your servants take pleasure in her stones and show mercy to her dust, [16]then shall the nations fear the name of יהוה and the kings

abandon faith in God altogether? How many of us are truly prepared to declare that, if our suffering makes us more aware of God's presence in our lives, great blessing can come from totally unwanted infirmity? How many of us are aware of the degree to which faith can be a healing balm . . . or of the reality of a God who exists in a relationship of potential intimacy with *every* human being, no matter how weak or ill? How many of us have the strength of character to internalize the awful truth that frailty can be a blessing if it brings us to invite God into our lives, to call out and seek healing from its

את־כבודך׃ 17 כי־בנה יהוה ציון נראה בכבודו׃
18 פנה אל־תפלת הערער ולא־בזה את־תפלתם׃
19 תכתב זאת לדור אחרון ועם נברא יהלל־יה׃
20 כי־השקיף ממרום קדשו יהוה משמים ׀
אל־ארץ הביט׃ 21 לשמע אנקת אסיר לפתח בני
תמותה׃
22 לספר בציון שם יהוה ותהלתו בירושלם׃
23 בהקבץ עמים יחדו וממלכות לעבד את־
יהוה׃
24 ענה בדרך *כחי קצר ימי׃
25 אמר אלי אל־תעלני בחצי ימי בדור דורים
שנותיך׃
26 לפנים הארץ יסדת ומעשה ידיך שמים׃
27 המה ׀ יאבדו ואתה תעמד וכלם כבגד יבלו
כלבוש תחליפם ויחלפו׃
28 ואתה־הוא ושנותיך לא יתמו׃
29 בני־עבדיך ישכונו וזרעם לפניך יכון׃

v. 24 כחו כתיב

only real Source? How many of us truly believe that *whatever* brings an individual to God is, almost by definition, an instance of divine kindness?

Balancing this set of truths with the natural disinclination all people feel to avoid disability, pain, and weakness is the challenge inherent in the 102nd psalm. The psalmist is not suggesting, after all, that there is something peculiar or base about wishing not to suffer, but only that the unavoidable instances of ill ease and misfortune that characterize the lives of all people (at least some of the time) can be profitably exploited to yield real spiritual growth in those open to learning their potentially profound lessons.

Growth towards God, the poet is telling us, is neither simple nor easy for most people. Coming to faith involves a good deal of emotional and intellectual effort . . . and some of that effort is going to involve the wrenching decision to jettison some of our most treasured illusions about ourselves and the place we occupy in the world. Other aspects of the spiritual journey will involve coming to terms with the natural confines of human intelligence and with the limits imposed on the living by life itself—by its brevity, by its ephemeral nature, and by its fragility. None of these steps forward will be especially pleasant, but all have the capacity to bring human beings just a bit closer to the knowledge of God—which is, after all, the great goal of all reli-

of the world, Your glory—[17]for יהוה built Zion, then appeared there in full glory.

[18] God responds favorably to the prayer of solitary desert trees, never despising their prayer.

[19] Let this be written out for the last generation so that the people created by God might praise יה; [20]when God who looks down from holy heights, when יהוה looks down to earth from heaven, [21]it is to hear the moaning of the imprisoned, to free the manacles of those approaching death, [22] to tell of the name of יהוה in Zion, and to tell of God's praises in Jerusalem [23]when nations gather together, when kingdoms come together to worship יהוה.

[24] God afflicted my strength in mid-course, shortening my days.

[25] I say, "My God, do not lift me out of the world at what should be the midpoint of my life, while Your endless years of divine existence go on from generation to generation."

[26] In ancient times, You laid the foundation of the world; the heavens themselves are the work of Your hands.

[27] They will eventually pass away, while You Yourself will exist forever; they shall become threadbare like an old garment . . . and when You replace them as one would an old cloak, they shall simply be gone.

[28] You are the permanent One, O God, the One whose years go on without end.

[29] May the children of Your servants live on, and may their progeny be established in Your presence.

gious endeavor. No one wants to suffer, but if unhappy circumstances help us to acknowledge how things really are in our world, then they cannot be evaluated totally negatively.

The poet, judging from his own testimony, has suffered greatly and sees no end to his misery. That he remains steadfast in his faith is impressive. But that he had the courage and the fortitude to turn his plight into a kind of conduit capable of leading others towards the attainment of their own spiritual goals, *that* is what makes the poet into a spiritual prototype still able, even after all these many centuries, to inspire others to seek God even in the least wanted corners of their humanity.

קג

לְדָוִד ׀
בָּרְכִי נַפְשִׁי אֶת־יְהוָה וְכָל־קְרָבַי אֶת־שֵׁם קָדְשׁוֹ׃
2 בָּרְכִי נַפְשִׁי אֶת־יְהוָה וְאַל־תִּשְׁכְּחִי כָּל־גְּמוּלָיו׃
3 הַסֹּלֵחַ לְכָל־עֲוֺנֵכִי הָרֹפֵא לְכָל־תַּחֲלֻאָיְכִי׃
4 הַגּוֹאֵל מִשַּׁחַת חַיָּיְכִי הַמְעַטְּרֵכִי חֶסֶד וְרַחֲמִים׃
5 הַמַּשְׂבִּיעַ בַּטּוֹב עֶדְיֵךְ תִּתְחַדֵּשׁ כַּנֶּשֶׁר נְעוּרָיְכִי׃
6 עֹשֵׂה צְדָקוֹת יְהוָה וּמִשְׁפָּטִים לְכָל־עֲשׁוּקִים׃
7 יוֹדִיעַ דְּרָכָיו לְמֹשֶׁה לִבְנֵי יִשְׂרָאֵל עֲלִילוֹתָיו׃
8 רַחוּם וְחַנּוּן יְהוָה אֶרֶךְ אַפַּיִם וְרַב־חָסֶד׃ 9 לֹא־לָנֶצַח יָרִיב וְלֹא לְעוֹלָם יִטּוֹר׃ 10 לֹא כַחֲטָאֵינוּ עָשָׂה לָנוּ וְלֹא כַעֲוֺנֹתֵינוּ גָּמַל עָלֵינוּ׃
11 כִּי כִגְבֹהַּ שָׁמַיִם עַל־הָאָרֶץ גָּבַר חַסְדּוֹ עַל־יְרֵאָיו׃
12 כִּרְחֹק מִזְרָח מִמַּעֲרָב הִרְחִיק מִמֶּנּוּ אֶת־פְּשָׁעֵינוּ׃
13 כְּרַחֵם אָב עַל־בָּנִים רִחַם יְהוָה עַל־יְרֵאָיו׃
14 כִּי הוּא יָדַע יִצְרֵנוּ זָכוּר כִּי־עָפָר אֲנָחְנוּ׃

In the contemplation of God, every individual will find one specific aspect of divine reality that speaks to his or her consciousness with special force or clarity. The author of the 103rd psalm, for example, is especially moved by the concept of divine mercy. As he contemplates his life, everything seems to point him back to that one concept: it is the defining germ of an idea from which his faith has sprouted and grown. He was ill, but he recovered . . . and he sees God's healing power as the source of his recovery. When he found the strength to abandon sin and overcame the temptation to continue in his iniquitous way, however, he identified the moral courage he needed to do so as a blessing of God . . . and an unearned one at that. Knowing himself to be basically corrupt and drawn to wrong, decadent, and contemptible behavior rather than to decency, the poet feels overwhelmed at the countervailing force within his breast that somehow keeps him, at least most of the time, from straying too far from the path of righteousness and goodness. And he feels driven to identify that force as the influence of God's everlasting mercy in his own life.

In the context of his encomium to divine compassion, the poet pauses to consider the incredible implausibility of the larger picture. Human beings, the poet knows, are made of dust. They survive for a few years, then wither and die like blades of grass. That being the case, the poet is even more struck by the kindness inherent in the way God relates to humanity. What, the poet

103

(A psalm) of David.

O my soul, bless יהוה; all my innards, bless God's holy name.

[2] O my soul, bless יהוה and do not forget all the gracious deeds of God: [3]who forgives your sins, who cures your illnesses, [4]who redeems your life from the grave, who crowns you with mercy and compassion, [5]who fills your mouth with delicacies, who allows your youth to renew itself continually as though you were an eagle renewing its plumage.

[6] יהוה is the Doer of righteous deeds, the One who grants justice to all the oppressed, [7]who made God's ways known to Moses, who made God's exploits known to the children of Israel.

[8] יהוה is a gracious, compassionate, patient, and supremely merciful God [9]who neither stays angry forever nor permanently holds a grudge, [10]who neither deals with us in accordance with our sins nor punishes us in accordance with our transgressions.

[11] Indeed, divine mercy overwhelms those who fear God, just as the heavens tower over the earth.

[12] As far as east is far from west, so has God distanced us from our sins. [13]Just as a father behaves compassionately with his children, so does יהוה behave compassionately with those who fear God.

[14] Knowing our nature, God nonetheless recalls that we are but dust.

asks, can people do to respond, even inadequately, to such unexpected and unwarranted beneficence? His answer is rooted in the Hebrew word *levarekh*, usually rendered as "bless." Difficult to translate accurately, the term includes the idea of praise in it, but also suggests more than a bit of subservience and self-abnegation. There is no English word that brings all these ideas together well, but the poet's idea itself is simple enough: we should strive to live decently and to acknowledge God's grace in our lives, then respond to the experience with a sense of deep gratitude, with a frank sense of our inherent unworthiness, and with words that simply, elegantly, and wholeheartedly come together to form hymns of heartfelt praise.

15 אֱנוֹשׁ כֶּחָצִיר יָמָיו כְּצִיץ הַשָּׂדֶה כֵּן יָצִיץ׃ 16 כִּי
רוּחַ עָבְרָה־בּוֹ וְאֵינֶנּוּ וְלֹא־יַכִּירֶנּוּ עוֹד מְקוֹמוֹ׃
17 וְחֶסֶד יְהוָה | מֵעוֹלָם וְעַד־עוֹלָם עַל־יְרֵאָיו
וְצִדְקָתוֹ לִבְנֵי בָנִים׃ 18 לְשֹׁמְרֵי בְרִיתוֹ וּלְזֹכְרֵי
פִקֻּדָיו לַעֲשׂוֹתָם׃
19 יְהוָה בַּשָּׁמַיִם הֵכִין כִּסְאוֹ וּמַלְכוּתוֹ בַּכֹּל מָשָׁלָה׃
20 בָּרֲכוּ יְהוָה מַלְאָכָיו גִּבֹּרֵי כֹחַ עֹשֵׂי דְבָרוֹ לִשְׁמֹעַ
בְּקוֹל דְּבָרוֹ׃
21 בָּרֲכוּ יְהוָה כָּל־צְבָאָיו מְשָׁרְתָיו עֹשֵׂי רְצוֹנוֹ׃
22 בָּרֲכוּ יְהוָה | כָּל־מַעֲשָׂיו בְּכָל־מְקֹמוֹת מֶמְשַׁלְתּוֹ
בָּרֲכִי נַפְשִׁי אֶת־יְהוָה׃

The poet thus begins his paean of praise by calling, first of all, on his inmost self—his soul—and his internal organs to bless the name of God. The notion of someone addressing his own organs and calling upon them to praise their Maker may strike moderns as a bit peculiar, but the poet seems no less at his ease speaking to his liver and spleen than he does addressing his soul. God, he is suggesting, is the Creator of all that any human being is . . . and it is therefore perfectly reasonable for every part of every person to join together in the praise of the Almighty. Having called upon his body and soul to join in the praise of God, the poet goes off on a long exposition of the various ways in which he has experienced the mercy of God. At the end of his poem, though, he then invites others of God's creative handiwork to join in his hymn. The angels themselves are invited, then the other celestial beings that make up the heavenly legions, then every creature in every place of divine dominion. Finally, the poet imagines a world totally given over to the acclamation of God's great mercies, a universe in which all creatures, animal and human, join together with the celestial multitudes to express a deeply felt, truly universal

[15] Indeed, the days of a human being are like blades of grass: they blossom forth for a moment like a flower in the field, [16]until a wind blows by it and it disappears so totally that none can tell where it once sprouted.

[17] But the mercy of יהוה towards those who fear God is as ancient as it is everlasting. Indeed, God's righteousness extends even to the grandchildren [18]of those who keep the covenant and remember to obey its terms.

[19] יהוה set up the divine throne in heaven, but God's dominion extends to every earthly precinct.

[20] Bless יהוה, O angels, O mighty heroes who do God's bidding, who obey God's word.

[21] Bless יהוה all celestial legions, servants of God who act in accordance with God's will.

[22] Bless יהוה all creatures in every place of divine dominion. O my soul, bless יהוה.

sense of devotion and gratitude to God.

That spiritually sensitive moderns will be attracted to the image of a universe wholly given over to the exaltation of the Divine hardly needs to be argued. Nor is it hard to explain why there is something intensely appealing in the notion of a world in which all creation sings out to God in perfect harmony. But it is another thing entirely to say how precisely human beings, unsure of their own spiritual bearing, can find their place in the image the poet is conjuring up for his audience, however. It has to be possible . . . but to know exactly how to exploit one's spiritual desires to find one's place in the chorus is the great task the poet places before his audience to contemplate. It has to be possible . . . but the poet seems content to hint at his own answer by concluding his psalm with the same words he used to begin it. Look within, the poet is saying. Look within to your own soul and there, where your soul resides, you will find the beginning of the path that leads to your personal and private place in the great chorale of universal praise.

קד

בָּרְכִי נַפְשִׁי אֶת־יְהֹוָה יְהֹוָה אֱלֹהַי גָּדַלְתָּ מְּאֹד הוֹד
וְהָדָר לָבָשְׁתָּ׃

2 עֹטֶה אוֹר כַּשַּׂלְמָה נוֹטֶה שָׁמַיִם כַּיְרִיעָה׃

3 הַמְקָרֶה בַמַּיִם עֲלִיּוֹתָיו הַשָּׂם־עָבִים רְכוּבוֹ
הַמְהַלֵּךְ עַל־כַּנְפֵי־רוּחַ׃ 4 עֹשֶׂה מַלְאָכָיו רוּחוֹת
מְשָׁרְתָיו אֵשׁ לֹהֵט׃ 5 יָסַד אֶרֶץ עַל־מְכוֹנֶיהָ
בַּל־תִּמּוֹט עוֹלָם וָעֶד׃

6 תְּהוֹם כַּלְּבוּשׁ כִּסִּיתוֹ עַל־הָרִים יַעַמְדוּ־מָיִם׃

7 מִן־גַּעֲרָתְךָ יְנוּסוּן מִן־קוֹל רַעַמְךָ יֵחָפֵזוּן׃

8 יַעֲלוּ הָרִים יֵרְדוּ בְקָעוֹת אֶל־מְקוֹם זֶה ׀ יָסַדְתָּ
לָהֶם׃ 9 גְּבוּל־שַׂמְתָּ בַּל־יַעֲבֹרוּן בַּל־יְשׁוּבוּן
לְכַסּוֹת הָאָרֶץ׃

10 הַמְשַׁלֵּחַ מַעְיָנִים בַּנְּחָלִים בֵּין הָרִים יְהַלֵּכוּן׃

11 יַשְׁקוּ כָּל־חַיְתוֹ שָׂדָי יִשְׁבְּרוּ פְרָאִים צְמָאָם׃

12 עֲלֵיהֶם עוֹף־הַשָּׁמַיִם יִשְׁכּוֹן מִבֵּין עֳפָאיִם
יִתְּנוּ־קוֹל׃

13 מַשְׁקֶה הָרִים מֵעֲלִיּוֹתָיו מִפְּרִי מַעֲשֶׂיךָ תִּשְׂבַּע
הָאָרֶץ׃

Moderns, especially urban types, are used to dealing with creation in bite-sized pieces. We go to the beach and admire the sea. We go to a park and admire the trees. We go to a zoo and admire the animals. We go to an aquarium and admire the fish. Now and then, we may go camping in a national park of some sort, but even that experience is diluted by a dozen ancillary factors: the presence of hordes of other campers trying to have the same experience in the same place, the difficulty of coming across animals in their totally natural state, the presence of modern washrooms and shower houses, and even the knowledge that the park itself is an artificial preserve invented by bureaucrats rather than a *real* wilderness.

It is all the more moving, therefore, to encounter a poem like the 104th psalm. The poet's technique, simple and elegant, is to describe God as the Creator not in the past tense, but in the present. For example, the poet does not describe God as the One who made light on the first day of Creation all those millennia ago, but as the ongoing source of light in the world. Similarly, he doesn't describe God as the One who once made the mountains and the valleys, but as the One who sustains their existence in our world, who is the Creator of the things of the world not as they once were, but as they actually

104

O my soul, bless יהוה.

יהוה, my God, You are very great; You wear splendor and magnificence as Your garments.

[2] You are the One who wears light as though it were a robe, who hangs the heavens as though they were curtains, [3] who uses water to make the roofing for the uppermost chambers of the divine palace, who uses clouds as a chariot, who travels about on the wings of the wind, [4] who uses the winds as messengers, whose ministers are flames of burning fire, [5] who set the earth on its foundations so that it will never totter.

[6] The deep covered the earth as though it were its cloak. The waters rose over the mountains at that time, [7] then fled away at Your scolding command; indeed, they rushed away at the sound of Your thunder.

[8] The mountains grew and the valleys sunk to the precise foundation You laid for them; [9] You set a boundary for land and sea that neither will ever cross. The waters will never again cover the earth.

[10] You are the One who sends the water of subterranean springs into rivers that run between mountains and [11] give water to drink to all the animals of the field; even the wild donkeys, drinking of them, slake their thirst. [12] The birds of heaven dwell by them and sing out from the branches of nearby trees.

[13] You are the One who irrigates the mountains with waters stored in the upper chambers of heaven; the hunger of the earth is sated with the fruit You have made.

exist in the world in which the poet's audience lives. And the poet's task is made slightly simpler by the way verbs work in classical Hebrew: by artfully manipulating his tenses, the poet fuses past and future in a single, ongoing descriptive act. God, he suggests, is not to be celebrated simply as the one-time Creator of the world, but as the ongoing ordering force that grants all things the context in which they exist and may continue to exist in the physical universe.

Modern readers may wish to use this poet's psalm as a kind of meditative springboard for their own commu-

14 מַצְמִיחַ חָצִיר ׀ לַבְּהֵמָה וְעֵשֶׂב לַעֲבֹדַת הָאָדָם
לְהוֹצִיא לֶחֶם מִן־הָאָרֶץ׃ 15 וְיַיִן ׀ יְשַׂמַּח לְבַב־
אֱנוֹשׁ לְהַצְהִיל פָּנִים מִשָּׁמֶן וְלֶחֶם לְבַב־אֱנוֹשׁ
יִסְעָד׃ 16 יִשְׂבְּעוּ עֲצֵי יְהוָה אַרְזֵי לְבָנוֹן אֲשֶׁר נָטָע׃
17 אֲשֶׁר־שָׁם צִפֳּרִים יְקַנֵּנוּ חֲסִידָה בְּרוֹשִׁים בֵּיתָהּ׃
18 הָרִים הַגְּבֹהִים לַיְּעֵלִים סְלָעִים מַחְסֶה
לַשְׁפַנִּים׃
19 עָשָׂה יָרֵחַ לְמוֹעֲדִים שֶׁמֶשׁ יָדַע מְבוֹאוֹ׃ 20 תָּשֶׁת
חֹשֶׁךְ וִיהִי לָיְלָה בּוֹ־תִרְמֹשׂ כָּל־חַיְתוֹ־יָעַר׃
21 הַכְּפִירִים שֹׁאֲגִים לַטָּרֶף וּלְבַקֵּשׁ מֵאֵל אָכְלָם׃
22 תִּזְרַח הַשֶּׁמֶשׁ יֵאָסֵפוּן וְאֶל־מְעוֹנֹתָם יִרְבָּצוּן׃
23 יֵצֵא אָדָם לְפָעֳלוֹ וְלַעֲבֹדָתוֹ עֲדֵי־עָרֶב׃
24 מָה־רַבּוּ מַעֲשֶׂיךָ ׀ יְהוָה כֻּלָּם בְּחָכְמָה עָשִׂיתָ
מָלְאָה הָאָרֶץ קִנְיָנֶךָ׃ 25 זֶה ׀ הַיָּם גָּדוֹל וּרְחַב יָדָיִם
שָׁם־רֶמֶשׂ וְאֵין מִסְפָּר חַיּוֹת קְטַנּוֹת עִם־גְּדֹלוֹת׃
26 שָׁם אֳנִיּוֹת יְהַלֵּכוּן לִוְיָתָן זֶה־יָצַרְתָּ לְשַׂחֶק־בּוֹ׃

nion with God by focusing on the poet's exclamation, *mah rabu ma'asekha* יהוה *kulam behokhmah asita mal'ah ha'aretz kinyanekha* ("How great are Your works, יהוה! You have made everything with wisdom; the world is filled with Your creation.") But the poet writes not merely to enthuse, but also to instruct: to make ourselves capable of acclaiming God as the Creator, we must find a way to encounter creation up close and intimately, rather than being content to experience God's world as mere onlookers satisfied to observe the splendors of the natural world from a distance. To immerse ourselves in the glories of nature—to experience a virgin forest, to know eagles and owls not as pictures in a book, but as neighbors in the world, to see mountains rising in the mist—these are the tools moderns will have to gather before becoming capable of experiencing God as Creator. Absent these tools, the concept of God as Creator will remain a mere theological construct for most people—and, at that, one that by virtue of its undemonstrable nature may end up leading people away from faith. In the end, it comes to this: will the created world be a conduit leading us *to* God or a barrier keeping us *from* God?

One reasonable method for moderns seeking a way to know the Creator through the contemplation of Creation would be to think of themselves as part of the larger picture of the created universe. The psalmist sets the tone when he assigns humankind a place among the fauna of the world. Lions prowl the world at night looking for food, he notes. But then, when humans leave their

[14–15] You are the One who makes the grass grow for animals to eat and the vegetation necessary for humanity to bring forth bread from the earth through working the soil. Indeed, it is bread on which the heart of humankind feasts—and also wine, which gladdens the hearts of humankind and makes people's faces shine more brightly than if they were rubbed with oil. [16]The trees of יהוה are well nourished, the mighty cedars of Lebanon that God planted—[17]those trees in which birds make their nests—and the fir trees too, which are home to the storks. [18]And You also made the high mountains for wild goats and the great rocks that serve rabbits as their safe haven.

[19] You are the One who made the moon in all its phases and the sun in such a way that it knows to set in the evening. [20]You decree darkness and it becomes night, the time when the animals of the forest creep forth in safety, [21]when lions roar at their prey—for their roaring too is a way of asking God for food. [22]But when the sun shines again, they rejoin their prides and lie down in their lairs to rest, [23]just as humanity is ready to go to work, to labor until evening.

[24] How great are Your works, יהוה! You have made everything with wisdom; the world is filled with Your creation. [25]There is the sea, great and wide, filled with swimming things without number, small creatures and big. [26]There, ships make their way; there lives the Leviathan which You created to frolic in it.

homes to go to work and to labor until evening, the lions cease their nocturnal wandering and lay down in their dens to rest. The idea, therefore, is not simply to take note of the existence of lions, but to feel a kind of symbiotic balance between the leonine and human worlds: we share space in God's universe with lions not by struggling to dominate them, but by sleeping when they labor and by laboring when they sleep. The same could be said, just a bit more obscurely, of the flora of the world: the wheat grows across God's earth so that it can be harvested by farmers, then winnowed, ground up into flour, and baked into bread . . . that very bread that becomes the most basic food, enabling human beings to maintain the strength

27 כֻּלָּם אֵלֶיךָ יְשַׂבֵּרוּן לָתֵת אָכְלָם בְּעִתּוֹ׃ 28 תִּתֵּן
לָהֶם יִלְקֹטוּן תִּפְתַּח יָדְךָ יִשְׂבְּעוּן טוֹב׃ 29 תַּסְתִּיר
פָּנֶיךָ יִבָּהֵלוּן תֹּסֵף רוּחָם יִגְוָעוּן וְאֶל־עֲפָרָם
יְשׁוּבוּן׃ 30 תְּשַׁלַּח רוּחֲךָ יִבָּרֵאוּן וּתְחַדֵּשׁ פְּנֵי
אֲדָמָה׃

31 יְהִי כְבוֹד יְהוָה לְעוֹלָם יִשְׂמַח יְהוָה בְּמַעֲשָׂיו׃
32 הַמַּבִּיט לָאָרֶץ וַתִּרְעָד יִגַּע בֶּהָרִים וְיֶעֱשָׁנוּ׃
33 אָשִׁירָה לַיהוָה בְּחַיָּי אֲזַמְּרָה לֵאלֹהַי בְּעוֹדִי׃
34 יֶעֱרַב עָלָיו שִׂיחִי אָנֹכִי אֶשְׂמַח בַּיהוָה׃
35 יִתַּמּוּ חַטָּאִים ׀ מִן־הָאָרֶץ וּרְשָׁעִים ׀ עוֹד אֵינָם
בָּרְכִי נַפְשִׁי אֶת־יְהוָה הַלְלוּיָהּ׃

necessary to plant and tend to new crops. Here too the idea is not merely to notice the wheat waving in its field, but to feel a deep sense of partnership with even a part of God's creation as little able to respond in kind as a stalk of wheat. The point is not to struggle for dominion over it—and what, really, could make less sense than imagining human beings struggling to dominate plants?—but to feel a deep sense of connectedness in God's universe with even the plants that grow in our world: we tend their fields, they provide us with food, and that food in turn nourishes us and grants us the strength to tend their fields. This kind of thinking is what the poet whose poem became our 104th psalm had in mind when he wrote that the world is filled with God's creation. At first a bit

[27] They all look to You to give them their food in due course. [28] You give it to them and they gather it up; You open Your hand and they are sated with good. [29] But when You hide Your face, they are terrified; when You stop their breathing, they die and return unto they dust from which they came. [30] Then, when You send them Your breath to revive them, it is as though they are created afresh, just as You renew the face of the earth.

[31–32] May the glory of יהוה be forever. May יהוה —who can make the earth tremble merely by looking at it, who can touch mountains and make them smoke—forever rejoice in the work of divine creation.

[33] I shall sing to יהוה as long as I live; I shall sing hymns to my God as long as I exist.

[34] May my words be pleasant unto God, as it is in יהוה that I rejoice.

[35] May sinners be gone from the earth and may the wicked likewise vanish; O my soul, bless יהוה. Hallelujah.

of an odd thing to say—the world itself *is* God's creation, after all—the poet's point becomes clear in the context of his poem. Humankind is not merely the top of the food chain, he means for his audience to understand, but part of an infinitely intricate and immensely elaborate complex of shared space, shared destiny, and shared createdness in God. Seizing that and allowing it to become the intellectual path we travel along towards our effort to seize something of the Creator through the contemplation of Creation . . . *that* is the poet's point, and his poem's inspiring and stimulating message.

קה

הוֹדוּ לַיהוָה קִרְאוּ בִּשְׁמוֹ הוֹדִיעוּ בָעַמִּים
עֲלִילוֹתָיו:
2 שִׁירוּ לוֹ זַמְּרוּ־לוֹ שִׂיחוּ בְּכָל־נִפְלְאוֹתָיו:
3 הִתְהַלְלוּ בְּשֵׁם קָדְשׁוֹ יִשְׂמַח לֵב | מְבַקְשֵׁי יְהוָה:
4 דִּרְשׁוּ יְהוָה וְעֻזּוֹ בַּקְּשׁוּ פָנָיו תָּמִיד:
5 זִכְרוּ נִפְלְאוֹתָיו אֲשֶׁר עָשָׂה מֹפְתָיו וּמִשְׁפְּטֵי־פִיו:
6 זֶרַע אַבְרָהָם עַבְדּוֹ בְּנֵי יַעֲקֹב בְּחִירָיו: 7 הוּא יְהוָה
אֱלֹהֵינוּ בְּכָל־הָאָרֶץ מִשְׁפָּטָיו: 8 זָכַר לְעוֹלָם
בְּרִיתוֹ דָּבָר צִוָּה לְאֶלֶף דּוֹר: 9 אֲשֶׁר כָּרַת אֶת־
אַבְרָהָם וּשְׁבוּעָתוֹ לְיִשְׂחָק: 10 וַיַּעֲמִידֶהָ לְיַעֲקֹב
לְחֹק לְיִשְׂרָאֵל בְּרִית עוֹלָם: 11 לֵאמֹר לְךָ אֶתֵּן
אֶת־אֶרֶץ כְּנָעַן חֶבֶל נַחֲלַתְכֶם:
12 בִּהְיוֹתָם מְתֵי מִסְפָּר כִּמְעַט וְגָרִים בָּהּ:
13 וַיִּתְהַלְּכוּ מִגּוֹי אֶל־גּוֹי מִמַּמְלָכָה אֶל־עַם אַחֵר:
14 לֹא־הִנִּיחַ אָדָם לְעָשְׁקָם וַיּוֹכַח עֲלֵיהֶם מְלָכִים:
15 אַל־תִּגְּעוּ בִמְשִׁיחָי וְלִנְבִיאַי אַל־תָּרֵעוּ:
16 וַיִּקְרָא רָעָב עַל־הָאָרֶץ כָּל־מַטֵּה־לֶחֶם שָׁבָר:
17 שָׁלַח לִפְנֵיהֶם אִישׁ לְעֶבֶד נִמְכַּר יוֹסֵף:

Hardly any observation could be more banal than noting that the past and the future meet in the present. Nevertheless, the implications of such a statement are hardly banal at all. And its corollary—that the past flows endlessly into the present and gives shape and meaning to the future by casting the living as players in an ongoing pageant of creative human endeavor—is anything but ordinary.

Jews who read the 105th psalm will naturally be interested in the poet's take on the tales of ancient Israel. Interestingly, the poet doesn't follow biblical precedent too closely, referring to the plagues in a different order than the one in which they appear in the Book of Exodus and stressing some unfamiliar aspects of the story of Israel in Egypt. Still, the underlying message in his poem is clear enough: God brought forth Israel from Egypt not because slavery itself was an impossible institution to countenance, but for a specific purpose connected with the destiny of the Jewish people. God, the poet asserts, wishes to be known through the medium of law and legislation. Furthermore, the Almighty wishes not merely to be acknowledged, but actually to be worshiped, through fealty to a set of laws which transform daily life from a tiresome list of mundane chores into an endless series of opportunities to love God, to worship God, and to show deep allegiance to, and respect for, God.

105

Give thanks to יהוה, call out in God's name. Proclaim the deeds of God among the nations. [2] Sing out to God, sing hymns to God, speak of all God's wonders. [3] And derive praise for yourselves as well through your use of the holy name; may the hearts of those who seek יהוה be made joyous. [4] Seek יהוה through the contemplation of divine power; search out the face of God always. [5] Remember the wonders God wrought, the marvels of God and the judgments of God's mouth. [6] O seed of God's servant, Abraham, O chosen children of Jacob: [7] יהוה is our God, our God whose judgments pertain to the whole earth, [8] who recalls the covenant with Israel—that word bequeathed to a thousand generations [9] first established with Abraham, then reaffirmed by divine oath to Isaac, [10] and confirmed as law to Jacob as an eternal covenant with Israel, [11] saying, "To you do I give the land of Canaan as the substance of your inheritance."

[12] When they were just few in number and mere sojourners wherever they went, [13] wandering from nation to nation, from one kingdom to another people, [14] God did not permit anyone to oppress them. Indeed, God even took kings to task for behaving poorly to them, [15] saying, "Do not harm My anointed ones or hurt My prophets."

[16] God decreed famine on the land, destroying any trace of bread, the staff of life, [17] but then sent a man before them down to Egypt; Joseph was sold as a slave.

The poet does not explain the rather arbitrary choice of Israel as the nation destined to serve God in this way. But his assertion that the whole purpose of bringing Israel forth from bondage was *ba'avur yishmeru ḥukav*—so that they might keep God's laws—is nonetheless a stunning thought in its own right. Indeed, the poet has managed to suggest an exquisite confluence of history and national purpose in only a few words. And, at the same time, he suggests why the stories of Scripture are included in the sacred text in the first place: because they are part of a larger mosaic of memory and destiny intended to make living the Jewish life into a cosmic mission.

18 עִנּוּ בַכֶּבֶל *רַגְלוֹ בַּרְזֶל בָּאָה נַפְשׁוֹ׃ 19 עַד־עֵת
בֹּא־דְבָרוֹ אִמְרַת יְהוָה צְרָפָתְהוּ׃
20 שָׁלַח־מֶלֶךְ וַיַּתִּירֵהוּ מֹשֵׁל עַמִּים וַיְפַתְּחֵהוּ׃
21 שָׂמוֹ אָדוֹן לְבֵיתוֹ וּמֹשֵׁל בְּכָל־קִנְיָנוֹ׃ 22 לֶאְסֹר
שָׂרָיו בְּנַפְשׁוֹ וּזְקֵנָיו יְחַכֵּם׃
23 וַיָּבֹא יִשְׂרָאֵל מִצְרָיִם וְיַעֲקֹב גָּר בְּאֶרֶץ־חָם׃
24 וַיֶּפֶר אֶת־עַמּוֹ מְאֹד וַיַּעֲצִמֵהוּ מִצָּרָיו׃ 25 הָפַךְ
לִבָּם לִשְׂנֹא עַמּוֹ לְהִתְנַכֵּל בַּעֲבָדָיו׃ 26 שָׁלַח מֹשֶׁה
עַבְדּוֹ אַהֲרֹן אֲשֶׁר בָּחַר־בּוֹ׃
27 שָׂמוּ־בָם דִּבְרֵי אֹתוֹתָיו וּמֹפְתִים בְּאֶרֶץ חָם׃
28 שָׁלַח חֹשֶׁךְ וַיַּחְשִׁךְ וְלֹא־מָרוּ אֶת־*דְּבָרוֹ׃
29 הָפַךְ אֶת־מֵימֵיהֶם לְדָם וַיָּמֶת אֶת־דְּגָתָם׃
30 שָׁרַץ אַרְצָם צְפַרְדְּעִים בְּחַדְרֵי מַלְכֵיהֶם׃
31 אָמַר וַיָּבֹא עָרֹב כִּנִּים בְּכָל־גְּבוּלָם׃
32 נָתַן גִּשְׁמֵיהֶם בָּרָד אֵשׁ לֶהָבוֹת בְּאַרְצָם׃
33 וַיַּךְ גַּפְנָם וּתְאֵנָתָם וַיְשַׁבֵּר עֵץ גְּבוּלָם׃

v. 18 רגליו כתיב
v. 28 דבריו כתיב

The psalm, for its part, will provoke some profound questions for modern readers. Do we imagine that the past exists as more than mere recollective consciousness? Does the future exist as more than just theoretical potential? And what of destiny? Moderns tend to find the notion of kismet hard to seize, but do we actually think that personal fate and national purpose can successfully combine to create a nation of wholly conscious (rather than merely accidental) members of the House of Israel—or is that concept merely something we feel called upon from time to time to *say* we find self-evident? In the end, perhaps, it comes down to this: does the study of Jewish history merely interest us, or can we find a way to let it alter our spirituality from deep within by making us into willing links in the chain of dreams that is the history of Israel?

And more than merely studying history is called for. Acquiring a sense of familiarity with the personalities and events that constitute the pageant of Israel's past is essential, but moderns will need to go further if history is to become the actual context of their spiritual journeys, rather than simply a useful backdrop.

An analysis of how people live within their families will be instructive. Family is the setting for most human development: it is at home, more than in school or in the workplace or the marketplace, that we learn to love, to trust,

[18] They tortured his feet with chains, almost killing him with fetters of iron, [19]until the prediction concerning him came to pass, until the word of יהוה finally tested his mettle.

[20] God sent a king to release him from prison, a ruler of peoples who set him free, [21]who made Joseph master over his house and the ruler of all his possessions, [22]who gave him the right to arrest his princes at will and to make wise his elders.

[23] And so did Israel come to Egypt and Jacob lived in the land of Ham.

[24] God made the people increase there and wax more mighty than its enemies, [25]whereupon their enemies' hearts turned to hate the people of God and prompted them to scheme against God's servants. [26]God then sent Moses, the divine servant, and Aaron, God's chosen messenger.

[27] They wrought God's signs in the midst of those enemies, performing wonders in the land of Ham.

[28] God sent darkness to Egypt and it became dark, but Israel did not rebel against God's word.

[29] God turned their waters to blood and killed their fish.

[30] Their land swarmed with frogs, which came even into the chambers of their royalty.

[31] God spoke and there came wild beasts of all kinds, then came lice into every corner of their land.

[32] God made their rain into hailstones, a storm of fiery flames in their country.

[33] God smote their vines and their fig trees and destroyed the trees throughout their land.

to feel secure, and to develop and grow unimpeded by the expectations or assumptions of others. Knowing the details of one's family's history—the identities of one's relations, their origins and their ages, the specific relationship they bear to each other, and how they feel about each other—is essential, but *merely* acquiring and mastering the data will never be enough. Someone hoping to take his or her place in society as a member of a specific family, or to decipher human society by focusing its institutions through the lens of that specific family's matrix of complex interrelationships and

34 אָמַר וַיָּבֹא אַרְבֶּה וְיֶלֶק וְאֵין מִסְפָּר: 35 וַיֹּאכַל כָּל־
עֵשֶׂב בְּאַרְצָם וַיֹּאכַל פְּרִי אַדְמָתָם:
36 וַיַּךְ כָּל־בְּכוֹר בְּאַרְצָם רֵאשִׁית לְכָל־אוֹנָם:
37 וַיּוֹצִיאֵם בְּכֶסֶף וְזָהָב וְאֵין בִּשְׁבָטָיו כּוֹשֵׁל:
38 שָׂמַח מִצְרַיִם בְּצֵאתָם כִּי־נָפַל פַּחְדָּם עֲלֵיהֶם:
39 פָּרַשׂ עָנָן לְמָסָךְ וְאֵשׁ לְהָאִיר לָיְלָה:
40 שָׁאַל וַיָּבֵא שְׂלָו וְלֶחֶם שָׁמַיִם יַשְׂבִּיעֵם:
41 פָּתַח צוּר וַיָּזוּבוּ מָיִם הָלְכוּ בַּצִּיּוֹת נָהָר:
42 כִּי־זָכַר אֶת־דְּבַר קָדְשׁוֹ אֶת־אַבְרָהָם עַבְדּוֹ:
43 וַיּוֹצִא עַמּוֹ בְשָׂשׂוֹן בְּרִנָּה אֶת־בְּחִירָיו: 44 וַיִּתֵּן
לָהֶם אַרְצוֹת גּוֹיִם וַעֲמַל לְאֻמִּים יִירָשׁוּ: 45 בַּעֲבוּר
יִשְׁמְרוּ חֻקָּיו וְתוֹרֹתָיו יִנְצֹרוּ הַלְלוּיָהּ:

shared heritage, will need to go farther. The data is crucial, but without a deep sense of personal involvement in the fabric of family life, no amount of information—not even of the most intimate nature—will make anyone truly capable of living in the world successfully and meaningfully as a member of that family unit.

Similarly, seeking to know the Author of history by taking one's place in the history of one's people requires a great deal more than merely acquiring a certain amount of information about the past. Factual information is necessary, but it is only the prerequisite for transforming history from story to context, from an aggregate of facts regarding various things that once happened into a kind of framework for spiritual growth towards God. What the psalmist has to say about Israel can be easily translated into the contexts of other nations and cultures, but modern Jews will feel especially challenged to take the psalmist's words to heart: whatever implications his words may have for other nations and their national spiritual quests, it is the history of Israel that the poet is proposing as the model for learning to engage God in history. Indeed, the poet is convinced that God's presence in history is itself the great

[34] God spoke and there came locusts and grasshoppers without number, [35]who ate all the grass in their country and ate the fruit of their land.

[36] God smote all the firstborn sons in their land, the first fruits of all their fathers' strength.

[37] And God took them forth laden with silver and gold; none among the tribes failed to escape.

[38] Egypt rejoiced when they left, for the fear of Israel had fallen upon them.

[39] God spread out a cloud as a screen and sent fire to light up the night.

[40] They asked and God sent quail, and then made them sated too with bread from heaven.

[41] God split open a rock and out streamed water; rivers flowed through parched lands [42]as God recalled the holy word given to God's servant, Abraham.

[43] God brought forth the people in gladness, the chosen ones of God with joy, [44]giving them the lands of other nations so that they might inherit the fruit of other peoples' toil, [45]so that they might keep God's laws and uphold God's teachings. Hallelujah.

gateway to faith through which Jews sufficiently identified with the history of Israel must pass on their way to spiritual fulfillment.

Modern readers of the 105th psalm, and especially Jewish ones, will have to decide what it means to live inside history, to find within the almost infinite number of moments that stretches out between a people's origins and its national destiny a platform sturdy enough to support the encounter between the citizens of that nation and the God of history. That it can be done is certain. That it has been done, no less so. But how exactly to go about seeking the Author of history in the river of days that constitute a nation's past, present, and future—*that* is the question moderns seeking to use the 105th psalm as a springboard for useful meditation will find the most profitable to ponder.

הַֽלְלוּיָ֨הּ ׀
הוֹדוּ לַיהוָה כִּי־טוֹב כִּי לְעוֹלָם חַסְדּוֹ׃
2 מִי יְמַלֵּל גְּבוּרוֹת יְהוָה יַשְׁמִיעַ כָּל־תְּהִלָּתוֹ׃
3 אַשְׁרֵי שֹׁמְרֵי מִשְׁפָּט עֹשֵׂה צְדָקָה בְכָל־עֵת׃
4 זָכְרֵנִי יְהוָה בִּרְצוֹן עַמֶּךָ פָּקְדֵנִי בִּישׁוּעָתֶךָ׃
5 לִרְאוֹת ׀ בְּטוֹבַת בְּחִירֶיךָ לִשְׂמֹחַ בְּשִׂמְחַת גּוֹיֶךָ
לְהִתְהַלֵּל עִם־נַחֲלָתֶךָ׃
6 חָטָאנוּ עִם־אֲבוֹתֵינוּ הֶעֱוִינוּ הִרְשָׁעְנוּ׃
7 אֲבוֹתֵינוּ בְמִצְרַיִם ׀ לֹא־הִשְׂכִּילוּ נִפְלְאוֹתֶיךָ לֹא
זָכְרוּ אֶת־רֹב חֲסָדֶיךָ וַיַּמְרוּ עַל־יָם בְּיַם־סוּף׃
8 וַיּוֹשִׁיעֵם לְמַעַן שְׁמוֹ לְהוֹדִיעַ אֶת־גְּבוּרָתוֹ׃
9 וַיִּגְעַר בְּיַם־סוּף וַיֶּחֱרָב וַיּוֹלִיכֵם בַּתְּהֹמוֹת כַּמִּדְבָּר׃
10 וַיּוֹשִׁיעֵם מִיַּד שׂוֹנֵא וַיִּגְאָלֵם מִיַּד אוֹיֵב׃
11 וַיְכַסּוּ־מַיִם צָרֵיהֶם אֶחָד מֵהֶם לֹא נוֹתָר׃
12 וַיַּאֲמִינוּ בִדְבָרָיו יָשִׁירוּ תְּהִלָּתוֹ׃

Whether the 106th psalm had the same author as the 105th cannot be known, but the reason the former follows the latter in the Psalter is clear enough: the 105th psalm describes Israel's history from the age of the patriarchs and matriarchs through the exodus from Egypt, while the 106th describes the adventures of the people after leaving Egypt, first describing the miraculous deliverance of the people at the Sea of Reeds, then turning to their forty-year sojourn in the wilderness, and finally recounting their conquest of the Land of Israel.

But the two psalms are not merely two halves of the same story. The 105th psalm, for its part, is a hymn of thanksgiving for all the wondrous deeds God performed for the Israelites as the stage was set for their deliverance from Egyptian bondage. The 106th psalm, on the other hand, tells a different story entirely, one of rebellion and sedition played out and endlessly repeated against the background of God's patience waxing and waning in response to the people's behavior. Indeed, one could characterize the entire poem as a kind of extended meditation on the theme of human ingratitude and divine forbearance.

The poet most likely had no access to records of Israel's history other than the ones we find in the Bible. He is so anxious to describe Israel's history as an endless pas de deux of provocation and forgiveness, however, that he retells some of the Torah's stories in ways that seem inconsonant with the stories as they actually appear in the text of Scripture. Nonetheless, the poet—a philos-

106

Hallelujah.
Give thanks unto יהוה for God is good, for divine mercy is forever.

[2] Who can adequately describe the mighty acts of יהוה or express all the praise due God?

[3] Happy are those who keep God's law, who act justly at all times.

[4] Remember me, יהוה, when You show favor to Your people; visit me with Your salvation, [5]that I might see the goodness that accrues to those You choose to favor, that I might rejoice in the joy of Your nation, that I might glory in Your inheritance.

[6] Still, we continue to sin like our ancestors; we behave iniquitously and do evil.

[7] Our ancestors in Egypt did not become wise through the contemplation of Your wonders; they did not recall Your great mercies and they rebelled at the very banks of the Sea of Reeds. [8]Yet God nonetheless saved them for the sake of the divine name, so that they would come to know the might of the Almighty.

[9] God rebuked the Sea of Reeds and it dried up, then allowed Israel to pass through the depths on foot as though through a desert, [10]thus saving them from the hand of the adversary and redeeming them from the hand of the enemy.

[11] And as the waters covered their foes, sparing not even a single one of them, [12]they came finally to trust in God's promises and to sing hymns of divine praise.

opher of history, not a pedant whose goal was merely to record exactly how the events under discussion unfolded —should not be faulted for technical inaccuracies. And, indeed, he makes his real point entirely clear when he suggests that the Jews have been on a spiritual seesaw for as long as anyone can recall, first careening upward toward heaven as they are overwhelmed with gratitude for God's saving acts and then plummeting down away from God as they become stubborn and arrogant and forget the good deeds the Almighty has wrought on their behalf. The stories to which he refers may be familiar, but the profundity of the poet's message makes it clear that his point was not merely to retell some tales his audience already knew from other sources!

13 מִהֲרוּ שָׁכְחוּ מַעֲשָׂיו לֹא־חִכּוּ לַעֲצָתוֹ: 14 וַיִּתְאַוּוּ
תַאֲוָה בַּמִּדְבָּר וַיְנַסּוּ־אֵל בִּישִׁימוֹן: 15 וַיִּתֵּן לָהֶם
שֶׁאֱלָתָם וַיְשַׁלַּח רָזוֹן בְּנַפְשָׁם: 16 וַיְקַנְאוּ לְמֹשֶׁה
בַּמַּחֲנֶה לְאַהֲרֹן קְדוֹשׁ יְהוָה: 17 תִּפְתַּח־אֶרֶץ
וַתִּבְלַע דָּתָן וַתְּכַס עַל־עֲדַת אֲבִירָם: 18 וַתִּבְעַר־
אֵשׁ בַּעֲדָתָם לֶהָבָה תְּלַהֵט רְשָׁעִים:
19 יַעֲשׂוּ־עֵגֶל בְּחֹרֵב וַיִּשְׁתַּחֲווּ לְמַסֵּכָה: 20 וַיָּמִירוּ
אֶת־כְּבוֹדָם בְּתַבְנִית שׁוֹר אֹכֵל עֵשֶׂב: 21 שָׁכְחוּ
אֵל מוֹשִׁיעָם עֹשֶׂה גְדֹלוֹת בְּמִצְרָיִם: 22 נִפְלָאוֹת
בְּאֶרֶץ חָם נוֹרָאוֹת עַל־יַם־סוּף:
23 וַיֹּאמֶר לְהַשְׁמִידָם לוּלֵי מֹשֶׁה בְחִירוֹ עָמַד בַּפֶּרֶץ
לְפָנָיו לְהָשִׁיב חֲמָתוֹ מֵהַשְׁחִית:
24 וַיִּמְאֲסוּ בְּאֶרֶץ חֶמְדָּה לֹא־הֶאֱמִינוּ לִדְבָרוֹ:
25 וַיֵּרָגְנוּ בְאָהֳלֵיהֶם לֹא שָׁמְעוּ בְּקוֹל יְהוָה:
26 וַיִּשָּׂא יָדוֹ לָהֶם לְהַפִּיל אוֹתָם בַּמִּדְבָּר:
27 וּלְהַפִּיל זַרְעָם בַּגּוֹיִם וּלְזָרוֹתָם בָּאֲרָצוֹת:

Moderns reading the 106th psalm will want to ponder the course of Jewish survival in the post-biblical period to discover if the poet's pattern holds true throughout the successive epochs of Jewish history. Does something inherent in Israel's relationship to God somehow require—or appear to require—that the nation always be either approaching belief and trust in God or distancing itself from faith? Is there some reason that Israel cannot simply place its faith in God and leave it at that? And how are we who live after the Shoah to relate to the poet's image of God as endlessly forgiving, yet also endlessly disappointed by the behavior of the people? If the poet's image holds for today, then how can we break the cycle? How can we approach God without being doomed by our human nature to thwart our own efforts almost as soon as they begin to bear fruit?

Readers may wish to begin their contemplative study of the 106th psalm by comparing it to Psalm 78, the psalm with which it most prominently shares the theme of Israel's ever-alternating patterns of fealty and rebelliousness towards God. There, the poet puts forward the notion that God granted instruction to Israel specifically to assist them in breaking the cycle of obedience and disobedience: "God established testimony in Jacob and bestowed teaching upon Israel, a *torah* bequeathed to our ancestors so that they might make it known to their children, so that even the children born to the latest gener-

[13] However they quickly forgot all God's saving acts and they soon stopped waiting for divine advice; [14]giving in to their own desires in the desert, they tested God's forbearance in the wilderness, [15]whereupon God gave them their due and sent famine to them. [16]They became jealous of Moses in the camp and also of Aaron, the holy one of יהוה, [17]whereupon the earth opened up and swallowed Dathan, then covered up the congregation of Abiram; [18]a fire consumed both their congregations as flames engulfed the wicked.

[19] They fashioned a calf at Mount Horeb and bowed down to a molten beast, [20]thus trading in their glory for the image of an ox—an herbivore!—[21]and forgetting their God, their Savior who wrought such great acts in Egypt, [22]who wrought such wonders in the land of Ham, such awesome deeds at the Sea of Reeds.

[23] God then resolved to destroy them and surely would have, had Moses, God's chosen one, not stood in the breach before the divine presence to turn away God's wrathful desire to destroy.

[24] They then allowed themselves to be repulsed by a land of delight and did not believe in God's promise; [25]busy murmuring in their tents, they did not hear the voice of יהוה, [26]who accordingly raised a hand to cast them down in the desert, [27]to cast their progeny among the nations, to scatter them among foreign lands.

ation will rise up and tell of it to their own children, so that they will put their faith in God and not forget the deeds of God, so that they will keep the commandments of God, *so that they not become a stubborn and rebellious generation like their ancestors, a generation that did not make its heart right and whose spirit was not faithful to God* (Psalm 78:5–8)." That notion, that divine service and the study of God's teachings are meant to work in tandem as the dual antidotes for Israel's apparently systemic inability to follow the word of God faithfully and permanently, will sound reasonable to moderns schooled on the notion that the natural, yet destructive, inclination to sin can be best suppressed through some combination of Torah

28 וַיִּצָּמְדוּ לְבַעַל פְּעוֹר וַיֹּאכְלוּ זִבְחֵי מֵתִים׃
29 וַיַּכְעִיסוּ בְּמַעַלְלֵיהֶם וַתִּפְרָץ־בָּם מַגֵּפָה׃
30 וַיַּעֲמֹד פִּינְחָס וַיְפַלֵּל וַתֵּעָצַר הַמַּגֵּפָה׃
31 וַתֵּחָשֶׁב לוֹ לִצְדָקָה לְדֹר וָדֹר עַד־עוֹלָם׃
32 וַיַּקְצִיפוּ עַל־מֵי מְרִיבָה וַיֵּרַע לְמֹשֶׁה בַּעֲבוּרָם׃
33 כִּי־הִמְרוּ אֶת־רוּחוֹ וַיְבַטֵּא בִּשְׂפָתָיו׃
34 לֹא־הִשְׁמִידוּ אֶת־הָעַמִּים אֲשֶׁר אָמַר יְהֹוָה לָהֶם׃
35 וַיִּתְעָרְבוּ בַגּוֹיִם וַיִּלְמְדוּ מַעֲשֵׂיהֶם׃ 36 וַיַּעַבְדוּ
אֶת־עֲצַבֵּיהֶם וַיִּהְיוּ לָהֶם לְמוֹקֵשׁ׃
37 וַיִּזְבְּחוּ אֶת־בְּנֵיהֶם וְאֶת־בְּנוֹתֵיהֶם לַשֵּׁדִים׃
38 וַיִּשְׁפְּכוּ דָם נָקִי דַּם־בְּנֵיהֶם וּבְנוֹתֵיהֶם אֲשֶׁר
זִבְּחוּ לַעֲצַבֵּי כְנָעַן וַתֶּחֱנַף הָאָרֶץ בַּדָּמִים׃
39 וַיִּטְמְאוּ בְמַעֲשֵׂיהֶם וַיִּזְנוּ בְּמַעַלְלֵיהֶם׃ 40 וַיִּחַר־אַף
יְהֹוָה בְּעַמּוֹ וַיְתָעֵב אֶת־נַחֲלָתוֹ׃ 41 וַיִּתְּנֵם בְּיַד־
גּוֹיִם וַיִּמְשְׁלוּ בָהֶם שֹׂנְאֵיהֶם׃ 42 וַיִּלְחָצוּם
אוֹיְבֵיהֶם וַיִּכָּנְעוּ תַּחַת יָדָם׃

study and faithful observance of the commandments of Scripture.

The author of the 106th psalm, however, has a slightly different approach to the issue. For him, history is the canvas on which Israel's relation with God is to be drawn, not merely the frame around the drawing. Instead of noting the problem (that Israel is endlessly disobedient) and suggesting a solution (that Israel cleave ever more diligently to the word of God and to divine service), the poet whose song became our 106th psalm sees history itself as the medium in which Israel might grow towards God. "Many times did God save them," he wrote, "but they continually rebelled and sought instead their own counsel, sinking ever deeper into sin. God, however, took note of their peril when hearing their joyous hymns, remembering the covenant with them, and forgiving them in accordance with the vastness of divine mercy." He thus implies that the related experiences of feeling abandoned by God and then unexpectedly discovering that God is not distant, of realizing that the mercy of God can yet be activated by heartfelt prayer and joyous (or terrified) hymn, and of coming to understand that God is not so petty as to behave as though the human heart, with all its inadequacies and weaknesses, is not as God made it—that *these* lessons are collectively the path one may take successfully towards faith and a sense of security in God. Indeed, the poet is saying that each instance of being amazed by God's forbearance has the capability of bringing Israel one step closer to

[28] They attached themselves to Baal Peor and ate the sacrifices of the dead, [29] thereby enraging God by their actions. A plague raged in their midst [30] until Phinehas stood up and wrought justice, whereupon the plague stopped—[31] which deed came to be considered an act of true righteousness throughout the generations and for all time.

[32] They made God angry by the waters of Meribah and God punished Moses on their behalf; [33] they made him so bitter that he expressed himself about it aloud.

[34] They failed to destroy the nations as יהוה had ordered them to do, [35] but instead mixed together with them and learned their ways, [36] worshiping their idols, idols that became traps for them.

[37] They sacrificed their sons and daughters to demons, [38] thus spilling innocent blood; they spilled the blood of their sons and daughters whom they sacrificed to the idols of Canaan, whereupon the land became polluted with blood.

[39] They defiled themselves with their deeds, debauched themselves with licentious acts [40] so totally that יהוה, enraged with the people and disgusted with God's own inheritance, [41] gave them into the hands of alien nations—and thus did nations who hated them come to rule over them. [42] Their enemies oppressed them and, in time, they were crushed beneath the enemies' hand.

faith, one inch further along the path to national redemption.

The poets who wrote the 78th and the 106th psalms would probably not have found anything contradictory in each other's work. Moderns, on the other hand, may profitably compare the two poems by asking themselves which poet's approach strikes them as more cogent. Does the experience of seeking to break the cycle of human intractableness and divine clemency through study and observance resonate with moderns more deeply? Or does the notion of a people coming closer to spiritual maturity baby-step by baby-step through the experience of finding God in the contemplation of history sound more likely? The approaches are

43 פְּעָמִים רַבּוֹת יַצִּילֵם וְהֵמָּה יַמְרוּ בַעֲצָתָם וַיָּמֹכּוּ
בַּעֲוֺנָם׃ 44 וַיַּרְא בַּצַּר לָהֶם בְּשָׁמְעוֹ אֶת־רִנָּתָם׃
45 וַיִּזְכֹּר לָהֶם בְּרִיתוֹ וַיִּנָּחֵם כְּרֹב *חֲסָדָיו׃
46 וַיִּתֵּן אוֹתָם לְרַחֲמִים לִפְנֵי כָּל־שׁוֹבֵיהֶם׃
47 הוֹשִׁיעֵנוּ ׀ יְהוָה אֱלֹהֵינוּ וְקַבְּצֵנוּ מִן־הַגּוֹיִם
לְהֹדוֹת לְשֵׁם קָדְשֶׁךָ לְהִשְׁתַּבֵּחַ בִּתְהִלָּתֶךָ׃
48 בָּרוּךְ־יְהוָה אֱלֹהֵי יִשְׂרָאֵל מִן־הָעוֹלָם ׀ וְעַד
הָעוֹלָם וְאָמַר כָּל־הָעָם אָמֵן הַלְלוּיָהּ׃

v. 45 חסדו כתיב

not mutually incompatible and they are certainly both rational ways to analyze the flow of Jewish history over the millennia.

Nevertheless, moderns will find it a productive exercise to ask which psalm seems most in keeping with their own spiritual philosophy. Have instances of disaster and tragedy in their own lives, for example, impelled them to call out to God with a kind of security in God's ability to save that they may not have previously embraced? Or have they moved forward more decisively towards faith through the experience of devoting themselves to study and observance with an unprecedented degree of fervor in the wake of unexpected calamity or disappointment in their lives?

[43] Many times did God save them, but they continually rebelled and sought instead their own counsel, sinking ever deeper into sin. [44]God, however, took note of their peril when hearing their joyous hymns, [45]remembering the covenant with them and forgiving them in accordance with the vastness of divine mercy.

[46] God made those who had carried them off have compassion on them.

[47] Save us, יהוה, our God, and gather us in from among the nations so that we might give thanks to Your holy name and glory in Your praise.

[48] Blessed be יהוה, the God of Israel, for as long as the universe has existed and will continue to exist, and may the whole people say "Amen." Hallelujah.

קז

הֹדוּ לַיהוָה כִּי־טוֹב כִּי לְעוֹלָם חַסְדּוֹ׃ 2 יֹאמְרוּ
גְּאוּלֵי יְהוָה אֲשֶׁר גְּאָלָם מִיַּד־צָר׃ 3 וּמֵאֲרָצוֹת
קִבְּצָם מִמִּזְרָח וּמִמַּעֲרָב מִצָּפוֹן וּמִיָּם׃
4 תָּעוּ בַמִּדְבָּר בִּישִׁימוֹן דָּרֶךְ עִיר מוֹשָׁב לֹא מָצָאוּ׃
5 רְעֵבִים גַּם־צְמֵאִים נַפְשָׁם בָּהֶם תִּתְעַטָּף׃
6 וַיִּצְעֲקוּ אֶל־יְהוָה בַּצַּר לָהֶם מִמְּצוּקוֹתֵיהֶם
יַצִּילֵם׃ 7 וַיַּדְרִיכֵם בְּדֶרֶךְ יְשָׁרָה לָלֶכֶת אֶל־עִיר
מוֹשָׁב׃ 8 יוֹדוּ לַיהוָה חַסְדּוֹ וְנִפְלְאוֹתָיו לִבְנֵי
אָדָם׃ 9 כִּי־הִשְׂבִּיעַ נֶפֶשׁ שֹׁקֵקָה וְנֶפֶשׁ רְעֵבָה
מִלֵּא־טוֹב׃

10 יֹשְׁבֵי חֹשֶׁךְ וְצַלְמָוֶת אֲסִירֵי עֳנִי וּבַרְזֶל׃ 11 כִּי־
הִמְרוּ אִמְרֵי־אֵל וַעֲצַת עֶלְיוֹן נָאָצוּ׃ 12 וַיַּכְנַע
בֶּעָמָל לִבָּם כָּשְׁלוּ וְאֵין עֹזֵר׃ 13 וַיִּזְעֲקוּ אֶל־יְהוָה
בַּצַּר לָהֶם מִמְּצֻקוֹתֵיהֶם יוֹשִׁיעֵם׃ 14 יוֹצִיאֵם
מֵחֹשֶׁךְ וְצַלְמָוֶת וּמוֹסְרוֹתֵיהֶם יְנַתֵּק׃ 15 יוֹדוּ
לַיהוָה חַסְדּוֹ וְנִפְלְאוֹתָיו לִבְנֵי אָדָם׃ 16 כִּי־שִׁבַּר
דַּלְתוֹת נְחֹשֶׁת וּבְרִיחֵי בַרְזֶל גִּדֵּעַ׃

The fifth book of the Psalter opens with a long poem in which the poet imagines himself high up and aloft over the world in some sort of revolving lookout post from which he can observe the various ways God manages both to govern the world with mercy and kindness and also to grant to its inhabitants the right and ability to manage their own affairs and to choose freely between good and evil. The poet is not merely engaging in idle philosophical musing here, however, and imagines instead that he can actually see different groups of people passing before him, each affected in a different way by the liberating presence of God in their lives as they make their way forward in the world and forge their own destinies.

The first group the poet considers is made up of lost souls wandering aimlessly in a vast desert. Does the poet's mind wander to the plight of his own ancestors, the slaves who fled Egyptian bondage only to wander for decades in the wilderness? Perhaps it does, but the poet does not go off in that direction and his psalm reads just as easily if we imagine him simply looking down on the world and noticing a ragtag group of travelers who have become separated from their guide and who, therefore, must somehow fend for themselves in a very hostile, inhospitable environment. They have no money, no adequate provisions or clothing, no map, and no clear sense of which way to go. But God nonetheless takes pity on them and leads them to a city of decent, liberal

BOOK FIVE

107

"Give thanks to יהוה, for God is good, for divine mercy is forever"—[2]so let those who are redeemed in יהוה sing, those whom God has redeemed from the hand of the enemy, [3]those whom God has gathered from the lands of the east and west, from the north and from the sea.

[4]There was once a band of lost souls wandering in the desert, seeking a path in the wilderness, but finding no inhabited city. [5]Hungry and thirsty, their souls grew faint within them, [6]whereupon they cried out to יהוה in their distress. Then, when God saved them from their troubles [7]by directing them on a straight path to an inhabited city, [8]they proclaimed to all humanity the mercy of יהוה and the wonders of God, [9]who had sated their needy souls and filled their hungry souls with good food.

[10]Another group sat in darkness and gloom, imprisoned by misery and bonds of iron [11]because they had denied the words of God and scorned the counsel of God Most High. [12]God humbled them with suffering of the heart so grievous that none came to help them when they stumbled, [13]whereupon they called out to יהוה in their distress. Then, when God redeemed them from their troubles, [14]taking them from darkness and gloom and snapping their restraints, [15]they proclaimed to all humanity the mercy of יהוה and the wonders of God, [16]who had broken down doors of copper and split apart locks of iron.

people who will give them food and drink and, possibly, even allow them to live there in peace and freedom. They thus become the first group the poet notices who sing the praise of God's mercy and the wondrous way of the Divine in the affairs of humanity. (This becomes a constant refrain; indeed, the ability of each of the four groups to perceive God's governance in their affairs is what unites these four groups and makes them each other's counterparts.)

Having finished telling of the lost travelers, the poet now turns his attention elsewhere in the world and comes across a second group, this one consisting of escaped convicts. Languishing in prison because they lacked the merit to prompt God to help them avoid incarceration in the first place, the members of this second group were condemned to dwell in darkness and misery,

17 אֱוִלִים מִדֶּרֶךְ פִּשְׁעָם וּמֵעֲוֺנֹתֵיהֶם יִתְעַנּוּ׃
18 כָּל־אֹכֶל תְּתַעֵב נַפְשָׁם וַיַּגִּיעוּ עַד־שַׁעֲרֵי מָוֶת׃
19 וַיִּזְעֲקוּ אֶל־יְהֹוָה בַּצַּר לָהֶם מִמְּצֻקוֹתֵיהֶם
יוֹשִׁיעֵם׃ 20 יִשְׁלַח דְּבָרוֹ וְיִרְפָּאֵם וִימַלֵּט
מִשְּׁחִיתוֹתָם׃ 21 יוֹדוּ לַיהֹוָה חַסְדּוֹ וְנִפְלְאוֹתָיו
לִבְנֵי אָדָם׃ 22 וְיִזְבְּחוּ זִבְחֵי תוֹדָה וִיסַפְּרוּ מַעֲשָׂיו
בְּרִנָּה׃
*׆ 23 יוֹרְדֵי הַיָּם בָּאֳנִיּוֹת עֹשֵׂי מְלָאכָה בְּמַיִם רַבִּים׃
*׆ 24 הֵמָּה רָאוּ מַעֲשֵׂי יְהֹוָה וְנִפְלְאוֹתָיו בִּמְצוּלָה׃
*׆ 25 וַיֹּאמֶר וַיַּעֲמֵד רוּחַ סְעָרָה וַתְּרוֹמֵם גַּלָּיו׃
*׆ 26 יַעֲלוּ שָׁמַיִם יֵרְדוּ תְהוֹמוֹת נַפְשָׁם בְּרָעָה
תִתְמוֹגָג׃
*׆ 27 יָחוֹגּוּ וְיָנוּעוּ כַּשִּׁכּוֹר וְכָל־חָכְמָתָם תִּתְבַּלָּע׃
*׆ 28 וַיִּצְעֲקוּ אֶל־יְהֹוָה בַּצַּר לָהֶם וּמִמְּצוּקֹתֵיהֶם
יוֹצִיאֵם׃ 29 יָקֵם סְעָרָה לִדְמָמָה וַיֶּחֱשׁוּ גַּלֵּיהֶם׃
30 וַיִּשְׂמְחוּ כִּי־יִשְׁתֹּקוּ וַיַּנְחֵם אֶל־מְחוֹז חֶפְצָם׃
31 יוֹדוּ לַיהֹוָה חַסְדּוֹ וְנִפְלְאוֹתָיו לִבְנֵי אָדָם׃
32 וִירֹמְמוּהוּ בִּקְהַל־עָם וּבְמוֹשַׁב זְקֵנִים יְהַלְלוּהוּ׃

v. 23-28 נ׳ הפוכה

chained with bonds of iron and weighed down spiritually with deep, unyielding depression. It was precisely this sense of utter desolation, however, that led the prisoners back to God—and the divine response to *that* development was for God to grant them their freedom. How precisely did they escape from jail? The poet says that God took them forth, snapping their chains and breaking down the great iron bars across their windows and the enormous copper gates that kept them confined. We might imagine a simple scenario: the opportunity to escape presented itself and the convicts took it, recognizing the saving hand of God in their lives when it presented itself. They then joined the rescued travelers in singing hymns of thanksgiving focused especially on the incredible power of divine mercy and on the wondrous deeds God can bring about when sufficiently moved by earthly piety to do so.

The third group is made up of the sick. The poet imagines their diseases as being particularly virulent, so much so that they have become too weak either to eat or drink. The poet depicts them wandering ever closer to the gates of the underworld, but then, just as this ward of terminal patients actually approaches death, they come to the sudden, perhaps unexpected, realization that

[17] A third group, made up of villains in torment because of their iniquitous and sinful ways, [18]was so revolted by all manner of food that its members felt themselves approaching the gates of death, [19]whereupon they called out to יהוה in their distress. Then, when God redeemed them from their troubles, [20]sending a word to heal them so that they might escape their looming doom, [21]they proclaimed to all humanity the mercy of יהוה and the wonders of God, [22]offering thanksgiving sacrifices and telling of God's deeds with hymns of gladness.

[23] And then there were those who went down to the sea in ships to do their work in deep waters. [24]They saw the deeds of יהוה and the wonders of God in the depths, [25]for God spoke and the storm winds blew, winds that made tall the waves. [26]Sick with the fear of an evil end, they felt as though their ship was going up to heaven, then sinking down into the depths of the sea. [27]They circled about, reeling back and forth like drunkards, all their wisdom swallowed up by terror, [28–29]whereupon they cried out to יהוה in their distress. Then, when God brought them forth from their troubles, stilling the storm and quieting the waves, [30]they were struck dumb with joy. When, however, God brought them to their desired destination, [31]they proclaimed to all humanity the mercy of יהוה and the wonders of God, [32]exalting God in the assembly of the nation and singing God's praises in the council of elders.

their situation is the result of sin and iniquity. Therefore, instead of cursing God for not saving them, they turn to heaven in prayer and supplication so heartfelt that God, moved, actually saves them from their expected fates and sends a divine word to heal them and make them whole. For their part, the formerly sick are overwhelmed by their discovery of God's responsiveness to human prayer, and so they join the formerly lost desert travelers and the liberated convicts in singing the praises of God's mercy and in acknowledging the wonders that faith can bring about in the land of the living.

The fourth and final group is made up of sailors on a stormy sea. Both savvy

33 יָשֵׂם נְהָרוֹת לְמִדְבָּר וּמֹצָאֵי מַיִם לְצִמָּאוֹן׃
34 אֶרֶץ פְּרִי לִמְלֵחָה מֵרָעַת יֹשְׁבֵי בָהּ׃
35 יָשֵׂם מִדְבָּר לַאֲגַם־מַיִם וְאֶרֶץ צִיָּה לְמֹצָאֵי מָיִם׃
36 וַיּוֹשֶׁב שָׁם רְעֵבִים וַיְכוֹנְנוּ עִיר מוֹשָׁב׃ 37 וַיִּזְרְעוּ
שָׂדוֹת וַיִּטְּעוּ כְרָמִים וַיַּעֲשׂוּ פְּרִי תְבוּאָה׃
38 וַיְבָרְכֵם וַיִּרְבּוּ מְאֹד וּבְהֶמְתָּם לֹא יַמְעִיט׃
39 וַיִּמְעֲטוּ וַיָּשֹׁחוּ מֵעֹצֶר רָעָה וְיָגוֹן׃
*נ 40 שֹׁפֵךְ בּוּז עַל־נְדִיבִים וַיַּתְעֵם בְּתֹהוּ לֹא־דָרֶךְ׃
41 וַיְשַׂגֵּב אֶבְיוֹן מֵעוֹנִי וַיָּשֶׂם כַּצֹּאן מִשְׁפָּחוֹת׃
42 יִרְאוּ יְשָׁרִים וְיִשְׂמָחוּ וְכָל־עַוְלָה קָפְצָה פִּיהָ׃
43 מִי־חָכָם וְיִשְׁמָר־אֵלֶּה וְיִתְבּוֹנְנוּ חַסְדֵי יְהוָה׃

v. 40 נ׳ הפוכה

enough to realize the great danger they are in as the waves rise and also highly experienced in the ways of the sea, the sailors can barely stand upright; they look like drunkards as they careen back and forth on the deck of their ship. And then, terrified beyond the telling of it, the sailors suddenly perceive the hand of God in their disaster. Instead of blaming God for their predicament, however, they realize that the more appropriate response would be to lift up their voices in prayer to the Almighty. And when they do just that, the sea becomes still and the port towards which they were headed before the storm came upon them suddenly becomes visible on the horizon. The sailors, overcome with gratitude to God for their salvation from almost certain destruction, join the rescued travelers, the freed convicts, and the healed sick in praising the mercies of God and in recounting the wondrous salvation God has wrought on their behalf. And then the poet concludes his poem by describing the various ways in which God controls the destiny of people who are, somehow, nonetheless still endowed with the total freedom to choose their own paths in life.

Modern readers seeking to incorporate the recitation of the 107th psalm into their own devotional lives will want to dwell on the four groups of which the poet speaks so eloquently. No readers in today's world will be lost in vast, uncharted deserts as they contemplate the poet's psalm and only a small per-

[33] God can make rivers into deserts, water sources into arid land, [34]and fruited plains into salt flats because of the evil deeds of those who dwell therein.

[35] But God can also make deserts into lakes of water and parched land into sources of water, [36]then settle hungry people there so that they can establish inhabited cities, [37]sow fields, and plant vineyards that yield a harvest of fruit and grain.

[38] God can bless them such that their numbers increase and the number of their cattle not dwindle.

[39] But even if their cattle do dwindle and become burdened by oppression, evil, and suffering, [40]and even should God pour contempt on the gentry and lead nobles to wander in a roadless wasteland, [41]God can still lift the poor up from their poverty and increase their families like flocks of sheep. [42]In such a case, the upright of heart will look on and rejoice . . . but the mouths of doers of iniquity will snap shut. [43]Let whoever is wise ponder these truths and thereby come to understand the merciful deeds of יהוה.

centage will be incarcerated convicts, terminally ill patients, or sailors on a ship in danger of sinking in a storm. Nevertheless, the poet is challenging us all to imagine ourselves facing lives of endless, aimless wandering, imprisonment, incurable illness, or certain death on the high seas. Would we turn to God in prayer . . . or would we descend into a bottomless swamp of recrimination and blame, seeking with our last breaths to indict God for having brought suffering upon us in the first place? Is deliverance, predicated as it must be on calamity and disaster, a blessing or a curse? Does personal salvation from catastrophe testify more to God's caring mercy or more to the callous indifference of a God who could have spared us all our pain in the first place, but who instead brought us to such a calamitous state that we needed to be rescued from it? Can it possibly be that everything in the world is designed, somehow, to bring us closer to God?

קח

שִׁיר מִזְמוֹר לְדָוִד׃
2 נָכוֹן לִבִּי אֱלֹהִים אָשִׁירָה וַאֲזַמְּרָה אַף־כְּבוֹדִי׃
3 עוּרָה הַנֵּבֶל וְכִנּוֹר אָעִירָה שָּׁחַר׃
4 אוֹדְךָ בָעַמִּים ׀ יְהֹוָה וַאֲזַמֶּרְךָ בַּלְאֻמִּים׃
5 כִּי־גָדוֹל מֵעַל־שָׁמַיִם חַסְדֶּךָ וְעַד־שְׁחָקִים אֲמִתֶּךָ׃
6 רוּמָה עַל־שָׁמַיִם אֱלֹהִים וְעַל כָּל־הָאָרֶץ כְּבוֹדֶךָ׃
7 לְמַעַן יֵחָלְצוּן יְדִידֶיךָ הוֹשִׁיעָה יְמִינְךָ *וַעֲנֵנִי׃
8 אֱלֹהִים ׀ דִּבֶּר בְּקָדְשׁוֹ אֶעְלֹזָה אֲחַלְּקָה שְׁכֶם וְעֵמֶק
סֻכּוֹת אֲמַדֵּד׃ 9 לִי גִלְעָד ׀ לִי מְנַשֶּׁה וְאֶפְרַיִם
מָעוֹז רֹאשִׁי יְהוּדָה מְחֹקְקִי׃ 10 מוֹאָב ׀ סִיר רַחְצִי
עַל־אֱדוֹם אַשְׁלִיךְ נַעֲלִי עֲלֵי־פְלֶשֶׁת אֶתְרוֹעָע׃
11 מִי יֹבִלֵנִי עִיר מִבְצָר מִי נָחַנִי עַד־אֱדוֹם׃
12 הֲלֹא־אֱלֹהִים זְנַחְתָּנוּ וְלֹא־תֵצֵא אֱלֹהִים
בְּצִבְאֹתֵינוּ׃
13 הָבָה־לָּנוּ עֶזְרָת מִצָּר וְשָׁוְא תְּשׁוּעַת אָדָם׃
14 בֵּאלֹהִים נַעֲשֶׂה־חָיִל וְהוּא יָבוּס צָרֵינוּ׃

v. 7 ועננו כתיב

Either the 108th psalm is made up of sections of the fifty-seventh and sixtieth psalms that were put together to form a new hymn, or else sections of this poem were copied by the authors of those psalms for use in their own poems. Whatever the details of its literary history may be, however, the hymn we know as the 108th psalm has its own meaning as it now stands. The poet rises in the middle of the night, then fancifully calls to his musical instruments to wake up to assist him in using the power of music to channel the prophetic experience of God's presence into human language. He sings of God's truth and mercy, then reports to his audience that God has actually spoken to him and revealed some information. The specifics of that information will strike modern readers as obscure, but, whatever its original meaning may have been, the poet's point is clearly that God's existence as a real, communicative force in the world is

108

A psalm-song of David.

[2] My heart is ready, O God, as is my glorious soul; I shall sing and chant hymns of praise.

[3] Awake, lute and lyre, for I shall awaken the dawn.

[4] I shall acknowledge You among the nations, O יהוה, and I shall sing of You among the peoples of the world.

[5] For Your mercy reaches up to the highest heaven, Your truth, to the highest skies.

[6] Rise up over the heavens, O God, for Your glory is over all the earth.

[7] Let Your right hand save them as You answer me, so that those who love You might find relief.

[8] I rejoice that God has spoken in the divine sanctuary. "I shall divide Shechem," God said. "I shall survey the Valley of Sukkot. [9]For Mine is Gilead, Mine are Manasseh and Ephraim, my main strongholds; Mine is Judah, My terrestrial legislator. [10]Mine is Moab, My washing-tub. I shall stamp My shoe down on Edom and Philistia, which I shall make quake."

[11] Who will bring me to the fortified city? Who will lead me to Edom?

[12] Has God not abandoned us? Will You not go forth with our armies, O God?

[13] Grant us help against our enemies, since hoping for salvation from human beings is folly. [14]With God, we shall prevail; the Almighty will trample our enemies.

fact, not theory. Perhaps more to the point for modern readers, the poet wants us to understand, equally clearly, that God's word bears real meaning, and not the mere suggestion of significance . . . and, perhaps even more unexpectedly, that the word of God is actually audible, not merely perceptible in the vague way people sometimes say they can hear God speak through the contemplation of nature or love . . . or in the way our own prayers may reverberate audibly, yet also silently, in our heads as words are formed first in our hearts before being spoken aloud. And so the poet leaves us with a number of issues to ponder and with a deep and personal question to ask (and, if we can, also to answer): what exactly must the faithful do to be vouchsafed an oracle of God?

קט

לַמְנַצֵּחַ לְדָוִד מִזְמוֹר
אֱלֹהֵי תְהִלָּתִי אַל־תֶּחֱרַשׁ׃ 2 כִּי פִי רָשָׁע וּפִי־
מִרְמָה עָלַי פָּתָחוּ דִּבְּרוּ אִתִּי לְשׁוֹן שָׁקֶר׃ 3 וְדִבְרֵי
שִׂנְאָה סְבָבוּנִי וַיִּלָּחֲמוּנִי חִנָּם׃
4 תַּחַת־אַהֲבָתִי יִשְׂטְנוּנִי וַאֲנִי תְפִלָּה׃ 5 וַיָּשִׂימוּ עָלַי
רָעָה תַּחַת טוֹבָה וְשִׂנְאָה תַּחַת אַהֲבָתִי׃
6 הַפְקֵד עָלָיו רָשָׁע וְשָׂטָן יַעֲמֹד עַל־יְמִינוֹ׃
7 בְּהִשָּׁפְטוֹ יֵצֵא רָשָׁע וּתְפִלָּתוֹ תִּהְיֶה לַחֲטָאָה׃
8 יִהְיוּ־יָמָיו מְעַטִּים פְּקֻדָּתוֹ יִקַּח אַחֵר׃
9 יִהְיוּ־בָנָיו יְתוֹמִים וְאִשְׁתּוֹ אַלְמָנָה׃ 10 וְנוֹעַ יָנוּעוּ
בָנָיו וְשִׁאֵלוּ וְדָרְשׁוּ מֵחָרְבוֹתֵיהֶם׃
11 יְנַקֵּשׁ נוֹשֶׁה לְכָל־אֲשֶׁר־לוֹ וְיָבֹזּוּ זָרִים יְגִיעוֹ׃
12 אַל־יְהִי־לוֹ מֹשֵׁךְ חָסֶד וְאַל־יְהִי חוֹנֵן לִיתוֹמָיו׃
13 יְהִי־אַחֲרִיתוֹ לְהַכְרִית בְּדוֹר אַחֵר יִמַּח שְׁמָם׃
14 יִזָּכֵר ׀ עֲוֹן אֲבֹתָיו אֶל־יְהֹוָה וְחַטַּאת אִמּוֹ אַל־
תִּמָּח׃ 15 יִהְיוּ נֶגֶד־יְהֹוָה תָּמִיד וְיַכְרֵת מֵאֶרֶץ
זִכְרָם׃ 16 יַעַן אֲשֶׁר ׀ לֹא זָכַר עֲשׂוֹת חָסֶד וַיִּרְדֹּף
אִישׁ־עָנִי וְאֶבְיוֹן וְנִכְאֵה לֵבָב לְמוֹתֵת׃ 17 וַיֶּאֱהַב
קְלָלָה וַתְּבוֹאֵהוּ וְלֹא־חָפֵץ בִּבְרָכָה וַתִּרְחַק מִמֶּנּוּ׃

The author of the 109th psalm was a poet possessed of the deepest passions and the most unbridled hatred of his enemy. Who this enemy was, however, is left unsaid. Was it because the foe's identity—and the poet seems clearly to be speaking about a single individual throughout most of his poem—was considered so obvious in the poet's world so as not to require explicit statement? Or was the poet merely being prudent in trying to ward off the fury that a too-public indictment of his nemesis could possibly have provoked? We cannot answer these questions, but modern readers will find it more satisfying to consider the long list of imprecations with which the poet curses his adversary. The context here is important to consider, however, as the poet appears to feel that his misery is the specific result of a curse previously placed on him by his relentless antagonist. Twice, for example, the poet refers to his heart condition. His health is shot. His flesh is wasting away on his bones and he senses that the end of his life is drawing near. He refers to himself as a poor and wretched man whom the world considers no more consequential than an insect one barely pauses to shake off one's garment before squashing under one's heel. His poem, then, is both his response to his situation and his effort to repay in kind the man whose potent, unwarranted curse has brought him to death's door.

109

For the conductor, a psalm of David.

O God whom I praise, be not silent, [2]for mouths of wickedness and deceit have opened up against me; they speak to me with lying tongues, [3]surrounding me with words of hatred, attacking me for no reason.

[4] In exchange for my love, they loathe me, while all I can offer in return is prayer; [5]they offer me evil in exchange for good, hatred in exchange for my love.

[6] Place an evil man over my enemies' leader; let an accuser stand by his right hand.

[7] When he is tried, let him be convicted; may his prayer become naught but sinful words.

[8] May his days be few; may another take over his job.

[9] May his children be orphans, his wife, a widow; [10]may his children wander about begging, searching through the ruins of their homes.

[11] May his creditor put a lien on all that he has; may strangers seize the fruits of his labors.

[12] May there be no one to extend mercy to him, no one to show compassion to his orphans.

[13] Indeed, may his progeny be cut off from the people; may their name be erased as soon as the next generation.

[14] May the sin of his fathers be recalled to יהוה and may the iniquity of his mother not be erased; [15]indeed, may their sins be before יהוה always so that even their recollection be cut off from the earth. [16]For my foe did not remember to act with mercy and pursued a poor, wretched man; he is ready to murder a man with a faulty heart. [17]He loved speaking a curse—may it come back to him—and he takes no delight in blessing—may it be far from him.

Moderns may find it quaint that the poet apparently believed that one person can induce infirmity in another with a curse, but the more serious lesson to ponder is the poet's example of how one ought to respond to relentless, baseless, unyielding hatred. In the end, he turns not to violence but to prayer, thus declining to take matters into his own hands and instead placing the issue squarely in the hands of God. Moderns will want to consider that kind of response carefully. How many of us truly respond to misery and injustice by lifting our hearts in prayer to the Almighty?

It is also worth asking if we con-

18 וַיִּלְבַּשׁ קְלָלָה כְּמַדּוֹ וַתָּבֹא כַמַּיִם בְּקִרְבּוֹ וְכַשֶּׁמֶן בְּעַצְמוֹתָיו׃ 19 תְּהִי־לוֹ כְּבֶגֶד יַעְטֶה וּלְמֵזַח תָּמִיד יַחְגְּרֶהָ׃

20 זֹאת פְּעֻלַּת שֹׂטְנַי מֵאֵת יְהוָה וְהַדֹּבְרִים רָע עַל־נַפְשִׁי׃

21 וְאַתָּה ׀ יְהוִה אֲדֹנָי עֲשֵׂה־אִתִּי לְמַעַן שְׁמֶךָ כִּי־טוֹב חַסְדְּךָ הַצִּילֵנִי׃ 22 כִּי־עָנִי וְאֶבְיוֹן אָנֹכִי וְלִבִּי חָלַל בְּקִרְבִּי׃

23 כְּצֵל כִּנְטוֹתוֹ נֶהֱלָכְתִּי נִנְעַרְתִּי כָּאַרְבֶּה׃

24 בִּרְכַּי כָּשְׁלוּ מִצּוֹם וּבְשָׂרִי כָּחַשׁ מִשָּׁמֶן׃

25 וַאֲנִי ׀ הָיִיתִי חֶרְפָּה לָהֶם יִרְאוּנִי יְנִיעוּן רֹאשָׁם׃

26 עָזְרֵנִי יְהוָה אֱלֹהָי הוֹשִׁיעֵנִי כְחַסְדֶּךָ׃ 27 וְיֵדְעוּ כִּי־יָדְךָ זֹּאת אַתָּה יְהוָה עֲשִׂיתָהּ׃

28 יְקַלְלוּ הֵמָּה וְאַתָּה תְבָרֵךְ קָמוּ ׀ וַיֵּבֹשׁוּ וְעַבְדְּךָ יִשְׂמָח׃

29 יִלְבְּשׁוּ שׂוֹטְנַי כְּלִמָּה וְיַעֲטוּ כַמְעִיל בָּשְׁתָּם׃

30 אוֹדֶה יְהוָה מְאֹד בְּפִי וּבְתוֹךְ רַבִּים אֲהַלְלֶנּוּ׃

31 כִּי־יַעֲמֹד לִימִין אֶבְיוֹן לְהוֹשִׁיעַ מִשֹּׁפְטֵי נַפְשׁוֹ׃

sider the poet's approach to his misery to be entirely rational. Surely, there is nothing base in attempting to effect real change in the world through concerted, conscious effort. Protests and demonstrations all over the world, after all, have brought about dramatic changes for good in many different countries. And we see the same phenomenon on the individual level as well: moderns tend to admire, not to despise, people who stand up for themselves, who insist that the world listen when they perceive wrongdoing and injustice, and who become forceful advocates for positive change. Perhaps the best way to reconcile the poet's stance and our own would be to imagine that the poet isn't so much praying to God for the destruction of his enemy—for surely he has noted that God rarely, if ever, responds to such prayers directly and overtly—but rather for insight in how to deal the most productively and effectively with his enemy's apparently unbridled hostility. (Most moderns would feel far more reticent than the psalmist apparently did about expressing themselves in the openly vindictive terms put forward in this poem, but their need for divine counsel would be no less pressing.)

In the end, the poet has no recourse but to find some way to address his situation effectively and conclusively. He does curse his enemy, but he does so

[18] Indeed, let him wear that curse as his garment, let it come like water into his gut or like oil into his bones; [19]may it be like a cloak that he wraps on and cannot remove, like a belt he must always wear.

[20] Let this be the recompense from יהוה for those who hate me and speak ill of my soul.

[21] And as for You, יהוה-Adonai, deal with me for the sake of Your name; since Your mercy is genuine, save me, [22]for I am poor and wretched and my heart is hollow within me.

[23] I am going the way of a shadow as it lengthens; I feel like a locust someone might shake off without a moment's thought.

[24] My knees are weak from fasting, my flesh, devoid of fat.

[25] I have become an object of scorn for them, so much so that when they see me, they shake their heads in contempt.

[26] Help me, O יהוה, my God; save me in accordance with Your mercy [27]that they might know that this is Your hand that is acting against them, that it is You, O יהוה, who have done this.

[28] May You bless the very ones they curse; may they rise up and be shamed while Your servant rejoices.

[29] May those who hate me wear disgrace like a garment; may they wrap on their shame as though it were a cloak.

[30] I will give thanks to יהוה mightily with my mouth, praising God in public [31]for having stood up by the right side of a wretch to save him from those who would judge his soul.

in a psalm written to God, and not to his enemy's face. That being the case, moderns will do well to focus on the poet's actual response to his dilemma: he turns to God, vents his fury, calls out for help, and waits, presumably, for God to inspire him. He is fasting, he notes. He is praying, obviously. And by turning to God with his rage, he is also setting a noble example for moderns to follow. Can we learn to turn to God in the fullness of our unhappiness, out of the depths of our despair? Surely, we can . . . but how exactly to go about remembering to do so is, of course, another question entirely.

קי

לְדָוִד מִזְמוֹר
נְאֻם יְהֹוָה ׀ לַאדֹנִי שֵׁב לִימִינִי עַד־אָשִׁית אֹיְבֶיךָ הֲדֹם לְרַגְלֶיךָ׃
2 מַטֵּה עֻזְּךָ יִשְׁלַח יְהֹוָה מִצִּיּוֹן רְדֵה בְּקֶרֶב אֹיְבֶיךָ׃
3 עַמְּךָ נְדָבֹת בְּיוֹם חֵילֶךָ בְּהַדְרֵי־קֹדֶשׁ מֵרֶחֶם מִשְׁחָר לְךָ טַל יַלְדֻתֶיךָ׃
4 נִשְׁבַּע יְהֹוָה ׀ וְלֹא יִנָּחֵם אַתָּה־כֹהֵן לְעוֹלָם עַל־דִּבְרָתִי מַלְכִּי־צֶדֶק׃
5 אֲדֹנָי עַל־יְמִינְךָ מָחַץ בְּיוֹם־אַפּוֹ מְלָכִים׃
6 יָדִין בַּגּוֹיִם מָלֵא גְוִיּוֹת מָחַץ רֹאשׁ עַל־אֶרֶץ רַבָּה׃
7 מִנַּחַל בַּדֶּרֶךְ יִשְׁתֶּה עַל־כֵּן יָרִים רֹאשׁ׃

The 110th psalm is a difficult poem, but not to the point of being beyond reasonable interpretation. The poet appears to be reporting an oracle that he experienced in which God was not speaking to him, but to his king. In this context, the poet heard God inviting the king to be seated—surely among the greatest of honors—and predicting, as only the Author of History ever could, that the king will be victorious over all his enemies. The people themselves will act as God's holy agents by coming forward willingly to fight the king's battles, but God has more to say than merely offering a positive forecast for the king's military future. Indeed, there is also a secret God has to impart, one that will explain why the king is to be favored with good fortune. It turns out, the poet reveals, that there is more than one kind of priesthood in the world. Best known, of course, is the priestly caste of *kohanim* who serve in the Temple. But

110

A psalm of David.

The word of יהוה came to my master: "Sit by My right hand until such time that I make your enemies into a hassock for your feet."

[2] יהוה shall send your powerful staff out from Zion and thus shall it be as though God were to say to you, "Rule in the midst of your enemies."

[3] Your people are gifts to you on the day of battle; in holy splendor from the dawn of their lives, even from the womb, they are the dew drops that adorn your youth.

[4] יהוה swears and will never renege, "You are to be my priest forever, a priest at My behest belonging to the priesthood of Melchizedek."

[5] Adonai shall dwell at your right hand and will crush alien kings on a day of divine anger.

[6] God will judge nations soon to be filled with corpses; God will crush their heads on the great earth.

[7] Their blood will form a river in the street so that our king could actually drink from it; therefore will he hold his head up high.

God has other priests as well. Melchizedek, for example, was the king of Jerusalem in Abraham's day and is called a priest of God Most High by Scripture itself at the end of the fourteenth chapter of Genesis . . . and it is as a member of that shadowy priesthood, called after King Melchizedek, that the poet hears God acclaiming his king. Although the phraseology is obscure, the meaning of the poet's oracle is clear enough: the king is a servant of God and his life, for all its regal trappings, is meant to be a life of service to God. The poet implies—subtly, but unmistakably—that forgetting that simple truth would not only be folly, but the most tragically counterproductive of tactical errors.

קיא

הַ֥לְלוּ־יָ֨הּ ׀

אוֹדֶ֣ה יְ֭הוָה בְּכָל־לֵבָ֑ב בְּס֖וֹד יְשָׁרִ֣ים וְעֵדָֽה׃

2 גְּ֭דֹלִים מַעֲשֵׂ֣י יְהוָ֑ה דְּ֝רוּשִׁ֗ים לְכָל־חֶפְצֵיהֶֽם׃

3 הוֹד־וְהָדָ֥ר פָּֽעֳל֑וֹ וְ֝צִדְקָת֗וֹ עֹמֶ֥דֶת לָעַֽד׃

4 זֵ֣כֶר עָ֭שָׂה לְנִפְלְאֹתָ֑יו חַנּ֖וּן וְרַח֣וּם יְהוָֽה׃ 5 טֶ֭רֶף נָתַ֣ן לִירֵאָ֑יו יִזְכֹּ֖ר לְעוֹלָ֣ם בְּרִיתֽוֹ׃

6 כֹּ֣חַ מַ֭עֲשָׂיו הִגִּ֣יד לְעַמּ֑וֹ לָתֵ֥ת לָ֝הֶ֗ם נַחֲלַ֥ת גּוֹיִֽם׃

7 מַעֲשֵׂ֣י יָ֭דָיו אֱמֶ֣ת וּמִשְׁפָּ֑ט נֶ֝אֱמָנִ֗ים כָּל־פִּקּוּדָֽיו׃

8 סְמוּכִ֣ים לָעַ֣ד לְעוֹלָ֑ם עֲ֝שׂוּיִ֗ם בֶּאֱמֶ֥ת וְיָשָֽׁר׃

9 פְּד֤וּת ׀ שָׁ֘לַ֤ח לְעַמּ֗וֹ צִוָּֽה־לְעוֹלָ֥ם בְּרִית֑וֹ קָד֖וֹשׁ וְנוֹרָ֣א שְׁמֽוֹ׃

10 רֵ֘אשִׁ֤ית חָכְמָ֨ה ׀ יִרְאַ֬ת יְהוָ֗ה שֵׂ֣כֶל ט֭וֹב לְכָל־עֹשֵׂיהֶ֑ם תְּ֝הִלָּת֗וֹ עֹמֶ֥דֶת לָעַֽד׃

At first glance a simple hymn based on the Hebrew alphabet and filled with ideas familiar from other psalms, the 111th psalm concludes by presenting its readers with an unexpected challenge. The beginning of wisdom, the poet writes, is the fear of God. (This phrase will appear in slightly different words twice in the Book of Proverbs, but this is its only statement in the Book of Psalms and hence its first appearance in the canonical biblical text.) The poet puts forth this statement as though it were an obvious truth, but moderns will want to respond with their own questions. Must wisdom always grow out of the fear of God? And, for that matter, what exactly *is* wisdom? Is it the same as intelligence? Insight? Erudition? Knowledge? Acumen? And what, one might also ask, is the fear of God? Is it reverence? Respect? Fear? Terror? Is it the name we give to the deep sense of worry that will almost inevitably accompany the notion that God functions

111 Hallelujah.

I shall give thanks to יהוה with all my heart, both in the council of the just and in the wider congregation as well.

[2] The works of יהוה are great, sought after by all because of their desirability.

[3] Splendor and majesty characterize God's deeds; divine righteousness will stand for all time.

[4] God grants public recognition to divine wonders, for יהוה is compassionate and merciful, [5]giving food to those who fear God, perennially recalling the covenant.

[6] God has revealed the power of the Divine to the people so that they may have an inheritance among the nations.

[7] The works of God's hands are truth and fairness; all of God's laws are trustworthy, [8]permanently in effect, devised with truth and justice.

[9] God sends redemption to the people of God, bequeathing them an eternal covenant; holy and awesome is God's name.

[10] The beginning of wisdom is the fear of יהוה; it is the essence of intelligence to all who uphold the divine laws. The praise due God shall stand forever.

in the world as a supreme, cosmic Judge? Or is it merely the awe in which the pious hold even the idea, let alone the reality, of God functioning in their lives and in the world in the guise of absolute Sovereign? And another question suggests itself as well in the context of all these perplexing ideas: what does the poet's blithe tautology *really* signify? Is the human mind like an enormously sophisticated computer that, for all its theoretical power, still needs to be switched on, booted up, and made operative by an outside agent? And is the agent of wisdom, then, the deep respect in which God is held by the faithful? Can one be wise without God? The poet's answer is clear, but what will his readers' be?

קיב

הַֽלְלוּיָ֨הּ ׀
אַשְׁרֵי־אִ֭ישׁ יָרֵ֣א אֶת־יְהוָ֑ה בְּ֝מִצְוֺתָ֗יו חָפֵ֥ץ מְאֹֽד׃
2 גִּבּ֣וֹר בָּ֭אָרֶץ יִהְיֶ֣ה זַרְע֑וֹ דּ֖וֹר יְשָׁרִ֣ים יְבֹרָֽךְ׃
3 הוֹן־וָעֹ֥שֶׁר בְּבֵית֑וֹ וְ֝צִדְקָת֗וֹ עֹמֶ֥דֶת לָעַֽד׃
4 זָ֘רַ֤ח בַּחֹ֣שֶׁךְ א֭וֹר לַיְשָׁרִ֑ים חַנּ֖וּן וְרַח֣וּם וְצַדִּֽיק׃
5 ט֣וֹב אִ֭ישׁ חוֹנֵ֣ן וּמַלְוֶ֑ה יְכַלְכֵּ֖ל דְּבָרָ֣יו בְּמִשְׁפָּֽט׃
6 כִּֽי־לְעוֹלָ֥ם לֹ֣א יִמּ֑וֹט לְזֵ֥כֶר ע֝וֹלָ֗ם יִהְיֶ֥ה צַדִּֽיק׃
7 מִשְּׁמוּעָ֣ה רָ֭עָה לֹ֣א יִירָ֑א נָכ֥וֹן לִ֝בּ֗וֹ בָּטֻ֥חַ בַּיהוָֽה׃
8 סָמ֣וּךְ לִ֭בּוֹ לֹ֣א יִירָ֑א עַ֖ד אֲשֶׁר־יִרְאֶ֣ה בְצָרָֽיו׃
9 פִּזַּ֤ר ׀ נָ֘תַ֤ן לָֽאֶבְיוֹנִ֗ים צִ֭דְקָתוֹ עֹמֶ֣דֶת לָעַ֑ד קַ֝רְנ֗וֹ
תָּר֥וּם בְּכָבֽוֹד׃
10 רָשָׁ֤ע יִרְאֶ֨ה ׀ וְכָעָ֗ס שִׁנָּ֣יו יַחֲרֹ֣ק וְנָמָ֑ס תַּאֲוַ֖ת
רְשָׁעִ֣ים תֹּאבֵֽד׃

Many psalmists pondered the question of how to define human happiness, but when the author of the poem we know as the 112th psalm addressed himself to that issue, he came up with a composite response. Happiness, he concluded, exists—or may exist—in a human breast when an individual possesses both the fear of God and a willing readiness to worship with focused intensity, passion, and fervor. All the other blessings enumerated in the poem flow from this simple proposition, but even this simple exposition of how religious observance can lead to personal happiness will challenge modern readers to ask some interesting questions. If an individual fears God, for example, then would we not expect that person's ritual observance to be a function of awe and reverence rather than passion or desire? Conversely, if one's commitment to rite and ritual is based on the great pleasure one derives from worship, then would it not be natural for such an individual to relate to God as the cosmic source of well-being and delight,

112

Hallelujah.

Happy is the individual who fears יהוה, who desires God's commandments intensely.

[2] His progeny shall be heroes on earth, a generation of just people worthy of blessing.

[3] Wealth and fortune shall favor his home; his righteousness shall stand forever.

[4] Merciful, compassionate, and righteous, he shall function like a shining light in the darkness for the just; [5] he shall be known as a good person who lends funds kindly, who supports his own words with a sense of justice.

[6] Such a person shall never totter; he shall ever be known as righteous.

[7] He has no reason ever to fear slander; his heart, trusting in יהוה, is strong.

[8] Indeed, his heart is firm and he has no fear of being unable to stare down his enemies.

[9] He gives gifts to the poor; his righteousness stands forever, his horn ever held high in honor.

[10] The wicked see such a person and become enraged, grinding their teeth and shrinking away—for the desires of the wicked shall come to naught.

rather than as a force of awesome, fear-inspiring majesty? One could easily think so, yet the poet's point appears to be that precisely the opposite is true: happiness comes to most people from being so overwhelmed with awe of the Divine that they are moved to realize that the only true source of pleasure in life is the service of God.

הַֽלְלוּיָ֨הּ ׀
הַֽלְל֭וּ עַבְדֵ֣י יְהוָ֑ה הַֽ֝לְל֗וּ אֶת־שֵׁ֥ם יְהוָֽה׃
2 יְהִ֤י שֵׁ֣ם יְהוָ֣ה מְבֹרָ֑ךְ מֵ֝עַתָּ֗ה וְעַד־עוֹלָֽם׃
3 מִמִּזְרַח־שֶׁ֥מֶשׁ עַד־מְבוֹא֑וֹ מְ֝הֻלָּ֗ל שֵׁ֣ם יְהוָֽה׃
4 רָ֖ם עַל־כָּל־גּוֹיִ֥ם ׀ יְהוָ֑ה עַ֖ל הַשָּׁמַ֣יִם כְּבוֹדֽוֹ׃
5 מִ֭י כַּיהוָ֣ה אֱלֹהֵ֑ינוּ הַֽ֝מַּגְבִּיהִ֥י לָשָֽׁבֶת׃ 6 הַֽמַּשְׁפִּילִ֥י
לִרְא֑וֹת בַּשָּׁמַ֥יִם וּבָאָֽרֶץ׃ 7 מְקִימִ֣י מֵעָפָ֣ר דָּ֑ל
מֵ֝אַשְׁפֹּ֗ת יָרִ֥ים אֶבְיֽוֹן׃ 8 לְהוֹשִׁיבִ֥י עִם־נְדִיבִ֑ים עִ֝֗ם
נְדִיבֵ֥י עַמּֽוֹ׃ 9 מֽוֹשִׁיבִ֨י ׀ עֲקֶ֬רֶת הַבַּ֗יִת אֵֽם־הַבָּנִ֥ים
שְׂמֵחָ֗ה הַֽלְלוּיָֽהּ׃

The author of the 113th psalm begins his poem by commanding his audience to praise God, then answers their unheard question ("Why should we?") with reference to the paradox of God's existence in the world. God, the poet explains, exists at the end of innumerable axes of seemingly incompatible identities, but these paradoxes need not destroy faith. Indeed, the poet presents himself as a reasonable example of how they can be embraced as basic building blocks of belief. Although he is more than able to perceive God's role in the world as that of exalted Ruler present from one horizon to the other, for example, he also knows God in the guise of caring Friend, concerned Advisor, and devoted Confidant. Furthermore, although he accepts God as an omnipotent, cosmic Sovereign who rules existence, he also knows a God who stoops down from celestial heights to support a beggar faint from hunger as he trips and falls into a roadside ditch, who scruples to lend succor and support to a street person who falls into a trough of garbage while trying to retrieve some discarded table scraps, and who troubles to take time away from attending to a cosmic to-do list to grant children to a woman miserably childless, therefore deemed (in the poet's world) useless and superfluous. How, the poet prompts us to ask, can one deal with a God who functions simultaneously on such

113

Hallelujah.

Praise, O servants of יהוה, praise the name of יהוה.

[2] May the name of יהוה be blessed from now on and forever.

[3] From the place where the sun rises until the place where it sets, may the name of יהוה be praised.

[4] יהוה is exalted over all the nations; the glory of God is over the heavens.

[5] Who is like unto יהוה our God, who, while dwelling on high, [6] will yet stoop down low enough to see all that happens in the heavens and on earth, [7] who lifts up the poor person from the dust—indeed, who will even lift up an indigent from a pile of refuse—[8] and seats him among nobility, even among the nobles of his people, [9] who takes an infertile woman and makes her the happy mother of children? Hallelujah.

diverse levels—who rules the world yet hears the softest whisper of prayer, who governs all creation, yet who exists in a relationship of potential intimacy with every individual human being? His answer is simple: one simply asserts *both* aspects of God's being, declaring (and believing) both to be avenues of reasonable spiritual contemplation for people to travel down in the quest for personal redemption.

Do we find that answer practical and useful, or merely theoretically interesting? In either event, the 113th psalm can also prompt us to ask ourselves whether we find the concept that God exists on multiple levels of divine reality simultaneously stimulating or off-putting . . . and if we ever pause to feel grateful for the fact that the human heart is more than wide enough to accommodate the kind of faith that is not hemmed in by prior conceptions of how God *should* function in the world.

בְּצֵ֣את יִ֭שְׂרָאֵל מִמִּצְרָ֑יִם בֵּ֥ית יַ֝עֲקֹ֗ב מֵעַ֥ם לֹעֵֽז׃
2 הָיְתָ֣ה יְהוּדָ֣ה לְקָדְשׁ֑וֹ יִ֝שְׂרָאֵ֗ל מַמְשְׁלוֹתָֽיו׃
3 הַיָּ֣ם רָ֭אָה וַיָּנֹ֑ס הַ֝יַּרְדֵּ֗ן יִסֹּ֥ב לְאָחֽוֹר׃
4 הֶֽהָרִ֗ים רָקְד֥וּ כְאֵילִ֑ים גְּ֝בָע֗וֹת כִּבְנֵי־צֹֽאן׃
5 מַה־לְּךָ֣ הַ֭יָּם כִּ֣י תָנ֑וּס הַ֝יַּרְדֵּ֗ן תִּסֹּ֥ב לְאָחֽוֹר׃
6 הֶֽהָרִ֗ים תִּרְקְד֥וּ כְאֵילִ֑ים גְּ֝בָע֗וֹת כִּבְנֵי־צֹֽאן׃
7 מִלִּפְנֵ֣י אָ֭דוֹן ח֣וּלִי אָ֑רֶץ מִ֝לִּפְנֵ֗י אֱל֥וֹהַּ יַעֲקֹֽב׃
8 הַהֹפְכִ֣י הַצּ֣וּר אֲגַם־מָ֑יִם חַ֝לָּמִ֗ישׁ לְמַעְיְנוֹ־מָֽיִם׃

The author of the 126th psalm imagined that those who returned to Zion from exile in Babylon must have felt as though they were dreaming. The poet who wrote the 114th psalm addresses himself to a different journey to Zion, but his imagery is no less dreamlike—and considerably more fantastic—than his colleague's. He imagines the exodus of Israel from Egyptian bondage neither as a military maneuver nor as a helter-skelter race across the desert to freedom, but as a series of cosmic events. The liberation of Israel, after all, was not merely a geopolitical event in the normal sense of the term, but also, as Israel's giant step forward from clan to nation, the last hurdle necessary for the people to overcome before encountering God at Sinai. And the ever-sensitive earth responded in ways that suggested its own insight into the events taking place on its outer crust. Rivers flowed backwards. Mountains broke loose from their moorings and skipped about like rams frolicking in verdant meadows. The sea itself began to run in reverse, the breakers forming at the edge of the beach and rolling out to sea instead of the other, far more regular, way around. Perhaps more pertinently, the lands destined to become the Israelite homeland also underwent a change of status on that day: as the former slaves left Egypt,

114 When Israel left Egypt, when the House of Jacob left a foreign land, [2]Judah became God's sanctuary and Israel, God's dominion.

[3]The sea saw and fled; the Jordan turned backwards.

[4]The mountains danced like rams and the hills, like sheep.

[5]Why are you fleeing, O sea? Why are you turning back, O Jordan?

[6]Why are you dancing like rams, O mountains, and you hills, like sheep?

[7]Indeed, you do right to tremble, O earth, in the presence of your Ruler, in the presence of the God of Jacob, [8]who can turn a rocky crag into a lake of water or a flint into a fountain of water.

the entire Promised Land passed into the governance of the Jewish people and effectively became one immense sanctuary devoted to the worship and service of God.

The 114th psalm is a well-known hymn. Sung during the synagogue service on all holidays, chanted as part of the Passover *seder*, endowed (at least by Ashkenazic Jews) with a merry tune in four-four time that by its very meter evokes the image of a people on the march, this psalm may profitably be read as a challenge to reconsider the cosmic aspects of Jewish identity. Is Israel's covenant with God unique? Is it inviolate? Does it truly possess cosmic (as opposed to merely ethnic) importance? Is Israel chosen? Blessed? Special? Unique? Underlying all these questions, however, rests one so basic that it is rarely asked aloud: what precisely *is* God's role in the history of Israel?

קטו

לֹא לָנוּ יְהוָה לֹא לָנוּ כִּי לְשִׁמְךָ תֵּן כָּבוֹד עַל־חַסְדְּךָ עַל־אֲמִתֶּךָ׃
2 לָמָּה יֹאמְרוּ הַגּוֹיִם אַיֵּה־נָא אֱלֹהֵיהֶם׃ 3 וֵאלֹהֵינוּ בַשָּׁמָיִם כֹּל אֲשֶׁר־חָפֵץ עָשָׂה׃ 4 עֲצַבֵּיהֶם כֶּסֶף וְזָהָב מַעֲשֵׂה יְדֵי אָדָם׃ 5 פֶּה־לָהֶם וְלֹא יְדַבֵּרוּ עֵינַיִם לָהֶם וְלֹא יִרְאוּ׃ 6 אָזְנַיִם לָהֶם וְלֹא יִשְׁמָעוּ אַף לָהֶם וְלֹא יְרִיחוּן׃ 7 יְדֵיהֶם ׀ וְלֹא יְמִישׁוּן רַגְלֵיהֶם וְלֹא יְהַלֵּכוּ לֹא־יֶהְגּוּ בִּגְרוֹנָם׃
8 כְּמוֹהֶם יִהְיוּ עֹשֵׂיהֶם כֹּל אֲשֶׁר־בֹּטֵחַ בָּהֶם׃
9 יִשְׂרָאֵל בְּטַח בַּיהוָה עֶזְרָם וּמָגִנָּם הוּא׃

Readers familiar with the 115th psalm solely from its liturgical use as part of Hallel, the liturgy of festival praise, will be slightly surprised to encounter it in its biblical setting. Here, the first eleven and final seven verses are presented as the beginning and end of a single, unified hymn—rather than as separate literary units, as found in Hallel. Nonetheless—and the rousing beauty of the Hallel notwithstanding—the meaning of the poem only reveals itself when both its halves are read together as a single poetic work, which is undoubtedly how their author intended them to be read.

It's an us versus them kind of hymn. The poet begins with a scathing castigation of idolaters, and then presents Israel specifically as the nation that first had the sense to turn from idol worship and the absurdity of fetishism to worship God and bless the divine name directly.

This condemnation of the use of idols in worship is marred, however, by excess. Did the poet truly expect his readers to believe that the idolaters of his day were so naively foolish so as to imagine that the statues in their temples *themselves* were the gods who made the world? Modern observers of the religious scene know this is not the case in Catholic churches or Hindu temples. Surely, neither would it have been the case in the sanctuaries of antiquity, where educated pagans attempted to commune with the divine realm through the worshipful contemplation of plastic representations of their gods. Yet the poet's sarcasm is as scathing as his logic: because the statues in pagan temples can neither clear their throats nor walk nor see, all the worship conducted therein must, ipso facto, be utterly worthless.

But what if the poet is not *really* ascribing such unlikely gullibility to pagan worshipers after all? What if the poet's point is that the flaw in the faith of

115

Give honor not to us, יהוה, not to us—but to Your own name, because of Your mercy and Your truth.

[2] Why, after all, should the nations ask, "Wherever is their God?", [3]since even though our God dwells in heaven, the Almighty nevertheless does anything the divine will dictates; [4]indeed, it is their idols that are made of silver and gold, they are the work of human hands. [5]They have mouths, but cannot speak. They have eyes, but cannot see. [6]They have ears, but cannot hear. They have noses, but cannot smell. [7]They have hands, but cannot feel. They have feet, but cannot walk. They cannot even clear their throats.

[8] May those who make them—and all who trust in them—be just like them.

[9] Trust in יהוה, O Israel . . . for God is their help and their shield.

pagans is not that their statues are deaf and blind, but that the mythological aspects of God *represented* by those statues are not properly acknowledged within the cult as being mere metaphor and poetry? What if the poet's point is not that the *statues* are impotent, but that their *worshipers* are intellectually feeble? And that the superiority of Judaism over the ancient pagan cults rested in the Jewish willingness to acknowledge that, although language is not really any less artificial than any other medium of expression devised by human beings, refusing to attempt to define the nature of God within the limits of human language is just as wrongheaded as refusing to acknowledge the presence of the Almighty in the world—and that this is so even if one honestly feels incapable of ever saying anything at all accurate about God in any language at all.

In other words, the 115th psalm can best be read as an encomium to Jewish worship if we assume that the poet believed that Jewish people praise God and pray to God not because they can, but because they must. And his point is still deeply relevant for moderns hoping to worship with integrity. The poet's assertion is that the key, always, is to worship because one feels compelled to do so, because one considers oneself *commanded* by God to step out of reality long enough to attempt to address God with the only tools available to human

10 בֵּית אַהֲרֹן בִּטְחוּ בַיהוָה עֶזְרָם וּמָגִנָּם הוּא׃
11 יִרְאֵי יְהוָה בִּטְחוּ בַיהוָה עֶזְרָם וּמָגִנָּם הוּא׃
12 יְהוָה זְכָרָנוּ יְבָרֵךְ יְבָרֵךְ אֶת־בֵּית יִשְׂרָאֵל יְבָרֵךְ אֶת־בֵּית אַהֲרֹן׃ 13 יְבָרֵךְ יִרְאֵי יְהוָה הַקְּטַנִּים עִם־הַגְּדֹלִים׃
14 יֹסֵף יְהוָה עֲלֵיכֶם עֲלֵיכֶם וְעַל־בְּנֵיכֶם׃
15 בְּרוּכִים אַתֶּם לַיהוָה עֹשֵׂה שָׁמַיִם וָאָרֶץ׃
16 הַשָּׁמַיִם שָׁמַיִם לַיהוָה וְהָאָרֶץ נָתַן לִבְנֵי־אָדָם׃
17 לֹא־הַמֵּתִים יְהַלְלוּ־יָהּ וְלֹא כָּל־יֹרְדֵי דוּמָה׃
18 וַאֲנַחְנוּ ׀ נְבָרֵךְ יָהּ מֵעַתָּה וְעַד־עוֹלָם הַלְלוּ־יָהּ׃

worshipers—their breath, their intelligence, and the sounds they can make with their tongues and teeth. Worship should never come out of the conviction that one can actually ever say with precision that God is this thing or that, that God looks this way or that, or that God may be known as anything more substantial than the shadow of divinity that passes over the world from time to time when the ripples in the tide of being made by God's desire to be known bend the perimeters of reasonability for the briefest of

[10] Trust in יהוה, O House of Aaron . . . for God is their help and their shield.

[11] Trust in יהוה, O Fearers of יהוה . . . for God is their help and their shield.

[12] יהוה remembers us and shall bless us all: the House of Israel, the House of Aaron, [13]the Fearers of יהוה, both the young ones and the old.

[14] May יהוה grant that you increase, both you and your children.

[15] May you be blessed unto יהוה, Maker of heaven and earth, [16]for the heavens are the heavens of יהוה, but God gave the earth to humankind.

[17] And although neither the dead nor those who have gone down to Dumah can praise יה, [18]we, the living, shall indeed bless יה from now on and forever. Hallelujah.

moments. The sin in idol worship, then, is not rooted in the fact that the statues themselves are made of mud and plaster, but rather grows out of the belief that the gods those statues represent can grant knowledge of God to worshipers so mired in mythology so as to be totally devoid of any practical insight into the ineffable nature of the Divine.

A version of verses 4–11 of this psalm appears as verses 15–20 of Psalm 135.

קטז

1 אָהַבְתִּי כִּי־יִשְׁמַע | יְהוָה אֶת־קוֹלִי תַּחֲנוּנָי׃
2 כִּי־הִטָּה אָזְנוֹ לִי וּבְיָמַי אֶקְרָא׃
3 אֲפָפוּנִי | חֶבְלֵי־מָוֶת וּמְצָרֵי שְׁאוֹל מְצָאוּנִי צָרָה וְיָגוֹן אֶמְצָא׃ 4 וּבְשֵׁם־יְהוָה אֶקְרָא אָנָּה יְהוָה מַלְּטָה נַפְשִׁי׃
5 חַנּוּן יְהוָה וְצַדִּיק וֵאלֹהֵינוּ מְרַחֵם׃
6 שֹׁמֵר פְּתָאיִם יְהוָה דַּלּוֹתִי וְלִי יְהוֹשִׁיעַ׃
7 שׁוּבִי נַפְשִׁי לִמְנוּחָיְכִי כִּי יְהוָה גָּמַל עָלָיְכִי׃
8 כִּי חִלַּצְתָּ נַפְשִׁי מִמָּוֶת אֶת־עֵינִי מִן־דִּמְעָה אֶת־רַגְלִי מִדֶּחִי׃
9 אֶתְהַלֵּךְ לִפְנֵי יְהוָה בְּאַרְצוֹת הַחַיִּים׃ 10 הֶאֱמַנְתִּי כִּי אֲדַבֵּר אֲנִי עָנִיתִי מְאֹד׃
11 אֲנִי אָמַרְתִּי בְחָפְזִי כָּל־הָאָדָם כֹּזֵב׃
12 מָה־אָשִׁיב לַיהוָה כָּל־תַּגְמוּלוֹהִי עָלָי׃
13 כּוֹס־יְשׁוּעוֹת אֶשָּׂא וּבְשֵׁם יְהוָה אֶקְרָא׃ 14 נְדָרַי לַיהוָה אֲשַׁלֵּם נֶגְדָה־נָּא לְכָל־עַמּוֹ׃
15 יָקָר בְּעֵינֵי יְהוָה הַמָּוְתָה לַחֲסִידָיו׃
16 אָנָּה יְהוָה כִּי־אֲנִי עַבְדֶּךָ אֲנִי עַבְדְּךָ בֶּן־אֲמָתֶךָ פִּתַּחְתָּ לְמוֹסֵרָי׃ 17 לְךָ־אֶזְבַּח זֶבַח תּוֹדָה וּבְשֵׁם יְהוָה אֶקְרָא׃
18 נְדָרַי לַיהוָה אֲשַׁלֵּם נֶגְדָה־נָּא לְכָל־עַמּוֹ׃
19 בְּחַצְרוֹת | בֵּית יְהוָה בְּתוֹכֵכִי יְרוּשָׁלָם הַלְלוּיָהּ׃

The very first word of the 116th psalm, *ahavti* ("I love"), is tantalizingly ambiguous. Is the poet saying merely that he loves it when God listens to his prayers? The translation presented here reflects that interpretation, but could it also be that the poet is saying that he has some inkling of the nature and power of love when he cries out to God and believes that God hears him and enters into a kind of dialogue with him? Or is he perhaps saying that it is precisely *because* he believes wholeheartedly in the strength and power of love that God listens to him when he calls out and answers his prayers positively and faithfully?

Many people believe that we learn how to love God by first learning of love as it may exist between human lovers. But what if the reverse were the case?

116

I love when יהוה listens to my voice and hears my supplications, [2]for God has indeed inclined a divine ear to me whenever I have cried out.
[3] As the bands of death surrounded me, the straits of Sheol found me; I found naught but pain and agony. [4]And so in the name of יהוה I called out, "יהוה, I beg You, save my soul."
[5] יהוה is merciful and just; our God is the very essence of compassion.
[6] יהוה must take special care of fools, for although I was cast down low, God saved me nevertheless.
[7] Return to your restful state, O my soul, for יהוה has acted kindly towards you.
[8] And so indeed did You save my soul from death, my eye from tears, my foot from slipping.
[9] I walked about before יהוה in the land of the living; [10]I believed my own words as I spoke them, saying, "I am suffering greatly."
[11] I said in haste, "All people lie about God's ability to save the wretched."
[12] And now, what can I return unto יהוה in exchange for all that God has done for me?
[13] I shall lift the cup of salvation and call out in the name of יהוה; [14]I shall fulfill all my vows to יהוה in the presence of the people of God.
[15] Precious in the eyes of יהוה is the "death" of pious worshipers.
[16] יהוה, I am Your slave, the son of Your maidservant. You loosed my bonds, [17]and so I shall offer up a thanksgiving sacrifice to You and continue to call out in the name of יהוה.
[18] I shall fulfill all my vows to יהוה in the presence of the people of God, [19]in the courtyards of the House of יהוה, in the very center of Jerusalem. Hallelujah.

What if the ability to love another on earth ultimately were a function of the ability to love God and to know of love *from* God? What if the capacity to love were to stem from a willingness to accept that surrendering to God *and* embracing faith in God *and* serving God *and* giving oneself over totally to the worship of God are, in the end, all aspects of the same thing . . . and that this thing is the love the poet had in mind when he wrote the first line of the 116th psalm?

קיז

הַלְלוּ אֶת־יְהוָה כָּל־גּוֹיִם שַׁבְּחוּהוּ כָּל־הָאֻמִּים׃
[2] כִּי גָבַר עָלֵינוּ ׀ חַסְדּוֹ וֶאֱמֶת־יְהוָה לְעוֹלָם
הַלְלוּיָהּ׃

Is this little hymn a psalm unto itself or just a fragment of some longer poem no longer known to us? Or, perhaps, was it originally the closing strophes of the poem that precedes it in the Psalter or a kind of introduction to the next psalm, whose opening strophes resume its central idea? Any of these possibilities could be the case, but, at least according to Jewish tradition, the 117th psalm—however short—is its own poem and, as such, a psalm to be read and contemplated on its own. And, indeed, its shortness can be seen not as a defect, but as a riddle for moderns to try to unravel as they seek God in the narrow space between its two lines.

The poet begins with a forceful idea: the nations of the world, and not Israel alone, ought to sing the praises of God. Are not the other nations also populated by people created in the image of God? Did not God create the world they inhabit and the air that they breathe, the fish they catch in their rivers, and the antelope they hunt on their plains? The nations, therefore, have every reason to praise God, to sing hymns of homage and acclamation to the Creator who made them and their countries as well. The poet does not, however, develop any of the above ideas. Instead, he opts for a far more challenging one: the nations of the world should praise God because of the divine mercy shown to Israel: "Adore God, all peoples . . . for the mercy of God has overwhelmed *us*."

In other words, Israel exists in a relationship of intimacy and closeness to

117 Praise יהוה, all nations.
Adore God, all peoples.
[2] For the mercy of God has overwhelmed us and
the truth of יהוה is forever. Hallelujah.

God that logically ought to be impossible on any level. God is beyond the ken of even the wisest sage and beyond the understanding of even the most insightful of observer-poets. God, therefore, ought to be as totally unknown as divine reality is unknowable. But God is *not* unknown to Israel. Indeed, the Jewish people exists in a covenantal relationship with the Almighty that, for all its unlikelihood, transcends the inherent frailty of the human intellect and allows its human partners insight into God's nature. And for that reason alone, the poet suggests delicately, the nations of the world should be prepared to sing hymns of praise: were it not for Israel, God would either be totally unknown or else relegated to the sidelines of philosophical inquiry and absent from the daily lives of real people.

Both those who recite the 117th psalm as part of worship and those who choose it as a text for quiet contemplation need to ask themselves whether any of the above seems cogent to them. The languages of the world are merely different codes for describing the same things and can have, therefore, no relationship of superiority or inferiority to each other. Are the religions of the world in the same category? Or is Judaism different not only in terms of detail, but even in terms of its very essence, from the other faiths of the world? These are thorny, difficult questions for moderns schooled in the democratic ideal and by nature tolerant and respectful of others. We all know the party line, but what do we really think?

הוֹדוּ לַיהוָה כִּי־טוֹב כִּי לְעוֹלָם חַסְדּוֹ׃
2 יֹאמַר־נָא יִשְׂרָאֵל כִּי לְעוֹלָם חַסְדּוֹ׃
3 יֹאמְרוּ נָא בֵית־אַהֲרֹן כִּי לְעוֹלָם חַסְדּוֹ׃
4 יֹאמְרוּ נָא יִרְאֵי יְהוָה כִּי לְעוֹלָם חַסְדּוֹ׃
5 מִן־הַמֵּצַר קָרָאתִי יָּהּ עָנָנִי בַמֶּרְחָב יָהּ׃
6 יְהוָה לִי לֹא אִירָא מַה־יַּעֲשֶׂה לִי אָדָם׃
7 יְהוָה לִי בְּעֹזְרָי וַאֲנִי אֶרְאֶה בְשֹׂנְאָי׃
8 טוֹב לַחֲסוֹת בַּיהוָה מִבְּטֹחַ בָּאָדָם׃ 9 טוֹב לַחֲסוֹת
בַּיהוָה מִבְּטֹחַ בִּנְדִיבִים׃
10 כָּל־גּוֹיִם סְבָבוּנִי בְּשֵׁם יְהוָה כִּי אֲמִילַם׃
11 סַבּוּנִי גַם־סְבָבוּנִי בְּשֵׁם יְהוָה כִּי אֲמִילַם׃
12 סַבּוּנִי כִדְבוֹרִים דֹּעֲכוּ כְּאֵשׁ קוֹצִים בְּשֵׁם יְהוָה כִּי
אֲמִילַם׃
13 דַּחֹה דְחִיתַנִי לִנְפֹּל וַיהוָה עֲזָרָנִי׃ 14 עָזִּי וְזִמְרָת יָהּ
וַיְהִי־לִי לִישׁוּעָה׃
15 קוֹל ׀ רִנָּה וִישׁוּעָה בְּאָהֳלֵי צַדִּיקִים יְמִין יְהוָה
עֹשָׂה חָיִל׃
16 יְמִין יְהוָה רוֹמֵמָה יְמִין יְהוָה עֹשָׂה חָיִל׃

Jacob, upon awakening from a dream vision in which he saw God standing atop some sort of impossibly tall ziggurat in the presence of attending angels, declared the homely patch of ground on which he had lay down to sleep to be *sha'ar hashamayim,* the gateway of heaven. The poet whose hymn became our 118th psalm also found a gateway to God in his life, first declaring such a thing actually to exist and then noting that the righteous—those who pursue lives in God and of God—may pass through it as a means of coming closer to redemption in God. It is one thing, however, to note that there is a portal through which representatives of terrestrial humanity may step towards the reality of God's presence, and that, more than a door, this portal is a kind of path down which the faithful may travel to the empirically verifiable, sensually perceptible, intellectually unimpeachable experience of God's nearness *and* of God's willingness to communicate *and* of God's existence in the guise of Lover and Friend (as well as Sovereign, Parent, and Master). It is, however, quite another thing to say where precisely that sacred gateway might actually be located.

The poet writes that he has suffered mightily. His enemies have swarmed

118 Give thanks unto יהוה for God is good, for divine mercy is forever.

[2] May Israel say, " . . . for divine mercy is forever."

[3] May the House of Aaron say, ". . . for divine mercy is forever."

[4] May the Fearers of יהוה say, ". . . for divine mercy is forever."

[5] From dire straits I called out to יה, who answered me with the generosity of יה.

[6] As faith in יהוה is mine, I have no fear; what can a mere mortal do to me?

[7] If יהוה is among my helpers, I can stare down my enemies.

[8] It is better to trust in יהוה than to trust in human beings; [9] it is even better to trust in יהוה than to trust in noblemen.

[10] Alien nations of all sorts surround me, but I shall cut them down to size in the name of יהוה.

[11] They swarm about me, surrounding me completely, but I shall cut them down to size in the name of יהוה.

[12] They swarm around me like bees, spreading like fire through dried-out thorns, but I shall cut them down to size in the name of יהוה.

[13] You shoved me hard that I might fall, but יהוה helped me; [14] יה is my strength and my song and will always be the source of my salvation.

[15] The sound of joy and salvation is always heard in the tents of the righteous, for the right hand of יהוה is mighty.

[16] Indeed, the right hand of יהוה is exalted; the right hand of יהוה is mighty.

around him like angry bees and he has had the horrifying experience of feeling the world narrowing around him and leaving him in straits so dire that his only hope for safety lay in faith in God. Living through all that must have been horrific, but it was ultimately all for good: the experience of finding safety and security in God was so intense—and so palpably real and meaningful—to the poet that his life changed. He did not die, he writes, but lived . . . and now he will—he *must*—spend the remaining days of his life singing of God's saving power. More to the

17 לֹא אָמוּת כִּי־אֶחְיֶה וַאֲסַפֵּר מַעֲשֵׂי יָהּ׃ 18 יַסֹּר יִסְּרַנִּי יָּהּ וְלַמָּוֶת לֹא נְתָנָנִי׃
19 פִּתְחוּ־לִי שַׁעֲרֵי־צֶדֶק אָבֹא־בָם אוֹדֶה יָהּ׃
20 זֶה־הַשַּׁעַר לַיהוָה צַדִּיקִים יָבֹאוּ בוֹ׃
21 אוֹדְךָ כִּי עֲנִיתָנִי וַתְּהִי־לִי לִישׁוּעָה׃
22 אֶבֶן מָאֲסוּ הַבּוֹנִים הָיְתָה לְרֹאשׁ פִּנָּה׃ 23 מֵאֵת יְהוָה הָיְתָה זֹּאת הִיא נִפְלָאת בְּעֵינֵינוּ׃
24 זֶה־הַיּוֹם עָשָׂה יְהוָה נָגִילָה וְנִשְׂמְחָה בוֹ׃
25 אָנָּא יְהוָה הוֹשִׁיעָה נָּא אָנָּא יְהוָה הַצְלִיחָה נָּא׃
26 בָּרוּךְ הַבָּא בְּשֵׁם יְהוָה בֵּרַכְנוּכֶם מִבֵּית יְהוָה׃
27 אֵל ׀ יְהוָה וַיָּאֶר לָנוּ אִסְרוּ־חַג בַּעֲבֹתִים עַד קַרְנוֹת הַמִּזְבֵּחַ׃
28 אֵלִי אַתָּה וְאוֹדֶךָּ אֱלֹהַי אֲרוֹמְמֶךָּ׃
29 הוֹדוּ לַיהוָה כִּי־טוֹב כִּי לְעוֹלָם חַסְדּוֹ׃

point, it is exactly here that the poet locates his personal *sha'ar shamayim:* the experience of knowing God—and salvation *in* God—in the context of his personal life itself was the portal through which the poet stepped, the experience that ushered him into the divine presence more potently than anything else he had ever previously known. And so he now gives thanks to God for showing him the gateway only the pious may enter and through which he himself has also now also entered. The poet is now among those happy few who know God not as theory, but as fact, and his poem, therefore, is a song of intense joy, immense satisfaction, and unrestrained happiness.

The question the poet's ode to the joy of personal redemption challenges us to ask, then, is this: can moderns accept that, as much as the succor of a religious community may be essential for the maintenance of spiritual optimism and enthusiasm, the gateway to God will always be a private, personal one through which every seeker will have to pass as an individual?

[17] I shall not die, but live to tell the works of יה; [18]although יה afflicted me with grievous suffering, God did not put me to death.

[19] Open the gates of righteousness for me, that I might pass through them and give thanks to יה.

[20] This is the gateway to יהוה; the righteous alone may pass through it.

[21] I am thankful when You answer me, thus becoming the source of my salvation.

[22] The stone the builders despised has ended up serving as the cornerstone; [23]wondrous in our eyes, this can only have come from יהוה.

[24] This is truly the day יהוה has wrought, let us rejoice and be glad on it.

[25] We beseech You, יהוה, save us. We beseech You, יהוה, grant us success.

[26] Blessed be those who come in the name of יהוה; we bless you from the House of יהוה.

[27] יהוה is God and shall grant us light; loose the festival offering from its bonds and bring it up to the horns of the altar.

[28] You are my God and I give thanks to You, my God whom I exalt.

[29] Give thanks unto יהוה for God is good, for divine mercy is forever.

אַשְׁרֵי תְמִימֵי־דָרֶךְ הַהֹלְכִים בְּתוֹרַת יְהוָה׃ [2] אַשְׁרֵי
נֹצְרֵי עֵדֹתָיו בְּכָל־לֵב יִדְרְשׁוּהוּ׃ [3] אַף לֹא־פָעֲלוּ
עַוְלָה בִּדְרָכָיו הָלָכוּ׃ [4] אַתָּה צִוִּיתָה פִקֻּדֶיךָ
לִשְׁמֹר מְאֹד׃ [5] אַחֲלַי יִכֹּנוּ דְרָכָי לִשְׁמֹר חֻקֶּיךָ׃
[6] אָז לֹא־אֵבוֹשׁ בְּהַבִּיטִי אֶל־כָּל־מִצְוֹתֶיךָ׃ [7] אוֹדְךָ
בְּיֹשֶׁר לֵבָב בְּלָמְדִי מִשְׁפְּטֵי צִדְקֶךָ׃ [8] אֶת־חֻקֶּיךָ
אֶשְׁמֹר אַל־תַּעַזְבֵנִי עַד־מְאֹד׃

[9] בַּמֶּה יְזַכֶּה־נַּעַר אֶת־אָרְחוֹ לִשְׁמֹר כִּדְבָרֶךָ׃
[10] בְּכָל־לִבִּי דְרַשְׁתִּיךָ אַל־תַּשְׁגֵּנִי מִמִּצְוֹתֶיךָ׃
[11] בְּלִבִּי צָפַנְתִּי אִמְרָתֶךָ לְמַעַן לֹא אֶחֱטָא־לָךְ׃
[12] בָּרוּךְ אַתָּה יְהוָה לַמְּדֵנִי חֻקֶּיךָ׃ [13] בִּשְׂפָתַי
סִפַּרְתִּי כֹּל מִשְׁפְּטֵי־פִיךָ׃ [14] בְּדֶרֶךְ עֵדְוֹתֶיךָ שַׂשְׂתִּי
כְּעַל כָּל־הוֹן׃ [15] בְּפִקֻּדֶיךָ אָשִׂיחָה וְאַבִּיטָה
אֹרְחֹתֶיךָ׃ [16] בְּחֻקֹּתֶיךָ אֶשְׁתַּעֲשָׁע לֹא אֶשְׁכַּח
דְּבָרֶךָ׃

[17] גְּמֹל עַל־עַבְדְּךָ אֶחְיֶה וְאֶשְׁמְרָה דְבָרֶךָ׃ [18] גַּל־עֵינַי
וְאַבִּיטָה נִפְלָאוֹת מִתּוֹרָתֶךָ׃ [19] גֵּר אָנֹכִי בָאָרֶץ
אַל־תַּסְתֵּר מִמֶּנִּי מִצְוֹתֶיךָ׃ [20] גָּרְסָה נַפְשִׁי לְתַאֲבָה
אֶל־מִשְׁפָּטֶיךָ בְכָל־עֵת׃ [21] גָּעַרְתָּ זֵדִים אֲרוּרִים
הַשֹּׁגִים מִמִּצְוֹתֶיךָ׃ [22] גַּל מֵעָלַי חֶרְפָּה וָבוּז כִּי

Cast as a series of twenty-two sets of eight verses, each of which begins with the same letter of the Hebrew alphabet, this octuple acrostic has eighty-eight times as many verses as the shortest psalm and more than twice as many as the next longest psalm, and is thus by far the longest poem in the Psalter. Most of the poems of the Psalter actually are fairly short. Indeed, other than the 119th, only three have more than fifty verses and a full seventy of the psalms have a dozen or fewer verses. But it is not only a matter of length that sets the 119th psalm apart from the other chapters of *Tehillim;* there is the question of content to consider as well.

As even a cursory reading of the poem will reveal, the poet has law on his mind. Indeed, he seems to be intensely focused on the notion that God may be known through the medium of commandment and divine precept. For moderns familiar with the basics of Jewish life, this idea—that one can seek God through fidelity to ritual and ethical laws deemed to encapsulate divinely revealed, eternal principles—will seem commonplace, perhaps almost even banal. But within the context of the Psalter, this approach to communion with the Divine is, to say the very least, anomalous.

Perhaps the best way to make the point clearly would be to consider the matter from a lexicographical point of view. The poet uses five Hebrew words

119

Happy are they whose path is without guile, who walk in the way of the teaching of יהוה. [2]Happy are they who keep God's testimonies, who seek God with all their heart—[3]surely they commit no base acts as they walk in God's ways. [4]You commanded us to observe Your precepts diligently. [5]I pray that I remain firm in keeping Your laws, [6]for then I shall not be ashamed when I contemplate Your commandments. [7]As I learn Your righteous ordinances, I give thanks to You in all honesty. [8]I shall keep Your laws faithfully; do not abandon me.

[9] How shall a young man keep pure his path, if not by acting according to Your word? [10]With all my heart, I have sought You out; help me not to stray from Your commandments. [11]In my heart, I have hidden away Your word so that I not sin against You. [12]Blessed are You, O יהוה; teach me Your laws. [13]With my lips, I have spoken all the laws of Your mouth. [14]I have rejoiced in the way of Your testimonies as though I were possessed of all the wealth in the world. [15]I shall speak of Your ordinances; I shall look to Your paths. [16]I shall take pleasure in Your statutes; I shall never forget Your word.

[17] If You deal kindly with Your servant, I shall live and keep Your word. [18]If You open my eyes and I look out, I shall seize wonders of Your teaching. [19]For although I am a stranger in the land, do not hide Your commandments from me. [20]Since my own soul is consumed with longing for Your laws at all times, [21]You shall instead rebuke the accursed wicked who stray from Your commandments. [22]Remove from me shame and embarrassment, for I have kept Your testimonies.

to denote the laws and precepts with which he is so deeply involved: *mitzvot, pikkudim, ḥukkim, edot,* and *mishpatim.* The word *pikkudim* (when used to denote a set of laws) is more or less unique to this context: the word appears with that meaning twenty-one times in the 119th psalm and only three times elsewhere in the entire Book of Psalms. The word *edot* is similar in terms of its lexicographical scope: it appears with the meaning of "laws" only thirty-seven times in Scripture, all but ten of them in the Psalms. Yet, of those twenty-seven instances, only five are *not* in the 119th psalm. The word *ḥukkim* is a word

עֵדֹתֶיךָ נָצָרְתִּי׃ 23 גַּם יָשְׁבוּ שָׂרִים בִּי נִדְבָּרוּ עַבְדְּךָ
יָשִׂיחַ בְּחֻקֶּיךָ׃ 24 גַּם־עֵדֹתֶיךָ שַׁעֲשֻׁעָי אַנְשֵׁי עֲצָתִי׃
25 דָּבְקָה לֶעָפָר נַפְשִׁי חַיֵּנִי כִּדְבָרֶךָ׃ 26 דְּרָכַי סִפַּרְתִּי
וַתַּעֲנֵנִי לַמְּדֵנִי חֻקֶּיךָ׃ 27 דֶּרֶךְ־פִּקּוּדֶיךָ הֲבִינֵנִי
וְאָשִׂיחָה בְּנִפְלְאוֹתֶיךָ׃ 28 דָּלְפָה נַפְשִׁי מִתּוּגָה
קַיְּמֵנִי כִּדְבָרֶךָ׃ 29 דֶּרֶךְ שֶׁקֶר הָסֵר מִמֶּנִּי וְתוֹרָתְךָ
חָנֵּנִי׃ 30 דֶּרֶךְ־אֱמוּנָה בָחָרְתִּי מִשְׁפָּטֶיךָ שִׁוִּיתִי׃
31 דָּבַקְתִּי בְעֵדְוֺתֶיךָ יְהוָה אַל־תְּבִישֵׁנִי׃ 32 דֶּרֶךְ־
מִצְוֺתֶיךָ אָרוּץ כִּי תַרְחִיב לִבִּי׃

33 הוֹרֵנִי יְהוָה דֶּרֶךְ חֻקֶּיךָ וְאֶצְּרֶנָּה עֵקֶב׃ 34 הֲבִינֵנִי
וְאֶצְּרָה תוֹרָתֶךָ וְאֶשְׁמְרֶנָּה בְכָל־לֵב׃ 35 הַדְרִיכֵנִי
בִּנְתִיב מִצְוֺתֶיךָ כִּי בוֹ חָפָצְתִּי׃ 36 הַט־לִבִּי אֶל־
עֵדְוֺתֶיךָ וְאַל אֶל־בָּצַע׃ 37 הַעֲבֵר עֵינַי מֵרְאוֹת
שָׁוְא בִּדְרָכֶךָ חַיֵּנִי׃ 38 הָקֵם לְעַבְדְּךָ אִמְרָתֶךָ אֲשֶׁר
לְיִרְאָתֶךָ׃ 39 הַעֲבֵר חֶרְפָּתִי אֲשֶׁר יָגֹרְתִּי כִּי
מִשְׁפָּטֶיךָ טוֹבִים׃ 40 הִנֵּה תָּאַבְתִּי לְפִקֻּדֶיךָ
בְּצִדְקָתְךָ חַיֵּנִי׃

41 וִיבֹאֻנִי חֲסָדֶךָ יְהוָה תְּשׁוּעָתְךָ כְּאִמְרָתֶךָ׃
42 וְאֶעֱנֶה חֹרְפִי דָבָר כִּי־בָטַחְתִּי בִּדְבָרֶךָ׃

more regularly used in biblical Hebrew to denote laws of various kinds. It appears eighty times in the Bible, but only three times in the Psalms outside of the 119th psalm. Yet within the twenty-two stanzas of our poem, the word appears a full twenty-one times: clearly, our poet has *hukkim* on his mind in a way that the other psalmists did not.

The evidence relating to the other terms is similar in nature. The well-known word *mitzvot,* denoting the commandments of God, appears, for example, 117 times in the Bible, but only three times in the Book of Psalms outside of the 119th psalm. Yet within the 119th, the word appears a full twenty-one times, clearly suggesting that the whole concept of divine commandments was occupying our poet in a way that it failed to engage his colleagues in the psalmists' guild. The fifth term, *mishpatim,* functions just as the others: a fairly common word, it appears over 120 times in the various books of Scripture, but not even three dozen times in the Psalms. Yet, of these instances, over half appear in the 119th psalm. Even the word *torah* itself, used in classical Hebrew to denote a set of divine teachings presented, usually, as laws and statutes, fits the mold: the word (in both its singular and plural forms) appears well over two hundred times in Scripture, but of the three dozen instances within the Psalter, more than twice as many appear in the 119th psalm as appear in the

[23]Even though princes sit and speak against me, Your servant speaks only of Your laws. [24]Thus Your testimonies are my delights, my sources of wise counsel.

[25] My soul cleaves unto the dust; grant me life according to Your promise. [26]I have told of my ways and You have answered me: teach me, therefore, Your laws. [27]Make the way of Your ordinances comprehensible to me and I will speak of Your wonders. [28]My soul is ebbing under the burden of sadness; raise me up according to Your promise. [29]Remove the way of deceit from me; graciously make known to me Your teaching. [30]I have chosen the way of faith, I have contemplated Your laws. [31]I cleave unto Your testimonies; יהוה, do not put me to shame. [32]I run towards Your commandments, for You make wide my heart.

[33] Teach me, יהוה, the way of Your laws that I might follow them every step of the way. [34]Grant me understanding that I might keep Your teaching, that I might observe Your laws with all my heart. [35]Guide me along the path of Your commandments, for that is the path I desire. [36]Incline my heart to Your testimonies and not towards financial gain. [37]Turn my eyes away from gazing at vain things; grant me life in Your ways. [38]Fulfill Your promise to Your servant, who holds You in total awe. [39]Remove from me the shame that I fear, for Your judgments are good. [40]Behold: my longing is for Your ordinances; in Your righteousness, grant me life.

[41] May Your mercies come to me, יהוה. May Your salvation come according to Your promise [42]so that I might have a word with which to answer my tormentor, for I have trusted in Your word.

149 other poems combined.

All these numbers may appear a bit mysterious to readers inexperienced with this kind of vocabulary-based analysis, but the main point is this: the poet who wrote the 119th psalm was dramatically more involved with the notion of knowing God through the medium of law and commandment than were the other psalmists.

Readers will naturally wonder what historical circumstances might have prompted this preoccupation with law and legality. The precise situation that gave birth to the 119th psalm cannot be known, of course, but we can nonetheless make an educated guess

43 וְאַל־תַּצֵּל מִפִּי דְבַר־אֱמֶת עַד־מְאֹד כִּי
לְמִשְׁפָּטֶךָ יִחָלְתִּי׃ 44 וְאֶשְׁמְרָה תוֹרָתְךָ תָמִיד
לְעוֹלָם וָעֶד׃ 45 וְאֶתְהַלְּכָה בָרְחָבָה כִּי פִקֻּדֶיךָ
דָרָשְׁתִּי׃ 46 וַאֲדַבְּרָה בְעֵדֹתֶיךָ נֶגֶד מְלָכִים וְלֹא
אֵבוֹשׁ׃ 47 וְאֶשְׁתַּעֲשַׁע בְּמִצְוֺתֶיךָ אֲשֶׁר אָהָבְתִּי׃
48 וְאֶשָּׂא כַפַּי אֶל־מִצְוֺתֶיךָ אֲשֶׁר אָהָבְתִּי וְאָשִׂיחָה
בְחֻקֶּיךָ׃

49 זְכָר־דָּבָר לְעַבְדֶּךָ עַל אֲשֶׁר יִחַלְתָּנִי׃ 50 זֹאת
נֶחָמָתִי בְעָנְיִי כִּי אִמְרָתְךָ חִיָּתְנִי׃ 51 זֵדִים הֱלִיצֻנִי
עַד־מְאֹד מִתּוֹרָתְךָ לֹא נָטִיתִי׃ 52 זָכַרְתִּי מִשְׁפָּטֶיךָ
מֵעוֹלָם ׀ יְהֹוָה וָאֶתְנֶחָם׃ 53 זַלְעָפָה אֲחָזַתְנִי
מֵרְשָׁעִים עֹזְבֵי תּוֹרָתֶךָ׃ 54 זְמִרוֹת הָיוּ־לִי חֻקֶּיךָ
בְּבֵית מְגוּרָי׃ 55 זָכַרְתִּי בַלַּיְלָה שִׁמְךָ יְהֹוָה
וָאֶשְׁמְרָה תּוֹרָתֶךָ׃ 56 זֹאת הָיְתָה־לִּי כִּי פִקֻּדֶיךָ
נָצָרְתִּי׃

57 חֶלְקִי יְהֹוָה אָמַרְתִּי לִשְׁמֹר דְּבָרֶיךָ׃ 58 חִלִּיתִי
פָנֶיךָ בְכָל־לֵב חָנֵּנִי כְּאִמְרָתֶךָ׃ 59 חִשַּׁבְתִּי דְרָכָי
וָאָשִׁיבָה רַגְלַי אֶל־עֵדֹתֶיךָ׃ 60 חַשְׁתִּי וְלֹא
הִתְמַהְמָהְתִּי לִשְׁמֹר מִצְוֺתֶיךָ׃ 61 חֶבְלֵי רְשָׁעִים
עִוְּדֻנִי תּוֹרָתְךָ לֹא שָׁכָחְתִּי׃ 62 חֲצוֹת־לַיְלָה אָקוּם
לְהוֹדוֹת לָךְ עַל מִשְׁפְּטֵי צִדְקֶךָ׃ 63 חָבֵר אָנִי

what the issues may have been to which the poet was responding with his poem. As far as we can tell from the literary evidence left behind, there were two schools of thought to which different groups in society adhered throughout the entire biblical period. On the one hand was the position that the ideal medium for encountering and knowing God is obedience to law. This position was exemplified by the theology of the Torah itself, in which the possibility of surviving visual contact with God is mostly denied, and the possibility of auditory contact is limited to bona fide prophets chosen specifically by God to bear the divine word into the world. For the rest of the populace, however, the ideal way to know God is to follow the commandments, to adhere faithfully to the statutes and laws, and to seek the reality of God's presence in the experience of self-subjugation to even the most picayune detail of divine legislation.

However, although this became the dominant view (and eventually evolved into the cornerstone of rabbinic Judaism), it was not the only approach to spiritual endeavor in Jewish antiquity. The psalms themselves, taken as a whole, suggest the feel of the alternate approach. According to its theology,

[43]Banish not the truth from my mouth in any way, for I have yearned for Your laws. [44]I shall keep Your teaching for ever and always; [45]indeed, I shall walk about in ease for I have sought out Your ordinances. [46]I shall speak of Your testimonies before kings without shame. [47]I shall delight in Your commandments, which I love. [48]I shall lift up my hands to do Your commandments, which I love, and I shall speak openly about Your statutes.

[49] Remember the word spoken to Your servant, that word by means of which You have given me such hope. [50]It is my comfort in times of suffering, for Your remark has given me life. [51]Though the arrogant mock me ceaselessly, I have not turned away from Your teaching. [52]I have recalled Your laws always, O יהוה, and found comfort in doing so. [53]I have been seized by fury on account of wicked people who have abandoned Your teaching. [54]But as for me, Your statutes have become as familiar to me as the songs I sing at home. [55]I recall Your name at night, יהוה, and I keep steadfast to Your teaching. [56]This all has been mine because I have observed Your precepts.

[57] יהוה is my portion; I promise to observe Your words. [58]As I entreat Your face with all my heart, be gracious to me in accordance with Your promise. [59]I considered my ways, then turned my feet back to Your testimonies. [60]I hurried without tarrying to keep Your commandments. [61]The bonds of the wicked bound me, but I nonetheless did not forget Your teaching. [62]Indeed, I rise at midnight to give thanks to You for Your just laws. [63]I am a friend to all those who fear You

God's voice *can* be heard by ordinary people possessed of the spiritual bearing to call successfully on God to speak to them. In other contexts, the light of God's face *can* be experienced by those willing to create a context for it to shine forth onto them. More to the point, the sensory, physically real experience of God's presence was identified as the great goal of human spirituality . . . and as something totally available to those who call on God in truth, candor, and absolute spiritual integrity.

The author of the 119th psalm appears to have believed that a synthesis was possible between these two (only

לְכׇל־אֲשֶׁר יְרֵאוּךָ וּלְשֹׁמְרֵי פִּקּוּדֶיךָ׃ 64 חַסְדְּךָ
יְהֹוָה מָלְאָה הָאָרֶץ חֻקֶּיךָ לַמְּדֵנִי׃
65 טוֹב עָשִׂיתָ עִם־עַבְדְּךָ יְהֹוָה כִּדְבָרֶךָ׃ 66 טוּב טַעַם
וָדַעַת לַמְּדֵנִי כִּי בְמִצְוֺתֶיךָ הֶאֱמָנְתִּי׃ 67 טֶרֶם
אֶעֱנֶה אֲנִי שֹׁגֵג וְעַתָּה אִמְרָתְךָ שָׁמָרְתִּי׃
68 טוֹב־אַתָּה וּמֵטִיב לַמְּדֵנִי חֻקֶּיךָ׃ 69 טָפְלוּ עָלַי
שֶׁקֶר זֵדִים אֲנִי בְּכׇל־לֵב ׀ אֶצֹּר פִּקּוּדֶיךָ׃ 70 טָפַשׁ
כַּחֵלֶב לִבָּם אֲנִי תּוֹרָתְךָ שִׁעֲשָׁעְתִּי׃ 71 טוֹב־לִי
כִי־עֻנֵּיתִי לְמַעַן אֶלְמַד חֻקֶּיךָ׃ 72 טוֹב־לִי תוֹרַת
פִּיךָ מֵאַלְפֵי זָהָב וָכָסֶף׃
73 יָדֶיךָ עָשׂוּנִי וַיְכוֹנְנוּנִי הֲבִינֵנִי וְאֶלְמְדָה מִצְוֺתֶיךָ׃
74 יְרֵאֶיךָ יִרְאוּנִי וְיִשְׂמָחוּ כִּי לִדְבָרְךָ יִחָלְתִּי׃
75 יָדַעְתִּי יְהֹוָה כִּי־צֶדֶק מִשְׁפָּטֶיךָ וֶאֱמוּנָה עִנִּיתָנִי׃
76 יְהִי־נָא חַסְדְּךָ לְנַחֲמֵנִי כְּאִמְרָתְךָ לְעַבְדֶּךָ׃
77 יְבֹאוּנִי רַחֲמֶיךָ וְאֶחְיֶה כִּי תוֹרָתְךָ שַׁעֲשֻׁעָי׃
78 יֵבֹשׁוּ זֵדִים כִּי־שֶׁקֶר עִוְּתוּנִי אֲנִי אָשִׂיחַ
בְּפִקּוּדֶיךָ׃ 79 יָשׁוּבוּ־לִי יְרֵאֶיךָ *וְיֹדְעֵי עֵדֹתֶיךָ׃
80 יְהִי־לִבִּי תָמִים בְּחֻקֶּיךָ לְמַעַן לֹא אֵבוֹשׁ׃
81 כָּלְתָה לִתְשׁוּעָתְךָ נַפְשִׁי לִדְבָרְךָ יִחָלְתִּי׃ 82 כָּלוּ

v. 79 וידעו כתיב

apparently) mutually antagonistic approaches. The key to understanding his approach lies in yet another lexicographical insight, however, this one relating to the poet's use of the Hebrew verb *leḥayyot,* meaning "to grant life" or "to make alive." The poet's plaintive plea *ḥayyeni* ("grant me life!") is repeated nine separate times within the 119th psalm, but does not appear even once anywhere else in the Bible (including, obviously, in any of the other psalms). Yet the poet does not seem to have "life" in the regular sense of the word on his mind. (And, indeed, the word *ḥayyim* ["life"] itself does not appear even one single time within his poem.) Still, five of the six times the word *eḥyeh* ("I shall live") appears in the Psalter are in the 119th psalm. And the phrase *teḥi nafshi* ("may my soul live") also appears in the 119th psalm, but not in any other.

The poet seems to believe that knowing God through law and precept is possible not only in the quid pro quo sense of looking after one's legal obligations in order to provoke God into granting various blessings, but in a far more personal and spiritual sense. People, the poet seems to be suggesting, can be alive in different ways. There are those who live in the ordinary sense of the word: people who eat and sleep, whose hearts beat, whose internal organs function, who raise families, and who work in the way that normal people work throughout their long or short lives. But the poet also knows the possibility of living in God—of experiencing a kind of truly transformational revivification in God—through the performance of the commandments in a way that is no less sensually real than any other kind of personal experience of the Divine, and it is this kind of sensory experience of the Divine rooted in allegiance to law that the psalmist appears to be putting forward for his

and to those who keep Your ordinances. [64]The earth, יהוה, is filled with Your mercy. Teach me Your statutes.

[65] You have done good with Your servant in accordance with Your word, O יהוה. [66]Teach me good taste and knowledge, for I have placed my faith in Your commandments. [67]Before, when I erred, I was afflicted, but now Your promise guards me. [68]You are good and You do good; teach me Your laws. [69]The arrogant have smeared me with lies, but I nonetheless keep Your precepts. [70]Their hearts are clogged with fat, but I have found pleasure in Your teaching. [71]It was good for me that I was afflicted, for that experience prompted me to learn Your laws. [72]The teaching of Your mouth is more precious to me than thousands of gold and silver coins.

[73] Your hands made me and established me; grant me understanding so that I may learn Your commandments. [74]Those who fear You will see me and rejoice, for I have placed my hope in Your word. [75]יהוה, I know that Your laws are just and that You have afflicted me for good reason. [76]May Your mercy now comfort me in accordance with Your promise to Your servant. [77]Let Your compassion come so that I may truly live, for Your teachings are my delights. [78]Let the arrogant be ashamed, for they have sinned against me with lies, but I shall speak only of Your precepts. [79]May those who fear You return to me, along with those who know Your testimonies. [80]May my heart be guileless in its devotion to Your laws so that I never be ashamed.

[81] My soul is pining away for Your salvation, yet I continue to hope for Your word. [82]My eyes

עֵינַי לְאִמְרָתֶךָ לֵאמֹר מָתַי תְּנַחֲמֵנִי׃ 83 כִּי־הָיִיתִי
כְּנֹאד בְּקִיטוֹר חֻקֶּיךָ לֹא שָׁכָחְתִּי׃ 84 כַּמָּה יְמֵי
עַבְדֶּךָ מָתַי תַּעֲשֶׂה בְרֹדְפַי מִשְׁפָּט׃ 85 כָּרוּ־לִי זֵדִים
שִׁיחוֹת אֲשֶׁר לֹא כְתוֹרָתֶךָ׃ 86 כָּל־מִצְוֺתֶיךָ אֱמוּנָה
שֶׁקֶר רְדָפוּנִי עָזְרֵנִי׃ 87 כִּמְעַט כִּלּוּנִי בָאָרֶץ וַאֲנִי
לֹא־עָזַבְתִּי פִקֻּדֶיךָ׃ 88 כְּחַסְדְּךָ חַיֵּנִי וְאֶשְׁמְרָה
עֵדוּת פִּיךָ׃

89 לְעוֹלָם יְהוָה דְּבָרְךָ נִצָּב בַּשָּׁמָיִם׃ 90 לְדֹר וָדֹר
אֱמוּנָתֶךָ כּוֹנַנְתָּ אֶרֶץ וַתַּעֲמֹד׃ 91 לְמִשְׁפָּטֶיךָ עָמְדוּ
הַיּוֹם כִּי הַכֹּל עֲבָדֶיךָ׃ 92 לוּלֵי תוֹרָתְךָ שַׁעֲשֻׁעָי אָז
אָבַדְתִּי בְעָנְיִי׃ 93 לְעוֹלָם לֹא־אֶשְׁכַּח פִּקּוּדֶיךָ
כִּי־בָם חִיִּיתָנִי׃ 94 לְךָ־אֲנִי הוֹשִׁיעֵנִי כִּי פִקּוּדֶיךָ
דָרָשְׁתִּי׃ 95 לִי קִוּוּ רְשָׁעִים לְאַבְּדֵנִי עֵדֹתֶיךָ
אֶתְבּוֹנָן׃ 96 לְכָל תִּכְלָה רָאִיתִי קֵץ רְחָבָה מִצְוָתְךָ
מְאֹד׃

97 מָה־אָהַבְתִּי תוֹרָתֶךָ כָּל־הַיּוֹם הִיא שִׂיחָתִי׃
98 מֵאֹיְבַי תְּחַכְּמֵנִי מִצְוֺתֶךָ כִּי לְעוֹלָם הִיא־לִי׃
99 מִכָּל־מְלַמְּדַי הִשְׂכַּלְתִּי כִּי עֵדְוֺתֶיךָ שִׂיחָה לִי׃
100 מִזְּקֵנִים אֶתְבּוֹנָן כִּי פִקּוּדֶיךָ נָצָרְתִּי׃ 101 מִכָּל־

readers' appraisal. In its own way, it is a radical proposal. But whether our poet was a traditionalist seeking to bring together two opposing schools of Jewish spirituality or a radical innovator attempting to forge an idiosyncratic third way cannot be known, of course.

Modern readers wishing to encounter the poet on his own ground can sidestep the historical questions that arise from studying his poem, however, simply by asking themselves what they believe serves most effectively to motivate ritual observance in our day. Or, to phrase the question the way the poet himself might have, we can ask ourselves whether we see the commandments of Scripture as taxes owed to heaven or as the price we all must pay to provoke divine blessing . . . or perhaps as tools designed to fashion a life of communion *with* God and a life of intimacy *in* God, and to serve as a means of coming to live *within* God's love in a way that is as real as the way we relate to people we know well intellectually, sensually, candidly, and totally honestly.

The 119th psalm is unique not only because of its great length and its anomalous content, but also because of its unexpected octuple acrostic structure. Indeed, although other psalms are presented as acrostics (that is, as poems organized in such a way that each successive line begins with the next letter of the Hebrew alphabet), a poem with eight lines for each letter of the alphabet is so exceptional that the commentators (or at least some of them) felt compelled

are faint watching for the fulfillment of Your promise, as if to ask, "When will You comfort me?" [83]Although I am as dried out as a wineskin cured in smoke, I have not forgotten Your laws. [84]How many are the days of Your servant? When will You execute judgment against my pursuers? [85]For, contrary to Your teaching, the arrogant have dug pits to trap me. [86]All Your commandments are instruments of faith, but they pursue me with lies. Help me! [87]They almost managed to run me into the ground, but I have not abandoned Your precepts. [88]Grant me life in accordance with Your mercy, and I will continue to observe the testimony of Your mouth.

[89] Forever, יהוה, shall Your word stand firm in the heavens. [90]Your faithfulness is from generation to generation; You have set up the world such that it shall always stand. [91]Those faithful to Your laws stand up today, for they are all Your servants. [92]Indeed, if Your teaching were not my delight, then I would have perished long ago in my misery. [93]I shall never forget Your precepts, for through them You have granted me life. [94]I am Yours; save me, for I have sought Your precepts. [95]The wicked hoped to destroy me, but I nevertheless continue to ponder Your testimonies. [96]I have seen an end come to every measure, but the scope of Your commandments is exceedingly wide.

[97] How I have loved Your teaching; it is all I talk about all day long. [98]With Your commandments, which are with me always, You make me wiser than my enemies. [99]Indeed, I have become more wise than my own teachers, for Your testimonies are my sole topic of conversation. [100]I am more insightful than elders, for I keep Your precepts.

to attempt an explanation. The Meiri (Rabbi Menachem ben Solomon of Provence, 1249–1316), for example, imagined that the number eight was meant to suggest the poet's resolve to subjugate all five of his senses as well as the three aspects of his soul—his consciousness, his avidity, and his intelligence—to the service of God. Radak (Rabbi David Kimhi, also of Provence, 1160–1235), had had a slightly different approach, however. For him too, the first five lines of each eight-part stanza in the poem were reminiscent of the five senses people use to know and decipher the world around them—that is, the tools one uses to

אֹ֣רַח רָ֭ע כָּלִ֣אתִי רַגְלָ֑י לְ֝מַ֗עַן אֶשְׁמֹ֥ר דְּבָרֶֽךָ׃

102 מִמִּשְׁפָּטֶ֥יךָ לֹא־סָ֑רְתִּי כִּֽי־אַ֝תָּ֗ה הוֹרֵתָֽנִי׃

103 מַה־נִּמְלְצ֣וּ לְ֭חִכִּי אִמְרָתֶ֑ךָ מִדְּבַ֥שׁ לְפִֽי׃

104 מִפִּקּוּדֶ֥יךָ אֶתְבּוֹנָ֑ן עַל־כֵּ֝֗ן שָׂנֵ֤אתִי ׀ כָּל־אֹ֬רַח שָֽׁקֶר׃

105 נֵר־לְרַגְלִ֥י דְבָרֶ֑ךָ וְ֝א֗וֹר לִנְתִיבָתִֽי׃ 106 נִשְׁבַּ֥עְתִּי וָאֲקַיֵּ֑מָה לִ֝שְׁמֹ֗ר מִשְׁפְּטֵ֥י צִדְקֶֽךָ׃ 107 נַעֲנֵ֥יתִי עַד־מְאֹ֑ד יְ֝הוָ֗ה חַיֵּ֥נִי כִדְבָרֶֽךָ׃ 108 נִדְב֣וֹת פִּ֭י רְצֵה־נָ֣א יְהוָ֑ה וּֽמִשְׁפָּטֶ֥יךָ לַמְּדֵֽנִי׃ 109 נַפְשִׁ֣י בְכַפִּ֣י תָמִ֑יד וְ֝תוֹרָתְךָ֗ לֹ֣א שָׁכָֽחְתִּי׃ 110 נָתְנ֬וּ רְשָׁעִ֣ים פַּ֣ח לִ֑י וּ֝מִפִּקּוּדֶ֗יךָ לֹ֣א תָעִֽיתִי׃ 111 נָחַ֣לְתִּי עֵדְוֺתֶ֣יךָ לְעוֹלָ֑ם כִּֽי־שְׂשׂ֖וֹן לִבִּ֣י הֵֽמָּה׃ 112 נָטִ֣יתִי לִ֭בִּי לַעֲשׂ֥וֹת חֻקֶּ֗יךָ לְעוֹלָ֥ם עֵֽקֶב׃

113 סֵעֲפִ֥ים שָׂנֵ֑אתִי וְֽתוֹרָתְךָ֥ אָהָֽבְתִּי׃ 114 סִתְרִ֣י וּמָגִנִּ֣י אָ֑תָּה לִדְבָרְךָ֥ יִחָֽלְתִּי׃ 115 ס֣וּרוּ מִמֶּ֣נִּי מְרֵעִ֑ים וְ֝אֶצְּרָ֗ה מִצְוֺ֥ת אֱלֹהָֽי׃ 116 סָמְכֵ֣נִי כְאִמְרָתְךָ֣ וְאֶחְיֶ֑ה וְאַל־תְּ֝בִישֵׁ֗נִי מִשִּׂבְרִֽי׃ 117 סְעָדֵ֥נִי וְאִוָּשֵׁ֑עָה וְאֶשְׁעָ֖ה בְחֻקֶּ֣יךָ תָמִֽיד׃ 118 סָ֭לִיתָ כָּל־שׁוֹגִ֣ים מֵחֻקֶּ֑יךָ כִּי־שֶׁ֝֗קֶר תַּרְמִיתָֽם׃ 119 סִגִ֗ים הִ֭שְׁבַּתָּ כָל־רִשְׁעֵי־אָ֑רֶץ לָ֝כֵ֗ן אָהַ֥בְתִּי עֵדֹתֶֽיךָ׃ 120 סָמַ֣ר מִפַּחְדְּךָ֣ בְשָׂרִ֑י וּֽמִמִּשְׁפָּטֶ֥יךָ יָרֵֽאתִי׃

develop a sense of one's self in the context of one's world. Radak's interpretation of the other three lines of each stanza are quite different from the Meiri's, however. There are, notes Radak, three other ways that people come to interpret the world: through intellectual knowledge they acquire from others, through their own deductive insight into the nature of things, and through the traditions of faith they have received from their ancestors. The number eight, therefore, suggests the eight-fold bridge that exists between the inner self and the outer world that Radak calls the "highway to the acquisition of wisdom," a bridge made up of sensory and intellectual planks of different sorts that, taken together, make it possible for the faithful to know their Creator through deciphering and contemplating Creation. Indeed, the 119th psalm can be read just that way: as a paean to the ultimate truth that possessing divine wisdom means neither knowing of God *solely* from the testimony of others or from books (even sacred ones), nor knowing God *only* through an individual's conviction that God is present in his or her own personal ambit. Divine wisdom—the experience of knowing God—needs to be acquired through some amalgam of both experiences, then: the sensory *and* the intellectual. And, indeed,

[101]I have kept my foot from every evil path so that I might keep Your word. [102]I have not swerved from Your laws, for You have taught me well. [103]How eloquent on my palate is Your word, sweeter even than honey in my mouth. [104]I have become insightful through the contemplation of Your precepts; therefore do I loathe every path paved with lies.

[105]Your word is a lamp at my feet and a light on my path. [106]I took a vow and shall honor it—a vow to keep all Your righteous laws. [107]I suffered terribly, but You granted me life, יהוה, in accordance with Your word. [108]Please, O יהוה, accept the offerings of my mouth and teach me Your laws. [109]I may continually take my life in my hand by doing so, but I have never forgotten Your teaching. [110]The wicked set a trap for me, but I never strayed from Your precepts. [111]I have accepted Your testimonies as an eternal bequest, for they are the joy of my heart. [112]I have inclined my heart to follow Your statutes, to follow at their heel always.

[113]I hate hypocrites, but I love Your teaching. [114]You are my protection and my shield; I yearn for Your word. [115]Depart from my presence, doers of evil, that I might keep the commandments of my God. [116]Support me with Your words, O God, that I may live; make me not ashamed by my hopes. [117]Assist me and I shall be saved, so that I may forever contemplate Your laws. [118]You have rejected those who stray from Your laws, for their fraudulent beliefs are lies. [119]You pitch away the evil of the earth like so much dross; therefore do I love Your testimonies. [120]My flesh crawls out of the fear of You; I hold Your laws in awe.

by imagining the eight-fold nature of the 119th psalm to be reminiscent of that fact, Radak is teaching latter-day readers something profound and challenging about the unchanging nature of human spirituality . . . and suggesting that the great highway to God that existed in ancient times when the psalmists wrote their songs was no different than the road to divine communion that existed in his own medieval day. Presumably, he would grant that the same path he identified exists in our day as well, for those spiritually adept enough—and daring enough—to travel along it.

Regardless of how they evaluate Radak's or the

121 עָשִׂיתִי מִשְׁפָּט וָצֶדֶק בַּל־תַּנִּיחֵנִי לְעֹשְׁקָי׃
122 עֲרֹב עַבְדְּךָ לְטוֹב אַל־יַעַשְׁקֻנִי זֵדִים׃ 123 עֵינַי
כָּלוּ לִישׁוּעָתֶךָ וּלְאִמְרַת צִדְקֶךָ׃ 124 עֲשֵׂה עִם־
עַבְדְּךָ כְחַסְדֶּךָ וְחֻקֶּיךָ לַמְּדֵנִי׃ 125 עַבְדְּךָ אָנִי
הֲבִינֵנִי וְאֵדְעָה עֵדֹתֶיךָ׃ 126 עֵת לַעֲשׂוֹת לַיהוָה
הֵפֵרוּ תּוֹרָתֶךָ׃ 127 עַל־כֵּן אָהַבְתִּי מִצְוֺתֶיךָ מִזָּהָב
וּמִפָּז׃ 128 עַל־כֵּן ׀ כָּל־פִּקּוּדֵי כֹל יִשָּׁרְתִּי כָּל־אֹרַח
שֶׁקֶר שָׂנֵאתִי׃

129 פְּלָאוֹת עֵדְוֺתֶיךָ עַל־כֵּן נְצָרָתַם נַפְשִׁי׃ 130 פֵּתַח
דְּבָרֶיךָ יָאִיר מֵבִין פְּתָיִים׃ 131 פִּי־פָעַרְתִּי
וָאֶשְׁאָפָה כִּי לְמִצְוֺתֶיךָ יָאָבְתִּי׃ 132 פְּנֵה־אֵלַי
וְחָנֵּנִי כְּמִשְׁפָּט לְאֹהֲבֵי שְׁמֶךָ׃ 133 פְּעָמַי הָכֵן
בְּאִמְרָתֶךָ וְאַל־תַּשְׁלֶט־בִּי כָל־אָוֶן׃ 134 פְּדֵנִי
מֵעֹשֶׁק אָדָם וְאֶשְׁמְרָה פִּקּוּדֶיךָ׃ 135 פָּנֶיךָ הָאֵר
בְּעַבְדֶּךָ וְלַמְּדֵנִי אֶת־חֻקֶּיךָ׃ 136 פַּלְגֵי־מַיִם יָרְדוּ
עֵינָי עַל לֹא־שָׁמְרוּ תוֹרָתֶךָ׃

137 צַדִּיק אַתָּה יְהוָה וְיָשָׁר מִשְׁפָּטֶיךָ׃ 138 צִוִּיתָ צֶדֶק
עֵדֹתֶיךָ וֶאֱמוּנָה מְאֹד׃ 139 צִמְּתַתְנִי קִנְאָתִי כִּי־
שָׁכְחוּ דְבָרֶיךָ צָרָי׃ 140 צְרוּפָה אִמְרָתְךָ מְאֹד

Meiri's identification of the specific eight planks that constitute the bridge between the world and its God, moderns will want to develop their own theories of why the poet chose to structure his psalm in the particular way he did. And, although the exercise may not yield conclusive results about the psalmist's plan, speculating about the symbolism of the number eight in the 119th psalm can still be a useful opportunity to join with Radak, the Meiri, and many others in wondering what people can bring to the quest for God, other than their five senses. The answers will vary from person to person: some will favor the three parts of the Freudian psyche for the final three slots, others will prefer to assign them to the three parts of the Hebrew Bible (which certainly can and do function as planks on the bridge between the world of humankind below and God on high), while yet others will see a correspondence with the three daily opportunities Jewish tradition provides the pious to pray to God. There will be, perhaps, as many answers to the riddle of the eight-fold stanza as there are people who undertake to provide answers. The spiritual value of the exercise, however, will not rest in the promulgation of this or that theory, but in the experience itself of attempting to think cogently about there being such a bridge, fashioned of perception and

[121] I have acted justly and righteously; therefore, do not abandon me to my oppressors. [122]Guarantee Your servant for good; let not the arrogant oppress me. [123]My eyesight is growing dim as I wait for Your salvation and for Your righteous word. [124]Deal with Your servant according to Your mercy and teach me Your laws. [125]I am Your servant; grant me understanding that I might know Your testimonies. [126]It is time to act for יהוה, for the wicked have annulled Your teaching. [127]As for me, all they accomplish is to make me love Your commandments even more than the finest gold. [128]Thus, I have found every one of Your precepts to be wholly upright; I loathe every path of falsehood.

[129] Your testimonies are wonders and so my soul does keep them. [130]Your words are a lighted portal; passing through it grants understanding to the simple. [131]I open my mouth wide and breathe them in, so intently do I long for Your commandments. [132]Turn to me and be gracious, as befits one of those who love Your name. [133]Make steady my footsteps with Your word, thus letting no evil befall me. [134]Redeem me from the oppression of humanity that I might keep Your precepts. [135]Shine the light of Your face upon Your servant and teach me Your laws. [136]My eyes have wept rivers of water because others do not keep the laws of Your teaching.

[137] You are righteous, יהוה, and Your laws are just. [138]Indeed, You bequeathed us Your just testimonies and Your deep faith. [139]My zeal has almost destroyed me, however, because my enemies have forgotten Your words. [140]Your speech is utterly tested and Your servant loves

thought, between God and humankind in the first place.

Can moderns build such a bridge? If they can imagine themselves constructing such a span, then of what would they fashion it? The medievals cited above had a clear concept regarding the specific planks they thought would be necessary for the bridge actually to lead from earth to heaven, but some of the assumptions that led to their specific choices will probably not strike moderns as all that cogent. Perhaps the basic model of a bridge fashioned of the five senses and the different branches of the intellect or the soul

וְעַבְדְּךָ אֲהֵבָהּ׃ 141 צָעִיר אָנֹכִי וְנִבְזֶה פִּקֻּדֶיךָ לֹא
שָׁכָחְתִּי׃ 142 צִדְקָתְךָ צֶדֶק לְעוֹלָם וְתוֹרָתְךָ אֱמֶת׃
143 צַר־וּמָצוֹק מְצָאוּנִי מִצְוֹתֶיךָ שַׁעֲשֻׁעָי׃ 144 צֶדֶק
עֵדְוֹתֶיךָ לְעוֹלָם הֲבִינֵנִי וְאֶחְיֶה׃

145 קָרָאתִי בְכָל־לֵב עֲנֵנִי יְהוָה חֻקֶּיךָ אֶצֹּרָה׃
146 קְרָאתִיךָ הוֹשִׁיעֵנִי וְאֶשְׁמְרָה עֵדֹתֶיךָ׃
147 קִדַּמְתִּי בַנֶּשֶׁף וָאֲשַׁוֵּעָה *לִדְבָרְךָ יִחָלְתִּי׃
148 קִדְּמוּ עֵינַי אַשְׁמֻרוֹת לָשִׂיחַ בְּאִמְרָתֶךָ׃ 149 קוֹלִי
שִׁמְעָה כְחַסְדֶּךָ יְהוָה כְּמִשְׁפָּטֶךָ חַיֵּנִי׃ 150 קָרְבוּ
רֹדְפֵי זִמָּה מִתּוֹרָתְךָ רָחָקוּ׃ 151 קָרוֹב אַתָּה יְהוָה
וְכָל־מִצְוֹתֶיךָ אֱמֶת׃ 152 קֶדֶם יָדַעְתִּי מֵעֵדֹתֶיךָ כִּי
לְעוֹלָם יְסַדְתָּם׃

153 רְאֵה־עָנְיִי וְחַלְּצֵנִי כִּי־תוֹרָתְךָ לֹא שָׁכָחְתִּי׃
154 רִיבָה רִיבִי וּגְאָלֵנִי לְאִמְרָתְךָ חַיֵּנִי׃ 155 רָחוֹק
מֵרְשָׁעִים יְשׁוּעָה כִּי־חֻקֶּיךָ לֹא דָרָשׁוּ׃ 156 רַחֲמֶיךָ
רַבִּים ׀ יְהוָה כְּמִשְׁפָּטֶיךָ חַיֵּנִי׃ 157 רַבִּים רֹדְפַי וְצָרָי
מֵעֵדְוֹתֶיךָ לֹא נָטִיתִי׃ 158 רָאִיתִי בֹגְדִים

v. 147 לדבריך כתיב

(or some amalgam of the two) could still work for moderns. But even if we were to work with just that model, then how exactly *would* moderns go about preparing themselves to travel across such a bridge? It is, after all, one thing to say that one may—or that one must—travel towards spiritual fulfillment by utilizing the perceptive capabilities of the five senses, but saying how exactly to utilize them to that end is another thing entirely.

Radak writes that the senses are to be pressed into service to assist in the acquisition of knowledge. Sight, he wrote, is to be used to study holy books. Hearing is to be used to hear the lessons of great sages well-schooled in the ways of God and humankind. He even theorizes that the sense of smell can be successfully honed for the sake of spiritual growth because the nostrils lead directly to the frontal lobes of the brain, the specific part of the brain in which Radak locates the seat of human imagination. The scientific accuracy of this theory notwithstanding, Radak's model is worth considering because of the deep question it leaves moderns to ponder: is the point of having sensory planks on one's bridge of faith specifically to assist one in acquiring wisdom from others? What if the point were to use one's senses to perceive God's presence in the world on one's own—as the psalmists seem to believe possible? Radak was a medieval who lived more than a millennium after Judaism traveled a

it. [141]I am young and scorned, but I have not forgotten Your precepts. [142]Your righteousness is permanently just and Your teaching is truth. [143]Trouble and distress have found me, but Your commandments remain my delights. [144]Your testimonies are permanently just; grant me understanding that I may live.

[145] I call to You with all my heart; answer me, O יהוה, that I may keep Your statutes. [146]I call out to You; save me that I might observe Your testimonies. [147]I rise in the night and, crying out, I hope for Your word. [148]My eyes are already watching when the night watchmen come on duty, that I might speak, inspired by Your word. [149]Hear my voice in accordance with Your mercy; יהוה, grant me life in accordance with Your law. [150]Those who pursue debauchery are approaching to do me ill, even as they distance themselves from Your teaching. [151]You are close by, O יהוה, and all Your commandments are truth. [152]I have known since my earliest years that You founded Your testimonies in such a way that they might endure forever.

[153] Behold my affliction and grant me relief, for I have not forgotten Your teaching. [154]Plead on my behalf and redeem me; grant me life according to Your word. [155]Salvation is distant from the wicked, because they have not sought Your statutes. [156]Great is Your compassion, יהוה; grant me life according to Your laws. [157]Many are my enemies and pursuers, but I have not strayed from Your testimonies. [158]I saw traitors

path to spiritual fulfillment less rooted in sensory perception of the Divine, so he can hardly be faulted for presenting views of spirituality that were normative in his own time and place. Moderns, however, should feel free to consider other possibilities.

As noted above, the author of the 119th psalm used five main synonyms to denote the laws of God. To these, the Masoretes (in a note to Psalm 119:122) pointed out another five terms for divine statutes that also appear in the psalm: *derekh* ("way" or "path"), *imrah* ("statement"), *dibbur* ("remark"), *torah* ("teaching"), and *tzedek* ("righteous law"). Could that have been the psalmist's plan: to compose a long, majestic poem celebrating the fact that the commandments of

וָאֶתְקוֹטָטָה אֲשֶׁר אִמְרָתְךָ לֹא שָׁמָרוּ׃ 159 רְאֵה
כִּי־פִקּוּדֶיךָ אָהָבְתִּי יְהוָה כְּחַסְדְּךָ חַיֵּנִי׃
160 רֹאשׁ־דְּבָרְךָ אֱמֶת וּלְעוֹלָם כָּל־מִשְׁפַּט צִדְקֶךָ׃
161 שָׂרִים רְדָפוּנִי חִנָּם *וּמִדְּבָרְךָ פָּחַד לִבִּי׃ 162 שָׂשׂ
אָנֹכִי עַל־אִמְרָתֶךָ כְּמוֹצֵא שָׁלָל רָב׃ 163 שֶׁקֶר
שָׂנֵאתִי וָאֲתַעֵבָה תּוֹרָתְךָ אָהָבְתִּי׃ 164 שֶׁבַע בַּיּוֹם
הִלַּלְתִּיךָ עַל מִשְׁפְּטֵי צִדְקֶךָ׃ 165 שָׁלוֹם רָב לְאֹהֲבֵי
תוֹרָתֶךָ וְאֵין לָמוֹ מִכְשׁוֹל׃ 166 שִׂבַּרְתִּי לִישׁוּעָתְךָ
יְהוָה וּמִצְוֹתֶיךָ עָשִׂיתִי׃ 167 שָׁמְרָה נַפְשִׁי עֵדֹתֶיךָ
וָאֹהֲבֵם מְאֹד׃ 168 שָׁמַרְתִּי פִקּוּדֶיךָ וְעֵדֹתֶיךָ כִּי כָל־
דְּרָכַי נֶגְדֶּךָ׃

169 תִּקְרַב רִנָּתִי לְפָנֶיךָ יְהוָה כִּדְבָרְךָ הֲבִינֵנִי׃
170 תָּבוֹא תְּחִנָּתִי לְפָנֶיךָ כְּאִמְרָתְךָ הַצִּילֵנִי׃
171 תַּבַּעְנָה שְׂפָתַי תְּהִלָּה כִּי תְלַמְּדֵנִי חֻקֶּיךָ׃
172 תַּעַן לְשׁוֹנִי אִמְרָתֶךָ כִּי כָל־מִצְוֹתֶיךָ צֶּדֶק׃
173 תְּהִי־יָדְךָ לְעָזְרֵנִי כִּי פִקּוּדֶיךָ בָחָרְתִּי׃
174 תָּאַבְתִּי לִישׁוּעָתְךָ יְהוָה וְתוֹרָתְךָ שַׁעֲשֻׁעָי׃
175 תְּחִי־נַפְשִׁי וּתְהַלְלֶךָּ וּמִשְׁפָּטֶךָ יַעְזְרֻנִי׃
176 תָּעִיתִי כְּשֶׂה אֹבֵד בַּקֵּשׁ עַבְדֶּךָ כִּי מִצְוֹתֶיךָ לֹא
שָׁכָחְתִּי׃

v. 161 ומדבריך כתיב

God, known to him by ten different names, are precisely the planks the poet himself wished to propose to his latter-day readers? Perhaps the poet would have made his point more clearly if he had composed a ten-fold acrostic, instead of an eight-fold one. The basic notion, however, is still clear enough: the covenant sealed at Sinai with ten statements can yield the context for the faithful of any generation seeking to know the God of Sinai through the observance of laws called by ten different names. Indeed, according to the same masoretic comment mentioned above, there is only one single verse in the entire 119th psalm that contains none of these terms. That verse, Psalm 119:122 ("Guarantee Your servant for good; let not the arrogant oppress me"), could be interpreted simply as the poet's personal plea for safety in a world that esteemed his specific kind of spirituality hardly at all.

Moderns reading along with the poet will know all too well what he meant. Indeed, for all modern readers may insist they live in a world that values spiritual enterprise and esteems religious commitment, they will also understand

and argued with those who do not follow Your word. [159]See how I love Your precepts; יהוה, grant me life according to Your mercy. [160]From the very beginning, Your word was truth and all Your just laws, therefore, will stand forever.

[161] Princes have persecuted me for no cause, yet my heart fears Your word. [162]Indeed, I rejoice in Your word like one who has found great spoils. [163]I hate falsehood, finding it truly repulsive, but I love Your teaching. [164]Indeed, seven times a day do I praise You because of Your just laws. [165]There is great peace for those who love Your teaching and they encounter no stumbling blocks. [166]As one who performs Your commandments, I expect Your salvation, O יהוה. [167]My soul has observed Your testimonies and I love them greatly. [168]I keep Your precepts and Your testimonies, for all my paths are before You.

[169] Let my joyful song reach You, יהוה; grant me understanding in accordance with Your word. [170]Let my supplication come before You; save me in accordance with Your promise. [171]Let my lips speak Your praise because You teach me Your ordinances. [172]Let my tongue repeat Your promise, for all Your commandments are just. [173]Let Your hand be ready to help me, for I have chosen Your precepts. [174]I yearn for Your salvation, יהוה, and Your teaching is my delight. [175]May my soul live that it might praise You and may Your laws help me. [176]I wander this earth like a lost lamb; seek out Your servant, for I have not forgotten Your commandments.

perfectly clearly why the poet ends his poem with a reference to himself as a lost lamb hoping against hope that God will inquire after him. But even in that final verse, one of the ten terms for the commandments appears . . . and so we are left with the sense that, except for one brief cry for help untempered by any reference to the succor inherent in observing God's commandments, the poet wrote his very long poem to put forward a single, inspiring idea: that God may be known and experienced fully—and not merely intellectually—through the medium of obedience to divine law.

קכ

שִׁיר הַמַּעֲלוֹת
אֶל־יְהוָה בַּצָּרָתָה לִּי קָרָאתִי וַיַּעֲנֵנִי׃
2 יְהוָה הַצִּילָה נַפְשִׁי מִשְּׂפַת־שֶׁקֶר מִלָּשׁוֹן רְמִיָּה׃
3 מַה־יִּתֵּן לְךָ וּמַה־יֹּסִיף לָךְ לָשׁוֹן רְמִיָּה׃
4 חִצֵּי גִבּוֹר שְׁנוּנִים עִם גַּחֲלֵי רְתָמִים׃
5 אוֹיָה לִי כִּי־גַרְתִּי מֶשֶׁךְ שָׁכַנְתִּי עִם־אָהֳלֵי קֵדָר׃
6 רַבַּת שָׁכְנָה־לָּהּ נַפְשִׁי עִם שׂוֹנֵא שָׁלוֹם׃
7 אֲנִי־שָׁלוֹם וְכִי אֲדַבֵּר הֵמָּה לַמִּלְחָמָה׃

What could be simpler than the two-word assertion *ani shalom*? Readers hardly need to be fluent in Hebrew to understand the poet's declaration and its corollaries. I personally am peace itself, he is saying. My life is peace. My goal is to live in peace. Peace is at the center of my being. Peace is the rationale for the way I live my life, for the way I think of myself as being truly alive. Peace, for me, is not simply the absence of war, but the state of inner tranquility that is an absolute prerequisite for attaining the spiritual wholeness necessary for anyone who would live a life in God and of God.

For the poet, then, we may theorize that *ani shalom* was as much a theological statement as a personal or political observation. And indeed, the Bible's notion of peace is something moderns will find stimulating and challenging to contemplate. In the biblical view, for example, peace is not simply the absence of inner conflict, nor is it the sole property of those people of faith who do not succumb, ever, to doubt or insecurity. It is not a sign of a dull mind or a gullible spirit, but neither is inner peace the booby prize awarded to the intellectually spineless as a reward for their complacency. Inner peace—the kind

120

A song for the Levites to sing on the steps.
In my distress I cried out to יהוה, and God answered me.
2 "יהוה," I said, "save me from those who speak the language of lies, from those whose tongues speak slander."
3 What will you get or gain, O slanderous tongue?
4 Only this: a hero's sharp arrows together with brands of burning broomwood.
5 Woe is me, for I live in Meshekh and dwell among the tents of Kedar.
6 My soul has lived far too long with one who hates peace.
7 I personally am peace itself, but when I speak, my foes go to war.

of peace that the Bible calls *shalom*—is a function of self-knowledge and self-acceptance. It is the ability of a human being to love God wholeheartedly and with a fullness of spirit translated into the language of inner calm. It can be sought by any man or woman, but rarely can it be attained by those who do not know love in other parts of their day-to-day lives. The Hebrew word for peace is related to the verb used to denote the payment of various kinds of debt, so—at least for the Hebrew-speaker—being at peace also involves the sense of being quit of outstanding obligations towards God. It is the state attained by people whose spiritual lives are energized by longing rather than guilt . . . and by the desire to live bathed in the light of God's face, rather than by the hope of somehow obliging God to grant various blessings by paying for them, so to speak, in advance. Being at peace with God means loving God, but every human being who has ever loved another will know that loving, wishing to love, and insisting that one can simply not live without love are not at all the same thing.

קכא

שִׁיר לַֽמַּֽעֲלוֹת
אֶשָּׂא עֵינַי אֶל־הֶהָרִים מֵאַיִן יָבֹא עֶזְרִי: 2 עֶזְרִי
מֵעִם יְהוָה עֹשֵׂה שָׁמַיִם וָאָרֶץ:
3 אַל־יִתֵּן לַמּוֹט רַגְלֶךָ אַל־יָנוּם שֹׁמְרֶךָ: 4 הִנֵּה לֹא
יָנוּם וְלֹא יִישָׁן שׁוֹמֵר יִשְׂרָאֵל:
5 יְהוָה שֹׁמְרֶךָ יְהוָה צִלְּךָ עַל־יַד יְמִינֶךָ: 6 יוֹמָם
הַשֶּׁמֶשׁ לֹא־יַכֶּכָּה וְיָרֵחַ בַּלָּיְלָה:
7 יְהוָה יִשְׁמָרְךָ מִכָּל־רָע יִשְׁמֹר אֶת־נַפְשֶׁךָ:
8 יְהוָה יִשְׁמָר־צֵאתְךָ וּבוֹאֶךָ מֵעַתָּה וְעַד־עוֹלָם:

The poet stands alone, perhaps in one of the courtyards of the Temple in Jerusalem, and ponders the overwhelming security that comes from faith in God. Searching the horizon for a symbol of the trust he feels in the Almighty, his eyes fall on the mountains of the Judean wilderness looming in the distance. For a moment he contemplates these immense purple sentinels that appear to be guarding the approaches to the city, then concludes that they are perhaps the perfect symbol for God. Immense, immovable, scalable only by the most adept climbers, permanent, and utterly unchanging from year to year—even from century to century or millennium to millennium—the mountains suggest the kind of absolute presence that the poet connects with God. Secure in his faith, he lifts up his eyes to the mountains and sees not the stuff of geology, but of faith. Indeed, he looks out at the mountains, but what he sees are potent symbols of God's presence and of God's role in the lives of the faithful that represent—or that *should* represent—a never-failing source of security, hope, and well-being for those happy individuals who walk with God in the world. Then, as he stands in the cool dusk and continues to look at the mountains, other thoughts seize him as well. God, his Redeemer, is the source of the poet's salvation, but the Almighty is also other things: a guardian who never sleeps, a source of life-giving cool shade on

121 A song for the Levites to sing from the steps.
I lift up my eyes to the mountains, from whence my help will always come. [2]My help shall come from יהוה, Maker of heaven and earth.
[3] May God not let your foot slip; may your Guardian not sleep. [4]And, indeed, the Guardian of Israel needs neither to slumber nor to sleep.
[5] יהוה is your Guardian; יהוה is the shade on your right hand [6]that keeps the sun from hurting you by day and the moon at night.
[7] יהוה will guard you from all evil and guard your soul.
[8] יהוה will guard your going out and your coming in, now and for all time.

an unbearably hot day, a shield against the evils of the world . . . and against the onslaught of trouble and travail, described here as the machinations of a malevolent moon.

The poet, like so many of the other psalmists, lives in a world of fear, worry, and uncertainty. He sees the world as a basically hostile place in which men and women of faith are not only not welcomed with open arms, but are not even slightly esteemed. He lives in an unfriendly world, but faith in God is the antidote to all the poet's various woes. In God, he finds trust, faith, and security. When he promises his audience that God will guard their souls—and the poet uses words derived from the Hebrew verb *shamar*, meaning "to guard," six times in the last six verses of his eight-verse hymn—and serve as their faithful and watchful Guardian, he cannot mean to say that they will never encounter sadness or heartache in their lives. Neither can he seriously want to assure them that they will be able to avoid any misery or grief merely by believing in God. Instead, he writes to assure all who might eventually come to take his words to heart that they need never succumb to melancholy or troubling worry. Faith in God is what counts, he writes. No matter what, the poet clearly believes that God will always repay faith with kindness. And that, no matter what, the Guardian of Israel will never go off duty.

קכב

שִׁיר הַֽמַּעֲלוֹת לְדָוִד
שָׂמַחְתִּי בְּאֹמְרִים לִי בֵּית יְהוָה נֵלֵךְ׃
2 עֹמְדוֹת הָיוּ רַגְלֵינוּ בִּשְׁעָרַיִךְ יְרוּשָׁלִָם׃ 3 יְרוּשָׁלִַם
הַבְּנוּיָה כְּעִיר שֶׁחֻבְּרָה־לָּהּ יַחְדָּו׃ 4 שֶׁשָּׁם עָלוּ
שְׁבָטִים שִׁבְטֵי־יָהּ עֵדוּת לְיִשְׂרָאֵל לְהֹדוֹת לְשֵׁם
יְהוָה׃ 5 כִּי שָׁמָּה ׀ יָשְׁבוּ כִסְאוֹת לְמִשְׁפָּט כִּסְאוֹת
לְבֵית דָּוִיד׃
6 שַׁאֲלוּ שְׁלוֹם יְרוּשָׁלִָם יִשְׁלָיוּ אֹהֲבָיִךְ׃
7 יְהִי־שָׁלוֹם בְּחֵילֵךְ שַׁלְוָה בְּאַרְמְנוֹתָיִךְ׃
8 לְמַעַן אַחַי וְרֵעָי אֲדַבְּרָה־נָּא שָׁלוֹם בָּךְ׃
9 לְמַעַן בֵּית־יְהוָה אֱלֹהֵינוּ אֲבַקְשָׁה טוֹב לָךְ׃

No city has ever tugged at a people's heartstrings like Jerusalem does at the Jewish people's. No place has ever seemed more sacred to more generations of people, no square mile more redolent of the perceptible presence of God. The poet stands in one of the gates of the Holy City and peers inside. He marvels at the congestion, then pauses for a moment to translate what he sees into the image of the city packed with ancient Israelites gathered together on a national pilgrimage to seek God in a sacred place. Deeply moved by the image he has conjured up, he adjures his companions to work for the peace of the city, then composes his own prayer. "May there be peace on your ramparts, tranquility within your palaces," he says simply, addressing himself to God as he speaks directly to the city of God, the place that, more than any other, stands for God's presence in the physical reality of the sublunary world.

122

A song of David for the Levites to sing on the steps.
I rejoiced when others said to me, "Come, let us go to the House of יהוה."
[2] Our feet would stand in your gates, O Jerusalem, [3]in Jerusalem, that compact city built up as one densely populated precinct, [4]the place to which the tribes, the tribes of יה, would ascend to give testimony to Israel by giving thanks to the name of יהוה—[5]for it is there that the thrones of justice were set up, the thrones of the House of David.
[6] Seek out the peace of Jerusalem and may those who love her be tranquil.
[7] May there be peace on your ramparts, tranquility in your palaces.
[8] For the sake of my brethren and friends, I can only say, "May there be peace in you."
[9] For the sake of the House of יהוה, our God, I shall ask for good for you, O Jerusalem.

Readers touched, even perhaps moved deeply, by the poet's love of Jerusalem will feel prompted to ask themselves what precisely the concept of a holy city means to them. If, as we generally insist, God is truly everywhere, then what can it mean for a particular place to be said to possess intrinsic holiness different in quantity—and perhaps even in quality—from the holiness of other places where God just as surely exists? Can a God who is *everywhere* also be *somewhere*? Does the doctrine of divine omnipresence imply that God is equally present in all places, or can we maintain a reasonable distinction between the holiness of different places? And this as well: is the sanctity of modern-day Jerusalem solely a function of its ancient holiness or do moderns have a role to play in its constant re-establishment and maintenance?

קכג

שִׁיר הַֽמַּ֫עֲל֥וֹת
אֵלֶ֗יךָ נָשָׂ֥אתִי אֶת־עֵינַ֑י הַ֝יֹּשְׁבִ֗י בַּשָּׁמָֽיִם׃
2 הִנֵּ֨ה כְעֵינֵ֪י עֲבָדִ֡ים אֶל־יַ֬ד אֲֽדוֹנֵיהֶ֗ם כְּעֵינֵ֣י שִׁפְחָה֮ אֶל־יַ֪ד גְּבִ֫רְתָּ֥הּ כֵּ֣ן עֵ֭ינֵינוּ אֶל־יְהוָ֣ה אֱלֹהֵ֑ינוּ עַ֝֗ד שֶׁיְּחָנֵּֽנוּ׃
3 חָנֵּ֣נוּ יְהוָ֣ה חָנֵּ֑נוּ כִּֽי־רַ֝֗ב שָׂבַ֥עְנוּ בֽוּז׃
4 רַבַּת֮ שָֽׂבְעָה־לָּ֪ה נַ֫פְשֵׁ֥נוּ הַלַּ֥עַג הַשַּׁאֲנַנִּ֑ים הַ֝בּ֗וּז *לִגְאֵ֥י־יוֹנִֽים׃

v. 4 לגאיונים כתיב

The ancient poet lives in a world of slavery and indentured servitude, both of which institutions are sanctioned in the Bible and regulated by legislation of various sorts. The psalmist, however, is neither a jurist nor a slave and is not, therefore, interested in the legal niceties that apply to either institution. Looking instead to mine the world for suitable metaphors with which to describe how the faithful look to God for vindication, support, and kindness, however, our poet cannot allow himself to leave any potential metaphoric range unexplored.

To begin considering the 123rd psalm, then, we can imagine the poet looking around his world for a model to use to describe the relationship between human beings and God. At first, perhaps, his eye falls on a pet lamb waiting to be fed by its master, then on a child waiting for a parent to show interest in a newly acquired skill or a recently learned trick. After that, we can imagine him noticing a soldier being inspected by his superior, then a couple talking quietly as they walk hand in hand in the street. Another poet might find the right model in any of these images, but our poet continues to look about. Eventually, he comes across a slave and master together. And when he notices

123

A song for the Levites to sing on the steps.
To You have I lifted up my eyes, O God who dwells in heaven.
[2] For just as the eyes of slaves are fixed on their masters' hands and just as the eyes of a maidservant will naturally be fixed on the hand of her mistress, so shall our eyes be fixed on יהוה until our God is gracious unto us.
[3] Be gracious unto us, O יהוה, be gracious unto us for we have borne more than enough contempt.
[4] Our souls have become suffused with more than enough of the scorn of the comfortable, with more than enough of the derision of the arrogant.

that the slave has his eye on his master's hand, the poet has found his model: as he contemplates the slave's eyes, he realizes that a slave's main motivation in doing his master's will is to stave off the punishment that will inevitably follow from failing to obey his instructions carefully and faithfully.

What a stern model for the relationship of human beings and God! Does the poet really feel motivated to serve God only because of the potentially dire consequences of failing to do so? Is it in the desire to stave off divine punishment that he wishes us to find the most potent impetus to devote our lives to the service of God? The poet's goal here may be to prompt us to ask ourselves about the real reasons for embracing religion . . . or perhaps about the real reasons for which we personally are prompted to piety. We may claim, after all, to be motivated solely by the love of God, but what is the reality behind the claim? What motives really do lurk behind the willingness to pray to God, to worship God, and to obey the commandments of God for most of us? Is the specter of self-gain—of averting disease or unhappiness, or of getting some useful blessing in the bargain—always there somewhere behind even the most heartfelt act of ritual observance? The poet's answer is dour, but what will ours be?

שִׁיר הַֽמַּעֲלוֹת לְדָוִד לוּלֵי יְהוָה שֶׁהָיָה לָנוּ
יֹֽאמַר־נָא יִשְׂרָאֵל׃
2 לוּלֵי יְהוָה שֶׁהָיָה לָנוּ בְּקוּם עָלֵינוּ אָדָם׃ 3 אֲזַי
חַיִּים בְּלָעוּנוּ בַּחֲרוֹת אַפָּם בָּנוּ׃ 4 אֲזַי הַמַּיִם
שְׁטָפוּנוּ נַחְלָה עָבַר עַל־נַפְשֵׁנוּ׃ 5 אֲזַי עָבַר עַל־
נַפְשֵׁנוּ הַמַּיִם הַזֵּידוֹנִים׃
6 בָּרוּךְ יְהוָה שֶׁלֹּא נְתָנָנוּ טֶרֶף לְשִׁנֵּיהֶם׃
7 נַפְשֵׁנוּ כְּצִפּוֹר נִמְלְטָה מִפַּח יוֹקְשִׁים הַפַּח נִשְׁבָּר
וַאֲנַחְנוּ נִמְלָטְנוּ׃
8 עֶזְרֵנוּ בְּשֵׁם יְהוָה עֹשֵׂה שָׁמַיִם וָאָרֶץ׃

The poets of ancient Israel had powerful enemies. Indeed, terror of the enemy would have to be counted among the two or three themes that run throughout the entire Psalter and make a unified anthology out of its disparate and diverse poems. And that fear, it is stressed over and over, is not merely philosophical or intellectual in nature: the poets are afraid for their physical well-being and refer over and over to the fear of being ambushed, attacked, beaten, or kidnapped. Indeed, if God had not seen to their safety, our poet asserts openly, the psalmists' foes would have eaten them alive. Indeed, the fear of being totally consumed by an enemy—or, symbolically, of being overwhelmed by the irresistibly strong current of a swiftly flowing river—is obviously foremost in the poet's mind.

Is the 124th psalm about a specific incident? It could easily be read that way. The poet thinks of a bird flying over a trap. The fowler has left a mound of birdseed on top of what appears to be a thatch of grass, but it is really a trap designed to spring as soon as a hungry bird alights on it. The bird, tempted, sees the seed and falls into the trap, but it unexpectedly breaks, leaving the bird to enjoy the seed and then fly off to safety. What could have

124

A song of David for the Levites to sing on the steps: "If יהוה had not been there for us."
Let Israel declare as follows:

[2] If יהוה had not been there for us when our human foe rose up against us, [3]then they would surely have swallowed us up alive in their rage against us, [4]then the current would have washed us away as the waters of the river rose up over us, [5]then would the waters of enmity have risen up over us.

[6] Blessed be יהוה, who did not let us become a morsel between their teeth.

[7] Just to the contrary, our souls escaped the only way a bird could ever escape from a fowler's trap: the trap broke and we escaped.

[8] Our help rests in the name of יהוה, Maker of heaven and earth.

happened to the poet to make him consider this a compelling parallel to his own situation? Did he too fall into a trap of some sort, only to find himself miraculously able to walk away? Was he captured by hooligans who inadvertently left the door to his dungeon unlocked? Was he ambushed by criminals who tied the ropes they used to bind him so inexpertly that he was able to wriggle out of them as soon as his tormentors' backs were turned? We will never know the answers to these questions, but that hardly means that we cannot be impressed by the poet's faith in God's goodness. He escaped, he asserts, not due to his captors' incompetence, but because God was with him. He feels that he owes his freedom to the fact that God cared for him . . . and to the fact that God's mercies extend not only to the rich and famous, but even to poets who humbly acknowledge God's great saving influence in their lives.

שִׁיר הַמַּעֲלוֹת
הַבֹּטְחִים בַּיהוָה כְּהַר־צִיּוֹן לֹא־יִמּוֹט לְעוֹלָם
יֵשֵׁב׃ 2 יְרוּשָׁלַם הָרִים סָבִיב לָהּ וַיהוָה סָבִיב
לְעַמּוֹ מֵעַתָּה וְעַד־עוֹלָם׃
3 כִּי לֹא יָנוּחַ שֵׁבֶט הָרֶשַׁע עַל גּוֹרַל הַצַּדִּיקִים לְמַעַן
לֹא־יִשְׁלְחוּ הַצַּדִּיקִים בְּעַוְלָתָה יְדֵיהֶם׃
4 הֵיטִיבָה יְהוָה לַטּוֹבִים וְלִישָׁרִים בְּלִבּוֹתָם׃
5 וְהַמַּטִּים עֲקַלְקַלּוֹתָם יוֹלִיכֵם יְהוָה אֶת־פֹּעֲלֵי
הָאָוֶן שָׁלוֹם עַל־יִשְׂרָאֵל׃

In ancient times, cities built on open plains were especially vulnerable to attack by marauding enemies. Building thick walls around such cities helped make them easier to defend, but nothing man-made can ever compare favorably to the innate security that comes from the right natural setting. Different kinds of settings were useful in different ways, of course, but a city nestled into the space among tall mountains was safest of all: no would-be besiegers could ever approach such a city without having to climb up hills that were easily defended in a world in which most weaponry depended principally on gravity, thus inevitably granting the upper hand to those shooting their weapons downward.

Jerusalem, nestled in the Judean hills, was the poet's home. He spent his days contemplating those hills, considering how God made the world in such a way so as to guarantee the defensibility of his nation's capital city. And from those idle hours of contemplation came some powerful ideas. The situation of Jerusalem among the mountains, the poet came to realize, can symbolize the way in which God cares for and protects Israel from its enemies. Further-

125 A song for the Levites to sing on the steps.

Those who trust in יהוה will be like Mount Zion itself, which will never totter and which will always be inhabited. [2]Just as mountains surround Jerusalem, so does יהוה encompass the people of God now and forever.

[3] For the staff of wickedness will not come down on the fortunes of the righteous, lest the righteous despair and put their hands to iniquity.

[4] Render goodness, O יהוה, unto the good and the upright of heart.

[5] But may יהוה lead away those who lean towards corruption together with the other doers of iniquity. Peace unto Israel!

more, the Judean hills are Jerusalem's natural ramparts, but God, existing as a natural bulwark between Israel and its enemies, plays that very same role for the Jewish people. Indeed, the poet can take the mountain metaphor one step further: just as Mount Zion itself is unmovable, unshakable, and permanently fixed in its sacred setting, so are those who place their trust fully in God fixed permanently in their places, unflappable, unterrifiable, and un-unnervable. Theirs is the security that comes from embracing faith in the one God whose permanence they declare axiomatic and whose unchanging nature grants them some small measure of endurance in a world of endless change. Perhaps the poet was hoping to inspire his readers to ponder how normal people might ever go about acquiring that kind of faith. Is it a gift *from* God or the gateway *to* God? Is faith innate or acquired, learned or inherited? Or is it present in every human heart from cradle to grave, waiting patiently to be discovered when the individual in whose chest that heart beats acquires sufficient self-knowledge to know where, precisely, to look for it?

שִׁיר הַמַּעֲלוֹת
בְּשׁוּב יְהֹוָה אֶת־שִׁיבַת צִיּוֹן הָיִינוּ כְּחֹלְמִים׃
2 אָז יִמָּלֵא שְׂחוֹק פִּינוּ וּלְשׁוֹנֵנוּ רִנָּה אָז יֹאמְרוּ
בַגּוֹיִם הִגְדִּיל יְהֹוָה לַעֲשׂוֹת עִם־אֵלֶּה׃
3 הִגְדִּיל יְהֹוָה לַעֲשׂוֹת עִמָּנוּ הָיִינוּ שְׂמֵחִים׃
4 שׁוּבָה יְהֹוָה אֶת־*שְׁבִיתֵנוּ כַּאֲפִיקִים בַּנֶּגֶב׃
5 הַזֹּרְעִים בְּדִמְעָה בְּרִנָּה יִקְצֹרוּ׃ 6 הָלוֹךְ יֵלֵךְ ׀ וּבָכֹה
נֹשֵׂא מֶשֶׁךְ־הַזָּרַע בֹּא־יָבֹא בְרִנָּה נֹשֵׂא אֲלֻמֹּתָיו׃

v. 4 שבותנו כתיב

The poet, either historically or whimsically, writes as an exile pondering the eventual return of Israel to Zion. It will be, he imagines, like a dream. And, indeed, his poem has a certain dream-like quality to it as it shifts back and forth from past to future, ending up with a profound observation about the nature of the poet's present day. Modern readers can only concur: the return to Zion in our own day also has a kind of dream-like feel to it. Indeed, as we ponder the modest origins of political Zionism followed by the descent of the Jewish people into hell and the nation's subsequent revivification not *merely* as a living people, but as a living people with its own powerful and successful army defending a free Jewish state in the ancestral homeland of the Jewish people, we too cannot but feel that we are contemplating a dream of some sort rather than a set of historical facts.

The 126th psalm should be recited and pondered by Zionists of all stripes and varieties, both those who admire the triumph of the Zionist ideal from afar as well as those who have chosen to live in Israel. In addition to its challenge to evaluate and re-evaluate the way we relate to the modern State of Israel, however, the poem also challenges us spiritually when it declares that

126

A song for the Levites to sing on the steps.
When יהוה brings about the return of Zion from exile, we shall be like dreamers.
[2] At that time, our mouths shall be filled with laughter, our tongues with gladness. At that time, the nations shall declare, "יהוה has done great things with those people."
[3] Indeed, יהוה will do such great things for us that we shall be truly happy.
[4] יהוה, bring us back home as effortlessly as those desert streams flow through the Negeb.
[5] People who sow in tears shall reap in gladness; [6] one who goes out crying as he carries his bag of seed shall surely come back in gladness carrying mature sheaves.

the inevitable destiny of those who suffered exile in Babylon was to merit restitution to Zion—just as all who sow in tears are bound, at least eventually, to reap in gladness. What, the poet prompts us to wonder, is the precise relationship between the Shoah and the founding of the State of Israel? Was Israel some sort of ghoulish prize won by the Jewish people as a result of having survived the Holocaust? Does anyone really believe that God works in history by testing the staying power of peoples and then rewarding the ones who survive the most horrific tests with countries of their own? But if we bristle at that idea, shall we then assert that there is no relationship at all between the two events, that the worst debacle and the greatest political triumph the Jewish people ever experienced came *coincidentally* a mere three years apart? Surely that seems even harder to accept than the idea that a relationship of some sort exists between the two. But making that connection and attempting to describe it adequately—let alone to explain it rationally—will be another thing entirely for moderns used to talking vaguely about God's role in history, but almost never at ease trying to explain precisely what they mean.

שִׁיר הַמַּעֲלוֹת לִשְׁלֹמֹה
אִם־יְהוָה ׀ לֹא־יִבְנֶה בַיִת שָׁוְא ׀ עָמְלוּ בוֹנָיו בּוֹ
אִם־יְהוָה לֹא־יִשְׁמָר־עִיר שָׁוְא ׀ שָׁקַד שׁוֹמֵר׃
2 שָׁוְא לָכֶם ׀ מַשְׁכִּימֵי קוּם מְאַחֲרֵי־שֶׁבֶת אֹכְלֵי
לֶחֶם הָעֲצָבִים כֵּן יִתֵּן לִידִידוֹ שֵׁנָא׃
3 הִנֵּה נַחֲלַת יְהוָה בָּנִים שָׂכָר פְּרִי הַבָּטֶן׃
4 כְּחִצִּים בְּיַד־גִּבּוֹר כֵּן בְּנֵי הַנְּעוּרִים׃ 5 אַשְׁרֵי הַגֶּבֶר
אֲשֶׁר מִלֵּא אֶת־אַשְׁפָּתוֹ מֵהֶם לֹא יֵבֹשׁוּ כִּי־יְדַבְּרוּ
אֶת־אוֹיְבִים בַּשָּׁעַר׃

Only two poems in the Book of Psalms, this one and the seventy-second, are attributed to Solomon. Whether that simply means that one or two poets named Solomon wrote them, however, or that the author wished to dedicate his poem to the great King Solomon—or perhaps even to attribute it to him—cannot be known. The poem itself is as subtle as it is wise, however, and even in five short Hebrew verses manages to suggest a deep truth. The poet begins by noting that human endeavors will only succeed if they have the support of the Almighty. Humans may build houses, for example, but those houses will not stand unless their existence is in accordance with the will of God. Similarly, humans can stand guard on the ramparts of a walled city, but the city behind those walls will never be truly secure unless God wills it to be so. Even nighttime rest, the poet suggests a bit obscurely, can only come to a person as a blessing from God. And that is the reason the poet believes that rest in the wake of the worship of alien gods, no matter how vigorous or strenuous that worship might have been, can never yield to true serenity or tranquility.

When the poet launches into an encomium to the joy of having children, however, the end of the poem appears—at least at first blush—to have nothing to do with its beginning. Children, the poet asserts, are the arrows in a man's

127

A song of Solomon for the Levites to sing on the steps.
If יהוה does not build a house, then in vain do its builders labor; if יהוה does not guard a city, then in vain does its sentinel stand guard.
[2] In vain too do you exert yourselves, you who rise up early after staying up late to eat the bread of idolatry, for it is God who rewards those who behave as faithful friends with restful sleep.
[3] Moreover, children too are a bequest from יהוה; the fruit of a woman's belly is a divine reward.
[4] Children born in one's youth are like arrows in the hand of a hero; [5]happy is the man whose quiver is filled with them—they will never lose face when they speak with enemies in the city gate.

quiver and his advocates in instances of public dispute. Furthermore, they are a gift from a benevolent God—and that is the case no matter how capable human beings may appear to be of producing children on their own. One solution is to imagine that the break between the psalm's two halves is intentional and that the poet's goal was precisely to prompt his readers to ask how his poem's beginning and end fit together. Different people will find different answers, of course, but a simple one is this. People can produce children without God, just as they can build homes and guard their cities' walls. But manufacturing, be it of houses or babies, is not to be confused with creation: for something truly to exist, it must be as created by God as it is made by human beings. Without God, the poet seems to imply, things may indeed come into being, but they can never truly *exist* in any but a secondary, derivative sense of the word. That notion may sound almost platitudinous to moderns . . . but its implications for the way we live our own lives are anything but banal. Do *we* exist simply because our parents made us? Or have we transcended mere existence and struggled successfully to live lives truly suffused with divine reality?

שִׁיר הַֽמַּֽעֲלוֹת
אַשְׁרֵי כָּל־יְרֵא יְהוָה הַהֹלֵךְ בִּדְרָכָיו׃
[2] יְגִיעַ כַּפֶּיךָ כִּי תֹאכֵל אַשְׁרֶיךָ וְטוֹב לָךְ׃
[3] אֶשְׁתְּךָ ׀ כְּגֶפֶן פֹּרִיָּה בְּיַרְכְּתֵי בֵיתֶךָ בָּנֶיךָ כִּשְׁתִלֵי
זֵיתִים סָבִיב לְשֻׁלְחָנֶךָ׃
[4] הִנֵּה כִי־כֵן יְבֹרַךְ גָּבֶר יְרֵא יְהוָה׃
[5] יְבָרֶכְךָ יְהוָה מִצִּיּוֹן וּרְאֵה בְּטוּב יְרוּשָׁלָם כֹּל יְמֵי
חַיֶּיךָ׃ [6] וּרְאֵה־בָנִים לְבָנֶיךָ שָׁלוֹם עַל־יִשְׂרָאֵל׃

By declaring that true happiness always comes from surrendering to the fear of God and from walking in the ways of God—and then by detailing the blessings that he expects will subsequently come to the truly pious individual—the poet is merely choosing an especially provocative way of asking what constitutes real happiness. And, perhaps to prompt readers to do the same, he offers his own answer rooted in the details of his personal life.

Most of the psalmists reveal their gender, if they do at all, only obliquely through the use of gender-based pronouns or verbs. The author of the 128th psalm, on the other hand, was certainly a man and his list of blessings reflects that fact . . . and, although he is formally expressing wishes appropriate for a male reader (or rather, since the psalms are songs, a male listener), one gets the strong impression that he is thinking of precisely those blessings he wishes for himself. He wants, he obliquely says, for example, not merely to have a wife, but for his wife to be fertile and to bear children regularly and easily. He wants to sit down in the evening for supper at a table surrounded by those children and, at that table, he wishes to eat food either grown by his own hands or purchased with funds he has personally labored to earn. Furthermore, he wants to live long enough not only to produce his own children, but to see his children's children seated at his dinner table, enjoying the fruit of their grandfather's lifelong labors.

128

A song for the Levites to sing on the steps.
Happy are all who fear יהוה and who walk in the ways of God.
[2] If you are among them, then you shall be happy and content when you eat food that comes to you through the labor of your hands.
[3] Your wife shall be as a fertile vine spreading into every corner of your house; your children shall be like olive saplings growing around your table.
[4] For precisely thus shall the man who fears יהוה be blessed.
[5] May יהוה bless you from Zion that you see the goodness of Jerusalem all the days of your life . . . [6]and also that you live to see your children's children. Peace unto Israel!

The poet yearns, however, not only for the love of a fertile wife and for children who come home for dinner. To be happy, he also wishes to live in a world at peace, to see with his own eyes the peace of Jerusalem, and to witness the establishment of peace and security for Jewish people everywhere. The poet may frame his thoughts on happiness by declaring that all these are blessings from God, but he is also asking his readers to contemplate his list in terms of their own lives . . . and in terms of the society they have created.

For modern Jewish readers, a list of things that would induce happiness might include living in a world at peace, living in a world in which both the Jews of the diaspora and the Jews of Israel live in security and prosperity, enjoying vigorous and prosperous lives we share with healthy wives and husbands, and being blessed with healthy children and grandchildren. But if we want these things as fervently as we constantly insist that we do, then perhaps the poet is prompting us to ask why, precisely, it is that we generally exert ourselves so feebly—if, indeed, we exert ourselves at all—to inspire God to bless us with those things by devoting our lives to worship and service. It's a good question, but one the poet leaves as blithely unanswered as formally unasked.

קכט

שִׁיר הַֽמַּעֲלוֹת רַבַּת צְרָרוּנִי מִנְּעוּרָי
יֹֽאמַר־נָא יִשְׂרָאֵל׃
2 רַבַּת צְרָרוּנִי מִנְּעוּרָי גַּם לֹא יָכְלוּ־לִי׃
3 עַל־גַּבִּי חָרְשׁוּ חֹרְשִׁים הֶאֱרִיכוּ *לְמַעֲנִיתָם׃
4 יְהוָה צַדִּיק קִצֵּץ עֲבוֹת רְשָׁעִים׃
5 יֵבֹשׁוּ וְיִסֹּגוּ אָחוֹר כֹּל שֹׂנְאֵי צִיּוֹן׃
6 יִהְיוּ כַּחֲצִיר גַּגּוֹת שֶׁקַּדְמַת שָׁלַף יָבֵשׁ׃ 7 שֶׁלֹּא
מִלֵּא כַפּוֹ קוֹצֵר וְחִצְנוֹ מְעַמֵּר׃
8 וְלֹא אָמְרוּ ׀ הָעֹבְרִים בִּרְכַּת יְהוָה אֲלֵיכֶם בֵּרַכְנוּ
אֶתְכֶם בְּשֵׁם יְהוָה׃

v. 3 למענותם כתיב

The image of the enemies of Israel lying wasted on the ground like so many handfuls of brown, withered grass will be a deeply satisfying picture for any Jew—even one with only a cursory understanding of the course of Jewish history—to contemplate. The poet doesn't write merely to present his readers with an agreeable image, however, but to challenge them to ask some critical questions. For example, is the more crucial point about the Shoah that so many millions died or that so many other millions survived? Is the lesson of the medieval expulsions from Spain and Portugal that we should loathe the heartless villains who perpetrated this terror on innocent men, women, and children . . . or that we should marvel that the culture of Iberian Jewry somehow survived—both among the people who lived through the expulsion and, even in our day, among their descendants? The point of contemplating the horrors of Jewish history, the poet implies, is not to become depressed by the unbelievable depths to which human beings can sink when they let themselves be seized by

129

A song of David for the Levites to sing on the steps: "They have afflicted me greatly since the days of my youth."

Let Israel declare as follows:

[2] They have afflicted me greatly since the days of my youth, but they have not vanquished me.

[3] The plowmen have used their plows on my back to carve long, deep furrows, [4] but יהוה is righteous, cutting the bonds with which the wicked tied me up.

[5] May all those who hate Zion lose face and be forced to retreat.

[6] May they be like the kind of grass on a rooftop that begins to wither almost before it finishes growing, [7] like the kind of grass so sparse that no harvester can fill his arms with it, nor the gatherer of sheaves, his apron.

[8] May they be the kind of people of whom passers-by never say, "The blessing of יהוה being so evidently upon you, we too shall bless you in the name of יהוה."

anti-Semitism, but to be deeply moved by the degree to which God has kept faith with the ancient promise to preserve and protect Israel from total annihilation. And the poet's point is also that this is no less true on the level of the individual than it is on the national level. If villains were to run the sharp blades of a newly whetted plow across an individual's back and, instead of sinking into an abyss of despair, that person were to be moved to feelings of gratitude to God (by whose grace he or she would have survived the experience), then would that not validate the experience at least partially and grant it some degree of worth? To contemplate the searing pain of life and to be moved, not to recrimination or blame, but to abiding, honest, and ennobling humility before God—*that,* the poet is saying, is the great goal of human life lived *in,* rather than *despite,* history.

קל

שִׁיר הַֽמַּעֲלוֹת
מִמַּעֲמַקִּים קְרָאתִיךָ יְהֹוָה׃
2 אֲדֹנָי שִׁמְעָה בְקוֹלִי תִּהְיֶינָה אָזְנֶיךָ קַשֻּׁבוֹת לְקוֹל
תַּחֲנוּנָי׃
3 אִם־עֲוֺנוֹת תִּשְׁמָר־יָהּ אֲדֹנָי מִי יַעֲמֹד׃
4 כִּי־עִמְּךָ הַסְּלִיחָה לְמַעַן תִּוָּרֵא׃
5 קִוִּיתִי יְהֹוָה קִוְּתָה נַפְשִׁי וְלִדְבָרוֹ הוֹחָלְתִּי׃
6 נַפְשִׁי לַאדֹנָי מִשֹּׁמְרִים לַבֹּקֶר שֹׁמְרִים לַבֹּקֶר׃
7 יַחֵל יִשְׂרָאֵל אֶל־יְהֹוָה כִּי־עִם־יְהֹוָה הַחֶסֶד
וְהַרְבֵּה עִמּוֹ פְדוּת׃ 8 וְהוּא יִפְדֶּה אֶת־יִשְׂרָאֵל
מִכֹּל עֲוֺנֹתָיו׃

In a dark corner of the Temple forecourt, a lone Levite crouches down in the shadows and waits for God. The night is still and dark as a cold breeze passes overhead. A shiver of loneliness, resignation, and stifled hope travels down the poet's spine, where it tingles for a moment before vanishing into the night as the poet waits and hopes for God. The vigil may be long, but its point is entirely clear: the poet yearns to hear the voice of God speaking the word of God. We know nothing, really, of the circumstances that led to the composition of the 130th psalm. But if we allow ourselves, just slightly tendentiously, to draw on the large set of hints and allusions in other, similar psalms, a plausible portrait of the poet begins to emerge.

The reason the poet is prepared to wait for as long as it takes for God to speak also becomes clear: only the audible proof of the divine presence will make worthwhile all the suffering the poets must endure, all the ridicule they live through on a daily basis, and all the jokes of which their spiritual aspirations are the insulting punch lines. The moon rises and sets. The stars twinkle in the dark blue sky. The nighttime air becomes cold, then bracing, then frigid. The sounds of the city, only barely audible within the Temple compound even at midday, diminish and then vanish entirely. All is completely

130

A song for the Levites to sing on the steps.
From the depths, I call to You, יהוה.
[2] Adonai, hear my voice; may Your ears be open to the sound of my supplications.
[3] If יה were to keep track of all sins, Adonai, who could withstand the scrutiny?
[4] For forgiveness resides with You so that, in dispensing it, You may be properly feared.
[5] I hope, יהוה—my soul hopes—I truly long for God's word.
[6] My soul awaits Adonai more ardently than those who wait for morning await the morning.
[7] May Israel come to put its hope in יהוה, for with יהוה resides mercy, for the great power to redeem resides with God—[8]and God will surely redeem Israel from all its sins.

and utterly still as the depth of night descends on the Holy City. Then, suddenly, the poet has an unexpected nocturnal insight. Why, he suddenly thinks to ask, are human beings created with the capacity for sin at all? Surely, if the point of Scripture is to command people to avoid transgression, the problem could have been solved (or rather, pre-empted) had the Almighty created people without the propensity—or perhaps even without the ability—to sin. But the poet also knows that the inclination to sin brings regret in its wake . . . and that regret brings on the desire for forgiveness, repentance, and redemption in God. And there, in the realization that the yearning for forgiveness leads eventually to redemption, the poet finally has an answer to his question: the inclination to sin, for all it may bring villains to crime, also brings the pious—at least eventually—to God. In the end, it is this insight, somehow both comforting and distressing at the same time, that insinuates itself in the poet's consciousness. It strikes him that he need wait for God no longer . . . not because God has become less distant, but because God dwells permanently and accessibly within the labyrinthine byways of his own mind and can be found, therefore, merely by being sought with sufficient intellectual vigor and spiritual stamina.

קלא

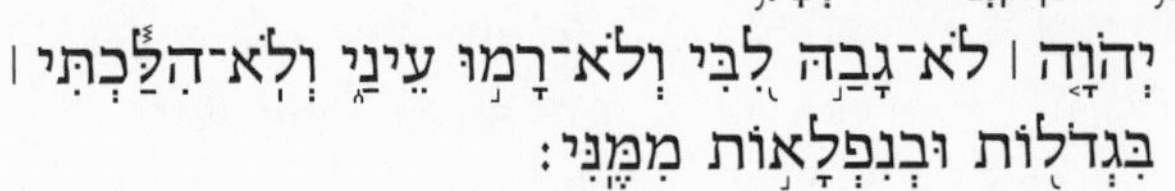

שִׁ֥יר הַֽמַּֽעֲל֗וֹת לְדָ֫וִ֥ד
יְהֹוָ֤ה ׀ לֹא־גָבַ֣הּ לִ֭בִּי וְלֹא־רָמ֣וּ עֵינַ֑י וְלֹֽא־הִלַּ֓כְתִּי ׀
בִּגְדֹל֖וֹת וּבְנִפְלָא֣וֹת מִמֶּֽנִּי׃
2 אִם־לֹ֤א שִׁוִּ֨יתִי ׀ וְדוֹמַ֗מְתִּי נַ֫פְשִׁ֥י כְּ֭גָמֻל עֲלֵ֣י אִמּ֑וֹ
כַּגָּמֻ֖ל עָלַ֣י נַפְשִֽׁי׃
3 יַחֵ֣ל יִ֭שְׂרָאֵל אֶל־יְהֹוָ֑ה מֵ֝עַתָּ֗ה וְעַד־עוֹלָֽם׃

The poet whose poem became our 131st psalm was a man possessed of an insight into the process of spiritual growth that may strike moderns as vaguely heretical—or at least iconoclastic. Religion in the poet's day, as in our own, was involved with complex regimens of prayer and ritual. The poet has realized, however, that the high road to redemption in God leads neither through the development and performance of elaborate rites nor through endless confessions of allegiance to even their most picayune details. Rather, the poet now understands true spiritual development to occur through the stilling of the spirit and the attainment of inner peace . . . and through calming of the internal ocean that, in the general course of things, rages ceaselessly within us from the moment we come into the world until the moment we depart for the world to come. The poet's truth, then, is as simple as it is unsettling: we come to know God best not by becoming like warriors facing the ultimate battle or like athletes facing the most grueling race, but by becoming like infants lying still, calm, quiet, rested, and totally content on their mothers' breasts as the nourishing milk they have suckled courses gently through their bodies, bringing total satisfaction to their every nutritional need.

131

A song of David for the Levites to sing on the steps.
יהוה, my heart is not arrogant nor are my eyes haughty, for I have not walked about in ways too great or too wondrous for me.
[2] Just to the contrary, I have looked to my soul and stilled it, making my soul within me as calm as an infant, as calm an infant lying on its mother's breast.
[3] May Israel put its hope in יהוה now and forever.

This is all quite natural to babies, but moderns seem generally inclined to assume just the opposite to be true. Indeed, the world almost always seems ready to label as truly religious those whose spirituality is all frenzy and fury, people for whom prayer without dramatic gesticulation and ostentation is somehow less worthwhile—perhaps even less real—than a single word breathed out almost silently by one who knows nothing of rules and regulations, but who yearns absolutely and wholeheartedly for God.

For the poet, then, the great goal of human spirituality is not to become a famous sage or a zealot for Jewish survival, however worthy these goals may be. The real goal of those who yearn for communion with the Divine is, rather, to become like infants sleeping contentedly on God's breast: filled up totally with the milk of God's presence and satisfied completely and utterly by the succor inherent in God's presence in their lives. We may respond, then, to this very short poem with a very difficult question: can we accept—and believe totally and without reservation—that the great goal of all religious observance, including communal and private prayer, is to sleep in total contentment within the sheltering presence of the Almighty, to feel secure in our faith to the point that we can know peace (rather than crippling doubt or uncertainty) through the rituals of Jewish piety? The poet declares it possible. But how exactly to go about attaining it, of course, is another question entirely.

שִׁיר הַמַּעֲלוֹת
זְכוֹר־יְהֹוָה לְדָוִד אֵת כָּל־עֻנּוֹתוֹ׃ 2 אֲשֶׁר נִשְׁבַּע
לַיהֹוָה נָדַר לַאֲבִיר יַעֲקֹב׃ 3 אִם־אָבֹא בְּאֹהֶל
בֵּיתִי אִם־אֶעֱלֶה עַל־עֶרֶשׂ יְצוּעָי׃ 4 אִם־אֶתֵּן
שְׁנַת לְעֵינָי לְעַפְעַפַּי תְּנוּמָה׃ 5 עַד־אֶמְצָא מָקוֹם
לַיהֹוָה מִשְׁכָּנוֹת לַאֲבִיר יַעֲקֹב׃
6 הִנֵּה־שְׁמַעֲנוּהָ בְאֶפְרָתָה מְצָאנוּהָ בִּשְׂדֵי־יָעַר׃
7 נָבוֹאָה לְמִשְׁכְּנוֹתָיו נִשְׁתַּחֲוֶה לַהֲדֹם רַגְלָיו׃
8 קוּמָה יְהֹוָה לִמְנוּחָתֶךָ אַתָּה וַאֲרוֹן עֻזֶּךָ׃ 9 כֹּהֲנֶיךָ
יִלְבְּשׁוּ־צֶדֶק וַחֲסִידֶיךָ יְרַנֵּנוּ׃
10 בַּעֲבוּר דָּוִד עַבְדֶּךָ אַל־תָּשֵׁב פְּנֵי מְשִׁיחֶךָ׃ 11 נִשְׁבַּע
יְהֹוָה ׀ לְדָוִד אֱמֶת לֹא־יָשׁוּב מִמֶּנָּה מִפְּרִי בִטְנְךָ

Each in its own way, every psalm challenges us to renounce some cliché or slogan that risks making faith something glib and easy. Perhaps that is why Jews have traditionally chanted, rather than simply studied, the psalms—so that the ideas they engender will be successfully acquired not quickly or efficiently, but rather in the slow, difficult way in which ideas are truly internalized by people blessed with introspective intellects and scrupulous intellectual integrity.

The author of the 132nd psalm, for example, presents us with an idea so often repeated in Scripture and liturgy that it sounds banal, almost ordinary: the notion that the Temple in Jerusalem was God's special residence on earth, the focus of divine presence intensely and profoundly concentrated in a way it has never been present in other, less sacred space. The poet imagines himself as David shortly after successfully conquering Jerusalem from the pagan Jebusites. The city, David has already determined, is destined for greatness: it is to be his capital city and the seat of his government. But a royal palace is not the ultimate adornment with which David wishes to glorify his new capital. The Holy Ark, the sacred box containing the tablets of the law, had been resting temporarily in a place called Kiriath-jearim after it had been in various other locations and, briefly, had been captured (but then returned) by the Philistines. It must have seemed obvious after the conquest of Jerusalem that the Ark needed to come there as well and eventually, as related in the sixth chapter of the Second Book of Samuel, David did indeed bring the Ark there. The biblical account of how that all happened is fascinating. And, indeed, it must have intrigued the psalmist no less than it does its modern

132

A song for the Levites to sing on the steps.
יהוה, remember all the suffering David endured [2]as a result of swearing to יהוה, as a result of taking this oath to the Mighty One of Jacob: [3]"Surely I shall neither enter my home tent nor climb up to my bedtime couch, [4]nor shall I grant sleep to my eyes or slumber to my eyelids, [5]until I find a place for יהוה, a residence for the Mighty One of Jacob."

[6] Now we heard of this in Efrat, we found evidence of it in Sede Yaar; [7]come, let us go to those sacred precincts, let us bow down to the place that is God's footstool.

[8] Rise up, יהוה, and come to Your resting place, both You and Your mighty Ark, [9]to that place where Your priests are garbed in righteousness and where Your pious rejoice.

[10] Do not turn away the face of Your anointed one for the sake of David, Your servant, [11]for יהוה swore an oath of truth to David, one from which never to turn back, saying, "I shall place one of

readers, because it was precisely in the context of these ancient events that the poet whose psalm became our 132nd chose to set his ode to the theological difficulty of locating God anywhere at all.

Does God exist everywhere? Everything we claim to know about God requires us to believe that the Almighty is everywhere, that the existence of God is unlike human existence precisely in that it does *not* require spatial coordinates to grant it physical reality. We say that so often—and repeat it so regularly in our prayers—that it eventually sounds as though it must be true. But what, really, does it mean? Our poet has David fearing that it was wrong, perhaps even sinful, for him to sleep in a warm bed in a gorgeous palace while the Almighty—not merely the Ark of the Covenant, but God fully present—had no place and no home. Put that way, the whole thought sounds naive, perhaps even slightly blasphemous. But David is merely giving voice to one of the deepest theological problems all people seeking to know and serve God must eventually face: that no matter how many slogans we mouth, we human beings are basically unable to conceive of (and, therefore, truly and unequivocally to believe in) existence without respect to the immutable coordinates of physical reality. As a result, the notion of God existing

אָשִׁית לְכִסֵּא־לָךְ׃ 12 אִם־יִשְׁמְרוּ בָנֶיךָ ׀ בְּרִיתִי
וְעֵדֹתִי זוֹ אֲלַמְּדֵם גַּם־בְּנֵיהֶם עֲדֵי־עַד יֵשְׁבוּ
לְכִסֵּא־לָךְ׃
13 כִּֽי־בָחַר יְהֹוָה בְּצִיּוֹן אִוָּהּ לְמוֹשָׁב לֽוֹ׃ 14 זֹאת־
מְנוּחָתִי עֲדֵי־עַד פֹּה אֵשֵׁב כִּי אִוִּתִֽיהָ׃ 15 צֵידָהּ
בָּרֵךְ אֲבָרֵךְ אֶבְיוֹנֶיהָ אַשְׂבִּיעַ לָֽחֶם׃ 16 וְֽכֹהֲנֶיהָ
אַלְבִּישׁ יֶשַׁע וַחֲסִידֶיהָ רַנֵּן יְרַנֵּֽנוּ׃ 17 שָׁם אַצְמִיחַ
קֶרֶן לְדָוִד עָרַכְתִּי נֵר לִמְשִׁיחִֽי׃ 18 אוֹיְבָיו אַלְבִּישׁ
בֹּשֶׁת וְעָלָיו יָצִיץ נִזְרֽוֹ׃

nowhere *and* everywhere *and* somewhere sounds enticing, but does not really mean anything at all to most of us . . . or at least nothing we can define with anything even remotely approaching precision.

When the poet writes that God has chosen Zion as a terrestrial *moshav,* then, the effect is both philosophically challenging and also slightly odd-sounding. Where is God? What exactly does it mean for God to have a *moshav,* a residence, on earth? If God has such a residence, then can (or must) we go

your own offspring on your throne. [12]Furthermore, if your children keep the terms of My covenant and the terms of the testimony that I shall teach them, then your progeny will sit on your throne forever."

[13] For יהוה, choosing Zion and desiring it as an earthly residence, said, [14]"This is to be My resting place for all time; here shall I dwell, for this do I desire. [15]I shall surely bless its provisions and satisfy its poor with bread. [16]Its priests I shall dress in salvation and its pious shall be very glad. [17]There shall I cause a horn to sprout for David, there shall I set up a lamp for My anointed one. [18]I shall dress his enemies in shame, but the crown on his head shall bring forth blossoms."

there to find God? How can God be both anywhere *and* everywhere? And if God is everywhere in equal measure, then how can we profess to feel the divine presence in a particular place without blaspheming against God's very nature? Is the search for God like the search for a missing key or is it like the search for love? Or is the search for God something utterly unique, something totally different from any other quest we might undertake in the course of our lives?

שִׁיר הַמַּעֲלוֹת לְדָוִד
הִנֵּה מַה־טּוֹב וּמַה־נָּעִים שֶׁבֶת אַחִים גַּם־יָחַד׃
2 כַּשֶּׁמֶן הַטּוֹב ׀ עַל־הָרֹאשׁ יֹרֵד עַל־הַזָּקָן זְקַן אַהֲרֹן
שֶׁיֹּרֵד עַל־פִּי מִדּוֹתָיו׃
3 כְּטַל־חֶרְמוֹן שֶׁיֹּרֵד עַל־הַרְרֵי צִיּוֹן כִּי שָׁם ׀ צִוָּה
יְהוָה אֶת־הַבְּרָכָה חַיִּים עַד־הָעוֹלָם׃

The opening verse of this psalm is a well-known and well-loved Jewish children's song. And, for many who sang it over and over as children, it may conjure up a set of semi-wistful memories as well. Summer camp. A chilly July evening in the country. Nine-year-olds gathered around a dying campfire. An odd mixture of conflicting emotions: longing for home, dreading the return home, loving the intimacy of friendship, being slightly afraid of the independence from one's family back home that the succor of such peer-based intimacy inevitably implies. And, indeed, the words of the song really are familiar—so familiar, in fact, that almost no one actually recalls learning them or the slightly boozy melody that goes with them, a melody somehow capable of encapsulating the sweetness of childhood friendship in a way few other songs or poems ever could.

But perhaps the 133rd psalm could be something else. It is, after all, a song from an ancient hymnal, not a summer camp songbook. Might it not be, then, the literary testimony, perhaps, of a Levitical poet struggling with conflicting emotions toward the priests among whom he works—and whom the world considers to be the *real* priests with their well-oiled Aaronic beards, their stylish haircuts, and their smart priestly outfits? Our poet feels a deep sense

133

A song for the Levites to sing on the steps.
It would surely be good and delightful if brothers were to dwell together in peace.
[2] It would be as though fine oil were drizzled down on their heads in such quantities that it drenched those beards, those Aaron-beards, in such quantities that the oil dripped down from there to soak the neck aperture of their priestly garments.
[3] It would be as though the great dew of Mount Hermon were to fall on the hills of Zion, for it is there that יהוה decreed that the blessing of life eternal be found.

of common purpose with his priestly brethren. But he receives back from them nothing other than the sense that he is unwanted . . . and that the spirituality of the Psalter is somehow second-best when compared with the exquisite worship-through-obedience theology of the Torah. The poet whose poem became our 133rd psalm knew that most of his co-citizens took his job merely to involve singing and serving without complaining and, even more to the point, without making waves. As someone with a sense of spiritual purpose and a religious orientation far deeper than most outsiders suspected, however, the poet feels betrayed and disliked by his priestly brethren—perhaps even despised by them—and his little song reflects his ambivalence and ill ease. What, he sings, if just for a moment, we were to find the courage to live together in peace? What if we set aside our differences for the sake of joining together in the worship of God? What if we really behaved like brethren instead of like teams of disgruntled employees ferociously competing for the boss's attention? What if the days of our lives were endless efforts to praise God instead of endless acts of self-aggrandizement?

קלד

שִׁיר הַֽמַּ֫עֲל֥וֹת
הִנֵּ֤ה ׀ בָּרְכ֣וּ אֶת־יְ֭הוָה כָּל־עַבְדֵ֣י יְהוָ֑ה הָעֹמְדִ֥ים
בְּבֵית־יְ֝הוָ֗ה בַּלֵּילֽוֹת׃
2 שְׂאוּ־יְדֵכֶ֥ם קֹ֑דֶשׁ וּ֝בָרְכוּ אֶת־יְהוָֽה׃ 3 יְבָרֶכְךָ֣ יְ֭הוָה
מִצִּיּ֑וֹן עֹ֝שֵׂ֗ה שָׁמַ֥יִם וָאָֽרֶץ׃

A cold night. A Jerusalem winter. The priests are asleep in the Hearth House on the northern wall of the Priests' Forecourt, the westernmost of the three adjoining courtyards that constitute the sacred inner space of the Temple in Jerusalem. The Levites are on duty throughout the night, guarding against intruders, against untoward events in the sacred precincts, and even against the specter of unwanted impurity. To the casual passer-by, they look like lumberjacks: big, burly men wearing padded winter jackets and holding pick-axes and other tools of the security trade. The priests treat them like servants. The people who frequent the Temple consider them doormen or, at best, minstrels. The Torah itself uses the language of slavery in describing how they were commissioned for divine service, but there is more here than meets the eye. Nighttime is the Levites' hour in the Temple: no one guards the sacred courts but they and, therefore, none to whom they grant access is ever turned away. As the moon rises and

134 A song for the Levites to sing on the steps.
Bless יהוה, all you servants of יהוה who stand throughout the night in the House of יהוה.
[2] Lift up your hands to the sanctuary and bless יהוה. [3] יהוה, Maker of heaven and earth, will bless you then from Zion.

the courts are bathed in its yellow light, a small group gathers. No one speaks. The night is totally still. The air is heavy with God. The hymns begin. Some of them are the famous "Songs of the Steps" that the Levites have composed specifically for recitation on the steps leading down from the Courtyard of Israel to the Women's Courtyard; others, however, are less familiar psalms taken from parts of the hymnal not everybody knows. The singing is muted, sometimes even whispered, lest it awaken any interest on the part of the outside world. The light of God will shine forth from the Holy of Holies . . . if those gathering in the Temple court can draw it out. A cold breeze sweeps through the courtyard. The Levites turn to the building that houses the innermost sanctum, the Holy of Holies. As if on signal, they raise their hands and in unison begin to bless God, the holy Source of light *and* night, Maker of heaven and earth, the God of Israel for whose communicative presence they yearn and whose protective succor they so ardently wish to solicit through their nighttime efforts.

קלה

הַֽלְלוּיָהּ ׀
הַֽלְלוּ אֶת־שֵׁם יְהוָה הַֽלְלוּ עַבְדֵי יְהוָה׃
2 שֶׁעֹמְדִים בְּבֵית יְהוָה בְּחַצְרוֹת בֵּית אֱלֹהֵינוּ׃
3 הַֽלְלוּיָהּ כִּי־טוֹב יְהוָה זַמְּרוּ לִשְׁמוֹ כִּי נָעִים׃
4 כִּי־יַעֲקֹב בָּחַר לוֹ יָהּ יִשְׂרָאֵל לִסְגֻלָּתוֹ׃
5 כִּי אֲנִי יָדַעְתִּי כִּי־גָדוֹל יְהוָה וַאֲדֹנֵינוּ מִכָּל־
אֱלֹהִים׃ 6 כֹּל אֲשֶׁר־חָפֵץ יְהוָה עָשָׂה בַּשָּׁמַיִם
וּבָאָרֶץ בַּיַּמִּים וְכָל־תְּהוֹמוֹת׃
7 מַעֲלֶה נְשִׂאִים מִקְצֵה הָאָרֶץ בְּרָקִים לַמָּטָר עָשָׂה
מֽוֹצֵא־רוּחַ מֵאוֹצְרוֹתָיו׃
8 שֶׁהִכָּה בְּכוֹרֵי מִצְרָיִם מֵאָדָם עַד־בְּהֵמָה׃ 9 שָׁלַח ׀
אֹתוֹת וּמֹפְתִים בְּתוֹכֵכִי מִצְרָיִם בְּפַרְעֹה וּבְכָל־
עֲבָדָיו׃
10 שֶׁהִכָּה גּוֹיִם רַבִּים וְהָרַג מְלָכִים עֲצוּמִים׃
11 לְסִיחוֹן ׀ מֶלֶךְ הָאֱמֹרִי וּלְעוֹג מֶלֶךְ הַבָּשָׁן וּלְכֹל
מַמְלְכוֹת כְּנָעַן׃ 12 וְנָתַן אַרְצָם נַחֲלָה נַחֲלָה
לְיִשְׂרָאֵל עַמּוֹ׃
13 יְהוָה שִׁמְךָ לְעוֹלָם יְהוָה זִכְרְךָ לְדֹר־וָדֹר׃
14 כִּֽי־יָדִין יְהוָה עַמּוֹ וְעַל־עֲבָדָיו יִתְנֶחָם׃

A shortened form of the four-letter, ineffable name of God, יה ("Yah"), appears on its own only two dozen times in Scripture, all but all five of them in the Book of Psalms. Together with the imperative form *hallelu* ("praise!"), however, it forms the most famous of all Hebrew words, *halleluyah* (written slightly differently in English, but pronounced exactly the same). This word appears another two dozen times in the Bible, all of them in the Psalter, and seems to have named a whole genre of ancient Israelite songs as well: ten psalms (this one plus the 106th, 111th, 112th, 113th, 146th, 147th, 148th, 149th, and 150th) begin with the word, sounding as though it were an indication of the specific genre of the hymn of praise that follows. Our psalm also ends with *halleluyah,* as do another dozen psalms (the 104th, 105th, 106th, 113th, 115th, 116th, 117th, 146th, 147th, 148th, 149th, and 150th), so the word also appears to have functioned as a kind of one-word doxology intended, presumably, to finish the song it concludes on a unison note of shared purpose in the praise of God. (Some psalms, like this one, both begin *and* end with *halleluyah.*)

It is no longer possible, of course, to know precisely what force the word had in ancient times or in the specific context of ancient Hebrew hymnody,

135

Hallelujah.

Praise the name of יהוה; praise it, [2]you servants of יהוה who stand in the House of יהוה, in the courtyards of the House of our God.

[3] Sing "hallelujah," for יהוה is good; sing to God's name, for it is pleasant.

[4] For יה has chosen Jacob as God's own, Israel as God's treasure.

[5] For I know that יהוה is great, our Ruler greater than the gods of all other nations: [6]יהוה acts solely in accordance with divine desire in the heavens and on earth, in the seas and in the depths.

[7] God brings up the rain clouds from the edges of the earth, makes bolts of lightning for the rain, brings the wind out of its storehouses.

[8] It was God who smote the firstborn of Egypt, both human and animal, [9]who sent signs and wonders into the midst of Egypt, into the circle of Pharaoh and his servants.

[10] And it was God who smote numerous nations and slew mighty kings—[11]Sihon, king of the Amorites, and Og, king of Bashan, and the kings of all the kingdoms of Canaan—[12]and gave their land as an inheritance, as an inheritance to Israel, the people of God.

[13] יהוה, Your name will forever exist; יהוה, Your appellation shall endure throughout every generation, [14]for יהוה shall judge the people and take pity on God's servants.

but the 135th psalm suggests how the *halleluyah* songs were actually used. The poet is not a lone bard sitting beneath a desert palm contemplating the nature of divinity, but a working Levite leading the chorus of song that accompanied the sacrificial service in the Temple in old Jerusalem. Choosing many familiar phrases from other psalms and biblical passages, he begins his hymn with a simple call to praise God. The Levites are in position on their risers. The priests are in place with the livestock in the innermost courtyard. The public is gathered in the other Temple courtyards, men and women together in the easternmost one and men alone in the one closer to the court of the priests. The song leader calls out for hymns of praise from all those standing in the Temple courts: they are to demonstrate their participation in the sacrificial

15 עֲצַבֵּי הַגּוֹיִם כֶּסֶף וְזָהָב מַעֲשֵׂה יְדֵי אָדָם׃
16 פֶּה־לָהֶם וְלֹא יְדַבֵּרוּ עֵינַיִם לָהֶם וְלֹא יִרְאוּ׃
17 אָזְנַיִם לָהֶם וְלֹא יַאֲזִינוּ אַף אֵין־יֶשׁ־רוּחַ בְּפִיהֶם׃
18 כְּמוֹהֶם יִהְיוּ עֹשֵׂיהֶם כֹּל אֲשֶׁר־בֹּטֵחַ בָּהֶם׃
19 בֵּית יִשְׂרָאֵל בָּרְכוּ אֶת־יְהוָה בֵּית אַהֲרֹן בָּרְכוּ אֶת־יְהוָה׃
20 בֵּית הַלֵּוִי בָּרְכוּ אֶת־יְהוָה יִרְאֵי יְהוָה בָּרְכוּ אֶת־יְהוָה׃
21 בָּרוּךְ יְהוָה ׀ מִצִּיּוֹן שֹׁכֵן יְרוּשָׁלָ͏ִם הַלְלוּ־יָהּ׃

service by chanting hymns of praise to God while the priests actually perform the animal sacrifices, disembowelling carcasses for immolation and preparing huge bowls of blood for libation. All are to join in: priests, Levites, ordinary citizens, even the class of (presumably) non-native "God-fearers."

For his part, the poet has a specific idea *how* they should praise their God: by combining various biblical references, the assembled are to acknowledge God not solely as the Sovereign of Nature or as the Author of History alone, but as both at once—as the God whose influence over the physical world and whose involvement in history only appear as separate categories to people anxious to embrace one aspect of God's governance of the world without inadvertently accepting the other.

Moderns readers will do well to respond to the 135th psalm by asking themselves why, precisely, it is so difficult to accept that the affairs of humanity and the reality of natural science are merely two sides of a very thin coin when

[15] The idols of the nations are made of silver and gold; they are the work of human hands.

[16] They have mouths, but cannot speak. They have eyes, but cannot see.[17] They have ears but cannot hear. And if they have no real noses, can there be breath in their mouths?

[18] May those who make them—and all who trust in them—be just like them.

[19] O House of Israel, bless יהוה. O House of Aaron, bless יהוה.

[20] O House of the Levite, bless יהוה. O Fearers of יהוה, bless יהוה.

[21] Blessed be יהוה who dwells in Jerusalem from Zion. Hallelujah.

viewed from the vantage point of faith in God. And they can also ask why this particular way of thinking appeals so little to moderns anxious to create a kind of faith for themselves that they can feel justified in pronouncing "reasonable." In the second part of his poem, the psalmist turns to the question of idolatry, using some familiar imagery but without explaining himself. Could it be that idolatry is, in the end, not so much the sin of making things into gods, but of making God into things? Of insisting that God stay well within what we conceive of as the boundaries of the divine realm instead of acknowledging that it is we, not God, who are shackled by the limits inherent in the nature of human perceptive consciousness? Is idolatry what happens when honest worship becomes so suffused with egotism and arrogance that it becomes meaningless . . . or possibly even blasphemous?

A version of verses 15–20 of this psalm appears (with some major and some minor changes) as verses 4–11 of Psalm 115.

קלו

הוֹדוּ לַיהוָה כִּי־טוֹב כִּי לְעוֹלָם חַסְדּוֹ׃
[2] הוֹדוּ לֵאלֹהֵי הָאֱלֹהִים כִּי לְעוֹלָם חַסְדּוֹ׃
[3] הוֹדוּ לַאֲדֹנֵי הָאֲדֹנִים כִּי לְעוֹלָם חַסְדּוֹ׃
[4] לְעֹשֵׂה נִפְלָאוֹת גְּדֹלוֹת לְבַדּוֹ כִּי לְעוֹלָם חַסְדּוֹ׃
[5] לְעֹשֵׂה הַשָּׁמַיִם בִּתְבוּנָה כִּי לְעוֹלָם חַסְדּוֹ׃
[6] לְרֹקַע הָאָרֶץ עַל־הַמָּיִם כִּי לְעוֹלָם חַסְדּוֹ׃
[7] לְעֹשֵׂה אוֹרִים גְּדֹלִים כִּי לְעוֹלָם חַסְדּוֹ׃
[8] אֶת־הַשֶּׁמֶשׁ לְמֶמְשֶׁלֶת בַּיּוֹם כִּי לְעוֹלָם חַסְדּוֹ׃
[9] אֶת־הַיָּרֵחַ וְכוֹכָבִים לְמֶמְשְׁלוֹת בַּלָּיְלָה כִּי לְעוֹלָם חַסְדּוֹ׃
[10] לְמַכֵּה מִצְרַיִם בִּבְכוֹרֵיהֶם כִּי לְעוֹלָם חַסְדּוֹ׃
[11] וַיּוֹצֵא יִשְׂרָאֵל מִתּוֹכָם כִּי לְעוֹלָם חַסְדּוֹ׃
[12] בְּיָד חֲזָקָה וּבִזְרוֹעַ נְטוּיָה כִּי לְעוֹלָם חַסְדּוֹ׃
[13] לְגֹזֵר יַם־סוּף לִגְזָרִים כִּי לְעוֹלָם חַסְדּוֹ׃
[14] וְהֶעֱבִיר יִשְׂרָאֵל בְּתוֹכוֹ כִּי לְעוֹלָם חַסְדּוֹ׃

Although its structure strongly suggests that it was composed as an antiphonal hymn, the 136th psalm does not bear any indication of how it actually was sung in ancient times, or even of how its author hoped that it would be performed. Still one can imagine the clarion voice of, say, an especially gifted Levitical tenor singing out the first half of each line while the citizenry, crammed into the Temple courtyards and led by the Levitical choir in place on their performance platform, responded in joyous response that, yes, divine mercy really is forever. The hymn itself is simply constructed. The poet took an apparently stock phrase—Psalms 106, 107, and 118 also begin with the same, or almost the same, opening line—and, after using it to start off his poem on a familiar note, then composed twenty-five alternate thoughts and plugged them into the last of those opening words so that all twenty-six verses of his poem end with the same three words: *ki le'olam ḥasdo* ("for divine mercy is forever").

Modern readers will find the poet's notion of divine mercy no less challenging than naive. Many centuries later, the kabbalists of medieval Europe would imagine the stuff of governance that flows through the godhead to the world below as being made up of equal or unequal parts of mercy and strict, rigorous justice. (The precise mixture of the two was thought to depend on the piety of God's terrestrial worshipers.) For the biblical poet, however, the idea was simpler and bolder: God is the absolute Sovereign of the world and can, therefore, govern humanity strictly or leniently at will. It would be feasible,

136

Give thanks to יהוה for God is good, for divine mercy is forever.

[2] Give thanks to the God of gods, for divine mercy is forever.

[3] Give thanks to the Ruler of rulers, for divine mercy is forever.

[4] To the One who alone does mighty wonders, for divine mercy is forever.

[5] To the One who made the heavens with wisdom, for divine mercy is forever.

[6] To the One who spread out the earth over the waters, for divine mercy is forever.

[7] To the One who made the great lights, for divine mercy is forever.

[8] The sun to govern during the day, for divine mercy is forever.

[9] The moon and stars to govern during the night, for divine mercy is forever.

[10] To the One who smote Egypt through her first-born sons, for divine mercy is forever.

[11] And who took Israel out from their midst, for divine mercy is forever.

[12] With a mighty hand and an outstretched arm, for divine mercy is forever.

[13] To the One who split the Sea of Reeds asunder, for divine mercy is forever.

[14] And who let Israel pass through it, for divine mercy is forever.

even perhaps reasonable, for God to punish humanity for its endless transgressions. There appears, however, to be a quality of mercy within the folds of God's ineffable nature that brings the world a kind of respite from the logical consequences of its impiety and its apparently endemic propensity to disobey the laws of God. And it is precisely this quality of mercy, the poet suggests, that rests at the core of God's relationship with the world. It was what prompted God to create the world in the first place, for example. And it was the aspect of the Divine responsible for Israel's liberation from Egyptian bondage and for the people's subsequent success in conquering the Land of Israel. In our day, it is the quality that prompts God to provide bread for the world.

The poet seems comfortable with the idea that nothing comes inevitably to people on account of their own merits. Indeed, the poet seems quite convinced

15 וְנִעֵר פַּרְעֹה וְחֵילוֹ בְיַם־סוּף כִּי לְעוֹלָם חַסְדּוֹ׃
16 לְמוֹלִיךְ עַמּוֹ בַּמִּדְבָּר כִּי לְעוֹלָם חַסְדּוֹ׃
17 לְמַכֵּה מְלָכִים גְּדֹלִים כִּי לְעוֹלָם חַסְדּוֹ׃
18 וַיַּהֲרֹג מְלָכִים אַדִּירִים כִּי לְעוֹלָם חַסְדּוֹ׃
19 לְסִיחוֹן מֶלֶךְ הָאֱמֹרִי כִּי לְעוֹלָם חַסְדּוֹ׃
20 וּלְעוֹג מֶלֶךְ הַבָּשָׁן כִּי לְעוֹלָם חַסְדּוֹ׃
21 וְנָתַן אַרְצָם לְנַחֲלָה כִּי לְעוֹלָם חַסְדּוֹ׃
22 נַחֲלָה לְיִשְׂרָאֵל עַבְדּוֹ כִּי לְעוֹלָם חַסְדּוֹ׃
23 שֶׁבְּשִׁפְלֵנוּ זָכַר־לָנוּ כִּי לְעוֹלָם חַסְדּוֹ׃
24 וַיִּפְרְקֵנוּ מִצָּרֵינוּ כִּי לְעוֹלָם חַסְדּוֹ׃
25 נֹתֵן לֶחֶם לְכָל־בָּשָׂר כִּי לְעוֹלָם חַסְדּוֹ׃
26 הוֹדוּ לְאֵל הַשָּׁמָיִם כִּי לְעוֹלָם חַסְדּוֹ׃

that existence itself can only be explained with recourse to the mercy of God . . . and that the fact that there is bread in the world proves the reality of divine mercy far more potently and profoundly than the fact that there are hungry people in the world denies it. In the post-Shoah world, we may consider this kind of theological thinking unsophisticated . . . but surely we have no reason to be less driven than our ancestors to find evidence of God's mercy in our world than they were in theirs.

Even so, there is something perplexing about the relentlessly optimistic cadences of the 136th psalm (called in Jewish tradition "the Great Hallel," the Great Song of Praise), something that will make its recitation and consideration occasion a sense of spiritual uncertainty for sensitive moderns. If, as the psalm says, God did all these great and helpful things for our ancestors because of the unchanging, steadfast, and constant influence of mercy within the panoply of divine qualities, then how could bad things *ever* befall the people of God? Is it possible that the very quality of divine mercy that the poet insists is *permanent* might not always be *operative*? Does God withhold the quality of mercy occasionally? It would be hard to explain the monstrous horrors that have befallen the Jewish people without arguing that divine mercy is *not* actually forever and always . . . but surely the poet whose poem became our 136th psalm must have known perfectly well that he was only singing about one side of the ledger. And he surely must also have known that other members of the poets' guild sang very different songs about the consequences of Israel's rebelliousness.

[15] And who pitched Pharaoh and his army into the Sea of Reeds, for divine mercy is forever.

[16] To the One who guided the people of God in the desert, for divine mercy is forever.

[17] To the One who smote great kings, for divine mercy is forever.

[18] And who killed mighty kings, for divine mercy is forever.

[19] To the One who killed Sihon, king of the Amorites, for divine mercy is forever.

[20] And Og, king of the Bashan, for divine mercy is forever.

[21] And who gave away their land as an inheritance, for divine mercy is forever.

[22] As an inheritance to Israel, God's servant, for divine mercy is forever.

[23] To the One who remembered us in our distress, for divine mercy is forever.

[24] And delivered us from our enemies, for divine mercy is forever.

[25] To the One who gives bread to all flesh, for divine mercy is forever.

[26] Give thanks to the God of heaven, for divine mercy is forever.

Indeed, by listing only the positive things that happened to the ancient Israelites in his song and by omitting reference to the various disasters that befell the people during the same years covered by his psalm, the poet is hinting that divine mercy, although theoretically forever existent, could still be overwhelmed by God's sense of strict, rigorous justice when circumstances warranted . . . or when the people's behavior left God with no choice other than to turn away and leave them to survive as best they could on their own.

Perhaps the poet's point is precisely that surviving on their own meant precisely fending for themselves without the protective balm of divine succor the poet knows normally to be Israel's defense against the rage of the world. And that for all divine mercy is forever *in theory,* the people of God will have to conduct themselves in a way consonant with the will of God if their descendants are going to sing about them in the same way the poet sang of his ancient forebears: by listing all the great and positive developments in their history and noting that, yes, the list itself proves that, divine mercy is forever present and permanently possible.

קלז

עַל־נַהֲרוֹת ׀ בָּבֶל שָׁם יָשַׁבְנוּ גַּם־בָּכִינוּ בְּזָכְרֵנוּ אֶת־צִיּוֹן׃
[2] עַל־עֲרָבִים בְּתוֹכָהּ תָּלִינוּ כִּנֹּרוֹתֵינוּ׃ [3] כִּי שָׁם שְׁאֵלוּנוּ שׁוֹבֵינוּ דִּבְרֵי־שִׁיר וְתוֹלָלֵינוּ שִׂמְחָה שִׁירוּ לָנוּ מִשִּׁיר צִיּוֹן׃
[4] אֵיךְ נָשִׁיר אֶת־שִׁיר יְהוָה עַל אַדְמַת נֵכָר׃
[5] אִם־אֶשְׁכָּחֵךְ יְרוּשָׁלָם תִּשְׁכַּח יְמִינִי׃ [6] תִּדְבַּק־לְשׁוֹנִי ׀ לְחִכִּי אִם־לֹא אֶזְכְּרֵכִי אִם־לֹא אַעֲלֶה אֶת־יְרוּשָׁלַם עַל רֹאשׁ שִׂמְחָתִי׃
[7] זְכֹר יְהוָה ׀ לִבְנֵי אֱדוֹם אֵת יוֹם יְרוּשָׁלָם הָאֹמְרִים עָרוּ ׀ עָרוּ עַד הַיְסוֹד בָּהּ׃
[8] בַּת־בָּבֶל הַשְּׁדוּדָה אַשְׁרֵי שֶׁיְשַׁלֶּם־לָךְ אֶת־גְּמוּלֵךְ שֶׁגָּמַלְתְּ לָנוּ׃
[9] אַשְׁרֵי ׀ שֶׁיֹּאחֵז וְנִפֵּץ אֶת־עֹלָלַיִךְ אֶל־הַסָּלַע׃

The poet reminds his readers that the Levites in the Second Temple were musicians, not mere versifiers, and that their psalms were therefore intended to be sung, not merely read or recited. In his mind's eye, he imagines himself back in Babylon during the period of exile in the sixth century B.C.E. and wonders what it would have been like to be ordered by the enemy to debase the hymns of Zion by singing them to entertain ruthless captors, rather than to elevate and instruct the faithful. He imagines his colleagues resisting the foe's command and going on strike as they hang up their instruments on the branches of nearby trees and declare that they simply cannot—and will not—sing songs of God's faithfulness and love for Israel in a context that would make a vulgar mockery of all that those hymns present as sacred.

Moderns will be impressed with the image of passive resistance presented in the 137th psalm, but less so by the vindictive, heartless curse with which the psalmist closes his poem. Does the poet cancel out his own virtuous sentiment

137

There, by the rivers of Babylon, we sat and wept as we remembered Zion.
[2] On the willows in her midst we hung our lyres [3]when our captors demanded to hear some songs, when our tormentors asked for some happy tunes, saying, "Sing us some songs of Zion."
[4] And just how shall we sing songs of יהוה on foreign soil?
[5] If I should forget you, O Jerusalem, let my right hand too forget how to function; [6]let my tongue cleave to my palate if I no longer remember you, if I do not place Jerusalem at the top of the list of things that bring me joy.
[7] Remember, יהוה, the "Day of Jerusalem" when You think of the Edomites as well, those who cried out, "Raze it, raze it down to its very foundation."
[8] O daughter of Babylon destined for plunder, happy will be the one who pays back to you just what you have done to us.
[9] Happy will be the one who seizes your infants and hurls them down on a rock.

by imagining that people who are prepared to resist tyranny so nobly could also wish for something so ignoble as the death of the enemy's innocent babes? It is probably foolish even to attempt to pass judgment on a poet without knowing any of the specific circumstances that led him to feel as enraged and vindictive as he apparently did feel. Reading the 137th psalm can, nonetheless, provide readers with a good opportunity to consider the conflict between baseness and nobility that rages within most human breasts. Must people be good or evil? Or is life an eternal battle between the two, one that saints acknowledge and sinners deny . . . but that no one can truly sidestep?

קלח

לְדָוִד ׀
אוֹדְךָ בְכָל־לִבִּי נֶגֶד אֱלֹהִים אֲזַמְּרֶךָּ׃
2 אֶשְׁתַּחֲוֶה אֶל־הֵיכַל קָדְשְׁךָ וְאוֹדֶה אֶת־שְׁמֶךָ
עַל־חַסְדְּךָ וְעַל־אֲמִתֶּךָ כִּי־הִגְדַּלְתָּ עַל־כָּל־שִׁמְךָ
אִמְרָתֶךָ׃
3 בְּיוֹם קָרָאתִי וַתַּעֲנֵנִי תַּרְהִבֵנִי בְנַפְשִׁי עֹז׃
4 יוֹדוּךָ יְהֹוָה כָּל־מַלְכֵי־אָרֶץ כִּי שָׁמְעוּ אִמְרֵי־פִיךָ׃
5 וְיָשִׁירוּ בְּדַרְכֵי יְהֹוָה כִּי גָדוֹל כְּבוֹד יְהֹוָה׃
6 כִּי־רָם יְהֹוָה וְשָׁפָל יִרְאֶה וְגָבֹהַּ מִמֶּרְחָק יְיֵדָע׃
7 אִם־אֵלֵךְ ׀ בְּקֶרֶב צָרָה תְּחַיֵּנִי עַל אַף אֹיְבַי תִּשְׁלַח
יָדֶךָ וְתוֹשִׁיעֵנִי יְמִינֶךָ׃
8 יְהֹוָה יִגְמֹר בַּעֲדִי יְהֹוָה חַסְדְּךָ לְעוֹלָם מַעֲשֵׂי יָדֶיךָ
אַל־תֶּרֶף׃

Although the modern Hebrew word for "thank you," *todah,* does not appear in the Bible with that specific meaning, the three-letter root at its core appears throughout the biblical text with two basic meanings, both of them evidenced in the 138th psalm. When, for example, the poet writes *odekha bekhol libi,* he means to say that he *gives thanks* to God with all his heart. When he writes just a line later, however, *odeh et shmekha,* he means that he wishes to *acknowledge* the sacred reality of God's name as an existent, effective, and holy force for good in the world. The poet may not even have noticed this feature of his own language, but modern readers may wonder why classical Hebrew sees the notions of confessing the reality of God and of feeling a formal need to express one's gratitude to God as the same

138

(A psalm) of David.

I give thanks to You with all my heart; in the presence of the celestial hosts, I sing to You.

[2] I bow down towards Your holy Temple and I acknowledge the sanctity of Your name because of Your mercy and Your truth, for You have made Your name, Your word, greater than all.

[3] You answered me on the day I called out to You, planting strength within my soul.

[4] All the kings of the earth will acknowledge You, יהוה, once they hear the words of Your mouth.

[5] And they shall sing of the ways of יהוה, for the glory of יהוה is great.

[6] Although exalted, יהוה still takes note of the lowly and identifies the arrogant even from a distance.

[7] If I were to walk into the midst of mortal danger, You would preserve my life by sending Your hand against the anger of my enemies; You would save me with Your right hand.

[8] יהוה will end my troubles for me. יהוה, Your mercy is forever. Forsake not the work of Your hands.

thing—or perhaps as two slightly divergent aspects of the same thing. And the corollary idea, that it should be impossible to acknowledge the reality of God without being overwhelmed with feelings of gratitude, is also well worth contemplating. For latter-day readers, the 138th psalm can prompt some other challenging questions as well. Is our faith the begrudging admission of a reality we feel, somehow, called upon to perceive? Or is it the joyous affirmation of divine goodness in the world the psalmist appears to find intrinsic to belief in God no matter what its origin? Can there even exist true faith in God that is begrudging and ungenerous?

קלט

לַמְנַצֵּחַ לְדָוִד מִזְמוֹר
יְהוָה חֲקַרְתַּנִי וַתֵּדָע:
2 אַתָּה יָדַעְתָּ שִׁבְתִּי וְקוּמִי בַּנְתָּה לְרֵעִי מֵרָחוֹק:
3 אָרְחִי וְרִבְעִי זֵרִיתָ וְכָל־דְּרָכַי הִסְכַּנְתָּה: 4 כִּי אֵין
מִלָּה בִּלְשׁוֹנִי הֵן יְהוָה יָדַעְתָּ כֻלָּהּ:
5 אָחוֹר וָקֶדֶם צַרְתָּנִי וַתָּשֶׁת עָלַי כַּפֶּכָה:
6* פְּלִיאָה דַעַת מִמֶּנִּי נִשְׂגְּבָה לֹא־אוּכַל לָהּ:
7 אָנָה אֵלֵךְ מֵרוּחֶךָ וְאָנָה מִפָּנֶיךָ אֶבְרָח:
8 אִם־אֶסַּק שָׁמַיִם שָׁם אָתָּה וְאַצִּיעָה שְּׁאוֹל הִנֶּךָּ:
9 אֶשָּׂא כַנְפֵי־שָׁחַר אֶשְׁכְּנָה בְּאַחֲרִית יָם:
10 גַּם־שָׁם יָדְךָ תַנְחֵנִי וְתֹאחֲזֵנִי יְמִינֶךָ:
11 וָאֹמַר אַךְ־חֹשֶׁךְ יְשׁוּפֵנִי וְלַיְלָה אוֹר בַּעֲדֵנִי:
12 גַּם־חֹשֶׁךְ לֹא־יַחְשִׁיךְ מִמֶּךָ וְלַיְלָה כַּיּוֹם יָאִיר
כַּחֲשֵׁיכָה כָּאוֹרָה:
13 כִּי־אַתָּה קָנִיתָ כִלְיֹתָי תְּסֻכֵּנִי בְּבֶטֶן אִמִּי:
14 אוֹדְךָ עַל כִּי נוֹרָאוֹת נִפְלֵיתִי נִפְלָאִים מַעֲשֶׂיךָ
וְנַפְשִׁי יֹדַעַת מְאֹד:

v. 6 פלאיה כתיב

The 139th psalm is filled with difficult turns of phrase, obscure words, and archaic expressions, but the poet's basic concept is entirely clear nonetheless: his God is neither theory nor dogma, neither philosophical construct nor emotional crutch, neither spiritual necessity nor article of theological faith. And, indeed, it is reasonable to imagine that the poet wrote specifically to express—to his audience, probably to himself, possibly even to God—the degree to which he feels the presence of God as a real, tangible, entirely existent presence in his life.

For all else that his faith may entail, the poet feels his God is utterly real and fully, palpably present—and not solely when he is engaged in prayer or poetry. Indeed, he perceives himself to be in the presence of God when he sits down to a meal or when he lies down to rest, when he sets out in the morning to walk to work and when he sets himself to contemplating the nature of things. The poet's God is within him no less totally than he, the poet, lives in his God. Indeed, when he declares that he simply cannot imagine that even the most banal word he utters is not somehow informed and shaped by the presence of God in his life, even the most skeptical listener cannot fail to be moved by his untroubled faith. But the poet's life is not lived in the company only of God—he also lives with villains and scoundrels who loathe him for his piety. Yet, like so many others of his colleagues in the poets' guild, he refuses to

139

For the conductor, a psalm of David.
יהוה, You have studied me, so You know what kind of person I am.
[2] You know when I sit and when I stand; You understand my thoughts from a distance.
[3] You scrutinize me when I go walking and when I lie down, examining all my paths in life; [4] there is not even a single word on my tongue that You do not know. O יהוה, You know it all.
[5] You fashioned me front and back, setting Your hand upon me to grant me life.
[6] Knowledge of You is too wondrous for me, exalted beyond my capacity to fathom.
[7] Where could I ever go to escape from Your spirit? Where could I go to flee from Your face?
[8] If I were to ascend to heaven, You would be there; if I were to spread out my bed in Sheol, You would be there too.
[9] Shall I sprout the wings of dawn and take up residence on the other side of the sea?
[10] Even there would Your hand guide me; even there would Your right hand grasp me.
[11] Shall I say, "Surely darkness shall hide me, surely night will keep light from me"?
[12] Even darkness will not keep me hidden from You, You for whom night is as bright as day, for whom darkness and light are no different.
[13] For You have made my kidneys; it was You who formed me in my mother's belly.
[14] And so I give thanks to You because of the awesome, wondrous way I am made; my soul well knows how wondrous are Your works.

blame his situation on God, preferring instead to consider his dilemma as a function of some disturbing character trait of his own, or perhaps some trace of unacknowledged sin he must beg God to help him avoid in the future.

Modern readers may well wish to ask themselves what it would mean to feel God's presence as deeply as did the author of the 139th psalm. What would it mean to embrace faith in God as a palpable part of the physical world in which we live, rather than merely as the result of philosophical inquiry or spiritual longing? Moderns are so used, after all, to explaining God as a noble philosophical theory that it comes almost as a disorienting surprise to find the poets of the Psalter writing about God as

15 לֹא־נִכְחַד עָצְמִי מִמֶּךָּ אֲשֶׁר־עֻשֵּׂיתִי בַסֵּתֶר
רֻקַּמְתִּי בְּתַחְתִּיּוֹת אָרֶץ׃
16 גָּלְמִי ׀ רָאוּ עֵינֶיךָ וְעַל־סִפְרְךָ כֻּלָּם יִכָּתֵבוּ יָמִים
יֻצָּרוּ *וְלוֹ אֶחָד בָּהֶם׃
17 וְלִי מַה־יָּקְרוּ רֵעֶיךָ אֵל מֶה עָצְמוּ רָאשֵׁיהֶם׃
18 אֶסְפְּרֵם מֵחוֹל יִרְבּוּן הֱקִיצֹתִי וְעוֹדִי עִמָּךְ׃
19 אִם־תִּקְטֹל אֱלוֹהַּ ׀ רָשָׁע וְאַנְשֵׁי דָמִים סוּרוּ מֶנִּי׃
20 אֲשֶׁר יֹאמְרֻךָ לִמְזִמָּה נָשֻׂא לַשָּׁוְא עָרֶיךָ׃
21 הֲלוֹא־מְשַׂנְאֶיךָ יְהוָה ׀ אֶשְׂנָא וּבִתְקוֹמְמֶיךָ
אֶתְקוֹטָט׃
22 תַּכְלִית שִׂנְאָה שְׂנֵאתִים לְאוֹיְבִים הָיוּ לִי׃
23 חָקְרֵנִי אֵל וְדַע לְבָבִי בְּחָנֵנִי וְדַע שַׂרְעַפָּי׃
24 וּרְאֵה אִם־דֶּרֶךְ־עֹצֶב בִּי וּנְחֵנִי בְּדֶרֶךְ עוֹלָם׃

v. 16 ולא כתיב

though the reality of the Divine were palpable and fully perceptible in the same way people perceive the world around them. Can moderns ever come to that kind of faith and belief in God, accepting it with the same kind of untroubled certainty with which they perceive things in their personal ambits? More to the point, *how* could moderns ever move themselves forward to that kind of serene faith? For most of us, philosophical inquiry—even of the most intense kind—can only yield a profound sense that God must logically exist. The psalmists seem to have felt the same way, which is why they apparently did not really buy into the idea that faith in God may be acquired solely through the performance of ritual. They do not speak disparagingly about the concept of ritual itself—and the psalms themselves are studded with references both to familiar rituals and unfamiliar, obscure ones. But the various poets whose songs were eventually united in the Psalter seem almost uniformly to have understood that, for faith in God to be totally real, it must derive from a root experience in which an individual perceives God to exist *truly,* in the regular way human beings per-

[15] I shall not hold myself back from You, neither the part of me conceived in secret nor the part knit together in the nethermost bowels of my mother, my earth.

[16] You saw my embryonic state, then had all the details of my development written down in Your book: all my days were thus charted, including every last one.

[17] From my own vantage point, how potent are Your minions, O God, how powerful the chief angels among them.

[18] Were I to count them, they would outnumber the grains of sand at the beach; but even if I eventually did finish, I would still be in Your company.

[19–20] O God, if You killed a wicked man, then would violent people—people who speak of You only to plot wickedness, whole cities of Your enemies given over to vain pursuits—would such people then stay away from me?

[21] Do I not hate those who hate You, יהוה? Indeed, I argue endlessly with those who struggle against You.

[22] I loathe them with ultimate loathing; they have become my personal enemies as well as Yours.

[23] Study me, O God, and know my heart; test me and know my innermost thoughts.

[24] See if mine is a path destined to bring me pain, then guide me instead on the path of eternity.

ceive their world and the things that *truly* exist within its boundaries.

God, the poets knew, will always be beyond the ken of human beings. But not being able to fathom something totally is not the same as not perceiving it at all . . . and the poets knew that as well. In our world, one may not fully understand just how cellular telephones work, but that will not affect the average person's unshakable conviction that telephones do indeed exist, or their ability to talk on the phone without feeling crippled by doubt or paralyzed by a sense of absurdity. The same, the psalmist is saying just a bit obliquely, should be true of God . . . if one can abandon the notion that God simply cannot be perceived, let alone truly and unshakably known, by human beings at all.

קמ

לַמְנַצֵּחַ מִזְמוֹר לְדָוִד׃

2 חַלְּצֵנִי יְהוָה מֵאָדָם רָע מֵאִישׁ חֲמָסִים תִּנְצְרֵנִי׃

3 אֲשֶׁר חָשְׁבוּ רָעוֹת בְּלֵב כָּל־יוֹם יָגוּרוּ מִלְחָמוֹת׃

4 שָׁנְנוּ לְשׁוֹנָם כְּמוֹ־נָחָשׁ חֲמַת עַכְשׁוּב תַּחַת שְׂפָתֵימוֹ סֶלָה׃

5 שָׁמְרֵנִי יְהוָה ׀ מִידֵי רָשָׁע מֵאִישׁ חֲמָסִים תִּנְצְרֵנִי אֲשֶׁר חָשְׁבוּ לִדְחוֹת פְּעָמָי׃

6 טָמְנוּ גֵאִים ׀ פַּח־לִי וַחֲבָלִים פָּרְשׂוּ רֶשֶׁת לְיַד־מַעְגָּל מֹקְשִׁים שָׁתוּ־לִי סֶלָה׃

7 אָמַרְתִּי לַיהוָה אֵלִי אָתָּה הַאֲזִינָה יְהוָה קוֹל תַּחֲנוּנָי׃

8 יְהוִה אֲדֹנָי עֹז יְשׁוּעָתִי סַכֹּתָה לְרֹאשִׁי בְּיוֹם נָשֶׁק׃

9 אַל־תִּתֵּן יְהוָה מַאֲוַיֵּי רָשָׁע זְמָמוֹ אַל־תָּפֵק יָרוּמוּ סֶלָה׃

10 רֹאשׁ מְסִבָּי עֲמַל שְׂפָתֵימוֹ *יְכַסֵּימוֹ׃

11 *יִמּוֹטוּ עֲלֵיהֶם גֶּחָלִים בָּאֵשׁ יַפִּלֵם בְּמַהֲמֹרוֹת בַּל־יָקוּמוּ׃

12 אִישׁ לָשׁוֹן בַּל־יִכּוֹן בָּאָרֶץ אִישׁ־חָמָס רָע יְצוּדֶנּוּ לְמַדְחֵפֹת׃

13 *יָדַעְתִּי כִּי־יַעֲשֶׂה יְהוָה דִּין עָנִי מִשְׁפַּט אֶבְיֹנִים׃

14 אַךְ צַדִּיקִים יוֹדוּ לִשְׁמֶךָ יֵשְׁבוּ יְשָׁרִים אֶת־פָּנֶיךָ׃

v. 10 יכסומו כתיב

v. 11 ימיטו כתיב

v. 13 ידעת כתיב

Unlike other psalmists who feared evil and violence in general, the author of the 140th psalm appears to have had experience with the real thing and has no qualms telling us how his wicked, violent enemies have stopped at nothing to harm him, how they have laid traps and dug pits to capture him, and how they have prepared snares to snap shut on his feet as he flees from their grasp. The poet, at least in theory, can give as good as he gets, however, and sounds quite pleased to list the specific ways he would like to see his foes punished. Modern readers either will or will not find his rage against his enemies

140

For the conductor, a psalm of David.

[2] Save me, יהוה, from evil men; guard me from men of violence [3]who, planning evil in their hearts, foment wars all day long.

[4] They have sharpened their tongues like a serpent's; the venom of a poisonous spider is under their lips, *selah*.

[5] Keep me from the hands of the wicked, O יהוה; guard me from men of violence who plot to shove my feet out from under me.

[6] The arrogant have laid a trap for me; they have spread out their ropes into a net beside the plaza. They have laid snares for me, *selah*.

[7] I say to יהוה, "You are my God. Listen, O יהוה, to the sound of my supplications.

[8] יהוה-Adonai, stronghold of my salvation, shield my head on the day of attack.

[9] יהוה, do not grant the wishes of the wicked; let their plot not come to fruition, lest they be exalted, *selah*."

[10] As for the leaders of those who surround me, may they be done in by the machinations of their own lips.

[11] May burning coals pour down on them; may they push them down into fire, into pits from which they will never rise.

[12] May slanderers not flourish in the land; may the evil that men of violence perpetrate itself hunt them down and topple them.

[13] I know that יהוה will provide justice for the poor and fair judgment for the indigent, [14]but it is the righteous who will give thanks to Your name and it is the upright who will dwell in the presence of Your face.

off-putting, but the more important point to ponder comes at the end of the poem when the poet makes it clear that his fear of physical violence has not led him to reject God. Indeed, if anything, he affirms his faith with all the more vigor in the face of terror. Does the fear of crime in our world likewise lead people to faith? Or does the mischief of villains weaken our confidence in God instead of making it all the stronger and more intense and urgent?

קמא

מִזְמוֹר לְדָוִד
יְהוָה קְרָאתִיךָ חוּשָׁה לִּי הַאֲזִינָה קוֹלִי בְּקָרְאִי־לָךְ׃

2 תִּכּוֹן תְּפִלָּתִי קְטֹרֶת לְפָנֶיךָ מַשְׂאַת כַּפַּי מִנְחַת־עָרֶב׃

3 שִׁיתָה יְהוָה שָׁמְרָה לְפִי נִצְּרָה עַל־דַּל שְׂפָתָי׃

4 אַל־תַּט לִבִּי לְדָבָר ׀ רָע לְהִתְעוֹלֵל עֲלִלוֹת ׀ בְּרֶשַׁע אֶת־אִישִׁים פֹּעֲלֵי־אָוֶן וּבַל־אֶלְחַם בְּמַנְעַמֵּיהֶם׃

5 יֶהֶלְמֵנִי־צַדִּיק ׀ חֶסֶד וְיוֹכִיחֵנִי שֶׁמֶן רֹאשׁ אַל־יָנִי רֹאשִׁי כִּי עוֹד וּתְפִלָּתִי בְּרָעוֹתֵיהֶם׃

6 נִשְׁמְטוּ בִידֵי־סֶלַע שֹׁפְטֵיהֶם וְשָׁמְעוּ אֲמָרַי כִּי נָעֵמוּ׃

7 כְּמוֹ פֹלֵחַ וּבֹקֵעַ בָּאָרֶץ נִפְזְרוּ עֲצָמֵינוּ לְפִי שְׁאוֹל׃

8 כִּי אֵלֶיךָ ׀ יְהוִה אֲדֹנָי עֵינָי בְּכָה חָסִיתִי אַל־תְּעַר נַפְשִׁי׃

9 שָׁמְרֵנִי מִידֵי־פַח יָקְשׁוּ לִי וּמֹקְשׁוֹת פֹּעֲלֵי אָוֶן׃

10 יִפְּלוּ בְמַכְמֹרָיו רְשָׁעִים יַחַד אָנֹכִי עַד־אֶעֱבוֹר׃

Like any poet worth the name, the author of the 141st psalm writes to lay bare his soul to his audience and to let them contemplate themselves in the image thus conjured up. Rejecting the hopeful notion that it is a simple thing to serve God by planting oneself firmly in the camp of the righteous, the poet writes of the riveting ambivalence he feels as he attempts to embrace goodness and eschew villainy. He prays that God place a guard of some sort on his mouth to keep him from speaking evil . . . and that the Almighty ignore his injudicious prayers for the destruction of any who dare rebuke him for his sins. He knows how overpowering the will to sin can be, but the poet truly wishes to be in the camp of righteousness because he realizes, perhaps intui-

141

A psalm of David.
I have called out to You, יהוה; hasten to me. Listen to my voice when I call out to You.
[2] May my prayer be as pleasant as incense before You; may you find my outspread hands as acceptable as the evening grain offering.
[3] O יהוה, place a guard at my mouth, a watchman at the door of my lips.
[4] Incline not my heart to do evil things, to become involved in wickedness with doers of iniquity; let me not be inclined to feast on the specialties of their houses.
[5] Let a righteous person strike me, mercifully taking the time to rebuke me; may my head not be denied such choice oil even if my prayer at the moment be that they suffer evil as a result of their candor.
[6] And as for the wicked, may their judges slip off rocky crags—while listening to my pleasant prayers.
[7] But what of us? Our bones are scattered at the mouth of Sheol like clods of earth when the plow blade cuts through the earth and breaks it up.
[8] Yet my eyes are still turned to You, יהוה-Adonai, and in You do I seek refuge; expose not my soul to harm.
[9] Guard me from the trap they have set for me and from the snares of the doers of iniquity.
[10] May all the wicked fall together into their leader's own net as I myself pass safely by.

tively, that only by embracing goodness can one ever hope to approach God. The question is: when we finally finish muttering the pious platitudes and shop-worn slogans of our faith—and when we are done forgetting that rituals are the *vehicles* of worship and not its point or essence—do we have enough strength left to analyze ourselves, and the trajectory of our spiritual journeys, as candidly and honestly as the poet who composed the 141st psalm was able to evaluate the worth and nature of his own religious life?

מַשְׂכִּיל לְדָוִד בִּהְיוֹתוֹ בַמְּעָרָה תְפִלָּה׃
2 קוֹלִי אֶל־יְהוָה אֶזְעָק קוֹלִי אֶל־יְהוָה אֶתְחַנָּן׃
3 אֶשְׁפֹּךְ לְפָנָיו שִׂיחִי צָרָתִי לְפָנָיו אַגִּיד׃
4 בְּהִתְעַטֵּף עָלַי ׀ רוּחִי וְאַתָּה יָדַעְתָּ נְתִיבָתִי בְּאֹרַח־
זוּ אֲהַלֵּךְ טָמְנוּ פַח לִי׃
5 הַבֵּיט יָמִין ׀ וּרְאֵה וְאֵין־לִי מַכִּיר אָבַד מָנוֹס מִמֶּנִּי
אֵין דּוֹרֵשׁ לְנַפְשִׁי׃
6 זָעַקְתִּי אֵלֶיךָ יְהוָה אָמַרְתִּי אַתָּה מַחְסִי חֶלְקִי
בְּאֶרֶץ הַחַיִּים׃
7 הַקְשִׁיבָה ׀ אֶל־רִנָּתִי כִּי־דַלּוֹתִי מְאֹד הַצִּילֵנִי
מֵרֹדְפַי כִּי אָמְצוּ מִמֶּנִּי׃
8 הוֹצִיאָה מִמַּסְגֵּר ׀ נַפְשִׁי לְהוֹדוֹת אֶת־שְׁמֶךָ בִּי
יַכְתִּרוּ צַדִּיקִים כִּי תִגְמֹל עָלָי׃

The poet, feeling alone and abandoned by people he once thought of as friends, writes from someplace he is being confined by enemies whose intentions for him he can imagine all too clearly. And his is a true nightmare. To be ambushed while walking along a familiar path and then to be dragged off to some hidden cell and forcibly imprisoned would undoubtedly have been upsetting enough. It must have been truly unbearable, however, for him to realize that no one seemed even to notice his absence, that no avenue of escape appeared to exist, and that the people of the poet's world were not only unconcerned with his fate, but were entirely ready to deny even being acquainted with him. Yet his faith remains strong as he lifts up his voice to call out to God, the ultimate refuge of the downcast and dejected, the force for good that the poet can still identify as his personal source of wealth and strength in the land of the living.

142

A wise-song of David: a prayer composed when he was in the cave.

[2] With my voice I cry out to יהוה; with my voice, I plead with יהוה for mercy.

[3] I pour out my plaint; I tell of my troubles before God.

[4] When my spirit was faint within me, they—You know my regular path—on that very path that I regularly travel, that is where they laid a trap for me.

[5] Look to my right and see how things are: no one knows me, my place of flight is lost to me, no one cares if I live or die.

[6] I cry out to You, יהוה; I declare that You are my haven, my portion in the land of the living.

[7] Hear my joyless hymn, for I am very downcast. Save me from my pursuers, for they are far stronger than I.

[8] Bring forth my soul from prison, that I might give thanks to Your name. Indeed, the righteous shall yet crown me as a chief beneficiary of Your goodness because of the way You deal with me.

Modern readers will wonder what the poet could possibly have done to provoke such a violent, sadistic response on the part of his enemies. Could they simply have been enemies of God who considered the faithful, almost by definition, to be foes worth ambushing and kidnapping, perhaps even murdering? Or was there another, more specific reason for their enmity? We will never know any more about the poet's private circumstances than his poem reveals, but we can still wonder what our own response to that kind of persecution would be. Would we, like the poet, think of ourselves as latter-day Davids, totally and absolutely secure about God's love for us, while contemplating our lots from caves and dungeons we dare not (or cannot) leave? Would we call out to God in our unhappiness or turn away from religion? Would we call God our haven and our strength or would we seek refuge elsewhere? Would we feel buoyed by our faith or betrayed by God in our lonely hour of misery?

קמג

מִזְמוֹר לְדָוִד
יְהוָה ׀ שְׁמַע תְּפִלָּתִי הַאֲזִינָה אֶל־תַּחֲנוּנַי
בֶּאֱמֻנָתְךָ עֲנֵנִי בְּצִדְקָתֶךָ׃
2 וְאַל־תָּבוֹא בְמִשְׁפָּט אֶת־עַבְדֶּךָ כִּי לֹא־יִצְדַּק
לְפָנֶיךָ כָל־חָי׃
3 כִּי רָדַף אוֹיֵב ׀ נַפְשִׁי דִּכָּא לָאָרֶץ חַיָּתִי הוֹשִׁיבַנִי
בְמַחֲשַׁכִּים כְּמֵתֵי עוֹלָם׃ 4 וַתִּתְעַטֵּף עָלַי רוּחִי
בְּתוֹכִי יִשְׁתּוֹמֵם לִבִּי׃
5 זָכַרְתִּי יָמִים ׀ מִקֶּדֶם הָגִיתִי בְכָל־פָּעֳלֶךָ בְּמַעֲשֵׂה
יָדֶיךָ אֲשׂוֹחֵחַ׃
6 פֵּרַשְׂתִּי יָדַי אֵלֶיךָ נַפְשִׁי ׀ כְּאֶרֶץ־עֲיֵפָה לְךָ סֶלָה׃
7 מַהֵר עֲנֵנִי ׀ יְהוָה כָּלְתָה רוּחִי אַל־תַּסְתֵּר פָּנֶיךָ
מִמֶּנִּי וְנִמְשַׁלְתִּי עִם־יֹרְדֵי בוֹר׃
8 הַשְׁמִיעֵנִי בַבֹּקֶר ׀ חַסְדֶּךָ כִּי־בְךָ בָטָחְתִּי הוֹדִיעֵנִי
דֶּרֶךְ־זוּ אֵלֵךְ כִּי־אֵלֶיךָ נָשָׂאתִי נַפְשִׁי׃
9 הַצִּילֵנִי מֵאֹיְבַי ׀ יְהוָה אֵלֶיךָ כִסִּתִי׃
10 לַמְּדֵנִי ׀ לַעֲשׂוֹת רְצוֹנֶךָ כִּי־אַתָּה אֱלוֹהָי רוּחֲךָ
טוֹבָה תַּנְחֵנִי בְּאֶרֶץ מִישׁוֹר׃
11 לְמַעַן־שִׁמְךָ יְהוָה תְּחַיֵּנִי בְּצִדְקָתְךָ ׀ תּוֹצִיא מִצָּרָה
נַפְשִׁי׃
12 וּבְחַסְדְּךָ תַּצְמִית אֹיְבָי וְהַאֲבַדְתָּ כָּל־צֹרְרֵי נַפְשִׁי
כִּי אֲנִי עַבְדֶּךָ׃

The 143rd psalm reflects a situation similar to the 142nd. There is no way to know with certainty if they have the same author, but both poems clearly speak of their authors being ambushed and imprisoned against their will. Moreover, both were the victims of vicious calumny and denunciation. And both responded to the experience of being confined against their will by violent fiends not by becoming enraged at God, but by turning in humble supplication to the Almighty in the hope that in so doing they might come to walk more faithfully in God's ways.

As modern readers of both poems, we will want to ask ourselves where we

143

A psalm of David.

יהוה, hear my prayer and listen to my supplications; answer me in Your faithfulness, in Your righteousness.

[2] Enter not into judgment with Your servant, for no living creature can ever be considered totally righteous before You.

[3] Still, the enemy has pursued my soul, crushing my living spirit into the ground, forcing me to dwell in darkness as though I were already among the dead of this world, [4]making my spirit faint and my heart within me stunned.

[5] I remember old times and meditate on all Your works; I speak constantly about the work of Your hands.

[6] I spread out my hands to You, my soul yearning for You like an arid wasteland yearns for water, *selah*.

[7] Answer me quickly, יהוה, for my spirit is waning. Hide not Your face from me, lest I truly feel like those who have already gone down to their graves.

[8] Let me hear of Your mercy in the morning, for I have put my trust in You; help me know on which path I should walk, for I have lifted up my soul to You.

[9] Save me from my enemies, יהוה; in You do I seek cover.

[10] Teach me to do Your will, for You are my God. Let Your good spirit guide me in a just land.

[11] Grant me life, יהוה, for the sake of Your name; in Your righteousness, bring forth my soul from trouble.

[12] Destroy my enemies with Your mercy and annihilate those who trouble my soul, for I am Your servant.

find the security that we crave so ardently in the world. Do we truly imagine that money—even vast amounts of it—can insulate us against the cruelties of the wicked? Or do we put our real trust in police forces or armies? Do we imagine that safety against life's perils can be purchased, if only the price we are prepared to pay is high enough? Or do we follow the psalmists' lead and turn wholeheartedly in earnest prayer and thanksgiving to God when faced with the prospect of grave calamity followed by unyielding, endless sadness?

קמד

לְדָוִד ׀
בָּרוּךְ יְהוָה ׀ צוּרִי הַמְלַמֵּד יָדַי לַקְרָב אֶצְבְּעוֹתַי
לַמִּלְחָמָה׃
2 חַסְדִּי וּמְצוּדָתִי מִשְׂגַּבִּי וּמְפַלְטִי לִי מָגִנִּי וּבוֹ
חָסִיתִי הָרוֹדֵד עַמִּי תַחְתָּי׃
3 יְהוָה מָה־אָדָם וַתֵּדָעֵהוּ בֶּן־אֱנוֹשׁ וַתְּחַשְּׁבֵהוּ׃
4 אָדָם לַהֶבֶל דָּמָה יָמָיו כְּצֵל עוֹבֵר׃
5 יְהוָה הַט־שָׁמֶיךָ וְתֵרֵד גַּע בֶּהָרִים וְיֶעֱשָׁנוּ׃
6 בְּרוֹק בָּרָק וּתְפִיצֵם שְׁלַח חִצֶּיךָ וּתְהֻמֵּם׃
7 שְׁלַח יָדֶיךָ מִמָּרוֹם פְּצֵנִי וְהַצִּילֵנִי מִמַּיִם רַבִּים
מִיַּד בְּנֵי נֵכָר׃ 8 אֲשֶׁר פִּיהֶם דִּבֶּר־שָׁוְא וִימִינָם
יְמִין שָׁקֶר׃
9 אֱלֹהִים שִׁיר חָדָשׁ אָשִׁירָה לָּךְ בְּנֵבֶל עָשׂוֹר
אֲזַמְּרָה־לָּךְ׃
10 הַנּוֹתֵן תְּשׁוּעָה לַמְּלָכִים הַפּוֹצֶה אֶת־דָּוִד עַבְדּוֹ
מֵחֶרֶב רָעָה׃ 11 פְּצֵנִי וְהַצִּילֵנִי מִיַּד בְּנֵי־נֵכָר אֲשֶׁר־
פִּיהֶם דִּבֶּר־שָׁוְא וִימִינָם יְמִין שָׁקֶר׃ 12 אֲשֶׁר בָּנֵינוּ ׀
כִּנְטִעִים מְגֻדָּלִים בִּנְעוּרֵיהֶם בְּנוֹתֵינוּ כְזָוִיֹּת

Almost all the main ideas presented in the 144th psalm appear in other psalms, but the poet has nonetheless brought them all together to create an original poem that is, somehow, both a plea to God for the defeat of the poet's personal enemies and an evocation of a grateful nation at peace with God and with the world. When it comes to his enemies, the poet is no less clear than the other psalmists who write on that topic about what precisely he wants from God: the annihilation of the foe by divine lightning bolts (which the poet calls God's arrows) and, for himself, absolute extrication from the net of fear and violence in which his enemies have forced him to live. Indeed, the poet suggests the depth of his fear and ill ease only by underlining the stark contrast between his own misery and the exceptional prosperity his country is enjoying: while the general populace thinks things are going terrifically well, the poet and his colleagues who spend their time seeking and serving God are living in abject terror.

No less deeply moving than his description of his own plight, however, is the poet's description of the prosperity of his country. This state of national well-being, he contends, rests on six particular points that would be the envy and desire of any nation. The young men of the nation are strong and well-

144

(A psalm) of David.

Blessed be יהוה, my rock who teaches my hands to do battle and my fingers to wage war.

[2] You are my mercy and my fortress, my place of refuge and my source of deliverance, the shield in whom I seek haven and who subdues my people beneath me.

[3] יהוה, what are human beings that You should bother knowing them? What are mortals that you should take them into any sort of account?

[4] Human beings are akin to a breath, their days like passing shadows.

[5] יהוה, bend the heavens and descend; touch the mountains and make them smoke.

[6] Cast forth lightning and scatter my enemies; send out Your arrows and make them quake.

[7] Send Your hands from on high. Rescue me and save me from deep waters, from the hand of strangers [8] whose mouths speak falsehood and whose right hands are stretched forth in lies.

[9] O God, I shall sing a new song to You; I shall chant hymns to You while accompanying myself on a ten-stringed *nevel.*

[10] O God who extends salvation to kings and who rescued David, servant of God, from an evil sword, [11] rescue me and save me from the hand of strangers whose mouths speak falsehood and whose right hands are stretched forth in lies. [12] Do this, for it is we whose sons are like saplings well-tended in their youth and whose daughters serve our families like well-hewn

educated. The young women are deeply dedicated to the service of their families. The storehouses are filled to overflowing with grain and every kind of produce. The sheepfolds are packed with tens of thousands of sheep destined to provide the people with enough mutton and wool to suit their needs. The corrals built to hold the nation's oxen are packed with docile, happy animals that will easily provide a hungry nation with sufficient meat for all its citizens. And the broad places of the nation's cities are oases of calm in which no innocent person is ever robbed or molested, and in which no one needs to cry out for help.

The picture may not reflect the precise roles men and women play in our

מְֽחֻטָּבוֹת תַּבְנִית הֵיכָל׃ [13] מְזָוֵינוּ מְלֵאִים מְפִיקִים מִזַּן אֶל־זַן צֹאונֵנוּ מַאֲלִיפוֹת מְרֻבָּבוֹת בְּחוּצוֹתֵינוּ׃ [14] אַלּוּפֵינוּ מְֽסֻבָּלִים אֵין פֶּרֶץ וְאֵין יוֹצֵאת וְאֵין צְוָחָה בִּרְחֹבֹתֵינוּ׃
[15] אַשְׁרֵי הָעָם שֶׁכָּכָה לּוֹ אַשְׁרֵי הָעָם שֱׁיְהֹוָה אֱלֹהָיו׃

society, but the image is still deeply moving and satisfying. Indeed, the poet's country sounds like a peaceful, wealthy place whose citizens must surely have felt lucky and privileged to have lived there. The contrast with the poet's own lot, however, is shocking . . . and all the more stark for being juxtaposed against such a rich description of the nation's enviable status.

Readers will want to ask themselves if we live in a world similar to, or totally different from, the psalmist's. Do those in our world who devote them-

cornerstones at a palace, [13]we whose storehouses are full of goods of every kind, whose sheep run to the thousands and tens of thousands in our pastures, [14]whose powerful oxen are held in unbreachable corrals from which none breaks out, and in whose broad places there are piercing calls for help.

[15] Happy is the nation whose lot is thus. Happy is the nation whose God is יהוה.

selves to God share equally in the prosperity of our nations? Do those whose lives are spent in prayer and contemplation end up with a fair share of their nations' wealth? Do we live in a world in which people are forced to choose between the pursuit of affluence and spiritual pursuits? Do the people who spend their lives teaching Torah to our children make higher or lower salaries than lawyers or dentists? Do we expect a life spent in search of God to be its own reward? If it is generally accepted that the way in which the salaries of workers vary within a given society reflects its values, then what precisely *is* our hierarchy of values?

קמה

תְּהִלָּה לְדָוִד
אֲרוֹמִמְךָ אֱלוֹהַי הַמֶּלֶךְ וַאֲבָרְכָה שִׁמְךָ לְעוֹלָם וָעֶד׃
2 בְּכָל־יוֹם אֲבָרְכֶךָּ וַאֲהַלְלָה שִׁמְךָ לְעוֹלָם וָעֶד׃
3 גָּדוֹל יְהוָה וּמְהֻלָּל מְאֹד וְלִגְדֻלָּתוֹ אֵין חֵקֶר׃
4 דּוֹר לְדוֹר יְשַׁבַּח מַעֲשֶׂיךָ וּגְבוּרֹתֶיךָ יַגִּידוּ׃
5 הֲדַר כְּבוֹד הוֹדֶךָ וְדִבְרֵי נִפְלְאוֹתֶיךָ אָשִׂיחָה׃
6 וֶעֱזוּז נוֹרְאֹתֶיךָ יֹאמֵרוּ *וגדולָּתְךָ אֲסַפְּרֶנָּה׃
7 זֵכֶר רַב־טוּבְךָ יַבִּיעוּ וְצִדְקָתְךָ יְרַנֵּנוּ׃ 8 חַנּוּן וְרַחוּם יְהוָה אֶרֶךְ אַפַּיִם וּגְדָל־חָסֶד׃ 9 טוֹב־יְהוָה לַכֹּל וְרַחֲמָיו עַל־כָּל־מַעֲשָׂיו׃
10 יוֹדוּךָ יְהוָה כָּל־מַעֲשֶׂיךָ וַחֲסִידֶיךָ יְבָרְכוּכָה׃
11 כְּבוֹד מַלְכוּתְךָ יֹאמֵרוּ וּגְבוּרָתְךָ יְדַבֵּרוּ׃
12 לְהוֹדִיעַ לִבְנֵי הָאָדָם גְּבוּרֹתָיו וּכְבוֹד הֲדַר מַלְכוּתוֹ׃
13 מַלְכוּתְךָ מַלְכוּת כָּל־עֹלָמִים וּמֶמְשַׁלְתְּךָ בְּכָל־דּוֹר וָדוֹר׃
14 סוֹמֵךְ יְהוָה לְכָל־הַנֹּפְלִים וְזוֹקֵף לְכָל־הַכְּפוּפִים׃
15 עֵינֵי כֹל אֵלֶיךָ יְשַׂבֵּרוּ וְאַתָּה נוֹתֵן־לָהֶם אֶת־אָכְלָם בְּעִתּוֹ׃ 16 פּוֹתֵחַ אֶת־יָדֶךָ וּמַשְׂבִּיעַ לְכָל־חַי רָצוֹן׃

v. 6 וגדולתיך כתיב

Although the 145th psalm does not actually contain the word *ashrei* ("happy is" or "happy are"), it is nonetheless almost universally known among Jews as "Ashrei" or "*the* Ashrei" because it appears in the traditional prayerbook preceded by two verses (Psalm 84:5 and Psalm 144:15) that do begin with that word. Presented in the prayerbook for recitation three times daily, twice in the morning service and once at the beginning of afternoon prayers, this psalm was greatly prized by the rabbis—so much so that the Talmud preserves a tradition (at Berakhot 4b) that anyone who recites this psalm three times daily can be assured of a place in the world to come. Modern readers will wonder why, of all the poems in the Psalter, this particular one was so intensely cherished. Indeed, the poem is so well-known by people who attend synagogue services that it is actually difficult for regular worshipers to read it slowly and carefully. (For their part, the later rabbis of the Talmud also wondered why their own predecessors had

145

A psalm of praise of David.

I shall exalt You, O my God and Sovereign,
and I shall bless Your name for ever and always.

[2] Each day shall I bless You; I shall praise Your name for ever and always.

[3] Great is יהוה and very worthy of praise; there is no limit to God's greatness.

[4] One generation lauds Your works to the next, telling of Your mighty acts.

[5] Glorious is the splendor of Your majesty; I shall speak of Your wondrous acts.

[6] Some will talk about the might of Your awesome deeds, but I shall tell of Your greatness.

[7] Others will attempt to express the essence of Your great goodness, singing joyously of Your righteousness: [8]"יהוה is gracious and compassionate, long-suffering and greatly merciful. [9]יהוה is good to all and compassionate to all humanity."

[10] Indeed, all Your creatures will give thanks to You, יהוה, and the pious will bless You as well; [11]they will talk of the glory of Your majesty and speak of Your might, [12]so as to tell humanity about Your might and the glorious splendor of Your sovereignty.

[13] Your sovereignty is sovereignty everlasting; Your governance endures throughout every generation.

[14] יהוה supports all who fall and raises up all those who are bent over.

[15] Indeed, the eyes of all are fixed on You, for it is You who give them food when it is most needed, [16]You who open Your hand and who willingly satisfy the needs of all living creatures.

felt so strongly about it. But their answer—that it is the only acrostic poem in the Bible that makes reference to God providing food for the world—will probably strike most moderns as less than convincing.)

The theme of the 145th psalm that sets it apart from the other psalms is talking. Indeed, no other psalm has more references in it to people speaking. One generation is portrayed as speaking to the next. The poet is portrayed as talking to his listeners. Unidentified others are said to be telling and retelling the glory of God. The pious bless God in the presence of the less pious. All

17 צַדִּ֣יק יְ֭הוָה בְּכׇל־דְּרָכָ֑יו וְ֝חָסִ֗יד בְּכׇל־מַעֲשָֽׂיו׃
18 קָר֣וֹב יְ֭הוָה לְכׇל־קֹרְאָ֑יו לְכֹ֤ל אֲשֶׁ֖ר יִקְרָאֻ֣הוּ בֶאֱמֶֽת׃ 19 רְצוֹן־יְרֵאָ֥יו יַעֲשֶׂ֑ה וְאֶת־שַׁוְעָתָ֥ם יִ֝שְׁמַ֗ע וְיוֹשִׁיעֵֽם׃
20 שׁוֹמֵ֣ר יְ֭הוָה אֶת־כׇּל־אֹהֲבָ֑יו וְאֵ֖ת כׇּל־הָרְשָׁעִ֣ים יַשְׁמִֽיד׃
21 תְּהִלַּ֥ת יְהוָ֗ה יְֽדַבֶּ֫ר־פִּ֥י וִיבָרֵ֣ךְ כׇּל־בָּ֭שָׂר שֵׁ֥ם קׇדְשׁ֗וֹ לְעוֹלָ֥ם וָעֶֽד׃

God's creatures proclaim the goodness of their Maker and speak openly of the splendor of divine majesty. Those in need raise their voices in prayer and God, moved by the sincerity with which they cry out in honesty and candor, grants them their wishes. Indeed, when the poet concludes by asserting that his own mouth will henceforth be dedicated solely to producing words of praise, he is only reinforcing the image he himself has conjured up of a world filled with people using language to lead them to God and to bind them to each other in a sense of exalted common purpose.

Modern readers may wish to respond to the ancient poet's words by asking

[17] יהוה is righteous in all ways and merciful in all deeds.

[18] יהוה is close to all those supplicants who call out to God in truth; [19] God does that which those who fear God wish, listens to their prayers, and grants them deliverance.

[20] יהוה guards those who love God, but destroys all the wicked.

[21] For all these reasons shall my mouth sing the praise of יהוה, and all flesh shall bless God's holy name for ever and always.

what we in our world spend our days talking about. Do we use language as a tool to bind humanity together in the service of God, or as a means to get whatever it is we want from the world? Does every word, even the most banal or ordinary, that comes out of our mouths sanctify the world and glorify God? Is language a holy path towards God for moderns or a value-neutral invention that separates human beings from animals in a way that leaves God completely out of the picture? How many of us can say *tehillat* יהוה *yedabber pi* with the poet and mean that, in the end, there will never exit from our mouths any words that do not, at least in some sense, praise God?

קמו

הַֽלְלוּיָהּ
הַלְלִי נַפְשִׁי אֶת־יְהוָה׃
2 אֲהַלְלָה יְהוָה בְּחַיָּי אֲזַמְּרָה לֵאלֹהַי בְּעוֹדִי׃
3 אַל־תִּבְטְחוּ בִנְדִיבִים בְּבֶן־אָדָם ׀ שֶׁאֵין לוֹ
תְשׁוּעָה׃ 4 תֵּצֵא רוּחוֹ יָשֻׁב לְאַדְמָתוֹ בַּיּוֹם הַהוּא
אָבְדוּ עֶשְׁתֹּנֹתָיו׃
5 אַשְׁרֵי שֶׁאֵל יַעֲקֹב בְּעֶזְרוֹ שִׂבְרוֹ עַל־יְהוָה אֱלֹהָיו׃
6 עֹשֶׂה ׀ שָׁמַיִם וָאָרֶץ אֶת־הַיָּם וְאֶת־כָּל־אֲשֶׁר־בָּם
הַשֹּׁמֵר אֱמֶת לְעוֹלָם׃
7 עֹשֶׂה מִשְׁפָּט ׀ לָעֲשׁוּקִים נֹתֵן לֶחֶם לָרְעֵבִים יְהוָה
מַתִּיר אֲסוּרִים׃
8 יְהוָה ׀ פֹּקֵחַ עִוְרִים יְהוָה זֹקֵף כְּפוּפִים יְהוָה אֹהֵב
צַדִּיקִים׃
9 יְהוָה ׀ שֹׁמֵר אֶת־גֵּרִים יָתוֹם וְאַלְמָנָה יְעוֹדֵד וְדֶרֶךְ
רְשָׁעִים יְעַוֵּת׃
10 יִמְלֹךְ יְהוָה ׀ לְעוֹלָם אֱלֹהַיִךְ צִיּוֹן לְדֹר וָדֹר
הַלְלוּיָהּ׃

The poet who wrote the 146th psalm was not privy to any secret information about the relationship between the eternal reliability of God and the ephemeral, transient nature of human life, but he was nonetheless prepared to build a life in God based on what he did know of that relationship. From his poem, we may surmise that the poet was surrounded by powerful noblemen—the ancient equivalent of politicians and elite business tycoons—who were constantly urging him to put his trust in them rather than in God and in the intangible trappings of divine support. But the poet was able to understand,

146

Hallelujah.

Praise יהוה, O my soul.

[2] I shall praise יהוה during my lifetime; I shall sing to my God for as long as I exist.

[3] Trust not in nobles, in human beings who have no capacity to effect deliverance, [4] who begin to turn back to dust on the day their breathing stops; on that day their thoughts—their memories—are lost.

[5] Happy are those aided by the God of Jacob, those whose hopes rest in יהוה, their God, [6] Maker of heaven and earth and the sea and all that is in them, eternal Guardian of truth.

[7] Purveyor of justice to the oppressed and Giver of bread to the hungry, יהוה grants the release of those who are imprisoned.

[8] יהוה grants sight to the blind. יהוה enables those who are bent over to stand erect. יהוה loves the righteous.

[9] יהוה guards the strangers among us, supports the orphan and the widow, and makes crooked the path of the wicked.

[10] יהוה will reign forever; your God, O Zion, shall reign in every generation. Hallelujah.

perhaps intuitively, that an essential part of living in God is feeling the trust and the hope that only faith truly engenders, and that neither can effectively be sought while one is busy placing one's confidence in other human beings, no matter how powerful or wealthy they might be. Modern readers may feel prompted to ask themselves where they themselves have placed their trust. If, as the poet observes, God is the eternal Guardian of truth, then must not faith always elude people who feel that embracing the truth about the world means placing their deepest trust not in God, but in even the most beneficent—and powerful—of human beings?

קמז

הַֽלְלוּיָ֨הּ ׀
כִּי־ט֭וֹב זַמְּרָ֣ה אֱלֹהֵ֑ינוּ כִּֽי־נָ֝עִ֗ים נָאוָ֥ה תְהִלָּֽה׃
2 בּוֹנֵ֣ה יְרוּשָׁלִַ֣ם יְהוָ֑ה נִדְחֵ֖י יִשְׂרָאֵ֣ל יְכַנֵּֽס׃ 3 הָ֭רוֹפֵא
לִשְׁב֣וּרֵי לֵ֑ב וּ֝מְחַבֵּ֗שׁ לְעַצְּבוֹתָֽם׃ 4 מוֹנֶ֣ה מִ֭סְפָּר
לַכּוֹכָבִ֑ים לְ֝כֻלָּ֗ם שֵׁמ֥וֹת יִקְרָֽא׃
5 גָּד֣וֹל אֲדוֹנֵ֣ינוּ וְרַב־כֹּ֑חַ לִ֝תְבוּנָת֗וֹ אֵ֣ין מִסְפָּֽר׃
6 מְעוֹדֵ֣ד עֲנָוִ֣ים יְהוָ֑ה מַשְׁפִּ֖יל רְשָׁעִ֣ים עֲדֵי־אָֽרֶץ׃
7 עֱנ֣וּ לַיהוָ֣ה בְּתוֹדָ֑ה זַמְּר֖וּ לֵאלֹהֵ֣ינוּ בְכִנּֽוֹר׃
8 הַֽמְכַסֶּ֬ה שָׁמַ֨יִם ׀ בְּעָבִ֗ים הַמֵּכִ֣ין לָאָ֣רֶץ מָטָ֑ר
הַמַּצְמִ֖יחַ הָרִ֣ים חָצִֽיר׃ 9 נוֹתֵ֣ן לִבְהֵמָ֣ה לַחְמָ֑הּ
לִבְנֵ֥י עֹ֝רֵ֗ב אֲשֶׁ֣ר יִקְרָֽאוּ׃
10 לֹ֤א בִגְבוּרַ֣ת הַסּ֣וּס יֶחְפָּ֑ץ לֹֽא־בְשׁוֹקֵ֖י הָאִ֣ישׁ
יִרְצֶֽה׃ 11 רוֹצֶ֣ה יְ֭הוָה אֶת־יְרֵאָ֑יו אֶת־הַֽמְיַחֲלִ֥ים
לְחַסְדּֽוֹ׃
12 שַׁבְּחִ֣י יְ֭רוּשָׁלִַם אֶת־יְהוָ֑ה הַֽלְלִ֖י אֱלֹהַ֣יִךְ צִיּֽוֹן׃
13 כִּֽי־חִ֭זַּק בְּרִיחֵ֣י שְׁעָרָ֑יִךְ בֵּרַ֖ךְ בָּנַ֣יִךְ בְּקִרְבֵּֽךְ׃
14 הַשָּׂ֣ם גְּבוּלֵ֣ךְ שָׁל֑וֹם חֵ֥לֶב חִ֝טִּ֗ים יַשְׂבִּיעֵֽךְ׃
15 הַשֹּׁלֵ֣חַ אִמְרָת֣וֹ אָ֑רֶץ עַד־מְ֝הֵרָ֗ה יָר֥וּץ דְּבָרֽוֹ׃

The author of the 147th psalm has a lot to say about God, but moderns will find the flow of ideas in his poem slightly mysterious. Moving from the concept that God is the true Builder of Jerusalem to the notion that God heals the broken hearts of the downcast and miserable among us, and then to the idea that God is also the Maker of the stars and the divine Assigner of their names, the poet gives no early indication as to what is prompting this particular chain of thoughts. But then, almost abruptly, he does: towards the end of his poem, the poet embarks on a list of references to God that have more and more to do with winter storms of snow and ice. At first, the poet only mentions that God covers the skies with clouds and sends the necessary precipitation to the world to make grass grow on the mountains. He then turns to other topics—how God makes the borders of Israel peaceful and provides the people with the choicest wheat—only to develop the concept of God's role in winter storms a few lines later. Indeed, one gets the sense that the poet has finally gotten to his point when he describes how God covers the land with snow so deep that the world looks as though it were covered with a woolen blanket, then sends a covering of hoarfrost so extensive that it appears to the casual onlooker as though somebody has sprinkled the landscape

147

Hallelujah.

It is good to sing to our God and pleasant to sing songs of lovely praise.

[2]The true Builder of Jerusalem is יהוה, Gatherer of the dispersed ones of Israel, [3]Healer of the brokenhearted and the Bandager of their wounds; [4]God counts the countless stars and assigns names to them all.

[5]Great is our Ruler and mighty of strength; there is no limit to God's understanding.

[6]יהוה encourages the humble, but casts the wicked down to the ground.

[7]Sing to יהוה with thanksgiving, play hymns to our God on a lyre, [8]for it is God who covers the skies with clouds, who prepares rain for the earth, who makes the mountains green with grass, [9]who gives animals their food, who even feeds the raven's young when they call out for nourishment.

[10]יהוה neither esteems the might of horses nor delights in the strong legs of human beings, [11]but rather delights in those God-fearers who hope continually for divine mercy.

[12]O Jerusalem, praise יהוה; O Zion, laud your God, [13]that God who has fortified the bars on your gates and blessed your children in your midst, [14]who has made peaceful your borders and satisfied you with the choicest wheat, [15]who sends divine speech to earth, the word of God that so quickly races along,

with white ash or, perhaps, with breadcrumbs. Who, the poet asks as he finally gets to the point, can withstand the frigid coldness that God sends to the world? Yet spring follows winter as inexorably as the mercy of God follows divine wrath: one word from God and blasts of warm air melt the ice and fill the land with flowing streams of cold water that irrigate the countryside as they run into the sea.

Had the poet just experienced a rare Jerusalem snowstorm when he sat down to write his poem? Modern readers won't ever know, but we can still allow the poet's words to prompt us to ponder the way we ourselves respond to the fury of nature. Is the kind of ice storm that can immobilize an entire city a curse (because it ruins business for a day or a week) or a blessing (because it reminds people of the power

16 הַנֹּתֵן שֶׁלֶג כַּצָּמֶר כְּפוֹר כָּאֵפֶר יְפַזֵּר׃ 17 מַשְׁלִיךְ קַרְחוֹ כְפִתִּים לִפְנֵי קָרָתוֹ מִי יַעֲמֹד׃
18 יִשְׁלַח דְּבָרוֹ וְיַמְסֵם יַשֵּׁב רוּחוֹ יִזְּלוּ־מָיִם׃ 19 מַגִּיד *דְּבָרָיו לְיַעֲקֹב חֻקָּיו וּמִשְׁפָּטָיו לְיִשְׂרָאֵל׃ 20 לֹא עָשָׂה כֵן ׀ לְכָל־גּוֹי וּמִשְׁפָּטִים בַּל־יְדָעוּם הַלְלוּ־יָהּ׃

v. 19 דברו כתיב

and majesty of the Creator of the world)? Do winter storms have negative spiritual value because they make it difficult to come to worship services? Or is that inconvenience mostly—or even perhaps wholly—negated by the fear of God a severe winter storm can strike in the hearts of

[16]who covers the earth with snow as though it were a blanket of wool, who scatters frost on the ground as though it were ash, [17]who hurls chunks of ice to earth as though they were breadcrumbs—and who can withstand the cold God sends to earth?

[18]But it is also God who sends a word to melt all the ice, who sends a warm wind that makes the ice into flowing water; [19]it is God who tells such divine words to Jacob and the divine statutes and laws to Israel, [20]something God does not do for other nations, peoples that consequently do not know those laws. Hallelujah.

people who, even if they are generally insensitive to God's role in their lives, may be stirred to piety through the contemplation of terrifyingly treacherous weather?

קמח

הַלְלוּיָהּ ׀
הַלְלוּ אֶת־יְהוָה מִן־הַשָּׁמַיִם הַלְלוּהוּ בַּמְּרוֹמִים׃
2 הַלְלוּהוּ כָל־מַלְאָכָיו הַלְלוּהוּ כָּל־*צְבָאָיו׃
3 הַלְלוּהוּ שֶׁמֶשׁ וְיָרֵחַ הַלְלוּהוּ כָּל־כּוֹכְבֵי אוֹר׃
4 הַלְלוּהוּ שְׁמֵי הַשָּׁמָיִם וְהַמַּיִם אֲשֶׁר ׀ מֵעַל הַשָּׁמָיִם׃
5 יְהַלְלוּ אֶת־שֵׁם יְהוָה כִּי הוּא צִוָּה וְנִבְרָאוּ׃
6 וַיַּעֲמִידֵם לָעַד לְעוֹלָם חָק־נָתַן וְלֹא יַעֲבוֹר׃
7 הַלְלוּ אֶת־יְהוָה מִן־הָאָרֶץ תַּנִּינִים וְכָל־תְּהֹמוֹת׃
8 אֵשׁ וּבָרָד שֶׁלֶג וְקִיטוֹר רוּחַ סְעָרָה עֹשָׂה דְבָרוֹ׃
9 הֶהָרִים וְכָל־גְּבָעוֹת עֵץ פְּרִי וְכָל־אֲרָזִים׃
10 הַחַיָּה וְכָל־בְּהֵמָה רֶמֶשׂ וְצִפּוֹר כָּנָף׃ 11 מַלְכֵי־אֶרֶץ וְכָל־לְאֻמִּים שָׂרִים וְכָל־שֹׁפְטֵי אָרֶץ׃
12 בַּחוּרִים וְגַם־בְּתוּלוֹת זְקֵנִים עִם־נְעָרִים׃
13 יְהַלְלוּ ׀ אֶת־שֵׁם יְהוָה כִּי־נִשְׂגָּב שְׁמוֹ לְבַדּוֹ הוֹדוֹ עַל־אֶרֶץ וְשָׁמָיִם׃
14 וַיָּרֶם קֶרֶן ׀ לְעַמּוֹ תְּהִלָּה לְכָל־חֲסִידָיו לִבְנֵי יִשְׂרָאֵל עַם־קְרֹבוֹ הַלְלוּיָהּ׃

v. 2 צבאו כתיב

The author of the nineteenth psalm wrote that the heavens, by virtue of their indescribable splendor, can be said to be telling constantly of the glory of the Divine. The poet whose hymn of praise is our 148th psalm goes a step further, however, and imagines all of creation as a vast orchestra of adoration, exultation, and homage. That, in fact, is the point of his poem: to declare that all that exists—from the moon and stars above to the lowliest reptile creeping along in the mud—is called upon to justify its existence by joining in the cosmic chorus of praise due to God.

Modern readers may respond to the stirring cadences of the 148th psalm by contemplating the poet's worldview and comparing it to their own. The world appears as a disorganized, quasi-violent place to most people, yet the poet's faith has allowed him to detect a common, ordering principle in all things, a principle that possesses the potential to unite all creation in the deep beholdenness he expects every creature—and, somewhat mysteriously, every created inanimate thing as well—to feel towards their common Creator. Modern readers of this ancient poem may respond to it most effectively by asking if we can see ourselves finding a place in the universal symphony of praise . . . and, if we can, then how exactly we should go about finding it.

148

Hallelujah.

Praise יהוה from the heavens; praise God from the celestial heights.

[2] Praise God all angels; praise God all celestial minions.

[3] Praise God, O sun and moon; praise God all stars of light.

[4] Praise God, O highest heavens and the waters that are above the heavens.

[5] Let them all praise the name of יהוה, for they were all created when God commanded it: [6]God set them up permanently with a decree that cannot be undone.

[7] Praise יהוה from the earth, sea-monsters and all depths, [8]fire and hail, snow and mist, winds of storm that obey God's command, [9]the mountains and all hills, fruit trees and all cedars, [10]animals and all beasts, reptiles and winged birds, [11]kings of the earth and all nations, princes and all judges of the earth, [12]young men and maiden girls, the elderly together with the young.

[13] Let them praise the name of יהוה, for God's name alone is truly exalted; the splendor of God is all over the earth and the heavens.

[14] The Almighty will raise up the horn of the people of God, thereby garnering praise for all the pious, for the children of Israel, for the nation closest to God. Hallelujah.

קמט

הַלְלוּיָהּ ׀
שִׁירוּ לַיהוָה שִׁיר חָדָשׁ תְּהִלָּתוֹ בִּקְהַל חֲסִידִים׃
2 יִשְׂמַח יִשְׂרָאֵל בְּעֹשָׂיו בְּנֵי־צִיּוֹן יָגִילוּ בְמַלְכָּם׃
3 יְהַלְלוּ שְׁמוֹ בְמָחוֹל בְּתֹף וְכִנּוֹר יְזַמְּרוּ־לוֹ׃
4 כִּי־רוֹצֶה יְהוָה בְּעַמּוֹ יְפָאֵר עֲנָוִים בִּישׁוּעָה׃
5 יַעְלְזוּ חֲסִידִים בְּכָבוֹד יְרַנְּנוּ עַל־מִשְׁכְּבוֹתָם׃
6 רוֹמְמוֹת אֵל בִּגְרוֹנָם וְחֶרֶב פִּיפִיּוֹת בְּיָדָם׃
7 לַעֲשׂוֹת נְקָמָה בַּגּוֹיִם תּוֹכֵחֹת בַּל־אֻמִּים׃
8 לֶאְסֹר מַלְכֵיהֶם בְּזִקִּים וְנִכְבְּדֵיהֶם בְּכַבְלֵי בַרְזֶל׃
9 לַעֲשׂוֹת בָּהֶם ׀ מִשְׁפָּט כָּתוּב הָדָר הוּא
לְכָל־חֲסִידָיו הַלְלוּיָהּ׃

The poet's basic idea is as shocking in its utter simplicity as it is challenging in its various implications and ramifications. Many psalmists, after all, wrote of the urge to sing the praises of the Almighty as the common thread that binds together all creation, but the poet whose ode to that notion became our 149th psalm chose instead to dwell on the incredible power that devolves upon those who truly choose to devote themselves to the celebration of God. And the power he has in mind is not insignificant: in his conception, such people are not merely pious hymn-singers and prayer-mutterers, but, taken as an aggregate, these individuals possess the ultimate in international power. It is they, and neither the world's generals nor warriors, therefore, who can prompt God to bring nations down, to depose kings, and to execute vengeance upon alien armies. And it is therefore they who, by virtue of the divine favor they garner

149

Hallelujah.

Sing a new song to יהוה; sing out the praise due to God in the congregation of the pious.
[2] Let the people of Israel rejoice in their Maker; let the children of Zion be glad in their Sovereign.
[3] Let them praise God's name in dance; let them sing to God with drum and lyre.
[4] For יהוה takes delight in the people of God and will make splendid the humble with divine salvation.
[5] Let the pious exult in glory; let them sing hymns even on their beds [6]with the high praises of God in their throats and a double-bladed sword in their hands, [7]a weapon with which to take revenge upon the nations, to chastise alien peoples, [8]to order their kings bound with shackles and their nobles with iron fetters, [9]to impose upon them the sentence decreed against them. God is the splendor of the pious. Hallelujah.

for themselves with their hallelujahs, are the true forces for political change in the world.

Modern readers of this penultimate psalm will want to ask themselves where they consider that true potential to effect change in the world lies. In the end, it feels rational—and entirely reasonable—to insist that the only kinds of power that really count in the world are political muscle and military might, but the psalmist insists that the real agents of change in the world are the pious individuals who devote their lives to singing hymns of praise to God . . . and that this is true even when they rest in solitary seclusion on their beds at night and direct their heartfelt thoughts and wishes towards heaven. Do we find that notion satisfying or outlandish? Are moderns capable of accepting that the faithful are the agents of God's governance on earth?

קנ

הַלְלוּיָהּ ׀
הַלְלוּ־אֵל בְּקָדְשׁוֹ הַלְלוּהוּ בִּרְקִיעַ עֻזּוֹ:
2 הַלְלוּהוּ בִגְבוּרֹתָיו הַלְלוּהוּ כְּרֹב גֻּדְלוֹ:
3 הַלְלוּהוּ בְּתֵקַע שׁוֹפָר הַלְלוּהוּ בְּנֵבֶל וְכִנּוֹר:
4 הַלְלוּהוּ בְתֹף וּמָחוֹל הַלְלוּהוּ בְּמִנִּים וְעוּגָב:
5 הַלְלוּהוּ בְצִלְצְלֵי־שָׁמַע הַלְלוּהוּ בְּצִלְצְלֵי תְרוּעָה:
6 כֹּל הַנְּשָׁמָה תְּהַלֵּל יָהּ הַלְלוּיָהּ:

The Book of Psalms culminates with a hymn to the praise of God that is as basic to the psalmists' worldview as it is simply put, yet which manages at the same time to say something fresh, inspiring, and challenging. The great goal of human existence, the poet implies, is to praise God by becoming lost in a web of exultation that makes the strangely intertwined feelings of significance and insignificance any sensitive human being will bring to the contemplation of the divine not the stuff of rare, occasional insight into the nature of things, but simply the way one comes to view the world. For most of us, language will fail miserably as a vehicle for conveying the deepest of our spiritual feelings even to ourselves, let alone to God. The poet suggests, therefore, that we abandon the notion that human speech is the sole acceptable vehicle for prayer and praise, and we should instead seek to communicate our most profound thoughts outside the realm of language: with blasts of the *shofar* and with the gentle music of the lyre, with the evocative clanging of cymbals and with the deeply effective experience of dancing, perhaps in the style of King David himself, before God. The precise meaning of some of the musical terms the psalmist uses has become lost to us—no one is really sure anymore precisely

תם ונשלם
שבח לאל בורא עולם

סכום פסוקי ספר תהילים אלפים וחמש מאות ועשרים ושבעה וחצים ויפתוהו בפיהם וסדריו תשעה עשר ומזמוריו מאה וחמשים.

150

Hallelujah.
Praise God in the divine sanctuary.
Praise God in the firmament of divine might.
[2] Praise God for acts of divine heroism.
Praise God as divine greatness requires.
[3] Praise God with a blast of the *shofar.*
Praise God with the *nevel* and the lyre.
[4] Praise God with drums and dance.
Praise God with the *minnim* and the *ugav.*
[5] Praise God with *shama*-cymbals.
Praise God with *teruah*-cymbals.
[6] Let every breath praise יה. Hallelujah.

what kind of instruments the *ugav* or *minnim* were or what the specific difference between *shama*-cymbals and *teruah*-cymbals was. The psalmist's basic point, however, is entirely clear: to praise God effectively, we must abandon the fantasy that we must formulate our thoughts within the boundaries of human language, and instead embrace the more primitive (and far more effective) method of speaking to God through music and sound. Can moderns ever learn to speak to God through the singing of hymns in which the words are the accoutrements and the melody the main thing? Since language is born of our experience in this world, yet God is totally other than the world, learning to speak without words is essential. Can moderns do it? The psalmist implies that his colleagues could and did, but the answer for moderns will clearly have to do less with intelligence than with humility . . . and less with any skill at prayer we may manage to acquire than with our will towards God and our love of God, as both exist independent of any words written, spoken, or sung.

Complete and done
Praised be the One

The Masoretic note at the end of the Book of Psalms records that it is complete in 2,527 verses divided down into 19 sedarim *comprising 150 psalms.*

יְהִי רָצוֹן אַחֲרֵי אֲמִירַת תְּהִלִּים

יְהִי רָצוֹן מִלְּפָנֶיךָ אֱלֹהַי וֵאלֹהֵי דָּוִד הַמֶּלֶךְ נְעִים זְמִרוֹת יִשְׂרָאֵל, שֶׁתְּקַבֵּל בְּרָצוֹן אֶת הַמִּזְמוֹרִים שֶׁקָּרָאתִי הַיּוֹם כְּמִנְחָה עַל מַחֲבַת וּכְבִכּוּרֵי כֶּרֶם שֶׁנָּטַעְתִּי לִכְבוֹדֶךָ וְלִכְבוֹד שְׁמֶךָ.
כִּי יִרְאָה וָרַעַד יָבֹאוּ בִי בְּעֵת שַׁוְעִי אֵלֶיךָ, בְּקָרְאִי עֲנֵנִי, אֱלֹהֵי צִדְקִי, וְאַל תְּשִׁיבֵנִי מֵחַצְרוֹת קָדְשֶׁךָ כִּי אֵלֶיךָ אֶקְרָא בֶּאֱמֶת וְאַתָּה לִי מַחֲסֶה וָעֹז.
אַל תָּשֵׁב פָּנַי וּשְׁלַח לִי אוֹרְךָ וַאֲמִתְּךָ בְּרַחֲמֶיךָ הָרַבִּים וְהוֹשִׁיעֵנִי.
בָּרוּךְ אַתָּה יהוה, מֶלֶךְ מְהֻלָּל בַּתִּשְׁבָּחוֹת.

A Prayer after the Devotional Recitation of Psalms

May it be Your will, O my God and God of David, king and sweet singer of Israel, to accept the psalms I have read today as an offering like those of ancient times or the firstfruits of a vineyard planted in Your honor and in the honor of Your name.

As fear and trembling seize me when I turn to You in prayer, answer me when I pray, O God of righteousness. As I call upon You in truth, turn me not away from Your holy precincts, for in You do I find haven and strength.

Turn me not away, but send me Your light and Your truth in accordance with Your abundant mercies and grant me salvation.

Blessed are You, Almighty God, Sovereign of the Universe to whom all praise is due.